LITERARY HISTORY OF CANADA

Canadian Literature in English

Second Edition

VOLUME IV

General Editor

W.H. NEW

Editors

CARL BERGER, ALAN CAIRNS, FRANCESS G. HALPENNY,
HENRY KREISEL, DOUGLAS LOCHHEAD,
PHILIP STRATFORD, CLARA THOMAS

Advisory Board

ALFRED G. BAILEY, CLAUDE BISSELL,
NORTHROP FRYE, CARL F. KLINCK, MALCOLM ROSS

UNIVERSITY OF TORONTO PRESS
TORONTO BUFFALO LONDON

© University of Toronto Press 1990
Toronto Buffalo London
Printed in Canada

ISBN 0-8020-5685-7 (cloth)
ISBN 0-8020-6610-0 (paper)

Printed on acid-free paper

Canadian Cataloguing in Publication Data

Main entry under title:

Literary history of Canada

2nd ed.
First ed. published in 1965 in 1 v. Vols. 2 and 3 are revisions of 1965 ed.; v. 3
contains new chapters covering period 1960–1973; v. 4 surveys the years 1972–1984.
Vols. 1–3 edited by Carl F. Klinck . . . [et al.];
v. 4 edited by W.H. New . . . [et al.].
Includes bibliographies and indexes.
ISBN 0-8020-5685-7 (v. 4 : bound). – ISBN 0-8020-6610-0 (v. 4 : pbk.)

1. Canadian literature (English) – History and criticism.*

PS8071.L57 1976   C810'.9   C76-007077-6   PR9184.3.L57 1976

Robert Bringhurst's 'Poem About Crystal,' quoted in Chapter 1, has been used with
permission from the author.

This book has been published with the help of a grant from the Canadian Federation
for the Humanities, using funds provided by the Social Sciences and Humanities
Research Council of Canada. Publication has also been assisted by the Canada
Council and the Ontario Arts Council under their block grant programs.

This volume is dedicated to
Carl F. Klinck

Contents

CONTENTS

Preface

The *Literary History of Canada* project began in 1957, under the direction of Carl Klinck and a group of distinguished colleagues. The first edition of the work appeared in 1965; a second edition, subdivided into three volumes, appeared in 1976, extending coverage to 1972. When Professor Klinck and his Board retired in 1977, I undertook to direct the preparation of Volume IV, a volume intended to focus on anglophone Canadian literature published in the years between 1972 and 1984. It will be the last supplement to the Second Edition.

Helpfully, Carl Klinck and his Editorial Board agreed to continue as an Advisory Board for this volume, and Dr Malcolm Ross joined them in this role. It is with regret, however, that I record the death in 1979 of Dr Roy Daniells, one of the original Board members, whose constructive contributions to the *Literary History*, both editorial and critical, were of lasting value.

I appreciate the continuing support which Carl Klinck and the Advisory Board have given me; I am also deeply indebted to the members of the current Editorial Board, whose hard work, scholarly advice, and unfailing enthusiasm have so markedly shaped this volume. Without their active involvement in the project, it would not have been possible.

Special thanks go to my wife, Peggy, who discussed the project with me, and who saw it take shape over an entire decade. For her love and encouragement I am especially grateful. I wish also to thank Beverly Westbrook for her secretarial assistance; Elizabeth Devakos for checking references; Carol McIver for further library research assistance and for patiently proofreading the text and preparing the index; Jean Wilson for editorial advice; and Nancy Palmer for typing the final version of the manuscript. Gerry Hallowell, of the University of Toronto Press, provided invaluable editorial guidance and support throughout the project.

The Canadian Federation for the Humanities, the Social Sciences Federation of Canada, and various Learned Societies generously answered requests for information, as did Tannis MacBeth Williams, Neil Guppy, and Cole Harris.

Support from the Strategic Grants and the Research Programmes Divisions of the sshrcc greatly facilitated the work and enabled it to be completed close to schedule. The University of British Columbia provided continuing encouragement, and the University of Toronto Press at several critical moments tangibly enabled the project to proceed. I am grateful to all these agencies and institutions, and to the particular people in them who have been involved with the *Literary History* over the past ten years.

I wish finally to thank the contributors to this volume for their scholarly care, and for taking the time and effort to share with others their sustained interest in literature and ideas.

W.H.N.

Introduction

This volume extends the second edition of Carl F. Klinck's *Literary History
of Canada* to survey the years from 1972 to 1984. At the same time it
redefines the field it surveys, partly by redefining the manner of surveying
it. Literary history, like many other fields of enquiry, has been undergoing
changes in presumptions and methodology, many of which will be apparent
in the chapters that follow. Implicit in Volumes I–III were several attitudes
about literature and authorship: among them, a belief in the progress of art
in Canada, an acceptance of prevailing belletristic definitions of what was
'literary' (conventional genres, history, philosophy), and a reliance on the
notion of individual genius. To a lot of people these ideas have not lost their
appeal. A recurrent notion in this volume, however, is indeterminacy. While
the 1970s generated an extraordinary amount of data, many scholars who
were eager to gather it were also resistant to it, recognizing that all sets of
questions and answers carry limitations. Among other things, such limitations
derive from social biases (such as culture, region, gender, race, age), from
the design of an enquiry itself (selectivity or omissions in the data collected),
from the subjectivity of interpretation, and from the privileging of certain
information by seeking it – rather than pursuing some other topic – in the
first place. Such limited data, ably orchestrated, can nonetheless convince
and persuade. Fascinated by the power of selection and arrangement, many
writers turned their attention to the workings of artifice itself. They questioned
the ability of art to 'represent' the empirical world and challenged empirical
limitations of reality. But that there existed connections between artifice and
the empirical world was not in doubt: the problem was fixedness, whether
of expectation or estimation, which it was the aim of artifice to alter and
undermine. Against this background, literary history shifted its attention from
'factual' discovery to the processes of interpretation, from received standards
of categorization and judgment to an acknowledgment of the biases inherent
in perception and cultural context, from the genius of individual person to
the trends and patterns that characterize a given selection of books, from the

implications of sequential progress to those of disjunction and uncertainty. In the remarks that follow, this introduction focuses on a number of issues that relate to these distinctions: issues involving the structure of Volume IV, the social and political character of the years it surveys and the contexts in which it was itself composed, and the intellectual ramifications of the literary data assembled here.

1

Observing publication trends during the 1970s, the Editorial Board determined that Volume IV of the *Literary History of Canada* could not follow exactly the pattern laid down by its predecessors. There were other genres to attend to, different priorities of subject, the immediacy of the literary experience, and the shifting character of the social framework. Referring more to the social sciences than had previously been possible, Volume IV emphasizes how people were writing and reading traditional literary genres from within several separate kinds of framework, and also recognizes that for a large number of readers the term 'literature' now extends to a variety of less traditional forms of communication. For their part, the chapter writers – all of whom have felt constrained by the restricted amount of space available – have variously addressed changes in methodologies, devised systems of classification, and exercised judgment both by direct statement and through their criteria of selection; they have emphasized books rather than authors, verbal and intellectual structures rather than individuals. Hence this volume becomes a book about patterns of discourse. It charts some of the patterns themselves; it also asks how they elucidate a number of social changes in Canada over twelve years, and how they reveal tensions between prevailing cultural attitudes and various minority views about power and marginality, society and language.

Inevitably, the pressures of size and circumstance have resulted in omissions. The choice of areas to be covered has been influenced by the previous volumes and further determined by practicalities; everyone regrets that it has not been possible to be comprehensive. As an extension of Volumes I–III, this book focuses on anglophone writing, though it does glance from time to time at the plurality of francophone culture in Canada. In doing so, it acknowledges the increasing connections between anglophone and francophone literatures. But the editors have had to omit any extended account of writing in French or the burgeoning literatures in indigenous and 'unofficial' languages. A longer book would have pursued these intercultural parallels and differences in more detail, and also considered such subjects as scholarship in other languages, writings on non-Canadian history (a general field in which over 100 books and monographs were published during these years), and connections between literature and science. Hindsight suggests that more room perhaps should have been found for Canadian linguistics and the philosophy of language study, and for examining connections between literature and art history; these subjects are acknowledged here primarily within the chapters on life-writing, anthropology, and criticism. There are, however, compensations. Departing from the practice of Volumes I–III has meant corresponding extensions of coverage in other directions.

For example, a chapter on translation looks both at historical accomplishments and at the politics and practice of the art. A separate chapter on the short story reflects a growing recognition of the importance of this genre. A chapter on writing for non-traditional media (radio, television, film) reveals not only the distinctive demands of each of these forms but also the degree to which changes in technology have invited writers to reach markedly different audiences. And chapters on the literature of anthropology, political science, and psychology address the intellectual strategies of other forms of communication, stress the disciplinary differences of these avenues of enquiry, and further emphasize the complexity of the social and intellectual framework within which writers write. Each of these new chapters, moreover, surveys the changes in genre or discipline that lie behind practice in the 1970s and 1980s, therefore overlaps with Volumes I–III in some measure and provides a different set of contexts within which to read some of the works those earlier volumes mention. Bruce Trigger, for example, traces the linear developments in anthropology that link present-day practice with nineteenth-century academics, critics, and scientists such as Daniel Wilson and John William Dawson; he also demonstrates the lateral branching that has made contemporary writing in anthropology a voice of historical reassessment – and sometimes (on issues like education and land claims) of social activism.

The focus, however, remains on the immediate rather than the distant past, a perspective which affected the composition and organization of the volume as a whole. Indeed, because of the immediacy of comment, the very notion of 'whole' came into question. The following chapters therefore constitute a plural series of readings, not a single, monolithic version of literary accomplishment during the years 1972–84. The chapter writers, though in contact with each other throughout the preparation of this volume, designed their chapters separately. They devised organizational structures appropriate to their own particular topic *as they saw it*; they made their own informed decisions about what to include, stress, and omit; they expressed their own judgments. For the most part they stressed 'serious' and 'academic' rather than 'popular' literature (though this distinction was in dispute). Not all of their judgments, furthermore, coincide – a degree of indeterminacy is a characteristic of any 'contemporary history.' Hence the arrangement of these chapters (which, like the initial selection of subjects, fell to the editors) may consequently seem arbitrary. Yet there is a pattern. As this is a book of reference, not all readers will read it from cover to cover – but the sequence of chapters constructs a kind of 'narrative' of the years under review, which in turn suggests some of the editorial principles that governed the selection of subjects in the first place. The main intention was to record how a group of commentators perceived the literature of their own time. Inevitably, the flexibility of 'perception' became an issue to contend with, as did the shifting character of 'context.' One answer to indeterminacy was to use statistics; another was to emphasize the notion of interconnection.

This volume begins with the familiar – though the surveys of conventional genres (poetry, fiction, drama) are not altogether conventional in themselves. These chapters give way to chapters on critically less familiar forms (radio and film, for example, and translation) and to discussions of the several ways that critical methodology, imposing shape upon meaning and meaning upon shape, is itself a form of 'translation' – or performance. ('Theatre' is a recurrent metaphor.) The continuity thus begun by the obvious link between stage drama and drama in other media is then extended in the survey of drama written for children. Subsequently, the discussion of other forms of children's literature leads into the commentary on folklore, which in turn leads into the discussions of anthropological, political, and historical literature. These chapters provide contexts against which to read accomplishments in conventional genres; they also open up the definition of literature itself, as the chapter on 'life-writing' makes clear. Positioned between discussions of history and psychology – and referring to diaries, letters, and journals, as well as to biographies and autobiographies – the chapter on life-writing mediates between 'fact' and 'fiction.' It draws on both history and psychology; it sheds light on both. All three chapters share an interest in the verifiability of fact, the fictionality of form, the indeterminacy of motive, the limitations of perception, and the selective interpretation of details. These interconnections construct a kind of paradigm of how to read this book. But they do not impose a single 'meaning' upon it. The running dialogue throughout the book – between 'text' and 'context' – argues for plural possibilities of interpretation. Yet the presumptions and expectations of interpretation are themselves, of course, constructed against a reader's or a writer's experience of a series of historical *events*. And these (being constructed) read as 'fictions': versions of reality, shaped in words, 'stories' shaped by the priorities and preoccupations of a place and time. Because this volume surveys a literature-in-progress, there can be no fixed 'conclusions.' The final chapter is therefore not designed as a formal closure to the book 'as a whole' nor as a capsule guide to an 'entire period.' Instead, it provides yet another angle of vision on the fluid subject of this book – 'writing' – another glimpse of what 'literary communication' meant during the 1970s and 1980s and of how it 'actually' took place.

2

During the early 1970s the Vietnam War continued to affect Canada, in that the nation was commercially if not politically involved in military action; at the same time Canada was perceived as a safe haven by Americans opposed to the war. In 1975, the war drew to a close, but other upheavals took its place as a focus of international political attention. Television cameras made North Americans daily witnesses to them: famine in Mali and Ethiopia, protest against South African apartheid, social unrest in Poland and the Middle East, civil war in Central America, the emergence of a fundamentalist Shi'ite government in Iran. Canadian radio and television interviewers – on programs such as *As It Happens* and *The Journal* – provided direct news links with the participants. Recurrently the media asserted a Canadian perspective on the world; just as often, world events – from peace movements to political violence to the technology of space exploration and satellite communication – touched daily Canadian lives. Everyone, moreover, was living under the shadow of nuclear threat.

Domestically, there occurred another series of social and political changes, from the threat of Quebec secession to the passing of the Constitution Act, which affected the way authors and others perceived their culture. Native rights groups protested land use policies and threats to cultural survival. Ethnic minorities (for example, the Japanese Canadians) asked for recognition, and for resolution to the wrongs they suffered during the 1940s – writers, critics, and historians such as Joy Kogawa, Roy Miki, Ken Adachi, and Roy Kiyooka were part of a protest against social discrimination and the implicit biases of linguistic norms. The politics and economics of gender differences were also at issue: the Women's Movement campaigned for equal rights and equal pay. Regional disparities focused still other social resentments. The boom-and-bust of the oil economy, for instance, briefly moved economic and political power to Alberta, though the forces of centralization were to prove the stronger over the decade as a whole. There were also signs of urban unrest not unlike that which occurred during the 1910s and 1930s. By 1980 the chief domestic problems were unemployment and recession, which in turn fuelled social unrest and latent racism. The high public tolerance, however, for levels of unemployment and inflation that fifteen years earlier would have been deemed insupportable, was but one sign of the growing neo-conservatism of the 1970s and of the apparent end of Keynesian expansionism.

Changes in immigration policy during the 1970s affected the ethnic character of Canada, especially in urban communities. To the waves of immigrants and refugees who had come to Canada during the 1950s and 1960s – from Hungary, Czechoslovakia, and elsewhere – were added an increased number of immigrants of South Asian, East Asian, Caribbean, and southern European origin. The 1985 *Canada Year Book* reported that people from Asia accounted for 2.5 per cent of all immigrants during the period 1945–54, and for 32 per cent of all immigrants since 1970; three-quarters of all Asian-born immigrants, moreover, arrived after 1970; and during the period 1978–81, 43 per cent of immigrants came from Asia, 29.7 per cent from Europe, and between 5 and 10 per cent from each of the following areas: the United States, the Caribbean, and Latin America. The new ethnic mix, the patterns of settlement, the numbers in any particular group and their cultural cohesiveness all affected literature and language. Writers such as Marco Micone, Mary di Michele, Neil Bissoondath, and Rienzi Crusz wrote of the difficulties of living with two cultures. Leon Rooke emigrated from the United States, Jeni Couzyn from South Africa, Marilú Mallet from Chile; they brought with them different kinds of literary training and different perspectives on political reality. Second-language education, moreover, became an issue of even greater magnitude than it had been a decade earlier, compounding existing tensions over the relative precedence of English and French.

To some degree these developments could all be seen as the social ramifications of the 1960s. The generation that was young and active then (it was a larger generation than others, constantly skewing demographic norms) had placed an empirical faith in the coming of the 'Age of Aquarius'; by the late 1970s this idealism simply ran up against the conservatism of suburbia, late parenthood, and middle age. A belief in unflagging progress waned; many rebellions lost their impetus. Natural food fads replaced the drug culture; 'security' replaced 'freedom' as an effective desire. In response to a competitiveness born of numbers, many of those who in the 1960s had 'opted out' were now 'opting in' again. Like the smaller and more conservative generation that followed them, they found they had to compete for jobs and security, and often looked for power by attaching themselves to the social norms that seemed the strongest. These norms were not necessarily Canadian. Economic and cultural nationalism both waned by the 1980s, when American business models and Friedmanite economic principles became for many a political ideology, a program for life. While some writers resisted these trends – among them, several of the writers who had emigrated to Canada from the United States during the Vietnam years and who had become champions of Canada's cultural difference, its need to preserve its distance from American systems – there were others who read North America in another way. To many immigrants from Eastern Europe, for example – among them the novelist Josef Škvorecký – such declarations about distance seemed naive. Of greater importance to them was the larger polarity between East and West, a binary system in which the idea of 'America' (or 'West') was to be embraced, not held apart. Hence the word 'America' came to mean at least two different things. Two systems of rhetoric came into conflict. Two definitions of cultural opportunity came to be seen as antithetical, as mutually exclusive political choices rather than overlapping ones. The distinction fed a climate of confrontation.

While Canadians quarrelled about the idea of America and the value of American alliances, the United States continued directly to affect Canadian economics and attitudes. Many Canadians embarked on American careers – from opening business franchises in the United States to scriptwriting for Hollywood films – and the American economic and political influence in Canada increased as the recession hardened. Some Canadians remained suspicious of American technology, politics, and ownership. George Grant's attacks on what he castigated as the 'liberalism' of technological progress, and Charles Taylor's enthusiasm for a 'Red Tory' tradition, attracted adherents: yet it became Conservative party policy in the 1980s to espouse closer economic ties with the United States. It was as though the 1890s rivalry between George Parkin and Goldwin Smith were being reactivated. In 1887, Sara Jeannette Duncan wrote of the prevalence of American magazines in Canada and opined that if American matters were thus becoming familiar then American methods would shortly follow. The 1980s suggested something of a reversal, partly traceable to the influence of American media: that if American methods were already so familiar, then Canadians would soon start to accept American attitudes as their own.

Whether the media have such control over public judgment remained a disputed question. When sociologists and psychologists investigated the impact of American television on Canadian communities newly exposed to it, their results were not altogether clear. Programming appeared indeed to have a measurable impact on individual attitudes, but the difference between CBC programming and American programming (at least between 1973 and 1975) was of less measurable consequence than was the physical habit of watching television instead of doing other things. *The Impact of Television* (1986), edited by Tannis MacBeth Williams and involving research by herself, Raymond Corteen, Meredith Kimball, and others, argues further that television interferes with the acquisition of reading skills, perpetuates sex-role stereotypes, and increases aggressive behaviour more readily *in cases where the community itself provides no countervailing models*. If parents and the community obviously read and value reading, for example, then it seems children will learn the skill whether they watch television or not; if the community daily acts out alternatives to sex-role stereotyping, then the models on television may be only marginally significant. But the research also suggests that Canadian communities are most ambivalent not on these two issues but when it comes to projecting a message about the acceptability of violence.

Across the country, a recurrent public outcry against television violence and the availability of pornographic magazines and films suggests that many people believed that a connection did exist between media violence and violent behaviour. A widespread tolerance for violence in televised sport, however, and for the more insidious attitudinal violence implicit in racist and sexist stereotyping, does not argue a consistency of attitude. Even some of the protests against violence took violent forms, whether through direct action against booksellers and film rental companies, or in books and films themselves. To the degree that it became publicly acceptable to print obscenities, or to discuss or graphically represent patterns of behaviour formerly deemed 'deviant,' then social and aesthetic norms were both changing. The tolerance of the market governed the availability of products. Yet the primary intent of many aesthetic rebellions was less to titillate than to shock. Films like Anne Claire Poirier's *Mourir à tue-tête* (1979) and the National Film Board Studio D production *Not a Love Story* (1981), for example, used visually horrific images of empirical reality in order to condemn the violence of rape. And the escalation of linguistic and behavioural violence in books was often designed (often unsuccessfully) as a measure of reform. A problem for civil libertarians dealing with 'obscenity' – whether of language, attitude, visual representation, or behaviour – lay in the difficulty of defining the terms: the moral absolutism of many proponents of censorship (who made no distinction between a Margaret Laurence novel and a 'snuff film') was as offensive to them as pornography or media violence was. In a related issue, however, a series of celebrated trials in 1985 argued that the propaganda of race hatred should not be justified by appeals to freedom of speech. One result of these controversies was that books and films worked not merely as the agents of entertainment, information, and reform, but also as the ground on which defences of civil freedoms took place. It might be argued that such issues transcend societies. By the subjects they raise, however, and in their particular manner of dealing with them, the arts and the media both reflect and affect the priorities that a given society attaches to social problems and solutions.

3

To turn to creative writing is to see that political and social events not only affected literary settings and subjects, but also helped modify literary form. In the 1960s, Canadian settings were the norm in Canadian books; the arts were a means of ratifying the social reality. Regional settings carried a similar political function during the 1970s. But as the 1970s advanced, a Canadian setting no longer seemed quite such a self-conscious choice. Canadian writing began to range through space and time as much as it had done in the 1890s and 1900s, and apparently more confidently, with an eye less for referential truth than for the textual effect of artifice and allusion. Canadian historians and political scientists, more extensively than their predecessors, wrote about the world beyond Canada, including studies of Bourbon France, Russian foreign policy in the Balkans, twentieth-century pacifism, the labour movement in Peru, Nazi Germany, and the spontaneous generation controversy in eighteenth- and nineteenth-century science. Canadian novelists, poets, and dramatists wrote of Kepler, Giordano Bruno, eighteenth-century explorers, and Lizzie Borden; they set their works in fourteenth-century Spain, twentieth-century Germany, Chile after the death of Allende, Sri Lanka, Trinidad, and the astral planes of the imagination. Such topics were not unrelated to Canada or to personal experience, but less and less was it seen to be the role of art to validate the culture. Artists repeatedly took it on themselves to probe the limits of power by probing the limits of language. With changes in literary intent came changes in literary form. (Even economists took up the literary strategies of modelling and game theory.) As Canadian writers were influenced by their co-writers from around the world – V.S. Naipaul and Salman Rushdie, Milan Kundera and Umberto Eco, John Gardner and Alice Walker, Nadine Gordimer and Gabriel García Márquez – they shifted further from empirical realism and turned to the postmodern and the surreal. To generalize, these were years of literary protest and literary play, sometimes in the same work.

'Play' took several forms: humour, parody, experimentation with sequence, structure, fantasy, voice, and visual arrangement. It is not an unusual response to social pressure. A sardonic wit frequently allows a writer to observe disparities between reason and behaviour, while providing a defence against despair. Surrealism is a verbal and visual reaction to perceived social chaos. Metaliterary texts are sometimes signs of a flight from social reality into the perceived enclosures of art. In these years language itself became a plane on which to act. But action in art need not imply flight; often writers attempted to deconstruct the social values that conventional language had somehow allowed to seem fixed. Hence the language of play frequently turned into a strategy of protest and reconstruction.

In her chapter on folklore, Edith Fowke refers to the surge of interest in craft and design; this interest, too, reflects an attempt to overturn conventional hierarchies of judgment. Just as conventional criticism, by classifying 'native art' as 'folk custom,' had distinguished it from an implied 'real art,' so had many judgments of 'women's art' been implicitly dismissive. One impact of the showing of Judy Chicago's 'The Dinner Party' in Canada during the early 1980s was to turn this judgment around. Viewers recognized that embroidery (or quilting, or tapestry design) could achieve artistic excellence; it had, moreover, its own aesthetic and sociopolitical implications. In art and writing by women, a dialectic was under way. The language women used and the language used about women particularly came under scrutiny. At the 1983 'Women and Words' conference in Vancouver, women writers attacked the gender hierarchies of language, turned 'history' into 'herstory,' pierced received meanings of words in order to turn the 'subtext' of a literary work into a 'sub-version' of canonical (therefore ideological) judgments, and called for alternatives, options, and a substitute system of values. 'Quand je lis je m'invente' announced the title of Suzanne Lamy's 1984 book. Fantasy was a way of inventing a more acceptable present or of imagining a continuing future; protest was as often as not an attempt to disrupt a reader's passive acceptance of the current rhetoric of social conventions. The former rearranged the language of reality; the latter disputed the fixed reality of language. 'Postmodern' forms of art sometimes brought the two together.

Canadian writers in the 1970s were willing to accept the influence of various literary schools of protest and postmodern play – of feminist theory and South American 'magic realism,' to name two of the most obvious – for several reasons. One was their perceived social relevance; another was the availability of translations; a third relates to the speed of international communication that satellite technology made possible; a fourth has to do with cheaper air fares and the jumbo jet, both of which encouraged personal travel and personal contacts. The situation of Bharati Mukherjee provides an illustrative example. Bengali-born, of Brahmin background, married in the United States to Clark Blaise, resident in Montreal and Toronto until she returned to the United States, unhappy and articulate about Canadian racism, she represents in her own life a variety of cultural influences. During the 1970s she visited China on a tour with Alice Walker and other women writers; her 1985 work *Darkness* acknowledges the influence of Bernard Malamud; when V.S. Naipaul travelled to New York, she interviewed him for *Salmagundi*. Like Margaret Atwood and many others, moreover, she was writer-in-residence at several universities in the United States and Canada and was supported on reading tours by the Canada Council. The literary world, long mobile, now relied on the speed of movement as well. Institutions like Arts Councils and authors' associations encouraged contacts. Events like the PEN conferences, the Amnesty International conference (in which Margaret Atwood was significantly engaged), and Greg Gatenby's Harbourfront festival and program in Toronto brought writers from around the world together for readings and discussions. Inevitably, such contacts influenced the range of experience on which authors came to draw.

The institutions that affect Canadian writers directly include the Canada Council, the government, and the universities. When in the early 1970s

T.H.B. Symons examined the state of Canadian studies in the academies, he found that they enjoyed minimal status both at home and abroad. His AUCC report, *To Know Ourselves* (1975), noted that Canadian literature accounted for only 8 per cent of undergraduate classes in Canadian departments of English. The argument that ensued did not bring about uniform changes, but Canadian literature did acquire a higher academic profile, and by 1985 the Canadian percentage of undergraduate offerings had doubled. Clearer developments took place outside the country. Partly as a result of Symons's recommendations, the Department of External Affairs embarked on a deliberate policy of highlighting Canadian culture abroad: by making Canadian books, films, and performing companies available to overseas audiences, by enabling Canadian writers to travel overseas to read and overseas critics to learn more about Canada, and by encouraging the establishment of Canadian Studies organizations internationally. A Canada Council-sponsored exhibition called *OKanada* opened at the Akademie der Künste in Berlin in 1982. The Council also entered into bilateral literary exchange prizes with Australia, Belgium, and Scotland. Industry, too, began to support the field; Northern Telecom endowed an international prize in Canadian studies. Canadian Studies organizations began in the United Kingdom and the United States, India and Japan, Australia and New Zealand, and several European countries, including Italy, France, Norway, and West Germany. Given access to Canadian writing, overseas critics were quickly enthusiastic. French committees placed Margaret Laurence's *The Stone Angel* on the agrégation examination. Italian and Korean committees nominated Irving Layton for the Nobel Prize (other Canadian writers nominated include Laurence, Škvorecký, and George Faludy). Antonine Maillet's *Pélagie-la-charrette* won the 1979 Prix Goncourt. Courses in Canadian literature proliferated all over the world. Overseas commentators produced many articles and books: from *Canada et canadiens* (1984), an introductory text by Jean-Michel Lacroix and his colleagues at the University of Bordeaux, to Hugh Brody's discussion of the hunting economy and culture of the North, *Maps and Dreams* (1981), to studies of short fiction, Quebec poetry, and Louis Riel.

European theories of genre, sign, and structure notably affected the course of Canadian literature in the 1970s. They were apparent in Quebec before they reached anglophone writing, but in both instances they marked literary composition as well as critical methodology. Often, indeed, writers were themselves critical theorists, anthologists, and editors (Robert Kroetsch with *Boundary 2*, Nicole Brossard with *La nouvelle barre du jour*, to name only two) as well as poets and designers of prose. What this connection further affirms is the academic base of a great deal of contemporary writing. Much writing stemmed from theoretical propositions; much publication was aimed at textbook use. Moreover, while the academic character of writing had certain ramifications regarding style, critical judgment, and audience, it led also to questions about politics and economic priorities. By 1984, there were vocal challenges to the involvement of academia in culture and to the role of government as arts patron. Some people argued that culture, even a national culture, should be surrendered to the exigencies of the marketplace. Those who adopted this position classified art as a commodity; those who defended the engagement between government, writers, and schools, however, identified culture with national independence.

In Quebec, many poets and novelists were directly involved in politics, radio, and television: the poet Gérald Godin, for example, became René Lévesque's Minister of Cultural Communities and Immigration. But academia and journalism have been the more characteristic homes for anglophone creative writers. That more middle-aged writers than younger ones are attached to universities does not argue a revolutionary shift in point of view; it mostly indicates the state of the job market in the 1980s. With few academic positions available, the young either remain unemployed or find different sources of income, or turn to writing mass consumption literature, seeking again to cross the American border. The local market apparently is still not sizable enough to sustain most writers by royalties alone. Instructive, too, is the disparity Brian Harrison noted in 1982: surveying the annual income of all full- and part-time writers who were members of writers' organizations, he found that the median wage that men earned was $21,805, but that the median wage for women was $8,000. The Canadian 'poverty line' for a family of four that year stood at $16,065. Such distinctions are symptomatic of a larger problem. They reflect deep-seated connections between aesthetics and class (and, more generally, between region, ethnicity, and power). They also relate to changes that took place during the 1970s in the structure of state and institutional politics.

4

If the time covered by this volume can be called a 'period' at all, it is in many ways the 'Age' of Trudeau and Lévesque. The lawyer Pierre Elliott Trudeau became Liberal prime minister in 1968 and, except for the short duration of the Conservative government of Joe Clark in 1979–80, he remained in office until his retirement in 1984. (He was succeeded by John Turner, who lost to Brian Mulroney's Conservative party in the election later that year.) The journalist René Lévesque became leader of the Parti Québécois in 1968, took the party to power in 1976, and remained in office in Quebec City until his own retirement in 1985. (He was succeeded by Pierre-Marc Johnson, who lost to Robert Bourassa's Liberals in the election immediately held.) Between Trudeau and Lévesque there existed an ongoing public ten-

plays were accepted as indirect declarations of the masks of identity that whole cultures sometimes wore. Other works – from the feminist politics of Louky Bersianik and the race politics of Dionne Brand to the popular songs of Bryan Adams (serving African famine relief) and Gilles Vigneault ('Gens du pays' becoming a political anthem of modern Quebec) – spoke to the cultural milieu as well as of it.

Publishers also occupied political roles. The journals *Atlantis* and *Room of One's Own* both began in 1975, focusing on women's studies and writing by women; *The Toronto South Asian Review* (est. 1982) drew attention to some of the complexities of multiculturalism in modern Canadian writing; *Canadian Children's Literature* (est. 1975) supported the academic study of writing for children; *The Ontario Indian* (est. 1978) became one of several outlets for sharp and sometimes militant indigenous writers. Workshops (like the one conducted by Maria Campbell, resulting in the 1985 publication of *Achimoona*) directly encouraged Indian and Métis writers. The Women's Press was established in 1972; Press Gang publishers in Vancouver became an all-woman print shop in 1973; the National Film Board established a women's production studio (Studio D) in 1974. Williams-Wallace Publications emerged in Toronto as a voice of black Canadian writers. James Lorimer of Toronto continued to address the economics of class. Hurtig of Edmonton reiterated the cause of cultural nationalism, a commitment that led in 1985 to the publication of 'Alberta's Centennial Gift to the Nation,' the substantial *Canadian Encyclopedia*.

Government agencies – from the Alberta Heritage Fund, which supplied some of the capital for the *Encyclopedia*, to the Canada Council, the national Research Councils, the Ontario Arts Council, and other provincial organizations (though not all provinces had developed sophisticated arts support policies by 1985) – contributed even in the face of economic recession to the continuing vitality of the arts, although there were signs by 1985 of impending cutbacks in levels of support. The arts community had become increasingly vocal in upholding the Canada Council's artistic independence from explicit state direction, and in resisting the more sweeping recommendations of the 1982 Applebaum-Hébert Federal Cultural Policy Review Committee (to the effect that the CBC and the National Film Board should be reduced in size and turned over in some degree to private industry). By early 1986, the CBC was itself floating a plan to Canadianize its programming, to reiterate its initial 1936 mandate by eliminating all American rebroadcasting (a policy which bears on the issues Robert Fothergill raises about script and screenplay writing). The Canada Council's policies during the 1970s, however – as Philip Stratford, Cyndi Zimmerman, Brian Parker, and Frances Frazer variously acknowledge – had clearly both supported and encouraged publication and performance. Direct support for the publication of children's literature, for example, not only attracted a number of writers to this demanding medium, but also enabled a number of publishers to contend with the expenses of illustration and fine quality printing. Direct support for translations brought more into existence (both between English and French, and from other languages into one or the other of these two). And while Murray Schafer complained (in one of the essays he collected in *The Tuning of the World*, 1977) that Canada Council policy was imbalanced, in that it supported musical performance more than musical composition, the latent parallel with drama does not hold. Theatre groups burgeoned, at least during the 1970s; they provided opportunities for Canadian plays to appear before the public, and with more performances there emerged more plays and more playwrights: indeed, Brian Parker notes that more plays were written in Canada during the late 1970s and early 1980s than in all the years before 1972 put together.

In 1978 another event occurred that shaped subsequent literary developments. The Canada Council subdivided, reserving its original name for the institution that supports the creation and performance of the arts (and which therefore draws on artists rather than critics as its peer assessors). A new institution was formed to support scholarly research. Called the Social Sciences and Humanities Research Council of Canada, this institution by the very sequence in its name suggests the priorities of the time. As Table 1 indicates, a growth in membership in scholarly societies (and a growth in the number of societies themselves) reveals the directions of disciplinary expansion, which in turn reflects the general interest in the problems and dimensions of society at large.

Much historical writing is still the preserve of private scholars. (Indeed, SSHRCC programs for the support of research by private scholars recognize the merit of such enterprise; they also constitute an institutional reaction to the number of trained scholars who have been unable to obtain academic employment.) But in this respect, the study of history stands essentially alone. Edith Fowke points to ways in which a subject like folklore is altered when it becomes the object of academic study. Raymond Corteen, Alan Cairns and Douglas Williams, and Bruce Trigger, writing respectively about research literature in psychology, political science, and anthropology, emphasize the degree to which such writing is primarily university-based, its character related to the specialized interests of particular schools. In some cases – psychology, for one – disciplines pride themselves on the freedom from cultural ideology that their 'international' methods allow; but in these instances researchers are nonetheless affected by the character of their own academic training, itself culturally based. These subjects, moreover, influence cultural understanding. Enquiries in a subject like psychology, for example – as in studies of laterality, memory, or imagemaking – will not only serve their immediate disciplinary purpose, but also, over time, affect how readers and

TABLE 1: Membership in selected Canadian learned societies

Society	Founding date	1951	1961	1971	1981
Assn for Can. & Quebec Literatures	1973	–	–	–	123
Assn for Can. Studies	1973	–	–	–	c400
Assn for Can. Theatre History	1976	–	–	–	200
Assn of Can. University Teachers of English	1957	–	171	530	867
Can. Assn for Commonwealth Literature & Language Studies	1972	–	–	–	108
Can. Assn for Irish Studies	1973	–	–	40[4]	180
Can. Assn of Univ. Teachers of French	1958	–	no data	no data	c300
Can. Comparative Literature Assn	1969	–	–	120	253
Can. Historical Assn	1922	800	850	1368	2002
Can. Assn of Geographers	1951	67[1]	390	890	1223
Can. Political Science Assn				1266	1182
Can. Sociology & Anthropology Assn[2]	1972	–	–	707	989
Can. Economics Assn[3]	1967	–	–	1232	1422
Can. Psychological Assn	1939	no data	815	1050	2405

1 Figure is for 1952
2 In CPSA until 1966; officially incorporated 1972
3 In CPSA until 1967
4 Informal group, formed 1969
Source: Canadian Federation for the Humanities, Social Sciences Federation of Canada, & individual societies

critics understand literary processes and the nature of their own connections with art and writing. The influences that shape perception, the biases that interfere with perception, the impact of media rhetoric upon the understanding of events, the accuracy of memory: these issues, for example, at once involve systems of literary communication and the functional workings of the judicial system. There exist connections between academic studies and the culture. (Even Marxist sociology, so influential in Quebec, demonstrates by its open opposition to the capitalist state its connection with the prevailing norm.)

But often there is less direct communication between the disciplines and the lay reader – or among even closely related disciplines themselves – than might be anticipated. Each discipline has developed its own paradigms that it accepts as 'proof,' its own technical language, its own filter as it were on the world. Moreover, this academic fragmentation of perspective attitudinally inhibits any holistic view of the world – interrelating with (though inherently different from) the tangible forms of fragmentation that have appeared in society itself. While comparative and interdisciplinary programs might in some sense be seen as countering this trend towards fragmentation, in another sense they reinforced the relativism implicit in comparison. Scholars in these quarters might seek to blur boundaries, to cross what they saw as the artificial perimeters by which academic categories circumscribe knowledge, but they were also creating new boundaries. At the same time, other scholars were celebrating disciplinary boundary lines as a defence of objectivity. Under these circumstances, when the amount of information multiplies and the technical language of a discipline becomes dense, then the results of research and the very principles that underlie each methodology are no longer easily shared.

5

What is less apparent from the bare statistics in Table 1 is the degree to which disciplinary studies have in turn reinforced the academic character of much literary creation, aligned as it often is with critical and political commentary. Nor does the table spell out the degree to which the structures of support for academic study have also helped shape the kinds of enquiry that have taken place. To turn to these issues is to begin to appreciate how notions of fluidity and fixity ('fiction' and 'fact,' 'wave' and 'particle,' 'motion' and 'place') come together in this volume in different ways to illuminate the complex relations between Canadian literature in the 1970s and 1980s and the society in which it was written.

'Cliometrics,' or statistically based economic and social history, had its proponents during these years. A similar interest among Quebec historians shows the impact of the methodology of Fernand Ouellet and Fernand Dumont. The degree to which television program planners and politicians alike rely on opinion polls in order to shape policy provides further evidence of an abiding reliance on number. Such a quest for exactness strikes literary research in a different way, and Balachandra Rajan rather sorrowfully remarks the conservative character of Canadian scholarship. The predominance of multi-volume projects that collect and reprint (often in the name of textual verification or 'definitive' edition) – rather than, say, theorize and argue – is something he relates to the existence of a program of support which gives priority to such enterprises. Tied up with the accounting need to justify expenditures is a belief that 'answers' take precedence over 'enquiries.' Opposing these presumptions about factuality, however, are the 'process poems' that L.R. Ricou discusses, the changing notions about historiography that Carl Berger addresses, and the critical process that Barry Cameron's chapter self-reflexively articulates. The idea of the 'classic' text implicity removes a work from the manner and time of reading it; the counter-argument declares that all history is read in the present, and that the present, changing, alters values and so alters history.

Research projects now depend largely for their textual accuracy on computer technology. (It is worth noting parenthetically that fourteen of the sixteen chapters in this volume were submitted in word processor format; none of the chapters for Volume III were, a small sign of a large technical revolution that took place between 1973 and 1985.) Computers now allow 'on-line' bibliographical updating, printing, and journal production (Frank Davey's *Swift Current*, a critical 'magazine' available – until 1987 – only by computer, warrants special mention). Computers also control robot manufacturing, and scores of other microengineering techniques that affect medicine, museum display, and visual design (computer analyses of stress, for example, have led to new variety in roof design, taking architecture out of the rectilinear blocks of an earlier industrial age). Literary people are involved. Dave and Ellen Godfrey's company Softwords, affiliated with Press Porcépic, designs computer software programs. Marco Fraticelli designs poems in the shape of computer program flow-charts. Technology has other effects on communication, too: the calculator has revolutionized the speed of computation, the video-cassette recorder has provided an optional system of control over the sequence of events and the use of time, the photocopier has given rise to further attempts to update the copyright act, the satellite has taken telephone and television communication into remote regions. The technology has modified common assumptions about the effects of distance and time.

Paradoxically, this technology on which people have come to rely for speed and accuracy itself depends on theories of indeterminacy. Computers work because quantum mechanics has a practical application. And not only were quantum theories becoming more widely understood during the 1970s and 1980s, they were also in their own right becoming the subject of literature and beginning to take literary form. 'Open endings' and 'discontinuous narrative' are but two signs of verbally crafted indeterminacy – the literary intent of such techniques usually being to disrupt (hence challenge) 'normative' presumptions about the fixity of language, expectation, order, and political structure. When a poet such as Christopher Dewdney further declares that

> The universe exists and does not exist in regular, rapid succession.
> A fixed point in time, or one quantum, stabilizes the continuum, which is how everything happens at once.
>
> ('Points in Time,' 1985)

he has moved from technological practice into cosmology, and indeterminacy has become associated with holistic interpretations of the biological and physical workings of the universe.

Hence in some ways one of the most emblematic events for an understanding of life and literature during the years covered by this volume may well be an experiment involving submolecular physics which took place in Paris in 1932. Called the Aspect Experiment (after its chief researcher, Alain Aspect), it appears to have confirmed theories about quantum uncertainty that were first postulated in the 1930s. When we speak of reality, the experiment suggests, we speak of an illusion created by what we are looking for: we cannot know the position and the speed of a particle simultaneously. While statistical probability provides a basis for predicting likelihood, 'facts' remain susceptible to the bias in the expectations of the beholder and the character of the system of measurement. Moreover, says the Aspect Experiment, the very action of looking at something (a particle, an event) constitutes an interaction or interference with it (a principle long appreciated by poets and anthropologists); consequent change affects not only the 'reality' we see but also the character of the reality enjoyed by other particles or events which collaboratively realign in accordance with the observer's measure, although they do not on the surface appear to have been involved in the interaction at all.

The several reactions to these conclusions raise issues that bear on literature. Some commentators now see in physics a parallel to the mysteries of Eastern religions; some suggest that the sciences have simply caught up at last with the humanities. Some give credence to ideas previously considered the threshold of fantasy, allowing the possibility (a common theme in 1950s science fiction) of there being co-existent alternative worlds, equally real worlds that occupy different dimensions. Some resist all hints at mysticism, and observe that the Aspect Experiment still remains attached to a mechanically imagined universe, offering not so much a 'proof' of alternative worlds as a demonstration of current limits to systems, or quanta, of physical measurement. All these are responses to the indeterminacy of 'fact.' But the relevance of a disputed notion of 'fact' to an interpretation of what history is – or of what we accept that a particular manner of recording history tells us – is more obvious still.

Carl Berger writes that historical methods have changed – not just by giving up the biographical fallacies that equated historical change with the lives of 'Great Men,' nor simply by turning to hitherto unremarked fields (urban, local, social life), but more fundamentally in the way they deal with data. What historians have become aware of is the indeterminacy of the event, the importance of the impact of the historian-observer on it. An analogous process characterizes determinations of the link between literature and society. Public images of the national culture (as represented in the country's institutional structures and in the declared values of its history and art) do not stay the same. When people are alienated from their culture – to the degree that they do not recognize themselves in its institutions or values – they protest, until a system emerges that will accommodate them, and a rhetoric emerges that will describe the new system. This process of re-recognition has long been a part of Canadian cultural experience. Hence the move towards Anglo-Protestant norms (recorded in Volume I of the *Literary History of Canada*) finds a reaction in Volumes II and III, in the years when English-Canadian culture sought a political distinctiveness instead of a racial and religious one. From the 1960s on, there have been further attempts to reshape cultural norms, to accommodate challenges to received codes of region, gender, language, and ethnicity: these are the very protests that recur as themes in this volume. There are current signs that some of the most striking changes to Canadian culture are yet to come. Books such as Edgar Wickberg's *From China to Canada* (1982) and Norman Buchignani's *Continuous Journey* (1985) (they appear in the History of Canada's Peoples series, funded by the Multiculturalism Directorate of the Secretary of State) suggest that these changes may well come from East Asian, South Asian, indigenous, and Caribbean sources, restructuring patterns of dominance, questioning terms of value, and reinvigorating language in action.

There are signs also of a counter-movement, taking several forms. Some people argue the need to preserve existing hierarchies. Some regard the economic and political status quo as the natural order, hence ideologically reactivate Social Darwinism a century after it had appeared to die out. Some people refuse to accept that a holistic view of the world is impossible and declare the desirability of continuing to seek one, or at least to seek usable fictions whereby to deal functionally with reality now. Some resist surrendering their cultural difference to what is usually called the 'mainstream' (the perceived agents of existing power), especially if by doing so they are only mimicking the mainstream power group and not in any tangible way joining it. Coupled with the impulse to preserve differences is a declared need for a persistent historical memory, occasionally to claim a nostalgic attachment to the past, more often to assert a sense of self-respect. A further obvious theme in this volume (one that had not been anticipated) is perhaps a sign of such resistance to historical relativism. Recurrently, writers have been declaring their continuing awareness of fascism and the Holocaust. Books appeared in these years – by Maria Jacobs and Alice Parizeau, for example – on war experiences in the Netherlands and Poland. Other books addressed the sociology of fascism (today as much as at the time of Auschwitz, as in Hugh MacLennan's *Voices in Time*). Irving Abella's history and the television play *Charlie Grant's War* both exposed the extent of Canadian discrimination during World War II. Timothy Findley's novels and Irving Layton's poems probed the attitudinal dimensions of the fascism of violence and power, and called into question various images of order. Margaret Atwood's 1985 novel, *The Handmaid's Tale*, enquired into the fascist dimensions of exclusivity and reconstruction, especially as they affect women and words. Although, in the face of oppressive order, chaos proved for many to be only a mixed blessing, it meant for many others the possibility of the survival of the self. And once preserved, such a sense of identification refuses to surrender its authority over history to the selective memories of subsequent generations. History, in this sense, must be daily relived.

But it still does not constitute the same history for all. As far as the 1970s and 1980s are concerned, historians essentially gave up any fixed notion of the 'whole' society; the whole was inapprehensible, in flux. Criticism, too, edged away from seeing literature as foremost an expression of a single national character. Recent research in psychology called into question a related notion about the wholeness of the self, an idea which bears upon some readings of interrupted literary sequences (whether in poetry or short fiction). It bears, too, upon Linda Hutcheon's treatment of the novel, and underlies all of Shirley Neuman's chapter on the writing of biography and autobiography. Such attitudes do not implicitly deny their own authority; they simply call attention to the shifting limits of knowledge. Extending Volumes I–III of the *Literary History of Canada*, this volume also enters thereby into a dialogue with them and with the versions of the past which they record. At the same time, conscious of its own moment, it waits to be in dialogue with histories yet to come.

For the Editors
W.H. NEW

LITERARY HISTORY OF CANADA
VOLUME IV

Canadian Literature in English

1 Poetry

LAURIE RICOU

In the years after 1972, Canada saw one of its best emerging novelists –
Robert Kroetsch – become one of its most audacious and influential poets,
and one of its best poets – Margaret Atwood – become one of its most
celebrated and successful novelists. While they were crossing genres, Kroetsch
and Atwood also became Canada's least conventional and most readable
critics: Atwood's entertainingly polemical *Survival* (1972) was the most influential critical work in the early 1970s; Kroetsch's avuncular deconstruc-
tionism, collected in *Open Letter* (1983), reflected the shift of interest in the
1980s from national themes to the forms and languages of Canadian writing.
In different ways these two major Canadian poets wrote criticism revealing
how history is a fiction; my own sense that this chapter is more story than
history no doubt reflects this historical context.

Kroetsch's *Seed Catalogue* (1977) is one high point of the story. In this
long poem Kroetsch ponders questions of how to grow (a prairie town, a
prairie history, a prairie poet) and how to grow up, by freely adapting the
language and format of some fifty-year-old seed catalogues he discovered in
Calgary's Glenbow Archives. Kroetsch's choice of form was exemplary: the
seed catalogue was the vital book of the farming people whose existence
depended, literally, on growing seeds. The poet was writing *about* a particular
community's text at the same time as he used the form of that text to shape
his subject. Kroetsch's poem, in turn, seeded many other attempts to make
art of unliterary verbal forms; it incorporated written approximations of the
vernacular – in the winging descriptions of the seeds, in taciturn testimonials
from readers and growers, in scraps of proverb and song. Many of the poem's
precedents are obvious – from *The Prelude* to Pound, Milton to Williams.
Indeed, the poem is a celebration of the other texts it deliberately – or
unconsciously – cites, parodies, distorts, or parrots.[1] Its fortunate fusion of
discourse and subject has made it both a powerful literary model and something of a work of literary criticism: within 'Seed Catalogue' are directions
for reading the poem itself, and thus, by extension, how to recognize other

languages, other voices, other structures in the Canadian poetry which precedes and follows it:

> This is a prairie road.
> This road is the shortest distance
> between nowhere and nowhere.
> This road is a poem.

The story of Canadian poetry since 1972 obviously does not begin and
end with Kroetsch and Atwood. 'When a billion people start writing,' David
McFadden notes of his own work, and of the proliferation of poets, 'someone
is bound to write something like this.'[2] Rather than list titles, I will concentrate on relatively few books which seem essential to an understanding of
the forms which poetry has taken during the 1970s and early 1980s, and
which might establish a context for reading many talented poets whose work
will not fit.

Kroetsch's description of his ideal poem as 'the shortest distance / between
nowhere and nowhere' defines both the short poem (the compact closed lyric),
and the long poem (the inclusive open epic), the forms whose dialectic
animated the history of poetry in this period. The 'shortest' poem demands
precision and exactness of language; but from 'nowhere to nowhere' describes
the aspiration of the contemporary long poem, the poem which speaks un-
endingly from birth to death. The definitive poem is at once a catalogue and
a seed; according to Kroetsch's poetic, genres blur. Atwood's and Kroetsch's
alternating from poem to novel is a small reminder of the extent to which,
in the decade after *Survival*, writers questioned conventional definitions of
genre and challenged received critical terminology.

Still, when everywhere closure, containment, and focus were on the defensive, Atwood continued to write with the most elegant control. She seemed
to allude to her peers in her story 'Loulou,' when the title character discovers
herself accidentally 'mixed up with the poets ... After the first one, the others
seemed to follow along naturally, almost as if they were tied onto each other
in a long line with a piece of string.' Despite the powerful influence of her
book-length *Journals of Susanna Moodie* (1970), Atwood refused to get mixed
up with the long line of poets trying to write the least conclusive, the most
inevitably *continuing* poem. But her own short poems continued to suggest
trends. *You Are Happy* (1974) and *Two-Headed Poems* (1978), in particular,
suggested that Canadian poets were becoming a little tired of the self, were
searching – as Atwood does in several poems (eg, 'Torture'), reflecting her
commitment to the work of Amnesty International – for less narrowly national
subjects. At the same time many readers noticed Atwood's poetry mellowing

towards domestic anecdote, particularly in poems to and about her daughter, such as ''You Begin' about a child's use of colour and words.

Atwood's subject-matter and Kroetsch's cataloguing of verbal forms suggest that the 1970s and early 1980s were essentially a period of consolidation. Canadian poetry seemed to be assimilating and promoting the experiments launched in the more frenzied 1960s. The poets who had emerged in the 1960s grew older. George Bowering, Daphne Marlatt, bpNichol, and bill bissett were *established* by the publication of retrospective selections intended primarily for the classroom. Many older poets who had seemed to fall silent, such as A.G. Bailey, R.G. Everson, and Robert Finch, reappeared. Consolidation of the work of senior poets – in collected editions from Earle Birney, Dorothy Livesay, F.R. Scott, Ralph Gustafson, Raymond Souster, Fred Cogswell, Robin Skelton, Douglas Lochhead, and in major Selected Poems from James Reaney, Eli Mandel, and Phyllis Webb – was the culmination of careers extending four decades and more. Poets barely at midcareer, such as Atwood and Dennis Lee, joined their older colleagues in having their papers housed in major public archives.

The establishment of writing which fifteen years earlier had been exceedingly marginal signalled not so much a change in the poets as a change in readers and publishers. Again, Kroetsch's example is instructive: he made readers receptive to postmodernism by publishing his letters in *Boundary 2* (1975) and his journals in *The 'Crow' Journals* (1980); he committed himself to many communities of writers and readers – in founding the periodical *Dandelion* in Calgary, in enthusiastically supporting NeWest Press and Turnstone Press, or in the more unlikely role of *éminence*/tease at a conference on writing in British Columbia ('the coast is only a line,' Simon Fraser University, 1981). Although highly visible, Kroetsch's activity was not unique. Eli Mandel published his travel journals in *Life Sentence* (1981); Bowering and Nichol wrote more essays of simplified explication. Poets gained, or took, more control over the criticism and editing of their own work.

Content and production grew closer together as the decentralization of publishing, which George Woodcock described in the *Literary History of Canada*, Volume III, became more pronounced in the 1970s. Major publishers either disappeared or concentrated more intensely on the marketplace. This shift affected poetry more than any other genre. More small presses were founded to publish more poetry chapbooks by local poets. Gradually such presses broadened their scope, first to poets beyond the local community, then to anthologies, and eventually to fiction and non-fiction. In most cases, such presses were also able to attract financial support (however limited) from provincial cultural ministries, as well as from federal bodies. The decentralization of economic power to the provinces, which followed on the OPEC oil crisis of the mid-1970s, led not only to a demand for more decentralization of political power, but, eventually, to a recognition of the merits of regional cultural definition. This trend was particularly pronounced on the prairies, where Coteau Books, Thistledown, NeWest, and Longspoon – to mention only the most prominent – grew from nothing to become major forces in poetry publishing. Kroetsch's *Seed Catalogue* provides a typical history. Turnstone Press in Winnipeg, then just emerging, published it; the format was spacious and handsome, with Kroetsch's text printed in beige over a blue and green reproduction of the source text. Turnstone went on to publish over fifty books by 1985, vigorously promoting poetry from all regions of the country, while retaining its enthusiasm for the prairie twang. The new publishing houses were at the centre of an enthusiastic interest in regional cultures. The intimacy of the regional communities of poets – however limiting they might be – seemed essential to a clarifying of purpose: within them poets listened for differences in dialect, and developed literary forms, which could claim to be rooted in the specific locale.

The pronounced regionalism of poetry, and poetry publishing, was itself a further sign of retrenchment. Poetry developed in parallel to what Linda Hutcheon describes (in Chapter 3) as historiographic metafiction: poetry whose subject is its own language and the mechanics of its own writing, having become almost orthodox, looked to combine with a poetry of place, historical document, and the anecdotes of daily routine. Jon Whyte's *Homage, Henry Kelsey* (1981), Dennis Cooley's *Bloody Jack* (1984), and the contrast between the early books of bpNichol's *Martyrology* and *Book 5* (1982) all illustrate the tendency: within an indeterminate genre, using an indeterminate language, articulated by an illusory self, the poet turns to autobiographical or documentary detail to give the inward spiral some sense of authenticity in the external world.

Many small local publishers began by fostering regional consciousness. In 1980 Breakwater Books in Newfoundland launched a series introducing 'Canada's Atlantic Poets'; Square Deal Press focused on the poets of Prince Edward Island; Lesley Choyce developed Pottersfield Portfolio to promote Atlantic writing especially in Nova Scotia. At the end of 1982 Fred Cogswell, whose prodigious efforts had encouraged so many young poets, retired from editing Fiddlehead Poetry Books. *Fiddlehead* magazine, and Fiddlehead/Goose Lane Editions, under the editorship of Peter Thomas, emerged, redesigned, renewed, and with an even more distinct turn of attention towards the Atlantic region. At the other end of the country presses such as Sono Nis and Oolichan Books demonstrated the same commitment to developing poetry in their own region. The energy of Montreal as a recurring centre of Canadian poetry has always come from the advantage of *two* poetries, two literatures evolving side by side. Ken Norris's Véhicule Press was the most visible force in a major, broadly based revival of English-language poetry in the Montreal region; Guernica Editions gave particular attention to translations, and to work in other languages (especially Italian) which bridge the two official languages, publishing some bilingual editions with the support of the Quebec Ministry of Cultural Affairs.

The renewed importance of Montreal indicated that the search for distinctive language and forms was most pronounced where compelled by concerns of gender rather than of region. The attempt to articulate women's concerns and perspectives was undoubtedly the most exciting because it embraced international and continental movements, and because, with these as currency, it sought to join the French- and English-language poets – Daphne Marlatt and Nicole Brossard, for example – with a common political purpose rarely seen in Canadian culture. Continental literary theory has been assimilated by many Canadian poets, and has become a key to understanding them. Yet in the mid-1980s the understanding continued to be slow in coming. Poetry continued to suffer, in comparison with prose fiction, by the very slight amount of criticism devoted to it. Given the Derridean dance of a Nichol or Whyte, a reader is especially aware of the necessity of intelligent criticism, the need to learn new ways of reading. A good reader of contemporary Canadian poetry often needs not only critical theory, but also immersion in anthropology, geology, linguistics, and computer science.

But the trend to a hermetic non-referential poetry, however strong by the early 1980s, was still found in a small minority. The dominance of open verse, the verse of spoken commentary as Munro Beattie described it in the *Literary History of Canada*, Volume II, in the tradition of Whitman, Pound, and Williams, became still more pronounced. This form might also be discovered – prodded and parodied – in Kroetsch's definition of poetry. His phrase, 'This is a prairie road,' implies a speaking voice, since there is no antecedent for the demonstrative pronoun. The poem repeats the bland copula verb three times in the same syntactical structure. The lyric is constantly curbed by the subject-verb-object deliberateness of prose. In 'Seed Catalogue' this tension is vital: the associative resonances set off by the names of flowers must be read into the most banal of kitchen chatter. But, more generally, this kind of poetry is dominant (in numbers of poems published) because it is so relatively easy to write, so relatively easy to get away with. In the short poem, the prose syntax encourages faddishness without necessarily requiring felicity; in the long poem, based on the same line, it encourages accumulation without necessarily requiring selectivity or organization.

PROSE LYRIC

The 'prose lyric' is the overwhelmingly dominant convention of contemporary Canadian poetry (the publication of Al Purdy's *Cariboo Horses* in 1965 established its dominance), as it is of contemporary poetry generally. This useful term apparently originates with Stanley Plumly as a description of 'the intersection of the flexibility of the free verse rhythm with the strategy of storytelling ... a form corrupt enough to speak flat out in sentences yet pure enough to sustain the intensity, if not the integrity, of the line.'³ In a period of rampant genre-blur, accelerated by the attractiveness of a Derridean philosophy of the indeterminacy of literary texts, this massive category provides a ground against which to describe the various features of poetry in Canada.

Because the prose lyric is relatively easy to practise competently, such poetry proliferated. Speaking flat out in sentences poses problems beyond mere massive accumulation of poems: a lack of selectivity, a blurring of significances between experiences, a diffident and understated cynicism, and a general lack of any sense of an active persona or speaker. Merely using contractions to suggest conversation, or restricting the line to two words or three or four syllables will not, on its own, make poetry. Hundreds of books published between 1973 and 1984 fell lazily into the category of prose lyric.

The prose lyric's attempt at the naturalness of conversation implies no prosody, no literary allusion, no figurative language. Meaning and feeling are carried by the subject as seen through a transparent language. The strategy demands extraordinary skill with repetition, lining, abbreviation, and punctuation. Such careful attention in Fred Wah's *Tree* (1972) and *Among* (1972) invests unexpected levels of significance in the generalized and commonplace vocabulary of place; more radically, in Wah's attempt to 'translate' Indian rock paintings in *Pictograms from the Interior of BC* (1975), he isolates the word, and arrangements of words, as picture. Too often, the prose lyric merely speaks 'flat out,' without the 'intensity' gained through severe honing. But in the best examples, the colour of speech and the commitment to the clear communication of prose invest the prose lyric with novelty and the energy of lives being lived.

Al Purdy continued to publish at better than a book-a-year pace through the early 1980s; his two retrospective collections, *Being Alive* (1978) and *Bursting into Song* (1982), and two vigorous collections of new poems, *The Stone Bird* (1981) and *Piling Blood* (1984), encompassed the work which has had more influence on contemporary Canadian poetry than that of any other Canadian writer. His poetry has, for example, significantly affected the subjects and vernacular methods of Atwood and Kroetsch, and is more popularly accessible than their poetry. Purdy himself insists on the value of the prose lyric: 'I'd prefer to be understood with a minimum of mental strain by people as intelligent or more so than myself. I'd like them to hear the poem aloud when they read it on the page.'⁴ Yet Purdy is so 'sideways-on to the big events' ('Mantis,' *The Stone Bird*), that it would be hard to *mimic* his voice or perception. His influence is more general and oblique: he made it possible for a generation of younger poets (to whom he has been an inspiration, and often a personal friend) to relax in their poems, to make their personal pasts and their doubts part of the subject and procedure of their poems. He has shown many younger poets the poetry in their most habitual experiences, and the life and meaning in their national and personal histories. Here is Purdy, for example, telling us what he did on 'May 23, 1980':

> I'd been driving all day
> arrived home around 6 p.m.
> got something to eat and slept an hour
> then I went outside
> and you know
> – the whole world smells of lilacs
> the whole damn world

This unpromising beginning leads to a poignant half-remembering of a 'girl with violet eyes' at 'some kind of party,' through Purdy's usual self-depre-cation, to a rather melancholy insistence on the world's beauty, which the aging poet still wants to celebrate. This is far from Purdy's best poem, but its sense of imagery (shading from lilac to violet) and its self-reflexiveness (a poem which doggedly lists the incidents of a daily tedium becomes a study of an obsession with lists) are the more striking for their being discovered in the naiveté of subdued and disorganized talking. The way Purdy combines present and past anecdote – his taciturn hesitation, the dashes, the interrup-tions, the digressions, the groping repetitions – give continuous expression to the flux of experience in which the speaker is caught.

Purdy uses the parentheses, and circlings, and hesitations of speech to signify the movement of a mind struggling. Imagistic tension lies beneath the apparent randomness: Purdy's prose lyric is an effective combination of talk and song. Patrick Lane's work shows the same virtue although his poetry inclines considerably more to narrative. Lane has published eight volumes since 1973, of which the most comprehensive is *Poems: New and Selected* (1978), the volume which established Lane by winning the Governor Gen-eral's Award. Anecdote, especially its political implications, is the key to Lane's poems. 'The Hustler,' which first appeared in *Unborn Things: South American Poems* (1975), describes a bus driver who, about to descend into a three-thousand-foot gorge, seeks coins from the passengers to be offered at a roadside shrine. The pleasure of such anecdotal poetry lies, first, in the characteristic turn of incident at the end, the reader's sense of sharing in a discovery: 'I relax because I saw him as he knelt there / ... pour the collected *sucres* in his pocket.' Again, as in Purdy, the prose narrative is enriched by a nearly unnoticed compact structure of images, from 'rainbow' and 'gorge' to Mary's 'beatific head' and the 'endless abyss.' Exploitation is entangled with humility, pettiness with spirituality. Many of Lane's later poems in, for example, *The Measure* (1980), turn to a shorter line, and a near-imagism, but his strongest poetry lies in the wonder of the story, which is compelling on first reading and is then extended or ironically complicated by the associations of his imagery.

Purdy and Lane are the most memorable of the poets working in the tradition established and developed by William Carlos Williams's principal representative in Canada, Raymond Souster. It is a tradition maintained, in various registers, by Milton Acorn's Marxist-inspired outcries on behalf of the powerless, John Newlove's meditations on history in place, Elizabeth Brewster's deftly naive diary-poems, Glen Sorestad's pub poems, Pier Giorgio Di Cicco's family narratives, and Don Coles's recognizing in photographs, statues, and painting a way of writing. Souster's own single-minded pursuit of the most demotic language, and his framing of the most banal incident, found handsome tribute in a five-volume set of his *Collected Poems* (1980–4) from Oberon Press. No writer in Canada has been more devoted, in method or in mind, to the significance of the particular fleeting moment, especially where that moment reveals a social or economic injustice. Yet in so determinedly denying the metaphorical or aural elements of language, Souster risks the tedium of an undifferentiated poetry – poems claiming to use the voices of various characters seem to be in the same language as those spoken directly by the observing poet, and the 'turn' at the end of most of his newer poetry more often seems gratuitous than focusing, since it seldom forces the reader to reassess the language of the poem. In *Jubilee of Death* (1984), perhaps himself sensing the limitation of his favourite form, Souster wrote a book-length sequence, in multiple voices, about Canada's own Gallipoli, at Dieppe.

In the prose lyric, either the narrative has to be compelling in its own right (as in Lane), or the lyric side of the poem must reveal a significance where none might otherwise lie (as in Purdy). Tom Wayman, probably the ultimate referential poet in Canada, would incline to the former tendency: 'What I try to do,' he explains in an afterword to *A Planet Mostly Sea* (1979), 'is to present as accurately as possible the conditions and quality of our contemporary life.' Wayman's passion has been to use poetry's absence of profit motive as a passage to examining and celebrating the world of daily work. The best of his poetry lies not in the occasional metaphorical resonance, nor in the sense of tedium conveyed in ballad forms, but in his recording of the dialogue on the job. 'Asphalt Hours, Asphalt Air' in *A Planet Mostly Sea* is a longer poem composed of the scraps of conversation, the intriguing parts of stories, which bind workers one to another. Wayman's strength is so obviously in dialogue, in speech, in the poem as a little play, that he even makes a character of himself, telling stories and fantasizing about himself: 'The day after Wayman got the Nobel prize / he discovered the problem was still there: / how good are his poems?' (*The Nobel Prize Acceptance Speech*, 1981). Poetry to Wayman is simply a form of talking: *Money and Rain: Tom Wayman Live!* (1975) has the format of a public reading, where the talky introductions to the poems hold equal status with the talking poems. As talker Wayman is almost always a pleasure to listen to, varied, committed, and humorous.

George Bowering's entertaining introduction to David McFadden's *My Body Was Eaten by Dogs: Selected Poems* (1981) describes the author as a 'comic metaphysician.' Bowering's most perceptive comment about McFadden is his riddling reference to the importance of the word 'and.' McFadden's favouring of 'and' in his later work, and in his long poems, marks his long, loping line, the going-on of his conversation, the filling of the silence while he is thinking; McFadden does not want to read significances, but to add on details. A poem such as 'Border Skirmish,' which describes his wife's attempt to get change for a laundromat from a McDonald's at 7:30 in the morning, is a delightful case in point. McFadden uses the understated weariness of the prose lyric as humorous comment, easy to read, wryly entertaining, politics with tongue in cheek.

Eugene McNamara seemed to be more the Robert Frost of the prose lyric in Canada. Many of his poems recount family anecdotes and banal incidents from the daily routine, often with a clear sense of message, or 'moral.' Poems such as 'Last Seen' in *Diving for the Body* (1974), or 'Airport Dreams' from *Forcing the Field* (1981), typified his observations made memorable by a resonant or witty sense of closure. The same control appeared in R.E. Rashley's delicate anecdotes of prairie life in *Rock Painter* (1978), and in William Bauer's fine sense of humorous dialogue in *The Terrible Word* (1978).

Purdy's impact surfaces repeatedly. Peter Trower, west coast logging poet, is Purdy's contemporary and protégé. The ornateness and hyperbole of his most representative volume, *Ragged Horizons* (1978), might at first glance be thought to separate him from his model. Yet the blunderingly mixed metaphors of a poem like 'Grease for the Wheels of Winter' are not so much a flaw as the signature of the voice of a logger, with a schoolboy's memory of Keats and Shelley, trying to be a beer parlour balladeer. Peter Christensen followed a similar approach to the poetry of the workers' dialect in *Rig Talk* (1981). And Gordon Turner, in *No Country for White Men* (1979), showed both the strengths and weaknesses of Purdy's inspiration; 'Bear-shit in the Berry Patch' has a documentary frankness, and, in its parody of Dylan Thomas, a welcome self-burlesque of the metamorphosis of the excremental, despite a disappointing ending. Purdy's influence, that is, seems to extend to subject-matter as well as to voice and form. Jim Green's *North Book* (1976) might be a rather spare version of Purdy's interest in the Inuit, and Brian Brett's *Fossil Ground at Phantom Creek* (1976) echoes Purdy's sensitivity to archeology, to the immediacy of the layerings of history and pre-history. Probings of family and community history, often among cultures uniquely different from the puritan, loyalist, Anglo-Saxon mainstream of Belleville, also take impetus from Purdy. Leona Gom concentrated on her Peace River family, Kristjana Gunnars explored her Icelandic heritage, Mary di Michele chronicled her Italian family, and Gregory M. Cook traced the lineaments of Nova Scotia communities.

Among the younger poets, the prose lyric can often seem the tediously predictable orthodoxy. But Eva Tihanyi can be elegantly simple and shrewd in *Prophecies: Near the Speed of Light* (1984). Gerry Shikatani follows the sparer imagistic side of the prose lyric in *A Sparrow's Food: Poems 1971–82* (1984). David Donnell's *Settlements* (1983) uses the longer line with dry humour and witty self-control. Peter van Toorn's *Mountain Tea* (1984) is zesty and inventive: his polyphonic poems remind one strongly of Wayman's method, especially in his enthusiasm for the vernacular of the workplace.

No doubt the prose lyric's combination of a naive perspective and crude talking makes it particularly attractive to contemporary Canadian poets. Alden Nowlan, who died in 1983, although sometimes described as essentially a Maritime regionalist, seems on the strength of books such as *I'm a Stranger Here Myself* (1975) – the title marks his uneasily innocent tone – more of a personal and domestic poet. Nowlan is a sensitive reporter of commonplace incidents, though a sense of wonder or a feeling for the magical play of words, either of which might complement his innocent stance, seldom has prominence. Sid Marty's *Headwaters* (1973) assumed a cruder aspect of talking, to narrate the life of climber, park warden, trail rider, labourer, and lover in the Rocky Mountains. The stories are compelling, and Marty, not surprisingly, had greater success as a prose writer. The prose lyric cannot depend merely on imitating the wandering banality of casual speech. The audience listens for an accompanying sensitivity to the aural echoes within words, as in the best of Fred Candelaria's *Foraging* (1979), or for the metaphorically suggestive verb, or the carefully chosen sound image, which extends the colloquial voice of Stephen Hume's *Signs Against an Empty Sky* (1980).

The influence of Al Purdy's colloquialism and love of story is perhaps best summed up in the poetry of Dale Zieroth. And Zieroth is memorable because he has avoided publishing too quickly the poems which especially seem to multiply in this form. First known as a prairie poet, on the basis of his simply told memories of childhood experience in *Clearing* (1973), Zieroth writes mainly what George Woodcock called 'geopoems' in a quiet, nostalgic tone: the geopoem begins with a careful description of a landscape and shifts to a personal response.[5] In *Mid-River* (1981), Zieroth's landscape changes to the Columbia Valley near Invermere. Here we find more attention to multiplying metaphors and more sense of assonance and alliteration. If his language is still relatively limited in the possibilities it calls up, his sense of a taut narrative line (particularly in some perceptive anecdotes about his growing daughter), feathered at its ends by lyric sensitivity, makes Zieroth one of the most satisfying of the prose lyricists, precisely because he is so carefully unspectacular.

NEO-SURREALISM

Wired up at the ankles and one wrist,
a wet probe rolling over my skin,
I see my heart on a screen
like a rubber ball or a soft fig, but larger,
enclosing a tentative double flutter,
the rhythm of someone out of breath
but trying to speak anyway; two valves opening
and shutting like damp wings
unfurling from a grey pupa.

(Margaret Atwood, 'Heart Test with an Echo Chamber')

Anyone having echo electrocardiography might see her 'heart on a screen,' might even use the simile 'like a rubber ball' to describe the image. But adding 'or a soft fig' to the analogy, and then abruptly seeing the heart as emerging butterfly (or, at least, as its disembodied 'damp wings') bumps the reader from potentially recognizable experience to squirming disorientation. In reporting, almost journalistically, on a 'Heart Test with an Echo Chamber,' in *Interlunar* (1984), Margaret Atwood at first makes the connections metonymically: staring at the screen she recognizes the 'heart as television,' and even – presumably because the test takes place in the afternoon – as 'softcore addiction' or soap opera's 'melodrama.' But when the image appears as a 'slice of textbook geology,' then as 'a glowing stellar / cloud' the reader begins to lose track of the sequence of associations. And the immediate turn from the cosmic zone to the orchard, where the heart is 'A pear / made of smoke and about to rot,' is as nightmarish as it is ineffable. The objectivity of reportage reaches an extreme when the speaker departs through the 'tiled corridors' with her heart in her hand: synecdoche creates a vision of the dead callousness of man and world. But apostrophe ends the poem – tone changes as abruptly as analogy – and the heart addressed ponders the communicating ability of the speaking voice itself.

Such a poem is the essence of neo-surrealism, a type of poetry closely linked with the prose lyric (and, at the edges, as is usual with literary taxonomy, indistinguishable from it). Often the speaking voice, and the spoken story, are essential to the neo-surrealist's effect: the flatness of a voice apparently unaffected by the most bizarre collisions of imagery is a key strategy, and one which differentiates the neo-surrealist from the surrealist, whose revolutionary claims lie in an overt immersion in the world of madness, dream, and the irrational.

Fundamental to the form, as Paul Zweig defines it, is 'an imagery of disparate realities; it proceeds by leaps and breaks in the logic of perception.' But, in contrast to the careless freedom of the original surrealists, the incoherent imagery of the neo-surrealist is contained by 'transitions [which] are artful, almost mannered.' Whereas the prose lyric so often aspires to an individuality of voice, the typical surrealist tone seems anonymous: it 'avoids giving any sense of personality, since what is being written belongs to the flow of pure chance, not to the needs and feelings of a "self".' The surrealist attempt to convey, in Zweig's phrase, the sense that the poems 'come from no place, and mean nothing,' indicates another way in which Kroetsch's prairie road describes contemporary poetry.[6]

Paradoxically, the more exaggerated such anonymity becomes, the more likely the personality of the playful poet is to assert itself. As Alan Williamson suggests, a reaction against the intricately logical tropes celebrated by the New Criticism results in a 'parody of imagination itself.'[7] In other words, what Robert Pinsky calls the 'dead-pan fantasy' of the neo-surrealist promotes the very distinctive persona (witness Atwood) it seeks to hide or obscure.[8] The combination of bizarre collisions of imagery and a seemingly uninvolved pedestrian presentation describes a convention of contemporary poetry perhaps even more attractive to the apprentice than the prose lyric because it allows the poet to have it both ways, on a whim. The convention is still clearer in Pinsky's recognition that, within the wildly leaping imagery, lies a peculiarly persistent cluster: ' "silence" and "light" and "water" and "breath" … flowing, particulate substances, shapeless and pure and, most of all, tacit.' The entrenchment of the neo-surrealist convention is further evidence of the consolidation of the 1970s and 1980s. The most radically disruptive impulses of surrealism are somehow domesticated, and what seemed exploratory in Atwood's *The Circle Game* (1966) came by the mid-1980s to seem often either nostalgic or parodic primitivism. At least in others: 'Heart Test with an Echo Chamber' shows the continuing novelty potential in the form.

The attractiveness of Atwood's surrealism is that the situation of her poems is at once so bizarre and so logical. 'Tricks with Mirrors,' one of her most celebrated poems from *You Are Happy* (1974), depends on a limpid syntax, and simple diction, to enumerate the characteristics of mirrors in a 'used / furniture warehouse.' On the one hand, the poem is filled with the blandest of declarative statements: 'There's a nail in the back // to hang it with.' On the other hand, an earlier analogy, 'Mirrors / are the perfect lovers,' offers the grotesque leap beyond rational discourse to a murder scene, or to visions of men and women walking about with nails protruding from the bases of their necks. The title suite from *Two-Headed Poems* finds the two heads of Siamese twins speaking singly, and together, in the most unaffected, commonplace language. The key to Atwood's disconcerting dualism – ordinary freakishness – seems to be her shrewd use of the open verse line, at once enjambed, and yet self-contained. The great majority of Atwood's lines can stand on their own as discrete units of meaning, yet they also typically run on from line to line. Thus, the poet builds a duplicity into her syntax which allows both the ordinary sequential movement and the unexpected juxtaposition of fantastic images.

Atwood is at one extreme of the neo-surrealist form, precisely because her imagery, however bizarre on one level, has a metonymic logic. But Atwood's prominence has, no doubt, contributed to the widespread taste for the neo-surrealist form. The more accomplished of the writers in this form include poets both new and well established. Anne Szumigalski, who has enthusiastically tutored a growing community of young poets in Saskatchewan, made her reputation with *Woman Reading in Bath* (1974); her poems typically begin with the abrupt narrative of domestic experience which turns and descends into unconscious netherworld. In 'Beyond the Alpha Screen' 'Mildred and my aunt' are touring aboard a glass-bottomed boat, when Mildred cuts through the glass 'with her fingernails': 'in she dived / into a forest of seaweeds' to end as 'bones' – yet, consistent with the detached tone which masks such a bizarre turn, the aunt continues to take home movies and exclaim the clichés of tourist delight. George McWhirter published a sequence of documentary lyrics on ship-building in his native Ulster, *Queen of the Sea* (1976); its strength lies not in documentary but in what could be called its *low* surrealist element. McWhirter's typical ploy is to contain the bizarre leap of imagery in a metaphor, or, more usually, a simile; the hair of children seen playing by a lake is 'White as spray / cut beneath a bowl of light' ('Odysseus at Sproat Lake'). Three of the four images, here, are conventional for the low surrealist; white, spray, and light are indeterminate images, and at the end of the poem work to blur distinctions, to diffuse rather than to give the definite outlines we associate with the imagist poem, or with the modernist revival of metaphysical wit. McWhirter, however, hints at a move away from this sort of simile in the sequence 'Training in the Language,' a series of poems on immigrants finding a new home in the language of Canada. Here McWhirter follows the trend to metalinguistic approaches; poetry about his own language reveals the varied languages within Canadian English.

Susan Glickman is a younger poet who made an impressive debut in the

surrealist mode in *Complicity* (1983), a book whose epigraph, equating relationships to ambiguity, summarizes a familiar stance. 'After Such Pleasure'
shows Glickman's usual approach: the poem begins as nominalist reportage,
naming a familiar surrounding, then drifts into a questioning, then resolves
itself by exclaiming a surreal displacement of the earlier images. 'Living
Alone' reveals the bemused profundity Glickman draws out of the genre as
it moves from a catalogue to a cool internal emptiness; 'You wake up dreaming you're asleep in the fridge, / there's so much white space beside you.'
Glickman dedicates a poem to Roo Borson and thus associates herself with
a poet whose reputation grew quickly after the publication of *A Sad Device*
(1981). Borson is more inclined to landscapes than is Glickman or Atwood,
as the sensitively shaped sequence *Rain* (1980) showed. Indeed, rain and
light and wind and the colours of sky figure in much of Borson's work, as
she moves sensitively in each poem from images of landscape (turned askew,
pushed beyond ordinary sensory perception, usually by means of simile) to
near-metaphysical pondering. Lorna (Uher) Crozier, especially in *Crow's Black
Joy* (1978) and *The Weather* (1983), bent a supple prose to fuse sexual
politics, an edge of the comic, and the darknesses just beneath the simple
lines of the prairie. Paulette Jiles did something similar with the Arctic in
Celestial Navigation (1984).

Among the hundreds of quests for the irrational knowledge buried in the
surrealist form, lie, of course, large variations in method. Marilyn Bowering's
poetry has a vaguely sinister mythic tenor, discovered in syntactic leaps which
leave one unsure what subject is attached to a given pronoun. Bowering's
images scream to be read symbolically because there is no referential or
literal context into which to place them. *The Killing Room* (1977), therefore,
is a more satisfying collection than her later books, where the poems are so
speakerless, and so placeless. M. Travis Lane's title *Homecoming: Narrative
Poems* (1977) suggests that the surreal vision needs some beginning in locale
and story, yet her use of the term 'narrative' seems almost self-mocking, so
slight is its trace in poems which 'look with mind into the mind' ('Letter').
Jeni Couzyn in *Life by Drowning* (1983), a distillation of four earlier volumes,
prefers a three-line stanza and loose, more lengthy lines to create brutally
memorable surrealist essays, often strongly feminist or satirical; the numbing
grotesqueries of a poem such as 'Preparation of Human Pie' often overwhelm
the subtler effects of Couzyn's tenderer poems. Don Domanski's *The Cape
Breton Book of the Dead* (1975) used the abrupt breaks of a very short line
to surprise the witches and wolves of his native island.

The fashion for neo-surrealism is perhaps nowhere more evident than in
the metaphor of the poet-as-shaman which has dominated recent poetry in
Canada. Tom Marshall, indeed, in *The White City* (1976) classifies all Canadians
as 'fanatics' or 'secular shaman[s].' His own poetry, which depends heavily

on imagist labelling, touches the surreal, either in the frequent use of the diction associated with 'dream' itself, or, most effectively, in connecting specific sharply delineated images to abstractions, so that the latter seem, in the manner of a tranced vision, to take on the sensory qualities of the former. Charles Lillard's work, like that of so many writers of the West Coast, makes more explicit use of shamanistic analogies especially in the strange, misty landscapes of *Drunk on Wood and Other Poems* (1973). In the more recent *A Coastal Range* (1984) he makes the surrealism more demotic by putting 'his ear to the stump of these anecdotal shapes' created from the 'bursting uprush' of the sea-forest. J. Michael Yates is perhaps the father of this shamanistic group; his poems 'speak[ing] of things / which go quickly / Through the shadow of consciousness / Like animals in the thicket' were gathered together in the handsome collection *Nothing Speaks for the Blue Moraines* (1973). Yates's more recent poetry, although it remains attached to visionary metamorphoses, is more inclined to approach these through the totems of language itself than through images located in some identifiable landscape. *Esox Nobilior Non Esox Lucius* (1978) 'plunges ... out of light toward the shadow-mind / of wilderness' ('muskanonga') through a book-long series of free associations on the word and concept 'muskellonge,' which is continually re-spelled and re-invented as the title of each poem.

Susan Musgrave's poetry is filled with 'dark magic' and 'shadow-shamans' (*The Impstone*, 1976). Hers is often the black and nightmare side of surrealism, where something neurotic intersects with something religious. Typical of many of the neo-surrealist poets, Musgrave's at first remote and unidentifiable 'I' retreats before a more accessible syntax, and more rooted anecdote in books such as *A Man to Marry a Man to Bury* (1979). Yet her most impressive and distinctive work is still to be found in *Kiskatinaw Songs* (with Sean Virgo, 1977), which are included in *Selected Strawberries and Other Poems* (1977). In the introductions to these volumes Musgrave speaks regretfully of the 'Indian Bandwagon' rolling through Canadian literature. But the mass of trite poems about Indians could not obliterate the many satisfying attempts to hear the voices in the trees and stones by adopting the styles and forms of the Indian songs (however imperfectly translated) themselves. Other notable affiliates of this group (there is nothing like a 'school' involved) are Pat Lowther, Theresa Kishkan, and Linda Rogers. Lowther, who was murdered in 1975, left a varied collection of strong poems published posthumously in *A Stone Diary* (1977). Consistent with the shamanistic metaphor, her stones breathe, her mountains talk, and her slugs make love. The second half of the book moves towards more urban settings and a more sensational violence – the surreal element is particularly noticeable in the constant startling use of a diction associated with electricity. Theresa Kishkan's *Arranging the Gallery* (1976) is an evocative version of the Lowther/Musgrave mindscape, in which the echoes of Theodore Roethke's style and diction link exploding growth and tangled imagery in the Pacific Northwest. In *Queens of the Next Hot Star* (1981) Linda Rogers combines a straightforward narrative of her friendship with an old Indian woman, Maggie Jack, and a surrealist dreaming of the voice and dreams of Maggie, her people, and her spirit. The result is a rich blend of folk story and native myth.

The neo-surrealist poem differs from the prose lyric in its frequent dimension of parable. The poem's leaping from one complex of imagery to another is underpinned by some trace of story; it is not primarily anecdotal, nor situated in specific time or place, but generalized and universalized – sometimes to illustrate a message, more often to pose a question than to answer one. Such parable extends character portraits and reflections on the world of work in Erin Mouré's best book *Wanted Alive* (1983), shapes the aggressive allusiveness of Alexandre Amprimoz, and gives political point to Joy Kogawa's enquiry into her Japanese-Canadian heritage in *A Choice of Dreams* (1974). Cathy Ford mingles the shamanistic aspiration with West Coast landscape and feminist parable in *The Murdered Dreams Awake* (1979). Even in Myron Turner's *The River and the Window* (1974), which is much more purely surrealistic than any of these, the desire for ironic parable is clear.

At the other extreme from the surface of quotidian logic in Atwood's neosurrealism is the poetry of Leonard Cohen, which has always seemed to argue towards living within a dream, to becoming a parable. He, too, made much of his impact as a darling of the media, especially as a broodingly mysterious folksinger whose lyrics had more music than his voice. In *Death of a Lady's Man* (1978) his quest for the dream life seemed to dictate going beyond whatever reality is in poetry itself: the poems are in pairs – two poems, of a poem and a comment, with the same title – and each rejects the vision and even the existence of the other. In *Book of Mercy* (1984) Cohen assumed the role of contemporary psalmist, removed from the sensory world, chanting in an intensely private field of abstraction: 'Defeated by silence, here is a place where the silence is more subtle. And here is the opening in defeat. And here is the asp of the will. And here is the fear of you' ('no. 45').

Michael Ondaatje, who wrote the critical study *Leonard Cohen* (1970), shares Cohen's predilection for the edge of consciousness and the landscape of dream. But as his titles – *Rat Jelly* (1973), or 'King Kong meets Wallace Stevens' from that volume – show, Ondaatje gets there not through abstract drift, but by compressing contrasting colours, or textures, or characters into a short phrase. He has been, like Atwood, a model and an inspiration for the development of the neo-surrealist method in Canadian poetry. But whereas Atwood maintains a monotone in order to emphasize a bizarre shift in image, Ondaatje combines unpredictable juxtapositions with shifting voice registers, so that the speaker(s) becomes a primary surrealist element, in short lyrics as in his best-known book, the long poem *The Collected Works of Billy the Kid* (1970). At the same time Ondaatje's work, like Atwood's, moved in the 1980s towards the family anecdote side of the neo-surrealist form. The title *Secular Love* (1980) implied the direction. Hockey 'goalies' may have 'webbed feet,' and live in 'caves and castles,' but when he writes 'To a Sad Daughter,' who makes the goalies her ideal, the poem is more admonition than dream vision: 'You step delicately / into the wild world / and your real prize will be / the frantic search.' The poet's own combination of delicacy and wildness found its own most beautiful expression in *Running in the Family* (1982), a travel book, a prose poem, a collage of voices tracing Ondaatje's two return journeys to Sri Lanka in 1978 and 1980. In his Sri Lankan family lie the summation and inspiration of the neo-surrealist approach: 'My aunt Dolly stands five foot tall, weighing seventy pounds. She has not stopped smoking since the age of fifteen and her 80-year-old brain leaps like a spark plug bringing this year that year to life. Always repeating the last three words of your question and then turning a surprising corner on her own.'

METAPHYSICAL LYRIC

Look at it, stare
into the crystal because
it will tell you, not
the future, no, but
the quality of crystal,
clarity's nature,
teach you the stricture
of uncut, utterly
uncluttered light.
(Robert Bringhurst, 'Poem About Crystal,'
The Beauty of the Weapons, 1982)

Robert Bringhurst's beautifully conceived 'Poem About Crystal' is at once a manifesto proclaiming his own poetic objective, and a definition and embodiment of the modernist lyric. It is short, epigrammatic; you almost feel you have it memorized after the first reading. It urges, implicitly, the etymological identity of seeing and knowing: it seeks a visual clarity which is an intellectual clarity. Some would call this the *high* modernist tradition, to distinguish it from the demotic and democratizing impulse that has been so dominant in post–World War II Canadian poetry. Much of the best of the modern metaphysical lyric is certainly elitist: it is usually highly intellectual and wears its learning confidently, unapologetically. It is concerned, as A.J.M. Smith urged in 1936, 'with ... the emotional effect of ideas that have entered so deeply into the blood as never to be questioned.'[9] Such poetry may be

written in free verse, but it is more likely to use intricate patterns of sound
and metre. 'Poem About Crystal' is not rhymed. But the studied exactness
of the aural echoes, especially at the end of the poem, conveys to the ear
the 'stricture' of the fine crystalline poem: 'utterly' contains within it part of
the 'uncut,' and in turn is partly heard in the sound of 'uncluttered.'

The clarity of Bringhurst's poem contrasts with the inconclusiveness of
open verse: this poem is evidently and satisfyingly *closed*. The adjective
metaphysical – the precision of the form derives from earlier twentieth-century
interest in seventeenth-century metaphysical verse, hence its appropriateness
– is probably the best shorthand to isolate a form which is neither prose lyric
nor neo-surrealist, one whose most distinguishing features are a sense of
closure, and its variations on the conceit – the sustained, intellectual, witty
manipulation of a figure, which appears to exhaust the possibilities of a given
metaphor. Twentieth-century versions of the form are not restricted to the
conceit narrowly defined; often the concision and cleverness of the conceit
is manifest, as in Bringhurst, in sound patterns. The writer of the metaphysical
lyric will value Wallace Stevens over William Carlos Williams, Emily Dick-
inson over Walt Whitman.

In the 1960s when Robert Fulford was telling the readers of *The Toronto
Star* to buy Al Purdy's *Cariboo Horses* and *North of Summer*, to discover
a national history and idiom, the metaphysical lyric flagged in popularity,
and P.K. Page was being remaindered. Bringhurst's *Beauty of the Weapons*
signalled new recognition for the kind of poem of which Page is a master.
That the metaphysical lyric is less evidently national, in subject or intention,
is obviously significant: a decline in public nationalism, political and economic, created an acceptance of a poetry both receptive to the world at large,
and eclectic in subject-matter.

Robert Bringhurst's utterance has the uncluttered spareness of the conceit,
and yet it will seem, as 'Poem About Crystal' does, 'uncut,' as it manipulates
the discourse patterns of unconsidered conversation: 'Look at it' or 'not / the
future, no.' Here the best of the prose lyric seems united with the best of
the imagistic/metaphysical tradition. Mathematical and geometrical imagery
figure prominently. In ranging from contemporary Israel to Aztec cosmology,
from West Coast lichens to Egypt in the Fifth Dynasty, Bringhurst's poetry
often gives great pleasure simply for the sheer detail it contains. 'A Lesson
in Botany' gives a fascinating account of a twenty-four-pound Malayan flower;
'Xenophanes' combines mesmerizing design with superb insight into pre-
Socratic metaphysics. At the same time, Bringhurst is sensitive to the oral
traditions of indigenous cultures. Anyone who hears his deliberate and pray-
erful public readings appreciates how the intellectual challenge of the metaphysical lyric can be extended by that dimension of the prose lyric which
respects the unique ways of knowing possible in a pre-literate culture.

At the extreme of those poets who seek the poem as aesthetic artifact is Daryl Hine, an expatriate who edited *Poetry* (Chicago) for a decade ending in 1978. His tenuous connection to poetry which is 'Canadian' in subject-matter represents the detachment of the metaphysical lyric in its purest guise. The first twenty-five years of Hine's poetry is conveniently comprehended in *Selected Poems* (1980). Here the typical Hine poem emerges as a display of the ardours of the imagination for their own sake – its music is often masterful, its allusiveness daunting, its diction the essence of preciosity. 'Form is recognition / Of an underlying / Symmetry in something'; thus 'A commonplace is sacred if it scans' ('My Optics,' 'Linear A'). It is, of course, as Bringhurst's work shows, possible to put a more public and political face on the modern lyric – without adopting the epic aspiration of the long poem. P.K. Page has something of Hine's passion for overt pattern and various kinds of rhyming (as is evident in the retrospective *P.K. Page: Poems Selected and New*, 1974), but her concern for human suffering is closer to the surface. Her *Evening Dance of the Grey Flies* (1981) has, furthermore, many poems which move away from the ironic polish of 'The Stenographers,' to the very short lines of the imagist lyric. The book's title poem is a crisp expression of Page's strongest poetry: it tests the intellect, and then confronts the carefully reasoning mind with the meaninglessness of a painful death. The poem develops a conceit, that the movements of the grey flies in the twilight make a kind of writing ('a pencilled script,' 'a gold calligraphy'). Then, when light changes direction (is 'refracted') so does the poem, to contemplate the uniquely painstaking and rare form of writing ('silverpoint') seen in the face of a dying man. The poem seems tense with an unbearable suffering, yet it confronts the reader abruptly with a language of randomness, and with the triumph of making: 'your face // shone suddenly like the sun.'

Miriam Waddington has moved in the opposite direction; her indictment of the social system, which she worked as a social worker to improve, has given way, largely, to the poetry of the family musical and fabular evening. The music of lyric dominates *The Price of Gold* (1976), sometimes descriptive, more often introspective. Waddington consistently writes poems in which song seems to sing out over the barbarism she struggles to address. Dorothy Livesay, another poet about whom the same might be said, especially in *Feeling the Worlds* (1984), nevertheless continued in her seventies to keep political concerns from disappearing into the symmetries of song. The poems in *Ice Age* (1975), the powerful book which succeeded *Collected Poems: The Two Seasons* (1972), rediscover, often with intense eroticism, the politics of being a woman, and combine these with a new politics of aging: 'I had yet to discover / how even in old age / a woman moves with freshness' ('Breathing').

The very nature of the metaphysical lyric implies relative obscurity. It must take scrupulous care with every detail of pattern; the poem is the product of multiple rewritings. Since the successful poem takes such a long time to craft, the poets tend to drift out of the eye of a public eager for story and sizzle. D.G. Jones, whose control and co-ordination in the modernist lyric are admirable, is such a poet. If he jokes, and addresses friends in his poems, he has more love for the spareness of haiku than for the rambling vernacular anecdote of Al Purdy. If he likes bizarre surprise, he is more concise and overtly national than any neo-surrealist. He is much more obviously touched by the imagist dimension of the modernist tradition. He is the most natural successor to F.R. Scott (d1985), in his wry nationalism, his spareness, his bilingualism, his translations, his feeling for the land – although he is not obviously engagé. His triumphant volume *Under the Thunder the Flowers Light Up the Earth* (1977), was largely reissued in a volume of selected poems, *A Throw of Particles* (1983), which also contained some thirty-five new poems. Jones's 'A Garland of Milne' establishes the lovely balances found throughout *Under the Thunder*:

> All space came out in flowers
> miraculous, erupting from a void or mouth
>
> And every breath
> a wind or sun, a season or delight
> drew colour from the earth.

Jones's revealing reading of David Milne's paintings also becomes a description of his own work: the subtle absences of a Milne canvas, where delicate sweeps of colour shine against patches of raw canvas, somehow parallel the awed silences of Jones's poems, where a few images are set off by the spaces of the page. It is the mystery of silence (which demands, of course, its own ratiocinative detective work) which leads, also, to the important sequence 'Kate, these flowers ... (The Lampman Poems),' in which Jones imagines the love affair between Archibald Lampman and Katherine Waddell in contemporary idiom, providing one version of what was unspoken in their relationship: 'Loneliness becomes us, we / advance through separations.'[10] Thus Jones makes Lampman a genuine poetic predecessor, saluting his dream vision by discovering the shades of a love affair more natural, in nature, than sexual. The sequence establishes, like Atwood's *Journals of Susanna Moodie*, its most famous antecedent, the sense of a national tradition, not by cooking with maple syrup, but by evidently embodying the discourse of one phase of Canadian poetry in another.

In the context of a rediscovery of Moodie and Lampman, the accelerated reputation of Phyllis Webb was hardly so spectacular. Yet it is a striking affirmation of the renewed prominence of the metaphysical lyric that, especially since the publication of *Wilson's Bowl* (1980), she has been the poet most frequently hailed as an essential antecedent by a generation just slightly younger than herself. At the same time, Webb's own poetry has generally moved away from the intricacies of a tradition saluted in 'Marvell's Garden' to a more restrained form. Like Pound's introduction of the haiku's discipline into English, so Webb's enthusiasm for the anti-ghazal, her version of the ancient Persian series of couplets, shows the potential of restraint and of vertical juxtaposition: 'Winter breathes in the wings of the last hummingbird. / I have lost my passion. I am Ms Prufrock.'[11] Webb's inspiration to experiment with the form was John Thompson's *Stilt Jack* (1978). Michael Ondaatje introduced Webb to the ghazal; several other Canadian poets subsequently tested the intellectual surprises inherent in the form. Webb's work is crisp with solitude and glimpses of compassion, in touch with, yet not restricted to, the West Coast island on which she lives. The mysterious austerity and emotional charge of the earlier *Naked Poems* (1965) seems sustained, albeit more humorously, in the ghazals collected in *Water and Light* (1985). 'Wilson's Bowl' – the almost incantatory sequence which Webb describes as her attempt to deal with the suicide of her friend Lilo Berliner and with Berliner's interest in West Coast anthropology (Berliner discovered the petroglyph bowl on Salt Spring Island and named it in honour of Wilson Duff) – contains this neat summary of the principle of her lyrics: 'This is meditation's place / cold rapture's.'

The appearance of Margaret Avison's *Winter Sun / The Dumbfounding: Poems 1940-66* (1982), a reissue of two earlier volumes in McClelland and Stewart's Modern Canadian Poets series, was another sign of a reviving interest in the more cerebral side of modernism. Avison's *Sunblue* (1978) – its very slimness after a twelve-year absence an indication of the scrupulous reworking characteristic of this form – showed both the sustaining of Avison's commitment, and (although to a far lesser degree than in Bringhurst) some rapprochement between the discipline of the metaphysical conceit and the apparent offhandedness of the prose lyric. Even the book's title, of course, contains something of a conceit. Indeed the conceit concentrated within a single word is the most essential feature of Avison's poetry. Compound words proliferate, either with hyphen (the 'apple-spring-perfume' of 'Hid Life'), or without. Her 'March' has a 'deepwarm look' and is 'soaked in sunwash': these are two of the nine compounds (some coined, some familiar) which blend sensations and images in this vision of spring. She also makes energetic use of portmanteau words as in the pivotal centre of her 'SKETCH: Thaws':

> Swepth of suncoursing sky
> steeps us in
>   salmon-stream

                              crop-green
                      rhubarb-coloured shrub-tips:

Compounding and alliteration remind us first of Hopkins, an appropriate
analogy given Avison's eloquent Christian commitment to 'the achieve of,
the mastery of' God's world. At the same time, we can see in the freer use
of the space of the page, and the tentativeness suggested by the sketch (a
form used frequently in *Sunblue*), another blurring of generic distinction.

   In discussing the metaphysical lyric I am inevitably dealing with many
poets whom the previous volumes of this history have identified as the establishment. What strikes me now is how these writers have been honoured
for their continuing relevance, and have embraced aspects of evolving poetic
forms. Irving Layton is an exception. While poets such as Lochhead and
Birney have obviously continued to change forms, and Scott, Smith, Livesay,
and Brewster have been saluted for continuing to explore the same forms
that made them important influences on the direction of Canadian poetry,
Layton has changed less from first poem to last than any of the others. He
continued to trumpet his own magnificence, as if to set himself off from
everything else labelled Canadian poetry. Canadians, he would say, distrust
achievement.

   Although he seemed to be the slightly irrelevant voice of a previous generation, he continued to be important for determined promotion of the musical
dimension of poetry. The impulse to sing is expressed by Layton in the grand
Hebraic manner. His poetry can be summarized in the terms Northrop Frye,
in *Anatomy of Criticism* (1957), links to the *charm*: 'hypnotic incantation ...
pulsing dance rhythm ... the sense of magic, or physically compelling power ...
Invective or flyting, the literary imitation of the spell-binding curse ...' Layton
is the Canadian proprietor of flyting. Since *For My Brother Jesus* (1976),
most of Layton's invective has been directed at Xianity (ie, Cross-tianity),
at a complacent, pseudo-Christianity seen against a background of the Holocaust, 'the central moral and psychological fact of our times' (*Europe and
Other Bad News*, 1981). Many of the poems are addressed lamentingly to
Joshua (Hebrew name for Jesus) or adopt the persona of Joshua, as in this
ritualized cursing of Saul, the man most responsible for turning a 'Hebrew
revolutionary' into a victim of Jews:

               I curse you, Saul of Tarsus.
               I curse you, O epileptic Hellenized sod
               And the vile dolts who call me Jesus.
                         ('Jesus and Saint Paul')

The spellbinding element of Layton's curses usually resides in the sheer
linguistic bravado of jamming together words from radically different speech

registers: 'epileptic Hellenized sod.' A remarkable talent for smashing not-quite-assimilated hip colloquialism into erudite and remote mannered phrase is no doubt hypnotic. Yet the reader (prim Canadian, Layton would fume) still longs for more of the magic of the simple rhymed *charm*, such as 'A Song for Ancients.' Layton never seems to realize that the curse, no matter how incantatory, is a genre necessarily limited in duration. When the flyting continues book after book, the spell dissipates, and the listener simply tries to avoid the noise, or turns from the poetry to the more absorbing subjects – the man himself and his oracular prose.

Robert Bringhurst's ability to combine the grammar of orality with the tightly constructed witty lyric apparently restores to Canadian poetry the touch of Eliotesque conceit which waned in the 1960s. Publications by Page, Avison, Waddington, Livesay, even Layton, and especially Phyllis Webb have consolidated a modest revival. The difference between the metaphysical and the prose lyric, or the surreal lyric, is important to describing the topography of recent Canadian poetry. For each poet whom I have discussed as a surrealist or prose lyricist, several hundred – many of them very competent and readable poets – have had to be left out. In other words, these genres are the pervasive and fashionable ones. They are the bedrock – and the dung heap – on which most of the achievements of recent Canadian poetry are based. By contrast, the metaphysical lyric is comfortable home to a relatively few very patient and careful poets. Among the other poetry that sustains this form are the 'poised' and 'balance[d]' rhyming tetrameters of Richard Outram's *Turns and Other Poems* (1975), the gracefully whimsical imitations of classical seventeenth-century and early modern predecessors in David Solway's *Selected Poems* (1982), and the formal exercises, from sonnet to haiku, along George Woodcock's symbolic *Mountain Road* (1980). R.A.D. Ford, whose work was collected in *Needle in the Eye* (1983), uses his travels as distinguished diplomat to find his subject-matter in many places. And yet there is a sameness in it, which tends towards platitudes, and weak rhymes: 'Maybe there is a pill to take / Against this century / But I think our conscience is too bad / For any remedy' ('Sleeplessness of Our Times'). Among these restrained craftsmen, Robin Skelton is the most prolific. In 'The Arrangement' (*Limits*, 1981) the witty patterns of sound show off his continual effort to make 'of disorder order':

> of pebbles, petals,
> parapets and bees,
>
> descants and harmonies;
> I harmonize.

Robert Finch, one of the pioneering Canadian modernists included in *New*

Provinces (1936), appeared in two volumes of restrained elegance, *Variations & Theme* (1980) and *Has and Is* (1981), demonstrating that the discipline of the sonnet still shapes a teasing comparison: 'The only definition that defines, / Though inexpressible, informs these lines' ('Definitive'). Harmonies which harmonize and definitions which define: these are the disciplines of a modernist lyric which we can now, strangely, call traditional. In this work Canadian poetry finds its mind – the sense, that is, of conscious mind in isolated rationality playing with the inexpressible, in metaphors juggled, and in sound entrained.

THE LONG POEM

In the 1970s a growing awareness, under the tutelage of Saussure, that *langue* has no meaning except as *voiced* by a particular speaker, both described and created an impetus for the poem to expand to incorporate many voices, because we can only approach the meanings of *parole* if we hear multiple voices using the *langue*. Polyphony often drowned out the lyric. When language is a questionable community activity, the poet must locate us in a society, by enabling us to understand the way we talk. With the relation between object and word continually shifting, and history having to be continually rewritten, the poem's response is to lengthen into infinity. Poets appropriate more literary conventions, more forms of discourse, more voices to their repertoires.

To paraphrase Kroetsch's aphorism, the extension makes us real. The proliferation of the long poem is the most obvious change in Canadian literary history in the 1970s and 1980s. The lyric swells with the powerful feelings of a single self-absorbed singer; fiction and drama thrive on character and plot, and on their connection to the outside world of other people and public events. The long poem's incorporation of the narrative and dramatic might be thought of, then, as poetry's quest for mimesis. Mikhail Bakhtin's argument that 'in the presence of the novel, all other genres somehow have a different resonance' is a peculiarly apt comment on contemporary Canadian poetry. We are witnessing a 'battle for the novelization of the other genres; a search for genres which [structure themselves] in the zone of direct contact with inconclusive present-day reality.'[12] As the novel abandons the convention of realism, we detect the increasing novelization of poetry; the developing long poem absorbs the realistic convention, along with many others.

The novelization of poetry begins with making the poem longer – by three general means of extension. The most conservative is to link a series of conventional lyrics usually along a narrative line, creating the *serial long poem*. The most radical method is to find form (or, paradoxically, formlessness) in the unending movement of the poet's mind at the moment of composition – the *process-poem*. The third, and superficially most 'realistic,' method of extension is to adapt historical narrative, and to draw out in one of myriad ways the poetry within unliterary documents – the *documentary long poem*.

SERIAL LONG POEM

The serial long poem frequently takes an artist's life as its subject. Kevin Roberts in *Stonefish* (1982), for example, evokes both the powerful primitivism of Gauguin's paintings, and the agonized poverty and desperation in the painter's letters. The frustration of 'words I must turn to / colour' is met in mingled metaphors of fruit and flower (of the Tahitian vision), stonefish, and the breast/brown of the local sexuality which so mesmerized the painter. Judith Fitzgerald's 'Past Cards' in *Split/Levels* (1983) combines dated journal and pop song in order to 'remember / ... what we choose to be.' But it, like attempts to test the intersections of lyric and journal in several of Fitzgerald's books, seemed a groping towards the biography of an actual historic artist – *Beneath the Skin of Paradise: The Piaf Poems* (1984). This sequence of exceedingly spare lyrics often seems too flat to touch the emotion of Piaf's songs, but its progression through songs, voices, borrowings from William Carlos Williams, towards an incantation reminiscent of bill bissett, effectively mimics the chronology of Piaf's mounting nervous and mental breakdown. An undoubted tour de force in this genre is E.D. Blodgett's book-length apostrophe to Vincent van Gogh, *Sounding* (1977). I use the term apostrophe not only because the poem is, like all poems about artists, a cry to the muse, but also because the figure implies 'radical interiorization and solipsism.'[13] In the interstices and ellipses where Blodgett's verse characteristically operates, the singing of van Gogh's colours is a sounding of the limits of the poet's own voice: 'birds never yellowed there / but yellow aired / alone as never.' Van Gogh's biography – his places, his subjects, his madness – is no more than a palimpsest in Blodgett's poem. But the synthesis of colour and sound, of image and abstraction, in this brief excerpt, shows what the serial lyric attempted to add to narrative.

We find the same aspiration in poems about a historical event. Ted Plantos, whose collage (containing photographs, stories, found poems, and even a map) *The Universe Ends at Sherbourne & Queen* (1977) somewhat relentlessly documented Toronto's Cabbagetown neighbourhood, makes more effective use of the potential of lyric in *Passchendaele* (1983). Although the poems are chronologically dated, it is the echoing patterns of startling images, not the progress of battles, that compels the interest: particularly fascinating is the lyric web linking war as a fecund living organism, war as a sexual experience, and – most audaciously – war as magic: 'We are the demon

vegetation, stumps of new / lost in woodnymph dreams, eyes dripping or-
chards / and imagined fruit' ('The Fire Beginning'). Gwendolyn MacEwen
tells of a more distant war in *The T.E. Lawrence Poems* (1982), a chilling
sequence which brings together her career-long interest in the Middle East,
violence, and visionary mysticism. Gary Geddes imagines an imagined war
in *The Terracotta Army* (1984), his inspired discovery of the voices and
personalities of the 8000-strong sculptured army which Ch'in Shi Huang Di
(third century BC) commissioned to be his imperial bodyguard in the afterlife.
Geddes exploits the paradoxically riddling talkiness of the run-on couplet
(nine to each poem) as some two dozen soldiers comment on themselves as
models, and the poet contemplates the mystery of violence and art. In the
sequence of books which Fitzgerald, Blodgett, Plantos, MacEwen, and Geddes
have published we might trace a movement, not rigidly linear, from the
collection of occasional lyrics to the serial long poem which makes possible
more lyric variation and more prosaic interlude. The poet can slip into a
slacker prose, as Plantos does when the obscenity of talk in the trenches
takes over his poems, and then explore the poetry (the metaphorical extensions, the incantatory hypnosis) latent in that prose.

This technique lends itself as readily to a historical subject, with an established narrative shape, as to what we might call domestic narrative, behind
which, in one way or another, lies Wordsworth's ultimate autobiographical
long poem *The Prelude*. Robert Currie's *Diving into Fire* (1977) is his lyric
Bildungsroman of growing up in Moose Jaw. Currie's strength lies in anecdote, story, local voices, and dramatic monologue. But he is seldom able
to extend these into a metaphysical abstract significance, or a paradoxical
play of connotations. *Yarrow* (1980) was a marked improvement, a brisk
series of prairie stories, almost a novel, again in poems focused on a single
imagined character and family. If the poem has little verbal intensity, it does
show how the very unpretentiousness of prose lyric can be effectively extended to a narrative whose theme is unpretentiousness. Ron Smith, who has
developed the remote Oolichan Books into an important publisher of poetry,
quietly rediscovers his own growing up in a sentimental (in the best sense)
sequence of variations on the sonnet tracing his daughter's acquisition of
language in *Seasonal* (1984). Again, each poem has a specific date; Smith
uses the carnivalizing element of holidays, festivals, and anniversaries to
organize this year/lifetime of poetry, letting his daughter's discovery of language both humble the poet's ambition and reanimate the poet's dream:

> In summer the sun ascends from the sea,
> a silent verb of morning, and the song of birds
> sits on your tongue: 'Why is tomorrow, tomorrow?'

Or, 'When I grow up, do you grow down?'
('Nicole: August 20')

The limit of the lyric sequence is perhaps found in E.D. Blodgett's *Arché/
Elegies* (1984). This is a long poem which contains structural traces of
autobiography, travelogue, and history (obviously with emphasis on its archeological dimension). But it is perhaps best described as a metalinguistic
serial, since it shows where the lyric sequence will go under the influence
of semiotics (and sheer erudition). Blodgett's poem moves trans-Canada, to
translate Canada. The poem is based on the conviction that the codes which
shape our perceptions are by definition unrecognized. By doubting, and par-
odying, and translating these codes, Blodgett reveals the preconceptions of
a nation. Unlike *Sounding*, this poem touches the poet's local landscape: the
language of national mapping and national mythmaking, from Louisbourg
through Mackenzie King to Craigellachie. The poem is unforgivingly poly-
lingual and allusive and demands a reading capacious as the man who wrote
it. It is one of the major works of contemporary Canadian poetry. Canada
is alphabet: to find it we might begin by looking 'somewhere under *Ca-*,
perhaps, or other / sounds, mirrored gasps growing old, / frozen hiatus, spaced
into solecisms // of slow expirations, winter's one / harvest' ('O Canada').

PROCESS-POEM

By looking at words as an alphabet, Blodgett put the sequence of lyrics to
work at deconstruction. Examining a text as an infinite series of intertexts
proved to be enormously creative. Yet somewhere behind Blodgett's play lies
a sense of the first-ness of things, a nostalgia for the referential function of
language. Not so, perhaps, with bpNichol, whose multi-volume *The Martyrology*, undoubtedly the longest long poem in Canadian literary history, is
especially and totally immersed in a language that has no – that cannot have
– definable referents. *The Martyrology* is the central phenomenological long
poem of Canadian poetry. I am not sure it is the best (I prefer Blodgett's
allusiveness and Marlatt's etymology), but it is the most radical as well as
the most sustained. The phenomenological long poem is the poem which
attempts to present, somehow, the process of the mind – and the body – as
they are, moment by moment, implicated with language articulating themselves and creating the text. In outline, *The Martyrology* is a journal of self-
discovery through the poet's leisurely intense examination of the language
he is using. When Nichol made retroactive discovery of his formal model,
the Japanese poetic diary *utanikki*, he seemed to shift from the saints' books
and legends, and from his own uneasiness with the sainthood of words,

manifest especially in his play with words beginning in 'st' – (St And, etc.), which gave form and purpose to the early books of *The Martyrology*. Increasingly the poem talked of the identifiable friends and people, and of the personal travelling – *Continental Trance* (1982) – that the poetic diary implies. Even here, within a single long poem, we detect a trend to novelization. But the saints are never far away: 'I want the absolute precision / of fluid definition / the saints learned / long ago' ('Book 4'). For Nichol that fluid precision lies in the discoveries inherent in breaking words up into phonemes, morphemes, individual letters: break-up reveals the spiritual significance of language: 'every letter / invokes a spell / ing is / the power / letters have / over me' ('Coda: Mid-Initial Sequence Book 3'). This spell is powerful because it is revealed to be so commonplace. Everyone who uses language has been struck by such concealed meaning as Nichol discovers. In showing us the childlike fascination with the building blocks of language he makes the poem fundamentally demotic; he shows the simple, humorous, and exciting insight possible when we pull out a sequence of letters from 'thought,' to make a theory which itself breaks apart and turns to something different before it is complete:

> to rid me of
> the ugh in
> thought
> i spell anew
> weave the world
> out of the or
> binary
>   ('Book 4')

Many Canadian poets have learned this potential from Nichol, but none went quite so far as he did in denying language its referential function (although, as I have noted, the poem's evolving toward a more identifiable biography is its own internal consolidation). Roy Kiyooka kept the autobiographical process-poem much closer to document in *transcanada letters* (1975), a hefty catalogue of his letters and lyrics. Voyeuristic appeal – and often tedium – lie in this extreme of a private-correspondence-made-public-poem. The book is a travelogue, an autobiography, an epistolary novel, especially an exploration of family roots, of Japanese heritage in Canadian context. The letters' claim on authenticity is ambiguously asserted; they are 'the only things I write sometimes and they happen to be written out of the same concern I would bring to bear if I were writing something else.' An intellectual biography, given worldly familiarity because it incorporates everything he writes to the people and institutions in his life, thus claims its link to the verifiable external world.

More conventionally autobiographical in form is Dennis Lee's 'The Death of Harold Ladoo,' in *The Gods* (1978), where, consistent with the form of elegy, the poet identifies with the murdered Trinidadian writer. The title of George Bowering's 'Autobiology' (1972; collected in *The Catch*, 1976) suggests the phenomenological premise of so many of these attempts to contact an immediate personal reality. Written in short titled 'chapters,' which appear to be prose, he combines the form of autobiography with the empirical discourse of biology – both human and plant. He is at once recounting his growing up, and the physical and intellectual movements of his body at the ever-changing moment of composition: 'She wanted to have me ask / about her childhood was it generally a happy / childhood or generally an unhappy childhood / but I would say it depends on the reason you / would want to say whether it was a happy child- / hood or not.' George Bowering became established in the late 1970s as a prolific anthologist, critic, lecturer, and computer expert – not to mention writer. He is perhaps the best representative of the consolidation of Canadian poetry during the 1970s. Bowering's long-time interest in the local, for example, is embodied in *Kerrisdale Elegies* (1984), a deliberate imitation of a major European long poem. Bowering's shift from *auto*-biology to 'parody' of Rilke, like Kroetsch's from seed catalogue to Salonika, or Daphne Marlatt's from Vancouver poems to Malaysian poems, was yet another sign of the broad move away from the more insular nationalism of the 1960s.

Many of the characteristics of Rilke's *Duino Elegies* are found here: the basis in notebook (which Rilke always carried), the response to the perplexity of war ('Not to understand ... was my whole occupation'), the form of a poem forming itself around fragments of memory, the (middle-aged?) yearning to 'bear our own distress more passionately,' the attempt to find ' "external" equivalents for experiences that were becoming ever more "inward" and incommunicable,' the coming up repeatedly against the limitations of language. But Bowering's is a parody, in its reverence and respect for Rilke, and in its burlesque. He smiles where Rilke mourns, he chastises or urges where Rilke questions (Rilke's 'But were you equal to it?' becomes Bowering's 'You should know by now'). Often in theme, as well, Bowering reverses Rilke, so that in Elegy ix 'Is it not your [Earth's] dream / to be one day invisible?' becomes Bowering's 'It is time to speak now, / ... to name the world we can still see.' And yet, of course, Rilke emphasizes the numinous importance of the present moment or object observed: 'But because being here amounts to so much, because all / this Here and Now, so fleeting, seems to require us and strangely / concerns us.'[14] This here and now is central to Bowering's poetic/aesthetic. Thus the Elegy 5, a meditation on Picasso's 'Les Saltimbanques' (Acrobats), becomes Bowering's evocative celebration of the art of baseball.

In *What Matters: Writing 1968–70* (1980), Daphne Marlatt's journal quotes
Maurice Merleau-Ponty, the influential phenomenological thinker: 'the perceived thing ... exists only in so far as someone can perceive it. I cannot
even for an instant imagine an object in itself.' The phenomenological poet
is obliged to incorporate both the thing and the multiple process of perceiving
it. The objective necessarily results in a *long* poem: 'the writing takes so
long because it is attempting to get the whole field of consciousness (*not*
linear logic) of any given "I" or "he".' Thus this book itself is, in a sense,
an extension of an earlier poem, *Rings* (1971), which it incorporates in a
context of journal and other poems as it attempts to include the whole range
of consciousness surrounding the birth of Marlatt's son. Marlatt's work demonstrates how completely the phenomenological poem has questioned the
notion of book as continuous unfolding of some logical train of thought.
Throughout her poetry our attention is on the problem of representation, of
the necessity of continually rereading the language itself. The obscurity of
such poetry often intimidates even the dedicated reader of poetry; but *What
Matters* and the reissue of *Steveston* (1974, 1984) were signs of a gradual
mainstreaming of the phenomenological long poem. Marlatt's journal and her
afterword to the new edition of *Steveston* were ways of making the phenomenology of writing accessible to readers accustomed to linear forms.

Marlatt first attracted widespread attention with *Steveston*, perhaps because
it was both a long poem and a recognizable documentary. Illustrated with
photos by Robert Minden, it is at one level a sympathetic record of the
history and people and work and social conditions of the small Japanese
fishing community just south of Vancouver. It records – elliptically, discon-
tinuously – but it is also constantly aware 'that I persist, also, in seeing
them' ('Work'). And that phenomenological awareness constantly interferes
with the poem's anticipated structures, documenting the impossibility of documentary, following an aural association into another word and words, so
that the text repeatedly confounds itself. Similarly *How Hug a Stone* (1983)
shapes Marlatt's 1981 journey with her son to see her grandmother and visit
the mother's side of her family. Again, the process of the poem-journal's
own composing de-centres the journey, as if the poet at once recognizes her
self-deceptions and repeatedly tries to ignore them:

> *to feel at home*, even on unfamiliar ground, stand
>
>   [on your own
> (two feet, two eyes, ears, nose, ten tactile fingers
>
>   [go where
> the wind goes ...
>
>   be unnamed, walk

unwritten, de-scripted, un-described. or else compose
                                  [make
it say itself, make it up.
        ('leaning out at twilight rolling in on Dartmoor hills:')

The search for the mother and the mother-language continued in *Touch to My Tongue* (1984), the most overtly feminist of her books, where Marlatt again tries to include the whole field of consciousness of woman, being at home and de-scripted (ie, unwritten). That consciousness increasingly articulated through connections with the French language (long an interest of Marlatt), and especially with the experiments towards a women's language in such Quebec writers as Nicole Brossard and Louky Bersianik, by the mid-1980s promised a radical shift in gender and genre in Canadian writing; creating an alternative language from two tongues was especially evident in Lola Lemire Tostevin's *Color of Her Speech* (1982), in Anne McLean's *A Nun's Diary* (1984), in Smaro Kamboureli's *in the second person* (1984), in Phyllis Webb, and in Sharon Thesen.

Marlatt's work is a model for many Canadian poets who are magnetized by the temptation of narrative (the sequential pattern of a journey, the *Bildungsroman* implying a rediscovery of one's family), yet want to write the long poem which will undo the narrative and remove the putty and twine which hold it together. A whole subgenre of the process-poem as genealogy might be identified. Fred Wah's *Breathin' My Name with a Sigh* (1981) and *Grasp the Sparrow's Tail: A Poetic Diary* (1982) – later incorporated into the longer *Waiting for Saskatchewan* (1985) – mixed poetry and prose, as it mixed the sound of his own voice and a '*haiku* sensibility' to rethink his own Chinese and Scandinavian heritage and his memories of his father. The model for this form might be the poetry of Andrew Suknaski, who has given his whole career to exploring his family, community, and linguistic roots. But Suknaski's work is the model in subject rather than in phenomenological method, since his forte has been to tell anecdotes of Wood Mountain, Saskatchewan, and to tell them in convincing replications of the dialect voice of its people. Yet in *Montage for an Interstellar Cry* (1982), Suknaski, too, seems to incorporate the phenomenological method, which has perhaps always been implicit in his unapologetic and revealing multilingualism: 'the edge of mind evolves / to grasp / or print itself / on a cave's ceiling / ME THIS HAND.' Less linear than Suknaski's work, Dennis Cooley's *Fielding* (1983) is also underpinned by the narrative of his journey to his father's deathbed and his attempt to connect to his heritage, with its prairie fields, and its baseball games (with their essential fielding). Cooley is fascinated with the spoken voice, with the essential truth of untutored talk, with the poetry of cliché, curse, and dead metaphor – and with the disruption of these (as the epigraph from Heidegger to his volume suggests), recognizing the gap between what is spoken and what is said.

Cooley's *Fielding* insists that the long poem, with its continual attention to how the writer writing perceives his or her world, is by definition genealogical. Barry McKinnon's *I Wanted to Say Something* (1975) was one of many other examples which seemed to root in the emerging prairie regionalism of the 1970s. 'Continued stories as scattered history' is a phrase from the poem that might describe the form of many another poem exploring family roots. The poem is certainly less metapoetic than the process-poems just discussed, but both its use of women's discourse (the women reminisce while looking at a photo album), and its reaching for the punning possibilities of language link it to the familiar process: going down into family is also to become aware of one's own language. Patrick Friesen, in *The Shunning* (1980), uses the general diffuseness of the long poem to make possible a network of voices chronicling the families and lives of two fictional Mennonite men in southern Manitoba. Joining haiku, official documents, and monologues in various voices, the continuing mingling of codes makes the whole implicitly metalinguistic.

The genealogical process-poem focuses on the question of how to grow within a self-conscious collage such as Kroetsch assembles in *Seed Catalogue*. Kroetsch's example is behind all the poems I have mentioned here, except perhaps Marlatt's (although Kroetsch did edit *How Hug a Stone*). But the most marked example of a writer who used Kroetsch's inspiration to change his direction is Eli Mandel, whose genealogical poem *Out of Place* (1977) explores his Saskatchewan roots in a continual questioning of the once sacred connection between word and world, between text and self. Mandel's punning title implied how Mandel had come to feel out of place even within his own earlier poetry (metaphysical and mythic lyrics, compressed imagism). Catalogues, found poems, photographs, and scraps of diary overlaid one another in an exploration of the double, which became the obsessional centre of Mandel's self-questioning, continuing poem. *Out of Place* doubled *Seed Catalogue*; Mandel and Kroetsch talked to one another – out of print and in – and 1977 seemed a pivotal year in the development of the long poem.

DOCUMENTARY LONG POEM

To say 'This road is a poem' is to claim, as deliberately blandly as possible, that roads, in the perceivable world, have their own intense expressiveness and rhythm – it signals the artist's unending desire to look at the world afresh, to see the unusualness of the ordinary. But to recognize that the road 'is the shortest distance between nowhere and nowhere' is to admit that the poem is unending: there's no distance but infinity. The novelization of poetry is, of course, in Mikhail Bakhtin's sense, also its carnivalization. And carnival is intoxicating. This extension makes us reel.

Dorothy Livesay, Frank Davey, and Stephen Scobie make the most articulate claims that Canadian poets have been endlessly attracted to the documentary poem, with its implicit interest in the tension between the predicated naming and the infinity of language. They see that the documentary poem seeks to combine the merits of the prose lyric with the merits of encyclopedia and novel. Scobie finds an essential – and 'prophetic' – definition of the form in what Livesay calls the 'dialectic between the objective facts and the subjective feelings of the poets.'[15] If the documentary poem, as Scobie claims, is usually book-length and 'narrative in structure,' the crucial ingredient is 'an actual, documented character ... historical rather than literary or mythological. The appeal is to *the authoritativeness of fact*, to a category of reality which exists outside and independent of the text – admitting, of course, that as soon as it enters the text it becomes mediated, and "part of" the fiction.'[16]

Scobie's own *McAlmon's Chinese Opera* (1980) is the perfect case in point. It adopts the fiction that it is the autobiography of Robert McAlmon, an intriguing American modernist writer who disappeared in the shadow of the more famous Hemingway, Stein, and Pound with whom he was associated in the 1920s. Scobie's poem is, thus, in several ways 'nobody's autobiography'; hence, for this poem, the documentary is crucial to establishing a sense of the personality of the subject. Where the chronological sequence of lyrics slackens into catalogue and list, Scobie, and his character, are begging to be authenticated: this nobody was, and is, a somebody. You know, when you're reading this poem, that you must recognize a historical figure in it. As much as this poem – and so many other long poems – is absorbed in Steinian word play ('Glow, glaux, glaucoma'), and as much as it acknowledges the non-referentiality of language (frustrated with words, McAlmon retreats to live 'for three weeks a pure / non-verbal existence'), Scobie's 'abundance' must rest on reality; he must append a biographical essay and protest: 'my inventions have been modest: the more bizarre the event ... the more likely it is to be accurate.' Scobie's remark acknowledges that readers will be more interested in his poem if they appreciate the historical reality of his central figure.

The compulsion to authenticate seems to have a great deal to do with a caution about the public's willingness to accept 'pure' fiction. Since many poets in Canada can make more out of reading their poems publicly than from selling books of poems, the need for such recognizable subject-matter, or for a strong narrative line, becomes increasingly evident. Florence McNeil's poems are representative in several senses (she is a reluctant performer who, in the 1980s, accepted more and more offers to read publicly). Most of her poetry is firmly rooted in document. *Emily* (1975) is a sequence of lyrics which continually and overtly alludes to incidents and expressions in Emily Carr's journals and autobiographical fictions. *The Overlanders* (1982) is a long poem whose factual observations are gradually taken over by metaphors, linking landscape details and fantasy, as McNeil attempts to suggest the psychological torment of a woman who conceals her pregnancy while on a male quest for gold: 'goats and sheep rush / kaleidoscopic / through the sunlight.' But in including the (imagined) voices of factor, hunter, or nun, the poet still insists that 'the facts are real,' and the fascination of the chronological historical narrative is primary. Photographs have always been the most staple documentary element of McNeil's work; the most ordinarily representational of art forms leads, paradoxically, away from the actual world into mysteries of flatness and framing. The prosaic catalogue of the town *Barkerville* (1984) matches the dreams in the accompanying historical photographs. The primary accomplishment of the book is to present the diversity and fantastic history of the goldrush town, rather than the diversity and history of echoing language. The 'problem' of the documentary poem is defined in McNeil's work: the amusing *fact* of a particular man's using cognac on his hair is more *poetic* (more suggestive) than McNeil's poetic interpretation: 'as / the priest uses oils and chrisms / in the Mass' ('Cataline the Packer').

Something of the opposite limitation is found in Don Gutteridge, who may be the most resolutely documentary historical poet of the 1970s. *Borderlands* (1975) and *Tecumseh* (1976) completed what Gutteridge conceived of as a pan-Canadian historical tetralogy which began with *Riel: A Poem for Voices* (1968) and *Coppermine: The Quest for North* (1975). *Tecumseh*, like a term paper, ends in a bibliography of twelve sources, many of which are quoted verbatim in excerpts throughout the poem. *Borderlands*, a history of 'the northwest coast of America from 1778 to 1805' contains some evocative poems, such as an opening poem linking Maquina's distinctive perceptions with landscape and compass directions: 'Looking out is West / where Ocean begins // Looking in is East / where Forest has his root.' The scraps and fragments of documents, however, seem stuck on rather than integrated. When he turned to personal/family history in *God's Geography* (1982), Gutteridge used an even wider range of documents, including taped interviews, collages of items from the *Sarnia Observer* and, inevitably, photographs. But again, the integration of such material, even admitting the polyphonic aspiration of the collage, must run in two directions. Phrases from the poems are interestingly attached to the documents, but the language of the documents does not seem to echo much in the poems. A contrast with Kroetsch's *Seed Catalogue* is revealing. Kroetsch creates a verbal context which alerts the reader to the poem's intertextuality: we become aware of the presuppositions, and hence of the unexpected potential, of the language rediscovered in the source documents.

Frank Davey assimilates his source material much more thoroughly than Gutteridge in *The Clallam, or Old Glory in Juan de Fuca* (1973). Davey's subject is the absurd posturing which sinks a ship on its short run between Port Townsend, Washington, and Victoria in 1904: the captain of the *Clallam* will not allow his storm-battered ship to fly distress signals, and rescuers from Victoria watching the floundering vessel refuse to set out until they see a distress flag. The fuming anti-American curses of the narrator are anti-poetic, but they firmly establish authenticity – Davey's passionate involvement in his subject. This is narrative with the least possible amount of poetry; it is anti-E.J. Pratt in that special sense – Davey includes nothing to detract from the politics, no heroism of individual or group. The authentic poem is flat: 'For Capt. George Roberts / even goddamn Ned Pratt would have put away / the Scots metaphor –.'

Davey distrusts documentary, but asserts a stylistic spareness which inevitably claims the factuality of his subject's vicious arrogance. Such overt declaiming is, to be sure, the exception in the documentary narratives, where the speaker's voice is generally more reflective. As in John Ferns's *Henry Hudson or Discovery* (1975), the collage of document and the *readings* of the material by the poet is more commonplace. But the poetry of fact is more effectively evoked when the source documents are incorporated in the overt documentary method of the writer's diary. Dennis Gruending's *Gringo* (1983), for example, links his Saskatchewan home with touristic discoveries of South America by setting his prose lyrics in the context of journal entries which, if interesting for themselves, do little to elaborate the language of the lyrics, but merely serve to reinforce their journalistic flatness.

Such blurring of the line between journal and poem, which has a heritage in Canadian literature going back to Samuel Hearne, was reasserted in Daphne Marlatt's *What Matters*. Similarly, in Eli Mandel's *Life Sentence: Poems and Journals: 1976–1980*, travel journals (although all packed at the back of the book, separate from the poems) seem to revive a lyric impulse in the poems which was absent in most of Mandel's poetry published in the 1970s. A more thorough fusion of journal and poem appeared in Douglas Lochhead's *High Marsh Road: Lines for a Diary* (1980). And in *The Panic Field: Prose Poems* (1984), Lochhead superbly used documentary language to express the unease of 'over-trained' soldiers waiting endlessly for battle. In trying 'to translate the unheard language [that is, the silent fear, the inarticulate boredom] into words,' Lochhead discovers the aptness of plainly presented fact: 'Let me be spare with all this. The economy of barrack, clothing, the new rules should make it simple.'

Even the documentary long poem, with its affection for the conventions of realism, moved to incorporate reflections on its own making. The journal's self-consciousness is integrated with history's demand for fact (witness the many archival and contemporary illustrations) so that the text constantly questions its own authenticity. Thus George Bowering rewrote his poem *George Vancouver* (1970) as the novel (some would call it a long poem) *Burning Water* (1980), also about George Vancouver's voyage of discovery on the North West coast. Novel questions poem, George Bowering writing questions George Vancouver writing: such awareness of the writing process results in a strange form we might call the metadocumentary. An effective combination of document and documenting the writing process is Lionel Kearns's *Convergences* (1984), a venture into the poetry of explorers' journals, centring on Captain Cook's encounter with the Nootka in 1778, which inevitably reflects the poet's long association with Bowering. The book, like Gutteridge's, is anchored in documents and conventional works of history. Although Kearns uses little poetry – in the sense of image patterns, rhyme, several types of ambiguity – he assembles an intricate polyphony of the explorer's imperializing language, words in native Indian tongues, and a writer's awareness of audience: 'What you bring to this occasion I cannot even dream of.' The correspondences Kearns seeks to create, or to open up for discovery, make this an intellectually exciting work; it is part of that excitement that the metafictional aspect of the poem challenges the reader directly with the crucial issue of the poem *as poem* which is a constant undercurrent in writing that tests this boundary between document and lyric.

In its desire to incorporate multiple centres, and their langauges, their voices, the long poem yearns to be a list of facts, a history text, especially a novel. The tendency became apparent in the 1980s with such books as Frank Davey's *Capitalistic Affection* (1982), a six-part long poem revisioning the comic strips the poet grew up with. Davey's *Edward and Patricia* (1984) was promoted as a novel made of poems – a love story, which, like the novel, is also a study of an evolving society. The dream's realism is affirmed here by the cause-and-effect linearity of a chronological story. It is continuously humorous and (parodically) erotic, and like so many of the poems I have been discussing, it makes its claim on *authenticity* by appearing not to be, except very occasionally, *poetic*.

FRINGE FORMS

The long poem, by definition, is omnivorous. It takes everything in: it can accommodate many forms of discourse and competing theories of language. As *The Martyrology*, pre-eminently, shows, the unending poem of a lifetime is polysemous, polyvalent, polylinguistic. Because this roly-poly poem absorbs all kinds of poetry, it is, like the encyclopedia, a form of consolidation.

In the long poem highly technical vocabulary, unconventional transliteration, and sequences of syllabic sounds become more accessible in contexts of straightforward descriptive prose and familiar talk. I have, therefore, rather reluctantly used the term 'fringe' to embrace the poetics of science, the forms of translation, and the poem as public performance. They are certainly off the centre represented by the prose lyric and the surrealist song, that is to say the centre determined by sheer numbers of practitioners. But as the long poem grew in popularity, especially after the publication of *Seed Catalogue* in 1977, it seemed to establish a centre of its own which contained the tangents and peripheries. It is crashingly trite to say that in the twentieth century our concept of what the universe is made of and how it moves has fundamentally altered. Yet the persistence of Newtonian and Cartesian models to explain the sensorily apprehensible world makes the modern revolution in physics continuing news, and a continuing surprise to non-scientists. I would hardly argue that the implications of relativity theory and quantum theory made no impact on Canadian writing until 1970. But, as I have already remarked in discussing bpNichol, writing in the later 1970s indicated a greater willingness to explore the poetics of science. How does particle physics, which postulates a vast subatomic world, inaccessible to sensory perception and operating on principles different from the world accessible to the senses, affect a sense of poetic form and of language?

These questions found particular focus in the baffling, yet compelling poetry of Christopher Dewdney, brother of science writer Alexander Dewdney, and the son of Selwyn Dewdney, both novelist (*Wind Without Rain*, 1946) and anthropologist/archeologist. Dewdney adopted a technical vocabulary more completely than any other Canadian writer since Pratt (and what an interesting comparison they would make), extended radically the sense of what region is, and of its place in poetry, and especially attended to the connections between modern science and language.

Dewdney's books are collages illustrated throughout by the author's drawings, sometimes as precise as engravings, sometimes crudely freehand. Photographs, illustrations from other works, and Dewdney's own whimsical visual collages add to the eclecticism. These last usually serve to collapse zones of time: 'Paris Ontario 1951' in *A Palaeozoic Geology of London, Ontario* (1973), for example, shows what appear to be shards of limestone in a contemporary mine site overshadowed by drawings of plants that would have flourished in or near the tropical sea which created the limestone formations several hundred million years ago. Verbal collages are also characteristic: at the top of a page is a fragment of a prose poem, typically without syntactical indication of beginning or ending; the scrap of prose is (un)balanced by a more conventionally lyrical (ie, lined) poem at the bottom of the page.[17] The multiple collages suggest the poetics of science, in that the cryptic jottings, the puzzled questions, the mini-essays, the glossaries of specialized terms, sketchy illustrations, and the photos of fossils, represent the archeologist-psychologist's *log entries* (a title Dewdney uses frequently). Each book is presented as the observer's field notes, sometimes simply declarative, sometimes speculative, sometimes bemused, sometimes firmly convinced of an important discovery.

What seems to underpin all Dewdney's thinking, and his manipulations of language, are the discoveries of quantum physics. For a system of language, the second law of thermodynamics (that for any closed system the entropy always increases) implies that, over time, structure and order disappear, leaving a murky blend of signifiers all with a sort of grey uniformity. Yet the complement of the second law of thermodynamics is that 'for the creation of new order, the workings of the random, the plethora of uncommitted alternatives ... is necessary.'[18] Dewdney's challenge is to revitalize the system by encouraging the random. The potential of the random is encouraged by his collage of other systems of signs.

Two crucial dimensions of modern particle physics are incorporated in Dewdney's poetry. First, Heisenberg's uncertainty principle tells us that there is no such thing as a particle of matter – that is, an electron – that has a precise momentum and a precise position. It is then a 'fundamental truth about the nature of the universe' that 'we cannot know the position of even *one* particle precisely.' As physics has explored and identified more and more minuscule subatomic particles, our entire perception of solid matter has been destroyed. Any solid object is 'almost all empty space ... seething with activity, a maelstrom of virtual particles.' That there are 'vast reaches of empty space within a solid object' is still bewildering for the layman to contemplate.[19] And it is bewildering precisely because of the ways in which our language has structured our sense of actuality, the 'isness' of object implied by the referentiality of language.

As the title *Alter Sublime* (1980) implies, Dewdney honours both the divine sublimity of a world of empty space, and a reverence for the innate uncertainty of human perception:

> It is the, it is
> like a hole
> that runs through everything.
> Seen
> it is altered.
> Grasped it is broken.

Here Dewdney exploits the fundamental subject-verb-object principle of pre-dication in the English language. His 'it' has no antecedent, no object or concept to which it refers. What *it* 'is' is 'the,' an article (a particle?) that is supposedly *definite* but has no inherent semantic content. Dewdney, then, claims that this syntactical absence can be apprehended by analogy with something (even everything) in the supposedly physical world, but that something is a hole (a whole?) and therefore an absence of matter. As in so much of Dewdney's work, one senses a good deal of comic pleasure here. Anyway, if it could be seen, the very process of seeing it (as with the uncertainty principle) would alter it.

And so it runs through everything. At one point in his 'Log Entries,' Dewdney speculates that each word is a particle, an electron with 'a negative or positive end, according to the placement of the consonants (positive) and vowels (negative).' Then he proceeds, on the facing page, to construct a space poem showing how particles of 'stencil' attract and repel one another. More conventionally, in a study called 'The Parenthetical' (*Fovea Centralis*, 1975), Dewdney presents a proposition which makes some kind of absurd or surreal sense, then gradually interpolates parenthetic words into it, after almost every word, destroying all glimmers of conventional meaning, as he shows the infinite spaces inherent within language.

The other area in which the potential of science makes an overt appearance in Canadian poetry is in the 'Number Grid' poetry of Wilfred Watson, and in Paul Dutton's *Book of Numbers* (1979). Watson introduces a new dimension into what is otherwise poetry based on the syntax of the prose lyric, in *I Begin with Counting* (1978) and *Mass on Cowback* (1982). Watson explains that his system differs from traditional metrical verse in its counting words rather than syllables, and in using a predetermined grid rather than the line as the basic structural unit. Since, in the case of *I Begin with Counting*, each number but nine has two slots, he may be suggesting that each numeral is both exact number (a purely arbitrary verbal sign) and an inexact quantity (only understood in terms of another word). However conventionally the poem reads, one can't escape the influence of the numbers printed on the page; the reading of the text becomes an interplay between the codes of colloquial speech written, and the code of the decimal system (although there is no zero) with its programmatic, rationalistic, automatic, infinite replication.

Numbers, as contrasted to quantity, can be 'accurate because there is a discontinuity between each integer and the next.' Another crucial property of number, especially of the smaller and commoner numbers that Watson uses exclusively, is that they are 'often not counted but recognized as patterns at a single glance.' These numbers recognized as pattern are fundamental to the construction of the biological world where 'an organism, having chosen a number for the radial symmetry of some set of parts, will repeat that number in other parts.'[20] For Watson the use of various number grids is a way of exploring these multiplying symmetries in the organisms of language as well, and of establishing connections between the natural world and the mental world.

Paul Dutton's *The Book of Numbers* is less graphically puzzling, but more semantically obscure. In twenty-four 'chapters' Dutton writes a novel about the numbers as personalities, as characters ('seven dances quietly with two / all that's heard is their breathing'). The impact of John Cage's minimalist verbal abstractions seems evident, though Dutton seems most interesting – poetically – when his poem shows how his numbers (which elsewhere seem to have personalities) permeate the community dialect both as homophones (two/to/too), and as metaphor ('six's being at sixes and sevens over seven and eight').

As with revival of the metaphysical lyric, so the contemporary Canadian poetry which exploits the potential (both in vocabulary and in general conception of language) of the hard or exact sciences, points to some consolidation of tradition. The learned poet, reaching beyond his reader's knowledge (contrast the auto-didact Purdy concealing or apologizing for his learning) gained respectability. During the 1970s many writers, as well as critics, became increasingly interested in literary (especially post-structuralist) theory, with its principle of intertextuality, which argues that any text is 'comprehensible only in terms of other texts which it prolongs, completes, transforms, and sublimates.'[21] This theory of the generation of texts led to a lively interest in notions of translation, since all texts are, from this perspective, 'translations.' The principles and possibilities of homolinguistic translation were best summarized in Douglas Barbour and Stephen Scobie's *The Pirates of Pen's Chance* (1981), a collection of translations from English to English, which the authors note was inspired by Steve McCaffery's and bpNichol's earlier ventures into shifting codes. Barbour and Scobie give a clear explanation of the systems of their translation: the freest, and least 'meaningful,' metonymic system, various systems of acrostics, and structural translations. The book makes these strategies more accessible by including notes on the source texts and the systems used. Inevitably, especially in the metonymic mode, homolinguistic translation often resulted in self-indulgent blather. In the mid-1980s, it is less the accomplishment than the potential that seems important. The procedure of structural translation was especially satisfying in providing an alternative reading of source texts, as well as a reading of the translators. In his 'The Love Song of J. Alfred Prufrock' Scobie provides a surprisingly informative map of Eliot's poem by showing how frequently, and with what interruption, the word 'I' occurs: '/six words I / thirty-six lines three words I / three words I ... [etc.].'

Steve McCaffery used a metonymical system which he calls 'allusive referential' to make the most wholly satisfying 'translations from the English' to date. Working from Mary Barnard's translations of Sappho, McCaffery created *Intimate Distortions* (1979), a book with the coherence of a lyric sequence paying tribute to a single author. The method seemed ideal to illuminate Sappho in contemporary language, and to send readers back to Sappho (which the book necessarily does). McCaffery's intimacy is appropriate to the emotional commitment in Sappho's poems, to the adventures in sexuality associated with her name, and to the allegiance of those followers who learned from her how to sing. But McCaffery's distortions are essential, too, since what we have of the Greek poet's work is in fragments, presumably altered from her originals (the available texts date from about 300 years after her birth): 'Same's not / similar // & long ago / is now // in this / remembering' ('Fifty'). At the other limit to the valuable reinterpretation found in McCaffery was Sandra Braman and Paul Dutton's *Spokesheards* (1983), a package of postcards, whose metonymic translations of one another issued only in self-serving insularity.

Dewdney's poetry of physics and neuro-chemistry, and McCaffery's displacements of Sappho, embody radical shifts in poetics or poetic structure provoked by contemporary theories on the nature of language and matter themselves. In the main theirs were isolated gestures, rich in potential, but, at least by the mid-1980s, certainly not widely imitated or promising to become a *movement*. Sound poetry, however, under this and several other labels, did grow into a movement as it sought to reassess the bases and possibilities of language and text.

The growth of sound poetry seemed to be part of a general rise in emphasis on poetry as performance. When the Canada Council introduced, over considerable protest, a quota and ranking system to its generous program of assistance for public readings, the marketplace began to demand the effective performer. The poet with a commanding theatrical presence, like Robert Bringhurst or (if more restrained) Phyllis Webb, received more attention. Poetry, very much a minority art form, surfaced in more spectacular public occasions often integrated with music: Warren Tallman attracted thousands to a series of benefit readings in Vancouver; Earle Birney continued his life-long experimenting by performing publicly and on radio with the jazz group *Nexus* (eventually resulting in the valuable three-LP set, *Nexus & Birney*, 1983).

In international forums, only one literary form will invariably oblige mention of Canadian writers. Canadian sound poets are always thought of as essential contributors, if not leaders, in the development of their elusive art. This attention has a good deal to do with the fame of Marshall McLuhan as media guru, and more immediately with the influential adventures into aural wordscapes made by Murray Schafer, and by renowned pianist Glenn Gould. (Gould called his influential CBC Radio programs, 'The Idea of North' [1967] and 'The Latecomers' [1969], 'contrapuntal radio.')[22] bill bissett's almost twenty-five years' persistence with innocent incantation made him the most frequently cited Canadian sound poet. Among his various experiments in alternative spelling and visual forms, bissett especially developed the poem as insistent repetition – either of single word or phrase. Anyone who has heard him chant (to the pulsing rhythms of his hand-held rattles) a single word, such as 'honey,' will recognize his power as sound poet. The effect is at once holistic – as the incantation empties the sound of meaning and induces an entranced suspension of left-hemisphere activity – and meaningful, as different shades of volume and intonation explore the possible meanings layered in a single word.

This description is shorter than its historical significance dictates only because of the extraordinary difficulty of holding on to the performances. Sound poetry is, of course, written to be performed. In written form – as, for example, in sean o'huigin's *The Inks and the Pencils and the Looking Back* (1978) – a reader finds it difficult to imagine a performance, and ends groping for the few poems that contain glimpses of conventional lyric or narrative structure. The most prominent sound poetry *group*, The Four Horsemen (Rafael Barreto-Rivera, Paul Dutton, Steve McCaffery, and bpNichol) performing in various permutations, resist book publication, not to mention tape recorders and even microphones. Some limited sense of their work can be found in book form in *Horse d'Oeuvres* (1975), and on some difficult-to-obtain records. (The best indications of the breadth of Canadian sound poetry, and of recorded material available is in *Sound Poetry: A Catalogue* [1978], prepared by Steve McCaffery and bpNichol for the Eleventh International Sound Poetry Festival in Toronto.) Douglas Barbour and Stephen Scobie performed effectively as *Re-Sounding* in the early 1980s, and Penny Kemp made an impressive debut in *Animus* (1984), punning on the separate phonemes that make up a word. The sound poet most accessible in print is Joe Rosenblatt, whose energetically surrealist poems are almost invariably enriched by alliterating insects or exotic polysyllabics.

CONCLUSION

To emphasize the energies of consolidation in Canadian poetry while beginning with poets as different as Kroetsch and Atwood and ending with bissett and The Four Horsemen will appear either whimsical or perverse. The impetus to consolidation consists of a good deal more than the tendency to 'Collecteds,' 'Selecteds,' and classroom anthologies, or the increasing caution of major publishing houses. The impetus holds good in spite of the undoubted (and bewildering) proliferation of books of poetry, even into the recession-strained, restraint-plagued 1980s. I share Gary Geddes' wonder, in the 'Preface' to *The Inner Ear* (1982), about what kind of culture publishes so many books, so many decent, sincere, informative books of poetry which are destined to go unread, both in the marketplace and in the 'readings' which critical journals or literary histories provide. The myriad small, regional publishers, which could have been subversive, seemed generally conservative, both in their poetic naming of local place and history, and in their need to grow beyond region. Despite the radical dismemberment of language(s) and codes which I have discussed as 'fringe,' the growth of post-structuralist methods (in writing, but especially in criticism) changed our perceptions. The disruptive, mad poets, archetypally on the edge of society, moved towards the solid centre of the establishment – at least of the prestige establishment, as defined by the academic and civil servant determiners. Where are the belligerent innovators a literary culture depends on? Many of those whom we recognized in the 1960s – Bowering, Cohen, Rosenblatt, and others – were, in the 1980s, writing thematic studies and flying to New Zealand or Sweden to tell the world how Canada writes. They were also in the forefront of the computerization of Canadian writing. The very writers who were once the *tish*-disturbers are now the disciples of middle-class faddism. The emergence of a distinctively feminist poetry promised the most fundamental reassessment of the nature of language. But only a disappointing few of the deliberately feminist poets fulfilled their potential to write radical political poetry, or, more important, to dismantle the language to expose its gender bias. And the most obvious novelty among the younger writers is a sprightly tendency to the comic (and perhaps to comedy, the most profoundly conservative of literary genres). But in a postmodern ambience, where the bizarrely marginal becomes the establishment's chic, the artist will still find provocative stimulation. Where nothing is said to exist outside of language, the ultimate champions and lovers of language, the poets, can only be exhilarated by the absence. And begin to write their way inside out of it.

2 Short Fiction

DAVID JACKEL

Introducing *Canadian Short Stories* in 1928, Raymond Knister suggested that the Canadian short story, until then slow to flourish despite the recognized merit of writers such as E.W. Thomson, D.C. Scott, and Stephen Leacock, was about to enter a new era. Knister's brave hopes were not realized, although his own achievements and, of more distinction, those of Morley Callaghan, Thomas Raddall, Sinclair Ross, Hugh Garner, Ethel Wilson, Mavis Gallant, and Margaret Laurence, showed that individual authors could use the form skilfully. Canada's most gifted writers were, however, generally seen to be its poets and novelists. By 1965, in the first edition of the *Literary History of Canada*, Hugo McPherson was pessimistic about the future of short fiction, his views similar to those Robert Weaver expressed in his 'Introduction' to *Canadian Short Stories* (1960): 'There are few short-story writers in Canada these days and even fewer markets'; the form had a 'fugitive existence' in small periodicals (including Weaver's own *The Tamarack Review*) and in broadcast form on CBC Radio (also as a result of Weaver's efforts). More Canadian short stories, Weaver noted with irony, reached a Canadian audience through American magazines: 'It is an unhealthy situation.'

If Knister's optimism proved unwarranted, so too did the pessimism of the early 1960s. Margaret Atwood, Clark Blaise, Matt Cohen, George Elliott, Dave Godfrey, David Helwig, Hugh Hood, Norman Levine, John Metcalf, Alice Munro, Alden Nowlan, Ray Smith, Audrey Thomas, Rudy Wiebe – these and others had ensured by the early 1970s that the Canadian story no longer led a 'fugitive' existence. Numerous anthologies (created in part as a response to the increasing attention paid to Canadian literature in schools and universities) and new Canadian periodicals provided more opportunities for publication and helped to form something akin to that 'appreciative and representative audience' Knister had hoped for. Editors, too, could no longer comfortably accept Weaver's then generally accurate assertion of 1960: 'There have been so few collections of Canadian short stories that there is no tradition which an editor is required either to follow or to explain away.' Tentative, and sometimes apologetic, description began to give way to academic analysis and polemical judgment. Criticism of the short story, left until the late 1960s largely in the hands of reviewers, made a belated appearance in scholarly journals now that several authors had created a body of work requiring serious attention.[1] When Weaver's *Canadian Short Stories: Second Series* (1968) appeared, the confident and enthusiastic tone of his introduction reflected the prevailing atmosphere.

If the years after 1972 had permitted time for reflection, more considered discussion of the quality of short fiction would have been possible. Rebirth, however, was followed by inundation. Serious criticism could not keep up. Numerous collections, anthologies, and periodicals presented Canadian readers with an increasing number of short stories each year. Although keeping track of publications became well-nigh impossible, the obvious quantity did at least do away with the need to offer statistical proof of the vitality of the form.[2] And yet critical judgment was rendered difficult by markedly conflicting views of the nature of the form itself, of the proper critical methods to be employed, and of the directions in which various writers and their proponents thought that the development of the short story ought to proceed. Any discussion of Canadian short fiction after 1972 is inextricably linked to larger and naggingly persistent issues: what is 'Canadian' about Canadian literature, and what are the standards by which critics ought to judge it? Further complications were introduced by developments in literary criticism, developments that at times gave matters of theory priority over the careful reading of particular texts.

Many short story anthologies of the period were seemingly random assemblies of the better-known stories by the better-known writers, aimed primarily at a classroom market. These anthologies were often indistinguishable from each other, and few reached a second printing. Other anthologies served more ambitious, and sometimes more useful, purposes. The work of earlier writers was resurrected; collections of short fiction by Isabella Valancy Crawford, E.W. Thomson, Robert Barr, L.M. Montgomery, Mazo de la Roche, Norman Duncan, and Raymond Knister, although presenting work of uneven quality, provided some sense of the history of the form in Canada, as did David Arnason's *Nineteenth Century Canadian Stories* (1976), which argued in its introduction for the need to recognize continuities in the themes and concerns of writers of short fiction: 'Canadians are prone to the danger of forgetting the past and its influence on the present ... Modern Canadian writing is far more rooted in the past than we usually care to admit.' This position was to be under severe attack before the end of the decade.

A number of collections sought to convey a sense of place or region, most of them unsuccessfully, though there were notable exceptions. Macmillan's series of *Stories from Western Canada* (1972), *Stories from Atlantic Canada* (1973), *Stories from Ontario* (1974), and *Stories from Pacific & Arctic Canada* (1974) did, collectively, provide a good perspective on the differing histories and cultural characteristics of Canada's regions and on the differences within regions themselves. By contrast, collections intended to document social conditions or to offer social criticism were rare. Donna Phillips's *Voices of Discord* (1979) usefully compiled some neglected short fiction from the 1930s dealing with the anguish of the depression. Some of this material was interestingly experimental for its time; many of the stories were, however, too resolutely didactic, and the writers too often seemed intellectually rather than emotionally engaged with the working people and social concerns presented. No equivalent to Hugh Garner emerged after 1972; larger social and political issues were dealt with obliquely or hesitantly (if at all) and usually in the context of private rather than communal experience. The exception to this pattern is the increasing number of anthologies of short fiction by women writers (Rosemary Sullivan's *Stories by Canadian Women*, 1984, is a good example), which became one vehicle in which to argue feminist theory and to examine the specific concerns and characteristics of fiction by women.

Important also were anthologies that collected the work of individuals, several of them substantial writers (who influenced younger authors) for whom such collections were long overdue, among them Howard O'Hagan, A.M. Klein, Joyce Marshall, Sheila Watson, and Henry Kreisel. O'Hagan received more general recognition with the publication of *The Woman Who Got on at Jasper Station & Other Stories* (1977). Watson's short stories were collected in a special number of *Open Letter* (1974–5), and Kreisel's in *The Almost Meeting* (1981). M.W. Steinberg's edition of A.M. Klein's *Short Stories* (1983), with introduction and notes, assembled another body of fugitive publications; and in *A Private Place* (1975), Joyce Marshall selected from among her own work. Klein, Watson, and Kreisel showed that the Canadian writer's sensibility could be sophisticated and cosmopolitan as well as national or regional, and these collections were to provide some balance to the claims that the history of the short story in Canada had nothing much to offer the writers of the 1970s. Still other collections served to keep the work of major authors in print and accessible to a new generation of readers. D.C. Scott, Sinclair Ross, Callaghan, Laurence, and Hugh Hood (his earlier works) were among those whose stories made it unnecessary to denigrate or displace the old in order to welcome the new.

Two other kinds of anthology served more clearly to define the course of the short story during this period and to focus discussion of the merits of individual writers and particular approaches to the form. One might be termed the 'consensus' or 'representative' anthology, in which editors presented authors whose achievement seemed generally to be well recognized and used their introductions to set stories and authors in some relation to each other, their cultural context, and the Canadian tradition. The other was more likely to present stories of an 'innovative' or 'experimental' nature; editors, themselves often writers of short fiction, used their introductions to argue a distrust of tradition and urge the pursuit of the new. Although the division, in the choice of authors, was not absolute between the two kinds, it was usually distinct.

From the most prominent (if not always the most carefully titled) representative anthologies there emerges a sense of agreement as to which writers deserved attention and respect. Alice Munro is nearly always included, and is usually accompanied by Margaret Atwood and W.D. Valgardson, with Hugh Hood and Dave Godfrey (whose new collection, *Dark Must Yield*, appeared in 1978) also well represented. Audrey Thomas, Alistair MacLeod, Jack Hodgins, Clark Blaise, and Matt Cohen were among those who found a place in the anthologies of the late 1970s and early 1980s. Surprisingly, given the tendency of most critics and reviewers to be wary of or even ignore so-called expatriate writers, Mavis Gallant is as frequently included as Alice Munro, while Norman Levine appears more often than Hugh Hood. The editors' choices appear to reflect a consensus about the achievement of those writing in what might be termed the admittedly broad range of modernist realism, with the later inclusions of Thomas, Hodgins, and Cohen reflecting the number of authors associated with 'experimental' or postmodernist tendencies.

These anthologies provide relatively similar justifications for the inclusion of authors and stories; their comments about the form itself do not hint at controversy. Robert Weaver presented *Canadian Short Stories: Second Series* (1968) as a collection that illustrated both continuity and the shift 'from a rural to an urban sensibility' and an 'international outlook'; the stories were, however, chosen because of the 'high standard' of the contributors' work. Alec Lucas's introduction to *Great Canadian Short Stories* (1971) also noted similar tendencies, and commented on the increasingly subjective, poetic, and psychological tendencies of short fiction; nevertheless, Lucas added: 'I made my selections with no particular theme or thesis in mind.' Donald Stephens selected the material for *Contemporary Voices* (1972) simply on its merits as good writing. Ivon Owen and Morris Wolfe noted that while all but one of their selections in *The Best Modern Canadian Short Stories* (1978) were 'traditional in form' this had not been the result of any particular set of criteria for inclusion.[3] Robert Weaver's third series of *Canadian Short Stories* (1978) collected short fiction from the late 1960s and early 1970s (with the result that of the eighteen authors represented, only four[4] had made appearances in his earlier volumes); the material was selected primarily on its 'literary merit.' Weaver also took note of the number of new contributors who had immigrated to Canada. The introduction to John Stevens's *Best Canadian Short Stories* (1981) shows the influence of mythopoeic criticism, but his final argument for presenting the selections is not their mythic qualities, nor even their Canadian ones: the stories 'are too good to miss.'

In the 'Preface' to *The Penguin Book of Canadian Short Stories* (1980), Wayne Grady argues that 'realism' is the 'most characteristic feature' of Canadian short fiction, a tradition continued in the 'semi-autobiographical' work of later writers such as Laurence, Munro, and Hood. Grady also asserts that 'by interpreting for us the complexities of human life, by helping to bring the unarticulated soul of an entire community into sudden and radiant being, the short story can be said to have assumed a social responsibility left vacant by poetry since the late 1950s.' Grady's 'Preface' to *The Penguin Book of Modern Canadian Short Stories* (1982) defines the contemporary short story in Canada in terms of two thematic phases. In the first phase the past is tyrannical and oppressive, and freedom is achieved by rejecting it. In the second phase the freedom brought by rejection is questioned. That such themes 'are resoundingly the major themes of the second half of the twentieth century' he takes to demonstrate the maturity of the contemporary Canadian short story. Robert Weaver makes a similar point in his 'Preface' to the Fourth Series of *Canadian Short Stories* (1985), pointing out that 'more and more ... [Canadian] stories are being published internationally' and that by the 1970s the form occupied 'a central position in Canadian writing.' These 'representative' short story anthologies, moreover, despite the almost complete lack of any references to serious critical studies of the writers anthologized, generally convey a sense that the Canadian short story flourished and that its evolution in relation to a well-defined tradition was clearly describable. Other developments from the late 1960s onwards gave a quite different impression.

The majority of collections and anthologies from this period were avowedly to-the-moment in their emphasis. A sense of a Canadian tradition was often ignored, or denigrated, or seen as a detriment to the proper recognition of contemporary authors of short fiction. The effect of these compilations was not always salutary. Attention was deservedly drawn to the work of many active writers, particularly in the annual series begun by Oberon Press with *14 Stories High* (1971), edited by David Helwig and Tom Marshall, and continuing first as *New Canadian Stories* (1972–5) edited by Helwig and Joan Harcourt, and subsequently as *Best Canadian Stories* edited by John Metcalf and Harcourt (1976–7), by Metcalf and Clark Blaise (1978–80), and by Metcalf and Leon Rooke (1981–2). The range of writers included in the Oberon series was commendably wide, from the well-known (Garner, Atwood, Hood, Munro, Thomas) to those who would soon establish or significantly extend their reputations and publish collections of their own work (Don

Bailey, Beth Harvor, Andreas Schroeder, W.D. Valgardson, Matt Cohen, Kent Thompson, Jane Rule, W.P. Kinsella, Jack Hodgins, Elizabeth Spencer, Merna Summers). In general terms, the series displayed the eclectic approach exemplified in Weaver's anthologies – to publish good stories without demanding that authors adhere to specific expectations in subject-matter and style. Other kinds of anthology also made their mark, for other reasons. In these, the intention to publish good work was accompanied (or even overshadowed) by statements of critical principle. Aggressive and often doctrinaire editorial stances tended to generate more controversy than illumination, and the work of various authors was anthologized and discussed less for its intrinsic merits than as purported evidence in support of arguments over the directions in which the Canadian short story ought – or ought not – to be moving.

The two most active and influential figures here have been Geoff Hancock and John Metcalf. *Canadian Fiction Magazine* (est. 1971; Hancock editing after 1974) has published work by writers both new and established, but the editor has also used the magazine to champion writers such as Michael Bullock, Brian Fawcett, and J. Michael Yates, and as a forum to present his own (and others') views on the current state of fiction and on its future. The introduction to Hancock's *Magic Realism* (1980), an anthology composed largely of short stories first published in *Canadian Fiction Magazine*, offers a useful summary of these views: 'This anthology owes everything to international literary influences. Contrary to the thematic and historical studies of Canadian stories as taught in schools and universities, the writers of short stories use all kinds of literary methods. In the past decade, the modernist mode in Canadian short fiction has far exceeded the conventions of so-called realistic fiction.' For Hancock, the most important mode is magic realism, 'a blend of fantasy and everyday reality ... the conjunction of these two worlds in one place.' To those who would argue that magic realism can work only in an oral tradition and a pre-technological society, Hancock responds that this causes no difficulty for Canadian writers: 'Canada is an invisible country in the same way that Colombia, Peru, Argentina, and Paraguay are invisible, and the art of the magic realist is to make it real for us on their terms.'

Hancock gazes resolutely on the future; social and documentary realism are backward-looking, current Canadian literature is 'pallid brickwork,' and its authors drive 'ochre coloured compact cars.' Magic realism is, indeed, just one of the possibilities for writers 'looking for a way out'; anti-stories, fantasies, stories 'without any fidelity to social fact,' 'even stories without books' are all possibilities in the 'stratosphere' of innovation. Magic realism itself has other 'profound' implications for Canadian writing: 'It pulls away from mimetic realism and points towards the imaginative unknown which

still remains in a recognizable place. Magic realism opens up possibilities of
language, of imagery, of literary conventions that can ... elevate Canada's
prose writers to international stature.'

Not, like Hancock, an enthusiast, John Metcalf nevertheless has come to
hold some similar views. These are not evident in two anthologies he edited
in the early 1970s – *Sixteen by Twelve* (1970) and *Kaleidoscope* (1972) –
where writers such as Callaghan, Garner, Ross, Laurence, Munro, Hood,
Ray Smith, and Kent Thompson mingle in the customary eclecticism of most
collections. Yet a decade later Metcalf would flatly state: 'Our major short
story writers are Mavis Gallant, Norman Levine, Hugh Hood, Alice Munro,
Leon Rooke, and Clark Blaise.'[5] Hugh Hood's *Flying a Red Kite* (1962), he
continues, is 'the first book of modern short stories published in this country.'
(Metcalf explains that he means 'traditionally modern' rather than 'postmodern.') Hancock asserted that the realist tradition was not merely finished,
it had in fact been 'an illusion'; Metcalf goes farther in claiming that there
had been *no* 'native Canadian tradition in short story writing' and takes
Arnason and Grady vigorously to task for daring to suggest its existence. To
Metcalf – in his words 'an immigrant teacher of literature in the early sixties'
– 'there was precious little literature in evidence' in Canada. His *Kicking
Against the Pricks* goes on: 'Callaghan struck me as an extremely *clumsy*
writer ... The stories, which were accounted better than the novels, seemed
to me even worse. They were badly written and mawkish. The language was
plodding.' Sinclair Ross 'is a writer who, in his stories, was poised for flight
but remained earthbound, weighted down by traditional baggage he was unable to jettison.' 'Hugh Garner's writing is primitive and uncouth.' Before
Hood, it seems, Canadian writers generally laboured in a country 'isolated
from the rest of the world by some inexplicable time-lag.' It was only after
1962 that writers of short fiction in Canada joined the rest of the world in
taking formal concerns seriously: 'Where twenty years ago Canadian stories
stressed content – what a story was *about* – the main emphasis now is on
the story as verbal and rhetorical *performance*. Our best writers are concerned
with the story as *thing to be experienced* rather than as *thing to be understood.*'

Elsewhere, in an essay entitled 'The Curate's Egg' (*Essays on Canadian
Writing*, 1984–5), Metcalf explains the relation between formal concerns and
the desired effect of a story:

The desired final purpose of stories is to move the reader emotionally, to extend the
boundaries of his emotional world. Stories are not puzzles to be solved. Nor do they
convey simple moral messages. They are not sermons; they are not propaganda for
any cause. Their primary purpose, I must insist, is emotional. But that emotional
impact will not be felt until the reader has responded with great skill and knowledge
to all the nuances of a highly complex performance. *Reading a story is a purely
literary activity.*

Like Hancock, who describes magic realists as 'part of a second Romantic Rebellion in human artistic nature,'[6] Metcalf is, if less aggressively so, rejecting the 'realist' tradition in favour of a literature of *expression*. Expressive theories of literature usually place the artist in the centre of the picture, as Hancock and Metcalf do; their emphasis on the present and the future, combined with a denial of continuities and denigration of the past, is similarly to be expected.

Readers and critics of other persuasions may find themselves less comfortable with this position. Furthermore, the prescriptiveness of Hancock and Metcalf is no more justified than the long-vanished recipe for a 'well-made play' or the dogma that writers must *show* but never *tell*. Readers, writers, and critics will all suffer if, before getting on with their work, they must declare their allegiance to a particular and circumscribing theory.

Canadians have other reasons to hesitate before accepting the views of influential editors such as Hancock and Metcalf. The beginnings of Canadian literature, the Canadian novel, Canadian poetry and the Canadian short story have been announced and then reannounced so often as to suggest that the country is in a perpetual state of colonial inferiority. Although one can understand the reasons why authors of any period are motivated to shout 'Read me!' their accompanying dismissals of earlier writers imply both arrogance and insecurity: insecurity because setting aside the past as all but worthless shows a reluctance to allow comparisons; arrogance because dismissal carries with it the claim that their work will not in turn be similarly dealt with. To date the appearance of the 'modern' short story in Canada by citing *Flying a Red Kite*, and to denounce or ignore the work or the influence of Callaghan, Ross, Knister, Ethel Wilson, Watson, and Kreisel, whether they had or had not published collections of their work, is to deprive Canadians of their past.

To resist what T.D. MacLulich has termed 'the homogenizing tendency of international modernism,' we must insist that Canadian writers have made 'significant statements about life in particular parts of our country, at particular times.'[7] Awareness of literary trends outside Canada does not mean that an attention to Canadian distinctiveness must be abandoned. To do so, as John Sutherland argued in opposing A.J.M. Smith's approval of 'cosmopolitanism,' is to substitute one form of colonialism for another. 'International standards' are not truly international. Like dominant economic theories, or the price of gold, they are established by imperial powers. They are *trans*national at best, not *inter*national, for few functional exchanges take place *between* (*inter*); what happens instead is that the dominant centres assimilate the peripheries.

Hence there is no need to exalt experimentation and language-centred fiction at the expense of the regional or the mimetic. The 'poetic' qualities in work by Alice Munro do not require readers to ignore the regional and the realistic. Leon Rooke's skill need not be asserted by denying the merit of W.D.

Valgardson. Metcalf's own good judgment in selecting authors to praise and anthologize does not entail an acceptance of his critical and polemical positions. Dogma cannot deny achievement, and the study of Canadian short fiction written after 1970 reveals an achievement both praiseworthy and varied.

Margaret Atwood, Matt Cohen, Jack Hodgins, Hugh Hood, Audrey Thomas, and Rudy Wiebe, known to most readers as novelists (and Atwood as poet and critic as well), all published important collections of short fiction after 1972. Although the stories in Atwood's *Dancing Girls and Other Stories* (1977), her first collection, deal for the most part with strained personal relationships, severed connections, and desperate characters on the verge of madness, these lives of bleakness and moral emptiness are set in perspective by Atwood's mordant wit, through the cool control of a narrative voice, the careful structuring of a story, or the pointed arrangement of what might first seem trivial detail. *Bluebeard's Egg* (1983) presents, in part, a similarly blighted emotional landscape, in which victims and victimizers play out their shoddy (and sometimes savage) games. Characters live in confusion, fear or emptiness. Sometimes, however, as in 'Significant Moments in the Life of My Mother,' the tone is warmer and less detached. In other stories, too, there are notes not perhaps of affirmation but at least of acceptance and even affection. Placing Atwood's stories in relation to her poems and novels is difficult and probably premature. In some ways the best comparison would be with her essays: varied in tone, sometimes tentative and speculative, or provocative and playful, sometimes irritatingly quirky and cryptic – the product of an intelligence still setting itself in order behind a series of what seem to be necessary masks.

The short stories of Matt Cohen rarely convey the strong sense of place and history characteristic of his best novels; their moral perspectives, moreover, are often less clearly focused. Many of these stories are resolutely experimental: multiple points of view, disarranged chronologies, and varieties of tone ranging from wit and whimsy to calculated flatness, combine to challenge the reader's expectations. The stories in *Columbus and the Fat Lady and Other Stories* (1972) and *Night Flights* (1978) – collected in *The Expatriate* (1982) – are often disconcerting, occasionally bizarre and surrealistic. Characters search for self-awareness or grope their way towards an understanding of their relationships with others; they seek to evade traps, or set traps for themselves; they pursue some sense of purpose while at the same time doubting their own ability to grasp it. These quests are usually unsuccessful, sometimes disturbingly so. What is found is often deserved, but also unexpected. Meaning must, apparently, be sought, yet experience is replete with incongruities and deceptions. Even in the stories which are not experimental ('Death of a Friend,' for example, and 'Brothers'), where Cohen's vision of life is less ambiguous, meaning is still uncertain. 'Who knows what people do,' says the narrator of 'Death of a Friend.' This is a statement, not a question.

Some of the experimentation in these stories seems forced, and the shifting tones can at times seem evasive. *Café Le Dog* (1983) shows Cohen more consistently at his best. Experiments continue, but are here, as in the title story, more controlled and seldom distracting. Characters and their contexts are more fully realized; the reader's perspective on persons and events is more subtly directed and focused. The humour of the stories is also more subtle; true comedy and pointed irony are more common here than laconic whimsy. 'The Sins of Tomas Benares' and 'Golden Whore of the Heartland' are much closer to the world of Cohen's novels than that of his earlier short stories. They are longer, richer in detail, and complex without being inconclusive.

Margaret Atwood, in reviewing *Ladies & Escorts* (1977) in *The Globe and Mail*, noted 'the fascination with language for its own sake' that characterizes the work of Audrey Thomas; Thomas's stories are also 'about language: the impossibility, and the necessity, of using it for true communication.' For most of her characters, true communication is impossible. Men are obtuse and insecure, their relationships with women self-centred and parasitic. The female characters lead more intense emotional lives, yet their sensitivity leaves them vulnerable or alienated – inhabitants of a solipsistic universe. In *Real Mothers* (1981), the women who attempt to assert their independence and break free of relationships that have isolated and frustrated them find themselves new difficulties in trying to order their lives in a world that seems at best fragile and on the verge of collapse.

Thomas's concern with order in life, and order in art – the connections between self and other, between form and content – was evident in her first collection, *Ten Green Bottles* (1967), and has persisted. When aesthetic control is not exercised, her obsessively self-absorbed characters can seem to be figures in a fictional autobiography obscurely motivated. But in her most successful stories, Thomas uses a range of cultural contexts (Canadian, African, Mexican), irony of situation, and carefully crafted dialogue, to detach the reader from the emotional preoccupations of her characters. Here the reader becomes involved in the stories' language, and so experiences something of the communication that conventional language paradoxically inhibits.

Readers impressed by the sweeping vision of history in Rudy Wiebe's major novels will find many of his short stories disappointing. The longer form gives Wiebe the space he needs for his epic recreations of the past. In the short story, even when dealing with similar themes, Wiebe's material seems unduly truncated. 'Games for Queen Victoria,' for example (a reworking of William Francis Butler's account, in *The Great Lone Land*, of his meeting with Louis Riel), and 'The Year We Gave Away the Land' (which recalls scenes better located in a historical context in *The Temptations of Big Bear*), alike ask for extended treatment. By contrast, two stories from Wiebe's first collection *Where Is the Voice Coming From?* (1974), the title story and 'The Naming of Albert Johnson,' work much better because the doomed Johnson and Almighty Voice have significance primarily in the brief and violent episodes that lead to their deaths. Both stories are also good illustrations of Wiebe's interest in the processes of 'story-making' and useful therefore to critics of his work.

Wiebe's religious convictions, and his critical examination of them, are also less convincingly evident in his short stories. 'All on Their Knees' and 'Chinook Christmas' are superficial and sentimental in comparison to *Peace Shall Destroy Many* or *The Blue Mountains of China*, although 'Did Jesus Ever Laugh?' (*The Angel of the Tar Sands and Other Stories*, 1982) is more ambitious and far from sentimental. Frequently anthologized, Wiebe has himself edited several useful collections.

Jack Hodgins, too, is a better novelist than writer of short stories. While *Spit Delaney's Island* (1976) and *The Barclay Family Theatre* (1981) include stories that may appear capable of standing on their own, their significance is fully seen only when they are read in relation to the other stories in each volume. Hodgins's concerns in them are those of his novels: the idiosyncrasies of Vancouver Island life, the temptation to flee from reality to mythology, the contemporary compulsion to find ways of escape from meaning, the incoherently justified importance of privacy at the expense of community. But his novels render these concerns with a control not always visible in particular stories. Hodgins's comic sense, appealing as it is, can at times override his wider purposes. While some critics read his farcical humour as part of his moral vision, others find that zaniness too often obscures it.

By the early 1970s Hugh Hood had established himself as both a major novelist and one of Canada's finest writers of short stories. Although his most substantial achievement since then has been the several novels of his continuing series *The New Age*, Hood has also greatly enhanced his already distinguished reputation as a writer of short fiction with the publication of *Dark Glasses* (1976), *None Genuine without this Signature* (1980), and *August Nights* (1985). Characteristically, these are more than 'collections'; the stories in each volume, while individually impressive, also illuminate the others, showing the various manifestations of the divine in a seemingly secular world. Hood's stories, more persuasively than those of any of his contemporaries (with the possible exception of Mavis Gallant's), convince the reader of the author's intelligence. He knows the world we live in, knows the obsessions and self-deceptions of its inhabitants. From the banal to the serious, from popular music and sports to consumerism and philosophic error, Hood's subject-matter shapes a chronicle of our age; and his didactic impulse, his moral vision (which very seldom declines into sententious moralizing commentary), invokes dramatically what (in an 'Afterword' to *Trusting the Tale*, 1983) he has called 'the primal guarantee of the actual, the authentic certificate of its existence which God provides, the signature in the heart of the existent.' This statement, and others like it, warn the careful reader of the need to know how firmly Hood's art is grounded in his Roman Catholicism and in an accompanying desire to question the shallow thinking of his time. Love and faith are not mere abstractions; Hood makes their redemptive power plain to his audience, even when presenting characters who cannot grasp this significance.

For Hood, the experience of life is where we must begin if we are to find the presence and meaning of divinity. In 'The Hole' (*Dark Glasses*), philosophical abstractions detached from actuality are shown to be morally destructive. 'The Woodcutter's Third Son' (*None Genuine*) depicts the disastrous consequences of falling into that 'interminable sea of myth in which nothing can be apprehended as of final, resting significance,' in which we put off 'presence' and defer 'actuality.' 'Weight Watchers' (*August Nights*) transforms a mundane ritual into a vision of spiritual hunger. Fable and allegory, given modern complexity, are well-suited to Hood's purposes, as these and other stories excellently show. The shaping power of true art, informed by intelligence, judgment, compassion, and a dry and subtle sense of the human comedy, are Hood's strengths in his quest to trace the 'Divine Intelligence' in the 'immense social forces ... swirling around [us].' His novels may prove to be the outstanding monuments of his work, but his short stories are also the work of a gifted artist who has observed the details of life precisely and also given his readers the means to transcend and evaluate the 'rain of matter upon sense.'

That John Metcalf's short fiction has attracted increasing attention is only in part the consequence of his public and frequently controversial role as editor, critic, and gadfly. Serious critics have responded favourably to his short stories for other reasons. The amount of Metcalf's collected work is not large: between 1972 and 1984, two books appeared: *The Teeth of My Father* (1975), and *Selected Stories* (1982). (In addition, the two novellas of *The Girl in Gingham*, 1978, were reprinted as *Private Parts*, 1980.) Metcalf insists that short stories should be as intense, complex, and well written as poems are.[8] His ability in his best stories to invest objects, times, and places with a moral and cultural significance and his preoccupation with the relationships between art and life command a reader's respect when they are effectively combined in stories such as 'The Strange Aberration of Mr Ken Smythe' and 'Gentle as Flowers Make the Stones' (*The Teeth of My Father*).

Robert Lecker, in *On the Line* (1982), calls Metcalf's artistry 'relatively traditional in form.' Readers must be attentive, but not necessarily familiar with current trends in literary theory. His concern with the details of his art is, however, both a strength and a weakness. The painstaking attention to words and phrases, and to the rhythms of sentences, can lead to the creation of delicate and subtle effects. It can also leave readers marooned among these effects. Metcalf, describing his concern with the 'bits and pieces' of a story (in *Making It New*), goes on to say: 'Writing is very hard work, but at the same time it is delightful play. When I think about the act of writing, I often think it's like the play of small children on the beach absorbed in building sandcastles and towns with roads and tunnels all decorated with flags made from popsicle sticks and bits of cigarette packets.' Metcalf's position leaves him at risk of producing fine writing about persons and issues of no compelling concern to any but the artist himself and those who find the artist's predicament fascinating. In his weaker stories he does little more than play with small effects; at his best he builds more than sandcastles. A Metcalf more consistently at his best would be a short-story writer of lasting importance.

Clark Blaise was one of the writers associated with Metcalf's attempt in the early 1970s to create a wider audience for short fiction. The Montreal Story Teller Fiction Performance Group, which also included Hood, Ray Smith, and Ray Fraser, was united less as a combination of writers who shared similar views of literary art than as writers who agreed that a wider forum than the limited circulation of magazines, journals, and small press publication was needed.[9] Blaise and Metcalf were later to collaborate as co-editors of three volumes of *Best Canadian Stories*, but while their standards of judgment may be similar their stories are not. In *A North American Education* (1973), Blaise declared and depicted the concerns that have informed all his writing: the search for meaning and identity in an uncertain and sinister world. This quest is sociological, artistic, and personal. In his first collection, and later in *Tribal Justice* (1974) and *Resident Alien* (1986), exile and dislocation are the dominant themes, and his characters find their sense of self and place threatened or shattered by the disorderly, surprising, even terrifying, reality that they encounter when the surface of ordinary life is tested or taken for granted. As Blaise – interviewed for *Canadian Fiction Magazine* in 1980 – has said of the central character in 'At the Lake' (*Tribal Justice*), to deny reality is to invite catastrophe; the character desires 'to place a faith in names rather than reality, so that eventually reality comes, eventually what happens to him is that he is forced to pay the price for his preference to live in a world of aesthetics rather than realities so he ends up with bloodsuckers around his body.'

Blaise's attention to 'identity' attracted serious readers in a time when this issue had been given prominence by Margaret Atwood's *Survival* (1972) and other works. But Blaise was more than topical; he was an artist intent on representing the disorder of life with a breadth of vision and through the careful structuring of narrative and arrangement of details. In a 1982 interview in *Essays on Canadian Writing*, Blaise also declared himself a moralist. The writer, in dealing with the questions arising from our 'cultural dilemma,' opposes his moral vision to the seeming disorder of nature: 'Doesn't morality oppose nature? It's our only way of fighting back. Otherwise, our very "natural" deaths would make a mockery of all human activity.'

The parallels between the characters and events in his stories and the experience of Blaise himself have led some reviewers and critics to describe his fiction as autobiographical. Blaise has disagreed, saying that his writing is more 'created' than personal. The personal is, nevertheless, an important element. If his characters are not to be taken as figures in an autobiographical fiction, their central problem is that of Blaise himself. 'What it is that I am, fundamentally, is a matter of earnest agony to me,' writes the narrator in one of the essays in *Resident Alien*; and in the introduction to this collection Blaise calls the book 'a journey into my obsessions with self and place.' The emotional conviction his stories compel is, in no small way, the product of their author's own sensibility. Barry Cameron has stated that Blaise has given us 'some of the most rewarding books of fiction ever produced in Canada,' that the 'extraordinary richness and intensity' of his work, 'the sheer consistency of good writing, suggests that on qualitative grounds Blaise might be considered a major Canadian writer of fiction.'[10] Yet Blaise still has not shown that his moral stance can firmly control the seeming chaos of contemporary experience. In *Resident Alien* he expresses his own uncertainty: 'there is nothing more wonderful, more relaxing, more expectant to me than the interior of my car or a train or even a plane and the thought of just *moving*. Going somewhere, anywhere, for no special purpose. Time stands still, life is suspended, and if mystical union is possible in this life, I achieve it.' Blaise knows and feels the temptations to escape reality and the difficulties of judgment. Whether he can consistently and forcefully reject these temptations is yet to be seen.

Leon Rooke had published more than twenty stories and one collection, *Last One Home Sleeps in the Yellow Bed* (1968), before leaving the United States to settle in Victoria in 1969. Subsequently, more than twenty other stories appeared in Canadian and American periodicals, followed by two collections, *The Broad Back of the Angel* (1977) and (the first volume published in Canada) *The Love Parlour* (1977). Although Rooke's writing career extended by this time over almost two decades, his work had received what now seems unduly limited attention. Neglect was followed by a sudden and remarkable enhancement of Rooke's reputation. Blaise favourably reviewed the two collections in *Canadian Literature* (1979); Metcalf and Blaise in-

cluded his work in *Best Canadian Stories;*[11] *Canadian Fiction Magazine* made
him the subject of a special issue in 1981. By the mid-1980s, Rooke had
become for many readers and critics one of the most important writers of
short fiction in Canada, notwithstanding that his most significant public recognition came in the form of a Governor General's Award for his second
novel, *Shakespeare's Dog* (1983).

Rooke's short stories have been seen as quintessentially postmodern, the
'latest in fabulation and metafiction,' and his experiments with form, narrative
method, and language do encourage such an approach.[12] In a 1981 interview,
the author himself stated his position somewhat more carefully: 'I'm a traditional writer, but at times a more experimental one ... My position isn't
fixed, it isn't firm. It's always at the mercy of whatever material I'm dealing
with. Some stories demand a traditional form. I don't think the traditional
form is exhausted or ever can be. Because it always changes. Frequently,
the two come together in an amalgamation that is both traditional and
"experimental".'

Rooke uses one of his most successful stories, 'Adolpho's Disappeared
and We Haven't a Clue Where to Find Him' (*Cry Evil*, 1980), to illustrate
his point. He finds nothing truly 'experimental' in its framework, method of
narration, arrangement of material, or even its content. 'If a work is successful
then it is no longer "experimental",' he concludes. 'It is the New Traditional.' Rooke is, perhaps, closest to tradition in his unwillingness 'to relinquish character,' although his characters are often abnormal, or even disturbingly
grotesque; he is most distinctive in the impressively wide and authentic range
of voices he creates for these characters, from the gospel-inflected and boisterous
in 'Mama Tuddi Done Over' (*Death Suite*, 1981), to the carefully managed
juvenile colloquialisms of 'Why the Heathens Are No More' (*A Bolt of White
Cloth*, 1984).[13]

Despite the attention it has recently received, Rooke's complex body of
short fiction still awaits proper critical assessment. Although the characters
and situations he presents are for the most part unpleasant or absurd, they
are redeemed by the author's wit and intellectual detachment. In what larger
vision all of this coheres remains to be shown. Rooke's own voice, 'somewhere underneath all those others,' awaits description and definition.

Some critics, and some writers (including Rooke himself), urgent in their
support of complexity and innovation, make their case in part by disparaging
the more conventional work of other authors, such as W.D. Valgardson. Like
Blaise, Metcalf, and Rooke, Valgardson established his reputation in the
1970s. Like them, too, he is a self-conscious artist, but his painstaking
craftsmanship ('I rewrite thirty and forty times') produces stories more obviously traditional in form, and he rejects experimentation because it would
weaken 'the bond of understanding' he wishes to achieve with his audience;

the unfamiliar locales of many of his stories require 'a very authoritative tone,' and first person narration is also unsuitable for his moral purposes: 'I also have a strong Lutheran, and conservative, background that needs to make the statement of belief that the omniscient voice has.'[14] Valgardson's first collection, *Bloodflowers* (1973), contains stories set (for the most part) in the bleak northern Manitoba of his upbringing; there are few moments of triumph or affirmation to set against his dark vision of life. The violence of the natural world, the emotionally crippling effects of family and social life, shape the brutal actions and destructive or self-destructive destinies of characters who cannot understand or transcend their environment. *God Is Not a Fish Inspector* (1975) offers similar themes and settings, in a tone often grimmer. Violent death, deformity (literal and spiritual), and a thwarted instinct for survival are pervasive in a world whose inhabitants construct or confront their fates, unwilling or unable to recognize any redemptive power. *Red Dust* (1978), although not departing significantly in its themes from the previous collections, does present a less dark, if still not optimistic, view of human experience. A wryly comic acceptance of one's fate or circumstances is sometimes possible.

Some reviewers of this third collection criticized Valgardson for his unwillingness to attempt different styles and treat different themes. Some critics and writers asserted that his specifically Canadian locales and concerns might lead him to be unfairly 'exalted' to the disadvantage of writers less directly concerned with such social or historical issues, or that his seeming to work 'out of the textbook rules of long ago and far away' might encourage readers to undervalue those writers whose short stories are deliberately intended to test the presumed limits of the form.[15] Valgardson may at times descend to melodrama and monotony of style, and these lapses should be noted, but his essentially conservative forms and firm moral position are not invalidated by the more indirect and elusive approaches adopted by some of his contemporaries; as Atwood noted, writing in *Essays on Canadian Writing* (1979–80), 'Writers' universes may become more elaborate, but they do not necessarily become essentially different. Popular culture, based on the marketing of novelties, teaches us that change is desirable in and for itself. Valgardson is its antithesis.'

Alistair MacLeod is, like Valgardson, unabashedly traditional. Even more than Valgardson, he is a regionalist. His 1976 collection, *The Lost Salt Gift of Blood*, depicts Cape Breton society, its historical sense of community embodied in folktales and ballads, its fragile culture that survives with difficulty if it survives at all given its own impoverishment and the homogenizing forces of the twentieth century. The author writes sympathetically and with a convincingly intelligent understanding of the individual's actions as they are shaped by historical and social contexts. To succeed in public or profes-

sional life in Canada often means that one's regional origins must be subordinated, that intellectual fulfilment can deny emotional fulfilment; a 1986
Books in Canada interview quotes MacLeod: 'you have to leave your environment, and this may mean leaving your parents, or leaving your landscape, or leaving lots of other things. This is a tension that's felt by a lot
of people in Canada because of the nature of the country. What you want
to do with your mind may be at variance with the yearning of your heart.'

Few contemporary writers of short stories have conveyed so effectively the
ways in which the sense of place haunts people even in another environment.
Few have so well depicted the seasonal and cultural effects of a particular
region. MacLeod finds in Cape Breton no sentimentalized retreat from modern
confusions; the impacts of tradition may be compelling for his characters but
they are not always aware of the traps and deceptions that tradition may
invite. Their problem, as MacLeod shows, is to adjust the traditional and
the modern, to find some way of making the past live in the present and
enact the strengths of tradition in a world inclined to accept the superficial
comforts (themselves deceptive) of modernity. The view here of Canadian
life is serious and compelling; like the best regional writing, it transcends its
time and place.

A sense of place persists in Canadian literature, but since the 1960s writers
seeking to create it have seldom been working from any narrowly documentary impulse to name, define, describe, and explain the characteristics of
landscape and society in a particular region or locale. The aim is more usually
to analyze the ways in which human experience is significantly affected by,
and sometimes affects, specific environments and traditions. This is nowhere
more apparent than in the best work of Alice Munro. The details of ordinary
life are there in profusion, and from them a social historian could reconstruct
Munro's knowledgeable vision of times and places, especially of that part of
southwestern Ontario from which she comes. Yet she is much more an artist
than a recorder, one who was 'excited' by the regional writers of the American
South – she observes in a 1973 interview with Graeme Gibson – because
they suggested ways in which she could render her understanding of her own
territory: 'I felt there a country being depicted that was like my own ... I
mean the part of the country I come from is absolutely Gothic. You can't
get it all down.' Munro's distance from that country is not only aesthetic,
it is personal, the result of growing up 'feeling very alienated' from a 'very
traditional rural community': 'I almost always felt it. I find it still when I
go back. The concern of everyone else I knew was dealing with life on a
very practical level ... but I always realized that I had a different view of
the world, and one that would bring me into great trouble and ridicule if it
were exposed. I learned very early to disguise everything, and perhaps the
escape into making stories was necessary.'

The materials of Munro's fiction often seem autobiographical in their origins, and the development from the concerns and perspectives of youth in her first collection, the Governor General's Award-winning *Dance of the Happy Shades* (1968), to the motif of journey and return which controls *Who Do You Think You Are?* (1978), which also received a Governor General's Award, to the concentration on the experience of middle-aged or older women in *The Moons of Jupiter* (1982), may serve to encourage a critical approach that would seek the motive and meaning of her fiction in the writer's personal life. Munro describes herself, however, as a 'writer who uses what is obviously *personal* material ... as *opposed* to straight autobiographical material,'[16] one who is compelled by a 'need' to write and a 'need' to arrange her chosen materials as she does:

Yes, I use bits of what is real, in the sense of being really there and really happening, in the world, as most people see it, and I transform it into something that is really there and really happening, in my story. No, I am not concerned with using what is real to make any sort of record or prove any sort of point, and I am not concerned with any methods of selection but my own, which I can't fully explain. This is quite presumptuous, and if writers are not allowed to be so – and quite often, in many places, they are not – I see no point in the writing of fiction.[17]

The intensely felt personal experience of ordinary reality, which needs to be transformed by the artist and on the artist's terms into something more real, is both the starting point and the justification of her art.

The stories collected in *Something I've Been Meaning to Tell You* (1974) are generally less retrospective, less concerned with the experience of growing up in a small town in southwestern Ontario. Seven of the stories adopt an urban and contemporary setting, and even those stories located in Jubilee depict, in their references to events and issues of the late 1960s and after-wards, a more recent and altered version of the small town seen in *Dance of the Happy Shades*. Personal experience, felt and observed, is now primarily that of adult characters, warped by selfishness or cowardice or misunder-standing, whose deceptions and self-deceptions entrap them in isolation or despair. The title of the volume, and its title story, make clear the theme that is most prominent in this collection: the near impossibility of commu-nication. Men and women, particularly women, inhabit a world in which sexuality is exploited or denied, in which pretension and hypocrisy and an inability or unwillingness to 'tell' (as in 'Material,' 'Tell Me Yes or No,' and 'The Spanish Lady') are pervasive. The careful arrangement of detail in these stories and the frequent irony invite the reader to take the title of this collection literally: her characters may not be able to find appropriate words, but the author herself has something to tell us.

Who Do You Think You Are? is a collection of ten linked stories about one character, similar in structure to Munro's novel, *Lives of Girls and Women* (1971), and similar, too, in its depiction of a girl's development to maturity. But the central figure of these stories, Rose, moves much further into the adult world than does Del Jordan in the novel, and the world she encounters as child, adolescent, and adult is more ambiguous and more distressing. The Canadian title of the book – it was called *The Beggar Maid* in American and British editions – is again significant. Rose is in search of her identity, carrying with her into an urban adult life her impoverished and guilt-ridden youthful experience in a small town, acting many parts to disguise her origins (and eventually becoming an actress), adeptly assuming identities that circumstances seem to demand. Her journey brings her back to her beginnings, but it does not finally and clearly reveal whether she has acquired a true sense of who she is or whether, in Hallvard Dahlie's words (*Canadian Writers and Their Works*, 1985), 'imitation, duplicity, deceit, dissimulation – stratagems she casually utilizes to resolve momentary crises – have become by the end of the book indistinguishable from other aspects of her operative reality.'

The quest for identity, and the burden of the past, are present again in the stories collected in *The Moons of Jupiter*. The 'ordinary' lives of girls and women in a world disordered by chance, change, and accident are presented with a cool and understanding intelligence. The narrator of the title story, watching an astronomical show in a planetarium, reveals in her response to it an understandable distrust of an age too assured of the truth of supposed 'facts' to recognize its own inconsistencies, its own wayward shifting of the grounds of certainty: 'I set my dodging and shrinking mind sternly to recording facts ... Moonless Mercury rotating three times while circling the sun twice; an odd arrangement, not as satisfying as what they used to tell us – that it rotated once as it circled the sun. No perpetual darkness after all. Why did they give out such confident information, only to announce later that it was quite wrong?' The stories in this collection also persuasively convey what feminist critics (and not only feminist critics) have seen as Munro's concern to present 'the [physical, emotional, and intellectual] experiences and perceptions of women.'[18]

Commentators on Munro's work have noted her fondness for the paradoxical and for the juxtaposition (not the resolution) of dualities; an analogy with the art of the twentieth-century photographer has also been suggested,[19] one that references in the stories and her own comments would seem to support: 'I like looking at people's lives over a number of years [she said to Geoff Hancock in 1982] without continuity. Like catching them in snapshots. And I like the way people relate, or don't relate, to the people they were earlier ... I think this is why I'm not drawn to writing novels. Because I don't see that people develop and arrive somewhere. I just see people living in flashes.

From time to time.' This way of 'seeing' is characteristic, and it also indicates why the coherence of the stories in *Who Do You Think You Are?* – and the consistency of attitude – is subject to question. 'I never,' Munro said in 1983, 'worry at all about whether I'm being sympathetic.' This deliberate and measured detachment, together with a concern for 'the surface of life' that accompanies what seems (in her interview with Gibson) an anti-intellectual stance, have still to engage serious critical notice.

Notwithstanding the reputation he has acquired in England and Europe, and despite the championing of his work by such editors as Robert Weaver, John Metcalf, and Wayne Grady, the short stories of Norman Levine have been inexcusably ignored or superficially treated by the great majority of Canadian critics of the form. That the autobiographical *Canada Made Me* (1958) did engender some misguided resentment because of its exposure of Canadian complacency and meanspiritedness, or that Levine made England his home for thirty years before returning to Toronto in 1980, are not satisfactory or reasonable grounds for this neglect. Claims that Levine's stories are too often superficial depictions of ordinary life, too obviously fragments of autobiography, too predictable in their reworking of a narrow range of themes, are equally unpersuasive. In a few of his stories readers may find that while the surface of experience has been precisely and faithfully rendered, the final effect is one of flatness and inconsequence. Yet this is not often actually the case. Levine is a meticulous craftsman, concerned indeed with the 'visible world,' with setting his stories in 'a particular, physical landscape,'[20] but committed as well to illuminating the mundane, to revealing the significance and meaning that lie behind the apparent surfaces of contemporary existence.

Levine is no mere recorder of mundane events. Like Graham Greene, whom he admires for his similar intention, Levine wants to make his readers 'see': 'When I write I write very quickly, and then I revise and revise. The revisions are to make things clear, lucid.' Vision and revision, purpose and craft, are for Levine the ways in which seeming simplicity becomes in his art a form of discovery, a recognition of connection and coherence: 'although it sounds like it just comes off the end of the pen, this is all deliberate. I write for myself, and what's the point of telling myself things I already know?' So 'By a Frozen River,' collected in *Thin Ice* (1979), presents the artist's transformation of two actual and apparently unrelated events – a burial in a long disused Jewish cemetery in Penzance, and an unhappy marriage encountered in Fredericton – into an understated but moving story about dying traditions and contemporary insecurity, set in a small northern Ontario town. Levine finds his materials in such 'confrontations' arising out of his own experience: as traveller in search of his past ('In Lower Town,' *Thin Ice*), as husband and father ('Boiled Chicken' and 'I'll Bring You Back Something

Nice,' collected in *Why Do You Live So Far Away?*, 1984), as writer ('The Man with the Notebook,' *I Don't Want to Know Anyone Too Well, and Other Stories*, 1971, and 'We All Begin in a Little Magazine,' *Thin Ice*). These latter two stories suggest that readers should not be persuaded by claims that Levine's stories are patently autobiographical, claims that his preference for first person narration might seem to justify. 'The Man with the Notebook' is a third person account of a writer who asks of his experience questions which, unlike Levine, he cannot answer; 'We All Begin ...,' a striking depiction and a subtle analysis of the modern artist and his milieu, was inspired in part by a meeting that never occurred. Levine's own comment on the stories collected in *Champagne Barn* (1984) more appropriately directs our attention: they 'form a kind of autobiography.' But, as in 'By a Frozen River,' it is 'autobiography written as fiction.'

The style through which the author attempts to make sense of the apparently random juxtapositions that experience provides – particularly his concern with the relationships between past and present – does not immediately invite attention. Appearances are, however, deceptive. Levine avoids 'sentimental nostalgia,' but the language of his best work, in its 'evocation of mood and scene and its poetic use of implication,'[21] is the product of a deliberate if self-effacing artist. Not only does language 'make things clear' but structure also: 'unless you have this structure, unless it holds together [Levine said to Grady], then people reading that story who have different backgrounds won't understand it ...' Levine's concern for his audience is matched by his respect and affection for his materials: 'I've found that things I like writing, that give me satisfaction, have to do with the world and the people I know. And after I finish them I sort of fix them. A lot of writing is paying tribute to people and places that have meant something to me.' He is a writer who, regardless of his place of residence, thinks of himself as Canadian, feeling in England 'much more Canadian than I did in Canada'; a writer unusual in his willingness to let time make its judgment on his work.

'I often have the feeling with Canadian readers that I am on trial.' There is an acerbic quality to this and other comments that Mavis Gallant makes in the introduction to *Home Truths: Selected Canadian Stories* (1981), the collection that finally gained her some deserved public recognition (a Governor General's Award). Because she has spent nearly all her writing life in Paris, because most of her stories have first appeared in *The New Yorker*, and because she has not limited herself to the treatment of overtly Canadian issues, Gallant has, until quite recently, either been ignored or treated as if she were one of the 'displaced' persons so frequently at the centre of her stories. Like Norman Levine, she is viewed as somehow having implicitly renounced her nationality and distanced herself from Canada. In *Home Truths*,

Gallant herself has rejected, with justifiable irritation, the assumption that an author's place of residence determines sensibility and point of view:

I am constantly assured that Canadians no longer know what they are, or what to be Canadian should mean; for want of a satisfactory definition, a national identity has been mislaid. The most polite thing I can say about this is that I don't believe it. A Canadian who did not know what it was to be Canadian would not know anything else: he would have to be told his own name ...
    I suppose that a Canadian is someone who has a logical reason to think he is one. My logical reason is that I have never been anything else, nor has it occurred to me that I might be.

For Gallant, 'the national sense of self' is 'quite separate from nationalism ... and even patriotism ... The accident of birth does not give rise to a national consciousness, but I think the first years of schooling are indelible. They provide our center of gravity, our initial view of the world, the seed of our sense of culture. A deeper culture is contained in memory. Memory is something that cannot be subsidized or ordained. It can, however, be destroyed; and it is inseparable from language.' Memory and language are not only at the heart of Gallant's 'sense of culture,' they are also central concerns in her short fiction.

    Characteristically, Gallant's stories are ordered by what George Woodcock, in *Canadian Fiction Magazine* (1978), has termed a 'helical patterning of memory.' The people of these stories – usually exiles or expatriates, figures somehow alienated, literally or figuratively – are shown in the process of reconstructing, distorting, and evading their pasts; they adjust personal and political history to their present settings and situations, creating 'fictions' that become, as they do for the central character in 'Ernst in Civilian Clothes,' collected in *The Pegnitz Junction* (1973), a means of avoiding confrontation with the truth of experience:

Ernst, on his feet, stiff with the cold of a forgotten dream, makes a new decision. Everyone is lying; he will invent his own truth. Is it important if one-tenth of a lie is true? Is there a horror in a memory if it was only a dream? In Willi's shaving mirror now he wears the face that no superior officer, no prisoner, and no infatuated girl has ever seen. He will believe only what *he* knows. It is a great decision in an important day. Life begins with facts: he is Ernst Zimmerman, ex-Legionnaire. He has a ticket to Stuttgart.

Ernst invents his truth, selects his facts. The truth of his experience in Nazi Germany is, nevertheless, revealed by the narrator's shaping of his patterns of memory. 'The Moslem Wife,' in *From the Fifteenth District* (1979), presents with even greater force and vividness what Neil Besner (*Essays in*

Canadian Writing, 1986) has termed 'the revelatory collision of history with memory.' Netta Asher, 'the Moslem wife,' has her moment of insight, but the reality of history is unbearable and she subsides finally into the deceptive comforts of a habitual relationship. More impressive still are the six Linnet Muir stories collected in *Home Truths*. Again the past is juxtaposed with the present, but Linnet realizes that memory cannot provide a comfortable escape from immediate reality: 'My dream past evaporated. Montreal, in memory, was a leafy citadel where I knew every tree. In reality I recognized nearly nothing and had to start from scratch' ('In Youth Is Pleasure'). Linnet Muir's experience may seem to invite autobiographical comparisons with Gallant's own years in Montreal, particularly with respect to Linnet's spirit of rebellion against restrictive traditions. She is, however, a created character, decided and even dogmatic in the earlier stories, growing more tolerant and less assured in her quality of understanding as the sequence progresses. She is the product of an intelligent and mature imagination, a displaced person shrewdly and ironically rendered.

Gallant's stories have at their centre characters who are exiles or aliens. Their displacement is, however, not primarily a matter of physical or spatial separation, but as David O'Rourke has observed (*Canadian Literature*, 1982) more an exile of time. (One of the Linnet Muir stories is entitled 'Varieties of Exile'; the words could serve as well to describe collectively the main subject of most of Gallant's stories.) The awareness of time – time as record, time as irrevocable movement, time as shaping force – is also central to Gallant's views of style and structure, recorded in John Metcalf's *Making It New*:

[Style] is not a last-minute addition to prose, a charming and universal slipcover, a coat of paint used to mask the failings of a structure. Style is inseparable from structure, part of the conformation of whatever the author has to say. What he says – this is what fiction is about – is that something is taking place and that nothing lasts. Against the sustained tick of a watch, fiction takes the measure of a life, a season, a look exchanged, the turning point, desire as brief as a dream, the grief and terror that after childhood we cease to express. The life, the look, the grief are without permanence. The watch continues to tick where the story stops.

'Like every other form of art,' Gallant adds, 'literature is no more and nothing less than a matter of life and death.' Although this comment was made with reference to the writer's duty to aim at nothing less than 'the inborn vitality and tension of living prose,' the statement also directs us to the moral seriousness of her work, to her concern with the essential questions that existence and experience should compel us to ask. Her complex style, even more than her themes, makes demands on the reader, requires a considered attention that must strive to match the author's own standards of dedication and discernment. Gallant's subtly crafted use of dialogue in dramatic scenes, her precise use of particular detail and historical references in her depiction of manners, situations, and places, the blended tones of urbanity, wit, erudition, irony, and compassion, the indirect yet forceful social analysis and criticism: these in combination have daunted or baffled many readers unwilling to meet her demands, readers who find her work on first acquaintance to be opaque or pretentiously sophisticated. Those who admire her fiction do so by accepting the challenge and the rewards offered by a writer whose style 'is, finally, the distillation of a lifetime of reading and listening, of selection and rejection.'

In her short stories the novelist Jane Rule occasionally suggests something akin to Gallant's cosmopolitanism, but her best work tends to be focused more specifically on the subject of female sexuality, and on the naturalness of homosexual love and the problems involved (within the conventions and usual orderings of society) with its expression. It would, however, be inaccurate and unfair to say that Rule's concerns are limited to these issues, either in her novels or her short fiction. *Theme for Diverse Instruments* (1975) presents a variety of personal relationships, with careful attention to their complexity and considered attention to the tensions between freedom and restraint; several of the stories present children as central characters, sensitively and for the most part unsentimentally. *Outlander* (1981) is somewhat narrower in its range. Lesbian issues dominate, and the book has at times a didactic, even somewhat polemical, quality. These issues appear again in *Inland Passage and Other Stories* (1985), but the stories collected here consider a broader range of human concerns as well. Rule's sympathetic, tolerant, and perceptive treatment of everyday pleasures and problems is appealingly evident.

Elizabeth Brewster has been honoured for her poetry, and in her short stories her style is similarly direct, clear, and understated. Her two collections, *It's Easy to Fall on the Ice* (1977) and *A House Full of Women* (1983), deal primarily with the lives of women, presenting for the most part an impressive but quietly rendered depiction of the loneliness, frustration, and difficult day-to-day survival of characters whose experience and memories limit their enjoyment of life or detract even from the comfort that might be afforded by small satisfactions. Brewster is also particularly effective in her treatment of the relationships between women, their hesitant and often frustrated searching for companionship and affection. Too frequently considered a regionalist and a writer of limited range, Brewster has yet to be recognized as a writer who seriously and forcibly, albeit in a style that does not call attention to itself, examines and, at her best, movingly presents the common concerns of people who, if not remarkable, nevertheless matter not just to themselves but to everyone.

Sandra Birdsell did not begin a serious writing career until the mid-1970s, but her work was thereafter prominent in important magazines and journals, and her first collections, *Night Travellers* (1982) and *Ladies of the House* (1984), were well received by reviewers. The first of these is a collection of linked stories (Birdsell has expressed her admiration for Alice Munro, who has organized some of her collections in a similar way) about the Lafreniere family in the fictional small prairie town of Agassiz (and this allusion to the Swiss-American zoologist and geologist is not without purpose). The analysis of the complex social and moral issues of small-town life in this collection is careful and convincing. The second collection also deals in most of its stories with members of the same family, but the settings are both rural and urban (the working-class areas of Winnipeg). Birdsell deliberately chose to link her stories, yet she did not see them as fragments of a novel. The 'closed' story required an ending, in her view, and this was 'too contained.' 'Yet I knew as I was writing,' she says of her first collection, 'that it wasn't a novel, because I need to work with so many different voices at one time.'[22] Birdsell is also convincing in many of her stories in presenting the ways in which men in general show 'a complete lack of understanding of the female perspective or the female condition.' On some occasions, inadvertently no doubt, women display similar failures of understanding. Moreover, Birdsell's generally effective presentation of the inner lives of her characters is sometimes achieved at the cost of a lack of clarity in the focus and direction of her narratives. Her work is nevertheless more than promising, and its quality indicates the possibility of lasting achievement in the form.

David Adams Richards, like Birdsell, has at times been too narrowly seen as a 'regional' writer. Although his several novels, and his collection of short stories, *Dancers at Night* (1978), all use the Miramichi Valley of New Brunswick as their setting, Richards's concerns are more than local. He does establish a firm sense of place, and displays an acute ear for the idioms and the dialogue of the region. His stories convince as social documents. But the careful attention given to the psychology of his characters is also important. Richards has a vision of life that has correctly been described as bleak, yet it is not pessimistic. His characters are often victims, inarticulate products of degradation, poverty, and despair, violent in their actions and language, or at the mercy of indirect violence in their manipulation by others. The author's attitude to these characters is a combination of measured detachment and controlled sympathy. The dispossessed, the failures, the hopeless, the violent, and the self-destructive, are all treated as if their lives mattered, while at the same time their weaknesses are presented in an unsentimental and forceful way.

While Richards continues to explore and map the territory of his origins,

Neil Bissoondath's first collection, *Digging Up the Mountains* (1985), offers a variety of settings (Canadian, West Indian, Japanese, and Central American). The Trinidadian-born Bissoondath (a nephew of V.S. Naipaul) acknowledges the importance of his West Indian experience in his formative years, yet at the same time insists that his work should not be approached or defined primarily in terms of his Caribbean origins. He has firmly expressed his dislike for 'professional ethnics,' those who cannot grow beyond their 'old country' experience, those who in the name of multiculturalism trivialize their own cultural traditions. The policy, he argues, even works against the achievement of quality in the arts, 'because multiculturalism is an attempt to freeze people into what they have been, and an artist has to be open to everything.'[23] These views have not won Bissoondath friends in some quarters, but they are consistent with the themes and concerns of his stories. Exile, isolation, and misguided attempts to find a true homeland are recurring issues, combined with a perceptive analysis of social and political realities. The titles of many of the stories ('The Cage,' 'Insecurity,' 'An Arrangement of Shadows,' 'Continental Drift') indicate clearly Bissoondath's focus on those who are trapped, deceived, and displaced in a world of shifting loyalties and uncertain values. The variety of characters and settings, the convincing presentation of differing voices and circumstances, the critical, coolly compassionate, and often subtly satiric control of his narration, show Bissoondath to be, for a young writer, impressively mature and accomplished.

Another young writer, Guy Vanderhaeghe, achieved public recognition remarkably quickly, by winning the Governor General's Award for fiction with his first collection, *Man Descending* (1982). Alienation, loneliness, and the difficult struggle to establish and maintain some sense of personal integrity are Vanderhaeghe's usual concerns: 'It's not within my capability to dissect the society and act as sociologist, but I think there's enormous fragmentation in our society and a tremendous feeling of rootlessness, a tremendous feeling of lethargy.'[24] His view of the world is for the most part a bleak one, and perhaps this has been overemphasized by reviewers and critics who have taken their cue from the book's title, which was not Vanderhaeghe's own choice.[25] He has asked that the small triumphs of some of his characters be given due recognition, yet at the same time concedes (in interview with Andrew Garrod) that his concern is primarily with characters who do not succeed: 'I think some themes recur in my work – the theme of the outsider, for instance, or the theme of obsession of one kind or another – but I'm not certain why I'm drawn to those themes ... I'm interested in people who are "wounded" in some way, people who are failures, people who have difficulty fitting in.' Vanderhaeghe's stories show a keen attention to the patterns of speech by characters from different social classes, a skilful use of dialogue, and an indirect but effective attention to the essential qualities of various settings. His success as a writer of short stories is surprising in one way; Vanderhaeghe's preferred form is the novel.

Just as Vanderhaeghe's work won a major award, so too did the collections by Alice Munro (1978) and Mavis Gallant (1981). The short story in Canada had become, belatedly, what Knister had predicted it would. Magazines and anthologies and collections testified to the vitality and achievement that the form was capable of realizing.[26] The recognition given within Canada was accompanied by serious international attention to the work of Gallant, Munro, Atwood, and others. Less encouraging was the tendency to find the short story a ground on which to battle over the merits of experimental and self-reflexive fiction at the expense of more traditional forms. As well, the promotion of a vague and rootless cosmopolitanism which would somehow accord with 'international standards' invoked but never defined, seemed to deny the Canadian-ness of Canadian short fiction. Such a quality does not require the blatant parading of Canadian settings and issues; it can, as many writers have shown, be made apparent in the ways various themes are presented and considered. Hood, Atwood, Munro, Gallant, Vanderhaeghe, and others, know their country, its regions, its concerns, its peculiar points of view, even when their stories use non-Canadian settings or deal with human issues that transcend the local or the national. T.D. MacLulich has properly observed that Canada's continued existence, as George Grant claimed, has traditionally been based on an assertion of particularity against the homogenizing claims of continentalism and universalism. 'Canadian fiction,' MacLulich asserts, 'has provided some of the most eloquent expressions of our devotion to such particularity.'[27] Writers who seek to attune themselves with currently fashionable theories of art, and neglect the realities of their time and place, add to the risk that literature will become merely source material for social scientists and cultural historians. Fortunately, the variety, the substance, and the quality of many short stories published between 1972 and 1984 give some reason to hope that dogmatic, doctrinaire, and ill-grounded 'international' views will not in the end prevail.

3 The Novel

LINDA HUTCHEON

One of the most significant influences on the fiction of these years (and on this chapter[1] about it) was the unsettled literary critical climate in which they were both written, a climate that revealed an increasing suspicion even about the value and authority of literary histories in their role as creators of the so-called canon. The once familiar notion of a 'great tradition' of writers was dissolving, as the supposedly universal culture and values upon which it was based were seen to be rooted, in fact, in a very particular place, time, class, and sex. Canadians became particularly aware of the normative power of the notion of canon through an attempt to draw up a list of Canadian 'classics' at the 1978 Calgary Conference (the papers later collected in Charles Steele's *Taking Stock*). But what constitutes a 'classic'? Is it a matter of simple critical consensus? If so, who is to be involved in this evaluation and when will it take place? The history of the novel is especially full of examples of best-sellers becoming great unknowns in a few decades' time. Undoubtedly, the very act of selecting novels for mention here is going to be seen as evaluative in effect. Nevertheless, since the great number of novels written during this period precluded reference to all of them, the criterion used for this (obligatory) selection was adherence to the dominant modes of writing that appeared in these years; in other words, examples cited were considered those that best illustrated the formal and thematic characteristics being considered.

The chapter on fiction in the last volume of this history remarked on the 'palpable effect' of the decade of the 1960s on Canadian writing. Interestingly, this effect continued to be felt because many of the novels in the 1970s and 1980s were written by those 'formed' in that decade when considerable attention was paid to broad social and political concerns: ecology, peace, civil, and women's rights. Although the years to follow brought economic recession and a return to more conservative values and politics, the novels of the period generally continued to reflect the ideological climate of the 1960s in their broadly political orientation. Writings by Joy Kogawa and

Timothy Findley illustrate the vast range of formal, tonal, and thematic possibilities within the 'novel of ideology.' Kogawa's *Obasan* (1981) was a personal and poetic evocation of the fate of Japanese Canadians, whose search for assimilation and economic security was met by evacuation and internment at the hands of the government of their own country during World War II. In Findley's *Famous Last Words* (1981), the same kind of mixture of the fictional and the factual served as the background for a more general investigation into the relation between fascism and aestheticism, between public history and private fantasy, in what purported to be the 'writing on the wall' for our century. While Margaret Atwood's *Bodily Harm* (1981) was specifically ideological in combating forms of political tyranny, other novels fought more local oppression – the more subtle, but no less ideological repression exerted in the name of bourgeois middle-class values. Many of these novels appeared to be psychological studies, but the constant implied matching of the private with the public dimension suggested a broader perspective in which such fiction should be read: for instance, the focus on the puritanical ethics of a certain class and age in Janette Turner Hospital's *The Tiger in the Tiger Pit* (1983), or the personal *and* public rebuilding after moral and physical devastation in Elizabeth Spencer's *The Salt Line* (1984). In addition to influences from outside the country, some of the impetus to politicize the English-Canadian novel – in both form and content – likely came from the example of Québécois revolutionaries and writers such as Hubert Aquin. The novelist *engagé* also appeared in the new cultural, or at least new media, roles that Canadian novelists adopted in these years. Not only did many of them actively participate in the 1981 Amnesty International 'Writer and Human Rights' congress in Toronto, many – Atwood, Findley, Rudy Wiebe – also took upon themselves the responsibility of giving voice to the oppressed or of acting as the conscience of power. This ethical sense of community became increasingly an international one.

The 1960s in Canada were also years marked by a heady Canadian nationalism (cultural and economic) of the sort portrayed in Harry Boyle's *The Great Canadian Novel* (1972). The government, partly through the CBC and the Canada Council, partly through direct grants to publishers, launched a long and largely successful campaign to create a literary community in Canada. One of the important manifestations of the existence of this community was the creation of new presses to champion experimental or non-commercial novels: House of Anansi, Oberon, New Press, Coach House, ECW, Talonbooks, NeWest Press, among others. Many of these flourished; some merely survived. Some went under (Virgo); others rose in their place (fittingly, Groundhog Press). Some tried innovative marketing techniques; Quadrant first sold only by subscription. All this activity outside the 'establishment' culture made possible the existence of other than what are known as 'commercial' novels. Increasingly the larger publishing houses found that they had to play to the big book chains and clubs in order to survive in the face of a bleak economic climate and a more fragmented readership. Some presses, such as McClelland & Stewart and Anansi, deliberately balanced their solid sellers with more daring (that is, less commercially viable) novels. The smaller presses often found that they could not afford to print novels without government subsidies: fiction did not always pay for itself in the marketplace. However, more positive signs appeared in the book market as well. Three publishers introduced mass-market paperback series of 'Canadian classics' to be made available to the large number of Canadian literature courses in the schools and universities. The media paid considerable attention to new novelists who would normally have been ignored, and in some provinces (Alberta, Manitoba) and in *Books in Canada*, there were annual contests and awards for the best first novel.

The steady increase in the number of 'popular' novels written, published, and purchased in Canada marked another kind of continuity with the publishing changes begun in the 1960s. 'Popular' fiction generally means light entertainment, those works which tend to confirm, and rarely challenge, dominant social beliefs. For this reason, they can often exemplify cultural patterns more overtly or stereotypically than 'serious' fiction does. This kind of novel frequently relies on preformulated narrative structures and, for this reason, is often referred to by the collective title of *genre* or *formula fiction*. The Seal First Novel Award, with its prize money, publicity, and international publishing contract, did much to make the Canadian public aware of the existence of its own brand of 'popular' fiction, as did, at another level, Pulp Press's annual international three-day novel writing contest. New possibilities for apocalyptic disasters provided subjects for new possible docu-thrillers: nuclear dangers and their politics, ecological hazards, terrorist plots, domestic hostage-taking, or the conspiracies of multinational conglomerates. In all, power was what was at stake. Other formulas involved domestic soap opera and soft-core pornography. Topics ranged from courtroom drama to costume drama, and from gambling to sports. The growth of an indigenous Canadian 'popular' fiction industry reached its height in Harlequin Enterprises, which cornered a romance market both inside and outside Canada.

The publishing industry affected the history of the novel in Canada in other important ways. If there were certain clear trends in the novel, they might well exist because some publisher thought a market was developing for historical novels, for instance, rather than because more historical fiction was statistically being written. On the whole, the Canadian novel was well served by the many national and regional publishers who were deeply committed to the advancement of Canadian literature,[2] and by governments willing to provide generous subsidies and even bail out floundering companies. Despite this good will, however, the future of Canadian fiction publishing by no means looked assured in the mid-1980s.

Many other social and cultural developments which had begun in the 1960s continued to affect the novels of the 1970s and early 1980s: for instance, the obvious and constant strong influence of American culture in general, and more specifically, of such institutions as the Iowa Writers' Workshop, whose impact on the Canadian novel, through writers such as Clark Blaise and W.P. Kinsella, was considerable. Another development, this time common to both the United States and Canada, was the increasing institutionalization of fiction within the academy. Most of the novelists in Canada are, or at one time were, academics or writers-in-residence at universities. The results for the fiction written were varied. Academic *romans à clé* ranged from Jack MacLeod's amusing *Zinger and Me* (1979) and *Going Grand* (1982) to Robertson Davies's didactic and gossipy *The Rebel Angels* (1981). Political and diplomatic arenas were bared in novels like *A Very Political Lady* (1979) and *A Right Honourable Lady* (1980) by Judy LaMarsh and *First Lady, Last Lady* (1981) by Sondra Gotlieb. Academic institutionalization meant, most significantly, a new enthusiasm for experimentation in form. As the work of Robert Kroetsch, among others, revealed, Canadian fiction and poetry both paid considerable attention to contemporary literary theory and to theories of communication – from those of Innis and McLuhan to structuralism and semiotics.

The 1960s also witnessed the so-called sexual revolution, and Leonard Cohen's early novel, *Beautiful Losers* (1966), was likely the archetype of this challenge to both sexual mores and novelistic form. The questioning of sex and gender roles has been a major force behind the continued development of the novel about women – written by both men and women. This heritage of the 1960s later promoted increased investigation of the consequences of what some novels (such as Jane Rule's *Contract with the World*, 1980) saw as a very Canadian refusal or reluctance to face sexuality (heterosexual or homosexual). The novels of Keith Maillard (*Two Strand River*, 1976; *The Knife in My Hands*, 1981; *Cutting Through*, 1982) studied male and female sexual identity and gender confusion.

These were among the once muted voices to be heard more loudly in Canadian fiction by the late 1970s. But they were not the only ones. This period also saw the coming of (writing) age of a generation of immigrants or children of immigrants, some writing in English, others in their native tongues. Their novels, frequently fictionalized autobiographies, often took the form of either a generational saga or a *Bildungsroman*. They dealt with the problems faced by any newcomer to any society, problems within the self and the family structure, and also with the new world to be confronted. These works were obsessed with social, psychological, and physical displacement;

their tales were of struggle for survival and against alienation. One might well imagine the many tensions to be resolved before these writers could face – in print – their past, perhaps especially because that past involved a major cultural uprooting. Canadians have traditionally prided themselves on their multiculturalism, their ethnic 'mosaic' that allowed cultural diversity. But this liberal concept of a mosaic could turn into a tyrannical model as well; as the fiction revealed, it demanded that one retain one's ethnic roots *and* become a Canadian too (Jan Drabek's *Report on the Death of Rosen-kavalier*, 1977). And arrival in liberal-thinking Canada did not always mean a total escape from racial prejudice. An ironic narrative pattern can thus be seen in novels such as Michael Cullen's *Goodnight, Sammy Wong* (1983) and Saros Cowasjee's *Goodbye to Elsa* (1974); and the immigration pattern was turned amusingly upside down in the inverted missionary tale of Harold Sonny Ladoo's *Yesterdays* (1974). In general, the writers who could explore (with some distance) the immigrant pains of dislocation and the exhilarations of new possibilities were not first-generation immigrants, but second. In this context, however, their novels could be read as variants of a familiar enquiry into the nature of national and cultural identity.

Unfortunately for that process of identity-seeking, there continued to be little extended fiction actually written in the Inuit, Indian, or Métis communities, perhaps because of the strength of the oral tradition in these societies. Many white writers, however, attempted to take the mythology and history (both past and present) of the native peoples as their subject-matter in their own search for roots. The culture of the Inuit was the focus for James Houston's *Spirit Wrestler* (1980) and Harold Horwood's *White Eskimo* (1972). Peter Such's *Riverrun* (1973) raised ethical issues involving the fate of both the Arctic and its people. Other fiction focused more directly on the often disastrous interaction between native and white cultures, including W.O. Mitchell's *The Vanishing Point* (1973) and Rudy Wiebe's *The Temptations of Big Bear* (1973). In some novels a strong anthropological documentary quality dominated the presentation of Indian culture. Nan F. Solerno and Rosamond M. Vanderburgh's *Shaman's Daughter* (1981) was perhaps the extreme of this mode. In others, such as Wayland Drew's *The Wabeno Feast* (1973), this impulse was wedded to a concern for the ecological and sociological fate of the native peoples. When white and Indian worlds met in fiction of this period, they did so in any number of forms and tones: from the comic irony of James Polk's *The Passion of Loreen Bright Weasel* (1981) to the solemn polemic embedded in David Williams's *The Burning Wood* (1975) and Matt Cohen's *Wooden Hunters* (1975). Although the second half of Susan Musgrave's *The Charcoal Burners* (1980) went in a surreal and horrifying direction, the first half certainly shared these concerns.

The Indian mythic figure of the trickster continued to prove attractive to the Canadian novel, which was searching, as always, for its own mythology. Alan Fry's *The Revenge of Annie Charlie* (1973) and Robert Kroetsch's *Gone Indian* (1973) both made interesting, if different, uses of this figure. T.D. MacLulich, writing in the *University of Toronto Quarterly* (1982–3), noted that, in general, the Canadian use of native characters in fiction differed from the American. According to this argument, American novels have tended to see in the contact with the Indian a meeting with one's true self. Canadian novels, by contrast, have related the Indian and the Inuit to the wilderness in which they live: both native and nature have come to embody some eternal spiritual essence. This is an image of the native who has managed integration with nature, who can live in harmony with natural forces in a way admired and sought after by whites. In short, these novels could still be seen as grappling with topics that have long dominated Canadian literature: identity and the relation of man to nature. The need to feel rooted in the land has often taken on primitivist or romantic associations through the process of identification that Terry Goldie has called 'indigenization,' but equally often the message presented was ideological, as in the white historian hero's dealing with the Cree Maskepetoon in Rudy Wiebe's *My Lovely Enemy* (1983) or, again, in Kroetsch's more daringly parodic *Gone Indian*.

This particular concern clearly takes us beyond the context of one decade, the 1960s, and into the more general continuum of literary history in Canada. Many novels in the 1970s and 1980s adhered to that strong sense both of place and of the potency of nature that resulted in the general labelling of Canadian fiction as regional. But it is a truism of the novel as a mimetic genre that it is set in a particular place and time. Hence what novel would not be regional in some way? The density of realistic social and geographical detail in David Adams Richards's Faulknerian novels about the Maritimes have earned those works the label of regionalist. But what does this mean? In the 1960s, Henry Kreisel argued that the landscape had a particularly important social and psychological impact on the western novel, where, to use Laurie Ricou's evocative phrase, vertical man met a horizontal world. But surely the very specifically rooted Manawaka novels of Margaret Laurence, like those of Richards, transcend geography – as do the novels of Joyce, Dickens, and Balzac. In the novel form, it is difficult to write about individuals without placing them in a geographical and social setting, and thus writing about an entire society, with its communal history and values. Novels as diverse as Wiebe's *The Scorched-Wood People* (1977) and David Williams's *The River Horsemen* (1981) revealed an interest in places and communities that had some spiritual anchor, some vision of the world that belonged particularly to them.

In all these 'universal' regional novels, a double pull operated. There was a clear attraction to an almost National Film Board-like documentary realism.

There was also a pull towards the presentation of the local and natural as symbolic or metaphoric. This could be seen as one way of domesticating or taming the unknown, but it could also be a way to give voice to a relation with the land. Both impulses focused on the two obvious settings of city and country. The country here usually meant the small town or sometimes the family farm, or it could also mean the Canadian wilderness, where the attractions of a kind of modified mythic and romantic mode were never far away, even in tales of survival like John Buell's *Playground* (1976), Thomas York's *Snowman* (1976), and Rudy Wiebe's *The Mad Trapper* (1980). According to Margaret Atwood's thesis in *Survival* (1972) and Gaile McGregor's in *The Wacousta Syndrome* (1985), Canadians were seen in their literature as the victims of hostile natural forces. Allan Pritchard argued (*Canadian Literature*, 1984) that, in novels from British Columbia at any rate, the pattern was reversed: it was the wild paradise that was victimized by Canadians and their American-inspired machine civilization. Perhaps, then, the typical Canadian model for a response to the wild was ambivalent. Some novels suggested this ambivalence in (paradoxically) clear terms: in Marian Engel's *Bear* (1976), a citified and literary woman confronted nature and sexuality in the form of a bear, while the more destructive forces of that nature were faced – in the same bear form – by the literary hero of W.O. Mitchell's *Since Daisy Creek* (1984). Yet, from evocations of symbolic meaning to tales of the ecological, these novels all used the wilderness as both setting and subject, often more primitive than pastoral. Another version of this Canadian sense of place seemed to have been created specifically for and by women – novels that took place at a cottage or cabin, a domesticated home in the wilderness: Joan Barfoot's *Abra* (1978), Engel's *Bear* again, Atwood's *Surfacing* (1972), and even Margaret Laurence's *The Diviners* (1974). Susanna Moodie's and Catharine Parr Traill's experience in the bush provided the literary antecedent of the lives of the women these novels portrayed. The contemporary characters coped with a 'wilderness' that was both outside and inside: a wilderness of physical nature and of their human and sexual identities as women and, often, as creatrix-figures as well.

During these years, however, the major locations in which to set novels (for realistic and symbolic purposes) were the big city and the small town: Alice Munro's Jubilee, Robertson Davies's Deptford, Margaret Atwood's Griswold, Margaret Laurence's Manawaka, Matt Cohen's Salem, and Jamie Brown's Shrewsbury. Occasionally these small towns were presented as idyllic places of rural felicity or as refuges from urban madness. Most frequently and powerfully, the small town in Canadian fiction came to represent a limited and limiting society from which protagonists yearned to escape. Matt Cohen's communities in southeastern Ontario took on gothic proportions as human desire was transmuted into puritanical sin (*Flowers of Darkness*, 1981;

and even, to some extent, *The Sweet Second Summer of Kitty Malone*, 1979). The intellectual, psychological, and emotional confinement of Deptford in Robertson Davies's trilogy (*Fifth Business*, 1970; *The Manticore*, 1972; *World of Wonders*, 1975) drove the characters out into the wide world of experience.

In much of this small-town fiction, the harshness of the land and the disintegration of traditional values that once bound the community to that land were reflected in the people who had to inhabit it. The varying degrees of human and geographical sterility and desolation of Susan Kerslake's *Middlewatch* (1976), Terrence Heath's *The Last Hiding Place* (1982), or M.T. Kelly's *The Ruined Season* (1982) were more than matched by the economic and physical violence wrought by and upon the people of the logging community of Richards's Miramichi Valley in New Brunswick (*Lives of Short Duration*, 1981; *Blood Ties*, 1976). These are all examples of what Leslie Fiedler (*The Return of the Vanishing American*, 1968) once called, in an analogy with the Western genre, the Northern. Here the small town, dwarfed by a hostile environment, was the setting for the struggle of the often (but not necessarily) sensitive individual against a puritanical society, often symbolized or incarnated in some patriarchal figure of authority, whose weight of guilt was internalized by the would-be rebel. The legacy of the earlier rural chroniclers – Grove, Stead, Buckler, Ross – was clear in the writing of Richards or Marian Engel, whose *The Glassy Sea* (1978) showed that to grow up plain, smart, and female in small-town Ontario was to face the repressive consequences of rebellion early in life. Other novels – Atwood's *Bodily Harm* and Laurence's *The Diviners* – offered less negative visions of female futures from similar pasts, through a mature acceptance of the pain of living and of having lived.

Urban novels of the period showed less cause for optimism. Here the same double pull could be seen between the documentary impulse and the drive toward symbolic universalization (that is, toward the presentation of the Eliotian Unreal City). Not surprisingly, the most common image during the 1970s and early 1980s was of the city as the final place of social and psychological alienation. Austin Clarke's moving trilogy about Barbadian immigrants in Toronto (*The Meeting Point*, 1967; *Storm of Fortune*, 1973; *The Bigger Light*, 1975) showed the city's racial diversity in a less than flattering light; for instance, it provides the excuse for hierarchies of power that even money cannot move. Attacks on the mores and values of Canadian urban society could take the form of hallucinatory surreal fantasy, as in Juan Butler's *The Garbageman* (1972), or of documentary and didactic realism, as in the Cabbagetown and suburban novels of Hugh Garner (eg, *Death in Don Mills*, 1975; *The Intruders*, 1976; *Murder Has Your Number*, 1978). The Vancouver streets of Helen Potrebenko's *Taxi!* (1975) and the Victoria subculture of britt hagarty's *Prisoner of Desire* (1979) were equally unappealing (though likely naturalistic) portrayals of one side of urban Canada. The city was also usually seen as the cause, as well as the scene, of middle-class marital breakdown, of lives of quiet desperation, as in some of the carefully crafted, rather low-key novels of Richard B. Wright: *In the Middle of a Life* (1973), *Final Things* (1980), and *The Teacher's Daughter* (1982). These tales of sociological horror and cosmic despair contrast sharply with Adele Wiseman's *Crackpot* (1974), deeply rooted in the concrete world of the north end of Winnipeg, yet reaching mythic dimensions as the author exploits, yet inverts, some of the most grotesque of ethnic and cultural stereotypes.

The hearty humour of Wiseman's novel located it within a long tradition in Canadian letters: since Leacock and Haliburton, satire and laughter have been standard ways for Canadians to come to terms with where and how they live. Rick Salutin (*Marginal Notes*, 1984) once implied that the trick in covering Canadian culture was to figure out what to do *besides* satirize. Mordecai Richler continued to expose his own generation of urban middle-class Jewish professionals and intellectuals in *Joshua Then and Now* (1980) – without leaving the Protestant establishment unscathed. The novels of Morley Torgov (*A Good Place to Come From*, 1974; *The Abramsky Variations*, 1977; *The Outside Chance of Maximilian Glick* 1982) and of Seymour Blicker (*The Last Collection*, 1976) continued this familiar North American vein of Jewish satire and comedy. In the comic novels of Max Braithwaite, Ontario cities and towns came under the same satiric scrutiny. In fact, much Canadian humorous writing was in the traditional moralistic or satiric mode which affirms 'the good and true' (John Moss, *A Reader's Guide to the Canadian Novel*, 1981). And hardly a Canadian institution escaped ironic or satiric investigation: the RCMP (Ken Mitchell's *The Meadowlark Connection*, 1975), the literary and academic communities (Rachel Wyatt's *Foreign Bodies*, 1982), politics (Ian MacNeill's *The Battle for Saltbucket Beach*, 1975; Eric Koch's *The Leisure Riots*, 1973), tourism (Richard B. Wright's *Tourists*, 1984), or Canadian education and its effects on the culture (John Metcalf's *Going Down Slow*, 1972; *General Ludd*, 1980). The humour ranged from the genially playful to the condescendingly withering. Often satiric fiction of this period took the structure of the modern picaresque: Ken Mitchell's *The Con Man* (1979), Richard Wright's *Farthing's Fortunes* (1976), and Anthony Brennan's *The Crazy House* (1975).

It was not just urban novels that had the so-called sophistication to poke fun at themselves in the spirit of witty, but cogent, criticism. The fictive small town of Plum Bluff, Manitoba, was the scene of Helen Levi's trilogy (*A Small Informal Dance*, 1977; *Tangle Your Web and Dosey-Do*, 1978; *Honour Your Partner*, 1979), a sharp, ironic portrait of middle-class innocence and decency. And it was in a similar social milieu – though in the

Ottawa Valley – that was born one Bartholomew Bandy, the foolish, feckless hero who goes to war and returns to adventures in Donald Jack's continuing series of *The Bandy Papers* (1962–). Out of the Canadian *farm* experience, however, little such variety of tone seemed possible. Whether the farm was in Quebec (Jean-Guy Carrier's *Family*, 1977), northern Ontario (Gail Henley's *Where the Cherries End Up*, 1978), or Saskatchewan (Mary Ann Seitz's *Shelterbelt*, 1979), it was equally a lure and a burden. It was the place where a family – often an immigrant family – put down its roots, and was also the place from which the family could never escape. This ambivalence was as strong in the novels about Ukrainian new arrivals on the prairies as it was in those about multigenerational farms in Loyalist southern Ontario. In Matt Cohen's powerful *The Disinherited* (1974), the farm novel took on the dimensions of the family saga, of the conflict between generations, between the older one that was firmly rooted in the mythic and mundane reality of the soil and the younger one, willingly exiled from the land, but disinherited and rootless. Of course, this kind of generational novel of family conflict could be, and was, set in cities as well: witness Robert Harlow's *Paul Nolan* (1983). T.D. MacLulich has suggested that the frequency of this generational conflict novel in Canada may reflect a transferred exorcism of Canadian writers' own relations to a utilitarian, materialistic, pragmatic society against which they must define themselves. Novels like David Williams's *Eye of the Father* (1985) or F.G. Paci's *The Italians* (1978), *Black Madonna* (1982), and *The Father* (1984) were, in this light, more than tales of specifically immigrant displacement and assimilation; they also became allegories of the artist's struggle with Canadian society at large.

What was perhaps most noteworthy about all this 'regional' Canadian fiction was that it seemed to retain, for the most part, the accepted forms of traditional realism. Novelists themselves offered a number of theories to account for this constant in Canadian fiction. George Bowering, for instance, writing in *Canadian Fiction Magazine* (1979–80)), blamed 'good old puritanism' – realist novels somehow seem more useful, for they reflect Canadian values and culture. Matt Cohen, defining the realist novel rather basically as one that is about 'reality' (and 'in which not only does thought or action lead to subsequent connected thought or action, but does so in groups of words organized into logical sentences, paragraphs, chapters, etc.'), explained this realist impulse in terms of the Canadian need to invent, not just reflect, reality. (Cohen, along with the several other writers assembled in *Canadian Literature*'s 25th Anniversary issue, 1984, was discoursing on a favourite topic.) The realist conventions allow novelists, he argued, to fill a gap in their consciousness – the gap caused by the lack of a country. For Cohen, Canada is a concept too large to hold in the mind, too diverse to unite in the imagination or in reality, and so the manageable and familiar conventions of the realist novel allow writers to invent a country which they *can* imagine. Perhaps. It is nevertheless difficult to avoid noticing that contemporaneous American, French, British, and Italian novels also continued to find the realist mode congenial. In other words, whatever the local theory about the geographic size or the puritan mores of Canada, Canadian literature did not exist in a *literary* vacuum. It shared its formal and often thematic preoccupations with the literature of many other nations. Like the European and American novel, Canadian fiction was heir to both nineteenth-century realism and twentieth-century modernism. The constant staples of the novelistic tradition – of social analysis and psychological investigation – buttressed the Canadian novel, too. Robert Kroetsch may have speculated (in *Labyrinths of Voice*, 1982) that, because we lacked an Eliot or a Pound, we skipped modernism in Canada and went right from the Victorian to the Postmodern, but the *Bildungsroman* of the 1970s and 1980s was clearly the offspring of the modernist concern for psychological realism. Not that there was any obvious uniformity in the use of this convention. Some tales of growing up were quite radically experimental (David Young's *Incognito*, 1982). And, even among the many comic versions, there was a range from the light, sentimental irony of Ted Allan's *Love Is a Long Shot* (1984) to the darker humour of W.O. Mitchell's *How I Spent My Summer Holidays* (1981) to the comic verbal exuberance of Armin Wiebe's subversion of English syntax and lexicon in the Mennonite dialects of his *The Salvation of Yasch Siemens* (1984).

Frequently, the story of the coming of age of the protagonist took place in a small town – the grim New Brunswick mill town of David Adams Richards's *The Coming of Winter* (1974), the Nova Scotian frontier community of Alden Nowlan's *Various Persons Named Kevin O'Brien: A Fictional Memoir* (1973), Stan Dragland's more comically treated Depot, Alberta, in *Peckertracks: A Chronicle* (1978), or small-town Ontario in documentary poet Don Gutteridge's *Bus Ride* (1974) and *All in Good Time* (1981). In most cases, the limitations (geographical, emotional, and moral) of the town did not make growing up any easier. In many, the village took on the power of potential destruction. Whether the *Bildungsroman* was set in the country or the city, or both (as in Betty Wilson's tale of a Métis youth, *André Tom Macgregor*, 1976), the experience of coming to maturity was almost always one that transcended the individual. Often the quest for self involved a coming to terms with the public and private past, as in W.D. Valgardson's *Gentle Sinners* (1980) and T.F. Rigelhof's *The Education of J.J. Pass* (1983). Sometimes that past was a European one that was never really left behind: the Venice of Caterina Edwards's *The Lion's Mouth* (1982), the war-torn Poland of Ann Charney's *Dobryd* (1973) or Abraham Boyarsky's *Shreiber* (1983), or the omnipresent Ukraine in Maara Haas's *The Street Where I Live* (1976). Maria Ardizzi's *Made in Italy* (1982) was typical of many of these *Bildungs-*

romane written by those who emigrated to Canada, in that it was a tale of dislocation and isolation (linguistic, cultural, familial) and of the desperate desire to integrate and communicate. These were themes familiar to many stories of youthful development, but made more acute by the immigrant status of the protagonist.

Although many of the novels of growing up dealt with particularly male experience – Keith Maillard's *Alex Driving South* (1980), Barry Dickson's *Home Safely to Me* (1973), Dennis T. Patrick Sears's *The Lark in the Clear Air* (1974), or Peter Gault's *Golden Rod* (1983) – none explored more dramatically the dark side of maturing in an alien and sexually dangerous landscape than Clark Blaise's *Lunar Attractions* (1979). But one of the most interesting developments during the 1970s and early 1980s was that young women, as well as men, became the focus of the *Bildungsroman* form. Shirley Faessler's *Everything in the Window* (1979), Cecelia Frey's *Breakaway* (1974), Sylvia Fraser's *Pandora* (1972), Nessa Rapoport's *Preparing for Sabbath* (1982), Sondra Gotlieb's *True Confections or How My Family Arranged My Marriage* (1978), and, in a more Proustian vein, Oonah McFee's *Sandbars* (1977) were among the many novels that dealt with a woman's experience of coming of age. In the female variant of the *Bildungsroman*, in contrast to the traditional male form, familial ties were often rejected in the name of broader social and personal possibilities for women: the maternal, as associated in patriarchal culture with subservience and impotence, had to be redefined as either matriarchally powerful or as more positively feminine.[3]

The *Bildungsroman* was only one of the many forms taken by the fiction that followed the general questioning of gender and of sexual roles by a growing body of feminist criticism. Most, but certainly not all, of the novels about these issues were written by women. Some men did deal sensitively and provocatively with feminist political and personal themes: Ian McLachlan's *Helen in Exile* (1980) or the novels of David Helwig, especially *Jennifer* (1979), *It Is Always Summer* (1982), and *The Only Son* (1984), all concern sexual wars and the power relations between men and women. Some male writers told the stories of women, with varying degrees of credibility, from the inside: David Lewis Stein in *The Golden Age Hotel* (1984), Leon Rooke in *Fat Woman* (1980), Jack Ludwig in *A Woman of Her Age* (1973), Howard O'Hagan in *The School-Marm Tree* (written in the 1950s, but published in 1977). The acute portrayal of the sensibility of a perfectly ordinary young woman in Kent Thompson's *Shacking Up* (1980) followed upon his equally incisive presentations of the male psyche in *The Tenants Were Corrie and Tennie* (1973) and *Across from the Floral Park* (1974).

Domestic dramas, whether by men or women, about the decline of modern marriage or about sexual politics in general, abounded in this period, some written by old hands like Brian Moore (*The Doctor's Wife*, 1976; *The Mangan*

Inheritance, 1979; *The Temptation of Eileen Hughes*, 1981; *Cold Heaven*, 1983), and others by newcomers like Wayne Tefs (*Figures on a Wharf*, 1983) and Sharon Butala (*Country of the Heart*, 1984). John Marlyn's *Putzi, I Love You, You Little Square* (1981) and George Jonas's *Final Decree* (1981) were novels that gave the distinct impression that the women's liberation movement had had very few positive effects on human relations – at least from a European male perspective. However, more thoughtful fiction analysed the consequences of change: for instance, the results of switching family roles in George Szanto's *Not Working* (1982). Among the novels written by women on these sorts of subjects, the range of tone and approach was broad: at one end of the spectrum were the overtly anti-male novels[4] of Aritha van Herk (*Judith*, 1978, and *The Tent Peg*, 1981); at the other appeared a novel like Janette Turner Hospital's subdued study of the female condition in different cultures, *The Ivory Swing* (1982).

However, it was the *everyday* life of women, both with and without men, that was the staple of Canadian fiction written by women during these years. Family life, from both the female and male perspectives, was the occasion for considerable complex psychological analysis in *Small Ceremonies* (1976), *The Box Garden* (1977), and *Happenstance* (1980), all by Carol Shields; it was also the excuse for the almost pathological solipsism depicted in Joan Barfoot's *Abra* (1978) and *Dancing in the Dark* (1982). Other novels, such as Betty Lambert's *Crossings* (1979), Elizabeth Brewster's *Junction* (1982), and Katherine Govier's *Random Descent* (1979), suggested that the search for present identity could be undertaken, for women as for men, only through coming to terms with the past. These different modes and perspectives should serve to dispel the cliché of some sort of monolithic entity called the 'feminist novel.' Fiction centred on professional women (Doris Anderson's *Two Women*, 1978, and *Rough Layout*, 1981) differed in theme and tone from fiction about motherhood or old age; Constance Beresford-Howe wrote about all three subjects in *A Population of One* (1977), *The Marriage Bed* (1981), and *The Book of Eve* (1973). Novels by women also varied in form, from the self-reflexive parable about a prehistorical creatrix, in Pegeen Brennan's *Zarkeen* (1982), to the satiric extravaganza of Rachel Wyatt's *The Rosedale Hoax* (1977), to the bizarre mixture of tall tale and history, of fantasy and biography, in Susan Swan's *The Biggest Modern Woman of the World* (1983).

In Swan's novel, the reader is told: 'to be from the Canadas is to feel as women feel – cut off from the base of power.' The relation of the individual female experience of powerlessness (so insightfully explored in all the fiction of Audrey Thomas) to a more generalized social and cultural experience was an issue that novels like Marian Engel's *Bear* and Jane Rule's *The Young in One Another's Arms* (1977) also investigated in some depth. In these novels, as in Atwood's *Surfacing, Life Before Man* (1979), and *Bodily Harm*, a broader rebellion emerged, not just against the patriarchal structures that controlled sexual politics, but against the paternalistic patterns of modern post-industrial capitalism. In Atwood's novels, this protest moved more and more into the public arena. Many of these women's novels also revealed an intense awareness of the relation between bonding and bondage: that is, between a woman's need for connection with others and her equally strong need for freedom and independence. It was this theme that made novels such as Audrey Thomas's *Intertidal Life* (1984) and Margaret Clarke's *The Cutting Season* (1984) political novels in the broadest sense of the word.

Other novels, by both men and women, went beyond sexual ideology to use the male/female structure as a way of self-consciously investigating the eternal question (recently declared to be the new question of postmodernism) of the relation between art and life. But there was a most interesting difference in the way men and women used this metaphorical space. The writer figures in the women's fiction – in Audrey Thomas's *Latakia* (1979) or in Margaret Laurence's *The Diviners* – saw in the physical and passionate attraction of the sexes (and in its possible result) a model for the energy of creation, with a strong emphasis on maternal images of birth, of potential generation. However, in the men's novels – Robert Kroetsch's *Alibi* (1983), Clark Blaise's *Lusts* (1983), Rudy Wiebe's *My Lovely Enemy* – the relation between sex and art was a more ambivalent one: while sexuality was still linked to the creative urge, there was also a strong awareness less of the birth than of the death impulse inherent in it.

Such novels signalled Canadian fiction's arrival at another '-ism': at what we seem to have decided to call postmodernism. Some critics have seen this development as representing – finally – a loss of faith in the realist story (George Bowering in *Canadian Fiction Magazine*, 1979–80). Others explained that Canada's national discontinuities made us ripe for the discontinuities of postmodernism (Kroetsch, in *Labyrinths of Voice*). Still others sought to deny the change. Matt Cohen felt that in Canada there had been only isolated postmodernist experiments by only a few writers: 'although these experiments have often been enthusiastically welcomed by critics eager to see the emergence of a "post-modern" Canadian literature, postmodernism in Canada is more alive as a critical theory than as a group of books.' *Pace* Cohen, many books written in the 1970s and 1980s *were* 'metafictional' or postmodernist. Indeed, this movement toward fiction about fiction was perhaps the biggest development in Canadian fiction – long or short – during the 1970s and 1980s. Interestingly, the Canadian novel by no means lost faith in the realist story; what was striking about the fiction of this period was that the postmodernist challenges to convention all came from *within* the conventions of realism itself. Canadian fiction rarely took on that familiar American or French mode of increasing self-reflexivity or of increasing focus on literary materials (narrative or linguistic) in and for themselves (that is, outside the context of some sort of realism or, at least, of a direct parody of its conventions). Such an unwillingness to jettison realism might well be analogous to what Laurie Ricou has called the nostalgia for the referential function of language in contemporaneous Canadian poetry. In fiction, we need only think of those Canadian novels about the artistic process, such as H.R. Percy's *Painted Ladies* (1983), Keith Harrison's *Dead Ends* (1981), Leo Simpson's *The Peacock Papers* (1973), Robert Harlow's *Scann* (1972), or even Guy Vanderhaeghe's *My Present Age* (1984) where, as in *Don Quijote*, characters learned that they could not live in, or even as in, books.

Yet many determinedly experimental novels were written in Canada in those years. Elegant productions came from Coach House Press, such as Geraldine Rahmani's *Blue* (1981), where each of the three narrators was given a horizontal piece of the page, and Robert Sward's *The Jurassic Shales* (1975) with its distorted photographed heads of the Queen and equally distorted play with plot and character conventions. Other verbal and graphic effects were achieved in Ann Rosenberg's *The Bee Book* (1981). The visual collage form that Cozette de Charmoy played with in *The True Life of Sweeney Todd* (1973) was brought to a surreal extreme in the discontinuous form of written collage and fragment of Audrey Thomas's *Blown Figures* (1974). Yet, even in Thomas's formal play, the experimentation was presented as a sort of mimetic analogue of the psychology of a distressed woman. The challenge to the linearity of print, the breakdown of convention on a formal level, was echoed in the difficulties that both character and reader faced in trying to understand. The linguistic play in her *Intertidal Life* was also not pure post-structuralist 'dissemination' of language: it was thematically motivated by the fact that Alice, the aptly named protagonist, was a writer. That she was also a mother provided the focus, not only of the plot, but also of the verbal associations that tied the novel together, as well as of the many echoes of other texts that gave such resonance to the work (echoes, eg, of Virginia Woolf, Margaret Atwood, George Bowering, Lawrence Durrell, D.H. Lawrence, Radclyffe Hall). Among other novels to use fragmentary forms of composition, Sinclair Ross's *Sawbones Memorial* (1974), with its many unnumbered episodes, recalled the interior monologues of British and European modernist fiction, interwoven as they were with speeches and conversations. The overlappings of theme, character, and plot worked to pull together four generations of the fictive town of Upward. Helen Weinzweig's *Passing Ceremony* (1973) constantly altered the narrative perspective, providing the reader with a formal illustration of the failure of human relations that was the subject of the novel. Her *Basic Black with Pearls* (1980) took us into a mind and a fragmentary form that did not distinguish between realism and fantasy in the 'fun-house of appearance and illusion.' That many of these explorations of psyche and form were of and by women might not be coincidental, for it was women writers who perhaps most obviously questioned the thematic and structural inheritance of the novelistic patrimony.

Postmodernist (and modernist) possibilities of perspective also invited self-conscious play. Once again, realist conventions were contested from within the conventions themselves. Leon Rooke's *Shakespeare's Dog* (1983) was a comic realist novel, even if the perspective was that of a dog and the language that of Elizabethan England. In Ken Ledbetter's *Too Many Blackbirds* (1984), sixteen retellings of a story (a tale that was itself an unsolved mystery) asserted the impossibility of telling reality from fiction. The seven episodes of Ray Smith's experimental *Lord Nelson Tavern* (1974) altered point of view and narrative time in such a way that the readers' involvement in piecing together the relationships among the characters made manifest – in a postmodern way – the task readers have always had in the novel genre: the imaginative creation of a world of fiction.

In other words, many of these novels made explicit the conventionality of fiction; they were examples of 'metafiction,' fiction about fiction-making. At times, as with Robert Allen's two-part novel *The Hawryliw Process* (1980 and 1981), the cleverness and inventiveness seemed to be victorious over any narrative power, but in general in Canada, this auto-referentiality was seldom achieved at the expense of narrative interest. For example, Clark Blaise's *Lusts* was basically an epistolary novel, but his more postmodern version of that canonical (and realist) form is enacted in the changing shapes of the relationship between the letter writers. Kroetsch's *Alibi* was in some ways a traditional journal novel, but it had a totally metafictional twist. In each of these novels, as in many others, it was the role of the reader – and his or her surrogate within the novel – that made these novels different from modernist ones (with their primary emphasis on the act of *writing*). In postmodernist fiction – long or short (see Geoff Hancock's 1983 anthology *Metavisions*) – it was the politics of how and why we read that came to the foreground. Reading became an act of co-creation. Given that so many Canadian novelists have been academics, it was not surprising that they should have been self-conscious about the material nature of their work and about the interpretive power of the reader. The fact that many of these novelists have also been poets (for example, Atwood, Kroetsch, Ondaatje, Bowering, and Musgrave) might well have contributed to opening up the novel to new possible forms.

Aside from the continuing strength of Canadian 'regionalism' and realism (though not without alterations), this kind of broader international trend in fiction had the greatest impact on the Canadian novel of the 1970s and 1980s. Perhaps most apparent was the internalized challenge offered by Latin American fiction, a challenge that was often called magical realism (Angel Flores, writing in *Hispania*, 1955). This kind of realism was less a rejection of the realist conventions than a contamination of them with fantasy and with the conventions of an oral story-telling tradition. This very mixture seemed to prove especially congenial to the Canadian novel, itself working within, but questioning and pushing realism's limits. Among the many heirs of Gabriel García Márquez's *One Hundred Years of Solitude* (1967; trans. 1970) in Canada were Kroetsch's *What the Crow Said* (1978), Susan Swan's *The Biggest Modern Woman of the World*, Jack Hodgins's *The Invention of the World* (1977) and *The Resurrection of Joseph Bourne* (1979), and Michael Ondaatje's *Running in the Family* (1982). The fact that this last work was also a biography and autobiography, in a sense, raised the question of the limits of the *novel* genre. In fact, one of the results of postmodernism was that textual self-reflexivity led to a general breakdown of the conventional boundaries between the arts, and, by extension, between genres. Borders between the novel and forms of what had been traditionally considered non-fictional genres were constantly being crossed; the metafiction of the 1970s and 1980s played with the boundaries between fiction and history, biography, and autobiography. In other words, there was not just a deliberate confusion between the novel and the short story collection (in the work of Alice Munro and Ray Smith) or the novel and the long poem or poem sequence (Derk Wynand's *One Cook, Once Dreaming*, 1980; Stephanie Nynych's *...and like i see it*, 1972; Frank Davey's *Edward and Patricia*, 1984), but it appeared that fiction and non-fiction were interpenetrating in forms that differed from the usual fictionalized biography or historical novel. The difference from these traditional forms would appear to rest in the degree of metafictional self-consciousness within the work itself; these works were unabashedly fictional artifice – stories made up of words – but they also laid claim to a historically verifiable context. As in the documentary long poem of the same years, there was a strong pull towards the authoritativeness of fact. Sometimes these were Canadian historical facts: George Bowering's *Burning Water* (1980) told the tale of the writer writing *and* of the analogous process of discovery of the West Coast by George Vancouver, and in *A Short Sad Book* (1977), also by Bowering, figures of the modern Canadian literary scene mingled with Sir John A. Macdonald. Sometimes it was not really a Canadian historical context at all: in both Chris Scott's structurally complex *Antichthon* (1982) and Mark Frutkin's *The Growing Dawn* (1983), the metafictional focus was on the reading and writing about two more distant figures – respectively, Giordano Bruno and Marconi.

The writing of history had itself, of course, come under considerable scrutiny in the same decade, and its links to fictional narrative forms were among the main foci of attention. Historiography was redefined as a poetic construct. To write history (as Hayden White's *Metahistory*, 1973, demonstrated) was to narrate, to reconstruct by means of selection and interpretation. History began to be seen as being *made* by its *writer*, even if the events seemed to speak for themselves. Narrativization was seen (Fredric Jameson's *The Political Unconscious*, 1981) as a form of human comprehension, a way to impose meaning and form on the chaos of historical event. Given this new historical self-consciousness, it was not odd that when the Canadian novel chose to represent actual, historic personages – the Duke and Duchess of Windsor in Findley's *Famous Last Words* or Riel and Big Bear in Wiebe's *The Scorched-Wood People* and *The Temptations of Big Bear* – it should have done so equally self-consciously. Like history, the novel had to use emplotting strategies of exclusion, emphasis, and subordination of the elements of the story, and it had to deal with the chaos of already constituted events. But it also had another set of conventions to confront: those of fiction. So, in this period, a paradoxical new form emerged, one that might be called 'historio*graphic* metafiction,' with the stress on the processes of writing both fiction and history. These processes could be overtly thematized, as in Robert Harlow's *Scann*, or they might be presented more allegorically, as in Graeme Gibson's *Perpetual Motion* (1982).

The reason for the attraction to historical modes might well have been, as Gibson claimed in *The Globe and Mail* (1983), a late post-colonial need to reclaim the past. Such a theory might account for the large number of historical novels (as well as of historiographic metafictions) written in the dozen years following 1972. A very short list would include Sara Stambaugh's *I Hear the Reaper's Song* (1984), Janet Hamilton's *Sagacity* (1981), Morley Callaghan's *A Time for Judas* (1983), Brian Moore's *Black Robe* (1985), and Matt Cohen's *The Spanish Doctor* (1984). This theory might also account for the comprehensive reportage or 'Documentary Fantasy' of recent Ontario history in Hugh Hood's multi-volumed series of 'novels of ideas' called *The New Age/Le nouveau siècle* (1975–). The same impulse seemed to be behind Abraham Ram's 'novel of its time' (three volumes were published by 1984). Or this attraction to historical modes might have reflected the lure of 'alterity' that each writer had to come to terms with (Stephen Scobie in *Canadian Literature*, 1984), even if only by actual personal appearances within the work itself: the narrator entering at the end of Ondaatje's *Coming Through Slaughter* (1976). Or such novels might have intended to challenge – in a conscious way – the formal borders of generic distinctions, to push realism as far as it could go: that is, into document, on the one end, and into metafictional mimesis of the process of writing and reading, on the other.

In the emerging postmodern fiction, the genres of history and biography overlapped considerably. In both, an overt dialectic opposed the 'fact' of historically verifiable document to the structuring and interpreting acts of writer and reader. Unlike the more or less traditional fictionalized biography

(William Goede's *Quantrill*, 1982; Roy MacGregor's *Shorelines*, 1980, about Tom Thomson; Heather Robertson's *Willie: A Romance*, 1983, about Mackenzie King), metafictions like Ondaatje's *Coming Through Slaughter* deliberately forced the reader to separate life and art, biography and fiction, at the same time as they structurally united them. Timothy Findley's *The Wars* (1977) was a variant of this form: a war novel (a familiar fictional genre) and, at the same time, a novel very much about the writing of history and biography, just as John Mills's *Skevington's Daughter* (1978) was about the writing of both biography and fiction. The relation between metafiction and autobiography was perhaps less problematic, given that there has always been an accepted fictionalizing (or at least ordering process) built into the concept of the writing of the story of one's life. The self-reflexive *Bildungsroman* appeared in a number of forms, from the straightforward structure of Lorris Elliott's *Coming for to Carry* (1982) to the more self-dismantling use of convention in Audrey Thomas's *Songs My Mother Taught Me* (1973). But these were not quite the same as a metafictional autobiography, a self-aware and self-reflexive fictionalizing of one's own life, or of the roots of the personal past. A striking example of this mode in this period was certainly Ondaatje's *Running in the Family*, in which the author sought to write the history of the people of his familial past in Sri Lanka, to 'touch them into words.'

To overlap with history, biography, and autobiography, to challenge the boundaries of the novel genre, was one way for novels to work within the conventions of realism and still contest them. Another way was to take the major structures of the realist novel and work variations on them, play with them, parody them. The realist novel, for instance, pretended to present 'reality,' usually authorized by either written or oral sources. In Canadian metafiction after 1970, an interesting split developed between the use and awareness of these two kinds of sources, specifically between the written chronicle and the oral tale. Many novels dwelled almost obsessively on the written product of history as something fixed and fixing; others also played with the overt fictionality and the transience (if immediacy) of the oral tradition. The chronicle, the mode of written history, was clearly an attractive structuring device for even the most self-reflexive of metafictions. But it was not just at the level of structure that this model had its impact. In this fiction, new 'trappings' of realism were made possible by modern technology. There was no need to rely only on historical documents of the old kind, because newspapers and, especially, photographs, films, tape-recordings, videos, and data banks also provided 'facts.' Novels duly used these devices as ways to suggest the verification and, by implication, verifiability of even their most fictive creations: witness Becker's tape-recording transcripts and scrapbook in Jack Hodgins's *The Invention of the World* (1977). However, these new trappings of realism were not presented in the usual realist fashion; their contexts often suggested something rather sinister, while at the same time paradoxically suggesting that the act of taping or photographing was the direct analogue of the novelist's act. The fixity of the photo (in Findley's *The Wars*; Kroetsch's *Badlands*, 1975; Munro's *Lives of Girls and Women*, 1971; Ondaatje's *Coming Through Slaughter*), the illusory kinesis of the moving picture (in Atwood's *Surfacing*), the deceiving orality of the tape-recording (*The Wars* and *The Invention of the World* again) – all these were compared to the fixing on paper that constituted the act of writing. All were acts of reducing open, imaginative immediacy to framed form. It took, argued these metafictions, the reverse, dynamizing process of the act of reading to resurrect the creative immediacy that once lived in the imagination of the writer.

The post-structuralist literary theory contemporaneous with such fiction suggested that writing had been historically undervalued by Western society, that it had been degraded as the petrified, ossified form of oral speech. Canadian novels were extremely self-conscious of the paradox of looking, within a written genre, for new, specifically oral narrative forms that might grant them both more immediacy and a broader social context. In Margaret Laurence's *The Diviners*, the oral Scottish narratives and Métis songs were set against Morag's writing – and implicitly, against Laurence's own. In Wiebe's *The Temptations of Big Bear*, the oral (immediate and transitory) power of Big Bear's speeches was opposed to the written (fixed and permanent) power of the white treaties and the trial evidence. But neither novel could escape one final irony: the only way to explore the oral/written dialectic was in print. Big Bear's dynamic oral presence lived on in static print, just as his historical existence lived on, in part at least, in a fiction.

Perhaps these two poles – the oral tale and the written chronicle – reflected as well the legacy of the theories of Marshall McLuhan's work, including *The Gutenberg Galaxy* (1962). For McLuhan, oral cultures were collective, simultaneous, auditory, and oriented towards the present, while written cultures were individual, signed, linear, visual, and under the control of the past, of the causality and succession imposed by history (*Counterblast*, 1970). But McLuhan, like Wiebe, Hodgins, Laurence, and so many others, could only express these ideas, could only pass them on to us today, through the written medium of print. Even the metafictions most based on oral traditions of narrative only existed as written, individual, signed works – as, of course, did that paradigm of postmodern fiction, *One Hundred Years of Solitude*. In Canadian fiction, this paradox was often explored by polarizing the two extremes. One model took its form and modality specifically from oral gossip and communal, often mythic, memory; the other was modelled on the historical chronicle and the individual need to record in writing. The first, the oral model of communal gossip, was tied to myth, legend, fairy stories, and the tall tale; the written one was linked, instead, to the cause-and-effect rationality and realism of historical narrative. In the latter were found most often those new technological trappings of literary realism – the tape-recording transcripts, the (descriptions of) photographs and films, or the more traditional historical archives. None of these resolutely *written* novels really seemed to manifest what Kroetsch saw as a terrible longing for validation by stasis. Rather, they were more likely open acknowledgments of the problematic nature of those conventions of realism that were usually taken for granted. In works using the other model, however, instead of this serious earnestness, there was the Rabelaisian scatology and obscenity of Kroetsch's *What the Crow Said*, with its emphasis on animal and animal-like noises, on folk legend, and, in general, on the traditions of story-telling (story in the sense of a lie, as well as a narrative). Metafiction met oral history, with all the paradoxical implications which that might suggest.

Canadian postmodernism was characterized not simply by metafictional self-consciousness about genre and the conventions of realism, however. The important role of parody in challenging accepted modes and themes *from within* them was another strategy that Canadian fiction shared with many other nations. Some novels were overtly ludic and parodic: John Mills's *The October Men* (1974) was an example of what Louis MacKendrick (*English Studies in Canada*, 1984) has called 'centripetal comedy' in parodic forms. Novels by women used parody in a much more ideological fashion; all 'intertextual' echoing of other works (parodic or otherwise) implicitly acted to contest the (male) Romantic belief in aesthetic uniqueness and originality. Parodic play, in particular, implied a kind of ironic distance and difference at the very heart of similarity, a distance that allowed a text to speak *to* its culture, from *within* that culture, but without being totally co-opted by it. Parody could be a weapon against marginalization, for it literally incorporated that upon which it ironically commented. It could be both inside and outside the dominant discourses whose critique it embodied. For example, Marian Engel's *Lunatic Villas* (1981) offered an ironic parody of the picaresque form, a form more usually used by men to write about men. Here the usual male rogue-figure – footloose and fancy-free – travelling 'on the road,' was inverted to become the woman into whose house and life various rogues enter. As in Thomas's *Intertidal Life*, male models, whether of explorers or rogues, did not adapt to the common female reality of children and social responsibilities. Many novels of these years investigated the available alternatives – both aesthetic and ideological.

Similarly, in an attempt to question the class-inspired highbrow/lowbrow hierarchies of an Arnoldian classification of art, contemporary metafiction also challenged some of the assumptions of the 'serious' novel form; it assimilated history, biography, autobiography, poetry, and the short story collection, but also incorporated 'popular' or formula modes of fiction that were otherwise usually shunned. In these novels the structures of the 'popular' forms of fiction – the mystery story, the sports tale, the romance – were internalized and used as markers of metafiction: they overtly signalled that these works were fictive. Often this play was parodic, as in Atwood's use of the costume gothic in *Lady Oracle* (1976). There, when life (in fiction) began to imitate art, parody took on an important structural role and also offered a mode of voicing a social and cultural critique of the destinies of women: as characters, as authors, and as readers. Other forms usually considered as lowly and 'popular' that were used to metafictional ends include the spy story (Chris Scott's *To Catch a Spy*, 1978, and *Hitler's Bomb*, 1983) and the sports tale, be it about horse-racing (Robert Harlow's *Making Arrangements*, 1982) or baseball: both Paul Quarrington's *Home Game* (1983) and W.P. Kinsella's *Shoeless Joe* (1982) were delightful metafictional mixtures of fact and fantasy.

In her essay on 'Canadian Monsters' (*Second Words*, 1982), Margaret Atwood claimed that the supernatural was not part of the mainstream of Canadian fiction. Yet fantasy was well represented in the fiction of the 1970s and 1980s, both in its regular and in its metafictional variants. On topics as diverse as the Canadian identity (Stephen Franklin's *Knowledge Park*, 1972) and computerized two-dimensional worlds (Alexander Dewdney's *The Planiverse*, 1984), fantasy emerged as an important mode. Sometimes such fabulation was presented in more or less realist narrative forms (Ruth Nichols's *Song of the Pearl*, 1976); other times it appeared in a more experimental surrealist style (Frances Duncan's *Dragonhunt*, 1981), or set in an indeterminate time and space (Leon Rooke's *The Magician in Love*, 1981). Frequently these modes of fantasy also involved mythic dimensions, especially in their metafictional forms. Often, once again, the influence of that Latin American 'real maravilloso' (Alejo Carpentier's term) could be seen in the bizarre mixture of fact and mythic fantasy that is possible in a society that has enough 'peasant' faith to grant plausibility to the whole (R.R. Wilson in *The Compass*, 1979). The hero of Leo Simpson's *Kowalski's Last Chance* (1980) had an innocent faith, of sorts, in leprechauns, and the people of Port Annie (in Jack Hodgins's *The Resurrection of Joseph Bourne*, subtitled *or A Word or Two on Those Port Annie Miracles*, accepted the 'Peruvian seabird' and the bizarre consequences of her arrival with an equanimity worthy of the inhabitants of García Márquez's Macondo. In Hodgins's novel, the fantasy – or imagination – of the characters and of the reader makes communication possible (in both art and life). Frequently this metafictional concern for the power of the creative imagination took on psychological dimensions. In Brian Moore's *The Great Victorian Collection* (1975), a Montreal history professor found exactly that – a collection of Victorian memorabilia – outside his

California motel. Was it real? hallucination? fantasy? The novel never fully resolves the mystery. In other fiction, we seemed to enter a fairy-tale or dream world with metafictional links to our own (through concentration on the acts of creating and interpreting), but in which the unconscious and the irrational seemed to take over, as in part of David Helwig's *The King's Evil* (1981). Comparably, in Graham Petrie's *Seahorse* (1980), were we in the nightmarish world of the id? a Kafkaesque fantasy of deadly magic? The allegorical temptations of this novel, like those of the more satirically distopic *The Carbon Copy* (1973) by Anthony Brennan or those of the adventure tale variant in Guy Gavriel Kay's *The Summer Tree* (1984), suggested further dimensions which metafictional fantasy could possess. In all of these self-reflexive forms, despite their formal introversion, parodic play, and often totally unrealistic plots, the connection to the mimetic and realistic tradition was never quite totally severed. In a novel like Leo Simpson's *The Peacock Papers*, no matter how overtly authorially manipulative, no matter how absurd the plot and its resolution, no matter how parodic (of Thomas Love Peacock's style, of the mock heroic genre), the satiric drive in the name of saving 'civilization' from the barbarians of technocratic efficiency maintained the mimetic link.

Fantasy could clearly be used as a vehicle for many kinds of messages. It could allow a novel to escape linear history and plunge into visionary, mythic dimensions, as in Geoffrey Ursell's *Perdue: or How the West Was Lost* (1984). It could also be used to confront moral issues of the present in allegorical form. Perhaps the most daring such use of fantasy in the 1980s was Timothy Findley's *Not Wanted on the Voyage* (1984). The apocalyptic vision of Findley's earlier work here took on more comic yet still very moving and serious form in his parodic retelling of the story of Noah's flood, this time as a story about evil and destruction, both biblical and future. In this novel, as in Hodgins's *The Invention of the World*, the power of imagination and legend, of fiction and myth, confronted the stubborn tenacity of fact and document – and of final responsibility.

To write self-reflexively and often parodically of fantasy and imagination, of games and of play, of history as process in progress (instead of as completed product) – all these were ways to break down the finality of narrative closure that was a legacy of the realist novel. They challenged that closure *from within*. None of these modes of writing denied the mimetic connection between art and life; they merely relocated its site of operation, from the products of fiction to the processes. The 1970s and 1980s may have been times of theoretical suspicion and critical questioning but they were also times when new voices demanded to be heard, and were. But it was perhaps the formal consequences – for the shape of the novel as a genre – of technically significant works like *Running in the Family*, *Famous Last Words*, *The Temp-*

tations of Big Bear, Lady Oracle, Intertidal Life, The Diviners, Alibi, and *Antichthon*, to name but a few, that revealed best what Canadian fiction did to open up the borders, to challenge the boundaries, not just between narrative genres, but between the world and the word.[5]

4 Translation

PHILIP STRATFORD

In 1972 Gérard Pelletier, then Secretary of State, inaugurated a Canada Council Translation Grants Programme in the hope that making the best writing in French or English available in the other language would foster mutual understanding and cultural exchange. Since then over six hundred Canadian books have been translated, almost twice as many as in all the years before. So the history of literary translation in Canada might well be said to begin in 1972.

Of course, there is a long pre-history.[1] Cartier's kidnapping of Chief Donnaconna's two sons to train as interpreters is the first recorded act, one that backfired and earned the French the undying enmity of the Iroquois when the two princes died in captivity. Champlain's strategy seventy-five years later was more enlightened: he sent Étienne Brulé to live with the Hurons and learn their language. This scheme misfired too, for Brulé began to live almost exclusively with his hosts, and after twenty years was totally assimilated when he was assassinated and his tongue was ceremonially eaten. The Nipissing Indians called interpreter-explorer Jean Nicolet 'he who is twice a man' or 'double man'; behind the compliment lurks the perennial suspicion that all translators are double-dealers.

For centuries translation continued to be more functional than literary. Accounts of explorations published in Europe are the oldest examples. John Florio's 1580 translation of Cartier's first voyage (from the Italian of Ramutius, since the original French was lost) is the earliest text. Similarly, our knowledge of the third voyage (1541–2) comes not in French but in English from Hakluyt's *Voyages*. Interest in reports from the New World is demonstrated by the fact that Lescarbot's *Histoire de la Nouvelle France* (1609) appeared in English the same year, as did Hennepin's *Nouvelle découverte d'un très grand pays* ... (1697) and Lahontan's *Nouveaux voyages* ... (1703). But Champlain's *Voyages*, the *Jesuit Relations*, and accounts of discoveries by other explorers like La Salle, La Vérendrye, and Charlevoix had to wait until the late nineteenth century for translation. Here the work of American scholars should be signalled. John G. Shea translated Charlevoix and Le Clercq, and Reuben Gold Thwaites edited and provided translations from French, Latin, and Italian for a seventy-three-volume edition of the *Relations*. Definitive translations of Champlain, Lescarbot, Sagard, La Vérendrye, and others were sponsored by the Canadian Champlain Society in the early years of this century. It is worth noting that none of the works of great western or northern explorers (Kelsey, Henday, Hearne, Henry, Cook, Mackenzie, Thompson, Fraser, Franklin, or Frobisher) is available in French.

With the fall of New France and British occupation, a new era opened: the printing press came to Canada and government translation services became a necessity. The recent Supreme Court ruling requiring all Manitoba laws to be put into French has dramatized the translation issue, but since 1760 an increasingly large, costly, and indispensable group of anonymous translators has been at work turning hundreds of thousands of government documents into French and English. With such expertise at hand, it is anomalous that literary translation remained such a late starter. In the nineteenth century several well-known Quebec writers – Philippe-Joseph Aubert de Gaspé (author of *Les anciens canadiens*), historian François-Xavier Garneau, novelist Antoine Gérin-Lajoie, and poets Louis Fréchette and Pamphile Le May did a stint as government translators, but only the last two turned their professional skills to artistic ends. Fréchette wrote an English version of his own collection of short stories *Le Noël au Canada* (1900), and Le May produced the most celebrated French translation of the century with his 1884 version of Kirby's *The Golden Dog*. *Le chien d'or* has been called 'both a French translation and a French-Canadian adaptation of Kirby's original,'[2] a task Le May ingenuously described as 'ardue pour un traducteur qui ne sait pas l'anglais.'[3]

Several other English novelists were turned into French in this period. Frances Brooke's *The History of Emily Montague* had appeared in a French version in Amsterdam and Paris in 1770, making it the first Canadian literary translation in either language. From 1859 to 1873 five of Rosanna Leprohon's works were translated, the best known being *Antoinette de Mirecourt*, whose French-Canadian characters were so well portrayed that the author was often taken to be French. The same mistake was made for Missouri-born John Lesperance, who nevertheless wrote in English: three of his works were translated, the most popular being *The Bastonnais* (trans. 1896).

This flurry of activity was not matched on the English side in quantity or substance. Most nineteenth-century translations had the sensationalist appeal of Anger's *The Canadian Brigands: An Intensely Exciting Story of Crime in Quebec, Thirty Years Ago!!* (1867), Poutré's *Escaped from the Gallows* (1862), or Chevalier's *Legends of the Sea: Thirty-Nine Men for One Woman* (1862). The one really distinguished literary work was *Les anciens canadiens* (1863), rendered first as *The Canadians of Old* by Georgiana Pennée in 1864, then under the same title by Charles G.D. Roberts in 1890 but later reprinted as *Cameron of Lochiel*, and finally in a revision of the Pennée version by T.G. Marquis in 1929 as *Seigneur d'Haberville*, making it 'the only Canadian novel to have been translated by three separate hands and under three distinct titles.'[4]

The spurt of interest in translation – coincident with the literary awakening of the 1860s – was not long-lived. Using fiction as a gauge, one sees a relapse into general indifference for almost a century. American publishers skimmed off the most famous French titles for translation, including *Maria Chapdelaine, Trente arpents, Au pied de la pente douce*, and *Bonheur d'occasion*, while three times more English-Canadian works were translated and published in France than in Quebec, among them *Literary Lapses, Jalna, Anne of Green Gables, Two Solitudes*, and *The Apprenticeship of Duddy Kravitz*. Only slightly more than one hundred Canadian novels were translated in the first seventy years of this century, almost 60 per cent commissioned and marketed abroad. Quebec's lack of curiosity was due to a new cultural self-interest and an old xenophobia. English-Canadian publishers were a little more intrepid (they translated thirty-three novels to Quebec's eleven), but on the whole they observed a branch plant attitude to American initiatives, hardly surprising when most Canadian writers at the time had their sights trained on the u.s. market. (Buckler, Callaghan, de la Roche, Grove, MacLennan, Montgomery, Raddall, and Ross all had first novels published in the United States.)

On the French side, since translation policy was largely dictated in Paris, three writers – Mazo de la Roche, Malcolm Lowry, and Arthur Hailey – accounted for over half the novels translated, while in the opposite direction two Canadians, Gabrielle Roy and Marie-Claire Blais, and two Frenchmen, Louis Hémon and Maurice Constantin-Weyer, supplied a quarter of the fiction. This tendency to favour a few sure names is understandable economically but it results in a distorted view of the other culture. Even today many English readers might excusably think that in Quebec Blais, Carrier, Roy, and Tremblay were all the law and the prophets.

It should also be noted that while Quebec translated far less fiction than English Canada, in non-fiction the two were nearly equal. Quebec publishers are traditionally drawn to non-fiction: McLuhan and Frye, for example, with half a dozen titles each, rank with the most frequently translated novelists. As for other genres, very little poetry or drama was translated in either direction before 1970. In the aggregate about twice as many books were translated into English as into French, but in world terms Canadian output was piddling. During the decade ending in 1972 Canada ranked between Iceland and Albania in annual production.

This was the situation the Canada Council was empowered to improve.

Already in the early 1960s as part of its new mandate to support the arts, without much fanfare or system, the Council had begun to make a few translation grants. Centennial exuberance aiding, the number steadily increased over the decade. A new impulse and orientation had been given; concrete acts were quick to follow.

The first was the appearance in 1969 of *Ellipse*, a quarterly dedicated to the translation of poetry. The English Department at l'Université de Sherbrooke, already committed to the comparative study of Quebec and Canadian literatures, now launched this new venture. Each issue featured the work of two poets, one French, one English; the original poem appeared on the left, the translation on the right. The face-to-face format, the quality of the translations, the intelligent and provocative juxtapositions of poets made this a unique publication. By 1984 *Ellipse* had introduced the work of over sixty modern poets, had initiated dozens of young writers to the art of translation, and had set standards for much of the poetry translated elsewhere. This included some two dozen books, headed up by several important anthologies: *Poetry of French Canada in Translation* (1970), edited and with an excellent introduction by John Glassco; Fred Cogswell's solo translations, *One Hundred ...* (1970), and then *A Second Hundred Poems of Modern Quebec* (1971), later collected as *The Poetry of Modern Quebec* (1976); Frank Scott's *Poems of French Canada* (1977), and the avant-garde bilingual collection *Les stratégies du réel / The Story So Far 6* (1979) edited by Nicole Brossard.

Poetry was not the only genre to feel the new impetus. In 1973 two Montreal publishers, Pierre Tisseyre with Cercle du livre de France's Collection des Deux Solitudes, and Maynard Gertler with Harvest House's French Writers of Canada series, began issuing translations in a concerted way. In five years these two published more translated novels than the whole Canadian production in French and English in the previous decade. Other publishers followed suit, some specializing in particular writers (Anansi in Roch Carrier, Musson in Anne Hébert, Exile in Robert Marteau), others in genres (Oberon in new fiction, Talonbooks and Simon & Pierre in drama, Coach House and Exile in experimental writing, University of Toronto Press in criticism and scholarship), while among the larger houses McClelland & Stewart remained the biggest publisher of translations and the most eclectic. The flow of nonfiction continued, children's books began to be translated in both directions, and drama, largely thanks to Bill Glassco and John Van Burek's translations of Michel Tremblay, began to appear in print and on stage. Several anthologies marked the growing interest in Quebec literature in translation: Stratford, *Stories from Quebec* (1974); Stratford and Thomas, *Voices from Quebec* (1977); Brunelle, *French-Canadian Prose Masters* (1978); Kalman, *Seven Authors from Quebec* [plays] (1978); Shouldice, *Contemporary Quebec Criticism* (1979); Wagner, *Canada's Lost Plays ... French-Canadian Drama,*

1606–1966 (1982); and Teleky, *The Oxford Book of French-Canadian Short Stories* (1983). No equivalent yet exists in French.

Encouraged by the favourable climate, translators themselves broke their customary solitude and in the summer of 1974 met to discuss the advantages of solidarity. The Literary Translators Association/Association des traducteurs littéraires, founded in 1975, was the result. (The Writers' Union of Canada dates from 1973; l'Union des écrivains du Québec from 1977.) The Association now numbers eighty members, half working from French to English, half the other way, while a dozen also translate from other languages. Additional visibility was given by the creation in 1974 of two Canada Council Translation Prizes to parallel the Governor General's Literary Awards. Its recipients make a roster of the country's most distinguished translators. In 1982 the Translators Association inaugurated its own award, the John Glassco Prize, for a first translation by a Canadian from any language into English or French.

To assess what had been done and what had been left undone, in 1975 Maureen Newman and Philip Stratford published a bilingual *Bibliography of Canadian Books in Translation* (revised 1977). On the basis of this survey various attempts were made in the late 1970s to rationalize translation activity: lists of untranslated works were circulated, grants were guaranteed for the translation of certain Canadian classics, an international wing was added to the Translation Programme, offering support for foreign translations of Canadian works in languages other than English and French. As in most Canada Council transactions, the pressure was gentle and generally the laws of supply and demand and personal initiative prevailed.

Some critical attention had always been accorded translations, for example, in *Canadian Literature* where increased interest was reflected in a doubling of the number of reviews after 1975, but such attention was still relatively scanty and the quality of the reviewing was uneven. A new phase began in 1977 with the addition of a 'Translations' section to the *University of Toronto Quarterly*'s annual survey of 'Letters in Canada.' John J. O'Connor assumed the virtuoso task of reviewing the year's work in both directions (he dropped translations into French after 1980). Such a reviewer must know the two cultures and languages intimately, must be able to set the original in its literary context, must be ready to examine the translation line by line if necessary, should show felicities as well as errors, and must give the review a structure and a frame. With sometimes as many as twenty translations to consider, the job is formidable. O'Connor performed it with meticulous zeal; Kathy Mezei, his successor since 1983, while less detailed is better versed in theory and operates with flair and finesse; both have provided exemplary answers to the vexing question of how best to review translations.

From critical attention it is only a short step to theoretical speculation, and with many writers and scholars involved in translating in the 1970s, the step was soon taken. Sessions on translation were held by various learned societies, notably ACQL and CCLA (1977) and APFUQ (1980); symposia were held – *Translation and Interpretation: The Multi-Cultural Context* (1975) at Carleton University and *Translation in Canadian Literature* (1983) at the University of Ottawa. Not only were special issues of many Canadian journals devoted to translations of writing from Quebec – *Contemporary Literature in Translation* (1971, 1975), *Canadian Fiction Magazine* (1976, 1980), *Matrix* (1982), *Prism* (1982), *Rubicon* (1984), and special notice due to *Exile* (1972–) – but different aspects of the theory and history of translation were examined in *Meta* (1977), in *Ellipse*, no. 21 (1977), in *Canadian Review of Comparative Literature* (1980, 1981), and in *Room of One's Own* (1983).

Turning from this overview to a closer look at modern translations into English, the pioneers in poetry were Jean Beaupré and Gael Turnbull, who in the early 1950s produced almost clandestine translations of Saint-Denys-Garneau, Roland Giguère, Gilles Hénault, and Paul-Marie Lapointe in a series of mimeographed pamphlets published by Contact Press. Peter Miller added selected poems by Alain Grandbois and Anne Hébert in the 1960s, and Ryerson Press issued *Twelve Modern French-Canadian Poets* translated by G.R. Roy in 1958, and Nelligan's *Selected Poems* by P.F. Widdows in 1960.

But it was the exceptional work of John Glassco that marked a major change. Three-quarters of the two hundred translations he collected for his *Poetry of French Canada in Translation* were unpublished or newly commissioned. All were done by practising poets, among them Frank Scott, A.J.M. Smith, G.V. Downes, Eldon Grier, George Johnston, and Jay Macpherson. Filling gaps and playing favourites, Glassco did seventy-three poems by thirty-eight poets himself. As a translator he was a classicist. Like Samuel Johnson, whom he was fond of quoting, he believed it inevitable, indeed preferable, that the translator's personality should show, felt that translation should be 'an equivalent, not a substitute ... faithful but not literal,'[5] and described his book as 'an anthology of poetic translations rather than of translations of poetry.'[6] His own talents paired best with the wry and witty verse of Gérald Godin, Éloi de Grandmont, and Paul Morin ('do not insist on gathering roses / it leads to arteriosclerosis'), but his chef d'oeuvre was his translation of Saint-Denys-Garneau, first the *Journal* (1962), then *Complete Poems* (1975). He was also an able translator of fiction with versions of *Lot's Wife* (1975) by Monique Bosco and *Creatures of the Chase* (1979) by Jean Yves Soucy, who reciprocated by translating *Memoirs of Montparnasse* (1983).

Glassco saluted Frank Scott as 'Canada's first artistic translator of poetry'[7] and admitted to having 'pillaged' lines and phrases from him for his own translations of Saint-Denys-Garneau. In all Scott translated only some three dozen poems, mainly by poets he met in Montreal in the 1950s, but his influence was considerable. He was a literalist, if we give the word the noble sense Frye does when he writes: 'the translation of any poem worth translating should be as literal as the language will allow, but it should be a literal rendering of the real and not of the superficial meaning.'[8] All the corrections Scott brought to his translation of Anne Hébert's *Le tombeau des rois* – revealed in a fascinating exchange, *Dialogue sur la traduction* (1970) – moved closer to the French text. In risking a certain awkwardness by preserving features of French vocabulary and syntax, then sublimating them into new English poetic tensions, Scott set a style and standard followed by many younger translators, for example, Marc Plourde in his translation of Gaston Miron's *The Agonized Life* (1979).

Fred Cogswell's one-man anthologies did not much overlap Glassco's book and so enriched the general stock in the early 1970s. A plain stylist, all his translations of DesRochers are excellent, as are many of his versions of poems by Miron and younger Quebec poets, but he was not as versatile as Glassco and unfortunately often chose, as in *The Complete Poems of Émile Nelligan* (1983), to render older poets in rhymed verse and period diction, sometimes at the expense of rhythm or clarity.

With so many hands now translating the same major poets it became possible to compare translations, an activity that Glassco referred to scornfully as turning the art into 'a playground for philologists or students of linguistics.'[9] But linguistics had arrived. Undoubtedly the most extravagant experiment in this direction was issue 29/30 of *Ellipse* (1982), entitled '8 × 8,' in which four French poets and four English translated each other in continuous rotation, with Byzantine results. It is interesting to see that nearly all second-generation poetry translators came to the art through the novel: Sheila Fischman's translation of Giguère's *Miror and Letters to an Escapee* (1976) was preceded by a score of translations of fiction, as was Alan Brown's 1975 version of Anne Hébert's *Poems*; Ray Ellenwood served an apprenticeship in the verbal ironies of Jacques Ferron before translating Gauvreau's *Entrails* (1981), and Raymond Chamberlain in the tumultuous prose of Victor-Lévy Beaulieu before trying Claude Beausoleil's *Concrete City* (1983). Genre divisions were blurring in English practice. The same was true in French, as translators of Nicole Brossard's *textes* – Larry Shouldice, *A Book* (1976) and *Daytime Mechanics* (1980), and Patricia Claxton, *Turn of a Pang* (1977) – were to discover. Whether the texts were poetry or novel, they could hardly have been more allusive or elusive. It took a team of four to tackle Louky Bersianik's triptych feminist novel *The Euguélionne* (1981). Barbara Godard is another fiction translator who has moved from the considerable challenge of Antonine Maillet's *The Tale of Don l'Orignal* (1978) to her ingeniously punning, multifaceted translation of Brossard's *These Our Mothers* (1983).

Spurred by the anthologists and paced by *Ellipse*, the period produced a fair corpus of Quebec poetry in translation, but there remained much to do. Despite D.G. Jones's fine rendering of Paul-Marie Lapointe's *The Terror of the Snows* (1976), the Hexagone poets were still undertranslated, as was much of the work of the *parti pris* group.

Fiction remained the dominant genre. Over one hundred novels were translated into English from 1972 to 1984. Perhaps it is more telling to say that ten new novels by Marie-Claire Blais appeared during this period, seven by Carrier, six by Ferron, five by Anne Hébert, four by Aquin, four by Beaulieu, and three each by Archambault, Major, Poulin, Roy, Thériault, and Turgeon. The most important Quebec novelists were finding their way quickly into English. The spectrum was also extended into the past with Vida Bruce's translation of Gérin-Lajoie's *Jean Rivard* (1874, trans. 1977), Sheila Fischman's of Tardivel's *For My Country* (1895, trans. 1975), Irène Currie's rather faulty version of the bowdlerized edition of Girard's *Marie Calumet* (1904, trans. 1976), Conrad Dion's rendering of Laberge's *La Scouine* as *Bitter Bread* (1918, trans. 1977), Yves Brunelle's translation of Grignon's *Un homme et son péché* as *The Woman and the Miser* (1933, trans. 1978), and David Carpenter's version of Bugnet's *The Forest* (1935, trans. 1976). A sign of health was the publication of several retranslations designed either to improve corrupt texts or to provide more modern versions. John Glassco retranslated Jean-Charles Harvey's *Les demi-civilisés* (1982); Savard's *Menaud, maître-draveur* was redone by Richard Howard in 1976; Roy's *Bonheur d'occasion* by Alan Brown in 1980; and Renaud's *Le cassé* by David Homel in 1984. In many cases translators supplied careful introductions; usually they went to considerable trouble to establish the most reliable source texts; often they corrected mistakes and oversights, and sometimes, with the author's consent (eg, Stratford's translation of Félix Leclerc's *The Madman, the Kite & the Island*, 1976), edited the original, so that in some cases the translation might be said to be the definitive version. Many translators initiated translation projects themselves. Recognizing the importance of close collaboration between writer and translator, the Canada Council agreed to pay travel expenses so that the two could meet and review the work together.

To represent the volume and variety of fiction translation in the late 1970s and early 1980s, one might focus on the work of Sheila Fischman, undoubtedly Canada's best-known translator. Beginning with Roch Carrier's *La Guerre, Yes Sir!* for Anansi in 1970, she has since translated nine other Carrier books and is responsible for the fact that he sells more in the rest of Canada than in Quebec. Because of her close acquaintance with the Quebec literary scene – she has been an editor of *Ellipse* and book editor of *The Montreal Gazette* – she has been able to choose some of the most fascinating Quebec titles of the decade to present to an English public. John O'Connor's review of 1979 translations began with five Fischman works, translations that year of Carrier's

The Hockey Sweater and Other Stories, Jacques Poulin's *The Jimmy Trilogy*, her brilliant version of Aquin's *Neige noire*, the second volume of Naim Kattan's fictional memoirs, *Paris Interlude*, and Marie-Claire Blais's novel, *A Literary Affair*. This demonstrates her range; only a detailed examination of her thirty-five translations could reveal her grasp of the art. She handles the page-long sentences of Marie-Claire Blais (*Anna's World*, 1984), the erotic symbolism of Hubert Aquin (*Hamlet's Twin*, 1979), the Joycean exuberance of Victor-Lévy Beaulieu (*Don Quixote in Nighttown*, 1978), the poetic prose of Anne Hébert (*Shadow in the Wind*, 1983) or the sensuous humour of Michel Tremblay (*The Fat Woman Next Door Is Pregnant*, 1981) with equal sensitivity. Not all translators share Fischman's insatiable versatility. Pre-Canada Council translators – Felix and Dorothea Walter (Ringuet's *Thirty Acres*), Glen Shortliffe (Gérard Bessette's first novels), and Harry Lorin Binsse (early Lemelin and Roy), translated a few favourite authors each. Most second-generation translators are part-time and, retaining the advantages of a committed amateurism, favour certain authors (Bednarski and Ellenwood – Jacques Ferron; Chamberlain – V.-L. Beaulieu; Stratford – Antonine Maillet), or select only compatible titles. A few – Alan Brown, David Lobdell, Joyce Marshall – have translated almost as widely as Fischman in the Canadian field. A dozen years is hardly long enough to form a permanent corps of professionals, let alone a tradition, but a new generation of young freelancers – David Homel (*Broke City*, 1984, by Jacques Renaud), Mark Czarnecki (*Surrealism and Quebec Literature*, 1984, by André G. Bourassa), and Patricia Sillers (several stories in Teleky's 1983 anthology) – seem ready to tackle anything from the sludgiest *joual* to the most abstruse poetical musings.

In drama one name stands out, that of Michel Tremblay who, by virtue of a dozen translated plays, is almost a fixture of the English-Canadian stage. Only a dozen other playwrights have been translated and this imbalance does not fairly represent the extraordinary vitality of contemporary Quebec theatre. Gélinas has been translated, four plays by Gurik, and two each by Barbeau and Dubé, but whether the reading public for plays is too small, or the plays are too topical, only a fraction of current Quebec drama has crossed the footlights in English. Some of the most controversial feminist plays have been translated – the collective drama *Le nef des sorcières* as *Clash of Symbols* (1979) and Jovette Marchessault's *The Saga of the Wet Hens* (1983), both by Linda Gaboriau, and an interesting twist is that sometimes new plays are published in translation before they are published in French (see Kalman's anthology), but this, too, is only scratching the surface.

I do not wish to imply by omission that no important work was done in non-fiction, but it must suffice to say that the most significant titles were translated into English even more readily than fiction, and that most fiction translators in the 1970s also had several non-fiction titles to their credit. If one were to single out one or two works of special literary relevance one should salute the unsung translators of the French entries to *The Oxford Companion to Canadian Literature* (1983) and the *Dictionary of Canadian Biography* (1966–), and in the other direction Maurice Lebel's monumental single-handed translation of the first edition of this *Literary History* (1970).

Speaking to a World Congress of the Fédération Internationale des Traducteurs held in Montreal in 1977, James Holmes compared literary translators to bumblebees, which fly although it has been scientifically proven that their bodies are too heavy for their wing span. By and large Canadians have been too busy translating to do much theorizing about what they do, but in 'The Translation of Poetry / Traduire notre poésie' (*Ellipse*, no. 21, 1977) Jacques Brault, D.G. Jones, and others addressed the subject, the former touting his '*nontraductions*,' the latter admitting the inevitability of mistranslation but arguing that the act is less important as 'efficient communication' than as 'effective communion' between peoples. At the University of Ottawa symposium of 1982, E.D. Blodgett, translating Brault's position as 'Translation if necessary, but not necessarily translation,'[10] and Jones's as 'translation as an act of love,'[11] proposed his own figures: 'translation as threshold' or 'translation as exposure'[12] and laid the groundwork for a broad discussion in terms of current European critical theory with special application to the Canadian context. Recent critical writing seems to be taken up with narrower concerns – how to convey in English certain sexist features of French, or how to render *joual* or *acadien* – but the larger discussion is bound to continue. And when it does, besides being able to draw examples from books like Irène de Buisseret's witty manual, *Deux langues, six idiomes* (1975), and L.G. Kelly's *The True Interpreter* (1979), a scholarly history of translation theory and practice, the debate undoubtedly will be enriched by resources that lie just beyond the horizon of this survey: Kathy Mezei's bibliography of Canadian critical and theoretical writing on translation; John O'Connor's third edition of *Canadian Books in Translation*; Jean Delisle's forthcoming history, *La traduction au Canada, 1534–1984*, and Milly Armour's *World Dictionary of Translators* now in preparation. With these tools, a discourse on translation may develop to reflect the increasing complexity of Canadian practice.

For it is no longer just a binary proposition. How to do justice to the profusion of Canadian translations from other languages? Should one begin with Barker Fairley's *Faust* (1970), David French's *The Seagull* (1978), George Johnston's translations from Icelandic and Old Norse, Anna Rist's *The Poems of Theocritus* (1978), R.A.D. Ford's poems translated from several languages, Barry Callaghan's *Singing at the Whirlpool* (1982), translations of Yugoslav poet Miodrag Pavlović, or Leila Vennevitz's translations of the novels of Heinrich Böll? Confining oneself to Canadian authors, nearly every language group has its own collection, witness *Paper Doors: Poetry by Japanese-Canadians* (1981), *Italian Canadian Voices* (1984), *Poems of the Inuit* (1981), or *Songs of the Indians* (1983). As editor of the last two and translator of many languages, John Robert Colombo has succeeded Watson Kirkconnell as anthologist extraordinaire of multilingual Canada. J. Michael Yates's anthology *Volvox* (1971) groups twenty-four poets of different backgrounds, many of whom, writing in their own languages (Walter Bauer in German, George Faludy in Hungarian, Wacław Iwaniuk in Polish, Pavel Javor in Czech, Yar Slavutych in Ukrainian) were important writers in and of exile. Much of their work has been translated by Canadians, and it was a tribute to them all when *Příběh inženýra lidských duší* by Josef Škvorecký won the 1984 Governor General's Award for the best novel in English – in Paul Wilson's translation as *The Engineer of Human Souls*.

So how does the balance stand after a dozen years?

– A great many new translations; very few sponsored by any agent other than the Canada Council.

– A good collection of Québécois writing now available in English; a relatively feeble reciprocity, though Quebec may be on the verge of change, for the old two-to-one ratio is a thing of the past and in recent years as many titles have been translated into French as into English.

– A considerable investment; incalculable returns, in both senses of the word: the books are published, but are they promoted? distributed, but are they displayed? reviewed, but are they read or remaindered?

There is no doubt that the experience of translating is a rich one. Glassco calls translation 'the strictest examination a poem's intimate structure can undergo.'[13] Frye describes the Scott-Hébert exchange as 'a creative achievement in communication, not just a necessary evil or a removal of barriers.'[14] Brault writes that translation is 'a truly disalienating odyssey'[15] though he refuses to be restricted to any bicultural canal, proclaims the need to navigate international waters, and dreams of Hubert Aquin translating Borges, Miron translating Neruda, and Chamberland translating Octavio Paz. Blodgett goes a step further and, noting the impact of Gabriel García Márquez on Kroetsch, Hodgins, Ondaatje, and Wiebe, imagines English and French writers discovering common bonds on South American ground.[16] There have been stranger scenarios: in 1977 Nicholas Catanoy persuaded Margaret Atwood, George Bowering, Dennis Lee, Gwendolyn MacEwen, and Tom Marshall to contribute translations to his *Modern Romanian Poetry*. Whatever the meeting place, if translation continues to be encouraged, one can be sure that its flux and reflux will be registered in future histories of Canadian literature.

5 Theory and Criticism:
Trends in Canadian Literature

BARRY CAMERON

This chapter on the theory and practice of criticism during the 1970s and early 1980s, with specific reference to Canadian literature, is ideological, self-reflexive, and post-Saussurean. It is ideological because it uses language and because no discourse (as theorists such as Michel Foucault and others have made clear) is ideologically innocent. It is self-reflexive because I am aware that 'I' am in language (because critics write from within language, because they are constituted by and in the words they use). It is post-Saussurean in that it emphasizes the structures of discourse and the paradigms of thought inscribed within them rather than accepts the referential presumptions of a 'realist' concept of how language functions. It is conscious that criticism is a process as much as a set of conclusions. Hence I evaluate, but question the validity of certain kinds of evaluation; I design categories, but question the presumptions of taxonomies; I resist any impulse to design a 'total' picture, yet presume to survey trends over an 'entire' period. Paradox and contrast are germane here; in this chapter they are both a subject and a methodology, for the presence of contradictory alternatives demonstrates some of the ways in which literary criticism and theory during the years under consideration both depart from and reconstitute critical trends of the past.

'RESIDUAL' CONTEXTS

Like all other discursive practices, the writing of literary history systematically forms the objects of which it speaks. History is not an objective category of thought; like literature, it is an object constructed by understanding. As Linda Hutcheon observes, writing about 'Canadian Historiographic Metafiction' (*ECW*, 1984–5), 'To write history – or historical fiction – is equally to narrate, to reconstruct by means of selection and interpretation.' The writer constructs the history 'even if events are made to seem to speak for themselves.' Literary critics and historians, moreover, are not 'objective,' because they have no objective place from which to view their subject; they use their subject –

language – in order to analyze or construct it. Hence they shape a network of textual relations from inside ideological, historical, and social frames.[1] Seldom, however, did Canadian critics between 1972 and 1984 consciously enunciate their assumptions, any more than the critics of the five-year period 1967–72 (whom Miriam Waddington surveyed in the *Supplement to the Oxford Companion to Canadian History and Literature*, 1973) had done. Exceptions include a number of self-reflexive articles, such as Barbara Godard's 'Other Fictions: Robert Kroetsch's Criticism' (*Open Letter*, 1984) and 'Redrawing the Circle: Power, Poetics, Language' (in Marilouise and Arthur Kroker, eds, *Feminism Now: Theory and Practice*, a special issue of *Canadian Journal of Political and Social Theory*, 1985), and W.H. New's 'Re:Visions of Canadian Literature' (*Literary Criterion*, 1984). 'Residual' criticism in Canada, however – the dominant descriptive-historical mode against which post-Saussurean practice reacted – remained in view during these years; it is represented by such works as Elizabeth Waterston's *Survey: A Short History of Canadian Literature* (1973), Clara Thomas's *Our Nature – Our Voices: A Guidebook to English-Canadian Literature* (1972), and David Stouck's *Major Canadian Authors* (1984).

But the general disposition of this chapter to privilege the book over the essay also blurs the situation somewhat; the hierarchy in Canadian critical discourse (which esteems the book more than the article, the article more than the review) is misleading. Book-length criticism frequently falls into the 'residual' category; but much of the resistance to received modes took place initially in the shorter form. Because some of the most interesting critical practice did not appear in book form and some of the least effective criticism did, I am compelled not only to distinguish among trends and accomplishments but also to assess the mixed reception certain texts received. My strategy here is deliberately more archeological than genealogical, for though this chapter creates a narrative out of its subject-matter (and therefore runs the risk of generating a self-confirming structure), it resists the notion that it can tell the *whole story* of Canadian criticism. A 'genealogical' approach would design a model (to my mind, suspect) of progress or continuity; an 'archeological' approach insists that its findings are a *fragment* of a larger discursive formation.

As the number of journals, small presses (NeWest, Longspoon, Turnstone), and university presses increased – all with some interest in Canadian writing – the critical milieu became more complex, particularly in so far as many of the most interesting articles (such as Godard's) appeared in non-traditional (often feminist, political, and interdisciplinary) contexts. And just as there was an increase in the number of journals addressing Canadian literature in some degree, so also did several established journals change editorship, with consequent alterations in content or format: Peter Thomas, long affiliated with

The Fiddlehead's fiction offerings, took over the general editorship in 1982, following Fred Cogswell, Kent Thompson, and Roger Ploude; Constance Rooke took over *Malahat Revew* from Robin Skelton in 1983, devoting more attention to Canadian writers. Among journals devoted solely or primarily to Canadian writing, the oldest, *Canadian Literature* (est. 1959), changed editors for the first time, with W.H. New taking over from George Woodcock in 1977. Under Woodcock – whose own critical practice, exemplified by his travel essays, his lucid enquiries into social history, and a collection of writer-and-society-centred articles called *The World of Canadian Writing* (1980), influenced a generation of readers and critics – *Canadian Literature* had encouraged the first sustained serious attention to Canadian writing, and the articles it published tended to be author-centred, thematic, and concerned with social matters. Under New, the journal opened more to structural and technical commentary, while special issues (particularly no. 100, separately released as *Canadian Writers in 1984*) foregrounded the voices of writers themselves. Woodcock himself was also the subject of a 1978 Festschrift edited by New, *A Political Art*.

While *Journal of Canadian Fiction* slowly fell silent, many other journals began publishing during the 1970s and 1980s, focusing on particular genres or subjects: *Canadian Children's Literature* in 1975 (ed. John R. Sorfleet, succeeded by Mary Rubio and Elizabeth Waterston in 1980), *Canadian Poetry* in 1977 (ed. Michael Gnarowski and David Bentley, Bentley taking on sole editorship in 1983), *Canadian Theatre Review* in 1974 (ed. Don Rubin, with several guest editors; Robert Wallace succeeded him in 1983). *Journal of Canadian Studies* (est. 1966) more uniformly stressed the social contexts of literature; *Studies in Canadian Literature* (est. 1976) undertook to challenge conventional critical attitudes towards Canadian writing and some of the received interpretations of literary texts; Frank Davey's *Open Letter*, and various publications by the women's editorial collective 'Tessera' (in *Room of One's Own* and *Canadian Fiction Magazine*, for example) provide some of the most articulate expressions of nascent Canadian literary theory; and several little magazines – among them *Descant, Mosaic, Malahat Review, Capilano Review, Line* (est. 1983), and *Prairie Fire* – often tried to combine creative with critical experiment. A particularly striking change in the character of periodical literature occurred with the appearance of *Essays on Canadian Writing* at York University in 1974, under the editorship of Jack David and Robert Lecker (whose ECW Press developed out of this collaboration). ECW Press rapidly expanded, taking Canadian literature as its primary critical, historical, and bibliographic subject. The journal *ECW*, however, more openly endeavoured to challenge the realist bias of 'residual' commentary by focusing on contemporary and postmodern forms.

'POETICS' VS 'CRITICISM'

The generic distinction between 'poetics' and 'criticism,' elucidated by formalist-structuralist theory in Europe (as, for example, in the writings of Tzvetan Todorov), provides one way to distinguish between trends in Canadian critical discourse. 'Poetics' (though it may take specific texts as models) concerns itself with literary discourse at large, elucidating ways in which, for example, texts differ or coincide with each other and textual patterns or systems allow meaning to be generated. It recognizes that texts exist within the empirical world, but rejects the idea that they are constituted by it. 'Criticism,' by contrast, interests itself in whatever is unique to a given text, describing a particular work and designating its meaning. Empiricism is allowed a more constitutive power. In Canada, the 1972–84 'period' was ruled by a modified poetics, a poetics constructed with not only theory in view but also an idea of nationhood. Most critics, that is, were concerned with establishing a general grammar of Canadian literature *as a whole*, and with discovering in Canadian literary texts certain kinds of pattern. These 'patterns' were, further, deemed to characterize the nation or reveal the national character. Of such 'poetics,' most influential and controversial were D.G. Jones's *Butterfly on Rock* (1970), Margaret Atwood's *Survival* (1972), Laurence Ricou's *Vertical Man / Horizontal World* (1973), and John Moss's two books, *Patterns of Isolation in English Canadian Fiction* (1974) and *Sex and Violence in the Canadian Novel* (1977).

All these studies devise taxonomies of image or theme, drawing on a wide variety of texts for their evidence, but frequently emphasizing one intertextual trace at the expense of the dynamics of the single work. Unlike structuralist taxonomies, however, which rest on the *forms* of literary content, these Canadian poetics for the most part favour designs that rest on the *substance* of literary content. (In so far as Atwood sets up a typology of forms of victimhood by which to organize her treatment of theme, *Survival* is in this respect an exception.) Their systemic ordering also differs from structuralist poetics by positing that the character of the text is undeniable, thus grounding itself in empiricism (presuming the subject/object structure of knowledge, and treating texts positivistically as verifiable data) or in phenomenology (giving weight to intentionality and consciousness).

These studies all, moreover, rest on presuppositions about 'Canada.' They view literary texts less as part of a larger, specifically literary system – eg, *genre* – than as part of the production of an entire culture with an assumed unity. They see this literary system, in turn, implicitly as a subsystem of a more general system of cultural productions. Literary history in these terms turns into Canadian Studies; through an analysis of 'Canadian' symbols, images, and myths, literature is able to function potentially as a means of national identification and a force for national unity. Such studies thus manifest, as Eli Mandel has suggested in 'Strange Loops' (*Canadian Journal of Political and Social Theory*, 1981), a cultural Freudianism, in that they attempt to tell us 'who we are' in their analogies between literature and personality, nation and person. But they also try to tell us, as Ricou does, 'where we are,' in their assumption that literature arises out of or reflects geographical place.[2]

Jones and Atwood were especially influential because they attempted to fulfil a demand for a Canadian literary tradition – a demand which is generally a 'desire for an origin that will authorize a beginning.'[3] Strongly influenced methodologically by Northrop Frye, they nonetheless implicitly repudiate one of the ideological elements that permeates Frye's 'Conclusion' to the first edition of the *Literary History of Canada* (1965) and also his 'Preface to an Uncollected Anthology' (reprinted in *The Bush Garden*, 1971): the view that imagines the Canadian writer as an unfinished European or American writer. Thus they also reject the definition of 'culture' that equates taste with imported bourgeois values, and hence (despite significant ideological differences) Jones and Atwood share with Robin Mathews – whose Marxist critical practice is represented by *Canadian Literature: Surrender or Revolution* (1978) – a desire to discover indigenous traditions and thereby repudiate colonial status. By their argument, tradition (not language) distinguishes a national literature; a 'colonial literature' achieves independence by discovering, constructing, or 'inventing' a tradition, whether grounded in historical experience or not. But the effort to construct a literary tradition in Canada is more problematic than these statements suggest. Conventionally, 'nation' equates with the area where the national language is used. But when the nation is linguistically and geographically fragmented, and when the (plural) languages are at once 'our own' and those of other quite different and powerful cultures, then such terms as 'place,' 'speech,' and 'identity' carry ambivalent meanings.

As a nation formed more by political agreement and desire than by linguistic inevitability, Canada has a greater sense of territorial integrity[4] than a commonality of symbolic language that would enunciate – or 'authorize,' define – the cultural parameters of a social identity. 'Absence' or 'lack' (rather than the 'presence' of a common speech) can consequently be said to describe one recurrent paradigm of Canadian culture. 'Contradiction,' moreover, accompanies 'lack' and might be expected in an environment where a common history and a common destiny do not necessarily coincide with common interests. Faced with this social paradigm, some systems of cultural poetics interpret the idea (and the state) of Canada pessimistically, reading a structure of conflict as a sign of cultural decay; others read it positively, accepting the process of change as an opportunity for creativity. Either way, the practice of this kind of criticism turns commentary into a sociopolitical act. Jones, Atwood, Ricou, Mathews, Moss: all attempt to raise a national consciousness in order to render intelligible and justify our living together. Their collective concern with country and self explains their dominant critical concern with authority, voice, place, and social position.

The cultural designs these critics devised range from the empirical to the theological. Ricou, for example, posits a unifying centre by means of a Cartesian image; he argues that the generative principle for prairie fiction is 'the primitive geometric contrast between vertical and horizontal,' the 'basic image of a single human figure amidst the vast flatness of the landscape.' Also concerned with themes, images, and attitudes of mind, Atwood centres her study in the more abstract notion of 'survival,' using it symbolically to postulate national unity. Jones places Canadian literature within archetypal patterns of the Old Testament and aligns those patterns with Western literature in general. Specifically, Jones argues that 'the Canadian temper' and a Canadian view of life manifest themselves in various literary patterns: 'a sense of exile, of being estranged from the land and divided within oneself,' a garrison culture confronting a hostile wilderness, and a sense of a lost or yet undiscovered world. This absent world is implicit in the recurring images of the drowned poet, the sleeping shepherd, and the dreaming Adam under the snow, all of which Jones finds permeating Canadian writing. Moss, too, accepts forms of exile (which he links with two other 'patterns': a geophysical imagination and an ironic consciousness) as one of the metonymic 'patterns of isolation' that reflect the indigenous character of the Canadian community. As in his first book, Moss argues in his second that fiction reveals a collective national preoccupation with identity and moral vision. But such collectivity and such versions of 'the' national character came under increasing scrutiny.

Critics of these five books (eg, Russell Brown in *ECW*, 1982) have argued that the central motifs each writer uses as an organizing principle (survival, sex and violence, the drowned poet, the vertical/horizontal paradigm) are all self-confirming. Despite Moss's apologia as a structuralist, moreover – in an interview in *Books in Canada* (1981) and in his essay 'Bushed in the Sacred Wood' (in David Helwig, ed., *The Human Elements*, 1981) – his later, encyclopedic study *A Reader's Guide to the Canadian Novel* (1981) provoked similar reactions. His comments on sex and violence contrast markedly with the remarks – particularly those of Hutcheon, Godard, and Kroetsch – collected in a set of conference papers called *Violence in the Canadian Novel since 1960* (1982), edited by Virginia Harger-Grinling and Terry Goldie. The conference papers treat both the psychology and the formal manifestations of the themes of sex and violence with more theoretical sophistication, and they focus on textual structure rather than on national character. Responses to Atwood's *Second Words* (1982), however, a chronologically structured collection of her occasional essays and reviews, were generally favourable. Some of Atwood's key pieces appear here: her response to Robin Mathews's critique of *Survival*, which originally appeared in *This Magazine*; her essays on Canadian humour, Gwendolyn MacEwen, John Newlove, and Northrop Frye; and her study of aspects of the supernatural in Canadian fiction. The last of these originally appeared in a collection of essays that David Staines compiled specifically for an American audience, *The Canadian Imagination* (1977), which also includes interesting essays by Brian Parker on the quality and contexts of Canadian drama, Marshall McLuhan on the appropriateness of the 'Canadian condition of low profile identity,' and Frye on patterns of imagery in Canadian poetry.

There is little evidence of the direct influence of Frye's seminal *Anatomy of Criticism* (1957) on Canadian criticism of Canadian literature – the only sustained example that comes to mind is Patricia Morley's 'naive' (Frye's term) application of Frygian concepts of comedy to the fiction of Hugh Hood and Rudy Wiebe in *The Comedians* (1977). But the essays in his *Division on a Ground* (1982) and especially *The Bush Garden* have been an inspiration for the general thematic and cultural thrust of all the contemporary Canadian criticism that tries to answer the questions 'Who am I?' and 'Where is here?' In Frye's work, the land is a hostile or indifferent wilderness, for which the North is an effective symbol; in *The Bush Garden*, Frye labels this concept 'the riddle of unconsciousness.' Encountering the riddle produces 'a garrison mentality' that takes several different shapes in Canadian literature. The problem is that such works treat landscape as a given, whereas the environmental determinism in which they base their arguments – reiterated in Allison Mitcham's *The Northern Imagination* (1983), an account of the Far North as an environmental determinant in Canadian fiction – is a *social construction of the landscape*, a semiotic coding of nature in terms of culture.

This general thematic/environmental tradition affects several other studies as well, among them the works of Ronald Sutherland and Clément Moisan, both involved in comparative studies of francophone and anglophone literatures. Moisan's *A Poetry of Frontiers* (published in a French version in 1979, which Moisan rendered into a different version when he translated it in 1983) is not solely thematic in orientation; but it remains concerned with revealing a 'mainstream' – in this case the common quest of selfhood in Canadian and Quebec poetry that consequently provides us with a glimpse of 'universal man.' Sutherland's two books, *Second Image* (1971) and *The New Hero* (1977) – both grounded in social realism – argue (as does his essay 'The Two Cultures in the Canadian Novel,' collected in Charles Steele's *Taking Stock*, 1982) for a shared 'sphere of consciousness' for English-speaking and French-speaking Canadians, an ideological 'mainstream' defined by 'an author's awareness of and sensitivity to fundamental aspects of both major language groups in Canada, and of the interrelationships between these groups.' The notion of 'fundamental,' however, like the notion of 'mainstream,' is problematic. For Sutherland such thematic categories as 'Divine Order' and 'Vital Truth' carry national significance because he perceives the nation in binary religious terms, or in what *The New Hero* characterizes as a 'pantomime' between Calvinist and Jansenist sensibilities. Still other critics cast a national model in different binary terms. Leslie Monkman's *A Native Heritage: Images of the Indian in English-Canadian Literature* (1981) probes the nation by means of ethnic dualities; while Margot Northey's *The Haunted Wilderness* (1976), though it does not set up its subject as a closed literary or cultural system, nevertheless also deals in dualities within one country's borders. Northey's account of varieties of the Gothic and grotesque within the two Canadian literatures, moreover, does not provide a methodology for distinguishing between their ideological and cultural differences. The failure of these studies to question the realist assumptions on which they rest meant that they, too, over the course of time, engendered critical resistance.

Although they do not comment directly on Monkman or Northey, Louis Dudek's three collections of essays – *Selected Essays and Criticism* (1978), *Texts and Essays* (1981), and *Technology and Culture* (1979) – provide one perspective in the debate over 'nationalist' poetics. These essays share Sutherland's social realist stance; they assume that literature is the product of experience, favour mimesis, and accept criticism as a mode of interpreting empirical reality. As one of the *Selected Essays* puts it: 'Literature ... contains objective relations to a world of actuality, which must be tested and discovered. The main job of criticism and of scholarship is to look for the objective relations.' But at the same time Dudek rejected the use of a metaphorical mode of social and literary analysis – the mythosymbolic mode favoured by Frye, Jones, Atwood, and Marshall McLuhan – finding it a reductive use of the imagination.

Other critics accepted the validity of structural analysis but challenged (from various cultural margins) received definitions of 'centre' and 'mainstream.' For example, in *Configurations* (1982), E.D. Blodgett points to what he sees as the basic problems in Moisan's and Sutherland's studies: their positing of an illusory unity in Canada, either political or cultural, and their unwillingness or inability to recognize that 'Binarism in Canada, while it is a violent stasis, masks in fact an anglophone hegemony.' This is one of the reasons Blodgett himself includes a discussion of German-language writing in Canada in his comparative study; implicitly he attempts to decentre the traditional anglophone/francophone binarism. Blodgett demonstrates that 'centrist' thematic studies in Canada adopt a metaphor of universal forms, but that this overriding metaphor (desiring unity, seeking similarities that signify sameness) obscures the metonymies of Canadian literature (the associative structures that demonstrate relationship without requiring unity or identity). Convergences do occur between the two founding literatures in Canada, Blodgett says, but these convergences do not signify a 'mainstream' of Canadian writing. Blodgett thus represents an important shift in comparativist studies in Canada, in that he moves away from a predominant thematics towards a knowledgeable grounding of critical practice in structuralist and post-structuralist theory. Such knowledge also informs two of Blodgett's essays: his assessment of Dennis Lee's *Savage Fields* (a 1977 book, subtitled 'An Essay in Literature and Cosmology,' that posits a distinction between 'earth' and 'world'), which appeared in a 1982 Lee issue of *Descant*, and his intriguing 1984 essay in *ECW*, 'After Pierre Berton What?' Blodgett here discusses and examines the homological relationships between Canadian (especially prairie) and Québécois fiction, arguing that ' "Canadian" must always connote an ambiguity' and that unnaming and renaming, a gesture of discovery, 'is the point of departure for the study of Canadian literatures' (in the plural).

A further demonstration of the tension between poetics and criticism manifests itself in the writings of W.H. New. Although his collection of essays, *Articulating West* (1972), exhibits considerable concern for non-thematic properties in a wide range of Canadian texts, the introductory essay and the chapter on Canadian literature in his comparative *Among Worlds* (1975) situates his work in the thematic/environmental tradition by positing landscape as the central generative principle of language and literature in Canada, a metaphoric centring not unlike the poetician's basic critical gesture and its less ambitious form in Sutherland and Moisan. 'West' is used in the figurative sense of exploration, openness, discovery: 'To speak the language of "West" is not to be merely regional in bias ... but to articulate the tension between order and disorder, myth and reality, that underlies Canadian writing.' But, unlike so many others, New recognizes a mediating structuration or semiotics in this process: 'What these writers are also doing is creating a rhetoric of landscape,' ' "sentencing" their landscape.' The mimetic in this way becomes figurative, and the binary oppositions that New establishes here are picked up and developed in significant ways by Eli Mandel, Dick Harrison, and Robert Kroetsch.

ANTI-THEMATIC POSITIONS AND REPRESENTATIONIST PRESUMPTIONS

The widespread reaction to this 'thematic' or 'nationalist' tradition of criticism – in some cases more properly described as a poetics grounded in cultural criteria – effectively began with Frank Davey's attack, 'Surviving the Paraphrase' (subsequently published in *Canadian Literature*, 1976, and as the title paper of Davey's 1983 essay collection), delivered at the inaugural meeting of the Association of Canadian and Quebec Literatures at York

University in 1974. Reacting to the legitimacy of cultural poetics as critical practice and exalting 'literariness' over other criteria, Davey deplored the emphasis on theme that dominated Canadian criticism to the mid-1970s – at the expense of linguistic and formal studies and analyses of individual works. Such cultural/nationalist critical practice, he argued, stemmed from a desire to avoid evaluation (a stance derived from Frye) and to forestall treating Canadian literature as serious literature. Extra- or anti-literary and reductionist in nature, such critical practice, he argued, did no more than paraphrase the national literature in terms of international themes. Dismissing the way it privileged metalingual representation (the assumption of an invariable 'content' to which words *refer*) over texture (the stylistic particularities of a work), Davey proposed a series of alternative critical practices: literary histories of technique, linguistic, regional, and generic studies, and phenomenological criticism.

Shortly after the publication of Davey's paper, there appeared what seemed like a direct response to Davey's call for a different kind of criticism: a special issue of *Studies in Canadian Literature* significantly entitled *Minus Canadian: Penultimate Essays on Literature* (1977), edited by Barry Cameron and Michael Dixon. Cameron and Dixon were actually working independently of Davey, having been preparing since 1973 a collection they hoped would represent 'a concerted effort to expand the scope of Canadian criticism.' But the overall effect of the issue, as their polemical introduction, 'Mandatory Subversive Manifesto: Canadian Criticism vs Literary Criticism,' made clear, was to reinforce the thrust of Davey's essay. Rejecting the popular sociology of Frye and others, which they said stereotypes the Canadian consciousness, Cameron and Dixon stressed the importance of *formal* comparative contexts. Like Davey, they posited that form is ideologically innocent *in order to ask what 'Canadian' means as a literary term*, and they argued that a critic's approach and choice of evaluative criteria should be appropriate to the work under analysis, thus directly precluding neither thematic nor structuralist practice.

Russell Brown's review article, 'Critic, Culture, Text: Beyond Thematics' (*ECW*, 1982), took one step further this movement towards a less content-based critical practice, by specifically advocating the potential available in structuralist criticism – whereby *theme* can be treated as cultural coding (a structural feature of the text) and *genre* as a horizon of expectations (within which a critic interprets formal possibilities).

Among subsequent tilts with the thematologists are W.J. Keith's paper at the controversial Calgary Conference on the Canadian Novel in 1978 (published in Charles Steele's *Taking Stock*), a second Keith essay, 'The Function of Canadian Criticism at the Present Time,' printed in the tenth anniversary issue of *Essays on Canadian Writing* (1984–5), and Paul Steuwe's *Clearing the Ground: English-Canadian Literature after Survival* (1984). Keith, not wishing to ban theme altogether but to retain it as 'a tentative first step towards mature literary-critical discussion,' argued in Calgary for an evaluative methodology based more on content than on form. In the *ECW* essay, he added that thematic criticism 'belongs ultimately to the sociology of culture – which may be a legitimate object of study in itself but is no substitute for genuine literary criticism.' Writing within an ideology of common sense grounded in an Arnoldian-Leavisian tradition – we must read, he says, with 'mature enjoyment which is a combination of emotional sensitivity and humane intelligence' – Keith is skeptical of postmodern literary practice and dubious of both post-Saussurean critical practice and theorizing about 'interesting patterns or semiotic subtleties.'

D.J. Dooley's *Moral Vision in the Canadian Novel* (1979) argues a more overt Leavisite case; that is, literature is an image of society; coherence, verisimilitude, and a 'convincing social and moral context' for character constitute acceptable evaluative criteria; and 'a vital capacity for experience, a kind of reverent openness before life, and a marked moral intensity' – 'the conviction of felt life' – are the tenets that distinguish good literature. Writing in the tenth anniversary issue of *ECW*, T.D. MacLulich openly approves this position, for he praises Keith as an 'old-fashioned critic' who resists the trend towards technical innovation, at the same time disparaging critics such as Mandel, Kroetsch, and Cameron. MacLulich deplores the post-Saussurean 'academic takeover' of the literary institution in Canada, an exclusion of the common reader from critical discourse, and an evaluative preference for technical innovation. 'The result will be not the cessation of literature in Canada, but rather the assimilation of our literature to the style of the international avant-garde.'

Paradoxically, this conservative acceptance of *received* 'international' standards and the concomitant resistance to technical experiment coincides to some degree with left-wing political attacks on a nationalist hegemony of theme. Paul Steuwe's *Clearing the Ground*, for example (though it misreads Frye, and though it reads as though Davey, Cameron/Dixon, Brown, and Keith had not already presented an anti-thematic case), argues that the ubiquity of the thematic approach influences literary production itself. Some writers are canonized and others excommunicated, Steuwe suggests, on the basis of a nationalist privileged criterion of evaluation. His most interesting and original discussion involves the material conditions of literary production: writing as work, publishing as an economic activity, literature as a commodity, the reader as a consumer. This aspect of literary studies is almost completely ignored in Canada despite the availability of much interesting theory by such European Marxist critics as Terry Eagleton and Pierre Macherey.[5] Only Paul Cappon, Robin Mathews, and Larry MacDonald have concerned themselves in any sustained way with situating criticism in socially and politically engaged historical materialism. Such criticism views literary texts as a means of understanding structure, change, and ideology in Canada; it is important because it recognizes that the social is the matrix which fleshes out any other critical context.

Cappon's *In Our House* (1978), which contains essays by other critic-sociologists (including Mathews) as well as several general essays by Cappon himself, manifests an activist sociology that views literature as a potential vehicle for social change. Several of the essays point out how pervasive liberal ideology, idealism, and empiricist-positivist stances are in Canadian literature and criticism. James Steele (in his essay in Cappon's book, 'The Literary Criticism of Margaret Atwood') argues, for example, that Atwood's *Survival* continues the idealist/elitist tradition of Frye by psychologizing or individualizing social phenomena that are, in reality, founded in concrete economic and political practices. When Atwood argues, through her typology of victim positions, that individuals are capable of resisting American imperialism, Steele says, she provides an instance of the 'bourgeois illusion of freedom.' Larry MacDonald argues in 'Psychologism and the Philosophy of Progress' (*Studies in Canadian Literature*, 1984) that such atomization of individuals also occurs in Atwood's fiction and in that of Robertson Davies and Hugh MacLennan, the last singled out by Mathews, too, in his 1978 book, *Canadian Literature*.

Mathews privileges social realism – community, social identity, collectivity – over personalism, individualism, psychologism. The group, the family, or the couple are exalted, Mathews says, in the Canadian tradition he articulates. But while he tries to deal with the relation between history and the social matrix on the one hand, and literature on the other, he does so only at the level of ideological content abstractable from the texts themselves. Like the other writers in Cappon's volume, he seldom if ever deals with literary form as an informing structure of social consciousness. Mathews also tends to read literary texts as the direct expression of the consciousness of a social class that is, in turn, the direct result of historical forces. As with bourgeois criticism, this sort of neo-Hegelian criticism treats the text as an object rather than as a social signifying practice with a material infrastructure. Like phenomenology, moreover, it privileges consciousness. Hence social realism may reveal the mimetic relation between economic structure and social behaviour, but it does not deal with literary form as a consequence of the technical and ideological conditions of the text's production. Only John Fraser's 'The Production of Canadian Literature,' an essay in Cappon's volume, gestures in this direction.

What seems to have disturbed most critics of the poeticians or thematologists, then, is that the traits they isolate emphasize theme and image in a peculiarly nationalist ideological configuration at the expense of discursive and generic conventions, or what the Formalists call 'literariness' or 'poeticity.' But resistance also stems from a repudiation of poetics itself: from a challenge to the credibility of the model and the indeterminacy of the taxonomies provided.

When critics delight in a realist fiction that manifestly denies its own material and historical construction, their criticism becomes what might be called 'expressive-realist.' It sees the literary text not as something that results from the process of producing an intelligible literary construct out of the available signifying systems of language, but as a 'natural' reflection of the (historical and geographical) world it supposedly delineates. It takes this world as inherently more real than its representations, and there is certainly no self-reflexivity in the critical act itself.

Those who hold such a representationist theory of language and literature – that is, a predominantly mimetic view of the relation between the text and a given preconstituted reality – tend to base their critical practice in the classic subject/object structure of knowledge, in the divorce between language and experience, central to empiricist epistemology. Such criticism presumes not that knowledge is a verbal production of meaning but that meaning lies outside language, in some objective or 'prediscursive' history or geography. It exalts referents (themselves constructs) over signs; knowledge of the object becomes part of the object itself. Mimetic adequacy, in other words, provides the normative knowledge of the text in which the 'image' is measured against the 'essential' or 'original' in order to establish its degree of representativeness and hence its 'authenticity' or correctness. Nationalist-thematic versions of this mimetic criticism frequently emphasize character as a sign of the national sociolect; a Canadian stereotype, that is, turns into an 'ideal image' – in relation to which Canadian texts are judged. Some anti-thematologists, however, given the decentred condition of Canada, dismiss this whole (covertly ideological) process as a normative fallacy.

Such reflective or expressive principles of language and literature characterize this 'corporate' Canadian criticism (I use Raymond Williams's term) as a form of cognition rather than as a discourse or a practice. The result is that criticism itself is privileged as a mode of knowledge over other forms of discourse, a conclusion which structures the critic as an arbiter of taste, and which – by giving the reader only the passive role of responding to the text (rather than any active role in constructing the text) – structures the reader as a consumer.[6]

POST-SAUSSUREAN PRACTICE

Emergent 'post-Saussurean' practice is represented most notably by the writings of Shirley Neuman, Linda Hutcheon, Barbara Godard, E.D. Blodgett,

Robert Kroetsch, and increasingly by Terry Goldie, Heather Murray, Stephen Scobie, Lorraine Weir, Sherrill Grace, Smaro Kamboureli, Barry Cameron, Frank Davey, and the other contributing editors to *Open Letter*, especially Steve McCaffery. Such critics focus on discourse, for they assert that the 'real' can only be constructed (created and organized) in a particular social formation, at a particular time, and in language. For post-Saussureans, any ostensible 'given object' or 'reality' therefore does not exist outside language; it is already 'written' (whether 'accurately' or not is tangential, for discursivity characterizes both the real and the imagined). Hence these critics argue that language 'precedes' geography and experience, in the sense that such concepts are only cognitively available to people when constructed in language. They are available only in the guise of signifiers. Consequently (to quote from Catherine Belsey's *Critical Practice*), 'To find a guarantee of meaning in the world or in experience is to ignore the fact that our experience of the world is itself articulated in language.' Within a Canadian context, post-Saussureans argue that the form and contents of Canadian literature derive from discursive practices, not from a preconstituted geography or social formation. To generalize: *signifiers* (words) always precede the *signified* (concepts); the signified then itself becomes a signifier for another signified; hence we can say that form produces or constructs content, and that this product in turn functions as signifier, produces another content, and so on, through a process that treats content as an effect of discourse.

The emergence of post-Saussurean critical practice in Canada – its structuralist and post-structuralist phases arrived at the same time – began to move criticism away from its orientation towards empirical referents, away from hermeneutic or interpretive impulses exclusively, towards a self-reflexive concern about methodology and theory. Critics became increasingly interested in the power of textuality and in the conditions of meaning: in the ways meaning is produced and the ways in which the conventions and operations of literature are the ideological products of a particular history.

SUBJECTIVE PHENOMENOLOGY: PROCESS, REGION, AND POLYPHONY

Until this development, the dominant alternative to empiricist criticism in Canadian literature was existential or subjective (as distinct from dialectical) phenomenology. Among its most noticeable and notable (though not always self-consciously so) practitioners were Frank Davey, George Bowering, Robert Lecker, Eli Mandel, and Warren Tallman.

In Davey's studies of Earle Birney (1971), Raymond Souster and Louis Dudek (1980), and Margaret Atwood (1984), as well as in *Surviving the Paraphrase* and *From There to Here* (1974), his guidebook of brief essays on writers since 1960 who mark the transition from modernism to postmodernism, his critical practice exhibits a New Critical concern with technique and form. This concern, however, is situated in an existential phenomenology mediated by Charles Olson and American (post)modernist poetics, especially the proprioceptive self of Olson that exalts consciousness – of which Warren Tallman speaks in his essay collection *Godawful Streets of Man*, a special issue of *Open Letter* (1976–7).[7] Heidegger and Merleau-Ponty are layered in Davey's critical writing, as they are in the work of other critics phenomenologically oriented. Man's being as a space of openness to the world, the self-motivation and self-mirroring of language, the disclosure of presence ('letting something be seen') through language ('unconcealment'), and pre-Socratic letting-be or Heraclitean authenticity: these are recurrent concerns.

Both Davey and Tallman are attracted to a common range of binary oppositions in which they privilege process over stasis, the open over the closed, fragmentation over wholeness, discontinuity over coherence, temporality over spatiality, speech over silence, region over centre, 'West' (as W.H. New uses the term) over 'East,' international over national, individual over corporate man, (post)modernism over humanism, postmodernism over modernism, self as subject (man as process, a temporality of action and decision) over self as object, and proprioception over perception. Similar binary oppositions emerge in *Criticism: The Silent-Speaking Words* (1966), in which Eli Mandel argues for the desirability of a phenomenological 'savage' criticism, at once subjective and unsystematic, that would experience the unmediated raw reality of the object-text – 'to become one with the work of literature' – by favouring perception and 'the meaning of the perceived moment' over abstraction/structure/pattern, and by eschewing interpretation, explanation, and evaluation.

Since phenomena are those things which show themselves to consciousness, criticism as language for a phenomenologist articulates the object-text as a phenomenon: a letting-be-seen of that which shows itself. From this critical perspective, there is no in-itself outside a perceiving consciousness (an awareness, incidentally, that signals the limits of Dennis Lee's study of 'earth' through 'world' in *Savage Fields*). In other words, the object-text becomes visible through 'my' perceptive critical act; if the text appears to mean or to speak in a given manner, it is for 'me,' in relation to 'myself,' that it does so. 'I' am the centre, in relation to which one text takes on its particularity, and others appear as different.

A phenomenology of reading, then, stresses not only the text but also, with equal force, the actions involved in responding to the text. In Davey and Bowering, however, the rhetorical strategies generate an apparent emphasis on the text, while in Mandel, Tallman, Lecker, and Lee, it more often falls on response: on a 'recounting'[8] of the adventures of the critics' own subjectivity, of their developing responses ('reflections,' 'impressions') to the succession of words on the page. That is why such criticism is so epideictic in nature – so highly performative and self-reflexively rhetorical – and why the object of criticism as an 'intentional object' is really the structure of that critic's experience. Obvious examples include Robert Lecker's discussion of reading Clark Blaise or his dilation on a single Hugh Hood story in *On the Line* (1982), Lee's response to Leonard Cohen's *Beautiful Losers* in *Savage Fields*, and Tallman's 'impressions' of Mordecai Richler's various texts.

The existential component is evident in such criticism when – as in Davey's study *Margaret Atwood: A Feminist Poetics* (1984), Bowering's essay on Lionel Kearns in *A Way with Words* (1982), or Lee's comments on Michael Ondaatje in *Savage Fields* – the critic attempts to characterize the nature of the writer's experience of world and self. These commentaries attempt less to describe particular objects of the writer's experience than to set particular experience within the context of the writer's whole being-in-the-world. That is why the replicating impulse in such criticism (which creates the performative effect) is so strong: it attempts to re-enact the author's prelinguistic, preconscious understanding.

Bowering, Tallman, and Lecker are much less concerned than Davey, Mandel, and Lee with cultural grounding in their discussions of literary texts, though there is a strain of environmental determinism in Tallman's treatment of Canadian writers which could be construed as a concern with culture. Davey reads form analogically in political or ideological terms in *From There to Here*, thus leading him, by way of McLuhan's influence, to identify regionalism with postmodernism and microelectronic technology and to identify centrism with modernism and mechanical technology. Lee, by contrast, drawing on the conservative philosophy of George Grant, sees all technology as a homogenizing international (American) colonizing force. Both Grant and Lee fiercely oppose bourgeois society (the priorities of liberal-democratic industrial capitalism); in this way, in the absence of a genuine revolutionary critique in Canada, it is radical conservatism that fills the void.

One of the modes that Davey proposed in 'Surviving the Paraphrase' as an alternative to thematic criticism involved the investigation of the regional consciousness – as a body of distinctive attitudes to language and form, of 'language and imagery that in some ways correlate with the geographic features of the region.' This last point, which Milton Wilson (following his argument in Mandel's *Contexts of Canadian Criticism*) would call 'the geographical fallacy,' derives from Tallman's far Western environmental determinism. It is a view that Mandel, preoccupied with Western regionalism, ultimately rejects in his struggle to come to terms with Northrop Frye's positions on nationalism, internationalism, and regionalism.[9] Mandel comes to see that the national context is political and the regional cultural; that 'region,' as both Sutherland and New imply, is a function of 'nation'; but that, perhaps, the nation 'Canada' itself is an 'American' region. Mandel thus reads 'region' not strictly as a place, a community, or a political entity, but as a cultural boundary, a set of social relations, or a language. 'Region' is thus a version of discontinuity and process in poetry (as it is for Davey) or a version of voice (as it is for Kroetsch) identified stylistically with oral and folkloristic tradition and formally with myth. From Mandel's perspective, regional cultures are established not by geography but by literary conventions. Such regionalism effectively works to move power from a received centre; it is a way imaginatively to undermine uniformity and centrism by paradoxically aligning itself with literary movements beyond the nation – ultimately continentalist movements, some would argue, not really as internationalist as they might at first seem.

It is this alignment that Mathews and Keith Richardson (in *Poetry and the Colonized Mind: Tish*, 1976) would resist. So, too, would Patricia Marchak, as her essay in *In Our House* makes clear; for her, such connections appear centripetal, a reinforcing of American power. These critics would also resist Stan Fogel's argument in *A Tale of Two Countries* (1984), which declares how impoverished, isolationist, and claustrophobic Canadian realist fiction is in contrast with the postmodernist, deconstructive American fiction of such writers as John Barth and William Gass. American metafiction seeks to deconstruct the monolithic American character, Fogel argues, in order to show that it is 'a bad fiction.' He bemoans the marginalization of such fiction in Canadian literature, tendentiously suggesting (via George Bowering and Edgar Friedenberg) that this condition might be due to the mythologized conservative character of Canadians, though Fogel does not really see it as myth. If Canada is still being constructed culturally, however, how can it be deconstructed vis-à-vis a politically motivated American deconstructive poetics? If a unified, centralized Canada does not exist, how can it be deconstructed at all? Problematically, Fogel accepts that a differential social condition separates the *fiction* of the two countries, but at the same time suggests that the absence of such differences between Canadian and American *poetry* is innocently due to poetic theory and tradition. Such 'innocence,' however, is undermined by the ideological base of literary forms.

Dennis Lee also is concerned with the problem of discourse and authenticity. In *Savage Fields* he explores in overt phenomenological terms the interaction of earth and world (Heidegger's terms here adopted and modified) in Ondaatje's *The Collected Works of Billy the Kid* and Cohen's *Beautiful Losers*. The savage strife between these two overlapping force fields, these two modes of being – the cosmology of 'savage fields' – is a model, Lee argues, that makes 'the terrible era of modernity intelligible.' As Blodgett points out in his *Descant* essay, 'Authenticity and Absence,' ontology and the metaphysics of presence (to use Jacques Derrida's locution) dominate the structure of Lee's thought. Lee wants to believe that language creates reality, that it articulates the world, that it is both what it names and what calls the named into being. As with Heidegger, Lee wants to believe that to be is to be in language, and that to be in language is to be shown to be, language and world having the same ontological features. But his fear is that there is no ontological referential reality, only an ontological structure of words: we cannot think of earth in earth's terms, for we can speak of earth 'only in terms of world's knowledge of it, because to speak at all is to assert our world-nature.' Another way of enunciating this problematic is to say that 'earth' is only available to us through a signifying system and that the ideology of that system is unconscious for us in that we are seldom aware of its mediating power. Thus there would be no 'earth' without signs, for then there would be no meaning for 'earth.'

Lee's concern with authenticity is also apparent in 'Cadence, Country, Silence' (*Open Letter*, 1973), an essay in which the poet struggles to come to terms with living in Canada in a borrowed language, by arguing that the impasse of writing in such language – its texture, weight, and connotations coming from abroad – must become its own subject, for 'to be authentic, the voice of being alive here and now must include the inauthenticity of our lives here and now.' As in *Savage Fields*, liberalism and empiricism are repudiated, but to speak of our inauthenticity is a way to break out of the silence imposed on us by our dissent from liberalism, thus allowing us to recognize that our condition under liberalism is only a muted one, not a silent one. Finally, in 'Polyphony, Enacting a Meditation' (*Descant*, 1982), Lee again discusses cadence or the press of meaning, of being, using the process of his own essay to argue in favour of the *polyphonic voice* of meditation.[10]

With much in subjective phenomenology, structuralism would quibble. For a phenomenologist, every conscious act involves intentionality, in which the subject constitutes the object with which he or she is concerned. But what is involved in the act of constituting? What is the subject? Is it unified and present to itself? How free is the subject? The structuralist would argue that if language is a social institution preceding and exceeding us as individuals, and if meaning is the product of the rules and conventions of different signifying systems such as language, there is no functional place for private meanings or intentions in this process. We do not have discretion over what our words will mean, and, so long as we speak a common language, we do not decide altogether separately on the 'meaning' of what we enunciate.

Both Marxism and Lacanian psychoanalysis would also repudiate this notion of conscious self. A culture, a social infrastructure, a personal unconscious, a literary system, a text – these do not simply provide conditions that make it possible to understand subjective consciousness in phenomenological terms; they are not merely an epiphenomenon of external forces. They in fact construct or determine subjective consciousness. Marxism and psychoanalysis would see a profound discontinuity between so-called self-understanding – that is, the understanding that all of us separately have, presumably, of what we do and why we do it – and an understanding of self provided by their explanatory analysis. At the limit, such analysis presents subjective consciousness as an 'imaginary' condition or 'false consciousness,' 'a consciousness systematically beset by illusions about its own autonomy' (to use Philip Pettit's wording in *The Concept of Structuralism*, 1975), exemplified, for instance, when a phenomenologist thinks that he or she gives meaning by his or her own intentional disposition. Phenomenology thus always runs the risk of reducing social life to the individual and textuality to the particular text – hence the structuralist's complaint about New Critical practice and the Marxist's about psychologism.

DIALECTICAL PHENOMENOLOGY

Some forms of structuralism, however, beg the issue of consciousness; and positivism or empiricism is not a viable alternative because it presupposes, as Lee notes, a separation of subject from object. Moreover, empiricism deals with 'subject' not in terms of a membership in a community but in terms of purposes and attitudes that originate with the individual rather than with a language community. Dialectical phenomenology attempts to resolve this problem because it 'treats consciousness not as originating with the individual and mediating the individual's relation to society, nor as an epiphenomenon of external social forces.'[11] Rather, it treats consciousness as an ongoing social and historical process.

As in subjective phenomenology, meaning in dialectical phenomenology is grounded in or internal to the relation of subject and object, critic/reader and text. It is not internal to the object-text nor is it internal to the subject/reader/critic. But, unlike subjective phenomenology, the object-text takes on meaning from a signifying practice, an interpretive/reading strategy within which the knower/critic/reader, historicized and socialized, stands. Dialectical phenomenology thus fuses certain features of phenomenology and structuralism. It is evident in the critical practice of Dennis Duffy, Dick Harrison, and Robert Kroetsch. All three of these critics treat consciousness as an ongoing social and historical activity and ground their reading of Canadian literature – both themselves and their texts – in cultural practices.

Inspired by Hugh Hood and George Grant, Duffy is concerned in *Gardens, Covenants, Exiles* (1982) with describing and analyzing the effects – on the literary culture of what is now called Ontario – of United Empire Loyalism: an attitude of mind that grows out of historical experience and the mythic representation of that experience, 'a process of defeat, exile, hardship, and struggle which is followed by eventual and righteous triumph,' and which in its displaced forms in various twentieth-century writers is 'a social mythology emphasizing stability and endurance.' More specifically, the 'form of the Loyalist myth suggests a Christian *typos* of suffering (the Revolution), redemption (the acquisition of Canada), and ultimate vindication (success in 1812, material growth), all in the service of a covenant (fealty to Crown and British institutions brings national survival under imperial aegis).' Interestingly, the book replicates the Loyalist myth in terms of Duffy's own phenomenological readings of its manifestations. The critic's own search for faith, for a personally sustaining myth, parallels his literary search for a Loyalist consciousness in the constructions and inevitable deconstructions of the Loyalist myth. Meaning inheres in the relation between critic-reader and text. The text's salience derives from the form of life, or purposive activity, in which the critic resides, and which constitutes for the critic the text as an object of knowledge.

Dick Harrison's *Unnamed Country* (1977) also concerns cultural formation, particularly the contradictions that arise when non-indigenous semiotic systems, whether homologically structured or not, are used to read the Western prairie. Canada's only archetypal 'region' (because it was the first region of Canada to be settled by Canadians themselves), the prairie is a ground where European or eastern Canadian culture (the named, the known, the mythic) confronted the geophysical territory (the unnamed, the unknown, the historical). For those who settled the prairie, the result was alienation.

The prairie was unnamed and therefore unknown for writers just as it was for settlers; it lacked the fictions, the literary and linguistic traditions, to construct it. As Robert Kroetsch observed in *Creation* (1970), 'In a sense, we haven't got an identity until someone tells our story. The fiction makes us real.' But how can one authentically have 'being,' given this contradictory situation, if language is 'always already' the grounds for any enquiry? This is the question such writers as Kroetsch and Rudy Wiebe have tried to answer. They want, in terms of both literary form and culture, to unname, demythologize, deconstruct – in order to rename, remythologize, and reconstruct the prairie and history more authentically. Wiebe says, in 'New Land, Ancient Land' (*The New Land*, 1978), that 'Human understanding is tied to language, whose primal expression is *naming*.' He speaks of the absence of indigenous memory, words, and myth that would help us understand the prairie and, echoing Kroetsch's 'Unhiding the Hidden' (*Open Letter*, 1983), of the necessity to disclose the hidden in imposed languages which must be read as palimpsests. (Beneath the politically motivated signifier 'Regina,' for example, is another signifier: 'where the bones lie.') Such criticism says that we must learn to read beneath the foreign myths carelessly attached to the

Canadian West – myths that come from the United States and British Ontario – so that we might be able to discover the concealed buried otherness of experience that is our own. For Kroetsch, we do this first by unhiding the hidden British or American experience in the Canadian *word* in order to remythologize it (as Kroetsch does in his novels) by mythologizing the quotidian commonplaces of prairie life.

Not only a prominent Canadian novelist, Kroetsch is also, as Shirley Neuman and Robert Wilson declare in *Labyrinths of Voice* (1982), a '*magister labyrinthorum,* an author who continually re/reads his own writing in the context of his current thinking.' But even when he is not dealing with his own writing, his criticism provokes because it is so charged with a knowledge of postmodern literary practice and post-Saussurean critical thought. Introducing his *Essays* – collected as one of two special Kroetsch issues of *Open Letter* – Frank Davey stresses the novelist-critic's McLuhan-like phenomenological orientation: 'Perception not only takes precedent over argument, but often replaces argument.' But this perception, whose meaning can only be produced through language, is situated in a consciousness conceived as an ongoing social and historical process. Text and writer/reader/critic are always on the move, shifting ground, but always within the Canadian problematic. Discontinuity and fracture recur as Kroetsch's technical strategies. And as with his writings, so with his speech. *Labyrinths of Voice* (Kroetsch in conversation with Neuman and Wilson), is another innovative mode of critical discourse; the form is of necessity discontinuous, while the presence of three speakers ruptures the conventions of the interview. And woven into this ongoing conversation (itself an instance of Heideggerian phenomenology) is a third form of fracture: a galaxy of stimulating quotations from other (usually critical) discourses which interact with the three speakers in a variety of ways. The result is a rich plurality of signification and discursivity as the text traverses four broad *topoi*: influence, game, narration, and myth.

IDEOLOGY, EVALUATION, AND AUTHOR-CENTRING

All three of the critics I have treated under the rubric of dialectical phenomenology – Duffy, Harrison, and Kroetsch – seem to be aware in their evaluation of texts that, no matter what the criteria, evaluation cannot be understood apart from the social conditions that shape both the text being evaluated and the critic engaged in the activity of evaluating. Such awareness is not always evident in three studies that concern themselves with the problematics of evaluation, particularly with regard to Canadian fiction: Wilfred Cude's *A Due Sense of Difference* (1980), B.W. Powe's *A Climate Charged* (1984), and John Metcalf's *Kicking Against the Pricks* (1982).

Inspired by F.R. Leavis, Cude's work represents one approach to evaluation. Overtly empiricist (appealing to induction and consensus), he attempts to isolate Canadian classics by 'arguing from a detailed explanation of why and how they might be deemed works of excellence.' Yet he does so by assuming that critical methodology is ideologically free and that literary and aesthetic criteria are universal, not grounded in history and particular value-laden cultural formations. Relying on Frye as an *authority*, moreover, he underestimates the complex power relations inherent in institutional canon-making.

Metcalf's work evaluates through a different form of polemic. Of the several Canadian novelists, poets, and short story writers who published collections of essays during the 1970s and early 1980s (among them A.J.M. Smith, Earle Birney, Irving Layton, Phyllis Webb, John Mills, and Hugh Hood), Metcalf is one of the most provocative. *Kicking Against the Pricks* addresses ways in which the difficulties writers face in Canada reflect on Canadian cultural conditions in general. 'We are mired ... in hopeless dishonesty about our literature,' Metcalf argues, going on to evaluate a number of Canadian writers he finds deficient in comparison with their contemporaries in the rest of the English-speaking world. More persuasive than Cude (whose performative purpose is praise), Metcalf uses the same rhetorical device Cude does (comparison-by-more), but he performs in order to blame. Especially, Metcalf bemoans the revisionist attempt to create what for him is a spurious indigenous tradition, which he sees as merely political nationalism in disguise. Such concerns have no place in literature, he says. Yet Metcalf's ideology of literary excellence is just as politically coded as 'nationalism' is. 'International' criteria are not ideologically neutral, and some readers even see them as evidence of colonial-mindedness and would argue that Metcalf is deceiving himself in thinking that human knowledge and technique are universal and apolitical.[12]

Metcalf's focus on the achievement of individual writers is not unusual, for much Canadian criticism continues to take if not 'reality' then 'the author' as a point of departure for interpretation. The numerous critical series that ground their various texts in an 'author' abundantly testify to this tendency: Canadian Writers and Their Work (Forum House), Canadian Writers (McClelland & Stewart), Studies in Canadian Literature (Copp Clark/Douglas and McIntyre), Critical Views on Canadian Writers (McGraw-Hill Ryerson), Reappraisals: Canadian Writers (University of Ottawa Press), Twayne World Authors: Canadian Literature (G.K. Hall), several Tecumseh Press anthologies, the Canadian Novel (NC Press), The New Canadian Criticism series (Talonbooks), Profiles in Canadian Drama (Gage),[13] and Canadian Writers and Their Works (ECW Press). Some of these series appear to be defunct; some are in limbo, and some, like the ECW Press series, are burgeoning. Several collections of essays outside these series also focused on single figures

– two on Alice Munro and Margaret Atwood, one each on Margaret Laurence, Rudy Wiebe, Robertson Davies, F.R. Scott, Hugh MacLennan, Sir Charles G.D. Roberts, Hugh Hood, and Earle Birney – and several guidebooks and general introductions to Canadian literature are organized according to authors.

Most of the 'special' issues of Canadian journals focused on authors as well: *Journal of Canadian Fiction* on Laurence; the *Malahat Review* on Atwood and Metcalf; *The Fiddlehead* on Metcalf; *Descant* on Lee and Ondaatje; *Journal of Canadian Studies* on Laurence, Callaghan, Davies, MacLennan, and Klein; *Essays on Canadian Writing* on Birney, Reaney, and Hood; *Capilano Review* on Audrey Thomas; and *Open Letter* on Sheila Watson, Tallman, Kroetsch, and Dudek. Finally, several individual studies (other than the volumes in the various series) were devoted to individual authors; there were books on Hood and Wiebe, on MacLennan and Cohen, on Atwood, on Robertson Davies, Rudy Wiebe, Alden Nowlan, Sinclair Ross, Mavis Gallant, Margaret Laurence, Gwendolyn MacEwen, E.J. Pratt, A.M. Klein, Susanna Moodie, and Malcolm Lowry.[14]

One ideological effect of these series, special issues, and author-centred studies is to reinforce the rhetorical and political power of the author-function in critical discourse: the role the 'author' serves is precisely to resolve the discontinuities or contradictions of discourse into a harmonious totality. Taken as a premise here is the concept that the originating *subject* stabilizes *meaning*. Even the one concerted book-length attempt to apply a European structuralist poetics, *Margaret Atwood: Language, Text and System* (1983), ed. Sherrill Grace and Lorraine Weir, takes not discourse but the individual subject as the source of the structures. 'System' is seen not as a differential semiotic process but hermeneutically as a thematic or 'organized network of obsessions' grounded in the writer as a phenomenological subject. 'Texts' are treated as the expressions of a 'structuring consciousness.' But to suggest that an individual subject is an authority for a single meaning is to ignore the degree to which subjectivity is itself a discursive construct. To seek in the world or in experience for a guarantee of meaning (as social realists such as Dudek, Sutherland, Keith, and MacLulich would do) is, further, to ignore the way language shapes our experience of the world.

This emphasis on author-function, along with the predominance of thematic/cultural critical practice, has contributed to the almost complete absence of major studies that treat Canadian texts in terms of the relative material autonomy of literature – treat poetry, say, in terms of verse forms, metre, and modes of representation. This is not, for example, how Joseph and Johanna Jones organized their survey, *Canadian Fiction* (1981). Nor is it how Tom Marshall organized *Harsh and Lovely Land: The Major Canadian Poets and the Making of a Canadian Tradition* (1979), the one exclusive, comprehensive, book-length study of Canadian poetry to appear between 1972 and 1984.

In this work, Marshall reads poems mimetically as organic microcosms or models of design in the universe, mediated through Canadian conditions; and he reads verse forms and metre in terms of what Yvor Winters called the mimetic fallacy, as expressions of environmental theme (for example, 'open verse' represents 'open landscape'). His primary concern, moreover, is to show that the themes and structures of Canadian poetry reflect multidimensional Canadian experience; and Marshall interprets this experience in geophysical terms: topography and climate, wilderness and space, psychological and physical garrisons. By contrast, Helmut Bonheim's *The Narrative Modes: Techniques of the Short Story* (1982), which pays considerable attention to Canadian short stories in a context which also includes English and American, is a noteworthy example of European criticism of Canadian literature[15] and an instance of the sort of semiotic study of conventions and genres now needed in Canadian criticism.

One further noticeable lack, during the period under review, is a major book of feminist literary criticism, though the publication of the papers from the Women and Words Conference in Vancouver in 1983 (as *in the feminine*, 1985, ed. Ann Dybikowski et al.), a special issue of the *Canadian Journal of Political and Social Theory* (1985), and two anthologies of feminist criticism – Barbara Godard's *Gynocritics/Gynocritiques* (1986), and *A Mazing Space*, ed. Shirley Neuman and Smaro Kamboureli (1986) – indicate increased activity.[16] Much interesting work has been published in feminist journals, however, and in social and cultural areas of research. It is important, too, to emphasize that feminist criticism signals a number of changes in critical direction in Canada – in methodology as well as in subject – and that it currently constitutes the leading edge of comparative anglophone-francophone critical theory and practice.

European criticism may have been more obviously semiotic and feminist than Canadian criticism was at least up to 1984. But if phenomenological criticism was one of the most influential forces in Canadian critical practice during the 1970s and early 1980s, overtaking and displacing systemic criticism, it is clear that structuralist and post-structuralist practice was becoming more frequent by 1984. It is clearer, however, what the growth of Canadian post-Saussurean practice argues than what it signifies: it may signify a change in critical expectations of literature, or suggest a different attitude to nationhood, or indicate the shift of critical practice away from the public forum (such as the newspaper review) to the academy. What it argues is that all language and all choices and definitions of language are ideological, in that they all structure a system of value. None of us in Canadian criticism, that is, can claim access to uncoded, pure, or objective experience of a real, permanently existing text. We re/construct what is given, if there is any given at all.

Because 'no language has an edge over any other' (as Roland Barthes tells us), because there is no metalanguage, writing or speaking in the form of a critical history cannot be undertaken (except smugly) as if the critic is external to the language he or she is describing. For the critic is also in language, constituted in and by it. Consequently no text, literary or critical, can transcend the discourses of literary criticism in which it is named, identified, and discussed, and every text is already articulated with other texts that determine its potential meaning.[17] These are issues raised by criticism during the years 1972–84. These issues are also evident in this chapter.

6 Scholarship and Criticism

B. RAJAN

In a paper read to the Royal Society in 1984, A.C. Hamilton found himself obliged to refer to the 'enormous conservatism' of Canadian literary scholarship.[1] Others, no more consumed by radicalism than Hamilton is, seem to concur in this bleak finding. Thus Russell Hunt, the *English Studies in Canada* reviewer of Linda Hutcheon's *Narcissistic Narrative* (1980), takes exception to the tone of the book but suggests that the tone is adopted 'because the author expects a significant proportion of its real audience to be hostile and contemptuous.' He adds that 'Literary theory does not have a good name among the traditional practitioners of literary scholarship in Canada,' and that 'only two or three articles' in *ESC* 'question, or propose alternatives to, the current paradigm of literary studies, and one of these [June 1983] had to be included as an "editor's choice" because it did not fit standard patterns of evaluation.' *ESC*'s record has improved since 1983 and may improve further as a result of Linda Hutcheon's appointment to its editorial board in 1985. Nevertheless, eighteen months later, Gary Kelly, in reviewing three books by Canadian scholars, found the following comment necessary: 'Dare one say that, like the country itself (my colleagues in "Central Canada" will forgive me) they [the three authors reviewed] seem to lack a centre, or else lack a sense that the centre they seem to have is no longer unquestioned, and that centredness itself is no longer beyond question? ... for our existence as a profession, such a lack can seem very damaging indeed in the present climate of radical scepticism in literary studies.'

It becomes important to ask how this 'enormous conservatism' and its imperviousness to the prevailing climate became decisive resistances in the inertia of Canadian scholarship. A decade ago one could have prophesied a different outcome. With the scholarship in the history of ideas and the attention to the text taught by Woodhouse, and with the innovativeness in critical theory of Frye and McLuhan, Canadian scholarship could have been seen as about to launch a new era in its self-realization. If such a consolidation had taken place the new developments in literary theory would not necessarily have imperilled it. Frye himself provided models for openness in his treatment of the Romance form and in his attention to biblical paradigms of process that can be read as inherently self-transforming. These opportunities within a system otherwise closed, precisely because of its formidable inclusiveness, could have enabled Canadian scholars inheriting Frye's understandings to meet the invitations of a post-structuralist world. There is some indication that the next decade may see some of these invitations accepted. *Centre and Labyrinth* (1983), a collection of essays honouring Frye, seems at least as concerned with the pleasures of the labyrinth as with the satisfactions of the centre. In the typical manner of revisionary theorizing the main interest of the system may be found to lie in the opportunities which the system offers for escaping from it. The future may surprise us but until now Canadian scholarship has been conspicuously reluctant to entertain the responses which make that future possible.

If some forms of systematization are suspect in contemporary literary theory, 'world-pictures' are suspect in historical studies. The new historicism participates in the skeptical temper by questioning the possibility of consensus, of assumptions shared so widely that they do not need to be stated. It exhorts us to see a work of literature as involved in ideology even in attempting to avoid it, as embedded in controversies towards which it is necessarily partisan, as a site of tensions rather than as a ground of unanimity. Such historicism, concerned not only with what the work assumes but as importantly with what the work conceals, is less than prominent in Canadian studies. Our scholars direct their attention to the text but to a text innocuously shaped by the forces of structure, genre, rhetoric, and other resources of literary organization. This is the eminently respectable and satisfyingly predictable trend of current interpretative scholarship. But even this trend is much the lesser part of a scholarly endeavour which is largely editorial.

Conservatism begins in the academies. During the 1970s, they were unable to make new appointments, and they remain frozen structures of personnel within and between which there is only minimal movement. Conservatism is strengthened by programs which we are comfortable in teaching, by a literary canon which we do not wish to question and which unfailingly provides the evidence for our conclusions about literature, and by the distressing but also protective presence of financial barriers to educational experiment. The graduate school, always the cutting edge of an advance in understanding, is slighted in comparison with an undergraduate effort that serves a community to which it is healthily answerable rather than a profession which is potentially narcissistic.

We might expect scholarship in such circumstances to concentrate on major works and major authors, to resist efforts to reshape that literary canon which authorizes and protects its own institutional identity, and to see literature as a field of its own rather than as a field in connection with other fields of study with which it may share primary characteristics. This is indeed the shape of much Canadian interpretative scholarship even if that shape is nearly always informed by civility, tempered judgment, and a concern for the humane in letters. (And though this chapter focuses on scholarship concerning literature in English, similar generalizations hold true for writings on French, German, Hispanic, and Italian literatures.) Books like Patricia Parker's *Inescapable Romance* (1979), which examines the poetics of dilation and deferral in Renaissance and Romantic literature, or Tilottama Rajan's *Dark Interpreter* (1980), which charts the parallel dynamics of Romantic poetry and German philosophy, are rare in their generosity of scope. Even more conspicuously absent are books which approximate the inclusive and synthesizing strength of M.H. Abrams's *Natural Supernaturalism* (1971), the innovativeness of Harold Bloom's *The Anxiety of Influence* (1971), or the educated and compendious eloquence of George Steiner's *After Babel* (1975). On the other hand, since the leading interpreter of high modernism retains Canadian citizenship, Hugh Kenner's associative brilliance and his unfailing sense of the crucial juxtaposition can be entered among our major credits.

2

The statistics of scholarly endeavour can be intoxicating when they are read in innocence of the reservations already made. Representative figures are offered by the Humanities Research Council of Canada: 700 books were supported by the Aid to Scholarly Publications Programme from 1971 to 1983, compared with 284 in the previous twenty-five years. The increase seems to indicate a burgeoning of Canadian scholarship – but the same burgeoning took place in other countries and may be largely a consequence of the world-wide growth of universities. The Council goes on to observe that half the books subsidized by the program in the mid-1970s were published abroad and that a decade later 90 per cent were published in Canada. The program has thus promoted the Canadianization of scholarly publishing. It is not clear that this accomplishment is to be greeted with unreserved applause. If the tone of Canadian scholarly publishing is set by a conservative academy – and there is much to suggest the harmonious chiming of the two institutions – then the Canadianization of scholarly publishing can come to mean a sealing off of Canadian scholarship from those newer critical approaches that are necessary for its invigoration.

The consideration of specific areas that follows does not seek to and cannot hope to provide an exhaustive listing of scholarly accomplishment in those areas. The endeavour is only to indicate the dispositions of scholarship within and between them, and to suggest how the characterizations offered at the beginning of this chapter are consonant with the evidence.

Medieval Studies

Most recent Canadian medieval studies have concentrated on textual, historical, and cultural concerns, although literary analysis has naturally had its place, not least in introductions to texts and translations. Another trend has been a high incidence of collaboration with scholars from other countries – a practice common in many areas of the humanities, but now especially frequent in medieval studies. Typical of these trends, and probably the most important Canadian-based international project, is the *Dictionary of Old English* at the University of Toronto, on which consultants from England, the United States, and Europe have played a major role throughout. Among the spin-off projects already published are *A Microfiche Concordance to Old English* (1980) by Antonette diPaolo Healey and Richard L. Venezky and *Old English Word Studies: A Preliminary Author and Word Index* (1983) by Angus Cameron et al.

The latter book appeared in the Toronto Old English series, itself an important by-product of the *DOE*, including, among other works, four editions of Old English texts and the important collection of essays on *The Dating of Beowulf* (1980), ed. Colin Chase. This series is only one of a number published in Canada, which has moved into a position of leadership in the publication of medieval texts and studies. Among other series published by the University of Toronto Press are the REED (Records of Early English Drama) series, the McMaster Old English Texts, the Toronto Medieval Bibliographies, and the Medieval Academy Reprints for Teaching. Several series of texts, translations, and studies, including the Toronto Medieval Latin Texts, are published by the Pontifical Institute of Mediaeval Studies (PIMS; Toronto), and the University of Toronto's Media Centre publishes an impressive medieval video collection of tapes on various subjects. Series published elsewhere in the country include the University of Manitoba Icelandic Studies series. To mention only one publication of interest from the vast number appearing in one or another of these series, the PIMS list includes *Piers Plowman: The Z Version* (1983), edited by A.G. Rigg and Charlotte Brewer.

English collaborators have also been involved in two notable recent textual editions: the Early English Text Society edition of Layamon's *Brut* (Vol. II, 1978) by R.F. Leslie and G.L. Brooke and *The Anglo-Norman Voyage of St Brendan* (1979) by Brian Merrilees and Ian Short. The Mediaeval Academy published *The Old English Vision of St Paul* (1978) by Antonette diPaolo Healey, and the Clarendon Press issued *The Poems of Robert Henryson* (1981) by Denton Fox. Two texts in the Anglo-Norman Text Society series edited by Canadians are *La Vie des Set Dormanz* (1977) by Brian Merrilees and *Mirour de Seinte Eglyse* (1982) by A.D. Wilshere. Among the editions published by other Canadian presses are *The Tiberius Psalter* (1974) by A.P. Campbell, the Old English *Christ and Satan* (1977) by Robert Emmett Finnegan, and *The Southern Version of the Cursor Mundi* (Vol. I, 1978) by Sarah M. Horrall.

A number of translations also appeared beyond those in the PIMS and Manitoba series, such as *Grettir's Saga* (1974) by Denton Fox and Hermann Pálsson, *The Faroe Islanders' Saga* (1975) by George Johnston, and the revised and enlarged *Beowulf and Other Old English Poems* (1982) by Constance B. Hieatt. An important recent reference work is the bibliography *Western Manuscripts from Classical Antiquity to the Renaissance* (1981) by Laurel Braswell, and Michael S. Batts has produced several bibliographies of importance to medievalists, including *The Bibliography of German Literature* (1978).

Literary studies produced during this period include *Nebuchadnezzar's Children: Conventions of Madness in Middle English Literature* (1974) by Penelope B.R. Doob; *The Early English Lyric & Franciscan Spirituality* (1975) by David L. Jeffrey; *Old Norse Court Poetry: The Dróttkvaett Stanza* (1978) by Roberta Frank; *Birds with Human Souls: A Guide to Bird Symbolism* (1978) by Beryl Rowland; and *Poets and Princepleasers: Literature and the English Court in the Late Middle Ages* (1980) by Richard Firth Green. Most of these works are of a cultural and historical, as against critical, nature, as is the case with most of the essays which have been published in Canadian collections, with the exception of *The Nature of Medieval Narrative* (1980), ed. Minnette Grunmann-Gaudet and Robin F. Jones: most of the contributors to that collection (including Eugene Vance, who has published a number of theoretical articles) take a structural or semiotic approach.

The only recent book-length study which can also be described as in the main stream of recent critical preoccupations is *Langue, Texte, Énigme* (1975) by Paul Zumthor, but a great variety of approaches will be found in journal articles. While these are too numerous to be adequately summarized, it is worth noting that two new Canadian journals have flourished as forums for the findings of medievalists: *Olifant*, devoted primarily to the Romance epic, has been edited by John Robin Allen at the University of Manitoba since 1973, and *Florilegium*, concentrating on the literature of Classical antiquity and the Middle Ages, has been published at Carleton University under the editorship of Douglas Wurtele since 1979. *English Studies in Canada*, which first appeared in 1975, has also included many articles on medieval literature, with, predictably, Chaucer outnumbering other subjects by more than two to one.

Renaissance Scholarship

Renaissance scholarship is dominated by the REED project and by the Erasmus project at Toronto. The former seeks to gather all the available material relating to performances of English drama, both in London and in the country, up to the closing of the theatres in 1642. The word 'drama' is generously interpreted so that the project is not simply to be an exhaustive theatrical history but also a detailed cultural record, fully documented in its economic and social aspects. The York records edited by Alexandra F. Johnston and Margaret Rogerson were published in 1979. The complete project is expected to take up more than twenty-five volumes. The Erasmus project is a fitting senior companion to the Yale edition of the works of Sir Thomas More. Two hundred scholars are involved in it and eighty volumes are to be published. Ten had been issued by 1986.

Books on the Elizabethan stage ally themselves naturally to the REED project. Foremost among such publications was John Orrell's *The Quest for Shakespeare's Globe* (1983), a meticulous attempt to reconstruct the physical dimensions of Shakespeare's theatre, using a variety of forms of evidence. Herbert Berry edited a collection of essays on the theatre in Shoreditch from 1576 to 1598 (1979); G.R. Hibbard, Canada's leading Shakespeare scholar, edited a group of essays on the Elizabethan theatre (1982); and John Ripley examined the stage history of *Julius Caesar* in England and the United States (1980). Standard editions include Anne Lancashire's presentation of *The Second Maiden's Tragedy* in the Revels series (1978) and Hibbard's *Bartholomew Fair* in the New Mermaids series (1977). J.A.B. Somerset edited *Four Tudor Interludes* for the Athlone Press (1974). The essays gathered by Anne Lancashire in *Editing Renaissance Dramatic Texts* (1976) deal with problems in English, Spanish, and Italian plays. Interpretative criticism includes Hibbard's *The Making of Shakespeare's Dramatic Poetry* (1981), Ralph Berry's *Changing Styles in Shakespeare* (1981), and Anthony B. Dawson's *Indirections: Shakespeare and the Art of Illusion* (1978). Frye's examination of Shakespeare's 'Problem Comedies,' *The Myth of Deliverance* (1983), further extends his study of the Shakespearean canon. Individual plays are studied by P.J. Aldus in *Mousetrap: Structure and Meaning in 'Hamlet'* (1977) and by John Reibetanz in *The Lear World* (1977). In *John Ford: Baroque English Dramatist* (1977), Ronald Huebert characterizes the plays in terms of a European movement.

Supplementing the Erasmus project are E.J. Devereux's *Renaissance English Translations of Erasmus: A Bibliography to 1700* (1983) and Marjorie O'Rourke Boyle's *Erasmus on Language and Method in Theology* (1977). *Contemporaries of Erasmus* is a biographical register of the Renaissance and Reformation edited by Peter Bietenholz and Thomas Deutscher; Volume II (F-M) was published in 1985. George Logan's *The Meaning of More's 'Uto-*

pia' (1983) treats that much-discussed text as involved in a debate within humanism rather than in a debate between humanism and its alternative.

Sidney is given his due in A.C. Hamilton's *Sir Philip Sidney: A Study of His Life and Works* (1977) and in Nancy Lindheim's *The Structure of Sidney's 'Arcadia'* (1982). In *The Triumph of Death and Other Unpublished and Uncollected Poems by Mary Sidney, Countess of Pembroke* (1977), Gary Waller collected over thirty psalms in versions very different from those found in Rathmell's edition. It is again A.C. Hamilton who gladdened the hearts of Spenser scholars with a sumptuous edition of *The Faerie Queene* (1977) in which the extensive annotation is handsomely displayed. A.K. Hieatt contributed to Canada's status in Spenser scholarship with one of the very few 'relationship' studies to be considered in this chapter (*Chaucer, Spenser, Milton: Mythopoeic Continuities and Transformations*, 1975). As the title indicates, the book is concerned with the persistence of patterns, notably temptation patterns, in the three authors. Other studies of Spenser are Thomas H. Cain's *Praise in 'The Faerie Queene'* (1978), and Zailig Pollock's *The Sacred Nursery of Virtue: The Pastoral Book of Courtesy and the Unity of 'The Faerie Queene'* (1977). The forthcoming *Spenser Encyclopedia*, a joint Canadian-American venture, with Hamilton, Hieatt, and W.F. Blissett among its principal editors, promises to be not merely a presentation of the existing state of knowledge about Spenser but an endeavour to advance that state through innovative articles.

Milton scholarship, by contrast, is not what it once was. Two books on Milton by John Spencer Hill and Dennis Danielson are commendable but do not suggest a revival of past glories. Of more promise, though not in the least revivalist, are Mary Nyquist's two articles, 'Reading the Fall: Discourse and Drama in *Paradise Lost*' (*English Literary Renaissance*, 1984) and 'The Father's Word / Satan's Wrath' (*PMLA*, 1985). The association of Lacan with Milton will horrify some Miltonists, but those who have read William Kerrigan's extraordinary book, *The Sacred Complex: On the Psychogenesis of 'Paradise Lost'* (1983), will be aware of what a psychoanalytical approach can accomplish when a literary intelligence controls its application. Poststructuralism would compound the complexity of the application but would not necessarily undermine its relevance. [BR]

Balachandra Rajan also continued his enquiry into seventeenth- and twentieth-century British poetry; it will be discussed all together here because it constitutes a remarkable single body of work, expanding during the 1970s to become more theoretical, particularly in *The Form of the Unfinished* (1985). His earliest book during the period under review was *The Overwhelming Question* (1976), in which he attempted to see the work of one writer, in this case T.S. Eliot, as a single macro-poem. This poem, he argued, is held together by a psychic narrative, which the book attempts to trace. Rajan also edited a book of essays, *The Presence of Milton* (1978), which is committed to the proposition that relationships between writers are not simply verbal but also thematic and structural. Milton and Eliot also figure largely in *The Form of the Unfinished: English Poetics from Spenser to Pound*, though the scope of the book ranges through all of English poetry from the Renaissance on and contains major discussions of Byron, Shelley, and Keats. The book's major argument is that, unlike 'the torso' and 'the ruin' which presuppose the existence of a whole and invite the reader to imagine that whole, 'the unfinished should not invite completion. If it falls short of finality (as *The Faerie Queene* and *The Cantos* do) or resists it (as *The Triumph of Life* does), it should do so because of forces that have been demonstrated to be grounded in its nature and that forbid arrival at a closure even when (as in *The Faerie Queene*) the gestures accompanying closure are richly invoked ... A poem that is properly unfinished should be less satisfactory if we were to pursue any of the conceivable ways of finishing it.' [HK]

The Metaphysical poets of the seventeenth century attracted more attention than Milton did. Anthony Raspa's 1975 edition of Donne's *Devotions* is a handsome book which should be well worn by scholars. Donne's sermons are studied in *Increase and Multiply: Arts-of-Discourse Procedure in the Preaching of Donne* (1976). Both this book and Heather Asals's *Equivocal Predication: George Herbert's Way to God* (1981) treat rhetoric as controlled by the author or as a reliable means of access to reality. Neither is discommoded by the agonizing questions about rhetoric which Paul de Man has embedded in critical theory. Terry G. Sherwood's *Fulfilling the Circle: A Study of Donne's Thought* (1984) bypasses notions of fragmentation by studying the 'drive towards coherence that animates Donne's thought from beginning to end.'

On the editorial side there is the Variorum Donne to be published by the University of Missouri Press. Though a predominantly American venture, its participants include Jeanne Shami and Barry Cameron. Their responsibility will be to bring together everything of significance said about Donne's *Epistles*. An important existing editorial accomplishment is Alan Rudrum's Penguin edition of the poems of Henry Vaughan, which, unlike some 'popular' editions, does not passively accept a standard text. It is also notable for the care and thoroughness with which it identifies the innumerable biblical allusions to be found in Vaughan's poetry. Rudrum has further assisted an understanding of Vaughan with his Clarendon edition of the works of Thomas Vaughan (1984). Marvell's tercentenary, celebrated in 1978, was marked by Annabel Patterson's *Marvell and the Civic Crown* (1978).

The school commonly differentiated from the Metaphysicals is represented by Douglas Duncan's *Ben Jonson and the Lucianic Tradition* (1979) and by Roman R. Dubinski's edition of the poems of Alexander Brome (1982).

Books more general in their scope include *Reformers and Babylon* (1978), in which Paul Christianson studies English apocalyptic visions from the Reformation to the eve of the Civil War. Patrick Grant, whose *The Transformation of Sin* appeared in 1974, surveys a wider landscape in *Images and Ideas in Literature of the English Renaissance* (1979). *Literature in the Light of the Emblem* (1979) is one statement of an interest which Peter M. Daly pursued indefatigably in more than one language. E. Ruth Harvey's *The Inward Wits* (1975) deals with psychological theory in the Middle Ages and the Renaissance. In *Science and the Human Comedy* (1976), Harcourt Brown deals with natural philosophy in French literature from Rabelais to Maupertuis. Rabelais is also the subject of a book by G. André Vachon (1977).

Canadian scholarship in the Renaissance is representative in its conservatism. It is not only in Canada that Renaissance scholars see themselves as the main defence against the post-structuralist onslaught, as maintaining a world in which traditional standards can await the return of an unfashionable gyre. But the dominance of the Renaissance in Canadian scholarship (a main part of the Woodhouse legacy) means that the Renaissance sets the tone of that scholarship to a greater extent than it is able to do elsewhere. Conversely, the reinvigoration of scholarship which elsewhere has come from other areas is likely in Canada to encounter a higher degree of institutional resistance.

Restoration and Eighteenth Century

Despite the work of scholars such as F.E.L. Priestley, the Restoration and Eighteenth Century has not so far been a major area of Canadian scholarly strength. Work during the 1970s and 1980s is more substantial than that indicated in earlier volumes of the *Literary History of Canada* but not considerable enough to change the picture greatly. The main effort again is editorial, with substantial participation in the Yale Johnson. Donald J. Greene has edited the political writings (Vol. x) and James Gray has co-edited the sermons (Vol. xiv). Canadian participation is also prominent in the Clarendon edition of the works of William Cowper. John D. Baird is a co-editor of the Poems, the first volume of which (1742–82) was issued in 1980. James King is a co-editor of the Letters and Prose Writings. Four volumes had been issued by 1984. The proceedings of a Toronto conference on the problems of editing eighteenth-century novels have been brought together by G.E. Bentley, and two such novels (Defoe's *Roxana: The Fortunate Mistress* and Richardson's *Pamela*) were edited for Penguin Books by David Blewett (in 1982) and Peter Sabor (in 1981) respectively. Sabor also produced *Horace Walpole: A Reference Guide* (1984). The commitment to editorial scholarship is augmented by the completion of the twelve-volume edition of *The Journals and Letters of Fanny Burney* by Joyce Hemlow with various scholarly collaborators. The final two volumes, covering the period 1818–40, were published in 1984. This ambitious project may be said to have initiated and aroused the Canadian passion for the epistolary, a passion which will be considered in some slight detail later.

Defoe seems to be the author who appeals most strongly to Canadian interpreters. David Blewett in *Defoe's Art of Fiction* (1979) considers his subject at an appropriate distance. Robert James Merrett moves closer in *Daniel Defoe's Moral and Rhetorical Ideas* (1980). Samuel Macey exposes some of the seamy reality in *Money and the Novel: Mercenary Motivation in Defoe and His Immediate Successors* (1983). On Swift there is A.B. England's *Energy and Order in the Poetry of Swift* (1980); on Goldsmith, Munro MacLennan's *The Secret of Oliver Goldsmith* (1975). Thomas R. Cleary studies Fielding as a political writer (1984). Ronald Rompkey's book on Soame Jenyns appeared in the Twayne English Authors series. W.K. Thomas's *The Crafting of 'Absalom and Achitophel'* was published in 1978. More recently, Judith Sloman's *Dryden: The Poetics of Translation* (1985) was posthumously edited by Ann McWhir. The book sees the texts which Dryden translated as deliberately chosen to constitute an œuvre. Drama is represented by Richard Bevis's *The Laughing Tradition* (1980), which considers stage comedy in the time of Garrick, and by L.W. Connolly's *The Censorship of English Drama 1737–1824* (1976). But in contrast to the centuries before and after, the eighteenth century has not attracted extensive critical attention.

The original Canadian establishment was Renaissance and Victorian, and older scholars are largely inhabitants of these two areas. Those who wish to reproach the lack of solidity of modern criticism and its penchant for casual generalization find the Renaissance an appropriate and largely unravished place for the display of scholarship's traditional splendour.

The Victorian era likewise has not been extensively subjected to the erosions of the postmodern, and its combination of affluence and uneasiness is reassuring to responsible minds. There is no strong reason for an older generation largely on the defensive to move from these areas into the eighteenth century. There is also no reason for a younger generation attracted to openness to respond enthusiastically to the tight containments, both cosmic and prosodic, which it sees as characteristic of the period. If the resultant vacuum is to be filled, it can only be filled by those within the area reconceiving the nature of the area in a critical idiom which can no longer be treated as merely fashionable or 'current.'

Romantic and Victorian Scholarship

The reinvigoration of criticism has originated more than once in Romantic territory. Frye's work began with a book on Blake that is still obligatory reading, before it moved on to the system that is the 'anatomy.' In the counter-statement that so powerful an organizational effort had to generate,

Harold Bloom (another Romantic) sought to replace Frye's Olympian taxonomy by a succession of existential and Freudian single combats. Displayed thus, the drama of literary history seemed to make unpredictability possible; but it remained implicitly taxonomical since there are a finite number of ways of killing the father. M.H. Abrams's *Natural Supernaturalism*, a book reminiscent of Frye in its strength of organization, was an impressively marshalled statement of Romantic affirmativeness. It was undermined almost immediately by a counter-movement, post-structuralist in its leanings, that stressed Romantic self-doubt and offered Nietzsche rather than Hegel as its philosophic emblem. In the contest of critical understandings, Romantic literature has been more than once in our time an area of creative dissensions from which the possibilities of change have spread to other areas. It is not extreme to argue that an academy in which the Romantic constituent is less than vigorous is likely to resist its opportunities.

Frye has more than once said that the eighteenth century never visited Canada, but Romanticism may be the real absence which Frye's own remarkable achievement has obscured. Scholars in the Romantics have published less than one-fourth the number of the books and articles published by their Renaissance colleagues. The problem is not simply one of productivity. While in the Romantic period the editorial component is less substantial than in the Renaissance, the editorial component is – given the much smaller volume of Romantic scholarship – dominant rather than prominent. This dominance is asserted in an area characterized outside Canada not simply by extensive interpretative criticism but by vigorous interpretative debate. The voices in this debate are not suppressed in Canada, but they are made to sound marginal.

To say this is by no means to denigrate the value of the work done by Canadian editorial scholars, particularly in the Princeton Coleridge (of which Kathleen Coburn is the director, and to which she has contributed the Philosophical Lectures and the series of notebooks still in progress). To this J.R. de J. Jackson has added the *Logic* (Vol. XIII) and George Whalley the first stage of the *Marginalia* (Vol. XII), on which he continued to work to the time of his death in 1983 (the second stage of *Marginalia* appeared a year later). Coburn's *In Pursuit of Coleridge* (1977) tells the story of a quest which, as Leon Edel observes, involves 'the very poetry of scholarship' and is part of a 'very sparse library of research history,' unlike anything 'in Canada's scholarly annals.' The mass of not simply unpublished but undeciphered and unknown work by Coleridge in the Princeton project obviously will profoundly affect our understanding of him. Coburn has looked into some of these possibilities in *Experience into Thought: Perspectives in the Coleridge Notebooks* (1979), drawing on the material which she herself made available. G.E. Bentley's long-lasting commitment to Blake has led to a two-volume edition of Blake's writings in the Oxford English Texts series (1979) and to

Blake Books, a catalogue of writings by Blake, books in Blake's library, and books about Blake.

Histories of literature are regarded by some critics as a genre approaching extinction but J.R. de J. Jackson surveyed the poetry of the Romantic period in Volume IV of the Routledge history. The single book history by the single mind is now beyond attainment and the multi-volume enterprise consents to a stratification by which it is thereafter constrained. The time may have come for the format to be reconsidered. Its main defect is that it makes it difficult to examine the nature of literary history within a work that is frustratingly a history of literature.

When the editorial component has been subtracted, the interpretative residue is less substantial than we might hope. Ronald B. Hatch's *Crabbe's Arabesque* (1976) examines how Crabbe created a dramatic structure 'which could express his deep-rooted ambivalence of feeling toward the society in which he lived and wrote.' In *Wordsworth's Metaphysical Verse: Geometry, Nature and Form* (1982), Lee M. Johnson finds deeply implanted in Wordsworth's poetry the mathematical forms that Blake despised. Jeffrey Baker published *Time and Mind in Wordsworth's Poetry* (1980). W.J. Keith's more far-reaching book, *The Poetry of Nature* (1980), begins with rural perspectives in Wordsworth and continues to the present. Nature in the first generation Romantics receives further consideration in Trevor H. Levere's *Poetry Realized in Nature: Samuel Taylor Coleridge and Early Nineteenth-Century Science* (1981).

The concentration on the early Romantics becomes apparent as we turn to their successors in whose work modern critical theory finds many of its favourite texts. Byron is represented by A.B. England's *Byron's 'Don Juan' and Eighteenth-Century Literature* (1975). Lloyd Abbey found Shelley's skepticism central to his poetry in *Destroyer and Preserver* (1979). The double nostalgia of Erika Gottlieb's title, *Lost Angels of a Ruined Paradise* (1981), refers to a study of themes of cosmic strife in Romantic tragedy. On the novel there is Juliet McMaster's *Jane Austen on Love* (1978) and David Ketterer's monograph, *Frankenstein's Creation: The Book, the Monster, and Human Reality* (1979). Less familiar territory is covered in Gary Kelly's *The English Jacobin Novel 1780–1805* (1976); Kelly also edited two of these novels: Mary Wollstonecraft's *Mary* and *The Wrongs of Women* (1976). Jane Millgate's *Walter Scott: The Making of a Novelist* appeared in 1984. In the category feebly described as 'prose' we have V.A. De Luca's *Thomas De Quincey: The Prose of Vision* (1981). Some of the most interesting work on the Romantics is by Ross Woodman who, in a series of articles published largely in *Studies in Romanticism*, examined the Miltonic presence and the feminine figure in Romantic poetry. These studies are Jungian rather than post-structuralist, but they are responsive to current ways of uncovering the text.

Recent Canadian work on Victorian letters falls into four main categories:

major editorial projects; biographies; studies in intellectual history; criticism. A great deal of the prestige and the funding has clustered around the editorial projects. Once again, the status of these projects can be taken as symptomatic of the conservative character of Canadian scholarship, which tends to demote critical activity to a mere service function. The critic has the lowly 'pastoral' role of annotating texts or of writing helpful commentaries. What cannot be computerized or what cannot aspire to the condition of editing, writing bio-graphies – or even producing excellent handbooks like Norman H. Mac-Kenzie's *A Reader's Guide to Gerard Manley Hopkins* (1981) – is somehow suspect. The Canadian criticism of Victorian letters is not always conceded to be a totally autonomous enterprise: novels, poems, and prose essays are often used as documents in intellectual and cultural history. Few practitioners have heard of the 'new literary history,' and would be scandalized by some recent suggestions that criticism has an authority of its own that supplements or invests the texts that it studies. The breakthroughs tend to occur when a biographer like Michael Millgate also draws upon the methods of the literary critic and upon the resources of the editor, or when an editor like Norman MacKenzie brings his knowledge as an editor to the close study of poems.

Most prestigious are the huge editorial projects, especially the editing of the *Collected Works of J.S. Mill* and the editing of Disraeli's letters. The *Collected Mill* (1977–) is the fist major editorial project undertaken in Can-ada. Twenty-one volumes had appeared by 1986, under the general editorship of J.M. Robson. The aim is to provide fully collated texts of those works which exist in a number of versions, both printed and manuscript, and to provide accurate texts of those works previously unpublished or which have become relatively inaccessible. The project has set high standards of schol-arship. Despite a local effort to revive interest in Mill by publication of *The Mill News Letter*, however, and despite efforts by David Shaw to relate Mill's *Logic* to an understanding of Victorian poetics, it cannot really be said that the publication of the twenty-one volumes has spurred a notable resurgence of Canadian interest in Mill's prodigious literary, political, and philosophic output.

Disraeli was a letter writer of astonishing prolixity. John Matthews has unearthed some fifteen thousand of his letters in the attics and coal cellars of England's stately homes: 694 letters from this stupefying total have so far been published. They take us up to the point of Disraeli's entry into the House of Commons in 1837. As one of the reviewers of these volumes observed, 'it is not possible within the canons of contemporary scholarship to question either the publication of the complete letters of such an eminent figure as Benjamin Disraeli or the ability of Queen's University to carry out such a project ... there can be no doubt that the edition will be very inter-esting, very professional and very handsome.' Some misgivings can be de-tected in this far-from-faint praise. The letters have consequences for the historian as well as the scholar, but one has to ask if the scale of the enterprise is proportional to the gain in understanding that may be expected to result from it. Moreover, to lay such a foundation is implicitly to prescribe a superstructure. Should Canadian scholarship be extensively directed to building this superstructure? The question goes beyond the Disraeli *Letters*.

With remarkably little capitalization from agencies aimed at promoting scholarship, the publication of John Pettigrew's edition of Browning's poems (1981) is a high-water mark in recent Canadian editing. Thomas Collins is really a co-editor of this edition, assuming responsibility since Pettigrew's death for supplementing and completing his work. 'Although the Ohio edition of Browning's poems, with its host of editors and complicated organization stirred up an interesting, and in the long run productive, debate on nineteenth-century editing,' as one reviewer notes, the problems of that edition, when compared with the achievement of the two Canadian scholars, suggest that authoritative scholarship does not necessarily thrive on committees, massive funding, and complicated divisions of labour. Also noteworthy are J.M. Gray's edition of Tennyson's *Idylls of the King* (1983), and Herbert Rosengarten's edition (with Margaret Smith) of *Shirley* (1979) and *Villette* (1984) in the Clarendon edition of the novels of the Brontës. A transcription of *George Eliot's 'Middlemarch' Notebooks* (1979) has also been made available by John Clark Pratt and Victor A. Neufeldt.

As in the editorial labours of Pettigrew and Collins, so in the biographies by Michael Millgate and Phyllis Grosskurth, much scholarship and learning have been unobtrusively assimilated. Apart from the inherent interest of the narratives, their respective biographies of *Thomas Hardy* (1982) and of *Havelock Ellis* (1980) may well serve as 'data banks' for future critics and scholars. Apart from Millgate's biography, Hardy is represented by Kristin Brady's *The Short Stories of Thomas Hardy* (1982); Brady emphasizes Hardy's achievement in this form by treating the stories not simply individually, but as three related groups each possessed of its own integrity. Hardy is studied both as a tale-teller and as a writer concerned with the formal problems of the genre. The age of Oscar Wilde is studied in J.E. Chamberlin's *Ripe Was the Drowsy Hour* (1977). Books on the Victorian novel include R.C. Terry's *Anthony Trollope: The Artist in Hiding* (1977) and Elliott B. Gose's *Imagination Indulged: The Irrational in the Nineteenth-Century Novel* (1972). 1975 saw the compilation of a bibliography of George Gissing by Michael Collie. *A Dickens Companion* (1984) was provided by Norman Page.

In the area of intellectual history and of Victorian non-fictional prose, one of the most thought-provoking contributions is William Robbins's *The Arnoldian Principle of Flexibility* (1979), a worthy sequel to his earlier book, *The Ethical Idealism of Matthew Arnold* (1959). In working with his own 'touchstone phrases' – 'imaginative reason,' 'ethical idealism,' 'humanism,' 'flexibility' – Robbins appropriates (and gives contemporary importance to) some of the Victorian's deepest concerns.

Yet Tennyson is clearly the major Victorian poet for the 1970s and 1980s. There are books by J.M. Gray (1980) and by David Staines (1982) on the *Idylls of the King*. F.E.L. Priestley's *Language and Structure in Tennyson's Poetry* (1973) and David Shaw's *Tennyson's Style* (1976) are close and notably perceptive studies of the rhetoric and language of Tennyson's text. In *Tennyson and Swinburne as Romantic Naturalists* (1981), Kerry McSweeney first views the earlier poet from the very different perspective of the later, and then proceeds to see 'romantic naturalism' or 'naturalistic vision' as an 'active principle' of 'central importance' in the work of both poets.

To bring before us the significant otherness of the Victorians is one way of invigorating our interest in the period. Donald S. Hair in his book on Tennyson does this by placing the poetry in a context of heroic and domestic norms that restores a sense of strangeness and otherness. Like William E. Fredeman's recent scholarship on the Pre-Raphaelites (including a special guest issue of *Victorian Poetry* which he edited in 1982), such critical thinking respects differences. It honours the peculiarity and unresolvable strangeness of what is studied. Such qualities are also to be found in Juliet McMaster's *Trollope's Palliser Novels* (1978), in R.D. McMaster and Juliet McMaster's *The Novel from Sterne to James* (1981), in W.J. Keith's work on the rural tradition in nineteenth-century poetry, and in Eleanor Cook's *Browning's Lyrics* (1974).

Estrangement assumes importance in the study of literature because it inhibits appropriation of the past by the present. By setting up the past as a meaningful otherness, by establishing a space of difference which problematizes communication across its alienating and yet inviting distance, it calls for a dialogue with the past rather than an absorption of it into the climax of the present or a dismissal of it as irrelevant to the present. A literary history based on successive estrangements would emphasize the suddennesses of change, the self-revisionary turns in the flow of literature. It would also remain aware of how the flow survives obliteration by the turns.

The Twentieth Century

Graduate dissertations have shifted sharply in the last decade to the period after 1800 and more particularly to the twentieth century. The record of twentieth-century publication reflects this movement, though not to the extent that might be imagined. Work on the poetry is scanty. Norman H. MacKenzie is the leading authority on the text of Gerard Manley Hopkins. His work on the poems is still in progress, but meanwhile it is helpful to have *A Reader's Guide to Gerard Manley Hopkins*, a book in which authoritative editorial work has sharpened and directed literary perception. Norman Page published a critical biography of A.E. Housman (1983). Among slightly more recent poets, Eliot continues to attract attention with Edward Lobb, Keith Alldritt, and Julia Reibetanz. The field becomes thinner thereafter. In *Beyond the Labyrinth* (1978), Christopher Wiseman studies Edwin Muir's poetry; Allan E. Austin contributed a book on Roy Fuller (1979) to the Twayne English Authors series. David Jones is a writer who has attracted attention – as much attention in fact as Eliot. *The Long Conversation: A Memoir of David Jones* (1982) by William Blissett is the most important of the books on Jones; in addition there is a book in the Twayne series by Samuel Rees (1978), and *An Introductory Guide to the 'Anathemata' and the 'Sleeping lord' Sequence of David Jones* (1979) by Henry Summerfield.

On the novel there is Ian Boyd's *The Novels of G.K. Chesterton* (1975) and Peter Thomas's *Richard Hughes* (1973). More contemporary, in their approaches as well as in their choice of subjects, are Evelyn Hinz's *The World of Anaïs Nin* (1978) and Shirley Neuman's *Gertrude Stein: Autobiography and the Problem of Narration* (1979). Jeffrey Heath's *The Picturesque Prison* (1982) studies Evelyn Waugh and his writings. S.P. Rosenbaum's invaluable compilation, *The Bloomsbury Group*, was published in 1975. John Graham's edition of Virginia Woolf's *'The Waves': The Two Holograph Drafts* (1976) handles a difficult editorial job with skill, and is essential in illuminating the creative procedures of a major writer. Susan Dick similarly edited the drafts of *To the Lighthouse* (1982). Michael Groden's first book, *'Ulysses' in Progress* (1977), established him as a leading Joyce scholar by its careful study of how our interpretation of the text of *Ulysses* needed to be controlled by fuller knowledge of the text's evolution. As general editor Groden also supervised the publication, in over sixty volumes (1977–9), of Joyce's works in their many existing states. Photostatic reproduction makes the material available; the editorial skill is exercised in the choice and ordering of those materials. Another Canadian book on Joyce is Elliott B. Gose's *The Transformation Process in Joyce's 'Ulysses'* (1980). Conrad is represented by Camille R. La Bossière's *Joseph Conrad and the Science of Unknowing* (1979) and Gary Geddes's *Conrad's Later Novels* (1980). E.M. Forster's *Posthumous Fiction* was published by Norman Page in 1977. The proceedings of a conference were edited by Judith Scherer Herz and Robert K. Martin as *E.M. Forster: Centenary Revaluations* (1982). In *Four Contemporary Novelists* (1982), Kerry McSweeney studied the work of Angus Wilson, Brian Moore, John Fowles, and V.S. Naipaul. He also edited a selection from the critical writings of Angus Wilson (1983). In *D.H. Lawrence's Nightmare* (1978), Paul Delany studied Lawrence and his circle during the years of the Great War.

Canada has been prominent in the study of Irish literature, and the proceedings of the annual meetings of the Canadian Association for Irish Studies were sometimes published with supplementary essays. Two such volumes are *Myth and Reality in Irish Literature* (ed. Joseph Ronsley, 1977) and *Literature and Folk Culture: Ireland and Newfoundland* (ed. Alison Feder and Bernice Schrank, 1977). The most important editorial project in this field (housed at Cornell University) is the task of selecting from, transcribing, and editing Yeats's innumerable drafts of his poems and plays (he wrote *Deirdre*, for example, twenty-two times over); Canadian participation in this project remains substantial though its results lie in the future. Editorial work already in print includes Ann Saddlemyer's *Theatre Business* (1982), which brings together the correspondence of the first Abbey Theatre directors. Saddlemyer is probably the foremost of Synge scholars; her two volumes of *The Collected Letters of John Millington Synge* had appeared by 1984. A series of conversations with Sean O'Casey was edited by E.H. Mikhail and John O'Riordan under the title *The Sting and the Twinkle* (1974). Interpretative work during the decade is scarcely in proportion to this considerable editorial activity. R.G. Skene studied Yeats's Cuchulain plays; Carol Kleiman in *Sean O'Casey's Bridge of Vision* (1982) examined structure and perspective in O'Casey's work; and Shirley Neuman in *Some One Myth* (1982) extended her interest in autobiography by considering the problems of Yeats's autobiographical prose. Shaw's *Saint Joan* is examined by Brian Tyson (1982).

Criticism of critics reveals a flurry of activity round the Leavises, including R.P. Bilan's *The Literary Criticism of F.R. Leavis* (1979) and P.J. Robertson's *The Leavises on Fiction* (1981). John Fekete's *The Critical Twilight* (1977) explores the ideology of Anglo-American literary theory from Eliot to McLuhan. Pamela McCallum's *Literature and Method* (1983) moves towards a critique of I.A. Richards, T.S. Eliot, and F.R. Leavis.

To sum up, scholarship in the twentieth century is dominated once again by editorial work, with interpretative criticism restricted very largely to the single author study and often to the kind of exposition that is likely to be useful in an Honours classroom.

American and Commonwealth Literature

The most notable work by a Canadian scholar on American literature is clearly Maqbool Aziz's edition-in-progress of *The Tales of Henry James*. Eight volumes are projected. The second was published in 1978. Aziz's accomplishment is meticulous and in the classic tradition – the largely unaided work of the single scholar. To accompany it there is Alwyn Berland's *Culture and Conduct in the Novels of Henry James* (1981). Turning to other novelists, David Stouck wrote *Willa Cather's Imagination* (1975) and Martin Kreiswirth wrote *William Faulkner: The Making of a Novelist* (1983). William R. Macnaughton's book on Mark Twain (1979) studies that author's last years as a writer. David Ketterer considers the rationale of deception in Poe (1979), and Gary Waller's *Dreaming America* (1979) investigates obsession and transcendence in the fiction of Joyce Carol Oates. Work on poets includes Charles Doyle on William Carlos Williams in the Critical Heritage series (1980) and Rosemary Sullivan's *Theodore Roethke: The Garden Master* (1975). Ross Labrie's *The Art of Thomas Merton* was issued in 1979. Labrie also published books on Howard Nemerov (1980) and on James Merrill (1982) in the Twayne United States Authors series. In a more general vein is Robert K. Martin's *The Homosexual Tradition in American Poetry* (1979). Stephen A. Black's psychoanalytical study of the creative process in Walt Whitman's poetry was published in 1975. In *A Light from 'Eleusis'* (1979), Leon Surette makes use of the Eleusinian mysteries to illuminate the structure of Pound's *Cantos*. The book is not a Procrustean appropriation of the Cantos to the mysteries; its balanced consideration of the problems of interpreting Pound's epic makes it one of the better books on that difficult work. A book dealing with a territory that deserves further exploration is James Doyle's *North of America: Images of Canada in the Literature of the United States, 1775–1900* (1983). Canadian scholarship on American literature is less abundant than it might be even though the *Canadian Review of American Studies* has been published for over fifteen years and has prospered sufficiently to become a quarterly.

When W.H. New published his selective bibliography of *Critical Writings on Commonwealth Literatures* (1975) he recorded a total of 6576 items up to 1970. The pace of commentary has quickened since then. Much of this activity is attributable to scholars in Commonwealth countries writing on their own literatures. Canada's involvement in writing about others was strengthened by the transference of *World Literature Written in English* in 1979 from Arlington, Texas, to Guelph. In addition, *Ariel*, once published jointly by Calgary and Leeds, has now been taken over by the former. It devotes at least one issue a year exclusively to Commonwealth literature. *The Dalhousie Review* also has a substantial involvement in Commonwealth writing.

G.D. Killam, the editor of *WLWE*, published books on Ngugi wa Thiong'o (1980) and Chinua Achebe (rev. ed., 1977). Rowland Smith's *Exile and Tradition* (1976) is a gathering of essays on African and Caribbean writing; and Anthony Boxill's *V.S. Naipaul's Fiction: In Quest of the Enemy* appeared in 1983. Work on Indian literature in English includes Saros Cowasjee's *So Many Freedoms* (1977), on Mulk Raj Anand, and Uma Parameswaran's *A Study of Representative Indo-English Novelists* (1976). *Stories from the Raj* (1982) is Cowasjee's prelude to his editing of a series of fictional works on the Raj which will serve both nostalgia and literary history.

The typical genres of Canadian work on Commonwealth literature are the single author study or the introductory survey. When the literature is unfamiliar these are the natural means of making it accessible. William New's *Among Worlds* (1975) is also introductory but differs from other books by being a study in translation – the translation of a common theme into different cultural discourses. The translations identify differences of perception rather than of stylization. Each culture is thus distinguished and set apart but connected to other cultures by the common preoccupation.

Scholarship in Commonwealth literature would make more rapid progress if facilities for studying it were more widespread and if departments of Asian, African, and Caribbean studies were not so hard to find. Unfortunately the Canadian political and economic commitment to these areas is still not sufficient to make such departments seem socially useful. Commonwealth scholarship also has not as yet responded sufficiently to studies of the relationship between dominance and discourse, of which Edward W. Said's *Orientalism* (1978) is a pioneering example. Exploration of this relationship has made it evident that freeing itself within the imposed discourse is only the first stage in the emancipation of the subjected voice. The second is to free itself from that discourse. Post-colonial literature may now be at the second stage. If so, a different and less familiar kind of scholarship may be required to address its problems.

Comparative Literature and Theory

The new movements in criticism have been largely French in origin and it would be perverse indeed if Canadian scholars in French literature did not respond to these movements. In fact the response has been inclusive, taking in semiotics, narratology, feminism, psychoanalysis, and more recently, the sociology of literature. Deconstruction, so far, has not been a notable presence. Such approaches affect many of the publications, therefore, that bear on the study of comparative literature.

For example, the strong interest in narcissism apparent in books on Camus and Gide is carried further in Valerie Raoul's *The French Fictional Journal: Fictional Narcissism/Narcissistic Fiction* (1980). Her deft title suggests not only narcissism but also its companion, reversibility. It seems only appropriate that Brian Fitch, the author of *The Narcissistic Text*, should also be the author of a work on reversibility (*Monde à l'envers: texte réversible*, 1982). Linda Hutcheon's *Narcissistic Narrative* is thus not an isolated statement but part of a shared understanding. Hutcheon's other books include *Formalism and the Freudian Aesthetic* (1984) and *A Theory of Parody: The Teachings of Twentieth-Century Art Forms* (1985). The first of these books seeks to re-evaluate formalism and psychology in twentieth-century literary theory through a study of the work and career of Charles Mauron.

As even the titles of many comparative critical works indicate, interpretative criticism looks behind and around the text and does not find peace in avoiding its own assumptions. The tone can be belligerent and the passions partisan, but Olympian scholarship is a nobleness given to few. When the alternative

to complacency is energy oftentimes wasted, the choice can be difficult but
it should also be clear.

Enquiry into the justification of the literary canon is active outside Canada and must inevitably lead to fuller consideration of the sociology of literature. Valerie Raoul's examination of the fictional journal looks at work
upon the margins of traditional literature. A stronger directive is provided
by Marc Angenot, who seeks to replace the notion of 'intertextuality' by
that of 'interdiscursiveness,' a term more fraught with social and ideological
implications.

When critical principles are in the process of formation, the article can be
better suited to the interim and anticipatory statement than the settled and
deliberated book. Much of the liveliness and the theoretical preoccupations
of Canadian scholarship in French are evident in articles published in *Voix
et images*, *Études françaises*, *Études littéraires*, and *RSSI* (*Recherches sé-
miotiques*). The founding of *Texte*, a new journal devoted to literary theory
and criticism, is indicative of interests to which scholarship in English has
seemed indifferent.

Although the balance between editorial and interpretative work is healthier
in French scholarship than in scholarship applied to other literatures, French
also has its share of large-scale projects, the most notable of which is the
Zola project. Its aim is to publish (by 1996) 5000 of the 12,000 letters of
Émile Zola. Canadian scholarship in German also displays an exceptionally
strong editorial presence. But in Hispanic studies, to conclude this partial
survey, three books on literary criticism and theory appeared. In 1976, the
dean of Canadian hispanists, Erich von Richthofen, celebrated his retirement
with a new book on criticism, *Límites de la crítica literaria*. In 1982 Antonio
Risco published the theoretical benchmark of contemporary criticism, *Liter-
atura y figuración*. The same year saw the publication of Mario J. Valdés's
*Shadows in the Cave: A Phenomenological Approach to Literary Criticism
Based on Hispanic Texts*. This is not Valdés's only encouragement of literary
theory in Canada. He has also edited (with Owen J. Miller) *Interpretation
of Narrative* (1978) and *Identity of the Literary Text* (1985).

Between 1951 and 1969 the Canada Council and the Humanities Research
Council of Canada sponsored only eight books under the classification of
comparative literature. Since then the *Canadian Review of Comparative Literature*, founded in 1974, has established an international reputation, and
comparative literature scholars have contributed significantly to making more
apparent that cohesion of the humanities which single author studies tend to
bypass. Apart from the several books mentioned elsewhere in this chapter,
publications by comparative literature scholars include such works as Zbigniew
Folejewski's *Futurism and Its Place in the Development of Modern Poetry*
(1980), Wladimir Krysinski's *Carrefour de signes: essais sur le roman mo-

derne (1981), Irving Massey's *The Gaping Pig: Literature and Metamorphosis* (1976), Timothy J. Reiss's *Tragedy and Truth: Studies in the Development of a Renaissance and Neoclassical Discourse* (1980) and his *The Discourse of Modernism* (1982). The last-mentioned book is concerned with the shift from Renaissance to modern discourse. Though influenced by Foucault, it seeks to replace the idea of epistemic 'rupture' by a model which provides for change as well as for severance.

Genre studies include Darko Suvin's four books (1976–9) on science fiction and its poetics. Studies of literary movements are represented by Edward Możejko's examination of socialist realism (1977). The presence of one country's literature in another's is considered in Ingrid Schuster's *China und Japan in der deutschen Literatur 1890–1925* (1977). The presence of economic forces in literature is examined in Marc Shell's *The Economy of Literature* (1978) and in his *Money, Language, and Thought: Literary and Philosophical Economies from the Medieval to the Modern Era* (1982).

Comparative literature studies are important in opening the boundaries of literary speculation at a time when these boundaries seem tightly drawn and zealously defended. Progress in this direction is held back by the paucity of graduate departments of comparative literature (the number is still in single digits) and by the misgivings with which these departments are regarded by the orthodox.

The passion for the epistolary which Canadian editorial scholarship exhibits deserves more than incidental attention. Apart from the 15,000 or so Disraeli letters, there are 12,000 or more by the hardly less prolific Zola. To these must be added the letters from the Helvétius project and the 2500 from the Graffigny project, currently under way. Ann Saddlemyer has worked on the correspondence of Synge, and Michael Millgate is assembling the letters of Thomas Hardy (five volumes were published by the Clarendon Press between 1978 and 1985). The journals and letters of Fanny Burney have been brought together in twelve volumes. In the Renaissance, Erasmus's more formal use of the genre is being placed before us in the collected Erasmus. Canada leads the world in correspondence-gathering, but without deprecating what letters can disclose to us, we can question whether this particular direction of editorial scholarship needs to be pursued to this extent.

If we wanted to point to the excellence of Canadian scholarship, we could note that the William Riley Parker Prize of the Modern Language Association has been won by Canadian scholars three times in a decade – by Evelyn Hinz (1977) for an article on types of marriage plots and their relationships to genres of fiction, by Hans Eichner (1982) for an article on the rise of modern science and the genesis of Romanticism, and by A.K. Hieatt (1984) for an article on Shakespeare and the *Ruines of Rome*, Spenser's translation of Du Bellay's poem. We could add the award to Beatrice Corrigan in 1975 of the Howard R. Marraro Prize of the Modern Language Association and the award of the 1985 prize of the International Association of Hispanists to Keith Ellis for his book on Nicolás Guillén. We could further add that three Canadians, still active, are Honoured Scholars of the Milton Society. If on the other hand we wanted to point to the modest aspirations of much Canadian scholarship we could note the remarkable extent of Canadian participation in Twayne's English, United States, and World Authors series.

3

After an enumeration of works of scholarship which, despite its length, is anything but exhaustive, it is time to come back to the opening remarks on the state of the academy. The evidence suggests that concentration upon a fixed canon, upon definitive editing of the canon, and upon expounding the canon in the classroom, are priorities not only established but fortified by Canadian academic commitments. Both the partitions and genres of scholarship seem immobile; rigorous adherence to the tried and tested is the reassuring sign of authentic accomplishment. Scholarship in these circumstances is formulaic rather than vital. Its obligation is to follow the rules and to show what can still be done by following them. The formidably strong editorial presence supports the idea of a fixed canon which is to be dealt with in fixed ways. Even though a very large part of the editorial effort has been devoted to documenting the evolution of the text, not only in printed versions but also in manuscript, and to gathering the correspondence of the authors of texts, the effect is not to open up the canon but rather to enrich its apparatus. In these circumstances the very substantial financial support which the Social Sciences and Humanities Research Council has given to editorial megaprojects does not operate to change the map of scholarship but rather to make change in it more difficult. The liberalization of the canon has to come from areas such as feminist studies and the study of post-colonial literature, both of which are involved in the relationship between discourse and dominance. Yet that very involvement and the skills of detection which it fosters can be seen as bearing disruptively on an academy which has defensively identified the forms of its discipline with the terms of its life.

Critical theory has a part to play in breaking down barriers and in invigorating the circulation of ideas. But critical theory has to be suspect in a conservative academy since it questions both the canon's composition and its legitimacy. Moreover, critical theory tends to regard the text not as a terminus but as a means of access to other understandings with which the text must be brought into relationship. The proposition that the text is a terminus, and that serving the text is the encompassing objective of the scholarly effort, has been instilled into us by more than a generation of new critical practice.

To question it is to throw open the very teaching of literature and the departmental programs that have been built around stubborn assumptions about how literature is to be taught. Finally, the concern of much of current critical theory is not with the overall text but with identifying and probing the confessional moment of the text's self-consciousness. The qualities of mind which these textual probings educate may not be welcome in an academy not as yet ready to reflect on its assumptions.

Comparative literature can also move across departmental borders, making conversation between different voices not only possible but productive. Because it is topic- and problem-oriented it may help to free traditional scholarship from its restrictive dedication to the single author and the single work. To say this is not to deprecate the single-author study, which must remain an important genre of criticism. Nevertheless the predictability of the genre needs to be reduced, and there must be room found in it for the surprises of scholarship. One possible way of achieving unexpectedness or, to put it more temperately, some opening for fresh thought, is to study the author's work as an œuvre rather than as a corpus, an activity rather than an artifact, and to speculate more freely on the poetics of the œuvre in relation to a variety of authors. In addition, the dominance of the genre, its widespread acceptance as a standard and therefore reassuring format, needs to be contested by the emergence of other genres if the single-author genre itself is to know its own potential. These expansions, which call both for the liberalization of boundaries and for more vigorous movement across those boundaries, tend to be construed by the academy as a sacrifice of depth to expansiveness. In addition, the alliance of comparative literature with critical theory makes its acceptance by a conservative academy more difficult. Its interdepartmental nature can then be seen as a threatening consolidation of reformist energies rather than as an innocuous crossing of borders.

It would be less than impartial not to recognize that much of the malaise we study has been intensified and may even have been brought about by financial constraints. The new appointments that might invigorate the academy are difficult to make, and middle-aged scholars cannot slip easily into strange new habits of thought. Computers can be welcomed in lieu of a more difficult retraining. New departments cannot be formed and the possibility of bringing about change in the academy by increasing its diversity of voices seems precluded. Graduate programs, the traditional forums in which revisionary scholarship is articulated before a prospective audience, are undercut by diminishing enrolments which in turn reflect sharply reduced employment possibilities. The combination of circumstances and their collusion with institutional inertia contribute strongly to bring about the 'enormous conservatism' noted at the outset of this chapter. But it is not sufficient to blame the environment. The academy is also to be rebuked for its failure to listen adequately to the voices of difference within itself which its own self-perpetuating energies may have minimized.

The very strong editorial component in the Canadian scholarly effort arouses ambivalent responses in this context. Distributed over the spectrum of literature, the major current editorial projects include such endeavours as the *Dictionary of Old English*, the records of early English drama, the Erasmus project, the Mill project, the Disraeli project, the Zola project, and the editions of Schlegel and Döblin. Outside Canada, Canadian scholarship makes a substantial contribution to efforts such as the Variorum Donne (Missouri), the Yale Johnson, the Princeton Coleridge, and the Cornell Yeats. Canadian editorial scholarship is not surpassed by that of any other country. In the accuracy and comprehensiveness of the editions it publishes, the University of Toronto Press could well be judged as second only to the Clarendon Press. Moreover, Canadian scholarship is prominent in at least five Clarendon Press ventures.

The achievement is impressive and important. The irony is that this enshrinement of texts comes at a time when the movement in criticism is away from texts and is concerned more with the presence in the text of paradigms or processes that penetrate all human activity and from which the text cannot claim to be immune. The financial aid and the employment opportunities that accompany editorial megaprojects tend instead to place the text at the imperial centre, reducing interpretative scholarship to colonial status with the 'service' function of expounding what the centre edits. Part of the effort of modern criticism has been to resist this diminution of the critic, and to install the critic not as the text's servant but rather as its mediator, as one who opens the text out – not to an audience of passive readers but to the entire world of scholarship and social change, which is invited to find in the text the embodiment and interplay of its major concerns. Such a specification must raise the question not only of what the text is but of what the text means beyond those formal principles of its coherence which have satisfied more than one generation of readers in the classroom. The latter question is in fact the dominant question which the humanities have immemorially continued to ask. One of the prime functions of the academy should be to make necessary the continuing pursuit and reformulation of the answer. To say that the answer is identical with what it was a generation previously is also to observe that there may have been no pursuit.

Northrop Frye began this decade with *The Secular Scripture* (1976). He ended it with *The Great Code* (1982). In closing the circle even in his titling, Frye puts it to us that the critical task is not simply the application and elaboration of the system but the reinstatement of that adventurousness which made the system possible in the first place. This adventurousness is not absent in the work of Jay Macpherson, Frye's most talented disciple, whose book

The Spirit of Solitude (1982) moves through literature and through work on the traditional margins of literature from Milton to contemporary Canadian with a sense of overall pattern and sensitivity to local detail. Adventurousness is certainly present in the work of Linda Hutcheon, Mary Nyquist, Patricia Parker, and Tilottama Rajan, all of whom think in the current idiom instead of using it as a fashionable finish for an all-too-conventional piece of scholarly furniture. It may be a simplification to think of these young critics as constituting a movement but they completed their doctorates within three years of each other and all have Toronto in their scholarly backgrounds. All four are women and their cumulative accomplishment is a reproach to an establishment in which women have been an insufficient presence. The interests they exhibit are diverse but not without their bearing on each other.

Hutcheon's three books deal with narcissism, parody, and formalism and the Freudian aesthetic. She describes her work as concerned with the manner in which literary theory is shaped by the conditions of production and reception of literature. Nyquist is a highly articulate representative of the combination of feminism and new historicism that has made rewriting the Renaissance its principal undertaking. Parker deals with the metaphysics of metaphor and, in *Inescapable Romance*, with deferral as a strategy that becomes its own objective. Rajan in *Dark Interpreter* combines deconstructive techniques with a strong sense of the historical relationship between literature and philosophy. Her current interest is the parallelism between nineteenth-century German hermeneutics and scenes of reading in Romantic poetry. Despite the wide spectrum (to which Pamela McCallum's Marxism could be added) these critics have interests in common. Narcissism, parody, and the Freudian aesthetic are all concerned with ways in which literature recognizes and organizes its self-consciousness. If the organization is diagnostic, if the purpose of literary self-consciousness is to reach back to the ground of its authority, the platonic dungeon of the body can become a new incarceration in the prison-house of language. The self must view the possibilities of otherness in the mirror of narcissism or the distorting mirror of parody.

If, on the other hand, the organization is repressive, the dynamics and circumventions of repression will have something in common with Marxism and feminism, both of which seek to investigate the uneasiness and disjunctions exhibited by works of literature in responding, whether affirmatively or resistively, to economic and social structures of dominance. Deferral links the secular scripture to the Derridean aesthetic. In erasing final causes from the space it creates to perpetuate, it substitutes play for purpose and eventually dissemination for deferral itself. Deconstructive evidence can thus be indicative of a fragmented culture, or a repressive ideology (repression, we might argue, is in the nature of ideologies), or ingrained in the very fabric that Penelope must weave on the loom of language. The common interest lies in the detection of the evidence and in the techniques by which it is gathered. Those differences of understanding which lie beneath the investigative alliances may be slurred over by the collective excitement of a common pursuit but should assert themselves more firmly as the evidence is interpreted. The danger is that we may stop short of interpretation and that the strategy may become the objective by a substitutive process that has already been noted. In seeking a philosophy we can be appeased by a method.

As we look at the picture of scholarship we find an academy protective of its investments and conservative to the extent of being sealed in by its safeguards. But we also find young scholars able to appropriate the skills of the establishment for understandings other than those the establishment wishes to nurture. They may persuade the academy into a dialogue with its future. [BR]

7 Writing for Radio, Television, and Film

ROBERT FOTHERGILL

Motion pictures and television and radio all depend upon the contribution of writers. In Canada, as elsewhere, these media have employed writers of every kind, celebrated and unknown, artists and hacks. From showcase dramatic productions through to *The Friendly Giant* and the weather report, the sheer volume of writing is immense. To speak of drama alone – the main focus of this chapter – a complete account of Canadian production would have to acknowledge tens of thousands of TV and radio plays, and many hundreds of movie films, feature-length and shorter. But how much of the writing generated for these media is to be regarded, for our present purposes, as Literature – either by virtue of deriving from acknowledged literary texts or authors, or as exhibiting the qualities and characteristics we call literary? And how can we intelligibly discuss it? How can we engage in a critical-historical dialogue about this writing, its forms and achievements, when in the great majority of cases there exist no published or even accessible texts? What, indeed, can be the point of such a discussion, when the films and tapes themselves are mostly unavailable to anyone but the accredited researcher, cautiously permitted to handle the sole archival copies? Unlike conventionally published literature, these works have no continuing existence in the public domain. They survive, not as texts perennially renewing themselves in collusion with readers or spectators, but as sketchy memories of things seen, heard, and sometimes reviewed. An enormous swatch of Canadian writing, the output of entire careers in one medium or another, has disappeared into a void.

In fact it's all still there, stored in the national memory-banks in perpetuity. Very little is deliberately thrown away. In various archives and libraries around the country can be found burgeoning collections of tapes and cassettes, kinescopes and prints, scripts, screenplays, and production notes, much of the material still only sketchily catalogued.[1] A fraction of this material does exist in the public domain. A handful of scripts have been published. Some work, particularly by the National Film Board, has a continuing life in dis-

tribution and through libraries. And long-forgotten items are sometimes resurrected, whether by the CBC for anniversary occasions, or to satisfy the
Canadian-content stipulations of pay-TV legislation.

All that writing, then, theoretically can be recovered, both in its original
written state, as it left the authors' hands, and in its realized forms as directed,
performed, recorded on tape or film, edited, and made public. And to make
this distinction is to point to a characteristic of what I shall, reluctantly, call
'media-writing' that complicates critical discussion. Everyone nowadays will
agree that even the traditional literary forms are to some extent affected by
external conditions of literary production and consumption – poetry probably
not very much, drama a good deal. The status of media-writing is different
perhaps only in degree, but the difference is nonetheless considerable. It
hardly needs to be said that writing for TV and for the cinema is crucially
governed by factors that have little to do with the integrity of the writer's
imagining.

Considerations of box-office and/or sponsorship affect not only how scripts
are transmuted by producers and directors, but which scripts are commissioned
for production in the first place, and even what conceptions, themes, and
styles writers will permit themselves to pursue. Radio programming by comparison, both dramatic and non-dramatic, has been remarkably free from
commercial considerations, being relatively inexpensive and, to an increasing
degree, an unsponsored minority interest. It should be stressed that in Canada
the various modes of public funding or financial participation, via the CBC,
the NFB, and the Canadian Film Development Corporation (CFDC, now Telefilm Canada), have deflected the impact on television and film production of
external conditioning factors – or have at least introduced a countervailing
set. More or less explicitly the productions of the CBC and the NFB – and
even, for a while, of the CFDC – have reflected a conception, however vague,
of a cultural 'mandate' that commends certain subjects and treatments and
precludes others, or leaves them to the private sector. Furthermore, almost
all media-writing is subject to the structuring constraints of arbitrary time-
formats – thirty-, sixty-, and ninety-minute blocks – and to the requirement
that it be readily consumable by a mass audience. This latter consideration
means that very little writing for TV and cinema, at least, is at all experimental; narrative, character, and theme must be quite broadly legible. While
at best this absence of experiment promotes a clarity and relevance that speaks
to the condition of the unsophisticated citizen, at worst it breeds a mechanical
handling of conventional situations, styles, and outcomes.

From another perspective one might make a distinction between a relatively
'pure' writer's medium, namely radio, and the 'impure' forms of television
and cinema. In radio drama the word is the paramount, and often the only,
element. Some scripts, and some writers, of course depend on elaborate

collages of music and sound-effects, but generally the material of a radio play is language – and silence. And whereas in stage and screen drama a pause is at least a silence visible, silence on radio is a living void. Writing for a screen, by contrast, reduces the importance of the word – or at least of the word-to-be-spoken. In many 'screen plays' the dialogue may be relatively slight, as the writer's effort has been concentrated on conveying the signifying appearances of things, the non-verbal behaviour of the actors, and the mediating activity of the camera. The written script is thus a highly elaborate text, sometimes evocative and eloquent, sometimes perfunctory and trite ('Their eyes meet and they smile warmly'), and sometimes a babble of shorthand directions to cut from an LS to an MCU (her POV). One task of the literary historian and critic, therefore, is to bring into focus those elements of media-writing – the manipulation of form, the structuring of story, the deployment of theme, the conception and exhibition of character, the composition of narrative and dialogue – that are the essential business of the writer, as distinct from the script editor. By the conventional criteria of literary criticism, who have been the most noteworthy among Canadian writers for the media? And more generally how, in the exercise of their 'mandate,' have the Canadian media – chiefly the CBC – nourished the national imagination?

2

To pick up in 1970 or thereabouts the story of Canadian radio and television drama, and even of feature film-making, is to arrive at the party after many of the guests have left. To do even minimal justice to a field of writing which this *History* has hitherto neglected one would have to reach back a number of years, even decades, to the so-called golden ages of the respective media. For radio drama this means the 1940s and 1950s, the era of the legendary producers Andrew Allan, Esse W. Ljungh, Rupert Caplan, and J. Frank Willis. With the introduction, in January 1944, of 'CBC Stage,'[2] and the addition of 'CBC Wednesday Night' in 1947, both national network series, a handful of producers were channelling the most creative energies in Canadian culture of that time into dramatic productions of astonishing originality, variety, and seriousness. Though mostly unpublished, the plays from that period by Len Peterson, Joseph Schull, Lister Sinclair, Mac Shoub, Patricia Joudry, and many more, challenge comparison with any of the work of their contemporaries in other genres. As Howard Fink reasserts, CBC radio drama during this period truly was the 'Canadian National Theatre on the Air.'[3]

With the spread of network television across Canada and the emergence of the Shakespeare Festival Theatre in Stratford, Ontario, radio drama undoubtedly lost its premier position in the theatrical life of the country. Many of the actors and actresses nurtured by a dozen or more years in radio moved to take up the expanding opportunities. Some producers, likewise, tried their hands at television directing; Allan and Ljungh, for example, did a season of 'Folio' productions for TV in 1958–9. And, of course, experienced dramatic writers were in demand by a new medium that had almost no national pool of stage or screen playwrights to draw upon. Some writers, naturally, continued to move happily between radio and TV for many years – George Robertson and George Salverson are outstanding cases in point – but more commonly they established themselves in one medium or the other, with occasional forays into the less familiar territory. From the late 1950s and through the 1960s, dramatic writing for radio was as prolific and probably as creative as ever, but in a condition of honourable obscurity. A new wave of producers, such as John Reeves (himself an eloquent and prolific poet, dramatist, and adapter), Peter Donkin, Jean Bartels, and Alan J. King, and in Vancouver Gerald Newman and Don Mowatt, emerged to succeed the founding generation, and new names appeared in the writing credits, particularly in series specifically entitled 'Introducing ...' While the audience for a new play on 'CBC Stage' might number a hundred thousand – beyond the envious imagining of a stage playwright or a novelist – the exposure brought little fame (though some fortune). By 1970 radio drama had become an art produced by and for a dedicated subculture.

Reviewing the past decade and a half, it is hardly an exaggeration to say that almost every Canadian writer of any repute has contributed to radio drama; and almost equally true that some of the very best of it has been by writers virtually unknown to the reading, or even the theatre-going, public. Some already recognized authors have found their way into radio through the adaptation of non-dramatic work. Others, for example John Murrell, Erika Ritter, Sheldon Rosen, George Walker, have had successful stage plays performed on the air. (And, of course, the process has worked in reverse, as plays originally conceived for radio have been adapted for the stage, as with James W. Nichol's *Feast of the Dead*, 1973, produced by Theatre London in 1974 as *Sainte-Marie among the Hurons*, and Sharon Pollock's *Generations*, 1978, produced in Calgary in 1980.) Among original radio scripts a distinction can be made between those commissioned for a thematic series, and self-contained plays appearing under a portmanteau title like 'CBC Stage,' 'CBC Playhouse,' or, from Vancouver, 'The Hornby Collection.' In the former category one might mention a series like 'The Bush and the Salon' which presented, over a number of years, literally hundreds of dramatizations of early Canadian episodes, by dozens of different hands. Some of these shows, as for example Michael Mercer's *Hope: The Colours of Time* (1974), were so imaginative as to warrant rebroadcasting on the prestigious 'CBC Tuesday Night' program.

More recently, and particularly since the shake-up of the Radio Drama

Department instituted by Susan Rubes when she took over as Head in 1980, thematic series and outright serials have been tending to displace the older format of unrelated weekly plays. In an effort to recapture an audience supposedly lost to television, radio drama has been trying to make itself more *like* television. Listeners, it is presumed, will more readily make a habit of attending at a particular time-slot if they know what to expect, or are hooked by a continuing story. And programmers can judge more accurately whether a particular formula works or not. The effect of this policy on the quality and character of writing is almost certainly to introduce a degree of uniform digestibility. Writers for series like 'The Scales of Justice' (dramatizations of famous Canadian legal cases) or 'Great Canadian Disasters' (self-explanatory) are largely writing to formula, if not actually on specifically prescribed subjects.

Likewise the six- or seven-part serials of the late 1970s, such as Harry Junkin's *The Chase* (1976) and Laurence Gough's *The Bright Red Herring* (1978), while they were professionally crisp and entertaining exercises in the private-eye style, provided little imaginative nourishment. *Johnny Chase, Secret Agent of Space* (Henry Sobotka and John Ferguson, 1978) was an unabashedly whiz-bang sci-fi thriller, with welcome doses of wit, while Marian Waldman's *Sussex Drive* (1978–80) – seasons in the public and private life of Canadian Prime Minister Macdonald Coleridge – was actually promoted by the CBC as a superior kind of soap opera. On the other hand, her five-part serial *Bloodroot* (1982), a breathtakingly florid saga of passion and betrayal from Ontario to the Yukon, from the death of Sir John A. to the Winnipeg General Strike, would be Canada's *Gone with the Wind* if published as a novel. And some of the thirty-minute tales of mystery and the imagination broadcast on 'Nightfall' and its successor 'Vanishing Point' have exploited beautifully the power of radio to mystify and disturb. Yet another packaging innovation has been the inclusion in 'Morningside' of serials running over several weeks in daily fifteen-minute segments. Among the most distinguished of these have been Linda Zwicker's *The Panther and the Jaguar* (1983), Ann Crosby's *Marriage in Three Movements* (1984), and *The Secret Life of Susanna Moodie* (1984) by James W. Nichol.

For all this, the staple of radio drama continues to be the self-contained 'thirty' or 'sixty,' and in this brief survey a select few of the most productive and distinct contributors of recent years will have to stand for the hundreds worthy of mention. Pride of place must go to the formidably prolific Len Peterson, credited with well over twelve hundred separate items for radio, as well as work for TV and the stage. Working in radio drama since the early 1940s, and author of some of the acknowledged classics of the genre, for example *Burlap Bags* (1946), *Lilith* (1959), *Joe Katona* (1961), and *The Great Hunger* (1962), Peterson continues to turn his hand to an extraordinary variety of subjects and styles. His facility is legendary and is sometimes achieved, it must be admitted, at the expense of some subtlety and depth. He regularly musters a passion and a vehemence which make for an arresting power when fully transmuted into dramatic terms, but which can also issue into assertive shrillness. Peterson has always favoured ambitiously complex structures, pressing to the limit radio's extreme fluidity with respect to time, memory, fantasy, inner and outer consciousness, in that boundaryless sound-space where voices mingle, echo, and recur. His work characteristically presses towards the surreal, and is distinguished by intense, even exorbitant, verbal energy. A theme that preoccupies him is the struggle of the heroic outcast, hounded within and without by demons, driven to extremities by the selfish complacency of the world around.

Peterson's *To Keep the Lightning Out* (1970) consists of a nightmarish collage of fragmentary encounters and recollections in the consciousness of a contemporary teenage girl, Tish. In the period following her father's death, Tish lives with her three siblings and demoralized, apathetic mother in the family car in a shopping plaza parking lot, and subsequently inside a department store, always on the run from security guards. In addition to fending for her beleaguered family, Tish is tormented by the shame and anxiety of their condition, and by unfocused sexual yearnings and an unresolved relationship with her father. Accentuated by the musical punctuation of Morris Surdin, the writing sustains an astonishing stream-of-consciousness energy, as snatched phrases catch at momentary thoughts and fling off to others. Another impassioned piece, dating from 1973, *The Trouble with Giants* constructs from a series of flashbacks and an inner dialogue the life story of a Lithuanian refugee from both Nazism and Communism whose demons catch up with him and propel him towards madness. His crisis of exile and alienation is brought to a head by the arrival in Canada of the wife he had been compelled to abandon in the chaos of war. Their reunion is unsuccessful and exacerbates Jonas's torment at having been ground between the giant millstones of nations and ideologies. In a kind of incantatory prose-poetry he frets at the question of *what coat to wear* against the storm, and comes at last to assert the individuality of men without any coats at all.

Peterson's output for radio continues through 1985, with contributions of every kind: to 'The Bush and the Salon,' to 'Nightfall,' to 'Morningside,' and to the drama showcase anthologies under their various metamorphoses. His reputation and his style were developed in a period when radio drama inclined towards the melodramatic and highly wrought, in contrast to the cooler and more spartan mode of recent years. In consequence, some of his recent work has come to seem peculiarly strident and overheated. Thus, for example, a 1983 play for 'Saturday Stereo,' *Évariste Galois*, comes across, with all its preachy passion, as awkwardly unrealized. Yuzyk, a high school math teacher, has a feverish, kaleidoscopic dream of being in turn all the benighted teachers and authorities who persecuted the young revolutionary math genius Évariste Galois in the 1820s and 1830s. Recognizing himself as an incarnation of the jealous conformity that stamps out courageous originality, Yuzyk launches into a hysterical tirade about the mathematics of weaponry bringing on the ultimate big bang, and concludes with a frenzy of Sieg Heils. For all its righteous passion, the play seems frantic and undigested, its rhetoric embarrassingly unstable.

Another playwright of the older school, George Salverson, has produced an impressive range of work, from the tight little thriller to the thought-provoking social problem play. In plays like *The Write-Off* (1969) and *The Expropriated* (1974) he created elaborate montages of quasi-documentary evidence with which to indict contemporary social abuses. *The Write-Off* exploits effectively the technique of radio-within-radio, as Walter Denning, fired at forty-nine from a senior executive's job, is interrogated by a bullying radio interviewer about the shock of being dumped overboard in mid-career. Equally elaborate in construction, blending public scenes and private confrontations, voices over and voices under, *The Expropriated* dramatizes the struggle of the 'People over Planes' movement to stop the building of a second Toronto airport in a region of prime farmland. 'Populist' in its hostility to government and officialdom, and in its sympathy for individualism and protest, the play builds to a critical point in the struggle and breaks off. Like *The Write-Off* it provides no resolution, leaving the listener indignant at the prospect of defeat. One more play to indicate Salverson's range: *The Jewel* (1973) develops a structure of feeling that the intrinsic properties of radio drama seem peculiarly apt to induce, namely a mood of poignant speculation about the unlived life, the ache of the unrecoverable, unredeemable past in which everything might have been different. A writer on his deathbed retraces in a kind of delirious flashback the nodal points in his life where everything began to go wrong. As he re-experiences the mistakes and miscalculations, the chances not taken, moves not made, he calls out desperately, 'Re-write!' – as if the script could somehow still be altered, the outcome averted.

Of the new school of leaner, more astringent radio drama, James W. Nichol and Marian Waldman must stand out for their consistent power to astonish. Nichol's large output can be divided for convenience into the 'Kingforks' plays and the others. Roughly based on Paris, Ontario, the fictional town of Kingforks is the setting for a series of bitter, beautiful tales from the decades around 1900, all linked by the shift of a marginal character from one play to the role of protagonist in the next. In several instances framed by a narrator's long look back to the traumatic events of half a century earlier, the plays unfold almost Brontëan tales of passions thwarted, punished, turned awry or murderous, in the harsh, Scots-Protestant climate. With careful economy of means, never resorting to extravagances of music or sound effects, Nichol concentrates almost entirely on starkly evocative speech, rich in imagery, breaking into a bleak and thorny poetry. To take only one, arguably the finest, of the Kingforks plays: in *The Austere Gwendoline Parker Elliott* (1972) old David Easton tells how, at the age of twelve, in 1907, he was drawn into a kind of amorous enchantment, erotic yet innocent, by the town's crazy lady, Gwendoline, who wanders the overgrown grounds of her dead father's house, a virtual pariah. Reading *Jane Eyre* with him, she makes him play Rochester and leads his blind fingers over her weeping face. When another Rochester appears, a travelling salesman named Parker, the heartbroken David rouses his father, old 'Pork' Easton, and a bunch of cronies, with reports of abuse to Gwendoline. In a horrifying climactic episode, David accompanies them as they horsewhip, with a weird sexual malevolence, the man who has acted out their guilty fantasy.

Beyond the realm of Kingforks, Nichol's imagination has moved in disparate directions. *Feast of the Dead* (1973), a two-hour narration for three voices, recounts from the points of view of the unresting spirits of one Blackrobe and two Indians the appalling tragedy of the Jesuit mission to the Hurons. In *Purr* (1973) an intensely withdrawn math prodigy, Billy, dubbed unimaginative by his parents, Twitter and Grunch, secretly nurtures a kitten while resisting all attempts by parents and teachers to communicate with him. 'Purr' grows bigger and bigger, and eventually devours everybody except Billy, who enters Purr's eye and descends into a velvety darkness. *Rapunzel* (1975) reimagines the classic fairy-tale in perturbing terms. More recently, in *Nova Scotia Brothers* (1980), Doug Westheffer from 'Looneyburg,' Nova Scotia, finds brother Billy down and out in Toronto and has to reveal that the family he has dreamed of returning to for twenty years are all dead. Finally, *Biko*, which was commissioned for CBC's 'Africa Week' in 1980, creates a powerful memorial to the Black African leader who died in 1977. Framed by scenes of Biko's interrogation and fatal beating by security police, the play interweaves flashbacks to his early career with a harsh paean of racial pride and indomitability by an Afrikaner: 'And does the world care for you Biko? I am the scapegoat. I am the whipping boy. I am the bitter ointment that salves the conscience of the white world.' But the voice is drowned out by an African anthem at Biko's funeral.

Marian Waldman's earlier plays draw on the rich resources of Jewish idiom and culture for their warmth, humour, and intensity. *Tinker's Dam* (1970) brings Saul, son of Aaron and Dasha, back from Asia with an Afghan baby that he bought at a roadside stall. Dasha's sister Goldie is back from Israel to find out if her husband really slept with Dasha. Daughter Eileen is married to a *schwarze* teacher, Harold. Aaron only wants Saul to follow him into the slaughterhouse business. And Dasha, a sculptor who used to make gods

by the river, and sit on them, is dying. In the welter of family turbulence
Saul learns that his paternity is unknown, his identity his own to create.
'Vimmins bisteh?' he has been asking of everybody; 'whose are you?' Dasha,
the source of wisdom in the play, tells him, 'It is beautiful not to belong.'
Another Jewish play, *Holidays* (1974), follows the mixed marriage of Alvin
the dentist, his wife Shirley, and his very Yiddishe mother, from New Year's
Eve, 1949, to 1970. Occurring on a series of holidays, religious and secular,
the play ends on an extremely upbeat note as Alvin and Shirley celebrate
the baby of their later years, their new 'son-rising.' And the poignantly
mysterious piece *Chain Letter* (1975) unfolds a brief and dreamlike idyll
between a woman on a lonely cliff-top farm and a passing Jewish pedlar. Is
he the luck that a chain letter has promised her? And when she breaks the
chain, does it cause his death under his overturned cart?

In another vein, Waldman's work can tilt into the absurdist, the bizarre.
A pair of plays, *Vision* and *Revision* (1974), take Carl, who lost his sight
in a car accident, on his first 'blind date' with Wanda from the CNIB who
resents the fact that he once could see. Subsequently, as some kind of
obsessive hobby, Carl takes up covering everything in sight (as it were) with
paint, to the hysterical horror of his mother, Flo. Back at Flo's place it
gradually emerges that her husband Gurney is not just maintaining a stubborn
silence, but has been dead for several days. Carl begins feverishly to paint
him, then Flo, then himself. Moving further still into an unbounded absurdity
only possible on radio, blending Ionesco with the Goon Show, *Incompletions*
(1974) and *Bokhara* (1977) revel in zany dialogue, ghastly puns, and situations utterly bizarre – as for instance in *Bokhara* the gradual reduction of
Harry Talisman to nothing but a pair of lips, 'not so much disembodied as
defaced.' One of her triumphs, *Twenty Years of Twilight* (1975), a black
comedy in a home for the elderly where the inmates plague their custodians
with an insubordinate carnality, culminates in a scene of surrealistic liberation
as old Mr Timmerman and Patty Pilsudski appear at the wedding that has
been coyly planned for them, stark naked.

A pair of playwrights active in the early 1970s, whose works bear some
resemblance, are Helen French and the inexhaustible Mavor Moore. While
Moore has been writing, producing, and acting for radio and TV since the
1950s, French is a relative newcomer. Both writers practise a spare, elusive,
Pinteresque style, as in French's *The Appointment* (1975) where Trevor –
fifty-seven, well-to-do, disgruntled, anxious – encounters Bill, forty-seven, a
nomadic self-sufficient wino, full of quirky wisdom; and in Moore's *The Pile*
(1969) in which two voices wonder what to do with an unidentified pile of
undisposable something-or-other; or, to take another pair, in *Charlie's Chair*
(1970) by French, in which sixty-year-old Charlie, who only coughs and
sucks his pipe, having shrunk almost to nothing behind his newspaper, is

put down the garburator by his nattering wife; and in Moore's *The Store* (1972), an interview between a complaining customer and a department store manager who turns the tables on her to the point of attacking and killing her while uttering wild owl cries, 'Who? Who?' – the whole thing reminiscent of Ionesco's *The Lesson*. One more play of Moore's, *Come Away, Come Away* (1972), establishes with delicate immediacy the gently surreal encounter between an old man and a little girl who personifies his death.

Highly prolific but somewhat uneven, Rachel Wyatt has been writing all through this period. In some work she reaches after experimental, intellectually ingenious conceptions – as in *Remaindered* (1975), set in the year 2003, in which two people argue before an Arbitrator as to why the other one should be liquidated by the codes of a futuristic totalitarian state; and in *Crash Landing* (1975), a cleverly constructed piece involving a ham radio operator chancing to pick up the talk, on an unsuspected open mike, of three survivors of an air crash facing death in the icy North and reviewing their suddenly unredeemable lives. Combining regret for the unlived life with the radio-within-radio effect, this is a quintessential radio play. In other work, however, and increasingly of late, Wyatt settles for a more ordinary kind of realism, sometimes touching and well observed, as in *A Chair to Sleep In* (1972) with its grainy recognition of the entrapment of the working poor; sometimes rather lacklustre and prosaic, as in *My House Tonight* (1977), *Twenty-One Days* (1982), or the two-part adaptation of her own novel about a difficult English couple on sabbatical in Toronto, *Foreign Bodies* (1983).

While some radio dramatists work almost exclusively in the one medium, others migrate busily between print, stage, sound, and screen, recycling their own conceptions as the opportunity presents itself. W.O. Mitchell's *Back to Beulah*, to take an egregious example, while not staged until 1976, managed in 1974 to be nominated as both Best TV Drama and Best Radio Play, and to win in the latter category. Certainly this struggle for power between a tyrannically liberal psychologist and her patients gains a special strength on radio, as the cries of the disputed 'baby' and Dr Anders's traumatic recall of her auctioneer-father are heard in a collective soundspace where authority over what is 'real' has been radically challenged. Mitchell's work in radio goes back to the early 1950s when he wrote several seasons of *Jake and the Kid* stories, as well as *The Black Bonspiel of Wullie MacCrimmon*. A version of *The Devil's Instrument* was aired in 1953, and a radio dramatization of his novel *The Kite* in 1965. In a version rewritten for the stage (1981), *The Kite* made it to radio again in 1983 in a two-hour feast of vintage W.O., as rambunctious old Daddy Sherry hopes to fart coast-to-coast on national TV, to celebrate his 117th birthday. (The script contains the following direction to the sound engineer: 'They embrace – however the hell you manage that!').

A fellow to W.O.M. in both habitation and name, Saskatchewan playwright

Ken Mitchell has similarly made the most of his material, producing stage and radio versions of *This Train* (1973/1973) and *The Shipbuilder* (1979/ 1981), a radio dramatization of his novel *The Con Man* (1979/1983), and a self-published novel *The Meadowlark Connection* (1975) out of a 1971 radio serial *The Meadowlark Caper*, featuring the fantastical misadventures of zealous RCMP constable James Ashwanden. Certainly the translation to radio of *The Shipbuilder* is magnificently effective in conjuring up, perhaps more vividly than could the stage, the mad epic of Jaanus Koronkola who builds a hundred-foot steamship in the middle of the prairie, in hopes of sailing home to Finland, by way of Hudson Bay. Touching in a way, but dramatically much less interesting, *The Promised Land* (1983) presents the tribulations and triumphs of a young Scots couple migrating from a highland croft to Moose Jaw in the 1880s. From initial revulsion and timidity, Colin McPherson comes to exult in the space and freedom of his promised land, and with the birth of a baby girl is doubtless destined to mature into one of the terrible Scots patriarchs of prairie literature.

With adaptations and original work, Michael Cook continues to return to the medium where he began, in 1966, with a string of radio plays produced out of St John's. The adopted playwright laureate of Newfoundland, he has produced radio versions of nearly all of his stage plays, from the anguished Beckettian threnody of *Tiln* (1971), raging at the senseless sea and proclaiming himself 'God ... of the tilting universe'; through the wry historical parable of *Colour the Flesh the Colour of Dust* (1972), re-enacting a sordidly farcical series of betrayals in 1762; to the circus brutality and pathos of Cook's atonement for the Beothuk extermination, *On the Rim of the Curve* (1977). Much of this material, with its vehement denunciation of the rapacity and vicious hypocrisy of Christian civilization, is assimilated into the broad and splendid symphony of *This Damned Inheritance* (1983). Richly exploiting the possibilities of stereo, this three-part epic ranges over the entire span of Newfoundland history, from the coming of St Brendan to the ascendancy of Brian Peckford. As witnesses to the depredations wrought upon their people by Vikings and colonists, the spirits of Shanadithit and Nonosabasut are resurrected from *Rim of the Curve* to mourn the extinction of an animist religion dedicated to 'the Maker of Arrows.' And in the present an aging fisherman, also the last of his tribe, wrestles with the curse afflicting his island, denounces the vapid palliatives of religion – 'There's nothin' else! There's nobody up there!' – and dies, in hospital, regretting that he can't go down in the cold arms of the sea – 'you Old Bitch!' And in a bitter epilogue his young partner, Billy, who had abandoned the fisheries for a more modern and lucrative career, goes down with all hands on the *Ocean Ranger*. A richly textured, tragic work, *This Damned Inheritance* deserves to be a Canadian classic.

A quite striking coincidence has old Eddy Nurlin, one of a dying breed of beleaguered prairie farmers in Sharon Pollock's *Generations* (1978), proclaiming in the final moments his defiance, not of the sea but of the farmer's equivalent loved enemy, the sun: 'Look at me, yuh Old Bitch! Look at me! ... I'm still here!' Pollock's play, while it has none of the historical scope of Cook's, is similarly occupied with the potentially crippling legacy of bondage to unconquerable Nature – in this case, the land. A naturalistic family drama, later adapted for the stage, it probes the ambivalence of the self-professed 'salt of the earth' in the face of a temptation to call it quits. Pollock's work for radio includes adaptations of her stage plays *Walsh* (1974) and *Whiskey Six* (1983), and a number of radio originals, notably *Sweet Land of Liberty* (1979), an ACTRA award winner. Structured as a series of flashbacks within a kind of inquest, the play circles towards revelation of the hideous episode in Viet Nam that drove a young marine from Montana to desertion, and that continues to haunt his exile in Canada. Befriended by a single mother and her son, he finds no lasting respite from his nightmare, and at last puts a shotgun into his mouth.

Turning to radio drama only lately, novelist David Helwig has contributed a number of works remarkable for their formal sophistication and dramatic power. *You Can't Hear What I'm Saying* (1978) creates a situation in which Morley, an Ottawa bureaucrat instrumental in the government's handling of the October Crisis of 1970, finds himself required by the terms of his mother-in-law's will to publish tapes of the clairvoyant nightmares in which she was able to 'see' what was happening to Pierre Laporte. By way of these tapes, and through a complex collage of flashbacks, Morley and the wife who was in the process of leaving him in October 1970 re-experience the public and private impact of those weeks. Also featuring tape-recordings, in a perfectly functional use of the medium, *Party Girl* (1981) consists entirely of the taped 'diary' of a small-town girl hitting the Toronto scene, and getting hit back repeatedly. A disjointed assemblage of reflective monologue, party chatter, pseudo-interviews, bits of song, even a vicious slapping-around, the play relays to the listener whatever Terry's microphone has 'heard' when she, or someone else, has chosen to switch it on.

Another formal experiment, *Moving In* (1980) eavesdrops on a couple carting their belongings into the rather dingy flat they are going to share. Taking to an extreme a kind of 'radio-vérité,' the microphone follows the couple back and forth, from truck to flat, in a series of long continuous takes, and hears the little drama of conflict and despondency that marks the start of 'living together.' One more play by Helwig, *Everybody Has Something to Hide* (1983) involves a husband's search for his missing wife, and her evasion of him. But when, after many months, the police appear to have located Catherine, he insists that they have found a different woman, a chance resemblance. Meanwhile, from subtly elusive scenes of Catherine's new life, the listener gathers something of the way her husband has always denied her reality.

Another latecomer, Michael Riordan, deserves mention for some original and arresting pieces. *Quiet in the Hills* (1982) follows a Canadian doctor in Guatemala to his reluctant realization that government forces are indeed bombarding peasants with poison gas. A passionately outraged piece of suspenseful drama, the play brings its doctor out alive to be a witness to atrocity. *Particles* (1983) constructs a wry, farcical, yet desperate don't-let-it-happen collage of life in a Canadian city in the hours before nuclear attack. And, in a different vein altogether, *The Other Side of the Moon* (1984) tells, in a retrospective first-person narrative from the year 2005, of growing up, and living a life, and growing old, gay. Dreamy, confiding, melancholy, the piece unfolds a life that never amounted to very much, in which the fact of being gay was of defining importance, yet somehow not really decisive.

One more dramatist, one more play: Vancouver playwright Betty Lambert, who died in 1983, was an infrequent but most distinguished contributor to radio. Her *Grasshopper Hill* (1979), a ninety-minute, three-voice drama of quite extraordinary richness and complexity, accompanies a woman in her pursuit of a baffling enigma – the man who has been her lover. Undertaking the affair as a kind of gamble, Susan, a university teacher, has lived with the arrogant, callous, cynical Gustav Gutke for a year of comradeship, pain, bewilderment, and a riveting curiosity about his past. Gustav survived Auschwitz. But what did he do there? He is Jewish. He was in the *Sondercommando*. 'I enjoyed Auschwitz enormously.' He admired the Nazis. He loved a German officer, Gastner, who saved his life. He witnessed 'experiments on love' in which parent or child could be saved from intensifying electric shocks only by administering them to the other. He got away and joined the Partisans. He broke a promise to report to the parents of a young German lieutenant whom he shot. He knows every degree of compromise and betrayal human nature is capable of. 'People do the unimaginable, and they go on living.' And now he testifies at the trials of Nazis, including his revered Gastner, hoping they will conduct themselves decently. 'A man without vanity is finished.' No brief account can do justice to this marvellously layered, eloquently disturbing play. One can only ask, why is such a work not *published*? Why is the tape of its superb production not offered for sale?

Finally, no survey of writing for radio should fail to mention, if only in a token way, first, the long contribution to Canadian literature of Robert Weaver's 'Anthology,' on which so much original fiction and poetry, by names later to become famous, was given its initial public presentation; and second, the wealth of documentary features, including the zealously researched and sometimes highly original presentations of 'Ideas Network.' To cite only a few titles: *The New Assassins* (1975) by Warren Wilson; *The*

Holocaust (1976) by Malka Himel; *Aftermath of Jonestown* (1979) by Terence McKenna; *Trotsky in Exile* (1981) by Jurgen Hesse; *The World after Nuclear War* (1983) by Jay Ingram, Anita Gordon, and Penny Park; and *George Orwell, a Radio Biography* (1984) by Edward Trapunski and George Woodcock.

3

To a much greater extent than for radio, drama written for television is conceived and organized in series and serials. The single sixty- or ninety-minute drama is a relative rarity, and is almost always a made-for-TV movie rather than a taped studio production. The best writing goes unquestionably into these drama specials, but the bulk of it goes into the shifting array of continuing interest series, whether long-running or ephemeral, serious or frothy. For the sake of convenience, three general modes of TV drama may be distinguished, loosely identified as comedy, dramatic fiction, and dramatized documentary – a spectrum running from pure entertainment to pure edification. The first two categories are usually in a series format (less commonly actual serials), and frequently studio-taped. The writing exhibits a high degree of professionalism but tends towards the formulaic. Most series are in fact scripted by several, if not dozens, of writers, each contributing episodes rather than writing as teams. The contribution here of the story editor or series co-ordinator is usually crucial, if unsung.

To distinguish more specifically: in almost every television 'season' at least one indigenous situation comedy has competed with American rivals for the loyalty of the Canadian audience. The most successful of these, *King of Kensington* (created by Perry Rosemond and employing, among many writers, Jack Humphrey, Louis Del Grande, and Anna Sandor), ran for 113 half-hour episodes, from 1975 to 1980, and established an engaging comic protagonist in the person of Larry King, the gregarious and ebullient Kensington Market storekeeper, played by Al Waxman. A Canadian cross between *Coronation Street* and *All in the Family*, the show mined a rich vein of domestic, ethnic, life-style humour and maintained a flow of verbal energy to the end. Another long-running series (since 1975) to which literally dozens of writers have contributed episodes, *The Beachcombers*, featuring Bruno Gerussi as Nick Adonidas, master of the *Persephone*, has allowed itself to absorb adventure, pathos, and what one of its writers, Lyal Brown, called 'little morality plays' into its rough-and-tumble comedy format. Writers for *The Beachcombers* have regularly been nominated for ACTRA awards, in recognition of the compact energy of these twenty-five-minute movies. More recently the sixty-minute segments of the *Seeing Things* series, many of them written by the team of Anna Sandor and Bill Gough, have walked an ingenious line between comedy and thriller, founded on the conception of a newspaper reporter (played by

Louis Del Grande) whose fitful bursts of clairvoyance permit him to 'see' tantalizing details of unsolved crimes. The frankly preposterous premise and predilection for wise-cracking dialogue draw the series into the comedy category, but the suspense format and cliff-hanger plotting make a claim for consideration as drama.

The admittedly cloudy distinction between comedy and dramatic fiction aims to differentiate between shows which seek mainly to entertain with humorous situations and laugh lines, and shows which offer to involve the viewer in emotionally charged relationships, structured on a conflict-climax-resolution format. The latter mode may be distinguished in turn from the dramatized documentary, not so much in terms of seriousness but in being overtly fictitious; while respecting the pseudo-realist conventions of almost all TV drama, it endows its dramatis personae with the acknowledged signs of fictionality – exorbitant individuality, idiosyncrasy, and fluency. They are 'characters,' creatures of the fictive imagination, rather than disguised or generalized case histories. Indeed, the main subgenres of TV drama may be seen to correspond more closely to types of popular prose fiction – period romance, family saga, mystery story, action thriller – than to types of contemporary drama for the theatre. Paradoxically perhaps, this fictionalizing process operates even on genuinely historical material, as figures and episodes from the Canadian past are appropriated for dramatic ends, as protagonists and antagonists, heroes and villains, crises and dénouements. Paramount among such works was the ill-starred *Riel*, scripted eventually by Roy Moore after several false starts, and accorded a very mixed reception when aired in 1979.

In the period under review several series call for appreciative notice. Running from 1976 to 1979, *A Gift to Last* picked up the recipe of a 1960s series, *Hatch's Mill*, in presenting dramatic episodes in the life of a rural Ontario family in days gone by. Gordon Pinsent wrote most of the series, with the occasional participation of Peter Wildeblood, and created for himself the role of Edgar Sturgess, boyish roustabout brother of the dour and narrow James. Coming back from the Boer War, Edgar opens the Mafeking Hotel in the little town of Tamarack where James owns and operates the local tannery. Their sister Clara, widowed in the first episode, marries John Trevelyan, the grocer's son, against the fierce opposition of Grandmother Lizzy Sturgess, whose Tartar exterior conceals a generous heart. The passage of life's crises and calamities – marriages and deaths, the loss of a child, a strike at the tannery, the persecution of a new teacher – provides a series of tests for the principal characters, who are found variously full and wanting. In conception the episodes are humane and frequently touching, with a generous sympathy for the predicaments and struggles of the characters. Pinsent's writing reaches towards peaks of unashamed eloquence, as characters are propelled into wholehearted declarations of love or loyalty, principle or pride.

In the benign, almost innocent quality of its life, Pinsent's Tamarack provides a striking contrast to Nichol's Kingforks of the same era, a contrast that testifies eloquently to the difference in ethos of television and radio drama.

Another popular series, *The Great Detective* (1978–81), reached back to a roughly similar epoch and locale, but in the adventures of Inspector Alistair Cameron, based on Ontario's first provincial detective, John Wilson Murray, it aimed for an increasingly fantastical style of comedy-melodrama in period costume. Written by many hands, including Peter Wildeblood, John Saxton, and Gordon Ruttan, the series provided a splendid if somewhat repetitious showcase for Douglas Campbell. Less remote in time but still a period piece, *Home Fires* (1980–3) took viewers back to the years of World War II. Novelist Peter Such, who conceived the series but was supplanted as writer by Jim Purdy, focused on the family of Toronto doctor Albert Lowe and his Polish-Jewish wife Hannah, meeting the challenges of life on the home front, as sons went off to fight, and refugees and wounded returned from the battle zones. A series set in the present, *House of Pride* (1974–6), followed the love and war among the descendants of old Dan Pride who died in the first episode and left the family farm outside Toronto, now worth a million dollars, to four of his five offspring. Endless permutations of family conflict took the series through fifty-two half-hour episodes, all of them authored or co-authored by the prolific George Robertson (widely respected for, among other things, the 1960s series *Quentin Durgens, MP*). *Backstretch* (1983–4) explored a rather different legacy – the failing Ettrick raceway which Marge Aylesworth, widowed in the first episode, determined to take on and manage for herself. Written by Wildeblood, Robertson, David Helwig, Bob Carney, and others, the series won a lot of praise for its salty authenticity. Like a good first novel, it took an overlooked corner of the world and brought it to life. Finally, to mention one more series of merit, in *Judge* (1983–5), writers John Maynard, Gordon Ruttan, George Robertson, and others produced a string of decently low-key, morally engaged court cases presided over by veteran Stratford actor Tony Van Bridge as His Honour Judge Humphries.

In addition to open-ended series like these, the CBC has also run a number of three- to six-hour productions in which a single complex story is sustained over several weeks in a serial format. Lyal Brown's *The Albertans* (1979) was an ambitiously panoramic composite portrait of contemporary Alberta, hinging upon a contested pipeline project. Spread over three hours, the story drew into a single orbit ranchers, financiers, construction magnates, politicians, a crooked Swiss speculator, and members of a radical Indian group intent on dynamiting the pipeline to bring attention to their cause. In the same general territory, *Vanderberg* (1983), by Rob Forsyth and others, was billed as a Canadian version of *Dallas*, featuring unscrupulous tycoons and proud unsatisfied wives. Young Hank Vanderberg, determined to beat out his corporate rivals in a bid to sell Alberta natural gas to Europe, rode roughshod over friend, foe, and family in six vigorous episodes. Unlike its American prototype, however, the script evinced intelligence and insight, the product of disciplined research and imagination. Two short series by Doug Bowie deserve mention, likewise, for their sophistication: *Empire Inc.* (1984) and *Love and Larceny* (1985). The former series dramatized, in six parts, the burgeoning of a Montreal commercial empire somewhat resembling that of the Bronfmans; while *Love and Larceny* (aired, perhaps unwisely, as a three-hour special) pursued the fraudulent get-rich schemes of Betsy Bigley, alias Pelvina de Vere, alias Mrs Chadwick, of Woodstock, Ontario, the last and boldest of which entailed representing herself to New York bankers as an illegitimate daughter of Andrew Carnegie.

Finally in the dramatic fiction category – but already nudging the dramatized documentary mode – there were the urban police-work series 'The Collaborators' (1973–4) and 'Sidestreet' (1975–8), the former focusing particularly on the collaboration between officers of the homicide squad and a team of forensic scientists, the latter on the mediating role of working cops in the Community Service squad. While still connected to each other by a recurring group of central characters, the sixty-minute screenplays for these series were virtually self-contained dramas, serious, humanistic, almost sociological in their depiction of crime and policing. Downplaying individual bravado or eccentricity, seldom resorting to the wise-cracking or shoot-outs of their American counterparts, the shows were often quite exemplary treatments of the seamier side of urban life. And the corps of writers for these series tended to be the same as that for the feature dramas, increasingly social-documentary in nature, that have appeared in the 'Anthology' and 'For the Record' programs since the late 1960s. It is appropriate, therefore, to take note of particular shows in these series as examples of the work of some of the major TV *auteurs* to whom this discussion now turns.

To speak of certain writers as 'veterans' is not to patronize their recent work but only to emphasize that their contribution to TV drama dates from long before the period covered by this volume. Still writing well into the 1970s, Charles Israel, M. Charles Cohen, and Leslie McFarlane all made their names two decades earlier with work under such prestigious umbrella titles as 'Festival,' 'Playdate,' 'On Camera,' and 'GM Presents.' More recently, in addition to a number of episodes of *House of Pride*, Israel wrote a couple of memorable 'Anthology' plays. *To Season with Time* (1972) takes a recurring subject of both radio and TV drama, relationships among the elderly, and probes the reluctance and fear, as well as the hope, which people in their late years face at the prospect of a last marriage – till death do them part. Avoiding easy sentimentality, and even allowing a daughter to express disgust at what she takes to be her mother's sexual involvement, the play confronts its couple with confusion and defeat, and ends ambiguously. *Lighten My Darkness* (1973) explores, with even an excess of thematic pointing, the situation in which a wife, blind from birth, gains her sight by means of a cornea transplant and becomes increasingly independent of the husband who has cherished her helplessness. A 1971 'Anthology' play by M. Charles Cohen, *The Golden Handshake*, takes the viewer rapidly down the slope from Rosedale to Skid Row in company with a high-priced executive, no longer young, who finds himself among the unemployed and unemployable, contemplating suicide. Like George Salverson's *The Write-Off* (radio 1969, TV 1975), the drama enforces a painful participation in the plight of a growing number of people to whom 'this sort of thing doesn't happen.' A third 'veteran,' Leslie McFarlane, noted for the *McGonigle Skates Again* series (1965–6), contributed a zany comedy to 'Anthology,' *Gold Is Where You Find It ... Maybe* (1970), in which a gold brick, the stock-in-trade of a phony promoter, falls into the hands of a succession of astonished recipients.

Originally a cameraman, who turned to writing and directing in the late 1960s in the *Wojeck* series, Grahame Woods bestows on his scripts a greater attention to visual detail and precise camera movements than probably anyone else writing for Canadian television. At the same time his writing consistently brings a dedicated seriousness to serious themes. Child abusers, abused children, psychiatric patients, strikebreakers, illegal immigrants, burned-out cops, rape victims, a missionary priest in war-torn Africa, a survivor of the Warsaw uprising: these are some of the subjects of Woods's investigation. Typically he dramatizes the predicament of ordinary people in desperate straits, struggling to keep their heads above water, to stay sane, to stay alive, fighting against the callousness, intransigence, or indifference of people with power over them. The style is what is loosely called 'documentary-realist': unglamorous everyday environments, straightforward exposition without teasing or mystification, self-effacing scene construction and camera work, minimal use of flashback, dream, subjective fantasy – in sum, the selective showing of what could be seen and heard by a privileged observer of 'actual' events. His outcomes tend on balance to be dispiriting; the odds are not in favour of people in desperate straits.

Two plays in the 'Anthology' collection – *Twelve and a Half Cents* (1970) and its sequel *Vicky* (1973) – tell the story of a beaten wife, once a beaten child, who beats and eventually kills her own children. The viewer is drawn into the situation by way of a well-intentioned social worker, Al Wicklow, who can see what is happening but who lacks the personal energy or legal authority to intervene decisively. As Vicky is led away by the police, Al passionately berates the prurient neighbours on the stairs of the dreary tenement for hearing, seeing, knowing the truth, and doing nothing about it. In the sequel, five years later, Vicky is released from psychiatric confinement to try and make a life for herself. Divorced by husband, denounced by father, evicted by landlord, and rejected by one-night lover when he learns her story, she ends up back inside. It's a harrowing depiction of a nearly inescapable cycle.

The general theme of the trauma of abuse and molestation is one that Woods returns to repeatedly. A 'Collaborators' episode, *Beyond All Reasonable Doubt* (1974) deals with the trial of an adolescent boy on a rape-murder charge in a small Ontario town – a situation strongly reminiscent of the Steven Truscott trial in the 1960s. And a 'Sidestreet' episode, *Section 143/144* (1975) explores both the paralyzing shock to the rape victim and the sickness of the rapist, in a show remarkable for the forthrightness of its social statement. In *Cop*, a 'For the Record' show (1981), the triggering event in Constable Heller's burn-out, disciplinary hearings, and attempted suicide is his clumsy intervention in a child-beating case. And in *Anne's Story* (1983), a ninety-minute drama special, Woods traces in scrupulous detail a growing girl's attempt to overcome the trauma of having been raped, at the age of six, by her teenage uncle, Bobby. This latter script, precise in its directions and eloquent in its dialogue, is one of Woods's finest achievements. We follow Anne through her parents' early separation, and their neglect of her which makes possible the rape, through her teenage years with her sleazy alcoholic mother, through a disastrous early marriage which her revulsion at sexuality renders her unable to consummate, to the slow growth of trust in a rather older man whose care allows her at last to confront, in a passionately written tirade, the now smugly married Bobby.

A work in a different key, which won for Woods the 1981 ACTRA award for TV drama, *War Brides* (1980) interweaves the experiences of four women arriving in Canada after World War II to join their wartime suitors. Of the three British girls, one finds much what she had expected and adjusts quite easily, one recognizes disaster from the moment she sees her fiancé in his natural habitat, and one, deserted at the outset, shifts for herself and marries her lawyer boss. Meanwhile, in Nova Scotia, Lisa, plucked from the ruins of defeated Germany, meets ostracism and abuse from her husband's family and community, but eventually confounds them all in a showdown speech at the Legion Hall. For all its human interest, and perhaps because of its backward gaze, *War Brides* seems rather softer than most of Woods's work, a swerving from his usual sources of strength.

Two writers whose careers intersect with that of Grahame Woods at several points are Lyal Brown and Tony Sheer. A contributor to radio since 1952, Lyal Brown has turned his talents to many kinds of TV writing. In addition to such work as *The Albertans* and various *Beachcomber* episodes, he has written for 'Anthology,' 'The Collaborators,' and 'Sidestreet,' and for the West Coast adventure series *Ritter's Cove* (1980–1) which he and his wife

Barbara scripted between them. His first TV script, *An Angel Against the Night* (1974) bleakly establishes the plight of the John Randall family, whose general store has been failing since the highway bypassed Randall's small Alberta home town. Putting his father in the nursing home, he takes his wife Helen and Jimmy, his child by the 'town squaw,' into the city to find work. But Jimmy is persecuted in school – 'squaw baby' – and, finding Helen in bed with a stranger, runs away to his grandfather. Together the old man and the boy flee to the hills, but old Jim falls mortally sick and has to instruct the boy on how to cope with his impending death. In a moving conclusion the boy's father finds him putting a crude cross on the grave he has lately dug. As examples of Brown's 'Collaborators' contributions, *Kiss the World Goodbye* (1974) features an extremely gripping hold-up and hostage situation, while *The Chance* (1974) shows an ex-cop attempting an armed robbery which leads to the death of the friend whose family he was trying to help. Under the 'Sidestreet' title Brown wrote, among others, *The Wife Beater* (1976), in which Community Service officers Raitt and Olsen assist a battered wife to a shelter and attempt to protect her against her enraged husband; and *Cry Wolf* (1976), in which Olsen is falsely accused of assaulting a pregnant woman during a demonstration. Investigative and humane, Brown's work blends sensitivity with versatile professionalism.

Another 'professional' writer, Tony Sheer, specialized initially in under-world-undercover stories, exploring a murky region of ambiguous loyalties, dubious legality, and dishonour among thieves. His screenplays combine skilful handling of thriller-craft with psychological insight and an attention to the detailed mechanics of both crime and police work. From a pair of 'Anthology' plays, *Rap City* (1972) and *The Changeling* (1973), he moved naturally into 'The Collaborators' with *A Little Something for Old Age* (1974) about an ex-con reluctantly drawn into one last safe-cracking job that turns out to be a homicide; and *Dark Children* (1974), a gaudily melodramatic showdown between rival gangs of bikers. After a couple of early 'Sidestreet' pieces Sheer moved in the direction of dramatic features and 'For the Record' plays. (He also wrote the dramatized sequences of the CBC's *October Crisis*, aired in 1975). Among his features: *The Man Inside* (1976) follows the infiltration of an undercover RCMP corporal into a heroin ring, and his fatal flirtation with the possibility of defecting to the enemy for a multimillion dollar haul; while *The Fighting Men* (1977), moving into new territory, has a pair of servicemen, one English-speaking, one Québécois, injured in a plane crash in Labrador, fighting for survival against cold, gangrene, wolves, and starvation, and intermittently fighting each other as representatives of the two solitudes. A heavily reworked script, *The Fighting Men* finally brings a search plane to its antagonists, although rejected endings had either called off the search, or led them to an Inuit hunter who, ironically, understands neither of the official languages. Sheer's 'For the Record' contributions, regularly nominated for ACTRA awards, include *Final Edition* (1981), which dramatizes most credibly the closing, for corporate reasons, of a major newspaper; *Maintain the Right* (1980), which pits radical lawyer Jane Kohl, and an idealistic rookie cop who has taken a fancy to her, against a dirty-tricks RCMP agent out to discredit Kohl for her involvement in militant unionism; and *Lyon's Den* (1980), wherein a crusading TV journalist, Pete Lyon, exploits the plight of welfare families for the sake of a sensational show on vandalism, while cynically shielding his own son from implication in a covertly filmed vandalistic act.

A recurring structure of 'For the Record' scripts, so common as almost to confer a thematic unity, pits individuals, armed with little but decency and a sense of right, against inflexible, relentless, and sometimes corrupt authority. To a degree that might be considered surprising in a publicly funded broadcasting system, these feature productions, the pride of the network, almost inevitably depict agencies of government – the RCMP, the Department of Defence, the Justice system, the Department of Indian Affairs, Farm Credit agencies, Employment and Immigration – as hostile to the citizenry, both as a matter of policy and in personal dealings. Shows repeatedly dramatize the predicament of people caught up in processes beyond their control, fighting oppression and indifference. Individuals display courage, integrity, and concern for one another; systems and institutions grind them down, sometimes with active malevolence, as in *Maintain the Right*, more often with bureaucratic impersonality. Against this tendency, however, a number of 'For the Record' scripts have dramatized purely individual predicaments.

One of the most distinguished contributors to 'For the Record,' Cam Hubert (Anne Cameron) has found a repeated theme in the suppression and reassertion of Canadian Indian culture. In the hauntingly beautiful *Dreamspeaker* (1976) she transcends the documentary-realist mode with a story of a 'delinquent' boy escaping from a government facility and stumbling into the care of an elderly Indian with the psychic and therapeutic power of 'dream-speaking.' With gentle wisdom he leads the boy through a critical struggle with his demons, but the boy is returned by the Mounties to the facility where, sensing the death of the old man, he hangs himself. In a much more documentary vein, *The Fred Quilt Incident* (1977) investigates the rigged inquest into the death from peritonitis of a BC Indian, allegedly the result of a police beating. And *Homecoming* (1979) rather sentimentally shows the adoption by a Cree family, in an elaborate 'name-giving' ceremony, of the teenage daughter of an injured rodeo rider. Beyond the native Indian theme, *A Matter of Choice* (1978) presents a furious diatribe against male sexual aggression, male proprietariness, male duplicity, and a male system of justice. And in *Drying Up the Streets* (1979), an ex-heroin addict, searching Toronto's underworld for his runaway daughter, is ruthlessly exploited by the RCMP narcotics squad to help them bust a heroin ring. A tense, hard-edged script in an expanded ninety-minute format, *Streets* was the scorcher of 1979.

Rapidly taking note of some other 'For the Record' contributions: *Every Person Is Guilty* (1979), by Roy MacGregor and Ralph Thomas, has the Department of Defence covering up a brutal assault by a British SAS man, imported to train Canadian servicemen in counter-insurgency techniques for use in Quebec; MacGregor's *Tyler* (1978) shows a young farmer scrabbling to raise $30,000 in an unsuccessful bid to buy his father's farm, while his *Ready for Slaughter* (1982) dramatizes the desperation of a cattle farmer caught in a credit squeeze; Rob Forsyth's *The Winnings of Frankie Walls* (1980) depicts the tumble down the ladder of unemployability of a laid-off machinist, and his battle to hang onto the bottom rung; in *A Question of the Sixth* (1980) Grahame Woods passionately endorses the decision of a fifty-year-old cancer victim to choose the day of his death, with the loving collaboration of his newly wedded second wife and against the moral outrage of his self-righteous family; *Running Man* (1981) by Anna Sandor explores the struggle of a secretly gay high school teacher – and husband and father – to confront the crisis of discovery; and perhaps the most controversial of all 'FTR' shows, *The Tar Sands* (1977), scripted by Peter Pearson, Peter Rowe, and Ralph Thomas, ran into a lawsuit for its instant-history depiction of a Peter Lougheed, under intense pressure from an international oil consortium, selling out the store rather than risking the collapse of his mega-projects.

Not all CBC drama specials are in the documentary-realist mode, of course, and there may be a trend, visible of late in the showcase work of Anna Sandor and Jeannine Locke, towards a more romantically fictive style of drama. Sandor's *A Population of One* (1980) traces the course of true love between Willy Doyle, a neophyte (female) Prof. of Eng. Lit., and crusty old Archie, the cantankerous, embattled, sixty-year-old chairman of the department. Taking Willy on as a student of bread-baking, Archie actually proposes marriage over the rising dough, and is accepted, but dies of a heart attack while visiting his sister in Florida. Willy smiles bravely over a new loaf as the credits roll. And even Sandor's much-touted TV feature *Charlie Grant's War* (1984), the true story of a Canadian's heroic effort to rescue Jews from Nazi Europe, and his spell in a concentration camp, has an ineffably dramatized air about it. *All the Days of My Life* (1982) by Jeannine Locke, another 'ninety,' introduces the genteel Christena to the Fairhaven Old People's Home, where she adjusts painfully to the abrasions of communal life. By the conclusion, however, she has come to appreciate working-class Vera, to feel a fondness for 'the Newfie,' to enjoy Grannie Nielsen's 100th birthday celebrations, and to care deeply for Hugh, who reads the Twenty-third Psalm

(King James Version) so movingly at the Newfie's funeral as to bring a tear to every viewer's eye.

Locke's spirited period piece from the early 1920s, *Chautauqua Girl* (1983) combines a campaign for election by a United Farmers of Alberta candidate, Neil, with the tireless promotion by Sally, the Girl of the title, of a touring culture-circus, and steers its way through two hours of sunshine to a romance-of-the-couple ending. And even *The Other Kingdom* (1985), depicting the impact of breast cancer on the career, family, and personal life of a forty-year-old woman, aspires to the meretricious pseudo-reality of TV commercials and conducts its heroine, Amy, to an inspirational conclusion. In so doing it compares unfavourably with a 1974 'Anthology' drama by Nika Rylski, *The Last of the Four-Letter Words*, in which a vulgar, gutsy, scared, self-pitying 'Hardy' struggles with the horror and fear of, in her case, a fatal cancer, in company with a husband largely paralyzed by his own fear and revulsion. Likewise, the overtly heartwarming project of *All the Days of My Life*, while not contemptible, looks shallow and glossy beside the more difficult insights of Charles Israel's *To Season with Time*. And a further comparison, with Marian Waldman's radio play *Twenty Years of Twilight*, points to an integral difference between the two media. Television drama in Canada spotlights the conditions of life of a wide variety of occupational, regional, and class settings, and it has a power actively to *disturb* the liberal optimist assumption that everything is more or less for the best in this best of all possible societies. But, in picturing recognizable people in recognizable places, television continues to confirm the commonality of human experience, behaviour, motivation. Neither the sponsored, mass audience format of its programming, nor the intrinsic properties of the medium itself, dispose television to *disorient* in the way that radio can. The very continuity of the TV image, a picture in the corner of the room – compared to the dislocations and silences of radio – confirms that *le monde visible existe*. On radio anything can happen, and sometimes does. Neither the conventions of human behaviour, nor even the continuities of time, space, and personal individuality can be depended upon.

One more dramatist, one more play: Timothy Findley's achievements as a novelist overshadow a contribution to television that includes *The Paper People* (1967), episodes of *The Whiteoaks of Jalna* (1972) and *The Newcomers* (1976), and an outstandingly complex and searching play about the treatment of emotional disturbance, *Other People's Children* (1980). A beautifully written script, in both its dialogue and its directions, it examines the crisis of professional competence of a zealous Children's Aid worker, Janis Anderson, determined to 'rescue' a wayward girl from her alcoholic, abusive – but loved – father. In tandem with this story the play views the unsuccessful attempts of Janis's mentor, Dr Pengelli, to invade the 'impenetrable aloneness' of an autistic boy under her care, whose decision to die she has to acknowledge. Going beyond television's conventional dilemma – will they be able to save their patients? – *Other People's Children* challenges the professional faith that justifies an imposed 'salvation.'

As with the discussion of radio, this survey must conclude by naming some distinguished examples of feature documentary work, by the CBC and NFB, separately or in conjunction: *Next Year in Jerusalem* (1974) and *Homage to Chagall* (1977) by Harry Rasky; *Minimata* (1975) by Warner Troyer; *Volcano* (1976) and *The Most Dangerous Spy* (1981) by Donald Brittain; *Just Another Missing Kid* (1981) by John Zaritsky; *War* (1983) by Gwynne Dyer; and *A Planet for the Taking* (1985) by David Suzuki, William Whitehead, and others. Finally a special acknowledgment should be made of Pierre Berton's drama-documentary-epic *The National Dream* (1973), surely the prime example of Canadian historical recreation for the mass audience, telling and showing the story of the Canadian Pacific Railway.

4

Compared to radio and television, the Canadian cinema can present relatively few claims to literary distinction. Since the late 1960s, when the creation of the CFDC made possible a surge in feature production, the film industry has been plagued by the apparent irreconcilability of authentically Canadian scripts, on the one hand, and commercial viability (ie, US distribution) on the other. For the first few years a number of Canadian films displayed a quixotic refusal to recognize commercial imperatives. The conditions for financial participation by the CFDC initially encouraged the production of idiosyncratic, personally authored films, inexpensively made, with a palpably indigenous style and subject. While a very few of these films, most notably *Goin' Down the Road* (1970), actually won critical and popular acclaim, most were swamped by the Hollywood competition, star-emblazoned, technically lavish, and distributed by an American-controlled system that never gave the Canadian suckers an even break (*pace* W.C. Fields). But there was also an intrinsic quality of Canadian films that contributed to their lack of appeal, a kind of self-defeating bleakness of outlook matching the austerity of their means. The best films of that period, the most honestly imagined, were also the most disheartening in their depiction of frustration and defeat. Few of them even recovered their costs. And since the mid-1970s a reorientation of CFDC policy in favour of big-name, big-budget, internationally co-produced, commercial movies has all but eliminated the authentically Canadian screenplay.

As befitted the offspring of the CBC and National Film Board, English Canadian film-makers recurrently favoured the 'documentary-realist' style, with a penchant for the unscripted and improvised. Among the first feature films of any merit, *The Drylanders* (1963), written by M. Charles Cohen, and *Nobody Waved Goodbye* (1964), written and directed by Don Owen, were both in their way dramatized documentaries. The style became definitive with William Fruet's script for Don Shebib's *Goin' Down the Road*. Growing out of a projected documentary to be called *Maritimers*, the script follows the misfortunes of Pete and Joey, who arrive in Toronto from Nova Scotia with high hopes and no marketable qualifications. With its rough humour and beery pathos, this extremely low-budget film has become a Canadian classic. In addition to another Shebib movie, *Rip Off* (1971), about four teenagers ludicrously failing to start a commune, and *Slipstream* (1973), featuring an unpleasant Alberta disc jockey, Fruet wrote, and also directed, the dismayingly bleak *Wedding in White* (1972), in which a dim-witted pregnant teenager is married off to the drinking crony of her bullying, loutish father.

Three screenplays featuring aging small-town roisterers: in *Rowdyman* (1972) Gordon Pinsent wrote for himself the role of an archetypal Newfie ne'er-do-well whose madcap antics cost him the life of a friend and the love of a good woman. Several thousand miles to the west, in Delisle, Saskatchewan, the antics of *Paperback Hero*'s protagonist cost him the love of two good women and his own life into the bargain. In the 1973 screenplay by Les Rose and Barry Pearson – authors of the fine, western-situated 'Anthology' shows *Rodeo Rider* (1971) and *Macleish's Wild Horses* (1971) – the fading star of the local hockey team swaggers his way into increasing isolation in a fantasy projection of himself as Matt Dillon of *Gunsmoke*. And finally in *The Hard Part Begins* (1974) a country-and-western singer, passing his prime, begins to feel the chilly winds of failure in the emptying bars of small Ontario towns. The gritty, deglamourizing script was written by John Hunter, who subsequently wrote a number of 'Sidestreet' episodes and, more recently, the distinguished 1983 movie *The Grey Fox*, about an old, gentle, but still practising train robber (circa 1900) for whom the hard part has already begun in earnest.

Still in the documentary-realist tradition, and working within the NFB, Robin Spry has written and directed several works with a strong vein of political concern. *Prologue* (1969) dramatizes the choice between the espousal and rejection of political commitment by taking a young man to the streets of Chicago in August 1968, while his girlfriend attaches herself to a rural commune. In 1973 Spry produced *Action* and *Reaction*, documentaries on the October Crisis of 1970 and its impact on the rest of the country. And his 1977 feature film *One Man* presents the struggle against vested interests of a crusading journalist who attempts to document a pollution scandal.

In marked contrast to the preceding works, three films written and directed

by Paul Almond, who launched into cinema after a distinguished career in
CBC drama, lean increasingly towards a kind of romantic idealism founded
on a mythicizing projection of his wife at the time, actress Geneviève Bujold.
In *Isabel* (1968) she is a troubled soul returning to her village in the Gaspé
to confront the perturbed spirits, living and dead, of her family. The scenario,
which Almond himself described as 'Gothic,' takes Isabel into scenes of
nightmare and hallucination from which she is rescued by a handsome stranger.
In *Act of the Heart* (1970) she is an ecstatic Christian who falls in love with
a priest and eventually makes for him the ultimate sacrifice of self-immolation.
And in the unabashedly surreal *Journey* (1972) she undergoes spiritual regeneration by removal to a commune dedicated to a primal relation to Nature
and existing on the ambiguous edge of some other dimension of Time.
Attempting a daring dramatization of psychic processes, Almond's conception
and writing here lurch close to pretentious bathos.

Several of the most successful Canadian films, as well as one or two of
the most disastrous (eg, *Surfacing*) have been adaptations of novels and short
stories. *The Apprenticeship of Duddy Kravitz* (1973), for which Mordecai
Richler shares the screenwriting credit with Lionel Chetwynd, takes advantage
of the largely dramatic quality of the original to reproduce very faithfully its
comic ethos, though arguably softening the image of Duddy himself. The
adaptation of Richler has continued with his 1985 screenplay of *Joshua Then
and Now*, while Chetwynd went on to write a creditable adaptation of Herbert
Harker's novel *Goldenrod* (1976), and to write and direct a version of Hugh
MacLennan's *Two Solitudes* (1978) which dramatizes only the first half of
the book. Patricia Watson came by way of sensitive adaptations of Margaret
Laurence's *A Bird in the House* (1973) and Alice Munro's *Baptizing* (1975)
to a feature-length version of W.O. Mitchell's *Who Has Seen the Wind*
(1977), directed by Allan King. An attractive tale of young Brian growing
up in a prairie town, the screenplay succeeds only faintly, however, in conveying the Wordsworthian-mystical apprehensions of the original.

Two more adaptations to conclude, both undertaken by the original novelists, and both issuing in films of considerable distinction: Ted Allan's screen
version of *Lies My Father Told Me* (1975) dramatizes vividly the love across
the generations between a young Montreal-Jewish boy and his exuberant,
horse-drawn, scrap-metal-dealing *zeyda*. A frankly sentimentalizing backward
look, directed by Jan Kadar, the film calls for comparison with *Duddy Kravitz*
and with the acknowledged masterpiece of Quebec cinema, Claude Jutra's
Mon Oncle Antoine (1970), screenplay by Clément Perron. And last, Timothy
Findley's adaptation of *The Wars* (1983), directed by Robin Phillips, while
it inevitably surrenders much of the narrative subtlety of the novel and omits
whole episodes which readers might regard as essential, captures most movingly the infernal pilgrimage of its protagonist. Especially effective are the

scenes away from the front, in the emotionally withheld Ross family in Toronto, and in the company of Barbara D'Orsey in England. The film succeeds also in supplying, with visual and aural images of a hallucinatory potency, something of the haunting poetry of Findley's writing.

8 Theatre and Drama

BRIAN PARKER and CYNTHIA ZIMMERMAN

By 1972 the revitalizing of Canadian theatre, urged two decades before by the 1951 *Report of the Royal Commission on National Development in the Arts*, had already achieved spectacular results.[1] The Stratford and Shaw festivals were thriving; the country had a network of regional theatres and a National Arts Centre in Ottawa; vigorous alternative theatres had begun to establish themselves; and 'In both the 1971–2 and 1972–3 seasons in Canada, more than 200 new Canadian plays received full-scale production.'[2] It was an exciting beginning to a period that was to experience some startling fluctuations as the theatre reacted to economic boom and recession.

Levels of Theatre

The period saw the establishment of six distinct levels of professional theatre, four of which were already in place by the mid-1970s, with the other two only coming fully into their own in the 1980s.[3] The oldest was *commercial theatre*, the road- and transfer-houses, dinner- and cabaret-theatres which run independently of subsidy and exist quite simply for a profit. Work in such theatres helped Canadian professionals earn a living, but otherwise made little contribution to the Canadianism of theatre and for the purposes of this study can largely be ignored.

Similarly, two of the *national theatres*, the Shakespeare and Shaw festivals, were of their very nature designed to showcase Canadian acting and production skills but not Canadian drama – though the former's Third Stage showed an intermittent interest in producing Canadian plays, especially while Urjo Kareda was the theatre's literary manager (1976–80). On the other hand, the mandate for the National Arts Centre was to serve as a showcase for the best Canadian theatre and drama across the country and to tour productions of its own; its failure to do so became a cause for bitter complaint later in the decade.

The third level, a network of *regional theatres* stretching right across the country, had been one of the most notable achievements of the late 1960s and early 1970s. These regionals were heavily dependent on subsidy and non-commercial in approach. They were designed to service specific communities, a responsibility which could include the touring of shows within their region, establishing theatre training, and creating special productions to visit schools; and their repertories were deliberately eclectic, balancing a classic with one or two West End or Broadway successes, at least one comedy, and perhaps the remounting of a proven Canadian play. At first a few of them also premiered Canadian plays, but in the period under review, with the exception of Montreal's Centaur, Regina's Globe, and Theatre Calgary from the late 1970s on, the regionals rarely attempted an original Canadian work.[4] Thus provoked, the two playwrights' conferences of 1971 and 1972 demanded that publicly subsidized theatres be compelled to produce a quota of indigenous drama. Though this never became public policy, the Canada Council let it be known that it would favour theatres which supported Canadian plays, which encouraged a number of the regionals to establish experimental second stages – Vancouver Playhouse's Waterfront Theatre, for example, the Citadel's Rice Theatre, or Manitoba Theatre Centre's Warehouse. These could program new Canadian work without much risk, but only recently have original scripts begun to reappear on regional main stages.

The development of Canadian drama was left almost entirely to a fourth level of production, the *alternate theatres*, which began to spring up in Toronto in the early 1970s and now exist from coast to coast. Excluded from the established theatres, and wishing not only to experiment with content and technique but also to produce their own work, the alternates worked on shoestring budgets and performed at first in deliberately non-theatrical venues. Initially, they tended to imitate the experiments of Off-Off-Broadway and the European avant-garde, but by 1972 'alternate theatre in Canada came [mainly] to be associated with the production of work – either collectively created or fully scripted – by Canadian authors.'[5] It was this level of theatre that underwent the greatest change between 1972 and 1984. Near bankruptcy to begin with, by the end of the period many were to find themselves coping with the benefits and burdens of success – with hit productions that were also toured and televised, costly buildings under mortgage, set seasons and subscription series, and an ever-increasing dependency on government support. In effect, the alternates had themselves become established; their urge to risk experiment faltered, and a new conservatism in programming threatened to make them nearly indistinguishable from the regionals. They, too, began to set up second stages to accommodate experiment, but their avant-garde status had already been pre-empted by yet another level of theatre, the *fringe*.

Most of the companies one would call fringe, with the exception of a few like the Playwrights' Workshop in Montreal and John Juliani's Savage God troupe, are products of the 1980s, standing in the same relation to that decade as the alternates did to the 1970s. Like the latter, they are poor, with too few productions to warrant subsidy; they have to improvise, borrow, or rent makeshift production space; many of them are committed to some kind of social protest – feminist, gay, ethnic, or Marxist; they alter their alliances and exchange personnel with a volatility that makes it difficult to keep track of them; and though their efforts are often undermined by inadequate rehearsal and low production standards, they are now the main seedbeds for new talent.

This is also true of a sixth level of production, *theatre for young audiences*, which Dennis Foon has called 'our distinctively invisible genre'[6] because, by being designed specifically for children and usually performed in school gymnasia, it is consistently overlooked. Only the Young People's theatre in Toronto has its own space and can provide large in-town shows as well as tours. Most TYA companies exist either as branches of the regional theatres (Theatre Calgary's Stage-Coach Players, for example, or Citadel-on-Wheels/ Wings), or more often, like Green Thumb and Kaleidoscope of British Columbia or the Mermaid Theatre of Nova Scotia, are independent companies which rely mainly on the schools for income. All of these companies have moved away from the old style of light entertainment for children: some mine veins of poetry and fantasy, others are committed to social relevance. In the last decade TYA has seen a 100 per cent growth; it now has the largest audience number in the country, the highest number of employees, and is producing the largest number of original scripts – despite which it remains undervalued and underfinanced.[7]

To these six kinds of theatre may perhaps be added summer and festival theatre, though this rather mixed grouping overlaps the other categories. In 1983 there were a dozen summer theatres in Ontario alone, not counting the Shaw and Shakespeare festivals, which also started in that format. Typically, summer theatres present three or four shows during a nine-week season; and though their repertories are usually limited to commercial favourites, they have increasingly found it worthwhile to include Canadian plays. Of particular note in this regard are the Charlottetown Festival in Prince Edward Island; the lamented Festival Lennoxville (1972–82), which pioneered revivals of Canadian plays in an attempt to establish a national repertoire; the Blyth Festival in Ontario, which concentrates on original works with local appeal, and the Port Stanley Festival, which stages only new Canadian plays; and, in a slightly different category, the annual DuMaurier Festival of one-act plays organized by the New Play Centre in Vancouver, which has given many current playwrights their first chance of production. Several festivals which are not themselves producers bring together other theatre groups, such as the International Theatre Festival for Young People which began in Vancouver in 1978 and now visits other major Canadian cities each May, and Edmonton's successful Fringe Theatre festival. To enrich the mixture still further there are also once-only festivals, such as the National Mime Festival (Toronto, 1978), or Toronto's 'Onstage 81,' a successful international gathering that gave impetus to local theatre interests.

Although there was no lack of varied professional theatre between 1972 and 1984, the relation of this activity to the production of original scripts is less encouraging. It seems obvious that playwrights, especially at the start of their careers, will write best when they can have a particular theatre in mind – as Rex Deverell composes specifically to be played in-the-round at Regina's Globe Theatre, or David French writes for the Tarragon audience – and this will be distinctly true when plays are directed at particular interest groups (feminist, gay, black theatre, theatre for young people) which are associated with specific venues. Of the six main levels of professional theatre, however, only the alternates, fringe, and TYA have consistently committed themselves to Canadian writers. Hits in the smaller theatres are rarely remounted by the larger ones, and this limiting of production possibilities has naturally affected the kind of plays that can be written: 'people wrote very limited, small plays, because they knew it was unrealistic to attempt anything else.'[8] Even this narrow market was put at risk when the national economy went into recession.

Boom and Recession

Though the Canada Council warned its clients as early as 1970 that a period of austerity was imminent, in 1972 box office boomed and was supplemented by lavish subsidy. Several of the big cities provided theatre grants, as did many, though not all, of the provinces; the federal government supported the national and regional theatres generously through the Canada Council, and primed the alternates with its Local Initiative Program and Opportunities for Youth grants. In addition, the private sector subsidized particular companies and productions and kept theatre before the public eye with such competitive annual awards as the DuMaurier trophy for the best short play in BC, a similar Clifford E. Lee Prize for Alberta, and the Chalmers Award for the best new Canadian play produced in Toronto (recently supplemented by a parallel award for the best play printed). The result of such bounty was that nearly every theatre overextended itself in the early 1970s, mounting increasingly ambitious seasons and taking out mortgages to expand and renovate its theatre plant.

When the economy slumped in the middle 1970s, the OFY and LIP grants were among the first to be eliminated, so that even by 1976 the number of plays eligible for the Chalmers Award had dropped by almost 50 per cent. Canada Council funds were frozen, with no regard for spiralling inflation or the larger number of applicants: 'from 1971 to 1980, federal grants to large theatre companies (budget over $400,000) declined from $1,964,000 to $1,428,000 in constant 1971 dollars – while the number of companies sharing those grants increased from 8 to 13.'[9] In 1984, after nine years of under-funding, the Council's budget was cut by 3.5 million dollars. For a time Ontario's Wintario Lottery and Alberta's Heritage Fund were able to take up some of the slack in those provinces, but they quickly reached their limit; the private sector, which the theatres began desperately to woo, did not substantially raise its support.[10]

One good consequence of this abrupt austerity was a boost in the number of co-productions and the touring of Canadian plays, but its bad effects were striking. Many companies folded: Edmonton's Theatre 3; Vancouver's West Coast Actors; Quebec's Festival Lennoxville; Ottawa's Penguin Theatre; and in Toronto, Open Circle, Phoenix, Theatre Compact, Theatre Second Floor, and New Theatre – to name just a few. Others retrenched and managed to continue in increasingly precarious circumstances. A *Canadian Theatre Review* survey of sixty theatres in 1978 indicates that they were releasing staff, cutting back on workshops and studio productions, shortening their season, and keeping to safer and smaller-cast plays. High morale gave way to internal dissent: a leadership crisis regarding the Board's repeated choice of non-Canadian artistic directors almost wrecked the Stratford Festival;[11] and there was bitter controversy about whether the Canada Council should give so much support to costly, established institutions or share its funds more equit-ably at every level of theatre. Finally, a federal investigation into the arts was launched in 1981 under the joint chairmanship of Louis Applebaum and Jacques Hébert, but its report in 1982 pleased no one. It gave scant attention to the achievements of the existing theatre network and 'The most disturbing aspect of the report [was] its tendency to respect the profit motive and its resultant lurching towards the more commercial aspects of the cultural industries.'[12]

Coast to Coast

The Atlantic Provinces are dominated by three regional companies, all sub-sidized and well established: the Neptune in Halifax, Theatre New Brunswick in Fredericton, and PEI's Charlottetown Festival. Neptune and TNB offer the usual regional fare, Charlottetown concentrates on original musicals (produc-ing thirty-eight in all, though only *Anne of Green Gables*, 1965, has proved a lasting success). Because of climate, most production takes place in summer but, as part of the theatres' mandate, shows are toured regularly to smaller communities, where it is always the locally based plays and performers that prove the most popular.

This preference for the home product is even more marked in Newfoundland, where Theatre Newfoundland and Labrador (1979) and the Stephenville Festival (1979) are limited to small summer operations. The most vital theatre in Newfoundland arises from an indigenous tradition of song and dance that lends itself easily to the collective creation process favoured by alternates; this has been developed by three companies in particular – the Mummers Troupe (1972–82), which mixed entertainment with populist social commentary; Codco (1973–6, re-emerging periodically), with their collaborative satiric-skit style of Newfie humour; and Rising Tide (1978), a splinter group from the Mummers which is currently the resident company at the St John's Arts and Culture Centre. Their collective shows have proved popular elsewhere in Canada, too, though in 1980 both Rising Tide and the Mummers decided to devote 50 per cent of their season to scripted works.

The other most lively Atlantic province is Nova Scotia, where Neptune's regional mandate is offset by three main alternatives: the Mulgrave Road Co-op (1977), a small touring company which performs both scripted and improvisational, collective creations; Seaweed Theatre (1975–?), which produces new Canadian plays; and the Mermaid Theatre (1972) of Wolfville, which specializes in native folklore and puppetry and is one of the most enterprising of Canada's theatres for young people. There have been other challenges to Neptune's mainstage dominance in the past (for example, Pier One Theatre and Neptune's own Second Stage Company, both of which did experimental work and early performances of Canadian plays, before they closed in 1976) and new companies are continually forming.[13]

There are particular difficulties for the anglophone theatre in Quebec, not the least of which is the fact that the community went through a decade of political disquiet. The Lennoxville experiment failed, mainly for lack of audiences. In Montreal, where the anglophone community is concentrated, two theatres slightly offset the Centaur's monopoly: Theatre Encore had a very brief tenure at the Saidye Bronfman Centre, and the Playwrights' Workshop has continued to develop new scripts and translations. Fortunately, the Centaur itself has proved an unusual regional theatre in its support of Canadian playwriting, its commissioning of original plays (David Fennario was writer-in-residence from 1973 to 1984), and its impressive record of shows toured to other Canadian cities.[14]

Theatres in Ontario can be divided into those located inside Toronto and those outside. In the nation's capital, the resident English-language theatre company of the National Arts Centre was disbanded in 1984. During John Wood's tenure as Artistic Director (1978–84) it had staged over forty Canadian plays; now, in line with the 'Applebert' Committee recommendation, the NAC will produce in-house plays only on an ad hoc basis and rely mainly on co-productions and on showcasing works from other companies across the country. Two out of the three Ottawa alternate theatres, Penguin Theatre

Company (1979–82) and Theatre 2000 (1978–83), both of which were founded to workshop and produce Canadian scripts, went bankrupt. Only the Great Canadian Theatre Company (1975), which focuses on Canadian material with a socialist bias, remains – and it, too, is experiencing financial difficulties. In Thunder Bay, Magnus Theatre (1971) presents a mixture of national and international work, while Kam Theatre Lab (1973) has committed itself to the support of local artists. Sudbury Theatre Centre and the Grand Theatre in London both restrict themselves to the tried and true, whereas the Blyth and Port Stanley summer festivals actively foster Canadian writing.

Most would agree that Toronto is the centre of professional English-language theatre in Canada and that this became true with the birth of the alternate movement. Commercial theatres there have also prospered, but what happens at the Royal Alex, the O'Keefe, the Bayview Playhouse, or Toronto Truck Theatre has little to do with the creative heart of things. The city's regional theatre, the St Lawrence Centre, is home to two theatre companies (Toronto Arts Productions, now CentreStage, and Theatre Plus) which have produced mostly modern mainstream material. Both companies have been criticized for costly shows and a failure to support Canadian drama. Alternate theatre companies have come and gone during the decade, but the five initiators of the movement have not only survived fiscal restraint but have positively flourished: Toronto Workshop Productions (1958), Factory Theatre Lab (1970), Theatre Passe Muraille (1971), Tarragon (1971), and Toronto Free Theatre (1972). United in their commitment to 'the development of new theatrical experiences, particularly in terms of new Canadian plays, which the regional theatre system had markedly discouraged,'[15] initially each had a special orientation to the alternate aesthetic: Toronto Workshop's group theatre with a political bias, Factory's focus on the early development of new work, Passe Muraille's democratic collective creations, Tarragon's nurturing of particular playwrights, and Toronto Free's hope for an ensemble acting company. Over the decade, as well as dealing with the recession, four out of the five managed to renovate their theatre spaces, and in the early 1980s they had a new influx of life with a change of artistic directors. It has become increasingly hard to tell one company's season from the next, but their commitment to Canadian material remains constant and is rarely lower than 50 per cent of the offerings. Also there is continuation, though not with the same emphasis, of workshopping, staged readings, and a series of backspace performances in the search for new voices.[16]

Toronto is also the nucleus of fringe theatre activity. The most important in Toronto is the Theatre Centre (1979), which began as an umbrella organization providing a venue for five experimental companies: AKA Performance Interfaces, Autumn Leaf, Buddies in Bad Times, Necessary Angel, and Nightwood Theatre. As a company became more established, it would move on, leaving space for others with nowhere else to go. Nine companies used the Centre in the first half of 1983 alone, a year in which approximately fifty professional companies altogether were performing in the city, including Black Theatre Canada (est. 1973).

On the prairies the four regional theatres dominate their respective cities.[17] Manitoba Theatre Centre in Winnipeg was the first of the modern community centres and, needing to offer something for everyone, its productions have been varied, traditional, and short on experimentation. In contrast, Regina's Globe mounts many new Canadian plays, has had a playwright-in-residence since 1972, and has been constant in its preference for plays with sociopolitical themes. The magnificent Citadel complex in Edmonton, now with five theatre spaces, unabashedly searches for potential Broadway hits and continues to stage the safe and stately. Once Rick McNair became artistic director, Theatre Calgary became identified with the plays of a number of Western playwrights including W.O. Mitchell, John Murrell, and Sharon Pollock. Between 1972 and 1983 Theatre Calgary commissioned ten new works.

Important smaller companies in Winnipeg, Saskatoon, Calgary, and Edmonton offer an alternative to the regional houses. In Winnipeg the Prairie Theatre Exchange (1973, formerly Manitoba Theatre Workshop) produces and tours Canadian scripts for adult and young audiences. Saskatoon, the second largest city in Saskatchewan, has two of the province's three professional companies (Regina has the Globe). Persephone (1974), the more traditional of the two, offers mainly contemporary, popular seasons; 25th Street Theatre (1972) remains committed to original prairie plays and collective creations. Both theatres have had a troubled history but so far have survived. In Calgary the popular Lunchbox Theatre (1975), performing one-acts from a wide repertoire, moved into larger quarters in 1979, and Alberta Theatre Projects (1972), with its emphasis on Canadian material, is to double its audience capacity with a 1985 move into the Calgary Centre for the Performing Arts. Edmonton has five professional 'alternate to the Citadel' companies. All are small, homeless, and struggling. Northern Light (1975), Catalyst (1977), Phoenix (1981; formerly Theatre 3), Theatre Network (1975), and Workshop West (1978) – the last two especially undertaking to develop and stage indigenous work – fit neatly into the national alternate perspective. August 1984 marked the third Edmonton Fringe Theatre Festival, which each year has doubled its attendance record and the number of its shows.

British Columbia's two regional theatres, Vancouver Playhouse and the Bastion in Victoria, perform mainly middle-of-the-road plays. Both are coping with deficits, and the Playhouse, particularly, has still not managed to regain the centrality it enjoyed in the early 1970s. Victoria's smaller Belfrey (1976) has a mandate to mount contemporary and new Canadian plays. In Vancouver, the province's theatre centre, the Arts Club (1963) dominates. Now successfully running three venues, it seems immune to the recession hitting everyone else. Moreover, begun as a commercial venture and currently on little subsidy, it is as likely to offer challenging plays as anyone and has introduced writers such as Tremblay, Fennario, Mitchell, and Salutin to Vancouver audiences. Tamahnous (1971), while no longer doing only collective original work, remains the oldest and best established of the alternates. The collective Westcoast Actors (1974) folded in 1982. Touchstone (1975) and the fringe companies, Headlines (1981) and Crossroads (1981), produce infrequently. The New Play Centre is still a unique institution. Since 1972 it has not only advised playwrights, but also does readings, workshops, some staging of new scripts by local authors, and annually mounts the DuMaurier Festival of original one-acts. Other notable companies in the province include the rurally based Western Canadian Theatre Company (1972) in Kamloops, West Kootenay's Theatre Energy (1976), and Nanaimo's Shakespeare Plus (1984). But the economy in BC is now exceptionally uncertain, and, there as elsewhere, any discussion of theatre inevitably comes back to money.

By the end of 1984, Canada had a varied and complex theatre network: roadhouses, regionals, alternates, an emerging fringe, and a booming theatre for young audiences. But the developmental-growth pattern traced for theatre in the first three volumes of this *Literary History* can no longer be applied so straightforwardly, for this period saw as many losses as gains. An increasing commercialism accompanied success; establishment status, together with funding cutbacks, encouraged a reliance on proven hits and safe selections as a strategy for survival; and as its commitment to new writing dwindled, concern grew that the once vital theatre was losing momentum.

Yet there was also a growing public recognition of Canadian talent during the period – to be seen in the proliferation of awards, the increase in media coverage, and the impact of sheer statistics. In 1976 Statistics Canada listed some 45 professional Canadian theatres; by 1982 that number had swelled to 133. Moreover, in the mid-1980s there were other encouraging signs of change, as some of the main alternate theatres were revitalized by new leadership and key figures from the previous alternate generation started to make their way to artistic directorships in the regional houses, taking their commitment to Canadian drama with them.[18] Nonetheless, if theatre is thriving it is doing so in spite of inflation and crippling cutbacks in subsidy. Perhaps the question at the moment is less how to move ahead than how to stop going backward. As John Palmer's Ibsen puts it: 'We have embarked on nothing less than a fight for our own culture. I can think of nothing sadder than inaction now ... We will produce well and badly but we must produce ...'[19] [CDZ]

DRAMA, 1972–84

More plays were written during this dozen years than in the whole of Canada's previous history. They take many different forms, and in different parts of the country drama still possesses distinct characteristics. Four main headings therefore structure this discussion: 'Social Focus,' 'Historical and Political Concerns,' 'Regional Influences,' and 'Dramaturgical Trends.' Unless otherwise stated, dates given in brackets indicate first Canadian productions.[20]

Social Focus

Between 1972 and 1984 theatre expanded to include aspects of Canadian experience neglected or ignored in previous periods, one of the most noticeable being theatre for young audiences. Much of this was unscripted clowning, mime and puppetry, but the texts of scores of children's plays reached print and many more were unpublished. Certain playwrights – such as Henry Beissel, Paddy Campbell, Dennis Foon, Isabelle Foord, and the partnership of Dodi Robb and Pat Patterson – specialized in this form, and several important writers of adult drama, such as Carol Bolt, Rex Deverell, Eric Nicol, Sharon Pollock, Gwen Ringwood, Betty Jane Wylie, and particularly James Reaney, also wrote for children. In the first half of the period many of these plays were influenced by Brian Way's theory of physical involvement of the audience, but by the late 1970s that element was diminishing and playwrights like Foon were starting to open up areas of social, political, and psychological comment that had earlier been thought too serious for non-adults.

Children's drama is difficult to evaluate because it addresses so specialized a group and there is no agreed-on criterion except audience response, which can vary enormously from performance to performance. A few texts are as interesting for adults as for the young, however, an exceptionally good example being the controversial *Dreaming and Duelling* (1980) by John and Joa Lazarus, which builds around a series of theatrically exciting fencing bouts a perceptive story of teenage idealism, fantasy, sexual tension, and the rival loyalties of love and friendship. It concerns two high school épée stars whose shared fantasy of being eighteenth-century swordsmen is shattered by their common lust and protectiveness for a girl who is painfully self-conscious about a birthmark that covers half her face. Besides exciting action and credible high school dialogue, the play conveys the agony of idealism and loss in adolescence, with all its intransigent refusal to compromise feeling; and its sympathy for the truths of dreaming recalls James Reaney's belief that drama should recover for adults the imaginative trust in 'play' they lost when they left childhood. By the end of the period this gap between adult theatre and theatre for young audiences was being bridged from both directions.

Another notable new aspect of drama was the emergence of a strong feminist voice.[21] A strikingly large proportion of Canada's ranking dramatists now are women: Mary Humphrey Baldridge, Carol Bolt, Anna Fuerstenberg, Joanna Glass, Linda Griffiths, Margaret Hollingsworth, Patricia Joudry, Betty Lambert, Sharon Pollock, Aviva Ravel, Erika Ritter, Beverley Simons, Judith Thompson, Betty Jane Wylie, to name only some of the most important. In addition, there have been several plays by men which successfully present events from a woman's point of view. George Ryga, who explored the desperation of an Indian girl in his most famous play, *The Ecstasy of Rita Joe* (1967), is also successful in *Sunrise on Sarah* (1972) in getting into the mind of a middle-class woman who is suffering mental breakdown because of ambivalent experiences with men; Paul Ledoux's *Rag Doll* (1976) is a horror story about a pregnant girl forced to bear her unwanted child; Larry Fineberg's *Eve* (1976) celebrates a grandmother who, tired of slaving for her family, leaves to take up residence in a ratty basement apartment and start a more equal friendship with the man in the flat above; in Hans Werner's bitter *Blessed Art Thou Among Women* (1978) the wife of a Nazi sympathizer is driven by him to suicide; and at least three of John Murrell's most successful plays explore specifically female experience: his *Waiting for the Parade* (1977), which tells the story of five Calgary women coping with loneliness, illness, war work, and family breakdown while their men are away during World War II, overlaps in content, though not in style, with Mavis Gallant's witty *What Is to Be Done?* (1983), about girls in wartime Montreal; *Memoir* (1977) features an aged Sarah Bernhardt re-enacting episodes from her life in order to get through a sleepless night; and *Farther West* (1982) is a sympathetic account of an actual Calgary prostitute of the 1880s who used profligacy as a means to personal freedom, escaping continually 'farther west' till she was murdered in Vancouver by an obsessed common law husband.

Of militantly feminist plays, three featured actual pioneers of the Women's Movement: Carol Bolt's *Red Emma* (1974) about Emma Goldman, the American anarchist; *What Glorious Times They Had* (1974) by Diane Grant (and company) about the Manitoba feminist Nellie McClung; and Wendy Hill's *The Fighting Days* (1983) about Francis Beynon, another Manitoba feminist. Equally militant in their various styles were Penny Kemp's ironically titled *Angel Makers* (1976), set in an abortion ward, Janis Rapoport's *Dream Girls* (1979), which takes place in a hostel for deserted and beaten wives, and *Jennie's Story* (1981) by Betty Lambert, which recounts the sterilization and seduction of a sixteen-year-old farm girl in Alberta on pretence of mental incompetence, under an act repealed only in 1971. More expressionistically, Elinore Simonovitch's *Big X and Little Y* (1974) presents the inequities a woman must face in birth, marriage, child-bed, child-rearing, employment, and politics through a lively agit-prop mixture of song, dance, games, and nursery rhymes; and three impressive collective creations on feminist topics were Nightwood Theatre's exploration of the history of witch persecutions, *Smoke Damage* (1984), *This Is for You, Anna* (1984) about a contemporary cause célèbre in Germany, and Mulgrave Road Co-op's *Another Story* (1981) about women's experience in Nova Scotia.

Women's drama was by no means always polemic, however; feminine experience also produced a great deal of comedy. Mary Humphrey Baldridge's *Bride of the Gorilla* (1974) satirizes marriage through the fantasies of a beleaguered housewife; and the situation of a middle-aged woman finally rebelling against domesticity is central to Aviva Ravel's *Second Choice* (1981), Anne Chislett's *The Tomorrow Box* (1980), and Charlotte Fielden's *One Crowded Hour* (1975). Erika Ritter's witty plays, on the other hand, dissect the difficulties of coping with the new sexual 'liberation' as a single, professional woman. Her first success, *The Splits* (1978), is about a twice-divorced scriptwriter whose attempt to cope with guilt about her marriages, her dependence on an unscrupulous ex-husband, and producers who want to turn her serious radio plays into sitcoms eventually sends her back to the psychiatrist. Sexual liberation is a topic for farce in Betty Lambert's offbeat *Sqrieux-de-Dieu* (1975) and Patricia Joudry's *A Very Modest Orgy* (1981). Warren Graves's *The Hand that Cradles the Rock* (1972) offers an equally comic male view.

Perhaps the most consistent writer of plays that probe female experience without militancy is Margaret Hollingsworth, who seems mainly interested in relationships between women. Her *Operators* (1974), for example, explores the need for non-manipulative friendship between women themselves, while *Ever Loving* (1980) sensitively traces the fortunes of three Canadian war brides as they struggle to adapt to very different circumstances after World War II. But the most striking woman's play of the period was Sharon Pollock's *Blood Relations* (1980), which examines the predicament of Lizzie Borden, acquitted of the murder of her father and stepmother in 1892 but condemned for it ever since in a popular children's rhyme. The play centres on the question 'Lizzie, did you?' with which it starts and finishes, and takes the form of a psychodrama ten years later in which Lizzie's role is played by her lover, an unnamed Boston actress, while Lizzie herself is displaced to the commentator role of Bridget, the maid. The re-enactment shows us an unconventional Lizzie stifled by her middle-class family and deprived by conniving step-relations of a farm to which she might have escaped, and we are left in little doubt that she killed in retaliation and as a final bid for freedom. But the psychodrama ends with the Actress as 'Lizzie' still poising the axe above the father's head, as the question is repeated, 'Lizzie, did you?' The Actress decides, 'Lizzie, you did,' but Lizzie herself replies, 'I didn't. *You* did'; and a final stage direction bids the Actress look first at the axe, then at the audience, associating both of them in guilty reconstruction. Thus, the cleverly oblique *relation* has involved the audience in *blood*.

Another play about female experience, Betty Jane Wylie's monologue *A Place on Earth* (1982), bridges to a third area that has become of increasing importance as the 1960s generation deals with aging parents: the isolation of the old. It depicts the life of an arthritic seventy-two-year-old widow in the firetrap of a Toronto roominghouse, with a squalid communal toilet, obnoxious children, and the threat of drunken intruders. She was mocked by the police when she tried to lay charges after sexual molestation, so now she fills her day with exercises, lingering over mementoes, deciding what to eat and what she can afford, telephoning her daughter in another city, and talking constantly to herself or via a glove puppet she once used as an infants' teacher. At the end, she tries to will the puppet to knife her, but suicide is against her fundamental beliefs. She must continue to endure. Alexis Bernier's *Centenarian Rhyme* (1982), Gwen Ringwood's *The Lodge* (1977), and Elinore Simonovitch's *There Are No Dragons* (1980) also consider the plucky independence of aging women, as do two plays by men – Fineberg's *Eve* and Christopher Heide's *I Ain't Dead Yet* (1985). And, of course, the same problem concerns old men: Fineberg's *Death* (1972) presents the suicide of a seventy-year-old, disillusioned with his selfish daughter and a world where life preys on itself and unable to accept the sympathy of a sixteen-year-old gardener. George Ryga's most successful recent play, *A Letter to My Son* (1981), recounts the memories of an old Ukrainian farmer as he tries to write a letter to his estranged son and at the same time cope with the unwelcome attentions of a friendly woman welfare worker – a similar situation to that explored in Frank Moher's *The Broken Globe* (1976). There are also plays about old couples: Gaëtan Charlebois's *Aléola* (1977), for instance, one of the few French-Canadian plays written in English, in which the isolated old folks finally drink poisoned wine; or Aviva Ravel's even more depressing *Dispossessed* (1977), where the problem is compounded by a retarded middle-aged son. Much more cheerful, though very subtle in its command of character nuance, is one of Gwen Ringwood's last plays, *The Garage Sale* (1981), a charming one-act in which an elderly man and wife worry about the reasons a young couple across the street may be selling their house, revealing in the process a great deal about their own relationship, their grown-up children, and their poignant desire still to be of use. Lazlo Barna's *Prisoners of Time* (1984) is a comic fantasy about what will happen when the hippie generation begins to enter nursing homes; this seems an area that is likely to be explored even more fully as the mean age of the population increases.

Such characters also fit in well with the long-established Canadian fascination with losers, survivors, and social outsiders, of which the period had its full quota. The way that society bullies the mentally unstable is the subject of David Freeman's *You're Gonna Be Alright, Jamie Boy* (1974), Ted Allan's *My Sister's Keeper* (1974), and W.O. Mitchell's *Back to Beulah* (1976), while Timothy Findley's *Can You See Me Yet?* (1976) suggests that life in an asylum was saner than the world that went to war in 1939; Judith Thompson's *Crackwalker* (1980) evokes the life of retarded alcoholics in downtown Kingston; and David French's *One Crack-Out* (1975) is set in the poolroom underworld of gamblers, petty crooks, prostitutes, and debt enforcers. Where the period went beyond its predecessors, however, was in the depths of degradation it was prepared to put on stage and the coarse naturalism of speech and action with which it represented them. Michael Hollingsworth's *Strawberry Fields* (1972) and *Clear Light* (1973) were pioneers here – the latter was closed by the police – but even more powerful were the plays that Tom Walmsley based on his personal experience of drugs, prostitution, sado-masochism, and crime: *The Working Man* (1975), *The Jones Boy* (1975), *The White Boys* (1982), and particularly *Something Red* (1980). Although several of these plays still have a satiric or reforming purpose, most seem more interested in recording the actual validity of such marginal experience, its independent truth; they no longer have much pull back to a Canadian 'norm.'

Another area opened up was the once forbidden theme of homosexuality, in plays by Robert Wallace, Louis Del Grande, Tom Hendry, Sky Gilbert, Paul Ledoux, Michael Hollingsworth, and especially the Quebec writer Michel Tremblay, whose influential works were translated into English and performed across the country. The subject of homosexuality was pioneered in John Herbert's prison play *Fortune and Men's Eyes* (1967), but the best known recent example is Tremblay's *Hosanna* (1974 in the translation by Bill Glassco and John Van Burek), in which an aging transvestite is tricked into impersonating Elizabeth Taylor's role as Cleopatra at a ball, then savagely mocked, but finds refuge with his biker lover when he sheds 'drag' to admit simply 'I'm a man.' Despite this sentimental ending, *Hosanna* conveys the complexity of gay experience successfully, and is remarkable for the tours de force required by the protagonist's long monologues before his mirror. Among the fewer plays specifically about lesbianism are *Blood Relations* and Margaret Hollingsworth's *Alli Alli Oh* (1977) and *Islands* (1978).

Family tensions and the war between the sexes continued to be staple topics, but again there was a slight shift in focus. Comparatively few plays concerned conflict between the generations. Though the motif appears in Michael Cook's *Jacob's Wake* (1975), Christopher Heide's *On the Lee Shore* (1977), Sharon Pollock's *Generations* (1980), and several of the plays of Michel Tremblay, the main interests here are regional; David French's *Of the Fields, Lately* (1973) continues the story of the Mercer family begun in

Leaving Home (1972), focusing again on the loving antagonism between father and son; and a similar situation, set in the Amish community of Ontario, is the subject of Anne Chislett's *Quiet in the Land* (1981) and, to a lesser extent, of her previous non-Amish play *The Tomorrow Box* (1980). More complex is Margaret Hollingsworth's *Mother Country* (1978), which on a naturalistic level presents an English-born mother's manipulation of her three Canadian daughters, but also has a dimension of what Hollingsworth herself has called 'magic realism' – that is, quasi-symbolic elements which suggest that the play may also be read as a metaphor for England's continuing influence in Canada. The location of the family house on one of the Gulf Islands near Vancouver suggests a peripheral commitment to Canada, as well as the isolation of any family unit; the house is shaped like a ship's cabin, moreover (à la *Heartbreak House*), but beds of chrysanthemums now separate it from the sea, each flower carefully protected by a plastic bag. The arrival of the estranged father's fiancée, an American girl younger than his daughters, acts as a catalyst to expose the mother's manipulations and enable the daughters finally to win free. As she leaves – by helicopter – the fiancée decapitates the chrysanthemums; but the mother's confident comment, 'As long as the roots are there, the blooms will be all the better next year,' suggests a more complex significance to her daughters' independence than mere repudiation. Whether serious or comic, most plays about the generational struggle were realistic in mode; but a splendid exception was Marc Diamond's *The Ziggy Effect* (1980), a black farce about the inability of hippie parents – Sylvia, an ex-commune groupie who works with 'spaced-out kids,' and Bill, a draft dodger now stocking his basement in expectation of Armageddon – to deal with their 'punk' son Ziggy and his friends, Moon, a New Wave science fiction freak in a perpetual drug haze, and Val, who is 'into performance art' – such as painting on air and throwing her cat out the window.

War-of-the-sexes also remained a central theme. There were good serious plays on the topic: Joe Wiesenfeld's *Spratt* (1978) is a vivid portrait of a destructive 'macho' loser; in his autobiographical play *Drift* (1980) Rex Deverell tries to understand why his West Indian mother allowed herself to marry and stay with a totally unsuitable husband; Alexis Bernier's *Court of Common Pleas* (1981) delicately maps out stages in the retrieval of a foundering marriage; and *Mark* (1972) by Betty Jane Wylie shows the strains imposed on a wife and daughter as the father of a family dies of cancer. On the whole, though, the theme was more notably handled as comedy of manners. Erika Ritter's plays are a good example, though in her most recent comedy, *The Passing Scene* (1982), the action seems contrived in comparison to its verbal wit. In this respect Sherman Snukal's *Talking Dirty* (1981) is its superior and is one of the best Canadian examples of that most difficult of genres, the classic farce. It depicts middle-aged restlessness among the sexually chic, a Vancouver professor newly separated from a long-time lover and his ex-school friend, a married Toronto lawyer footloose at a convention. Their competitive imbroglios with a variety of women produce a crackle of literate badinage and some hilariously improbable scenes – including a seduction during the composition of a paper on transformational grammar in *Paradise Lost* – but like all good farce, *Talking Dirty* also manages to convey the emotional pain beneath the comic surface, as the swinging professor ends up with neither friend nor lover.

By and large, there seems to have been proportionately more comedy than in previous periods. Besides the names already mentioned and the continuing work of such stalwarts as Robertson Davies, W.O. Mitchell, and Eric Nicol, other new writers specializing in comedy include Warren Graves, John Ibbitson, and Allan Stratton. Among successful single efforts, *O.D. on Paradise* (1980), by Linda Griffiths and Patrick Beamer, records the sexual confusions and traumatic encounter with Rastafarianism of a package tour of Torontonians in the Caribbean. A more ambitious, Chekhovian type of comedy was attempted by John Murrell in *New World* (1985), which has interesting parallels to *Mother Country*. Like the Hollingsworth play it brings together a family group of Britons on the extreme Pacific rim, and its central theme, keyed by references to *The Tempest*, is the need for Old World values to be adapted to new ways of life. Its Chekhovian lack of action is not made up for by a surfeit of self-conscious bon mots, however, and the characters are too schematized into national types to have Chekhov's endearing sense of oddity. One of the most successful comedies of the period was David French's *Jitters* (1979), detailing the production of a play like one of French's own family dramas at the Tarragon Theatre. Its aging star is hoping for a success that will enable her to get back to Broadway, and the conflict on this point between her and her leading man enables French to make some shrewd comments on the Canadian distrust of success and need for independence.

A particularly interesting aspect of comedy in the period was its frequent overlap with horror. 'Gothic' drama was popular in its own right: there were Dracula, Frankenstein, and several gory Donnelly shows;[22] as well as a series of plays about encounters with psychopaths, such as Peter Colley's *I'll Be Back before Midnight* (1980) or Tom Grainger's *The Injured* (1975). There was often an element of incongruous comedy involved, however, with the tone shifting from one to the other or held in tension throughout. In Carol Bolt's *One Night Stand* (1977), for instance, a woman's entertaining pickup from a singles bar proves to be a homicidal maniac, switching the tone from comedy to horror as he terrorizes her and she kills him; while in Jim Garrard's *Cold Comfort* (1981) a snowbound businessman on the prairies is lured into a rundown gas station by its psychotic owner, seduced by the owner's underage daughter, and the next morning finds himself shackled to the floor in front of a television set as father and daughter drive off together in his car. The play's effectiveness comes from the bland matter-of-factness with which it presents such lurid material. This taste for deadpan horror is central to the drama of George F. Walker, Bryan Wade, and Lawrence Jeffery, who specialize in situations of dominance achieved through psychic disorientation. In Jeffery's *Clay* (1982), for example, where the key character, Bobby, is once again a murderous psychopath, the technique is nicely epitomized in the opening image of a girl swinging in and out of a spotlight which dims a little each time she passes through it. All sorts of unacknowledged sexual obsessions are suggested obliquely by verbal hints and enigmatic action. What the audience is left to infer about the past is evil; what eventually occurs is shocking; but what is worst – yet at the same time grotesquely funny – is that no one will admit that anything untoward has happened, because each has still a secret to conceal. The play is like a semiotics test in reading contradictory signs, where the spare dialogue suggests much more than it says.

Historical and Political Comment

Among the many history plays written in the period only a handful dealt with non-Canadian history or with political allegory. Michael Cook's *The Gayden Chronicles* (1977), about a British naval mutiny in 1812, and George Ryga's *Paracelsus* (pub. 1974), which sets the career of the Renaissance holistic physician within the framework of an argument between modern doctors, are Brechtian attempts to use distanced history to comment on the present. Ken Mitchell's musical *The Great Cultural Revolution* (1979), set in 'a small theatre space at the Central Academy of Drama, Peking,' uses the translation of a Chinese work, *Hai Rui's Dismissal*, as a play-within-a-play to criticize Mao's cultural policy. And curiously there were three plays concentrating on Adolf Hitler's imaginative life: *The Life and Death of Adolf Hitler* (pub. 1975) by George Hulme is an overlong but intriguing interpretation of Hitler as a failed artist who pushed his fantasies into reality; while Wade's *Blitzkrieg* (1974) and Ken Gass's *Winter Offensive* (1977) concentrate on the element of sado-masochism which connects Hitler's political savagery with his sexual attitudes. The most fantastic of the allegorical plays is George Walker's *Rumours of Our Death* (1980), a confusing punk rock parable about the interconnections between sex and politics, totalitarianism and revolution. Steve Petch's *The General* (1972) and *Passage* (1974) are wartime fantasies set in South America that call for no specific application, but John Krizanc's *Prague* (1984) and Robertson Davies's *Question Time* (1975) are both overtly allegorical. At a time when the 'hands off' policy of the Canada Council was under attack because of fiscal austerity, *Prague* offered a slightly preachy satire about Czech censorship of the arts, using a play-within-a-play device that contrasts the humane clown world of a troupe called 'Bread and Dreams' with a corrupt political realism that combines artistic and monetary surveillance. More generally, in *Question Time* the spirit of a Canadian prime minister whose body is in a coma after an air crash wanders through a surreal landscape composed of Jungian Eskimo symbols and a burlesqued House of Commons, as he debates within himself the inner and outer truths of aridly intellectual success and a country still unable to define itself. The conclusion is that we should put more trust in intuition, in women, and in the folk wisdom of the country's indigenous inhabitants.

These rather cloudy implications overlap with a revisionary tendency in many of the plays on Canada's own history, which were apt to be populist rather than nationalist, siding with the losers in the settlement of the country and the struggles of early capitalism. Thus, Sharon Pollock's *Walsh* (1973) depicts the flight of the Sioux to Alberta in 1876 after the massacre at Little Big Horn, focusing on Sitting Bull's tragic relationship with Major James Walsh of the North West Mounted Police. This results (with some telescoping of time) in the eventual murder of Sitting Bull and his son, Crowchild, and the consequent alcoholic disintegration of Walsh himself, a humane man betrayed by his trust in a government that was more interested in good relations with Washington than in the plight of starving Indians. Ken Mitchell's *The Medicine Line* (1976) treats the same event, and a comparable position is taken up by Michael Cook's *On the Rim of the Curve* (1977), Herschel Hardin's *The Great Wave of Civilization* (1976), and James Nichol's *Sainte-Marie among the Hurons* (1974). A similar revisionism is also applied to more recent events: for example, whereas Rod Langley's *Tales from a Prairie Drifter* (1973) satirizes the era of Louis Riel itself, Carol Bolt's *Gabe* (1973) moves the criticism nearer home by contrasting the idealism behind Riel and Gabriel Dumont's rebellion with the hopeless, aimless law breaking of contemporary young Métis. A similar spirit informs Sharon Pollock's *The Komagata Maru Incident* (1976), a quasi-documentary that dissects the politics of racism behind the refusal to admit Sikh immigrants to Vancouver in 1914, while her more recent *Whiskey Six* (1983) contrasts the miseries of mining in Alberta of the 1920s with the affluence of illegal rum-running; and this same impulse to populist revision was behind most of the period's collective creations on historical events, which will be discussed later. A much more anarchic critical approach was adopted by Ken Gass in *The Boy Bishop* (1976) and Michael Hollingsworth in *The History of the Village of Small Huts* (1985), both about moral degradation in the early days of French settlement.

The other main impulse behind historical drama was to mythologize the past, focusing particularly on notable personalities, such as Rod Langley's *Bethune* (1974), Pauline Carey's *Anna Jameson* (1975), Ken Mitchell's *Davin: The Politician* (1978), Sandra Dempsey's *D'Arcy* (1979), or Rick Salutin's

Joey (1981). Of particular interest here are Allan Stratton's *Rexy* (1981), and *Maggie and Pierre* (1979) by Linda Griffiths and Paul Thompson. *Rexy* is a comic-strip presentation of Canada's most eccentric prime minister, Mackenzie King – who also figures in James Reaney's *The Dismissal* (1977) and Elizabeth Gourlay's *Isobel* (1978) – which carefully balances King's sanctimonious shrewdness as a politician determined to keep Canada united during World War II with his ruthless unreliability about conscription and eccentric behaviour as a spiritualist, dog lover, and lonely frequenter of prostitutes. *Maggie and Pierre* was a tour de force in which Linda Griffiths herself played the three roles of Pierre and Margaret Trudeau and a sympathetic reporter who feels guilty because of damage done the couple by overexposure in the press. And in a mythologizing class by itself was Rick Salutin's *Les Canadiens* (1977), in which Quebec independence is ingeniously presented through the victories of Montreal's famous hockey team, with its star of the 1950s, 'Rocket' Richard, equated with René Lévesque in the Parti Québécois election landslide of 1976.[23]

Regional Influences

The idea of writing for and about a particular region of the country was extremely influential between 1972 and 1984, but it was more important in some areas than others: in the Prairies predominantly, then in the Atlantic Provinces and the working-class society of Montreal, with smaller clusters representing rural Ontario and the Gulf Islands in BC. It was also another main concern of collective creations.[24]

Among the main prairie dramatists of the period were Baldridge, Deverell, Glass, Murrell, Pollock, Ken Mitchell, W.O. Mitchell, Frank Moher, and Gwen Pharis Ringwood. Mary Baldridge's *The Photographic Moment* (1974) exemplifies what came to be regarded as the prototypical prairie 'farming' play: it depicts a reunion of bitter brothers and sisters on an Alberta ranch one hot summer during the Depression, with physical hardship and emotional deprivation keeping some of them desperately single and driving others into unhappy marriages to escape a way of life that torments them but is their only refuge against indigence. Similar themes of entrapment and emotional deprivation mark Joanna Glass's *Prairie Gothic* (1975), *Artichoke* (1975), *The Last Chalice* (1977), and *Play Memory* (New York, 1984); Sharon Pollock's *Generations* also deals with the plight of a southern Alberta farm during drought, as well as fluctuating relations with Indian neighbours, women's subservience in a traditionally patriarchal society, and, as the title indicates, the differing attitudes of three generations to staying on the land. Ringwood's *Mirages* (1979), by contrast, more optimistically chronicles the survival of a Saskatchewan farm from its settlement in 1910 through two world wars to the affluent present. Other noteworthy prairie plays of the period were Ken Mitchell's *The Shipbuilder* (1978), about a Finnish home-steader in Saskatchewan who crazily defies the Depression and his family by building an ocean-going steamer on his farm, and *The Train* (1973, later retitled *Wheat City*), about forlorn survivors waiting for the daily train in a derelict prairie railway station. John Murrell's *A Great Noise, A Great Light* (1975), about the early days of 'Bible Bill' Aberhart's Social Credit party in Alberta, can represent the many plays based on historical fact; Frank Moher's very contemporary *Down for the Weekend* (1981) contrasts two oil workers, one married and resentful, the other single and ironic, journeying from Fort McMurray to Edmonton to see their girls and lose their money gambling; and the most popular of all the Western collective creations, 25th Street Theatre's *Paper Wheat* (1977), is a folksy musical play about home-steading days and the farmers' formation of grain co-operatives – a topic treated much more rebarbatively in Rex Deverell's collective with the Globe Theatre of Regina, *No. 1 Hard* (1978).[25]

In the Atlantic Provinces the major dramatist remained Michael Cook, but other interesting playwrights of the period were Al Pittman, Tom Cahill, Christopher Heide, Paul Ledoux, the partnership of Walter Learning and Alden Nowlan, Gordon Pinsent, and that Newfoundlander transplanted to Toronto, David French, whose *Salt-Water Moon* (1984) was a lyrical 'prequel' about the wooing of Jake and Mary Mercer, the parents in his *Leaving Home* and *Of the Fields, Lately*. Of all Cook's Newfoundland plays mixing salty dialect, folk song, ritualized stage business, and unobtrusive symbolism, the most successful was *The Head, Guts and Soundbone Dance* (1974), in which an old sea captain overrides his daughter to persuade his son-in-law and simple-minded son to continue their ancient rituals of deep-sea fishing, till his stubbornness permits the drowning of a child and alienates his followers. Tom Cahill's *As Loved Our Fathers* (1974) describes the break-up of a family by Newfoundland's decision to join Confederation; Paul Ledoux matches Cook's depiction of decaying outports with his play about a dying farm in the Annapolis Valley of Nova Scotia, *North Mountain Breakdown* (1978); an intelligent handling of history can be found in Walter Learning and Alden Nowlan's *The Dollar Woman* (1978), which refuses to simplify issues behind the harsh treatment of paupers in turn-of-the-century New Brunswick, while Rick Salutin's *Joey* is a more theatricalized, satiric comment on the career of Joey Smallwood; and of the many vigorous collective creations one might single out *They Club Seals, Don't They?* (1977), which Newfoundland's Mummers Troupe toured nationally to defend the seal industry, and from Nova Scotia the Mulgrave Road Co-op's *The Coady Co-Op Show* (1978) with Christopher Heide, about the founding of co-operatives in eastern Can-ada, or their *Tighten the Traces / Haul in the Reins* (1982) with Robbie O'Neill, about a songwriter's struggles against polio and prejudice.

Working-class Montreal found vivid representation in plays by David Fennario and Michel Tremblay, the latter in translations which skilfully transposed his joual into Anglo-Canadian slang.[26] Tremblay opposes the poverty, religiosity, alcoholism, and sexual ignorance that can make Québécois family life a trap to the equally self-destructive escapism of entertainers and prostitutes on the 'Main,' the honky-tonk strip of East Montreal, and presents these polarities in structures that are basically musical – nonlinear, disjunctive, overlapping, and intercut, with much reliance on monologue and chorus effects. *Les Belles Soeurs* (1973 in translation), for instance, is a funny-sad parable about a slum woman who wins a million trading stamps and gives a party for her female relatives and neighbours to help her paste the stamps into discount books. During the gossip and comic by-play the desperate sadness of each woman is revealed, and the Catholic myths of Québécois chastity and saintly motherhood are farcically discredited. The visitors end by stealing most of the books for themselves and leave bellowing the national anthem as stamps rain down expressionistically from the flies.

Tremblay resisted all attempts to co-opt his plays for separatist propaganda, but the political element he eschewed was emphatically present in David Fennario's left-wing drama about life in the tough Point St Charles district of Montreal, where anglophone and francophone workers mix. *On the Job* (1975) and *Nothing to Lose* (1977) concern abortive strikes that briefly unite the two groups, whereas *Moving* (1983) depicts a family torn apart by the province's political strife. Fennario's best-known play is *Balconville* (1979), still the only full bilingual play in the repertory. Its title is a bitter joke about the tenement balconies on which the unemployed must spend their stifling summers, with frustration enflaming the national antagonisms that are comically reflected in a display of rival flags and competitive television sets. Fennario's message is the familiar left-wing dogma that national differences are less important than the workers' common exploitation by employers and politicians, and accordingly the two groups unite at the conclusion to rescue furniture from a fire that threatens their tenement. Then, however, they turn to demand of the audience in both languages, 'What are we to do?' – the play recognizes its resolution as only temporary.

A sense of place also permeated several other plays. Small-town Ontario is the setting for many of James Reaney's plays, and the depiction of this community was also the specific mandate of the Blyth Summer Festival and its chief playwrights – Anne Chislett, Ted Johns, Peter Colley, and James Nichol – as well as the purpose of Paul Thompson's trend-setting collective with Theatre Passe Muraille, *The Farm Show* (1972). Similarly, there were plays that relied on the sense of isolation provided by British Columbia's Gulf Islands – Margaret Hollingsworth's *Alli Alli Oh*, *Islands*, and (to a lesser extent) *Mother Country*, Murrell's *New World*, and Charles Tidler's *The*

Farewell Heart (1983), which concerns the final collapse of hippie idealism. But though other plays may have a specific setting – for example, the Vancouver of Tom Walmsley's or Sherman Snukal's plays, the Kingston of Judith Thompson's *Crackwalker*, or the Toronto of Ritter, French, and Walker – they depend less on specific setting than on a more general sense of contemporary urban life.

Where regionalism too often fell short, in fact, was in failing to transcend itself. All good drama needs 'a local habitation and a name' – which, for most dramatists beginning their career, will usually be the community they are best acquainted with. But good drama also goes beyond specific setting: to function imaginatively, its location (or absence of location) must become a 'country of the mind.' Regionalism, important though it was in the period, always had two faces: a legitimate defence of cultural pluralism on the one side, but on the other complacent parochialism. It produced a substantial body of drama between 1972 and 1984, freed Canadian dramatists to concentrate on the experience and language they knew best, and encouraged them to experiment with non-traditional forms that could make immediate contact with audiences that were often theatrically unsophisticated. But, on the debit side, the originality of those experiments has tended to be exaggerated; vision and language frequently failed to rise above the commonplace; regions quickly produced their own stereotypes and clichés; and it was not long before some of the best regional dramatists – Pollock, Murrell, John Gray, interviewed in *The Work* (1982) – were themselves complaining that 'regional' should be a descriptive, not an evaluative, term.

Moreover, there was always a contrary pull against regionalism, a feeling of being uprooted that expressed itself in images of isolation and exile. Certain plays were given deliberately exotic settings – Prague, the south of France, New York, or nineteenth-century Lancashire – and the early plays of Tom Cone (Paris before 1914 and in the 1920s), Steve Petch (Turkey, the Greek Islands, South America, Mexico), and George Walker (Mozambique, Hong Kong, nineteenth century England, 'probably in Italy') are especially interesting in this regard. In place of regionalism's appeal to the familiar, they aimed to suggest imaginative freedom – the equivalent of 'a wood near Athens.' This reflects a major shift of dramaturgy in the period, away from realism to more consciously theatrical forms, and particularly to the collective creations and musical theatre that have usually been annexed too narrowly to regionalism.

Dramaturgical Trends

Realism remained a major mode in the period, but it was often qualified as 'magic realism' – a term borrowed from painting by Margaret Hollingsworth and Bryan Wade (with *Lifeguard*, 1973, and *This Side of the Rockies*, 1977, in both of which people return surrealistically from the dead, Wade seems to be interpreting 'magic' more literally) – or represented in the disjunctive format of a 'memory play.' 'Magic realism' implies that surface verisimilitude is presented in ways that suggest a further symbolic or mythic level of interpretation, as in *Mother Country*. A similar intensity of effect is gained by the combination of oblique dialogue and an unnaturally hard focus on ordinary behaviour in Wade's *Tanned* (1977), where three women at a summer cottage alternate between narcissistic oiling and sunbathing and febrile competitiveness over men, and Tom Cone's *Stargazing* (1978), in which a desultory, polyphonic conversation between two brothers and their wives while they watch for falling stars builds up an extraordinarily complex understanding of their relationships and the isolation of each of them. In the 'memory play' alternative, what is basically a realistic account of experience is presented in a fractured, non-linear form in which scenes from the past are re-enacted as they are recollected in the present. French's *Of the Fields, Lately* and Deverell's *Drift* use this technique, as do Warren Graves's *The Last Real Summer* (1981), in which a woman doctor visits her small home town with a troubled married daughter and remembers the summer when she lost the boy she really wanted to marry, and Sharon Pollock's *Doc* (1984), an autobiographical play about the damage inflicted on his New Brunswick family by her gifted but autocratic father.

The more dominant forms, and the more overt swings from realism, include collective creations, musical theatre, variations on the play-within-a-play device, and several kinds of formalism. Collective creation is a sort of theatrical poster art: it combines subject-matter that is usually (though not invariably) realistic with a self-consciously theatrical presentation. The actors themselves research the topic, then create a script by the improvisation of scenes exploiting their own personalities and any particular performance skills they may possess (a characteristic which makes the plays hard to recast). A writer may, or may not, be involved as a resource person or be brought in to help with the final draft. The actors invariably double many roles and also represent necessary props and scenery, using their bodies and voices to create ingenious stage metaphors and relying heavily on song, dance, and mime. The stage is never representational but is essentially a performance space, and the link between actor and audience is consequently very close, with each acknowledging the other's presence.[27] This basic technique was used for three main purposes in the period under review. One was to give a particular community a sense of its own identity, an approach to be seen at its best in Theatre Passe Muraille's *The Farm Show*, a kind of variety show or, as the director Paul Thompson described it, a 'Christmas entertainment,' recording his company's discovery of the farming community of Clinton, Ontario. (Michael Ondaatje's documentary film, *The Clinton Special*, records the creation of

The Farm Show.) Others with the same purpose were TPM's *Under the Grey-wacke* (1973) about miners, *The Immigrant Show* (1974, with Rick Salutin), *The West Show* (1975), and *Paper Wheat* from Saskatoon. Establishing a particular local 'myth' (to use Thompson's term) often involved some consideration of the community's past, so a second main focus for collectives was revisionary history.

The most popular of all the collectives, Toronto Workshop Theatre's *Ten Lost Years* (1974), was based on Barry Broadfoot's oral history of the Depression;[28] and this was also the period of Carol Bolt's *Buffalo Jump* (1972). Prairie Indians killed buffalo by stampeding them over a cliff, and this is used as a metaphor for the famous march of the West Coast unemployed to confront R.B. Bennett's government in Ottawa, which ended in the Regina riots. The play is built up of vignettes from the march and has clever agit-prop symbolism, such as a mock opera sung by townspeople feeding the marchers in the Opera House at Golden, BC, and a Calgary Stampede sequence in which the workers' leader is repeatedly thrown by a bull called R.B. Bennett, all narrated in typical Stampeder announcing style. Rick Salutin's *1837: The Farmers' Revolt* (1973) was another very successful collective; it caught the reforming mood of the early 1970s by recreating the wretched experiences of Upper Canada settlers that sparked William Lyon Mackenzie's rebellion. Rex Deverell's *Medicare* (1980) and *Black Powder* (1981) have much the same appeal.

Left-wing populism of this kind overlaps with a third main purpose of collective creations, which was to present current problems in such a way as to influence a community's actual decisions. Rudy Wiebe's *Far as the Eye Can See* (1977) was about Alberta farmers' attempts to stop the Dodds-Round Hill Power Development Project near Edmonton; the Mummers' *Gros Mourn* (1973) was put together in ten days to assist a Newfoundland community in opposing land appropriation for a state park; while their *Buchans: A Mining Town* (1974) overlapped all three categories, since it mythologized the community's past to raise morale in a mining town on strike. However, it should not be forgotten that collective creation techniques can also be used for other than sociopolitical purposes, though in the period this was comparatively rare. One of Tamahnous Theatre's most interesting creations, *Vertical Dreams* (1979, with Jeremy Long) was based on fantasy and dream material developed with the help of psychotherapists; and Richard Rose and Autumn Leaf Theatre also explored this area satirically in *Desire* (1985), a collage about sexual fantasy, and (more successfully) in *Mein* (1983) about power fantasies within a business corporation.

Collective creations between 1972 and 1984 were important more in terms of theatre than drama. Intellectually, they too often simplified complex situations; as texts they tend to be very loosely structured, with an inadequate sense of closure; and their inventive staging is seldom matched by any distinction of language. Even the best of them is dull to read; clearly it was their theatrical energy, perhaps even more than their content, that explained their success.

Closely related to collective creation was a vogue for 'workshopping' plays in which dramatists evolved their works-in-progress through playreadings and suggestions from actors and directors. As practised at the New Play Centre in Vancouver especially, this encouraged many new writers for the stage; and it is a technique particularly associated with the very distinctive drama of James Reaney, developed in workshops with his own NDWT company. Between 1972 and 1984 Reaney wrote ten plays, the most important of them being undoubtedly his Donnelly trilogy (1973–5) which has been called 'the masterwork of Canadian drama.'[29] It deals with an Irish family that immigrated to southwestern Ontario in 1844 and became embroiled with other Irish settlers, the local Roman Catholic Church, and the dominant Protestant political party, so that thirty-six years later a secret society of neighbours massacred them and burned their farm. The Donnellys seem to have been very chancy characters in real life, but Reaney transforms them to mythic exemplars of family love, independence, generosity, and joie de vivre, with the crippled violinist, Will Donnelly, representing the artist's impulse to resist parochial vulgarity. The trilogy is organized by recurrent themes, like poems or music, not by plot or character, and combines dense documentation from local archives with a free, theatricalist form in which actors frequently switch roles, talk to the audience, or represent props and scenery, and there is constant use of dance and song. Technically, it is very like a collective creation, with the important difference that language here is as inventive as the staging, with the same images constantly interchanged between words, set, and action; and the whole is unified by Reaney's powerful idiosyncratic vision.

The centrality of music to Reaney's plays and collective creations overlaps with the second major swing against realism, musical theatre. Besides Alan Lund's continuing productions at the Charlottetown Festival – including George Salven's *The Legend of the Dumbells* (1977), about the Canadian entertainment troupe of World War I – there was a spate of musical theatre which went well beyond traditional modes.[30] Paddy Campbell's *Hoarse Muse* (1974) presented turn-of-the-century Calgary through the mocking eyes of Bob Edwards, legendary editor of *The Calgary Eye Opener*; in *The Horsburgh Scandal* (1976) Betty Jane Wylie examined charges brought against a United Church minister in the 1960s of corrupting teenagers in Chatham, Ontario; and Campbell Smith's controversial *Juve* (1979) was a raw no-holds-barred depiction of juvenile delinquency adapted from three hundred interviews in the Greater Vancouver area. Tom Hendry's *Grave Diggers of 1942* (1973) and Peter Colley's *You'll Get Used to It* (1975) satirized Canada's involvement in World War II, while Morris Panych's *Last Call* (1982) was billed as a 'post-nuclear cabaret'; and there were two musical plays on unemployment: Chris Heide's *Pogie* (1980) using a cabaret-within-a-cabaret structure to interweave narrative and Nova Scotia songs, and the very innovative *Life on the Line* (1983) by Stephen Bush and Allen Booth, where New Wave music created 'an acoustic environment' and as much emphasis was given to the single performer's body language as to the script. Most fascinating of all was *Love Is Strange: A Courtroom Romance* (1984) by Paul Ledoux and David Young, which extrapolated from the recent prosecution of a prairie farmer for harassing the famous 'Snowbird' singer to explore the fantasy in all love relationships and the dangers of a public relations attitude to fans.

The most influential and widely produced writer of musical theatre in the period was John Gray. Stimulated perhaps by the success of Ken Mitchell's *Cruel Tears* (1976), a 'country opera' which transposed *Othello* to the world of Saskatchewan truck drivers, Gray's first success was a country-rock tribute to truckers and truck-stop waitresses entitled *18 Wheels* (1977). This was followed by *Rock 'n Roll* (1981) and *Don Messer's Jubilee* (1985); but the most successful of his musicals, indeed one of the most widely produced of all Canadian plays in the period,[31] was his collaboration with Eric Peterson on *Billy Bishop Goes to War* (1978), which they also performed together with Gray playing piano and doing the ironic narration and Peterson acting all the parts. It is based on the World War I air ace's autobiography, presented essentially as a story narrated by Bishop himself with illustrative songs, poems, 'letters to Margaret,' parodic recreations of encounters with the patronizing British, and mimed descriptions of aerial warfare, all laced with black Services' humour and Bishop's own anti-heroic irony. The central paradox of the man's career is brilliantly caught when he exultantly demonstrates his air battles with a toy plane, making the engine and machine-gun noises verbally like a small boy playing. This catches Bishop's essential naiveté, despite his colonial skepticism, his blood lust, and the guilt he angrily tries to repudiate for surviving more idealistic men like Albert Ball, the rival British air ace. The play makes no direct comment on war, however, and escapes the anti-imperialist cliché it could so easily have become because the contradictoriness of Bishop himself makes his presence as narrator-performer complex and alive.

Another aspect of this recurrent interest in the link between performance and personality was a concern with show business and the psychology of acting and writing. The play-within-a-play structure is central to such works as *Blood Relations*, *Jitters*, *Prague*, *The Great Cultural Revolution*, *Paracelsus*, *The Last Real Summer*, and *Pogie*. To these can be added Eric Nicol's *The Citizens of Calais* (1974), Warren Graves's *The Proper Perspective* (1977), and Carol Bolt's *Escape Entertainment* (1981), which did for the Canadian film industry what *Jitters* had done for theatre. Several plays probed the interrelation of life and performance: *Change Partners and Dance* (1977) by Patricia Carroll Brown was about the sterile relationship between two actresses on tour; while the symbiosis of pain and laughter, life and art, was the subject of Erika Ritter's funniest comedy, *Automatic Pilot* (1980), which also uses a performance-within-the-play structure to contrast the unsuccessful sex life of a woman comic with the hilarious stand-up routines into which she transmutes her pain. Similarly, Tom Cone's *Herringbone* (1975) debunks American showbiz by having its hero do a vaudeville routine which tells how he missed Hollywood stardom because at age thirty-five he had literally turned into the midget he started out merely pretending to be at the age of ten. Other plays were concerned with performers in real life: to *Memoir*, *Love Is Strange*, *The Legend of the Dumbells*, and *Don Messer's Jubilee* can be added Sheldon Rosen's play about the friendship between John Barrymore and the playwright Edward Sheldon, *Ned and Jack* (1977), Maynard Collins's *Hank Williams: The Show He Never Gave* (1977), and Leonard Angel's *Isadora and G.B.* (1976), in which Isadora Duncan tries to seduce G.B. Shaw. This category also overlaps with plays concerned with writers and the process of writing: Rick Salutin's *Nathan Cohen: A Review* (1981); Mary Baldridge's *The Mary Shelley Play* (1978), about events during the writing of *Frankenstein*; Michael Mercer's *Goodnight Disgrace* (1984), about the rivalry between Malcolm Lowry and Conrad Aiken; and two self-referential plays about the creation of the script itself: Rex Deverell's *Drift* and Margaret Hollingsworth's *War Babies* (1984).

Technically analogous are plays about the acting out of fantasies or the use of role-playing and memory games to dominate others. Mary Baldridge's *Bride of the Gorilla*, Aviva Ravel's *Tomorrow and Tomorrow* (1972), and Margaret Hollingsworth's *Apple in the Eye* (1983) all concern the imaginings of hard-pressed wives, with fantasy pushed to the point of schizophrenia in the last; and similar effects are exploited in Bryan Wade's *Nightshift* (1973) and Sheldon Rosen's *The Box* (1974). Charles Tidler's *Straight Ahead* (1979) is a one-woman bravura piece in which a farm girl conjures up memories and fantasies of the four men in her life; and in Deverell's *Boiler Room Suite* (1977), the fantasizing of two old winos in the cellar of a derelict hotel gradually involves a watchman whose first impulse had been to throw them out. Petch's *Victoria* (1979) and *Sight Unseen* (1979) both involve sadistic game-playing, as do Wade's *Aliens* (1975) and especially his *Underground* (1975), a fascinating experience in Pinter-like relativity whose three acts suggest totally different erotic relations between the two men and one woman who are its characters. Sexual dominance games are also central to Aviva Ravel's *Black Dreams* (1974) and, of course, Lawrence Jeffery's *Clay*; while

Jeffery's *The Tower* (1983), like Richard Rose's *Mein*, is about power-playing among the corporate elite, for whom sex is merely a tool of advancement. More expressionistically, Chris Heide's *Two Sisters/The Scream* (1976) is an account of one woman's dominance over another through the assumption of fictitious sisterhood; and his characters' use of dream-telling to impose or to evade corresponds to the tussle of rival 'memories' in Tom Cone's *Veils* (1974), as a seventy-year-old man struggles to maintain his own perspective on the past while his wife insists on reliving her version of their early years together.

This concern with self-referentiality and self-consciousness also manifests itself in various experiments with formalism, in which playwrights tried to imitate the effects of other arts. Tremblay's plays are organized musically, so it is appropriate that his *Forever Yours, Marie-Lou* (1972) was produced in 1983 with a counterpoint of rock, country-and-western, and Latin chants; Charles Tidler's *Blind Dancers* (1979) is written to match the jazz riffs with which it is interspersed; Hrant Alianak experimented with almost abstract rhythm and action in *Mathematics* (1972), in which six groups of carefully selected, highly associative objects are thrown one by one onto the stage at precisely timed intervals to the accompaniment of a constant, methodical beat. More verbally, Wilfred Watson's play about the Communist opponent of Mussolini, *Gramsci x 3* (1983), arranges the script on a 'number grid' that allows almost infinite permutations of overlap, counterpoint, and repetition of voices. Other plays reflected the visual arts, experimenting with what is called 'theatre of images.' Sheldon Rosen's *The Frugal Repast* (1974) was based on the Picasso painting of the same name, and in Tom Cone's *Beautiful Tigers* (1976) it is Picasso who directs Gertrude Stein, Guillaume Apollinaire, Alice B. Toklas, and others to form a tableau of Henri Rousseau's 'The Dream' as a surprise present for the painter; Nightwood Theatre's *Glazed Tempera* (1980) attempted to reproduce the effects of Alex Colville's work; while Cone's fascinating *Cubistique* (1974), which is set in the 1920s Paris of Eric Satie and is about a meeting after long absence between an American coquette and her stylish British hostess, finds equivalents for the multidimensional effect of Cubism by superimposing the women's faces in a spotlight, by overlapping their voices, by having each imitate what she remembers the other to have been like, and, most strikingly, by a climactic dance in which first one, then the other, faces the audience in rapid reversals – all thematically reflecting a shift of dominance between the two women.

Other writers have taken their cues from the electronic media or from popular cartoon books. Thus, Michael Hollingsworth experimented with a synthesis of rock, video, and live performance in adaptations of *1984* (1979) and *Brave New World* (1980); and, following the 'pop art' influence on Off-Off-Broadway, there was a spate of plays exploiting cartoon characters and the clichés of western and gangster movies: David Freeman's *Jesse and the Bandit Queen* (1975); Hrant Alianak's *Western* (1972), and his *Passion and Sin* (1976), a surrealistic gangster drama set in a shack in Havana; Ken Mitchell's *Heroes* (1972), in which the Lone Ranger and Tonto meet Superman and Lois Lane in a New York casting office; Bryan Wade's *Electric Gunfighters* (1973), and his hilarious *Alias* (1975), in which a cowardly Lone Ranger and red-power Tonto rescue Rebecca, a lady in distress who turns out to own a brothel, and one of her girls who is costumed as a gigantic phallus. Ken Gass provided a home-grown equivalent in his play about a Canadian comic book figure, *Hurrah for Johnny Canuck!* (1974). Equally image-oriented but more in the fashion of Sam Shepard was Judith Thompson's *White Biting Dog* (1984), which explored surrealistic extravagances more usually associated with the West Coast experiments of Tamahnous Theatre and Juliani's 'Savage God' troupe. The latter has also experimented with 'environmental theatre,' but the only significant text to come out of that particular approach has been John Krizanc's *Tamara*, evolved with the Necessary Angel company in 1981 and currently a great success in Los Angeles. This is a nineteenth-century melodrama of political intrigue, espionage, and romance, which Richard Rose staged in an old Toronto mansion with the audience separated into groups to follow different characters from room to room.

Such experiments were largely confined to fringe theatre, but one major dramatist who made the area his own was George F. Walker. Of all the major dramatists between 1972 and 1984 – Bolt, Cook, Fennario, French, Gray, Margaret Hollingsworth, Pollock, Reaney, and Tremblay – Walker is the one whose work reflects most clearly the ironic self-consciousness about media which was a distinguishing characteristic of the period. His plays are not based on 'Canadian' experience at all, but on amusing, sometimes unnerving, exploitations of previous literature and popular entertainment. After some early plays in the period based on strip-cartoon effects, such as *Sacktown Rag* (1972) and especially *Bagdad Saloon* (1973), Walker fixed on B-movies as his chief inspiration. The first result was a 'jungle' play, *Beyond Mozambique* (1974), in which a bizarre collection of Western decadents is isolated by rebellious natives, in a decaying colonial mansion, where they proceed to go horrendously to pieces; but Walker ultimately chose as his main model the kind of 'private eye' movie in which a disillusioned but sourly honest detective uncovers the corruptions of society, exploiting the sense of pervasive evil in the genre while at the same time making fun of it. At the centre of *Gossip* (1977), *Filthy Rich* (1979), and *The Art of War* (1983) is an inept but sharp-tongued 'investigative reporter' incongruously named Tyrone Power; and Inspector Cook, the detective who investigates the phantasmagoric Hong Kong brothel of *Ramona and the White Slaves* (1976), turns up again in

Theatre of the Film Noir, Part I (1981), which draws on Genet's *Pompes Funèbres*, Sartre's *The Condemned of Altona*, Greene's *The Third Man*, and Visconti's film *The Damned*, to create a marvellous pastiche of existentialist Europe after World War II. Beneath his generic burlesques and free-floating epigrams, Walker is clearly fascinated by the power of human evil to impose order on existence where idealism and pragmatism fail. He has said that what interests him in human behaviour is obsession, and particularly what happens when obsessions collide; and this can be seen in his best known play, *Zastrozzi: The Master of Discipline* (1977), a gothic melodrama inspired by Shelley's romance of the same name, in which the villainous swordsman Zastrozzi engages in a quest of retribution against his antithesis, the foolishly idealizing artist Verezzi. Yet, having killed his opponent's protector, the pragmatic 'ordinary man' Victor, Zastrozzi has to spare Verezzi himself, because without him he would have no 'occupation' for his life. A similar stand-off occurs between Power and General Hackman at the end of *The Art of War*, and between the good scientist Heywood and his evil manipulator Madeiros in Walker's pastiche of nineteenth-century science fiction, *Science and Madness* (1982). The serious, realistic issues raised by Walker's plays always twist back to humour because, first and last, he is a writer whose comedy appeals directly to the modern awareness of intertextuality and self-reference; but such humour, he has said, is his method of survival.

Besides increased production, plays were also more widely read and studied between 1972 and 1984 than previously. For the first time, it became usual for new plays to be published; forgotten plays were rediscovered and printed; and the neglected area of theatre history at last began to be mapped in. Two new journals, *Canadian Drama* and *Theatre History in Canada*, supplemented the excellent *Canadian Theatre Review* and *Performing Arts in Canada*; and basic research tools began gradually to appear: bibliographies of plays in print, of archival holdings, of companies, and of theatre history; collections of interviews with playwrights; and an illustrated national yearbook of productions up to 1982 – all making the serious study of Canadian theatre and drama a more exact endeavour. Solid historical and critical work followed, such as Betty Lee's book on the Dominion Drama Festival, Joyce Doolittle on children's theatre, Renate Usmiani on the 'Alternate' movement, and Ross Stuart on Prairie theatre, as well as several 'profile' series on individual playwrights and such useful collections of essays as the very recent *Contemporary Canadian Theatre: New World Visions* (1985), edited by Anton Wagner for the first meeting of the International Theatre Institute to be held in Canada.

And most significantly, the period ended with the publication of the first developmental anthologies of Canadian drama: by Richard Perkyns for the Irwin Publishing Company (1984), by Richard Plant for Penguin (1984), and by Jerry Wasserman for Talonbooks (1985).[32] All three provide good basic texts for the teaching of academic courses in Canadian drama, and will serve as excellent introductions for non-Canadians to the exciting theatrical activity going on here. But above all, they lay the foundation for an accepted repertory, a development of drama that is uniquely Canada's own.[33] [RBP]

9 Children's Literature

FRANCES FRAZER

Freedom and assurance characterized the Canadian children's literature of the late 1970s and early 1980s. New writers were able to enter a field formerly hedged by economic fears. Established and neophyte authors could essay untraditional subject-matter and experiment with fresh styles. Not long before, writers who hoped to win audiences in Britain and the United States had to be either self-consciously Canadian, exporting the recognized Canadian specialties – Indian and Inuit myths, animal stories, survival melodramas set in northern wildernesses – or carefully 'North American' rather than Canadian, so as not to repel or offend Americans. From the mid-1970s, Canadian authors could assume the universe, setting their stories in Toronto, Timbuktu, Outer Space, or boundless Faerie.

The moral support for this new confidence came principally from a wave of nationalism that acquired momentum in Canada's centennial year and surged on through the 1970s. Long-simmering resentment of foreign, especially American, cultural dominance in textbooks and the books available to children in Canada's bookstores and public libraries grew hotter. And fear of the mind-numbing potentialities of television (also dominated by American producers) moved parents, many of them older and better educated than the average parents of previous generations, to campaign for attractive Canadian books as alternatives to video fare.

Ultimately it was money that bought the freedoms. Publishing Canadian books for children did not suddenly become monetarily safe, but publishers' fears receded as houses such as Montreal's Tundra Books and Toronto's Annick Press ventured into the European market and achieved some noteworthy successes. Tundra's handsome picture books by artist William Kurelek (eg, *A Northern Nativity*, 1976) won international awards and healthy sales. Annick's colourful editions of surrealistic comic tales by Robert Munsch (eg, *Murmel Murmel Murmel*, 1982) and the best of its beguilingly illustrated books for toddlers (eg, *Red Is Best*, 1982; text by Kathy Stinson, artwork by Robin Baird Lewis) became bestsellers in Canada and abroad. The growing home market generated several specialist children's bookshops. The Children's Book Store, which opened in Toronto in 1975, had doubled its size and inventory by 1977.

Then, too, the Canada Council and other funding agencies (notably Ontario's arts council) loosened their purse-strings for writers and publishers of children's literature. The nation's schools offered a large market as they threw out set texts, usually 'Canadianized' American ones, and went looking for a choice of resource materials for their new, more flexible curricula. And a nationwide network of support systems for children's authors, artists, and publishers began to develop. In 1975, the National Library instituted a special section for Canadian children's books. Its dedicated, energetic librarian/consultant Irene Aubrey compiled and edited *Notable Canadian Children's Books* (1976) and subsequent supplements and annual addenda. The year 1976 saw the foundation of the Children's Book Centre, a non-profit association with headquarters in Toronto, to promote the development of Canadian children's books and disseminate information about them across the country.[1] A group of creative people organized themselves in 1977 into CANSCAIP, the Canadian Society of Children's Authors, Illustrators and Performers, to encourage the creation of art and literature for Canada's children. A critical quarterly, *Canadian Children's Literature*, made its debut in 1975 to meet an obvious need, obvious particularly after the demise of Irma McDonough's *In Review: Canadian Books for Children*, a journal funded by the government of Ontario from 1967 till 1982. Health and Welfare Canada acknowledged the power of the newly burgeoning genre by publishing an anti-drug treatise for the young in the form of a clever, entertaining vegetable fantasy, *The Hole in the Fence* (1976). Prizes and medals for children's authors and illustrators proliferated.[2]

In this hospitable climate, veteran authors such as James Houston, Christie Harris, and Jean Little produced some of their best work to date. Houston, artist and sculptor as well as writer, collected and edited a treasure-house of lore in *Songs of the Dream People: Chants and Images from the Indians and Eskimos of North America* (1972) and wrote spare but effective versions of native peoples' stories suitable for younger children (*Ghost Paddle: A Northwest Coast Indian Tale*, 1972; *Kiviok's Magic Journey: An Eskimo Legend*, 1973; *Long Claws: An Arctic Adventure*, 1981) and three short, workmanlike novels of hardship and adventure in the Far North for older ones (*Frozen Fire*, 1977; a sequel, *Black Diamonds*, 1982; and *River Runners*, 1979). He also produced a remarkable long novel, for adults but good reading for mature younger readers too, in *Eagle Song* (1983). The story of two Boston seamen who survived the 1803 massacre of their trading ship crewmates and were held captive by the Indians for two years has been told elsewhere – in Christie Harris's *The Trouble with Adventurers* (1982), for example. But Houston gives it an amusingly ironic perspective by assuming the voice of an earnest Nootka nobleman. In his northern adventure fiction, Houston's pro-Inuit sympathies are sometimes ostentatious. *Eagle Song* sustains an interesting conflict of sympathies.

Harris herself wrote ten books between 1972 and 1982, including an unusual collation of Indian heroines with European fairy-tale ones in *The Trouble with Princesses* (1980) and three particularly popular collections of good Northwest Coast Indian stories involving Mouse Woman, a busybody mouse narnauk that Harris discovered in Tsimshian mythology, *Mouse Woman and the Vanished Princesses* (1976), *Mouse Woman and the Mischief-Makers* (1977), *Mouse Woman and the Muddleheads* (1979).

Although her canvases are small and her action is typically low-keyed, Jean Little has had a devoted child following since the early 1960s, probably because her introspective young protagonists are reassuringly imperfect yet always victorious over a handicap or a complex. Little is not an easy sentimentalist. Crippled limbs remain crippled; mismatched moods produce squabbles and periods of alienation. But the novels' final implications are positive. In *From Anna* (1972), nine-year-old Anna, youngest of a German family who flee Hitler's Germany to settle in Toronto, learns to handle her just-discovered eyesight problems and stand up to her teasing siblings. In the sequel, *Listen for the Singing* (1977), she helps her despairing older brother survive the shock of sudden blindness. Most impressively, *Mama's Going to Buy You a Mockingbird* (1984) is a lively, heartening book despite its solemn theme: two children and their mother endure the father's fatal illness, his death, and its aftermath.

Of the established authors for adults who wrote for children in the 1970s, Mordecai Richler was the only one to produce a 'classic,' *Jacob Two-Two Meets the Hooded Fang* (1975), a short modern *Alice in Wonderland*. The small hero's dream adventures among flamboyant parodic versions of his relatives and acquaintances are both hilarious and satirical. Convicted of 'insulting behaviour to a big person,' Jacob is consigned to children's prison, where the Warden, the menacing Hooded Fang, alternately badgers and begs him to be terrified, meanwhile surreptitiously supplying him with candy. Beneath the semi-surrealistic action lie benign suggestions about the relations of a youngest child with his siblings and those of children with adults, most of whom, the book implies, are fake potentates with children's hearts and an abject fear of children's perceptive laughter.

After her British-oriented, anthropomorphic *Jason's Quest* (1970), a graceful failure, Margaret Laurence produced only three children's books, all for very young readers. *The Olden Days Coat* (1979) is a short, appealing tale of a youngster who travels back in time and meets her grandmother as a girl. *The Christmas Birthday Story* (1980) is a brief account of Christ's birth.

Her *Six Darn Cows* (1979) and Margaret Atwood's *Anna's Pet* (1980) were written for Lorimer's easy-to-read Kids of Canada series. Neither shows much of its author's skill, and both are badly served by ungainly illustrations. Atwood's *Up in the Tree* (1978) is a better blend, combining simple, vivacious nursery verses with the author's amusing drawings.

A host of new writers for the young rushed in where Canada's senior authors were stepping gingerly. Some wrote powerful books. Many, especially those whose work was published, apparently unedited, by thrifty presses, produced mediocre or bad ones. As Sheila Egoff has remarked, 'good writing does not ordinarily spring up in isolation from other kinds.'[3] Moreover, a contemporary taste for quick thrills, together with publishers' concerns about practicable book lengths, evidently persuaded a lot of authors to abridge or compress their material unduly.

Brian Doyle's splendid four novels escape this stricture. *Hey, Dad!* (1978), *You Can Pick Me Up at Peggy's Cove* (1979), *Up to Low* (1982), and *Angel Square* (1984) are all wise, funny books in which observant, humorously self-critical young narrators recount crucial episodes in their lives and educations. Eccentric secondary characters verge on caricature, but the emotions of the books are wholly convincing. *Angel Square* is a tour de force, a warm entertaining Christmas story that dramatizes a lesson in tolerance.

Barbara Smucker also casts a spell, albeit less with style than with gripping action. Smucker published fiction in the United States before moving to Canada in 1968, but her reputation was made by three novels written after immigrating: *Underground to Canada* (1977), an historical novel of flight from slavery; *Days of Terror* (1979), an account of a Mennonite family's sufferings in revolutionary Russia and their ultimate emigration to Canada; and *Amish Adventure* (1983), a contemporary story of an American-Canadian boy's accidental sojourn in an Ontario Mennonite community. All three, like Doyle's *Angel Square*, are persuasive attacks on man's inhumanity to man.

Monica Hughes, an inventive but uneven writer, completes the triumvirate of major children's novelists to appear upon the scene in the 1970s. At her best, as in *Hunter in the Dark* (1982), she demonstrates a sensitive intelligence and a formidable talent. *Hunter* is the story of a likeable young athlete compelled to face the sudden revelation that he has leukemia; it is also an adventure story as the boy defiantly goes hunting alone and makes a fundamental discovery about mortality. But fiction is stretched thin and themes are rather hackneyed in some of Hughes's work. Swift, clever narration and some daunting scientisms in *Earthdark* (1977) and *Ring-Rise, Ring-Set* (1982) do not compensate for an unconvincing plot or an unpersuasive thesis. Of the well-known *Isis* trilogy – *The Keeper of the Isis Light* (1980), *The Guardian of Isis* (1981), *The Isis Pedlar* (1982) – only the first novel merges reasonably credible science fiction premises with a completely absorbing story of complex characters.

Two other novels, designing future situations on the basis of current trends, represent Hughes near the height of her powers. In *The Tomorrow City* (1978), management of a city is recklessly handed over to a supremely logical computer which becomes increasingly ruthless. A blighted world is also portrayed in *Beyond the Dark River* (1979), set forty years after an undefined nemesis has ruined all urban centres. A Hutterite boy and an Indian girl with healing powers encounter crazed, murderous people in the remnants of a shattered city (recognizably Edmonton) as they search for pre-holocaust scientific wisdom to help immunity-less Hutterite children. Their experiences and the conclusions they draw from them compel attention, as do the book's implications about avidly technological societies and reactionary, enclosed ones.

In addition to addressing such subjects as multiculturalism and domestic relations, a surprising number of writers also tried their hands at fantasy, not a common mode in earlier Canadian children's literature. A combination of fantasy and history was the most popular compound, and in these novels history tends to dominate. It doesn't in Janet Lunn's *The Root Cellar* (1981), but the magic that connects the present with the past is more useful than intrinsically fascinating. *The Other Elizabeth* (1982) by Karleen Bradford is almost entirely a dramatized history lesson about the War of 1812; the time travel and 'possession' devices by which a twentieth-century girl temporarily usurps the life of an ancestress merely give fillip to the lesson. Similarly, Heather Kellerhals-Stewart's *Stuck Fast in Yesterday* (1983) appears to exist mainly for its evocation of Ontario in 1909. With a little more daring, Bradford transports latterday youngsters to an hypothesized, Druid-ridden Celtic Britain in *The Stone in the Meadow* (1984), and O.R. Melling injects modern Canadian teenagers into the epic clashes of legendary Irish warriors in her first novel, *The Druid's Tune* (1983).

No Canadian writer succeeded in creating an Other World with the distinctive character of a Narnia or a Middle Earth, but Ruth Nichols approached doing so in *The Marrow of the World* (1972) as she had in her earlier *A Walk Out of the World* (1969). Her witches, dwarfs, and embattled princes are familiar fantasy beings, but the half-witch, half-human heroine of *The Marrow of the World* provides unusual psychological complexity. William Pasnak also created his own special atmosphere in *In the City of the King* (1984) with its dancing-girl heroine, secret societies, and sinister priesthood.

Apart from Monica Hughes's futuristic novels, science fiction and space thrillers were comparatively rare. Douglas Hill contributed a competently written star wars saga in his five *Last Legionary* novels (1979–82).[4] Groundwood Books published (in 1982) *The City Under Ground* (c1964), an English translation of an engrossing story by Quebec author Suzanne Martel, about a subterranean metropolis under the ruins of a Montreal devastated by atomic warfare – and a refreshing departure from the conventional view that a highly organized, barricaded community must be a sick one. Most of the other novels that could be loosely categorized as science fiction were fanciful frolics for readers under twelve. Martyn Godfrey's *The Vandarian Incident* (1981) pits teenaged space cadets against intergalactic war-mongers. Clive Endersby's *Read All About It!* (1981) – based on a TVOntario series – and Elwy Yost's *Billy and the Bubbleship* (1982) are light-hearted farragoes of incredible adventures embroiling modern children with exotic extraterrestrials.

Historical fiction continued to flourish. Unfortunately many new books gave off a distinct classroom aroma. The short historical volumes in the Kids Canada series published by Kids Can Press and in Peter Martin Associates' Northern Lights series are patently aimed at the widening school market, although they appear on bookstore shelves. They are morsels of Canadian history skimpily frosted with fiction.[5]

A remarkable number of school-and-trade historical novels for older children focus upon the lamentable working conditions of factory hands and seamen in the late nineteenth and early twentieth centuries. Four much-publicized novels by Bill Freeman – *Shantymen of Cache Lake* (1975), *The Last Voyage of the Scotian* (1976), *First Spring on the Grand Banks* (1978), and *Trouble at Lachine Mill* (1983) – provide technical information about period logging, fishing, sailing, and manufacturing methods with an authoritative air, and they are illustrated with period photographs. Thus far they are unquestionably educational. But they are also blatantly one-sided and clumsily written (one's confidence is shaken when fines are *levelled* and a captain fears that his ship will *flounder*). Their heroine, a querulous adolescent perpetually crying 'It's not fair,' rallies her oppressed adult colleagues against a succession of ebony-hearted bosses. By comparison, frankly fictitious entertainments in colourfully described historical settings like Tony German's *Tom Penny* novels – *Tom Penny* (1977), *River Race* (1979), *Tom Penny and the Grand Canal* (1982) – seem almost credible. Far stronger cases for the union movement are made in more even-handed novels like *One Proud Summer* (1981) by Claire Mackay and Marsha Hewitt and *The Baitchopper* (1982) by Silver Donald Cameron.

Happily, a number of the historical novels of the time are free of the school aura. Jan Hudson's *Sweetgrass* (1984) contains a moving story of hunger and disease on the prairie during the terrible winter of 1837–8 as experienced by its narrator, a Blood Indian girl. In Raymond Bradbury's hilarious *The War at Fort Maggie* (1982), schoolchildren convey the tale of an actual 1726 French assault on New Brunswick's Fort Margaret in taped and written reports of their ill-fated attempt to re-enact it. Life in Canadian cities in the early decades of this century is warmly portrayed by Bess Kaplan in *Corner Store* (1975) and by Bernice Thurman Hunter in her touching, funny, semi-autobiographical novels, *That Scatterbrain Booky* (1981) and *With Love from Booky* (1983). Artist Tom Cummings does the same thing for rural prairie life just before World War I in the lightly plotted episodes of *Gopher Hills* (1983).

The tenor of these books is typical of most Canadian children's literature written before and during the later 1970s and early 1980s: fortifying rather than demoralizing, frequently poignant but almost never emotionally devastating, outward-looking rather than solipsistic, often quietly ironic. Strains that dominate in much British, American, and Australian young adult literature – raw violence, disillusionment, pessimism, outrage at conditions the innocent young have inherited, cynicism, self-pity – are comparatively rare, even in the most serious, realistic novels written for Canada's young adults. So is titillating exploitation of teenaged sexuality, the stock-in-trade of American young adult romances such as Scholastic's Wildfire and Wishing Stars series and Bantam's Sweet Dreams.

But in their quieter, more whimsical way, Canadian authors have tackled some of the social and domestic problems dealt with slashingly in other nations' bibliotherapeutic literature. Bereaved children, handicapped children, immigrant children, children of estranged or insensitive parents, and youngsters in the throes of puberty figure in many Canadian novels of recent years. In very few, however, are young protagonists portrayed as the wholly virtuous victims of wholly hostile environments. The aggrieved, rough-tongued young narrators of Kevin Major's *Hold Fast* (1978) and *Far from Shore* (1980) are sorry for themselves, but points of view other than theirs are implied or expressed. Normally, the 'problem novels' concern family love underlying schisms and the restorative effect of learning something well. Normally they have more to offer than problems – such as the evocative descriptions of the familiar yet mysterious bush country where a little girl hides from her feckless family in Jan Truss's *Jasmin* (1982).

As more and more immigrants have entered Canada, a number of authors have addressed the particular problems of minority groups.[6] Books for small children have promoted sympathy for newly arrived immigrant youngsters. *The Pillow* (1979) by Rosemary Allison, *The Sandwich* (1975) by Ian Wallace and Angela Wood, and *Michi's New Year* (1980) by Shelley Tanaka deal with homesickness, fear, and the suffering caused by thoughtless teasing. Books for older children have encouraged members of minority groups to cherish their old-country heritages. Examples are Frances Duncan's *Kap-Sung Ferris* (1977), Paul Yee's *Teach Me to Fly, Skyfighter!* (1983), and artist Ian Wallace's gorgeously illustrated *Chin Chiang and the Dragon's Dance*

(1984). Today's Canadian Indians have received sympathetic attention from writers like the late John Craig in *Zach* (1972)[7] and *No Word for Good-Bye* (1969; rev. ed. 1978), Mary-Ellen Collura in *Winners* (1984), and Joan Weir in *So I'm Different* (1981).

But the majority of the realistic, non-historical novels have been mainly entertainments. Sharon Brain gives an amusing twist to a feminist theme in *My Mother Made Me!* (1978) by portraying adolescent girls who don't want the right to play hockey that their mothers are demanding for them. Florence McNeil's *Miss P. and Me* (1982) treats potentially depressing subject-matter, maternal indifference and thwarted ambition, with humour. And two of Canada's most productive, commercially successful novelists have scarcely ever posed a theme. Gordon Korman began his first novel, *This Can't Be Happening at Macdonald Hall!* (1978), when he was thirteen. By 1984 he had published nine books all adhering to the same formula: irresponsible youngsters and eccentric adults collide repeatedly in slapstick actions narrated at breakneck speed. Eric Wilson started writing his fast-paced, undemanding mystery novels to create reading material that would hold the attention of backward readers. His youthful detectives, Tom and Liz Austen, travel widely after villains and clues, giving their author opportunities to inject local colour into his already highly coloured mysteries. Like Korman, Wilson has become something akin to a cult figure among young readers.

Beginning readers have acquired a more artful pied piper in Robert Munsch, an oral-storyteller-turned-author whose spare, emphatic, colloquial style suits his outré little fantasies. 'You look like a real prince, but you are a bum,' says his dragon-conquering princess (in *The Paper Bag Princess*, 1980) to the fastidious ingrate she has rescued. Munsch usually tells his audience genuine stories. In this respect his short, exuberant books stand out from a sea of glossy, cleverly illustrated ones that have appeared to supplement *Cinderella* and replace *Dick and Jane*. So do Patti Stren's sentimental, anthropomorphic animal tales with their Thurberish illustrations.[8]

Children's illustrators came into their own in the 1970s in picture books and even more markedly in a host of folktale and myth collections, many of them expensively produced. Artists trained abroad (Laszlo Gal from Hungary, Frank Newfeld from Czechoslovakia) contributed a cosmopolitan flavour to Canadian artwork. With Canadian-born Elizabeth Cleaver and Douglas Tait, Gal and Newfeld led a long roster of gifted artists who brought Canadian book illustration to the top levels of international competition – among the artists are William Kurelek, Ginette Anfousse, Vlasta van Kampen, Ann Blades, Lindee Climo, Kim La Fave, Olena Kassian, and Robin Muller.

Sadly, the folktale retellings and invented tales modelled on them seldom live up to the illustrations. Muriel Whitaker's *Pernilla in the Perilous Forest* (1979), a little allegory with a medieval air, is worthy of Jetske Ironside's emblematic artwork. Carole Spray's tall tale of pioneer days, *The Mare's Egg* (1981), is almost as good as Kim La Fave's richly colourful cartoons. Christie Harris's versions of Indian stories can sustain Douglas Tait's forceful drawings. But Elizabeth Cleaver's brilliantly coloured, neo-primitive collages overwhelm William Toye's terse texts in *The Loon's Necklace* (1977) and *The Fire Stealer* (1979) as they did in the pair's earlier collaborations. A similar problem besets Cleaver's own stories in *The Miraculous Hind* (1973) and *Petrouchka* (1980) and is compounded by some awkward phrasing. *Fox Mykyta* (1978), a translation by Bohdan Melnyk of Ivan Franko's Ukrainian classic, is candidly 'foreign' in subject and language and provides a better text for Kurelek's art – lively animal drawings this time.

In general, the most successful retellings of myths have continued to be those of Indian and Inuit stories rooted in Canada's past. Christie Harris's and James Houston's have remained the most popular versions for children. But there have been colourful supplements to their work, such as Yves Troendle's *Journey to the Sun* (1977) and *Raven's Children* (1979), novels interweaving Iroquois myths, and Garnet Hewitt's *Ytek and the Arctic Orchid* (1981), a romantic Inuit legend stylishly illustrated by Heather Woodall. And the descendants of the first native storytellers, following in the footsteps of George Clutesi and Markoosie, have pleased readers, especially cultural purists, with new stories like Basil H. Johnston's *Tales the Elders Told: Ojibway Legends* (1981) with eloquent illustrations by Cree artist Shirley Cheechoo, and Métis writer Maria Campbell's *Little Badger and the Fire Spirit* (1977), an Indian myth in a contemporary frame.

Canadian poetry for children remained scarce in the 1970s and early 1980s, apart from that of Dennis Lee, an award-winning poet for adults who produced his first full-fledged collection of modern, emphatically Canadian nursery rhymes, *Alligator Pie*, in 1974 and set his youthful compatriots chanting about Ookpik, Temagami, and 'Mississauga rattlesnakes.' In further collections – *Nicholas Knock and Other People* (1974) for slightly older readers, *Garbage Delight* (1977), and *Jelly Belly* (1983) – Lee continued to demonstrate the vital presence of the children within him,[9] their uninhibited emotions, their delight in rhythm and sound effects, mellifluous or raucous, their naughty pleasure in rude words ('Bitter batter bum'), and their alternating terror and bravado about the monster in the closet ('I EAT MONSTERS BURP!'). But even Lee's exuberance appeared to be flagging by 1984. *Lizzy's Lion* (1984) tells its tall burglar tale in fourteen occasionally perfunctory quatrains.

Mary Alice Downie and Barbara Robertson revised the contents of their *The Wind Has Wings* (1968), the first major anthology of Canadian poems chosen for children. However, *The New Wind Has Wings* (1984) contains no more poetry with distinctive appeals for children than its predecessor. Irving Layton's *A Spider Danced a Cosy Jig* (1984; edited by Elspeth Cameron) has a children's book format but consists entirely of previously published poetry for adults, much of it jaundiced. George Swede, bpNichol, and sean o'huigin[10] produced some amusing, fanciful trifles aimed principally at the very young. But aside from Peter Desbarat's three offbeat, metrically complicated narrative poems in *The Night the City Sang* (1977), verse written for children in these years tends to be deliberately light and ephemeral. Al Pittman's *Down by Jim Long's Stage: Rhymes for Children and Young Fish* (1976) represents the type at its unassuming best.

Serious children's drama was on the upswing. Between 1976 and 1984, the number of professional companies devoted partly or exclusively to young people's theatre increased from almost thirty to almost sixty, creating a need for plays that was met by some established playwrights such as Len Peterson, Gwen Pharis Ringwood, and Carol Bolt and by many new ones. Unfortunately, few of the new plays have been easily accessible to readers.[11] The Toronto-based Playwrights Canada and its successor the Playwrights Union of Canada published a lot, but chiefly in flimsy typescript editions unsuited to bookstores. Otherwise, publication has been limited to a few anthologies[12] and a handful of individual plays like those of Dennis Foon – *Heracles* (1978), *The Windigo & The Last Days of Paul Bunyan* (1978), *Raft Baby* (1978), *New Canadian Kid* (1982) – co-founder (with Jane Howard Baker) and from 1975 to 1988 artistic director of Vancouver's Green Thumb Theatre.

National and international communications about developments in young people's theatre have been much more effectively achieved by children's festivals. The Vancouver Children's Festival of 1978, based upon an idea proposed by Elizabeth and Colin Gorrie of Victoria's Kaleidoscope Theatre, led the way in Canada, featuring native and foreign entertainers and theatrical companies of various kinds. It has become an annual week-long event, and it proved so popular that by 1984 it was attracting some 80,000 spectators. Its success inspired children's festivals across the country, now regular spring events that have introduced plays to wide audiences, promoted cross-fertilization among regional theatre repertoires, including both anglophone and francophone ones, and brought several Canadian plays into the international limelight.

By comparison, trade publication of plays has lagged, but what there is of it confirms that beneath some regional differences (for example, Regina's Globe Theatre and its playwright-in-residence, Rex Deverell, have remained more dedicated than most to participatory drama) the clear trends have been towards realism and a polemicism that is sometimes stridently biased but more often healthily challenging. There is still a call for entertainment, magic, and poetry – for example, Henry Beissel's poetic *Inook and the Sun* has been a critical and popular success ever since its premiere on the Stratford Festival's Third Stage in 1973 – but increasingly dramatists have taken to 'child advocacy' theatre, plays which project child's-eye visions of the contemporary world. Children in Deverell's *The Copetown City Kite Crisis* (first produced in 1973) assail the adult greed and apathy that allow a kite-manufacturing plant to continue emitting poisonous fumes. Audiences cast as the plant's staff determine the play's conclusion: expensive, salutary reform or a future of business profits and toxic smog. Foon's *New Canadian Kid* (first produced in 1981; based on a concept by Jane Howard Baker) gives young playgoers a taste of immigrant experience with a simple, striking linguistic reversal: the young newcomer speaks English while his Canadian schoolfellows talk gibberish.

Threats to the ecology, playground cruelty, and other dark topics such as child abuse and the arms race have been treated more directly and more angrily in the children's drama of the time than in the fiction, despite the opposition of some adult spectators. In 1979, Joe Wiesenfeld's *Hilary's Birthday*, a frank play about a nine-year-old's conflict with her mother's new boyfriend, shocked Green Thumb's adult patrons. In its 1981–2 season, Toronto's prestigious Young People's Theatre incurred protests with *Dreaming and Duelling*, an intense psychological drama by John and Joa Lazarus. On the other hand, Green Thumb's collaborative production *Feeling Yes/Feeling No* (1981), a warning to children against sexual molesters, was swiftly reproduced by other companies and adapted for film by the National Film Board in 1984.

Verbal eloquence is seldom at home in realistic contemporary plays for and about young people. The new plays' claims to artistry frequently rest on other elements, such as movement, gesture, lighting, and sound effects. But some texts, especially ones on the borderline between drama for teenaged audiences and drama for adults, have real literary power. *Dreaming and Duelling* (published in 1982) approaches high tragedy, for all its vernacular crudities, as potentially lethal make-believe engulfs a gifted, troubled young fencer.

Writers of history, biography, and books on the sciences for young readers have also been productive in recent years, but their output is not widely known because most of it has little currency outside schools. Some good writing has been done for serviceable, school-oriented series like Fitzhenry and Whiteside's multi-volumed The Canadians, Douglas and McIntyre's How They Lived in Canada series, and Dundurn Press's ten Frontiers and Pioneers stories by Terry Leeder. A few biographies such as Kay Hill's lively *Joe Howe: The Man Who Was Nova Scotia* (1980) have had wider circulation. So have some imposing nationalistic books like George Woodcock's *100 Great Canadians* (1980), Janis Nostbakken and Jack Humphrey's *The Canadian Inventions Book* (1976), and Carlotta Hacker's somewhat arbitrary *The Book of Canadians: An Illustrated Guide to Who Did What* (1983). And a number of offshoots from *OWL* magazine – books of games, puzzles, and zoological lore magnificently illustrated in photographs – have been widely distributed.[13]

OWL, its sibling *Chickadee*, and *JAM*, all published in Toronto, were, however, the only impressive English-Canadian children's magazines to live on into the early 1980s. Three promising magazines published on a wave of enthusiasm between 1976 and 1980 soon foundered. *The Canadian Children's Magazine* (published in Victoria, 1976–9), *Ahoy* (Halifax, 1976–84), and *MST – Mountain Standard Time* (Edmonton, 1980–4) succumbed to high production costs, distribution problems, and competition from some seventy American periodicals. *Magook*, an eccentric combination of magazine and book, appeared sporadically between 1977 and 1980 and then expired.

OWL, a magazine specializing in natural science for older children, was founded by the Young Naturalist Foundation in 1976. *Chickadee*, a similar periodical for younger children, was initiated by the same foundation in 1979. These two magazines; their Quebec counterparts *Hibou* and *Coulicou*; *Vidéo-Presse*, a wide-ranging, informative periodical for francophone youngsters; and *JAM*, another science-oriented magazine, survived – some of them with the aid of subsidies. By 1985, they and Robert F. Nielsen's *Canadian Children's Annual*, which attained its tenth anniversary with the 1984 issue, were virtually the only distinctively Canadian periodicals available to young Canadian readers.

Canadian children's books did not suffer the special economic problems that beset the periodicals, but inflation sustained enough financial instability to keep Canadian authors aware that originality is not only a value in itself but also their best defence against the competition of imported books. Enough of them rose to the challenge to enlarge significantly the body of Canadian children's literature. There were also moves to keep that tradition fully visible. Good stories and novels from the past were republished, or at least preserved in part in anthologies like *Kanata: An Anthology of Canadian Children's Literature* (1976)[14] and Muriel Whitaker's story collections.[15] Stories and books – Richler's *Jacob Two-Two*, for example – acquired different kinds of currency in recorded readings and stage and film adaptations. Authors also diversified. Poet Dennis Lee, author-artist Tim Wynne-Jones, and playwright Carol Bolt all wrote for the CBC-TV puppet show *Fraggle Rock*, and Lee recorded his own readings of his children's verse. Francophone and anglophone children were assisted to discover more of their national literary heritage by a growing number of translations in both directions.

As Northrop Frye said in a Carleton University Convocation address (17 May 1957), 'Writers don't interpret national characters; they create them.' For much of Canada's history, Canadians – young ones in particular – were short of homegrown literature to 'create' Canada and Canadians for them as imaginative concepts. In the 1970s, fostered by nationalistic enthusiasm and dedicated pressure groups and fed by individual writers' inspirations, Canadian children's literature became a recognizable entity. By the mid-1980s it appeared to have developed a self-generating creative vitality of its own.

10 Folklore

EDITH FOWKE

The launching of a Folklore Department at Memorial University of New-foundland in 1968 and the founding of the Folklore Studies Association of Canada in 1976 gave a strong impetus to the study of Canadian folklore. Folklorists began turning to discussion and analysis, where earlier folklore publications had been largely collections or descriptions. Also noticeable was an increased tendency to study folk arts and crafts and other forms of material culture rather than oral traditions.

Three academic journals in this field are: *Canadian Folk Music Journal*, published annually by the Canadian Folk Music Society since 1973; *Canadian Folklore canadien*, a semi-annual published by the Folklore Studies Association of Canada since 1979; and *Culture & Tradition*, published annually by folklore students at Laval and Memorial universities since 1976. Several smaller periodicals are issued by universities to note the work of their students and scholars,[1] and journals published by related disciplines have sometimes focused on folklore in special issues. *Ethnomusicology*'s 1972 'Canadian Issue' included surveys of Anglo-Canadian and French-Canadian folk music, the music of some religious minorities and of Arab and East Indian communities, and useful bibliographies on Indian and Inuit music. In 1975 *Canadian Ethnic Studies* published a special issue on 'Ethnic Folklore in Canada,' providing articles on Icelandic, Polish, Ukrainian, Welsh, and Macedono-Bulgarian communities. The following year the *Laurentian University Review*'s issue on 'Folklore and Oral Tradition in Canada' discussed such topics as Ojibwa legends and the motif of the external soul in French folktales, surveyed archival collections, and outlined current research on French folktales in North America. Some Canadian folklorists have published in international periodicals such as the *Journal of American Folklore*, *Journal of the Folklore Institute* (now *Folklore Research Journal*), *Folklore Forum* in the United States, and *Lore and Language* in England. There are also several non-academic periodicals that publish some interesting folklore: *Cape Breton's*

Magazine; *Them Days: Stories of Early Labrador*; *Inuktitut*; and *The Livyere: A Newfoundland and Labrador Magazine.*

SURVEYS

The 1970s and 1980s saw the production of three comprehensive pioneering folklore books and a number of more specialized references. Edith Fowke's *Folklore of Canada* (1976) was the first extensive anthology of folklore materials. Divided into four sections on the native peoples, Franco-Canadians, Anglo-Canadians, and other ethnic groups, it presents folktales, legends, folk songs, folk speech, riddles, games, a folk play, square dance calls, jokes, superstitions, customs, and foodways, with introductory surveys for each section and background notes on each item. The aim was to sample Canadian folk culture (what Richard Dorson has termed 'the hidden submerged culture lying in the shadow of the official civilization about which historians write'), in the belief that this folk culture is just as important as high culture in understanding Canada's identity.

Carole H. Carpenter's *Many Voices* (1979) was the first extensive survey of Canadian folklore. This work, originally prepared as a doctoral dissertation at the University of Pennsylvania, draws on both library research and interviews. Dr Carpenter discusses the history of folklore studies up to the 1970s, and analyzes the past and current roles of folklore in relation to Canadian culture. She argues that 'a consideration of the past in terms of the nature of and motives for folklore study and interest in Canada cannot help but clarify the dominant themes and trends in Canadian culture ... Canadians cannot move into the unknown with assurance unless they have a feeling for what has gone before.'

Fowke and Carpenter then collaborated on *A Bibliography of Canadian Folklore in English* (1981), the first major bibliography of the fast-growing field, including nearly four thousand items. Sections cover Reference Materials, Periodicals, General, Folktales, Folk Music and Dance, Folk Speech and Naming, Minor Genres, Superstitions and Popular Beliefs, Folklife and Customs, Folk Art and Material Culture, Biographies and Appreciations, Records, Films, and Theses and Dissertations. Later they produced an anthology, *Explorations in Canadian Folklore* (1985), that ranges from an early account of life among the Haida, through personal reports of ballad-collecting, to surveys of tall tales, fiddle music, and folk medicine, and analyses of Buddhist dirges, ethnic jokes, and Quebec's folk culture.

A number of more specialized bibliographies and indexes also appeared, covering Inuit and BC Indian publications,[2] and three useful song indexes from Newfoundland.[3] In 1982 came a more important book, the *Dictionary of Newfoundland English* by G.M. Story, W.J. Kirwin, and J.D.A. Widdowson: the climax of a twenty-year project. Not only the first major Canadian dialect dictionary, this is a fascinating study of the history and culture of Newfoundlanders as revealed through their distinctive language. It records words created in Newfoundland and also words that acquired different forms or meanings there, or survived later. Of greatest interest to folklorists is the dictionary's extensive reliance on oral materials as a source of vocabulary items.

SONGS

Song books assembled since 1970 are less substantial than earlier ones (those of Mackenzie, Greenleaf, Karpeles, Creighton, Peacock, and Manny). In 1973 two small books from Prince Edward Island appeared, followed in 1979 by one from Cape Breton: *Folksongs from Prince Edward Island*, ed. Randall and Dorothy Dibblee; *Folk Songs of Prince Edward Island*, comp. Christopher Gledhill; and *Songs & Stories from Deep Cove, Cape Breton*, by Amby Thomas, edited by Ron MacEachern.

The lumbering lore of the Ottawa Valley inspired two other publications. Venetia Crawford's *Treasures of the Pontiac in Song and Story* (1979) contains historical anecdotes, legends, ghost stories, square dance calls, and songs. *The Rusty Leach Collection of Shanty Songs and Recollections of the Upper Ottawa Valley* (1984) collects personal narratives by local residents, among other items. Both books document a region particularly rich in lumbering lore, but they contain some inaccuracies and lack scholarly documentation.

Edith Fowke published *The Penguin Book of Canadian Folk Songs* (1981), an anthology that drew on earlier sources but also added a number of songs from her own Ontario material and from Kenneth Peacock's Newfoundland collection. She also edited *Sea Songs and Ballads from Nineteenth-Century Nova Scotia* (1981), made up of one sailor's collection of shanties, and a sea captain's notebook containing the earliest record of Anglo-Canadian ballads to come to light: it predates Mackenzie's pioneering collecting by some thirty years. In 1984 a revised and enlarged edition of her *Canada's Story in Song* (1960) appeared under the title *Singing Our History*. Discoveries in the last quarter-century made it possible to add sections on mining, transportation, and industrial conflicts.

One of the most important song books of this period also related songs to history: Philip J. Thomas's *Songs of the Pacific Northwest* (1979), the first substantial collection from west of Ontario. Assembling songs and verses composed by British Columbians, it emphasizes those that deal with the history and industries of the West Coast, providing detailed background notes on each. The Fraser, Cariboo, and Klondike gold rushes inspired verses such as these:

> Where mighty waters foam and boil
> And rushing torrents roar,
> In Fraser River's northern soil
> Lies hid the golden ore,

and the coal mines of Vancouver Island led to some early industrial clashes that were satirized in songs:

> Oh, did you see the kilties, boys?
> The laugh would nearly kilt you, boys,
> The day they came to kill both great and small,
> With bayonet, shot and shell
> To blow you all to hell,
> Did Bowser and his gallant Seventy-Twa.

Thomas's painstaking research has brought to light many details about British Columbia's history, and as few of the songs were well established in oral tradition, the book is more important as history than as folklore.

From the Atlantic side of the country came still another historically relevant collection: *Haulin' Rope and Gaff: Songs and Poetry in the History of the Newfoundland Seal Fishery* (1978) by Ryan Shannon and Larry Small.

Anthony Hopkins's *Songs from the Front and Rear* (1979), an anthology of Canadian servicemen's songs from World War II, also fits into this historical group. The songs are undoubtedly from oral tradition, but most were sung by British and American servicemen as well as by Canadians.

Two substantial collections of Gaelic songs with English translations appeared. Donald A. Fergusson's *Beyond the Hebrides* (1977) consists largely of Cape Breton songs, supplemented by some from other parts of North America, Australia, and New Zealand. Similarly, Margaret MacDonell's *The Emigrant Experience* (1982) includes Gaelic songs from different North American locales, and her notes on the bards and their verses give a vivid picture of the factors that forced the emigration in the sixteenth century:

> Landlords are enslaving
> Their people at this time,
> Evicting and forcing them
> To a land of prosperity for their children,

and of the conditions that faced them in America:

> We reached the land of promise,
> The frost was as hard as rock.
> More than twelve feet into the ground;
> Not even an ant could survive it.

Some of these compositions supply vivid details of emigration and settlement, and effectively suggest the emotional upheaval that attended the experience.

No major books presented new material on the songs of the native peoples, but that master-gatherer, John Robert Colombo, produced two important publications in this field. Through diligent research he compiled *Poems of the Inuit* (1981) and *Songs of the Indians* (1983), remarkably comprehensive anthologies that bring together most of the native songs that have been collected, with useful notes and references. Perhaps most importantly, they convey the natives' attitude to nature – an attitude revealed, for example, in this 'Prayer to the Spirit of the Slain Bear':

> You died first, greatest of animals.
> We respect you, and will treat you accordingly.
> No woman shall eat your flesh;
> no dogs shall insult you.
> May the lesser animals all follow you,
> and die by our traps, snares, and arrows!

TALES

Folktales still receive less attention than folk songs among Anglo-Canadians. One of the few Anglo-Canadian books in this period is Carole Spray's *Will o' the Wisp: Folk Tales and Legends of New Brunswick* (1979). Spray's introduction gives a lively account of her own collecting experiences, along with samples of New Brunswick's varied lore: superstitions, folk cures, children's rhymes, and lumbermen's games, as well as anecdotes about local characters. The tales include a number of international *Märchen* along with a good selection of local East Coast legends: 'The Burning Ship,' 'The Dungarvon Whooper,' 'The Man Who Picked the Gorbey,' and several local ghost stories. From the opposite end of the country came Michael Taft's lively *Tall Tales of British Columbia* (1983), an illustration of the continuing popularity of this type of yarn, which in Canada tends to emphasize the fanciful exploits of hunters and fishermen, and to exaggerate the already sufficiently extreme character of the climate.

Tales from other ethnic groups were more numerous. Two translations of Gaelic stories provide a cross-section of tale types from *Märchen* and legends to personal experience narratives. Calum MacLeod translated his previously published Gaelic collection as *Stories from Nova Scotia* (1974), and Margaret

MacDonell and John Shaw presented both Gaelic and English versions of the tales told by Hector Campbell in *Luirgean Eachainn Nill: Folktales from Cape Breton* (1981). Campbell's traditional repertoire includes, for example, a Highland Gaelic trickster tale, two international tales of the supernatural, a Celtic hero tale, and a story based on lucky accidents.

Robert Klymasz's *Folk Narrative among Ukrainian-Canadians in Western Canada* (1973) formed part of his 1970 doctoral dissertation, 'Ukrainian Folklore in Canada' (which was published in facsimile in 1980). The first comprehensive work on this topic, it shows what happened to traditional Ukrainian folktales some eighty years after the storytellers began settling the prairies in the 1890s. Klymasz investigates the circumstances of folklore change and describes the trends that these changes suggest. His material (like that in *Folktales of the Canadian Sephardim*, 1982, by André E. Elbaz) was drawn from the National Museum's folklore archives.

Native tales led to the largest number of books. But whereas earlier native tales had been compiled largely by whites, native peoples themselves are now publishing stories of their own experience and traditions. Norval Morrisseau had begun this practice with *Legends of My People: The Great Ojibway* in 1965, and more recently James Redsky wrote of the *Great Leader of the Ojibway: Mis-Quono-Quab* (1972); Edward Ahenakew produced *Voices of the Plains Cree* (1973); Beth Ahenakew and Sam Hardlotte compiled *Cree Legends* (1973); Mark Kalluak edited and illustrated *How Kabloonat Became and Other Inuit Legends* (1974); Patronella Johnston told *Tales of Nokomis* (1975); Basil Johnston described his *Ojibway Heritage* (1976); and Leoni Kappi produced *Inuit Legends* (1977). Especially noteworthy is the excellent collection by the famous West Coast Haida carver Bill Reid with poet Robert Bringhurst: *The Raven Steals the Light* (1984). A number of others are of less importance, but *Tales from the Longhouse* (1973) by Indian children of British Columbia, and *Stories from Pangnirtung* (1976) are valuable for their faithful representation of the oral tradition.

Visitors Who Never Left: The Origin of the People of Damelahamid (1974) is a valuable study of the relation of myths to the history and culture of a people. Kenneth Harris, a Gitksan chief, persuaded his uncle, Arthur McDames, to record the myths of his tribe, and then translated them. Versions of these tales were collected earlier by anthropologists, but as the editor, Frances R. Robinson, notes, 'None has hitherto appeared translated wholly by an Indian and from the Indian point of view.' Among the better stories by native storytellers presented by whites are *Indian Legends of Canada*, originally published in French by Claude Melançon, and translated by David Ellis (1967; trans. 1974); and *Legends of the River People* (1976), compiled by Norman Lerman. *Lillooet Stories* (1973) and *Shuswap Stories* (1979), edited by Randy Bouchard and Dorothy I.D. Kennedy, are literal transcriptions, and the British

Columbia journal, *Sound Heritage*, provided a cassette of the first. Of particular interest is *Tales from the Smokehouse* (1974) by Herbert T. Schwartz. This is one of the few books intended for the general reader that provides texts in unexpurgated form. The earthy nature of many Indian narratives causes them to be rewritten in order to make them suitable for children or inoffensive to adults, thus diluting the authentic flavour. Usually the tales as they were actually told are found only in collections published by anthropologists.

An important feature of the Indian tales is that they throw light on the different ways whites and Indians look at the world and themselves. Their most characteristic feature is the popularity of the trickster. The whites see characters as either good or bad, hero or villain, but to the Indians the same character can be at times hero, at times trickster who fools or is fooled, thus embodying different aspects of the human personality in the one character. Another difference, also noted in the songs, is that the Indians see themselves as part of the natural world, akin to the animals, which shapes their philosophy and their tales.

An innovative book that marks the transition from oral to written literature is *Paper Stays Put: A Collection of Inuit Writing* (1980) edited by Robin Gedalof. Here versions of old legends share space with more recent stories based on folktale themes and with reminiscences. Another book that combines traditional and literary material is Colombo's *Windigo* (1982), a fascinating collection of accounts of the dread cannibalistic spirit, ranging from the 1630s to the 1970s.

In French Canada many important song and tale collections appeared, but they were not translated into English. In *Les deux traditions: le conte populaire chez les franco-terreneuviens* (1983), however, Gerald Thomas brings together many Franco-Newfoundland tales with translations and with several tales told in English. Fowke's *Folktales of French Canada* (1979) provides straightforward translations of representative tales, mostly collected by Marius Barbeau. Some are Canadian adaptations of Old World *Märchen* featuring Ti-Jean; others are habitant legends of Rose Latulippe, the feux follet, the loup-garou, and the chasse-galérie. Margaret Low also directly translated a few French-Canadian tales in Richard Dorson's collection of *Folktales Told Around the World* (1975) which also contains a few Canadian-Jewish stories collected by Barbara Kirshenblatt-Gimblett. French-Canadian tales have, moreover, influenced several writers who are being read by an English audience. For example, Antonine Maillet's novels convey a strong sense of the Acadian folk, and Roch Carrier's books draw on many folk motifs and legends from Quebec.

Scholars recently have begun to study a different type of folktale: the recitation or monologue. Carole Spray includes a few of these in her New Brunswick collection, noting that 'Some verses were and still are recited at concerts and community entertainments.' In *The Blasty Bough* (1976), edited by Clyde Rose, Wilfred Wareham discusses 'The Monologue in Newfoundland,' observing that recitations have long formed part of the traditional Newfoundland 'times.' The main topics are history, local disaster, politics, religion, and bawdy scenes, which may take either verse or prose form.

OTHER FORMS

An area still rather neglected in Canada is that of children's folklore: the songs, rhymes, games, riddles, sayings, and customs that circulate among children without recourse to the adult world. Fowke's *Sally Go Round the Sun* published material of this kind in 1969; its successor, *Ring Around the Moon* (1977), included rounds, riddles, superstitions, and assorted songs, some from children and some from adults who used them to entertain children. These are primarily texts with sources and comparative references, but another book, *All in Together, Girls: Skipping Songs from Regina, Saskatchewan* (1980) by Robert C. Cosbey, goes farther, discussing the sources, transmission, and changes of the rhymes, describing the different skipping patterns, and analyzing the content and meaning of the texts. Despite its small size, this is an important book: the first genuine analytic study of Canadian children's lore. Another study relating to children, John D.A. Widdowson's *'If You Don't Be Good': Social Control in Newfoundland* (1977) investigates in detail the frightening figures parents use to threaten children who misbehave.

Several biographical books were of folklore interest. Edward D. Ives continued his excellent studies of individual east coast song composers with *Joe Scott: The Woodsman-Songmaker* (1979), in which he relates Scott's songs to his environment and analyzes the folksong creator as artist. Helen Creighton wrote *A Life in Folklore* (1975), recalling her experiences collecting Nova Scotia songs, stories, and superstitions. Victor Butler (fisherman) and Aubrey Tizzard (cooper) related their respective memories in *The Little Nord Easter: Reminiscences of a Placentia Bayman* (1977) and *On Sloping Ground: Reminiscences of Outport Life in Notre Dame Bay, Newfoundland* (1979). The novelist Adele Wiseman wrote movingly of her mother and her doll-making hobby in *Old Woman at Play* (1978).

In recent years more folklore students focused on material culture. Papers on folk arts and crafts frequently outnumber all others in folklore journals and at folklore meetings, and many theses and dissertations concentrate on material culture. This tendency may be influenced by the fact that few folklorists can find university positions, while more are being employed in museums, historical buildings, parks, and pioneer villages. Of the many books in this field, few so far have been by folklorists, although Marius Barbeau wrote of argillite carvings, totem poles, hooked rugs, the Assomption sash,

Laurentian wood carvers, and other subjects. Other early books included
Edwin C. Guillet's *Pioneer Arts and Crafts* (1968), Audrey Hawthorn's *Art
of the Kwakiutl Indians* (1967), and George Swinton's *Sculpture of the Eskimo*
(1965). A varied sampling of more recent volumes includes Harold B. and
Dorothy K. Burnham's *'Keep Me Warm One Night': Early Handweaving in
Eastern Canada* (1975), Ralph and Patricia Price's *'Twas Ever Thus: A
Selection of Eastern Canadian Folk Art* (1979), Selwyn Dewdney's *The Sa-
cred Scrolls of the Southern Ojibway* (1975), and Michael S. Bird's *Ontario
Fraktur: A Pennsylvania-German Folk Tradition in Early Canada* (1977).
Contemporary folklorists, especially in such journals as *Material History
Bulletin*, began to publish more in this field, adding contextual and interpretative material to existing descriptive accounts of such subjects as rug design
and stone-cutting. For a detailed listing of both French and English publications, see 'A Bibliography of Material Culture in Canada' (*Canadian Folklore canadien*, 1982).

Many important books originate with museums or art galleries, some of
the best being catalogues for exhibitions. For example, folklorists working
at the National Museum of Man produced *From the Heart* (1983), which
features items from the Canadian Centre for Folk Culture Studies. It begins
with artifacts representing aspects of traditional life, particularly pioneer farming and logging; the second section expresses commitment to the community
in the form of motifs, symbols, icons, and talismans; the third features works
of imagination, humour, and fantasy; the fourth concentrates on the work of
four Canadian folk artists. The compilers believe that folk art is in transition:
from tradition to innovation, from functionality to pure form, from collective
representations to individuality, and from ethnic origins to a more universal
view. They also note that it has become less traditional and utilitarian, moving
towards greater aesthetic appeal.

The most important regional book was Herbert Halpert's *A Folklore Sampler from the Maritimes* (1982). Halpert, the distinguished folklorist who
founded Memorial University's Department of Folklore, spent a year at Mount
Allison University, where he encouraged students to collect folklore of their
region; *A Folklore Sampler* represents the results of this unusual collaboration
between professor and students. While it is devoted largely to folk narratives,
it contains smaller chapters on folk 'dites' about weather, proverbial sayings,
folk beliefs, and childlore. Especially valuable is Halpert's extensive bibliographical essay. Halpert was honoured by a Festschrift, *Folklore Studies*
(1980), ed. Kenneth S. Goldstein and Neil V. Rosenberg.

Two other regional collections come from the prairies, a previously neglected area. Kay Stone, who teaches folklore at the University of Winnipeg,
compiled *Prairie Folklore* (1976), a sizeable mimeographed book covering
all the main genres, based largely on material submitted by her students.

Michael Taft, a freelance folklorist and oral historian, published *Discovering Saskatchewan Folklore* (1983), the first significant book from that province. It consists of three case studies: of a storytelling evening, of the St Laurent pilgrimage considered as a religious ritual, and of lace-making, a family craft tradition. In his introduction, Taft defines folklore as 'the common creativity of humankind,' and relates this definition to the various types of folklore. Then by discussing one singer's repertoire he shows how folklore is both universal and local, reflecting the culture of the people who use it.

RESEARCH ENTERPRISES

Much Anglo-Canadian folklore during this period came from Memorial University, an archival and study centre described in Herbert Halpert and Neil V. Rosenberg's *Folklore Studies at Memorial University* (1976). The University has been issuing a series of Folklore and Language Publications, of which three present articles by various scholars: *Literature and Folk Culture: Ireland and Newfoundland* (1977), ed. Alison Feder and Bernice Schrank; *Folklore and Oral History* (1979), ed. Neil V. Rosenberg; and *Canadian Folklore Perspectives* (1978), ed. Kenneth S. Goldstein. The first two look at folklore in relation to literature and history; the third and most significant relates folklore to the search for a national identity. Rosenberg considers regionalism and folklore in Atlantic Canada, Elli Köngäs Maranda surveys French-Canadian folklore scholarship, Ban Seng Hoe looks at Asian-Canadian folklore studies, and Carole H. Carpenter discusses the connections between folklore and government.

Memorial's Institute of Social and Economic Research (ISER) issues another series of publications, some of which have provided the best folklife material in recent years. Good examples are Widdowson's study of bogey figures and James C. Faris's *Cat Harbour: A Newfoundland Fishing Settlement* (1972). Folklorists at Memorial also have collaborated on *Folk Literature* (1983), a series of ten pamphlets designed for use in Newfoundland schools. These cover the various folklore genres, using local examples. The general editor is Larry Small; the writers include Goldstein, Widdowson, Rosenberg, and David Buchan.

A second major centre of folklore research is the National Museum in Ottawa. Several sections of the Museum issue Mercury series publications, which are reproduced from typed manuscripts to make the research available quickly. The most relevant come from the Canadian Centre for Folk Culture Studies, which by 1984 had published over fifty, based on field work among various ethnic groups. These are of uneven quality, and small print runs mean that they go out of print quickly, but they often provide material not available elsewhere. Those discussing folk music include studies of Korean, Black,

Polish, and Newfoundland communities;[4] a collection is Ellen Karp's *Many Are Strong among the Strangers* (1984).

More general volumes study communities of many ethnic origins: Norwegian, Korean, Danish, Hungarian, Swedish, Black, Italian, Greek, Chinese, Doukhobor, Gypsy, Mennonite, Romanian, Finnish, French, German, Polish, Scots, and Hutterite. Most of these contain some material of value; a few deserve to be issued in a more permanent form. One of the best is Klymasz's *Folk Narrative among Ukrainian-Canadians in Western Canada*. Other excellent studies include *People in the Tobacco Belt: Four Lives* (1975) by Linda Degh, *Traditional Doukhobor Folkways* (1977) by Koozma J. Tarasoff, *Békévar: Working Papers on a Canadian Prairie Community* (1980) edited by Robert Blumstock, and *The Newfoundland Mummers' Christmas House-Visit* (1984) by Margaret R. Robertson.

The Mercury series of the National Museum's Ethnology Service includes some valuable folklore papers dealing with the native peoples. Some are useful studies of particular groups,[5] and a number are particularly analytical, like Michael K. Foster's *From the Earth to Beyond the Sky: An Ethnographic Approach to Four Longhouse Iroquois Speech Events* (1974), Richard J. Preston's *Cree Narrative: Expressing the Personal Meaning of Events* (1975), Maija M. Lutz's *The Effects of Acculturation on Eskimo Music of Cumberland Peninsula* (1978), Ronald Scollon's *The Context of the Informant Narrative Performance: From Sociolinguistics to Ethnolinguistics at Fort Chipewyan, Alberta* (1979), and Anton F. Kolstee's *Bella Coola Indian Music* (1982).

Except for the work at Memorial, Anglo-Canadian folklore has been neglected recently in favour of minority cultures, mainly because of the Canadian Centre for Folk Culture Studies' emphasis on multiculturalism. This seems regrettable in view of the fact that Anglo-Canadians still form the largest group in Canada's ethnic mix. It is also doubtful whether the emphasis on material culture at the expense of oral traditions is desirable; a more even balance would probably produce a better cultural picture. Eastern traditions are still much better covered than western ones, and there is still more emphasis on rural than on urban lore. There are now a few publications dealing with occupational and children's lore, but more are needed. Some dissertations have been published, emphasizing the shift towards analytic study; these include Laurel Doucette's *Skill and Status: Traditional Expertise within a Rural Canadian Family* (1979), and Hilda C. Murray's *More than 50%: Women's Life in a Newfoundland Outport, 1900–1950* (1979). Most studies are local or regional: scholars are just beginning to produce some national and cross-cultural works. Much remains to be done, but, during the 1970s and 1980s, Canadian folklore became a much richer discipline.

11 Anthropological Literature

BRUCE G. TRIGGER

Anthropology developed from a romantic curiosity about human diversity that was stimulated by the Renaissance and the Age of Exploration. Europeans encountered societies throughout the world that had simpler technologies than their own and judged them to be 'primitive.' Naturalists slowly realized that equally 'primitive' cultures had existed in Europe in prehistoric times. By the eighteenth century these two perspectives were combined in an evolutionary synthesis that viewed all human societies as developing from simple to complex. Anthropology emerged in Western Europe and North America during the nineteenth century as a discipline that was devoted to the investigation of 'primitive' societies. It had four main branches: ethnology, which sought to record traditional cultures before they disappeared; prehistoric archeology, which documented such cultures prior to written records; physical anthropology, which explored the relation between physical and cultural characteristics among human groups; and comparative linguistics, which studied native languages. By means of these four approaches anthropologists sought to acquire a comprehensive understanding of the small-scale societies that were dominated by European colonists and to learn more about European societies in prehistoric times. In the eighteenth century, failure to progress had generally been attributed to environmental differences, a position that accorded with the Enlightenment's belief in the perfectibility of all human beings. Nineteenth-century anthropology was strongly influenced by a growing sense of European racial as well as cultural superiority. This view was reinforced by Darwinian evolutionism.

EARLY CANADIAN ANTHROPOLOGY

Until the late nineteenth century, there were no professional anthropologists in Canada. Yet three scholars published books that commanded international attention. Daniel Wilson (1816–92), who was already a renowned archeologist when he arrived from Edinburgh to teach history and English literature at

University College, Toronto, in 1853, found the living peoples of the New World as interesting as its archeology. His *Prehistoric Man: Researches into the Origin of Civilization in the Old and the New World* (1862; rev. ed., 1865; 3rd ed., 1876) compared the prehistoric development of cultures in Europe and America and studied the impact of European discovery on the Western hemisphere. He regarded what was happening to European and African immigrants and to racially mixed groups such as the Métis as being of as much anthropological interest as was the fate of native American peoples. John William Dawson (1820–99), who was born in Nova Scotia, educated at Edinburgh University, and Principal of McGill University from 1855 to 1893, was a geologist with broad scientific interests. His most important anthropological work, *Fossil Men and Their Modern Representatives* (1880; 3rd ed., 1888), sought to use the cultures of the contemporary native peoples of North America to illustrate European life in prehistoric times. Unlike Wilson, however, he opposed the concept of cultural evolution and argued that there was no evidence that all stages of human complexity had not co-existed throughout human history. The third outstanding amateur anthropologist was Horatio Hale (1817–96). He was born in New Hampshire and after graduating from Harvard University did important ethnological research in Oregon and the Pacific before becoming a lawyer in Clinton, Ontario. In 1883 he published his major work, *The Iroquois Book of Rites*, based on a study of oral traditions begun at the Six Nations Reserve near Brantford, Ontario, in 1870. All three anthropologists rejected the racist views about native people that were fashionable in the United States and, in keeping with the older ideals of the Enlightenment, stressed the inherent unity of the human race.

These pioneers influenced a second generation of anthropological researchers. Hale is credited with strengthening Franz Boas's aversion to the racist and evolutionary predilections of American anthropology, while he supervised the research that the young German ethnologist carried out for the British Association for the Advancement of Science among the Indians of British Columbia in the 1880s. Boas (1858–1942) quickly became the most influential anthropologist in the United States after he began to train graduate students at Columbia University.

Through his advocacy of archeology in the articles that he wrote for the *Canadian Journal*, published by the [Royal] Canadian Institute, Daniel Wilson encouraged the work of David Boyle (1842–1911), a teacher and bookseller of Scottish origin who, as a curator of what evolved into the archeological collection of the Ontario Provincial Museum, became the first salaried anthropologist in Canada. Boyle edited the *Annual Archaeological Report for Ontario*, Canada's first anthropological journal, in which he published his own reports on Ontario archeology and ethnology, as well as work by serious amateurs, many of whom he trained to do archeological research. While on the staff of the Geological Survey of Canada, George Mercer Dawson (1849–1901), son of John William, collected artifacts and wrote reports dealing with the native peoples of western Canada. Charles Hill-Tout (1858–1944), a British-born school teacher, published numerous studies of the Indians of British Columbia after he moved there in 1889. Ralph Maud reprinted some of these papers in *The Salish People* (4 vols, 1978).

The third phase in the development of Canadian anthropology began in 1910, when the Division of Anthropology was established within the Museums Branch of the Geological Survey of Canada, which later became the National Museum of Canada. Its chief until 1925 was Edward Sapir (1884–1939), an American student of Boas who was studying the native languages of western Canada. While in Ottawa, Sapir published his most significant theoretical work, *Language* (1921), as well as *Time Perspective in Aboriginal American Culture* (1916), which contains the best exposition of Boasian techniques for explaining changes within native cultures. Sapir built the Division of Anthropology into a major research centre. He hired the young Quebec-born, Oxford-trained ethnologist Charles Marius Barbeau (1883–1969), who remained at the National Museum for the rest of his life studying native languages and mythologies, West Coast Indian cultures, and French-Canadian folklore. Barbeau's numerous monographs include *Huron and Wyandot Mythology* (1915), *Folk-Songs of Old Quebec* (1935), and *Totem Poles* (2 vols, 1950–1). Diamond Jenness (1886–1969), who was born in New Zealand and trained at Oxford, was employed to study the Inuit and Athapaskans. Although he made some important discoveries concerning Inuit prehistory, he soon turned wholeheartedly to ethnological research. His *The Life of the Copper Eskimos* appeared in 1922 and a decade later *The Indians of Canada* (1932), a comprehensive survey of the traditional cultures of all the native peoples of Canada. This book has gone through seven editions and, although now sadly out of date, remains the only general coverage of Canadian ethnography. Frederick W. Waugh (1872–1924), a Canadian who was hired to study the Indians of eastern Canada, is best known for *Iroquois Foods and Food Preparation* (1916). William J. Wintemberg (1876–1941), who had been informally trained by David Boyle, carried out archeological research from Alberta to Newfoundland, although mainly on Iroquoian sites in southern Ontario. He published a distinguished series of monographs describing the sites he excavated as well as a number of important interpretative studies such as 'Distinguishing Characteristics of Algonkian and Iroquoian Cultures' (1931).

Although Wilson had taught courses in anthropology at University College as early as 1854, no anthropologist was employed full-time by a Canadian university until Thomas F. McIlwraith (1899–1964) was appointed lecturer at the University of Toronto in 1925. He was born in Hamilton, Ontario, and had studied anthropology at Cambridge University. His book *The Bella Coola Indians* (2 vols, 1948) was acclaimed as one of the most successful studies of the traditional culture of a native American group in the Boasian style, although a twenty-year delay in its publication diminished the full appreciation of his achievement. Anthropological research was severely curtailed by the economic depression of the 1930s and by World War II. The most important Canadian publication of that period was *The North American Indian Today* (1943), edited by McIlwraith and C.T. Loram of Yale University. Based on papers delivered at a conference held in Toronto in 1939, this book surveyed the current condition of native people in Canada and the United States. It reflected a growing preoccupation in both countries with the role that anthropology might play in formulating more humane and effective policies to administer native reserves.

CANADIAN ANTHROPOLOGY: 1945–72

World War II marked a major watershed in Canadian anthropology, with only Barbeau, Jenness, and McIlwraith surviving as major figures into the new era. After 1945 anthropology began to expand at an accelerating rate. The early phase of this growth reflected an optimistic postwar concern with the practical applications of anthropology. George Gordon Brown (1896–1955), a Canadian who had studied social anthropology (a school of ethnology influenced by the sociology of Émile Durkheim) at the London School of Economics and later been superintendant of education in Tanganyika, came to teach at the University of Toronto in 1946. His *Anthropology in Action: An Experiment in the Iringa District of the Iringa Province, Tanganyika Territory* (1935), co-authored with A.M.B. Hutt, had sought to ascertain how anthropologists and administrators might co-operate more effectively.

Harry B. Hawthorn, a New Zealander with a doctorate from Yale University, began to teach at the University of British Columbia in 1947. He had already published *The Maori* (1944) and soon became involved in research projects that had significant implications for formulating public policy in Canada. Major publications resulting from this research were *The Doukhobors of British Columbia* (1955), which he edited and co-authored; *The Indians of British Columbia* (1958), co-authored with Cyril S. Belshaw and the economist Stuart M. Jamieson; and *A Survey of the Contemporary Indians of Canada: Economic, Political, Educational Needs and Policies* (1966–7), co-edited with Marc-Adélard Tremblay. The last of these reports was based on a survey of the conditions of native people, carried out under Hawthorn's direction for the Indian Affairs Branch of the Department of Northern Affairs by an interdisciplinary team of fifty-two researchers, many of whom were anthropologists. It recommended greater self-determination for native people as well as the importance of improving their standard of living.

R. William Dunning's *Social and Economic Change among the Northern Ojibwa* (1959) examined the impact of external economic resources on the social organization of an Indian band in northern Ontario. Jenness's five-volume study of *Eskimo Administration* (1962–8) compared the policies used to deal with the Inuit by the Canadian, United States, and Danish governments and suggested how Canadian policies might be improved. In *Kabloona and Eskimo in the Central Keewatin* (1967), Francis G. Vallee studied relations between native people and white settlers, missionaries, and administrators in the Northwest Territories. *Patrons and Brokers in the East Arctic* (1971) was a series of essays that further explored grassroots political processes involving native people and whites. This book was edited by Robert Paine and published as one of the early volumes of the Institute of Social and Economic Research of Memorial University of Newfoundland. Although he had received his doctorate from Oxford University, Paine had taught and researched in Norway and was strongly influenced by the Norwegian social anthropologist Fredrik Barth. At McGill University, Norman A. Chance, the first director of the Programme in the Anthropology of Development, edited *Conflict in Culture* (1968) and *Developmental Change among the Cree Indians of Quebec* (1970). These reported studies of the effects of technological change on the social organization and values of the Indians of northern Quebec.

Marc-Adélard Tremblay, who had his doctorate from Cornell University, began to teach at Université Laval in the 1950s. His early works, such as *Les comportements économiques de la famille salariée du Québec* (1964), co-authored with Gérald Fortin, addressed the solution of contemporary social problems of Quebec. Later research was focused on the impact of industrialization and urbanization on traditional French-Canadian culture. *Rural Canada in Transition* (1966), co-edited with W.J. Anderson; *Les changements socio-culturels à Saint-Augustin* (1969), written with Paul Charest and Yvan Breton; and *Famille et parenté en Acadie* (1971), co-authored with Marc Laplante, continued a tradition of studying French-Canadian life begun by the American sociologists Everett C. Hughes and Horace Miner.

Anthropologists also began to pay more attention to change and development abroad. Cyril S. Belshaw, another New Zealander who came to the University of British Columbia in 1953, was a specialist in economic anthropology. His publications were marked by expanding theoretical scope: *Island Administration in the South West Pacific* (1950); *Changing Melanesia* (1954); *Under the Ivi Tree: Society and Economic Growth in Rural Fiji* (1964); *Traditional Exchange and Modern Markets* (1965); and *The Conditions of Social Performance* (1970), in which he argued that all societies should be analyzed as entities that seek to produce socially valued results.

The same year that he arrived at McGill University, Richard F. Salisbury, an English anthropologist who also specialized in economic studies, published *From Stone to Steel* (1962), which documented the far-reaching effects of recently introduced European technology among a highland New Guinea people. His next major publication, *Vunamami* (1970), sought to account for the successful integration of the Tolai of New Britain into an international market economy. In the late 1960s McGill University and the Université de Montréal became involved in a project to train graduate students to do research in the West Indies. Some of the results, focused mainly on economic development and social problems, appeared in *McGill Studies in Caribbean Anthropology* (1969), edited by Frances Henry, while a more diverse range of ethnographic topics was covered in *L'archipel inachevé* (1972), edited by Jean Benoist.

Traditional ethnographies produced during this period included Asen Balikci's *The Netsilik Eskimo* (1970); Richard Slobodin's *Band Organization of the Peel River Kutchin* (1962) and *Metis of the Mackenzie District* (1966); Norman Chance's *The Eskimo of North Alaska* (1966); and Bruce G. Trigger's *The Huron: Farmers of the North* (1969), which was based on seventeenth-century historical documentation. One of the finest products of a psychological approach in anthropology was Jean L. Briggs's *Never in Anger* (1970), a portrayal of native life based on an extended period that the author spent living as a member of an Inuit household.

In the 1960s the structuralist approach pioneered by the French ethnologist Claude Lévi-Strauss came to play a key role in the formal analysis of cultural patterning. It was introduced to the University of British Columbia in 1970 by Quebec-born Pierre Maranda, who was the co-editor with Jean Pouillon of *Échanges et communications* (1970), a prestigious two-volume Festschrift dedicated to Lévi-Strauss. The next year Maranda and his wife Elli Köngäs Maranda published a book of essays titled *Structural Models in Folklore and Transformational Essays* (1971). They also edited *Structural Analyses of Oral Tradition* (1971), a reader in symbolic anthropology. The structuralist approach became an important focus of anthropology departments at the University of Western Ontario and Université Laval as well as at the University of British Columbia.

While anthropologists at the University of British Columbia, Laval, McGill, and Memorial were strongly committed to the study of social change and development, the departments at the University of Toronto and the Université de Montréal emphasized the holistic Boasian view of anthropology; hence they paid more attention to archeology and physical anthropology. Separate departments of prehistoric archeology were founded at the University of Calgary in 1963 and at Simon Fraser University in 1971. A large number of archeologists employed by the National Museum of Canada also carried out archeological research across the country. Major works produced by the latter included Richard S. MacNeish's *Iroquois Pottery Types* (1952), which transformed Iroquoian studies by demonstrating that the cultures of Iroquoian-speaking peoples, such as the Huron, Neutral, and Iroquois, had slowly evolved in their prehistoric homelands rather than been brought to them by a series of migrations from the south as had previously been believed. James V. Wright's *The Ontario Iroquois Tradition* (1966) offered a more detailed account of prehistoric Iroquoian development in southern Ontario; and George F. MacDonald's *Debert: A Palaeo-Indian Site in Central Nova Scotia* (1968) was the first study of an early post-glacial habitation site in Canada.

Archeologists employed by universities also began to do research abroad. Philip E.L. Smith published *Le Solutréen en France* (1966) and in *Meroe: A Civilization of the Sudan* (1967) Peter L. Shinnie described the archeology of an ancient African kingdom. Trigger's *History and Settlement in Lower Nubia* (1965) and James A. Tuck's *Onondaga Iroquois Prehistory* (1971) were early applications of settlement pattern analysis in archeology. Trigger's *Beyond History: The Methods of Prehistory* (1968) attempted to synthesize increasingly discordant old and new trends in the discipline in the 1960s.

Canadian anthropologists started to create their own institutional structures and journals in the 1950s. *Anthropologica* (est. 1959), printed twice a year by the Canadian Research Centre for Anthropology in Ottawa, contained research in all branches of anthropology. The Canadian Sociology and Anthropology Association, which attracted many social anthropologists, published the *Canadian Review of Sociology and Anthropology* beginning in 1964. *Ontario Archaeology*, produced at irregular but increasingly frequent intervals by the Ontario Archaeological Society starting in 1954, provided an outlet for papers dealing with provincial prehistory, while the Canadian Archaeological Association, founded in 1968, soon established a *Bulletin*. These developments promoted a new level of collective awareness among anthropologists working in Canada.

The number of graduate students being trained in Canada was insufficient to meet the expansion of anthropology positions in universities during the 1960s. Many Canadians who filled these posts had received their graduate training in the United States or England. In addition, large numbers of foreign anthropologists, most of them Americans, found employment in Canadian universities. As a result of the competitive North American job market in the 1960s, many foreign scholars and even some Canadians left the country after brief stays. Those who remained came from many different backgrounds, were dispersed across a continent, and found themselves in departments that viewed anthropology from different perspectives. The choices made by established anthropologists in hiring new staff encouraged this diversity, although selectivity was inhibited by applicants being in short supply. In 1972 many anthropologists in Canada were close to the beginning of their careers. The next decade was to witness their florescence.

CANADIAN ANTHROPOLOGY: 1972–84

The 1970s saw a continuing interest in social change, in the impact of new technologies and expanding Western economies, and in using anthropology to solve social problems. By the start of that decade the world had been markedly changed. Most of the imperial possessions in which anthropologists had plied their trade on a global basis were now independent; this political change substantially affected the terms by which anthropologists could have access to these countries. Within Western nations, at the same time, native people were developing greater political consciousness and taking stock of their grievances. Anthropologists increasingly came to view their discipline as a medium by which the problems and viewpoints of marginal and powerless groups could be communicated to the dominant Euroamerican culture. In response to world-wide decolonization and native rights movements, they also grew more sensitive to the feelings and aspirations of the people they studied.

Many anthropologists became involved in land claims litigation and assessments of the impact of technological development, which was increasingly impinging on the independence and threatening the traditional ways of life of Canadian native peoples. Beginning in 1971 Richard Salisbury directed the research that provided basic information and suggested alternative solutions to both native people and the Quebec government that formed the basis for negotiating the settlement of the James Bay land claim. This experience led the McGill Programme in the Anthropology of Development to become increasingly engaged in social animation that involved researching and helping to solve problems identified by local people. Reports such as Salisbury et al., *Development and James Bay* (1972); Nathan Elberg et al., *Not by Bread Alone* (1972); and Ignatius E. La Rusic et al., *Negotiating a Way of Life* (1979) present the philosophy and results of the early research. Salisbury's *A Homeland for the Cree* (1986) documents in a broader historical perspective how the James Bay project forced the Cree to fight the project in the courts, negotiate with the Quebec government, build and staff a local administrative structure, and organize for economic development. He compares Cree society in 1971 with that in 1981 and provides an analysis of why this group's experience with development has been positive, in contrast to the negative experiences of most native groups in Canada and the United States.

In *The White Arctic* (1977), edited by Robert Paine, a group of anthropologists continued Vallee's and Paine's assessment of the interaction between

Europeans and Inuit by arguing that it was insufficient to try to alter native attitudes towards paternalistic government policies; change was more important in the policies themselves and in the attitudes of those who administered them. Human rights issues relating to native people and other minority groups were surveyed in Evelyn Kallen's *Ethnicity and Human Rights in Canada* (1982). A similar concern with native rights is evident in Rolf Knight's *Indians at Work: An Informal History of Native Indian Labour in British Columbia, 1858–1930* (1978) and Joan Ryan's *Wall of Words: The Betrayal of the Urban Indian* (1978). Native political consciousness was examined through case studies in *The Politics of Indianness* (1983), edited by Adrian Tanner. Sally M. Weaver analyzed the formulation of late 1960s government policy for dealing with native people in *Making Canadian Indian Policy* (1981), while Michael Asch's *Home and Native Land* (1984) sought to intervene in contemporary constitutional debates by arguing for a redefinition of the ideological framework of the native rights issue. Anthropologists no longer view native people as passive objects of study but as human beings struggling, often against heavy odds, to regain the power and resources necessary to make collective decisions concerning social, economic, and cultural matters that affect their lives.

In the 1930s the realization that native peoples were not becoming extinct encouraged some North American anthropologists to investigate how these peoples had responded to European domination in the past as a basis for formulating what were believed to be more humane and effective policies for dealing with them. By the 1950s these studies of acculturation had evolved into ethnohistory, which was recognized as a fifth major branch of anthropology concerned with understanding how native societies had changed since European contact. This development enhanced anthropologists' awareness of the dynamism and creativity of native peoples, whose cultures they had previously viewed only as disintegrating under European domination. The Canadian historian Alfred G. Bailey, influenced by the anthropologist T.F. McIlwraith and the economist Harold Innis, had pioneered this new approach with *The Conflict of European and Eastern Algonkian Cultures, 1504–1700* (1937; reprinted 1969). In anthropology Trigger's *The Children of Aataentsic* (2 vols, 1976) used the concept of interest groups to analyze the history of the Huron people from prehistoric times until their dispersal by the Iroquois after 1649. In particular, this book challenged the assumption that European nationalities and particular native peoples had confronted each other in a monolithic fashion. The positive role played by French traders in forging close relations with the Huron was documented for the first time and contrasted with the disruptive role played in these relations by Champlain and the Récollet and Jesuit missionaries. The methodological problems involved in this type of research and its implications for understanding EuroCanadian history have been examined in greater detail by Trigger in *Natives and Newcomers* (1985).

Daniel Francis and Toby Morantz documented the enduring economic independence of the Cree, despite the development of European trade, in *Partners in Furs: A History of the Fur Trade in Eastern James Bay 1600–1870* (1983). Robin Ridington's *Swan People: A Study of the Dunne-za Prophet Dance* (1978) examined the development of a religious revitalization movement among the Beaver Indians after European contact, while Gordon M. Day traced the origins of the Abenaki at Odanak in *The Identity of the Saint Francis Indians* (1981). J. Garth Taylor has used historical documentation to study factors influencing settlement size in *Labrador Eskimo Settlements of the Early Contact Period* (1974), concluding that weakness of authority and ensuing conflict in traditional Inuit society prevented their settlements from being as large as their subsistence economy would have supported. On the border between ethnohistory and archeology is Robert McGhee's *Beluga Hunters* (1974), which combined historical and archeological data to reconstruct the life of an Inuit group of the Mackenzie Delta prior to their near annihilation by European diseases around 1900. These studies, together with other ethnohistorical investigations by historians, such as Robin Fisher, and geographers, such as Conrad Heidenreich and Arthur J. Ray, are contributing to a better understanding of traditional native life and what has happened to native people since European contact. They are also rescuing Canadian history from an almost exclusive preoccupation with European settlers and their descendants.

Social anthropologists have also addressed many problems relating to non-native groups in Canadian history. Their research is generally distinguished from that of sociologists by relying on participant observation and informant interviews rather than on surveys. There have been further studies of French Canada, particularly of small towns and rural settings. Gerald L. Gold's *Saint-Pascal* (1975) investigates how postwar economic changes in a small town resulted in the replacement of its traditional elite, who were mainly members of the liberal professions, by a new generation of successful businessmen. In *L'identité québécoise en péril* (1983), Marc-Adélard Tremblay attempts to define what it means to be Québécois and to suggest how this broader sense of identity relates to the regional, social, and economic diversity of Quebec. He also analyzes internal as well as external factors that are promoting the development and dissolution of distinctive French-Canadian cultural values. *Communities and Culture in French Canada* (1973), edited by Gold and Tremblay, has made available in English many reports based on ethnological-style research by anthropologists and sociologists concerning facets of French-Canadian life in all parts of Canada. Frances Henry's *For-*

gotten Canadians (1973) sketches the social and economic history of the black population of Nova Scotia as well as life in two contemporary black communities. She also edited a substantial volume of papers dealing with *Ethnicity in the Americas* (1976). Canadian anthropologists have also published papers on regionalism, gender distinctions, and the treatment of immigrants.

Other books signal the concern of anthropologists with areas of life not conventionally associated with the discipline. Elliott Leyton's *Dying Hard* (1975) presents chilling oral accounts of the lives of Newfoundland miners afflicted by industrial illnesses. Other medically oriented studies include *Childbirth: Alternatives to Medical Control* (1981), edited by Shelly Romalis. This explicitly political book argues in favour of changing a system in which (the authors believe) professionals play too large a role in decision-making. Cyril Belshaw has used his anthropological skills to propose solutions for problems facing contemporary higher education in *Towers Besieged* (1974).

Research done within Canada is indissolubly linked to that carried out by Canadians abroad. Studies done in other countries encourage vital interaction with the international anthropological community and by doing so benefit the overall quality of work done inside Canada. In a complementary fashion, Canadian anthropologists bring to their foreign research the experience and theoretical perspectives gained from their work inside the country. The most comprehensive single Canadian contribution to understanding the value of anthropology for solving major problems confronting humanity is Belshaw's *The Sorcerer's Apprentice* (1976). While Belshaw castigates the foibles and shortcomings of anthropologists, he concludes that their broadly comparative understanding of human behaviour allows them to identify difficulties and suggest solutions more effectively than can more ethnocentric policy-makers. Richard Salisbury has edited an important set of papers examining the relation between *Affluence and Cultural Survival* (1984) in cross-cultural perspective. Peter C.W. Gutkind critically evaluates the ideas that have governed anthropological research in African cities in *Urban Anthropology* (1973). Two important collections of papers dealing with problems that modern developments are posing for pastoral peoples throughout the world are *Change and Development in Nomadic and Pastoral Societies* (1981), edited by John G. Galaty and Philip C. Salzman, and *The Future of Pastoral Peoples* (1981), edited by Galaty, Salzman, Dan R. Aronson, and Amy Chouinard.

Among the monographs reporting on specific ethnographic studies, Jacques M. Chevalier's *Civilization and the Stolen Gift* (1982) examines in detail the symbolic as well as the purely economic factors that are linking tribal and mestizo societies in the Amazon Basin of Peru with national and international structures, and that, in the course of doing so, are internally transforming these societies. Dan R. Aronson's *The City Is Our Farm: Seven Migrant*

Ijebu Yoruba Families (1978) offers a highly readable as well as a scientifically valuable account of modern urban life in Nigeria, while Stanley R. Barrett, in *The Rise and Fall of an African Utopia* (1977), traces the success and decline of a community of Yoruba-speaking fishermen who were persecuted because of their religious beliefs. Stuart B. Philpott examines the effects of massive emigration from a small island on those who remain behind in *West Indian Migration: The Montserrat Case* (1973); Margaret M. Lock the connections between traditional and modern healing in *East Asian Medicine in Urban Japan* (1980); Kathleen Gough economic and social change in two villages in *Rural Society in Southeast India* (1981); and Judith A. Nagata religious responses to radical social change in *The Reflowering of Malaysian Islam* (1984). In a special category because of its personal as well as its political significance is *Victims and Neighbors: A Small Town in Nazi Germany Remembered* (1984), by Frances Henry. This book, based on intensive interviews carried out in 1979, examines the full range of social relations between Jews and Christians in a town in which Henry grew up during the 1930s. Her account of the corrosive effects of state-encouraged hatred rises above conventional stereotypes with its documentation of acts of kindness that some Germans showed towards their Jewish neighbours.

Traditional ethnography, as distinguished from studies of change and development, has not been ignored in the past decade. The most authoritative and extensive compendium of information about the native peoples of North America to appear in this century is the Smithsonian Institution's *Handbook of North American Indians*, under the general editorship of William C. Sturtevant. By 1985 three regional volumes had been published that relate to Canada and contain many chapters written by Canadian anthropologists. Two of these have been edited by Canadian anthropologists, *Northeast* (1978) by Bruce G. Trigger and *Arctic* (1984) by David Damas, while the *Subarctic* volume (1981) was edited by June Helm. Each volume provides comprehensive information about the traditional cultures, languages, prehistory, post-European contact history, and current state of the various native groups inhabiting a major region of North America, as well as a thorough guide to the literature relating to these groups. These volumes supersede the old two-volume *Handbook of American Indians North of Mexico* (1907–10), edited by Frederick W. Hodge, as well as the extracts from that work that were reprinted as the *Handbook of the Indians of Canada* (1913).

One of the most important ethnographic studies by a Canadian anthropologist is Adrian Tanner's *Bringing Home Animals* (1979). It examines religious beliefs among the Mistassini Cree, especially in relation to their hunting and trapping practices in their winter bush life. Tanner concludes that among Cree hunters the ongoing activities of economic production play a major role in shaping religious ideology, although this process is constrained by the traditional Cree understanding of religious symbolism. Also of interest are Michael K. Foster's *From the Earth to Beyond the Sky* (1974), a study of Iroquois ritual speeches; Richard J. Preston's *Cree Narrative* (1975); and D. Lee Guemple's *Inuit Adoption* (1979). *Extending the Rafters* (1984), a Festschrift in honour of William N. Fenton edited by M.K. Foster, Jack Campisi, and Marianne Mithun, provides a comprehensive and interdisciplinary review of recent research on Iroquois prehistory, history, and culture in which Canadian contributions are prominent. David F. Aberle and the American linguist Isidore Dyen have published *Lexical Reconstruction: The Case of the Proto-Athapaskan Kinship System* (1974), a study of prehistoric social organization based on reconstructing the vocabulary of related prehistoric languages.

Numerous studies deal with the material culture and especially the artistic traditions of native North Americans. The most innovative of these is *Sacred Art of the Algonkians: A Study of the Peterborough Petroglyphs* (1973) by Joan M. Vastokas and Romas K. Vastokas, which interprets a magnificent manifestation of prehistoric rock art in southern Ontario in terms of the shamanistic beliefs of Algonkian-speaking peoples. This same art has been fantastically claimed by the American biologist Barry Fell in *Bronze Age America*, 1982, as evidence of Scandinavian visits to the New World during the Bronze Age. Among many works dealing with the spectacular native art of the West Coast are George F. MacDonald's *Haida Monumental Art* (1983), which maps, illustrates, and identifies the houses and totem poles from fifteen historically documented villages on the Queen Charlotte Islands; Marjorie M. Halpin's *Totem Poles* (1981), which explains the form and meaning of old and contemporary poles with special reference to specimens in the collection of the University of British Columbia; and *Indian Art Traditions of the Northwest Coast* (1983), edited by Roy L. Carlson, which surveys archeological as well as ethnological evidence. Exhibition catalogues of special interest are Ted J. Brasser's *'Bo'jou, Neejee!'* (1976), which discusses specimens of handicrafts from eastern Canada, many collected before 1850, and Wilson Duff's *Images, Stone, BC* (1975), dealing with West Coast native stone working.

Traditional ethnography done abroad by Richard B. Lee of the University of Toronto has provided the basis for what is probably Canadian ethnology's most important contribution to international debates. Ecologically oriented research among the Bushmen of southern Africa allowed Lee and his coworkers to demonstrate that these people could collect all the food that they required with very little effort. This contradicted the traditional interpretation of hunter-gatherers as being poor and hard-pressed because of their feeble technology. These views were widely disseminated through *Man the Hunter* (1968), the proceedings of an international symposium edited by Lee and Irven Devore. In particular, they influenced archeologists' interpretations of the nature of Paleolithic and more recent hunter-gatherer cultures. Lee's own ethnographic observations were presented in detail in *The !Kung San: Men, Women, and Work in a Foraging Society* (1979), which won the Herskovits Award of the American African Studies Association in 1980. Although the historical significance of his interpretation of the !Kung economy has been challenged (see especially Carmel Schrire, ed., *Past and Present in Hunter Gatherer Studies*, 1984), it has stimulated extensive debate. In *The Dobe !Kung* (1984), Lee has described the recent impact of other southern African cultures on the Bushmen – a theme that has been explored in cross-cultural perspective in *Politics and History in Band Societies* (1982), edited by Eleanor Leacock and Lee. Lee has also been the foremost exponent of a neo-evolutionary perspective in Canadian anthropology.

Other ethnographic studies done abroad that deal with traditional anthropological problems include Karla O. Poewe's *Matrilineal Ideology* (1981), which challenges the concept of universal male dominance by showing that relations between the sexes among the Luapula of Zambia and other matrilineal groups are characterized by female autonomy rather than dependence on males; Judith Nagata's *Malaysian Mosaic* (1979), which studies social change in a culturally diverse nation; and Elliott Leyton's *The One Blood* (1975), which examines how economic factors help to determine the importance assigned to kinship relations in an Irish village.

Much recent anthropological research in Canada has focused on problems of intergroup conflict, competition, and mutual accommodation. This is partly a continuation of the anthropology of development's concern with relations between dominant and less powerful groups. Those studies most closely linked to symbolic anthropology are concerned specifically with the relation between culturally conditioned perceptions and human behaviour. The latter orientation dominates a collection of essays edited by Robert Paine, *Politically Speaking: Cross-Cultural Studies of Rhetoric* (1981), which examines the underlying principles that make political speeches a flexible vehicle of persuasion. Paine further investigates the relation between politics and communication in *Ayatollahs and Turkey Trots* (1981), a spirited, if somewhat St John's-centred, examination of politicking in Newfoundland. Michael Lambek's *Human Spirits* (1981) examines the role of spirit possession in expressing and helping to manage interpersonal tensions, especially between men and women, in a Malagasy society. Phillip H. Gulliver's *Disputes and Negotiations* (1979), which attempts to generalize about how groups negotiate to resolve disputes, develops an interest already manifested in his *Neighbours and Networks: The Idiom of Kinship in Social Action among the Ndendeuli of Tanzania* (1971) and *Social Control in an African Society* (1963). In *A House Divided?: Anthropological Studies of Factionalism* (1977), Marilyn Silverman and Richard F. Salisbury have assembled a set of papers that examine the nature of conflicts within social groups and their significance for long-term change. One of the most interesting of these papers is Robert Paine's analysis of the role of friendship and antipathy in C.P. Snow's novel *The Masters*. Silverman examines factionalism in Guyanese village politics and shows how it affects the control of resources in *Rich People and Rice* (1980).

Other studies with a symbolic orientation deal with situations that are not of a confrontational nature. In *Exchange in the Social Structure of the Orokaiva: Traditional and Emergent Ideologies in the Northern District of Papua* (1974), Erik G. Schwimmer examines social structure as a 'web of mediation' and seeks to trace the role that notions of exchange play in Orokaiva thought and institutions. Symbolic anthropology also plays an important role in the work of Frank E. Manning. His *Black Clubs in Bermuda: Ethnography of a Play World* (1973) examines the role of associations in promoting adult male socialization and fostering black pride; while his *Bermudian Politics in Transition* (1978) stresses concerns with individual reputations and respectability as factors influencing political behaviour. In *The Celebration of Society* (1983) he edited a collection of papers that explore how rituals and celebrations permit groups to interpret and transform their social situation. By contrast, Christopher R. Hallpike's *The Konso of Ethiopia: A Study of the Values of a Cushitic People* (1972) argues that ritual expresses, rather than creates, basic moral unity.

Still other examples of symbolic anthropology are found in *Manlike Monsters on Trial* (1980), edited by Marjorie M. Halpin and Michael M. Ames. While this book is in part concerned with the seemingly intractable problem of whether such creatures actually exist, it is more interesting for its investigation of the role that the belief in them plays in the thinking of Western and non-Western societies. Tom McFeat's *Small-Group Cultures* (1974) reported on experiments in which small groups in laboratory situations organized themselves to carry out creative tasks. In *French Kinship* (1974) Pierre Maranda sought to account for major changes in kinship relations and terminology in France from medieval times to the present. He also promoted structural analysis by editing *Soviet Structural Folkloristics* (1974). Sylvie Vincent and Bernard Arcand employed anthropological perspectives to reveal systematic distortions in the portrayal of native peoples in French-language textbooks in *L'image de l'Amérindien dans les manuels scolaires du Québec* (1979).

A number of publications have specifically examined the viewpoints and objectives of social anthropology and therefore constitute examples of what has come to be called reflexive anthropology. Kenelm O.L. Burridge of the University of British Columbia has discussed the nature of anthropology at length in *Encountering Aborigines* (1973) and *Someone, No One* (1979). In these books he argues that anthropology is the result of a dialectical engagement between rational objectivity and the romantic attempt by Europeans to incorporate 'otherness' into their own being. He believes that the main impetus for studying anthropology is, and must continue to be, its moral significance and outlook. In *The Rebirth of Anthropological Theory* (1984), Stanley R. Barrett seeks to demonstrate that anthropological theory has failed to resolve its internal contradictions and can only do so by recognizing that it has the moral responsibility to make the analysis of power and privilege its central concern. Karla Poewe, under the pseudonym Manda Cesara, published an introspective personal account of her experiences doing fieldwork: *Reflections of a Woman Anthropologist* (1982). Finally, *Consciousness and Inquiry* (1983), edited by Frank Manning, is a set of papers that seek to deepen the critical self-understanding of Canadian ethnologists and to explore the relation between their work and Canadian society. Individual papers deal with the history of Canadian anthropology; Canadian research abroad; relations between anthropologists and native people, other ethnic groups, and the government; and various anthropologists' perceptions of what they are doing.

In a class by itself is C.R. Hallpike's *The Foundations of Primitive Thought* (1979). In the tradition of Lucien Lévy-Bruhl and Henri Frankfort, Hallpike argues that the thought processes of illiterate Third World peoples resemble those of Western children as defined by Jean Piaget's stage theory of cognitive growth. His concern with the nature of 'primitive thought' was already evident in his *Bloodshed and Vengeance in the Papuan Mountains: The Generation of Conflict in Tauade Society* (1977). Many anthropologists have rejected his conclusions as antithetical to an acceptable understanding of human behaviour. A spirited international debate has ensued.

Canadian publications in the fields of physical anthropology and anthropological linguistics have been more limited, and much of this work has appeared in journals. Linda M. Fedigan's *Primate Paradigms* (1982) challenges male-oriented views of primate behaviour. Joseph E. Molto's *Biological Relationships of Southern Ontario Woodland Peoples* (1983) and David K. Patterson, Jr's *A Diachronic Study of Dental Palaeopathology and Attritional Status of Prehistoric Ontario Pre-Iroquois and Iroquois Populations* (1984) demonstrate that detailed physical anthropological data may be more conclusive than archeological evidence for studying stability and movements of human populations in prehistoric times. These two studies offer evidence of population continuity that supports the local development of Iroquoian culture and of increasing reliance on maize as a food source after AD 500. Brenda Kennedy's *Marriage Patterns in an Archaic Population: A Study of Skeletal Remains from Port au Choix, Newfoundland* (1981) uses human morphological variations to indicate that female exogamy characterized the marriage patterns of a prehistoric hunter-gatherer band. Evolutionary studies include *Homo Erectus: Papers in Honor of Davidson Black* (1981), edited by Becky A. Sigmon and Jerome S. Cybulski, which contains the proceedings of an international symposium dedicated to the memory of a Canadian doctor who, while working in China, played a major role in studying fossil human beings.

The Social Life of Language (1980), a collection of essays written by Gillian Sankoff, traces the development of sociolinguistics: from its preoccupation in the 1960s with the way society channels the use of language, it has come to view society as an active force that shapes the internal structure of language. Many of these essays are based on her research in New Guinea and Montreal.

Prior to European discovery, all of Canada except southern Ontario after AD 500 was occupied by hunter-gatherers who had adapted to many different environments, temperate to arctic. Since 1972 archeologists across Canada have made considerable progress in charting the prehistoric development of these groups and in some cases they have been able to relate cultural changes to environmental ones that have occurred since the retreat of the last continental glaciers. More attention is also being paid to reconstructing patterns of social and political organization and to the religious beliefs of prehistoric peoples. In general, Canadian archeology has tended to stress a culture-historical orientation rather than the nomothetic, or generalizing, one that has predominated in the United States since the 1960s. Its primary aim has continued to be to understand what happened to native Canadians in prehistoric times.

Large numbers of reports on site surveys and excavations in Canada have been deposited in archives or published as scientific papers. Two collections of papers, Early Man in America from a Circum-Pacific Perspective (1978), edited by Alan L. Bryan, and Early Man in the New World (1983), edited by Richard Shutler, Jr, survey the still unresolved problem of when native peoples first arrived in the New World. Richard E. Morlan investigates bone fragments in order to determine if they have been affected by human use and hence to assess the possibility of an early human presence in northwestern Canada in Taphonomy and Archaeology in the Upper Pleistocene of the Northern Yukon Territory: A Glimpse of the Peopling of the New World (1980). Important publications relating to the prehistory of Atlantic Canada are James A. Tuck's Ancient People of Port au Choix (1976) and Prehistory of Saglek Bay, Labrador (1975); and Robert McGhee and James Tuck's An Archaic Sequence from the Strait of Belle Isle, Labrador (1975). William D. Finlayson's The Saugeen Culture (1977) has added to an understanding of the subsistence patterns of the hunter-gatherer populations that inhabited southern Ontario in the centuries prior to the introduction of a horticultural economy. Several monographs have transformed the archeological study of the semi-sedentary, horticultural Iroquoians. James V. Wright's The Nodwell Site (1974) demonstrated that much more could be learned about the social organization of these peoples by excavating whole village sites; while Peter G. Ramsden's *A Refinement of Some Aspects of Huron Ceramic Analysis* (1977) showed how some local clusters of sites could be interpreted as specific communities evolving over time; and Walter A. Kenyon's *The Grimsby Site* (1982) established a new level of excellence in the visual presentation of archeological data. Wright's *The Shield Archaic* (1972) was a first attempt to order the still limited archeological data from the boreal forest of northern Ontario and Quebec. Brian O.K. Reeves has examined *Culture Change in the Northern Plains: 1000 BC – AD 1000* (1983). Charles E. Borden's *Origins and Development of Early Northwest Coast Culture to about 3000 BC* (1975) offers a broad interpretation of early patterns of ecological adaptation on the West Coast, while *The Evolution of Maritime Cultures on the Northeast and the Northwest Coasts of America* (1983), edited by Ronald J. Nash, presents studies of prehistoric adaptations along both the Atlantic and Pacific coasts of Canada. Robert McGhee's *Copper Eskimo Prehistory* (1972) correlates major changes in Inuit culture with climatic fluctuations over the last millennium. He argues that altered sea-ice conditions, which affected the availability of food resources, especially during the 'Little Ice Age' of the seventeenth and eighteenth centuries, produced the sea-ice hunting culture of the historical Copper Eskimos.

Although no comprehensive synthesis of Canadian prehistory has been published, the National Museum of Man has sponsored a series of popular regional surveys. These include James Tuck's *Newfoundland and Labrador Prehistory* (1976) and *Maritime Provinces Prehistory* (1984); James Wright's *Ontario Prehistory* (1972) and *Quebec Prehistory* (1979); and Robert McGhee's *Canadian Arctic Prehistory* (1978). In the same series appeared George F. MacDonald and Richard I. Inglis's *The Dig* (1976), a popular account of archeological methods, and James Wright's *Six Chapters of Canada's Prehistory* (1976), a demonstration of how archeologists interpret their data.

Canadian publications dealing with archeology abroad have also increased in number. African research is represented by Peter L. Shinnie and Rebecca Bradley's *The Capital of Kush I* (1980), an account of excavations in the Sudan; Trigger's *Nubia under the Pharaohs* (1976); and substantial papers in Volumes I and II of *The Cambridge History of Africa* (1978, 1982), under the general editorship of J.D. Fage and Roland Oliver. East Asian research is presented in *Early Paleolithic in South and East Asia* (1978), edited by Fumiko Ikawa-Smith, and Jeong-Hak Kim's *The Prehistory of Korea* (1978), translated and edited by Richard and Kazue Pearson. Prior to returning to Canada, Richard Pearson published *Archaeology of the Ryukyu Islands: A Regional Chronology from 3000 BC to the Historic Period* (1969). Among the most important publications dealing with the New World are the first two volumes of David M. Pendergast's *Excavations at Altun Ha, Belize, 1964–*

1970 (1979, 1982), which document excavations by the Royal Ontario Museum at an ancient Maya site. David H. Kelley's *Deciphering the Maya Script* (1976) is an important contribution to one of the major breakthroughs in Americanist studies in the twentieth century, following in the wake of initial discoveries by the Soviet scholar Yuri Knorosov. That there is relatively little communication between anthropological archeologists working abroad and archeologists in fields such as Classics, Egyptology, and Assyriology may result from a significant difference in focus. Anthropological archeology is characterized by a broad concern to generalize about human behaviour rather than to understand the content of a particular ancient culture as an end in itself.

A few archeological works are primarily theoretical or methodological in orientation. Philip Smith's *Food Production and Its Consequences* (1976) is a significant addition to the international debate concerning the relation between population increases and the evolution of more efficient systems of food production. Brian Hayden edited *Lithic Use-Wear Analysis* (1979), a thorough review of techniques for understanding the manufacture and use of prehistoric stone tools. Hayden also used Australian ethnological data to interpret the use made of stone tools in *Palaeolithic Reflections* (1979). In *The Structure of Material Systems* (1984), based on the systematic survey of the material culture of modern Maya communities, he and Aubrey Cannon investigated the complexities involved in inferring social organization from the sort of evidence normally available to archeologists. *Time and Traditions* (1978) is a set of essays by Bruce Trigger that examine current problems of archeological theory in historical perspective.

The growing introspection about the nature of anthropology is reflected in a world-wide increase of interest in the history of the discipline. In Canada this trend is apparent in Richard Slobodin's biography of the English ethnologist *W.H.R. Rivers* (1978); Trigger's *Gordon Childe* (1980), which traces the intellectual career of the world's leading archeologist in the first half of the twentieth century; and *Readings in the History of Anthropology* (1974), edited by Regna Darnell, which covers mainly American anthropology; as well as numerous papers dealing with the history of Canadian anthropology. The historian Gerald Killan has written an excellent biography of *David Boyle* (1983).

Canadian anthropologists have generally been content to use foreign textbooks. An exception is *Challenging Anthropology* (1979), edited by David H. Turner and Gavin A. Smith. Its chapters, written mainly by young and self-styled radical anthropologists, were intended to provide an introduction to ethnology. Other texts of more limited scope are George K. Park's *The Idea of Social Structure* (1974) and Pierre Maranda's *Mythology: Selected Readings* (1972). Bruce Cox's *Cultural Ecology: Readings on the Canadian*

Indians and Eskimos (1973) reprints many ethnological studies that share an ecological perspective. John A. Price's *Native Studies* (1978) and *Indians of Canada* (1979) both contain large amounts of anthropological material. Knut R. Fladmark has produced *A Guide to Basic Archaeological Field Procedures* (1978).

There appears to be a trend towards greater specialization in anthropological journals in Canada. *Anthropologica*, which publishes papers dealing with all branches of anthropology, is attempting to revive after being moribund since 1982, while the *Canadian Journal of Anthropology*, which had been produced by the University of Alberta since 1980 and provided a similar broad coverage of the discipline, ceased publication in 1985. On the other hand, two successful journals devoted to ethnology and social anthropology have appeared in recent years: the first, *Anthropologie et sociétés*, published since 1977 at Université Laval, lags only slightly behind the Paris-based *L'homme* in terms of distribution numbers; the other, *Culture*, a bilingual journal published by the Canadian Ethnology Society since 1981, invites contributions relating to all aspects of anthropology but mainly contains articles and reviews of interest to social anthropologists and ethnologists. In addition, the Canadian Archaeological Association has published the *Canadian Journal of Archaeology* since 1977. Nicholas David, at the University of Calgary, has edited the *African Archaeological Review* for Cambridge University Press since this journal was founded in 1983. From 1975 to 1985, *Current Anthropology*, the leading international journal for the entire discipline, was edited by Cyril Belshaw.

The Mercury series, organized by James F. Pendergast for the National Museum of Man, has made good quality reproductions of the proceedings of conferences, research reports, and dissertations relating to Canadian subjects quickly available to scholars and libraries around the world. Mercury publications of interest to anthropologists are issued separately by the Archaeological Survey of Canada, the Canadian Ethnology Service, and the History Division of the Museum. The result has been of incalculable benefit to Canadian anthropology. The publications of the Institute of Social and Economic Research at Memorial University also continue to maintain the high standard they established in the early 1970s.

CONCLUSIONS

No Canadian anthropologist ranks alongside the leading figures of the profession, such as Claude Lévi-Strauss of France, Marvin Harris of the United States, or Fredrik Barth of Norway. Nevertheless a growing number have acquired world-wide reputations on the basis of their research and publications and have made substantial contributions to international debates. There is also no longer any obvious time-lag, as there was twenty-five years ago, between Canadian anthropology and that practised in the United States, England, or France. Both in quality and quantity, anthropology in Canada has drawn abreast of the highest international standards. There are now more full-time anthropologists employed per capita in Canada than in the United States. Anthropology also plays an increasingly important role in varied fields, such as development research, native studies, and history, as well as in the formulation and criticism of public policy.

Although the development of professional associations, journals, and informal research links has drawn Canadian anthropologists closer together and kept networks of English- and French-speaking colleagues in productive contact, it is uncertain whether Canadian anthropology can properly be distinguished from that found elsewhere. Anthropology as practised in Canada is a highly international discipline and contacts between Canadian anthropologists and foreign colleagues are often of greater intensity and importance than those linking anthropologists within Canada. Despite some calls for the creation of a distinctively Canadian approach to anthropology, the principal goal of most Canadian anthropologists continues to be to produce work that is good when judged by the best international standards. That much work by Canadian anthropologists is printed by foreign publishers and in international journals demonstrates considerable success in this endeavour.

Yet not all aspects of international anthropology are represented in Canada in the same proportions as they are elsewhere. Canadian anthropologists have generally avoided extremely deterministic interpretations of human behaviour. This is manifested in the general lack of impact that neo-evolutionary anthropology has had in Canada by comparison with the United States and by an absence of enthusiasm for deterministic versions of cultural ecology, although it might have been tempting to apply such theories to the climatic extremes found in Canada. There is perhaps little sympathy for any form of deterministic social science in a nation that has so long been told by foreign scholars that it is an historical absurdity.

One can note a connection with long-established traditions of Canadian social science, as epitomized in the work of Harold Innis, in the widespread convictions among anthropologists that human behaviour is complex, that explaining differences is as important as explaining similarities, that even the most esoteric studies should be relevant – although not necessarily in practical ways – to the society that sustains them, and that the study of humanity cannot, and should not, be morally or ethically neutral. Because of these attitudes, Canadian anthropologists have been able to consider at least the less dogmatic versions of Marxism with greater equanimity than do their American colleagues. Canada's regional diversity and complex ethnic mosaic also provide fertile ground for the application of semiotic or symbolic approaches that seek to understand how cultural symbols are manipulated as strategies of social interaction. Yet to what degree these features genuinely reflect the adaptation of anthropology to a Canadian intellectual milieu or result from random factors that have influenced the burgeoning of anthropology on a new frontier of employment only the future can tell.[1]

12 Writings in Political Science

ALAN C. CAIRNS and DOUGLAS WILLIAMS

INTRODUCTION

Contemporary political science in Canada brings together under one disciplinary label an eclectic cluster of subfields that share an analytical focus on the state and on the exercise of power in domestic and international arenas. Behind this common allegiance to a discipline exist multiple specializations, indifferent to national frontiers and often open to interdisciplinary ventures.

This chapter gives preferential treatment to publications dealing with Canada, partly because national political science communities invariably accord research priority to their own country. Except where it has been translated, the published research of francophone scholars, who constitute about one-quarter of the 700–800 academic political scientists in Canada, is not discussed.[1]

TEXTS IN CANADIAN POLITICS

Widely read texts in Canadian politics provide an entrée to the more specialized studies on which they build. The remarkable textbook ascendancy of R.M. Dawson, *The Government of Canada* (five editions, 1947, 1954, 1957, 1963, and 1970), ended in 1971. Dawson's text, revised in the fourth and fifth editions by Norman Ward, was a lucid, scholarly account of the historical evolution of Canadian government and politics. Its strength lay in institutional description, especially of parliament. It was unabashedly centralist, and paid negligible attention to Quebec or French Canada – two orientations which were natural to the first generation of its English-Canadian readers, but less so to succeeding generations.

James R. Mallory's *The Structure of Canadian Government* (1971), and Richard Van Loon and Michael Whittington's *The Canadian Political System* (1971) provided contrasting perspectives on how Canadian politics should be studied. Mallory's volume (revised in 1984), and Van Loon/Whittington (revised twice, 1976 and 1981), were joined in 1975 by Thomas A. Hockin's

Government in Canada. Ronald G. Landes's *The Canadian Polity: A Comparative Introduction* appeared in 1983, and Roger Gibbins's *Conflict and Unity: An Introduction to Canadian Political Life* in 1985, the same year as the multi-authored *Liberal Democracy in Canada and the United States,* ed. T.C. Pocklington.

Ward vigorously defended Dawson's institutional approach in his preface to the fifth edition. He could not 'conceive how one could understand the government of Canada without having at least some understanding of its main institutions.' Mallory's focus on the constitution reflected his commitment to the preservation of a viable constitutional order in which abuses of power can be prevented and rulers can be peacefully removed from office.

In contrast to the institutional and constitutional focus of Mallory and Dawson/Ward, Van Loon/Whittington stress the socio-economic, geographic, and cultural-linguistic environment of Canadian politics. Dawson/Ward and Mallory approach their readers as students who are also citizens; Van Loon/Whittington, building on what they call the 'great "behavioural revolution",' approach their readers as novitiates in a discipline. The change in focus from Dawson's 1947 edition to their own 1971 publication was due to developments in political science which, reflecting American leadership, have, in their words, 'meant a shift in the emphasis of political studies from the form and development of political institutions to the functional relationship of those institutions to society.' Accordingly, the formal institutions of government receive less attention and are relegated to secondary roles in the contemporary policy-making process. The diminishing significance of the elected side of government is dispassionately described as a by-product of the inevitable concentration of policy expertise in the appointed bureaucracy.

Government in Canada emphasizes the leadership role of government; Hockin was impressed with the predominance of the executive in the Canadian version of parliamentary government, the growth of both federal and provincial governments, and the capacity of governments to mould their respective societies. In *Conflict and Unity,* by contrast, Gibbins stresses the underlying dynamic of such recurring, deeply rooted concerns as language, regionalism, redistribution of wealth, Canadian-American relations, and intergovernmental relations. While the rules and institutions of political life – which he emphasized in *Regionalism* (1982) – are not ignored, he characterizes Canadian politics as driven by society-based forces. Like Hockin, he was concerned with the integrative capacity of the Canadian political system, believing that effective democratic political systems, such as Canada's, reduce the 'intensity and effects [of conflict] to a level compatible with a civil society.'

Pocklington's *Liberal Democracy in Canada and the United States* focuses on civic education and underlines the difficulty of the citizen's role in an era of big government. Landes is equally concerned with values. *The Canadian*

Polity, explicitly written from a liberal-democratic perspective, concludes with various reform suggestions to enhance the role of the citizen.[2]

In general, although they disagree about how to study Canadian politics, these texts reflect their authors' allegiance to liberal democracy.

POLITICAL ECONOMY, THE AMERICANIZATION CONTROVERSY, AND BEHAVIOURALISM

The adversarial nature of academic life and the impact of political cleavages on scholarship ensure that any status quo in the discipline will ultimately be challenged on the ground that it misapprehends reality or stands in the way of desired social change. The Americanization controversy of the 1970s bears this out, as does the related growth of support for a political economy approach, primarily Marxist in orientation.

Political Economy studies the linkages between the capitalist economic system and the political order, from a Marxist or a liberal perspective. Its revival in the 1970s drew sustenance from the earlier liberal political economy of Harold Innis, W.A. Mackintosh, Donald Creighton, and V.C. Fowke, and from the minority Marxist tradition of C.B. Macpherson, H.C. Pentland, and Stanley Ryerson. It was reinforced by the international reinvigoration of Marxist scholarship which, freeing itself from the ideological sterilities of Stalinism, made extensive inroads into bourgeois social science in many countries.

The intellectual allegiance to Marxism, which directed Canadian scholars to the European heritage of the social sciences, was combined with an antipathy to American social science which, Clement and Drache asserted in *A Practical Guide to Canadian Political Economy* (1978), had 'overwhelmed ... a uniquely Canadian tradition of [political economy] scholarship.' The rebirth of political economy, in both Marxist and liberal versions, reflected a nationalist desire for a political science with distinctively Canadian characteristics.

Marxist political economy challenged both the methodological assumptions of behaviouralism and the liberal pluralist lens through which it analyzed the relations between polity and society. Politically it worked for the survival of a Canada culturally and economically distinct from the United States. It aimed at a social science which was relevant to the interests of the working class and the disadvantaged. Specifically, it sought to make scholarship the servant of socialist change in Canada and the world.

In spite of this commitment to praxis, Marxist political economy is detached from any class or other significant base in Canadian society. The advance of Marxism in the social sciences coincides with the virtual disappearance of the Communist party in domestic politics and with the move of the New

Democratic Party – like its predecessor the CCF always more social democratic than Marxist – towards the centre of the party ideological spectrum. The social base of academic Marxism in Canada barely extends beyond the higher education system.

Marxist political economists have developed their own journals, including *Studies in Political Economy* (1979–), subtitled *A Socialist Review*, which publishes research from a left-wing political economy perspective; *Socialist Studies* (1979–), which provides a forum for debate on socialist theory and practice; and the *Canadian Journal of Political and Social Theory* (1977–), an outlet for various forms of critical theory.

Marxist political economy is a significant force in the social sciences. The 1985 *New Practical Guide to Canadian Political Economy*, ed. Clement and Drache, contains 3000 entries, twice as many as its 1978 predecessor, although not all were written within the political economy paradigm, Marxist or otherwise. Strikingly absent from this literature is specific research on the institutions of liberal democracy in Canada. The 1985 *New Practical Guide* pays no explicit attention to legislatures, cabinets, courts, civil liberties, elections, and the rule of law. In *The Federal Condition in Canada* (1987), Donald Smiley asserts that the relative autonomy Marxists now accord to the state seldom extends to the belief that differences in the institutional structures of the state are consequential. Although growth and legitimacy have contributed to a pluralism within Marxist political economy, and to more collaborative work with scholars who do not share its central assumptions, the institutions, procedures, and norms of liberal democracy remain little studied by Marxist scholars, with the exception of a critical literature advocating participatory rather than representative democracy.

The Marxist critique of bourgeois social science coincided with a political-academic controversy over the extensive migration of American political scientists to Canada, and an alleged intellectual hegemony of the American version of political science over its weaker Canadian counterpart. The 'Americanization' issue, which was not confined to political science, stimulated a wide-ranging debate about how much scholarly attention should be devoted to the domestic scene, and about the lens through which Canada should be viewed. Debate was most vigorous in those disciplines where national contexts seemed especially relevant to the selection of problems and the values which should guide their analysis.[3] The debate also had an international dimension, in response to the pervasive American social science presence around the world.

The opponents of 'Americanization' in Canadian political science disagreed over the nature of the 'enemy within,' and over the purposes and the meaning of Canadianization. Some of the opposition was based on anti-Americanism; some was little more than a desire to reserve jobs for Canadians; other concerns reflected disciplinary issues about the dangers to Canadian enquiry which, it was argued, would follow an uncritical assimilation of what a British scholar, Bernard Crick, called *The American Science of Politics* (1959). Fundamentally, it was a debate about how best to do political science in the different national contexts of its practitioners.

The fading of the Americanization issue in political science followed the virtual ending of faculty expansion in the late 1970s, thereby removing the most contentious issue – hiring – from the discipline's agenda. A more tolerant disciplinary electicism has replaced the frequently acrimonious debates of the late 1960s and 1970s. A thriving political economy orientation muted the critics who argued that an imported behaviouralism would stifle a rich indigenous tradition.

Inevitably, the encounter with American political science, as transmitted by American scholars teaching in Canada, by Canadians trained in American graduate schools, and by the sheer intellectual weight of the 70–80 per cent of the world's political scientists who live next door, influenced the research concerns of political scientists in Canada. In particular, election surveys and new research fields dealing with political culture and socialization were initially offshoots of earlier American studies.[4]

This research focus on the citizen base of political authority reflects the impact of democratic ideology on the research choices of American political scientists. In Canada, the salience of constitutional issues encouraged analyses of the relative strength of, and relations between, the provincial and national communities which lie behind the jurisdictional aspects of federalism. In the well-received *Public Opinion and Public Policy in Canada* (1986), Richard Johnston subtly examines the underlying support for the federal government and the national community, and explores public opinion in various policy areas. The recurrent Canadian attempts to monitor the regional dimension, to see whether the nation has yet appeared or disappeared, are only equalled in frequency by 'periodic attempts to monitor the class cleavage to see whether it has yet emerged.'[5]

The politically relevant cultural differences and similarities between Canadians and Americans are often explored through literature and comparative historical studies, as well as in survey research. In addition to the Canadian adaptation by Kenneth McRae and Gad Horowitz of the work of the American scholar Louis Hartz, and the continuing controversy it generated,[6] the American sociologist Seymour Martin Lipset has returned several times to the theme of Canadian/American convergences and divergences which inspired his earlier original work on *Agrarian Socialism* (1950). His most recent examination in Doran and Sigler, eds, *Canada and the United States* (1985), concludes that the 'United States and Canada remain two nations formed around sharply different organizing principles.'

FEDERALISM, FRENCH-ENGLISH RELATIONS, AND THE
CONSTITUTIONAL ISSUE[7]

The post–World War II hegemony of the federal government which a previous generation of English-Canadian scholars had expected to continue was undermined by Québécois nationalism and aggressive provincial governments in English Canada. Donald Smiley successively explored this buffeting of Canadian federalism by centrifugal pressures in the three editions of his major text, *Canada in Question* (1972, 1976, and 1980). J. Peter Meekison, ed., *Canadian Federalism: Myth or Reality* (1968, 1971, 1977), a comprehensive reader, often supplemented Smiley in university courses. Garth Stevenson's *Unfulfilled Union* (1979, 1982) applied a Marxist political economy analysis in a highly centralist text on Canadian federalism. Edwin R. Black's *Divided Loyalties: Canadian Concepts of Federalism* (1975), an historical analysis of the five major organizing concepts used to assess and describe Canadian federalism, indirectly suggested the multiple contradictions which the system had to manage. These texts intimated, both in their titles and in prefaces which anticipated the rapid obsolescence of the chapters to follow, that federalism was a contested, even threatened, institutional arrangement.

Understanding the new federalism required new academic perspectives. One of these focused on the complex pattern of intergovernmental entanglement which invalidated classic theories of federalism based on the independence of the two orders of government from each other. Richard Simeon's pioneering *Federal-Provincial Diplomacy* (1972) analyzed intergovernmental bargaining in three case studies illumined by the literature of bargaining in international relations. This was the precursor of a developing literature which explored the impact of federalism on policy. In a 1985 survey of some 150 general works and case studies on federal-provincial relations, Fred Fletcher and Donald Wallace (in an essay collected in Simeon's *Division of Powers and Public Policy*, 1985), concluded that federalism frequently incapacitated decision-makers in controversial areas, that intergovernmental negotiations often exclude relevant non-governmental interests from consideration, and that federalism is 'only moderately successful' in the management of conflict. Individual volumes by Banting, Careless, Dupré et al., Savoie, Schultz, Swainson, Taylor and Thorburn are helpful guides to the intergovernmental arena.[8] In *Quebec versus Ottawa* (1976), Claude Morin, a leading bureaucratic and political architect of the Quiet Revolution, and subsequently of the independence movement, analyzed Quebec-Ottawa controversies from a Quebec insider's vantage point seldom available to anglophone readers.

A second strand in the changed understanding of federalism explored the capacity of the state, viewed as an autonomous actor with its own interests and goals, to shape the society and economy under its jurisdiction. This statist approach, prominent in the works of Cairns[9] and Smiley, and from a different perspective in John Richards and Larry Pratt, *Prairie Capitalism* (1979), denied that the state was simply a puppet of socio-economic forces.

The steady growth of a rights consciousness in the years following World War II, and its embodiment initially in the weak 1960 Diefenbaker Bill of Rights and subsequently in the 1982 Charter of Rights, changed both federalism and the analysis appropriate to its understanding. The Charter, probably the most important constitutional change since 1867, alters the meaning of constitutional government in Canada, and redistributes status and power among the institutions of government to the benefit of courts and the judiciary. The competing interpretations which its ambiguities invite reinforce the relevance of academic commentary for constitutional development. Extensive analysis of the Charter's terms and a prescriptive literature on how judges should respond to their new responsibilities has already appeared.[10] Peter Russell, a constitutional specialist, convincingly argues in P.W. Fox and G. White's *Politics: Canada* (6th ed., 1987) that the Supreme Court's enhanced role makes it as important to Canadian political science as the US Supreme Court is to American political scientists. *The Supreme Court of Canada: History of the Institution* (1985), co-authored by the political scientist Fred Vaughan and the political historian James Snell, chronicles the history of an institution which was weakened by subordination to the Judicial Committee until 1949, and by the insensitivity of prime ministers to the principles of judicial independence. The pioneering volume by Carl Baar and Judge Perry Millar, *Judicial Administration in Canada* (1981), will lead to further research on the theory and practice of the kind of judicial administration required by the new burdens the Charter imposes on the Supreme Court.

The Charter challenges the academic disciplines that study courts by altering the nature of the questions which judges have to answer. Up to the 1949 ending of appeals to the Judicial Committee of the Privy Council, lawyers dominated the literature on judicial review of the constitution. Since then a few political scientists have begun to supplement the lawyers' analyses of courts and jurisprudence.[11] Donald Smiley contributed several incisive critiques of the developing political and intellectual support for an entrenched Charter and gave reasoned explanations for his own preference for leaving his fate in the hands of elected politicians.[12] Peter Russell edited and introduced three editions of *Leading Constitutional Decisions* (1965, 1973, 1982) to make constitutional cases more easily available to the non-lawyer. He also wrote *The Supreme Court of Canada as a Bilingual and Bicultural Institution* (1969) for the Royal Commission on Bilingualism and Biculturalism, and contributed to *The Court and the Constitution: Comments on the Supreme Court Reference on Constitutional Amendment* (1982), ed. Peter Russell et al.

While the constitutional tensions from the 1960s to the early 1980s had multiple sources and many actors, the contested relationship between French and English was undeniably central. Historically, that relationship had attracted negligible political science attention. The work of the Frenchman André Siegfried, *Le Canada, les deux races* (1906), reissued as *The Race Question in Canada* (1966), was the only in-depth political science analysis in the first half of the twentieth century.

This bleak picture of scholarly inattention was not transformed by the workings of the academic market, but by a massive government mobilization of resources behind the Royal Commission on Bilingualism and Biculturalism. Two political scientists, Michael Oliver and Léon Dion, were in charge of the extensive multidisciplinary research program which produced twenty-four published volumes and an additional 141 unpublished studies.[13] The Commission's Report and published research greatly enhanced the Canadian understanding of linguistic dualism and helped to transform language policy in the federal government and the national capital in the interest of francophones.

Subsequent research built on the Commission's legacy, partly in response to the major Quebec-Ottawa constitutional battles of the 1970s which kept French-English relations alive as an ongoing research concern for political scientists. The Annual Reports of the Commissioner of Official Languages (1970/1–) and the review *Language and Society* (1979–) reinforce the political and academic salience of French-English language issues.

Students of French-English relations have employed three distinct perspectives. The first, which goes back to Siegfried, stresses cultural differences between the two linguistic communities as the major source of inter-group conflict. Within this cultural orientation scholars have analyzed French-English differences in terms of Catholic vs Protestant, or following Louis Hartz, 'quasi-feudal' vs 'liberal' cultural fragments, and more recently in terms of explicit political values such as equality and the role of the state. In *The Roots of Disunity* (1979), David Bell and Lorne Tepperman reveal disturbing differences between anglophone and francophone political cultures in Canada which, they argue, are major barriers to political unity. However, although cultural differences may help explain historical instances of French-English conflict, they seem less relevant for the more recent past in which increased conflict coincided with their reduction. The sense of almost anthropological 'otherness,' of Quebec as another country, which the Tremblay Report (1956)[14] engendered in English-Canadian readers, was not repeated for those who, two decades later, read the familiar secular language of modern nationalism in the Parti Québécois advocacy of sovereignty-association or independence.

A second approach, a product of the 1960s, focused on the relative position of francophones and anglophones in federal institutions, ranging from the cabinet to the bureaucracy. Their respective numbers and influence were viewed symbolically as indicators of status, normatively as a measure of equity in the distribution of valued jobs, and politically as an indication of the capacity of a linguistic community to advocate its interests and values within government. In a contribution to Stanley M. Beck and Ivan Bernier, *Canada and the New Constitution* (1983), Smiley documents considerable progress since the findings of the Bilingualism and Biculturalism Royal Commission of the 1960s on francophone underrepresentation in the bureaucracy, especially in the higher ranks.

A more recent, and possibly the ascendant approach to the study of French-English relations, analyzes the competition between these two linguistic groups for demographic power and economic position. This approach focuses on the Canadian and Quebec governments as instruments to modify or preserve the relative power and status of the two linguistic communities. Three books – *Quebec's Language Policies* (1977), ed. John R. Mallea, *Conflict and Language Planning in Quebec* (1984), ed. Richard Y. Bourhis, and William D. Coleman's *The Independence Movement in Quebec 1945–1980* (1984) – are basic examples of this genre in the English language. Sandford F. Borin's *The Language of the Skies* (1983) is a gripping case study which graphically portrays the interaction of symbolism and economic self-interest in one of the most bitter French-English conflicts of the mid-1970s.

In a 1982 survey article, Kenneth McRoberts argues that the overall literature of French-English relations has been highly pragmatic and problem-oriented, only minimally comparative, and theoretically weak.[15] This negative assessment may be altered as further publications emerge from Kenneth McRae's ambitious examination of the social and political consequences of linguistic diversity in four multilingual democracies. Volumes on Switzerland and Belgium have appeared (1983, 1986), with Finland and Canada to come.

The work of Jean Laponce takes up theoretical issues in French-English relations. Laponce's many articles in both French and English, and a recent book, *Langue et territoire* (1984), explore the sociology of the interaction of languages and the territorial requirements for linguistic survival. In contrast to federal government policy, especially under Trudeau, which defined the coincidence of language and provincial borders as nation-threatening, Laponce asserts the needs of linguistic minorities for territorial security. The Swiss solution of territorial unilingualism is far more likely to reduce French-English tensions and Québécois separatism, he argues, than are the official policies which have inspired the Canadian government since the early 1970s.

The most widely diffused theoretical perspective of the last decade has been consociational democracy. Inspired by the work of Arend Lijphart (eg, *The Politics of Accommodation*, 1968, and *Democracy in Plural Societies*, 1977), introduced into Canada by Sid Noel in *Canadian Journal of Political Science* (1971) and given wider exposure in a valuable collection of readings by Kenneth McRae (*Consociational Democracy*, 1974), the theory asserts that culturally divided political systems can be held together by the accommodative practices of elites of the various subcultures. Later unpublished work, however, by Steven Wolinetz, which builds on McRae's initial reservations, has seriously questioned the applicability of consociational theory to Canada, either as a description of past practices or as a prescription for future intergroup harmony. Indeed, in the constitutional battles of the last decade and a half, impressionistic evidence suggests that the citizens were less divided than the governing elites who supposedly represented them.

The escalation of constitutional controversy leading up to the Quebec referendum of 1980 generated a striking concentration of effort on constitutional issues. English-Canadian political scientists explained the causes and possible cures of Canada's constitutional ailments at conferences; they acted as constitutional advisers to both orders of government, and they appeared before parliamentary committees. Québécois academics were even more intensely involved, with many articulately committed to independence.

Three volumes with evocative titles, produced by the Institute of Intergovernmental Relations at Queen's University, revealed the values, fears, and analytical capacities of political scientists: R.M. Burns, ed., *One Country or Two?* (1971), Richard Simeon, ed., *Must Canada Fail?* (1977), and Keith Banting and Richard Simeon, eds, *And No One Cheered* (1983). The first two, written entirely by English Canadians, display that uneasy mix of civic obligation and academic detachment which appears when academics see such a loved political object as their own country threatened. The commitment to Canada's survival in the first two volumes is accompanied by sympathy for Quebec nationalism and by a certain envy for the Quebec intelligentsia, which seemed to be making history. The third volume, following on the Constitution Act of 1982, and with five contributions from French-Canadian scholars, provides a sombre retrospective on opportunities missed and of the dangers considered inherent in a settlement which the government of Quebec rejected. A celebratory sense of national achievement is conspicuously absent in the English-Canadian chapters. Anger and an embittered sense of betrayal dominate the French-Canadian contributions.

In the period leading up to the 1982 Constitution Act, English-Canadian political scientists were prominent advocates of institutional and/or constitutional reform. In general, those institutions which appeared to be barriers to national unity or harmonious linguistic co-existence were critically examined for their reform possibilities. Political scientists singled out the electoral system, the Senate, the intergovernmental system, the Supreme Court, and the bureaucracy as candidates for reform.[16]

The overwhelming thrust of reform proposals was to make the political system, particularly the central government, more sensitive to regionalism.

Donald Smiley, writing in *Canadian Public Administration*, introduced this orientation into Canadian political thought in 1971 under the label of 'intrastate federalism.' Smiley later defined the term as 'the reflection of provincial/regional aspirations and interests in the structure and operations of the central government.' In *Intrastate Federalism in Canada* (1985) Smiley and Ronald Watts exhaustively canvassed the relevant literature and political discourse supporting the intrastate perspective. They gave qualified support for making federal institutions more responsive to regional values and interests, but asserted that the beneficial aspects of such reforms had often been overstated.

PARLIAMENTARY GOVERNMENT, PUBLIC POLICY, AND ADMINISTRATION

The institutions of parliamentary government experience constant scrutiny from scholars concerned about their historical development, current performance, and future evolution. Two journals, *Canadian Parliamentary Review* (1978–), and *Parliamentary Government* (1979–), help to focus discussion. Recent scholarship analyzes particular institutions and roles: governors general and lieutenant-governors, prime ministers, cabinets and senior bureaucrats, the House of Commons and the Senate.[17] Several volumes survey the parliamentary system from a reform perspective. In 1974, Eugene Forsey, an indefatigable commentator on parliamentary government and the constitution, published his collected essays under the title *Freedom and Order*.

The dramatic growth of both orders of government strained the institutional capacity of cabinets, legislatures, and bureaucracies, and seemed to threaten the values of indirect popular control on which responsible government was based. In 1978, writing in William A.W. Neilson and James C. MacPherson, eds, *The Legislative Process in Canada*, Robert Stanfield pleaded for 'recognition that democratic responsible government and all-pervasive government in Ottawa are not compatible.' The growth of state activities which lay behind this testing of inherited institutional arrangements and values was traced, analyzed, supported, and deplored in numerous publications, of which the most insightful were by Keith Banting, André Blais, George Lermer, Sharon Sutherland, and Bruce Doern.[18] The expanded public bureaucracies, and the public policy complexities of big government, were extensively studied.[19] The journal *Canadian Public Administration* (1958–), which monitored the bureaucracy, was supplemented by *Canadian Public Policy* (1975–) and *Policy Options* (1980–), which focused more explicitly on the substance and making of public policies.

The pervasive influence of the state quickened academic curiosity about what happened inside the 'black box' of government where policies were made. The study of public administration acquired a higher profile. The 1962

Glassco Royal Commission Report on government organization and the reforms it stimulated contributed to a concern with the management side of the public service, and to a difficult process of sorting out the differences and similarities between private 'business' administration and public administration. The study of public policy, which had hitherto occupied a peripheral place in Canadian political science, became a central research focus as scholars recognized the rigidities and inefficiencies which often attended the increased state role in market and society.

A spate of case studies relating to immigration, broadcasting, energy, foreign economic policy, old age pensions, health policy, the nuclear industry, the Columbia River treaty, and the welfare state indicated a relative transfer of disciplinary attention from the demand side to the substance of policy and the intragovernmental dynamics from which it emerged. The emerging thesis of the autonomy of the state, which suggested that what democratic governments did could not be entirely explained by an ever more refined examination of voters and parties, drove research in the same direction.

A related research focus analyzed the efforts by cabinets to assert collective control over and provide coherent direction to the multiple activities of the modern state. The Auditor General's 1976 concern that government expenditures were out of control also lay behind the creation of the Royal Commission on Financial Management and Accountability, the Lambert Commission, which reported in 1979. In 1980, *How Ottawa Decides*, by Richard French, graphically described the rivalry of competing central agencies charged with co-ordinating responsibilities from dissimilar perspectives. He concluded that what A. Paul Pross, writing in *Canadian Public Administration* (1982), called the 'cybernetic vision' had not been translated into effective performance. In a more elaborate and highly praised comparative study, *Governments under Stress* (1983), Colin Campbell analyzed the limited success which attended the Herculean efforts of political executives in Washington, London, and Ottawa to organize government in the service of greater policy coherence.

In the Canadian case the difficulties of imposing central political control were compounded by the proliferation of regulatory agencies and crown corporations which were deliberately distanced from legislatures and cabinets. While the separate reasons for the establishment of these 'structural heretics,' as Hodgetts called them, were no doubt individually convincing, their cumulative effect reduced popular control of government by the traditional means of competitive elections and parliamentary scrutiny of responsible ministers. As a consequence, the central government declined in legitimacy. ' "Ottawa",' stated the Pépin-Robarts Task Force on Canadian Unity (1979), 'is for many Canadians synonymous with all that is to be deplored about modern government – a remote, shambling bureaucracy that exacts tribute from its subjects and gives little in return.' The Canadian experience did not deny the conclusions of an American student (Richard Rose) that many problems of big government are conditions of existence.

A more intrusive state role generated more abrasive contacts between citizens and governments. A partial answer, the ombudsman institution which was widely adopted at the provincial level, presupposed that courts and representative institutions provided insufficient defence of individual rights.

This concern that citizens needed to be protected from their own governments was complemented by an efficiency critique of the state which advocated the 'downsizing' of government through privatization, and a greater reliance on the market, a position more congenial to economists and right-wing think-tanks than to political scientists, and one which pervaded the economic analysis of the Macdonald Royal Commission Report (1985).

Behind all the particular studies was the larger question of the success with which a historic system of responsible government was responding to the complex agenda of the modern state. The best answers came from scholars who know history and recognize the need for institutional adaptation. Two works stand out. *The Canadian House of Commons* (1977) by John Stewart, a former MP and now Senator, blends an insider's understanding with the training of a professional political scientist. Stewart identifies five functions for the House of Commons: 'first, to support a government; second, to prevent clandestine governing; third, to test the government's administrative policies and legislative proposals; fourth, to constrain the ministers; and fifth, to educate the electorate. The vital tension within the system arises from the need to balance the first of these functions against the other four.' J.E. Hodgetts's *The Canadian Public Service: A Physiology of Government 1867–1970* (1973), the first detailed academic overview of the public service, brought a historical perspective to a comprehensive analysis of 'the structures within which decisions affecting every citizen and every public servant are taken daily.'

The partly written Canadian Constitution, which gives a prominent role to the judiciary, also gives a special responsibility to the legal fraternity for its interpretation. F.R. Scott's *Essays on the Constitution* (1977) and W.R. Lederman's *Continuing Canadian Constitutional Dilemmas* (1981) assembled the most enduring essays of two senior constitutional scholars. Edward Mc-Whinney's *Constitution-making* (1981) brought a wealth of comparative knowledge to the subject, and Peter Hogg published two editions of a lucid text, *Constitutional Law of Canada* (1977, 1985). Canadian legal periodicals, increasingly scholarly in character, continued to provide an ongoing commentary and analysis of case law, the legal process, the system of courts, and the judicial role in constitutional development.

PROVINCIAL AND LOCAL GOVERNMENT AND POLITICS

Faculty growth transformed the study of politics from a central Canadian discipline to a pan-Canadian enterprise with sizeable university departments in every region of the country, a geographic dispersal which stimulated provincial studies. Various new interdisciplinary regional journals – particularly *BC Studies* (1968–), *Acadiensis* (1971–), and the *Canadian Journal of Regional Science* (1978–), which supplemented older journals such as *Ontario History* (1899–) – encouraged this research orientation.

The growth of provincial power required and received a new label – 'province-building' (examined by R.A. Young et al., in *Canadian Journal of Political Science*, 1984) – intended to remind researchers and others that the federal government was not alone in deploying government power in the service of extensive socio-economic transformation. The academic response was qualitatively and quantitatively impressive. A comprehensive survey by Rand Dyck, *Provincial Politics in Canada* (1986), contains a thirty-page 'Select Bibliography,' with over 600 entries, mostly recent. Although studies of individual provinces far exceed comparative provincial studies, two of the most impressive analyses were comparative. *Prairie Capitalism* by Pratt and Richards stands out, as does David Elkins and Richard Simeon, *Small Worlds* (1980).

Several high quality analyses by both French and English scholars were devoted to Quebec: Kenneth McRoberts and Dale Posgate, *Quebec* (1976; rev. 1980), is a perceptive account of political modernization and socio-economic change which analyzes the increased role of the Quebec provincial state and the social conflict produced by rapid change; Léon Dion's *Quebec: The Unfinished Revolution* (1976), a collection of translated articles by one of Quebec's leading scholars, analyzed a people in the grip of competing versions of nationalism; Dénis Monière's *Ideologies in Quebec* (1981), a translation of the 1977 Governor General's Award-winning study, surveyed the history of ideologies in Quebec from a perspective which highlighted the forces sympathetic to the working class. William Coleman's *The Independence Movement in Quebec 1945–1980* (1984) interpreted the Quiet Revolution and the political and social changes of the post-Duplessis years as a process which hastened the integration of Quebec into a framework of continental capitalism, and led to the decline of a culture integrated by Catholic social thought. In the new pluralist Quebec the French-language majority, no longer united by a shared past, became, like English Canada, increasingly multicultural and multiracial.

This literature on the provinces, much of it sympathetic to provincial aspirations, made an independent contribution to 'province-building,' especially in Quebec where the social science community was strongly supportive of Québécois nationalism. More generally, provincial studies changed the lens through which the country was viewed, and diminished the centralist bias in anglophone scholarship.

A small body of distinct scholarship addressed the unique social, economic, and constitutional concerns of Yukon and the Northwest Territories. By the late 1970s the fate of the North, with its considerable resources, plural society, and constitutionally dependent relationship with the rest of Canada, became a central policy issue for public officials and a handful of scholars. Government interest prompted a succession of enquiries headed by Thomas Berger and Kenneth Lysyk, both reporting in 1977,[20] and by C.M. Drury, whose report on *Constitutional Development in the Northwest Territories* appeared in 1979. These enquiries, supplemented by independent academic analyses, explored the political and constitutional options, the North's energy and resource potential, and the likely effect of development on the fragile ecology. The Berger enquiry underlined northern resentment at being viewed through the lens of resource policy.

Although both Yukon and Northwest Territories have elected legislative assemblies, and an approximation of responsible government, their status remains semi-colonial. Edgar J. Dosman, *The National Interest: The Politics of Northern Development 1968–75* (1975), is a powerfully argued critique of the closed, elite-dominated Ottawa decision-making process responsible for northern development policy. Dosman argues that policy development in the period 1968–75 was characterized by drift and responsiveness to big business interests. Gurston Dacks, in *A Choice of Futures: Politics in the Canadian North* (1981), held out little hope for constitutional development towards provincehood, which would deprive the Canadian government of powers it would be unwilling to sacrifice. He succinctly concluded that 'it will be for the North to react and the South to determine.' In *Northern Provinces* (1985) Gordon Robertson argued for constitutional experimentation in the form of 'Autonomous Federal Territories,' which could depart, where appropriate, from the norms and institutional practices of provincehood. *The North* (1985), ed. Michael Whittington, a research study for the Macdonald Commission, explored northern prospects from a multidisciplinary perspective.

This academic and Royal Commission analysis mirrored the larger constitutional reality in being undertaken overwhelmingly by outsiders. *Dene Nation: The Colony Within* (1977), ed. Mel Watkins, was a partial exception in its publication of briefs given by the Dene and their supporters to the Berger enquiry.

Although some have populations far in excess of the smaller provinces, the thousands of local governments under provincial jurisdiction are, like northern Canada, subject to the constitutional authority of a superior government. Neither their importance as providers of services deemed essential to contemporary citizens, nor the trend to urbanization which has progressively reduced the relative and absolute size of the rural population, has stimulated more than a trickle of interest from political scientists. Basic texts and books of readings on Canadian government and politics normally ignore this 'third order' of government. Authors of survey articles typically lament the paucity of publications and their theoretical weakness, which a recent spate of biographies of mayors does not alleviate. Few would strongly dissent from the scholar who characterized the statement that the study of urban politics was in transition ' "from infancy to the early stages of puberty" ... [as] an excessively complimentary progress report.'[21]

Donald Rowat, in *Canadian Public Administration* (1983), explains this weakness by the various factors which distinguish local government from higher level governments – the absence of responsible government, of overt parties bearing conventional labels, and of constitutionally based autonomy. These differences make this subfield alien territory to the scholar familiar with federal and provincial government. The lack of power at the local level also mutes interest, as in numerous areas local governments are little more than instruments to carry out specified provincial purposes.

Although some texts and readers have appeared in recent years,[22] along with a stimulating and controversial volume by Harold Kaplan, *Reform, Planning, and City Politics: Montreal, Winnipeg, Toronto* (1982), the field as a whole is underdeveloped. Some promising theoretical work by Warren Magnusson has recently appeared in professional journals.[23] In particular, his article 'The Local State in Canada: Theoretical Perspectives,' incisively disentangles the aggregation of governing authorities at the local level, including local agencies of superior governments, and special purpose local authorities, as well as the elected municipal government. He defines the local state as a 'network of special purpose agencies for local purposes, some locally and some centrally controlled, and none with any inherent authority over the others.'

PARTIES, ELECTIONS, AND PRESSURE GROUPS

The changing nature of the Canadian party system, its support base in the electorate, its efficacy as an instrument of change, the institutional factors which have influenced its development, and its relation to the constitutional crisis have attracted extensive scholarship. Four comprehensive overviews grappled with these and related questions: Hugh G. Thorburn, ed., *Party Politics in Canada* (3rd ed., 1972; 4th ed., 1979; 5th ed., 1985); Frederick C. Engelmann and Mildred A. Schwartz, *Canadian Political Parties* (1975); Conrad Winn and John McMenemy, *Political Parties in Canada* (1976); and Janine Brodie and Jane Jenson, *Crisis, Challenge and Change* (1980).

These texts confirm that students of parties in Canada agree on neither the facts nor their interpretation. The central thesis of Winn/McMenemy and their co-contributors that significant differences among the major national parties in ideology, organization, and electoral support have virtually no effect on policy has generated dissent since its appearance.[24]

Brodie and Jenson identify with the left-wing scholars who, since the 1930s, have seen the class cleavage as fundamental to advanced capitalist societies but, regrettably, as only weakly expressed in the Canadian national party system. They explain this non-event by the obfuscating strategems of the parties of the bourgeoisie which deliberately structure party competition on the more innocuous lines of 'bicultural and consensual definitions of Canadian politics,' which thwart the attempts of workers and farmers to organize on class lines. The bourgeois parties do not simply respond to voters' preferences, but are the social engineers of the false consciousness of the working class. Paradoxically, the proof that parties matter in the Canadian case is the success of the dominant parties in trivializing the agenda of competitive politics.

The need to enhance understanding of the links between parties and voters led to the large national voter surveys conducted after the federal elections of 1965, 1968, 1974, 1979, 1980, and 1984. John Meisel, a central figure in this development, initially published an interpretive account of the 1957 general election, *The Canadian General Election of 1957* (1962), stressing how the Liberals had lost touch with the electorate and with the federal nature of the country, thus paving the way for the Diefenbaker breakthrough. This was followed by an edited volume on the 1962 election, by several editions and revisions of *Working Papers on Canadian Politics* (1972, 1973, 1975), and by *Cleavages, Parties and Values in Canada* (1974), which explored the interaction between cleavages and the party system.

Harold Clarke and others analyzed the 1974 federal election in *Political Choice in Canada* (1979; abridged ed., 1980), the most extensive study of Canadian voting behaviour and partisanship at the time of its publication. *Absent Mandate* (1984), by the same authors, a provocative analysis of voting behaviour during the elections of 1974, 1979, and 1980, contends that elections rarely give governments the sort of mandate required to enact major policies, particularly with respect to the economy.

These behavioural contributions, which have broadened the substantive interests of political science in Canada, display a welcome concern for scientific method less evident in earlier research. While the creation of a distinct subfield is a notable achievement, various critics question the rigour of much of the analysis. Nelson Wiseman, in a 1986 *Journal of Canadian Studies* article, identifies major discrepancies in the survey data, in particular the often lengthy delay between the election and the administration of the post-election surveys, and concludes that the hard evidence on why people vote the way they do is meagre. Other critics agree on the theoretical weakness and excessive empiricism of much of the literature.

A separate literature explores the effect of institutions, rules, and regulations on the party system. As Allan Kornberg et al. underlined in *Citizen Politicians – Canada* (1979), political parties are heavily dependent on the voluntary labours of relatively few people. Yet those same political parties – incredibly amateurish from one perspective – are selectively shaped by a network of institutions and rules.

In 1978, in the *Canadian Journal of Political Science*, John Courtney refuted the proposition that political parties had a 'non-existence' in law and in Parliament, by documenting the various laws and regulations affecting parties in such areas as broadcasting, the tax system, and election finances, and their extensive recognition in the workings of Parliament. Two significant changes of the 1960s and 1970s – the Electoral Boundaries Readjustment Act of 1964 which provided for impartial, periodic reassessment of constituency boundaries according to known criteria, and the Election Expenses Act of 1974 to control election spending, provide public funding of parties, and require public disclosure of the income and expenditures of parties and candidates – have been subject to periodic scholarly assessment.[25] Many of the rules to control abuses, and to inject criteria of fairness into the adversarial party process, are explicitly designed to protect parties against their own baser instincts and thus preserve the overall legitimacy of the party system. The deliberate manipulation of the formal contexts within which parties manoeuvre weakens explanations of their behaviour based purely on socio-economic factors.

The contribution of the single-member plurality electoral system to a regionally fragmented national party system graphically underlined the consequences of rules. Many scholars argued that an electoral system which virtually shut the Conservatives out of Quebec and held Liberal representation from western Canada far below their voting support reduced the legitimacy of the national government. William P. Irvine's detailed monograph, *Does Canada Need a New Electoral System?* (1979), recommended a partial proportional representation system to make the elected representation of the major parties a more accurate reflection of their electorate and thus of the country.

The growing importance of the provinces increased academic interest in provincial parties and party systems. The scholarly response included Martin Robin, ed., *Canadian Provincial Politics* (1972, 1978); J.T. Morley, *Secular Socialists* (1984), a study of the CCF/NDP in Ontario from its depression origins; Nelson Wiseman, *Social Democracy in Manitoba* (1983); David Smith's superb study, *Prairie Liberalism: The Liberal Party in Saskatchewan 1905–71* (1975); and Donald E. Blake, *Two Political Worlds: Parties and Voting in British Columbia* (1985). Blake's volume lucidly explored the linkage between the different federal and provincial party systems in British Columbia and the different federal and provincial worlds of British Columbia voters, both produced by federalism. Federalism, which confronts the same electorate with two arenas for political expression, confirms the proposition that societies contain the potential for an indeterminate range of political activity which different institutional arrangements could activate.

Several additional publications deserve mention. Leadership selection received its first exhaustive analysis in John C. Courtney's *The Selection of National Party Leaders in Canada* (1973). William Mishler systematically explored *Political Participation in Canada* (1979). Notable studies of individual parties include works on the national Liberal party by Reginald Whitaker, Joseph Wearing, and David E. Smith, and on the Progressive Conservatives by George Perlin.[26] Perlin's phrase, 'the Tory syndrome,' has entered the public debate as a label for the destructive intra-party squabbles which flow from permanent minority status, and which inhibit successful performance during brief periods of government.

Whitaker's massive and brilliant volume, *The Government Party* (1977), focusing on party organization and financing of the Liberal party from the depression of the 1930s to the Diefenbaker breakthrough of 1957–8, was self-consciously an old-fashioned historical and descriptive account. The Quebec wing of the national Social Credit party was analyzed in Michael Stein, *The Dynamics of Right-Wing Protest* (1973), and Maurice Pinard, *The Rise of a Third Party* (enlarged ed., 1975). Ivan Avakumovic produced the first comprehensive history of the Communist party from a non-Communist perspective as well as a study of the CCF/NDP in federal and provincial politics.[27]

The proliferation of literature on parties, elections, and voters greatly increased understanding of a multitude of particulars, but did not add up to a coherent normative and empirical understanding of how they fitted into the collective political life of Canada. The traditional role of parties as intermediaries between society and the state was undercut by the emergence of social movements which saw political parties as only one, and not necessarily the most useful, instrument to influence public policy. The exceptional visibility of the women's and aboriginal movements owed little to parties. In general, their political aggressiveness was simply the Canadian version of the international politicization of gender and of indigenous peoples in the last quarter of a century. In Canada both groups profited from the prominence of the Charter in the federal government's constitutional strategy. In both cases their political visibility stimulated academic enquiry.

For the women's movement, the period began with the Royal Commission on the Status of Women in Canada which reported in 1970, and culminated in the successful campaign to exempt Section 28 of the Charter, guaranteeing its rights and freedoms 'equally to male and female persons' from the override clause, a victory described in separate accounts by Chaviva Hošek (in Banting and Simeon, *And No One Cheered*) and Penny Kome (*The Taking of Twenty-Eight*, 1983). For Indians, the 1960s ended with the publication of the federal government's 1969 White Paper on Indian Policy, which advocated the ending of special Indian status. Militant Indian opposition led to the withdrawal of the proposed policy and deprived the federal government of the initiative for the next decade. The anthropologist Sally M. Weaver describes this federal effort and its effective repudiation by organized Indian opposition in the superb volume, *Making Canadian Indian Policy: The Hidden Agenda 1968–70* (1981).

The development of aboriginal political skills, facilitated by extensive government funding of aboriginal organizations, led to the clauses of the 1982 Constitution Act which recognized aboriginal and treaty rights (s.35) and required the holding of constitutional conferences to try to identify and define those rights (s.37). The subsequent constitutional conferences of 1983, 1984, and 1985 are dissected in a detailed analysis by the University of Manitoba law professor Bryan Schwartz in *First Principles, Second Thoughts* (1986).

The political salience of aboriginal issues, which included land claims and self-government, in the context of a political climate influenced by anti-colonialism and affirmative action philosophies, elicited a small body of political science literature sympathetic to aboriginal demands. J. Rick Ponting and Roger Gibbins, in *Out of Irrelevance* (1980), analyzed the interplay between the federal administration of Indian Affairs and the National Indian Brotherhood, at that time the main Indian political organization. Two volumes of collected essays – Leroy Little Bear, Menno Boldt, and J. Anthony Long, eds, *Pathways to Self-Determination* (1984), and Menno Boldt and J. Anthony Long, eds, *The Quest for Justice* (1985), with chapters by aboriginal advocates, social scientists, and lawyers – provided a generally supportive platform for the expression and analysis of aboriginal demands. The appearance of the new journal *Native Studies Review* in 1985 underlined the rapidly growing scholarly interest in aboriginal issues.

The women's movement, the participation of women in politics and the economy, and the strategies to overcome gender-based inequities are analyzed in a literature primarily written by women and, as in the case of aboriginals, generally sympathetic to the cause. Introductions to this emerging research agenda are Sylvia Bashevkin's analysis of women in party politics in English Canada, *Toeing the Lines* (1985), and Sandra Burt's contribution to the research of Volume XXXIV of the Macdonald Commission, 'Women's Issues and the Women's Movement in Canada since 1970,' with a valuable bibliography. Other notable contributions include *Canadian Women in Politics* (1982) by Janine Brodie and Jill McCalla Vickers; Brodie's recent textbook,

Women and Politics in Canada (1985); and *Women and the Constitution in Canada* (1981), ed. Audrey Doerr and Micheline Carrier.[28] Mary O'Brien's *The Politics of Reproduction* (1981) made a well-received contribution to feminist theory.

The extensive resort of the women's and aboriginal movements to non-party channels was one indication of the decline of parties which John Meisel had eloquently argued in an essay in Thorburn's *Party Politics in Canada* (4th ed., 1979). Supplementary evidence was provided by the growing use of political consultants and lobbyists. The key instrument in that decline, however, was usually identified as the pressure group, whose larger numbers and increased political influence generated a scholarly literature which sought to evaluate the role of pressure groups in the Canadian system of representative democracy. A study by Robert Presthus, *Elites in the Policy Process* (1974), indicating that pressure groups disproportionately focused their attention on the bureaucracy rather than on backbenchers or legislative committees, suggested that the bridge between citizens and the state provided by elections and the party system could no longer carry the traffic of citizen demands.

In addition to the many case studies that appeared, from which David Kwavnick's *Organized Labour and Pressure Politics: The Canadian Labour Congress 1956–1968* (1972) stands out for its analytical rigour, the larger issue of the role of pressure groups in Canadian democracy was addressed by Robert Presthus in *Elite Accommodation* (1973) and *Elites in the Policy Process*; by Paul Pross, ed., in *Pressure Group Behaviour in Canadian Politics* (1975); and by Hugh Thorburn in *Interest Groups in the Canadian Federal System* (1985). The work of Pross culminated in *Group Politics and Public Policy* (1986). Pross documents the co-existence of and tension between two competing systems of representation. The traditional system, comprising elections, parties, and legislatures, is based on territory, the individual constituencies which send members to legislatures to act for all the citizens and interests within geographically circumscribed areas. The emerging system, based on groups of dispersed citizens and corporate actors with common concerns, is organized on sectoral and functional lines to interact with governments whose bureaucracies are similarly organized. 'A functionalist administrative structure,' as Paltiel put it in a 1982 *Canadian Public Administration* article, 'has produced a parallel structure of interest groups which has subverted the role of parties in the policy communication area.'

A more policy-oriented focus on pressure groups emerged in the Canadian discussion of the desirability and feasibility of corporatist practices, usually defined as the collaboration in tripartite settings of unions, business associations, and the state in the making of economic policy. The overt purpose of such practices, which are employed with varying success in Europe, is to transcend the conflicts between management and labour and involve both, along with government, in the determination of economic policy, the implementation of which should be facilitated by the prior agreement of the elites of the relevant economic interests. The Marxist political economist Leo Panitch is an influential contributor to this debate, and is frequently cited in the international literature. He wrote an impressive chapter in the Macdonald Commission research study *The State and Economic Interests* (1986), edited by Keith Banting. Both Banting and Panitch conclude that corporatism has little to offer Canadian policy-makers. Panitch, on the whole, distrusts corporatism, which he sees as a vehicle to control and manipulate the working class. Banting's reservations are more pragmatic – that the combination of federalism and the organizational fragmentation and weakness of the union movement, and to a lesser extent business, means that Canada lacks the prerequisites for its successful employment.

CANADIAN FOREIGN POLICY AND CANADIAN-AMERICAN RELATIONS

The series Canada in World Affairs goes back to World War II. The *International Journal* (1946–), an interdisciplinary vehicle comprehensible to non-specialists, has given a focus to Canadian foreign policy studies denied to most other policy areas. Two new annuals, *The Canadian Strategic Review* (1982–), published by the Canadian Institute of Strategic Studies, and *Canada among Nations* (1984–), published by the Norman Paterson School of International Affairs, Carleton University, provide additional monitoring of Canada's role as an international actor.

The escalating significance of international economic issues in the 1970s moved the agenda of students of international politics from the traditional 'high politics' of war, peace, security, and the balance of power to a host of new questions addressed to the 'low politics' of trade, international finance, the multinational corporation, and other indicators of a tighter global economic interdependence. The relevant literature is lucidly surveyed in a study by Jock Finlayson for Volume XXVIII of the Macdonald Commission research studies. More generally, the three Commission research Volumes XXVIII–XXX edited by Denis Stairs and Gilbert Winham, provide a political analysis of the options confronting Canada in the international economy, including a closer economic relationship with the United States. Extensive coverage of the legal and economic aspects of interdependence, focusing particularly on Canada-United States relations, is available in the seventy research volumes of the Macdonald Commission so far published. The Report itself makes the case for a bilateral Canada-United States free trade arrangement to strengthen Canadian economic performance. Canadian-American relations were also addressed in numerous other publications, of which the most widely debated was Stephen Clarkson's *Canada and the Reagan Challenge* (1982; rev. ed.,

1985), which analyzed Canadian-American confrontations over the economic nationalism of the National Energy Program and the Foreign Investment Review Agency, along with other challenges to the bilateral relationship.[29]

Prominent contributions to the study of Canada's postwar internationalism include the distinguished two-volume study by John Holmes, *The Shaping of Peace: Canada and the Search for World Order 1943-1957* (1979, 1982) and his *Canada: A Middle-Aged Power* (1972); three more volumes of James Eayrs's widely acclaimed study *In Defence of Canada* – ie, *Peacemaking and Deterrence* (1972), *Growing Up Allied* (1980), and *Indochina: Roots of Complicity* (1983); *The Diplomacy of Constraint: Canada, the Korean War, and the United States* (1974) by Denis Stairs; and a three-volume study by a senior diplomat of the 1940s, Escott Reid's *Time of Fear and Hope: The Making of the North Atlantic Treaty 1947-1949* (1977), *Envoy to Nehru* (1981), and *On Duty: A Canadian at the Making of the United Nations, 1945-1946* (1983). Hugh L. Keenleyside provides an additional personal account in his *Memoirs* (2 vols, 1981, 1982). The Canadian role in Bretton Woods and in the subsequent evolution of the international monetary order is analyzed in *Three Decades of Decision* (1977) by A.F.W. Plumptre, a prominent member of the postwar bureaucratic mandarinate who served for a time as Canadian Executive Director at the International Monetary Fund and the World Bank. The three volumes of Lester Pearson's autobiography *Mike* (1972-5), especially Volume III, which contains considerable information on Canadian-American relations, should not be overlooked.

Two recent incisive additions to the discussion of Canada's foreign policy during the Vietnam debacle are *In the Interests of Peace: Canada and Vietnam 1954-1973* (1984) by Douglas A. Ross, and *Peacekeeping in Vietnam: Canada, India, Poland, and the International Commission* (1984) by Ramesh Thakur. Ross's justly praised study explicitly challenges the Eayrs thesis of Canadian complicity in Vietnam.

The defence aspect of foreign policy is addressed by Colin Gray, *Canadian Defence Priorities* (1972), and in specific areas more recently by David Cox, *Canada and NORAD, 1958-1978* (1985) and Douglas A. Ross, *Coping with 'Star Wars'* (1985).

Bruce Thordarson's *Trudeau and Foreign Policy: A Study in Decision-Making* (1972) discusses the prime minister's role, and the environment of foreign policy decision-making. *The Canadian Condominium: Domestic Issues and External Policy* (1972), ed. Thomas Hockin et al., and *Canadian Foreign Policy and the Law of the Sea* (1977), ed. Barbara Johnson and Mark Zacher, explore the interaction between domestic political questions and priorities and the direction of Canadian foreign policy. *Canada and the Third World* (1976), ed. Peyton Lyon and Tareq Y. Ismael, is an informative collection of essays on a key strand in Canadian foreign policy.

Here, as elsewhere, textbooks help to focus discussion, synthesize scattered literatures, and occasionally try to change the terms of debate. *The Politics of Canadian Foreign Policy* (1985) by Kim Richard Nossal examines the 'ways in which the external and domestic environments constrain and impel Canadian foreign policy-makers,' paying particular attention to the apparatus of the state, or governmental politics, 'the interplay of the executive, the bureaucracy, the legislature and the provincial governments in the shaping of external policy.' In *Canada as a Principal Power* (1983), David Dewitt and John Kirton trace the decline of liberal internationalism in Canadian foreign policy against the changing international environment and the emergence of what they call 'complex neo-realism.' They contend that since 1968 Canada has been 'an ascending principal power in an increasingly diffuse, nonhegemonic international system,' an argument they illustrate with case studies. Valuable case studies also figure prominently in Michael Tucker's standard text, *Canadian Foreign Policy* (1980), which discusses 'The Third Option,' the Canadian response to the perceived demise of the 'special relationship' with the United States, the National Energy Policy, Canada and the law of the sea, the Garrison Dam confrontation, and the non-proliferation of nuclear weapons.

Three competing perspectives dominate the literature on Canadian foreign policy. The internationalist perspective, associated with Lester Pearson and adhered to by many academic students, views Canada as a middle power with a strong interest in collective security. The leading protagonist for this view is John Holmes, who published profusely after he resigned from the foreign service in 1960 and until his death in 1988.[30]

From an economic nationalist perspective, as in Clarkson's *Canada and the Reagan Challenge*, Canada is viewed as a dependent satellite of the United States – Canada–United States economic integration leaving only a limited margin of foreign policy autonomy. This perspective informed the various official reports on foreign investment in the 1960s and 1970s, and lay behind the third option search of the early 1970s for a diversification of Canadian international economic links. It is a natural perspective for the smaller of two partners caught in a continental economic and cultural embrace. The economic nationalist perspective is prescriptive, for it sees satellite status as psychologically demeaning and politically enervating.

To these rival interpretive schools has been added a third which goes back to a seminal article by James Eayrs, published in *International Perspectives* in 1975. His thesis, which views Canada as a foremost or principal power, has received its most elaborate expression in Kirton/Dewitt, *Canada as a Principal Power*. From this gratifying perspective for Canadians, Canada is one of the world's top states in the international status hierarchy and in its capacity to influence the international system. While this view strains the credulity of those who compare Canada only with the United States, it is more defensible when one objectively analyzes the comparative status and capabilities of all the world's states.

This threefold classification of Canadian foreign policy literature is elaborated in considerable detail in the valuable interpretive essay by Michael K. Hawes, *Principal Power, Middle Power, or Satellite?* (1984). Hawes also explores five additional perspectives which enjoy a lesser visibility and a more limited supporting literature.

COMPARATIVE POLITICS AND INTERNATIONAL RELATIONS

Faculty growth reduced the primary focus on Canadian politics characteristic of the much smaller Canadian political science community of the 1940s and 1950s and provided the resources to respond to an explosive increase in the number of states in the international system, from 51 in 1945 to over 150 in the mid-1980s. The retreat of Western imperialism from Africa and Asia and the emergence of dozens of new states altered the universe of comparative politics by adding a significant non-Western component.

At the end of World War II, comparative politics was largely restricted to the European world, including the white settler dominions of the British Empire, and to the Soviet Union. Most of the non-Western world was outside the vision of the small band of Canadian political scientists who were busily carving out disciplinary territory to call their own. Now, by contrast, developing areas have attracted many scholars, and interest in the Communist world has expanded to include Eastern Europe and China.

These new subfields developed simultaneously but somewhat differently in Canada and the United States. Canadian-American differences of intellectual culture and the marked difference of status and role of their respective governments in the global community sustain divergent intellectual orientations. Thus Canadian students of Communist politics, less influenced by Cold War considerations and removed from superpower concerns, have been less ideological and more detached; Canadian studies of the Third World have also questioned dominant American approaches, been skeptical of the American literature of modernization and political development and, in particular subfields (especially sub-Saharan Africa), been much more influenced by Marxist political economy than were their American counterparts.

The evolution of fields of study external to Canada partly reflected ethnic changes in Canadian society. Such changes, to which the 1971 official policy of multiculturalism was a response, diversified the international links between Canadians and the homelands to which the citizenry relate. For students of domestic politics the new ethnicity led to new journals, eg, *Canadian Ethnic Studies* (1969–), to state-sponsored studies of particular ethnic groups, and to studies of immigration and refugee policy.[31] From a comparative perspective it led to the multidisciplinary *Canadian Review of Studies in Nationalism* (1973–), which regularly publishes ethnic bibliographies, and to Canadian contributions to the comparative study of ethnically plural societies.[32]

Not only does domestic heterogeneity multiply the interest in foreign countries, but students of particular countries or political regions are often recruited from immigrant communities, from which they bring linguistic skills, cultural sensitivity, and political interest. While this is especially the case with scholarship on the Soviet Union and Eastern Europe where postwar immigrants from Eastern Europe (particularly Poland, Czechoslovakia, and Ukraine) are prominent, the phenomenon is widespread.[33]

Constitutional issues in Canada also led to an intertwining of domestic and comparative concerns. During the constitutional introspection from the 1960s to the early 1980s there was a selective intellectual ransacking of those political systems whose circumstances or governing arrangements elicited hopes that one or more of their institutions, suitably modified before transplantation, might be an answer to Canadian problems. This tendency was especially pronounced with respect to proposals for electoral and Senate reform. More generally, consociational theories, originally derived from studies of the smaller European democracies, intermittently informed discussions of recipes for the peaceful governance of an ethnically divided society, such as Canada. Comparative research on the corporatism employed with varying success in several European democracies was undertaken to assess its possible contribution to a more dirigiste state role as economic planner in Canada.[34]

While the individual volumes on particular countries, regions, and continents cannot be cited here, a few basic tendencies deserve comment. The research concentration on sub-Saharan Africa is remarkable. There are more domestic political scientists now studying this region than were studying Canada only thirty years ago. While this literature is not monolithic, much of it is influenced by a mix of Marxist political economy and political models ranging from social democracy to revolutionary socialism.

Israel excepted, there is a marked lack of attention to the Middle East, probably for language reasons. Thus the political influence of Islam in individual states and in the international system is relatively underexamined by Canadian political scientists. Islam is more likely to be studied in Canada from historical, cultural, literary, and religious perspectives. The attention paid to Western Europe is also surprisingly limited, given the European heritage of a majority of Canadians. The Commonwealth excites much less academic interest than formerly. Most remarkable is the almost complete absence of significant political science scholarship on the United States, although Roger Gibbins's comparative work, *Regionalism* (1982), is an impressive exception. By contrast, there has been continuing interest in the

United Kingdom, reflected in a number of major monographs, primarily written either by British academics now teaching in Canada, or by Canadians who did their doctoral work in the United Kingdom.[35] But it is noteworthy that Canadians completing doctoral work in the United States and Americans teaching in Canada have contributed little to the study of American politics. On the whole, Canadian scholarship in comparative politics can be explained neither by fidelity to practical concerns, nor as a mirror of the distribution of power in the international system.

The study of international politics, as with comparative politics, has been challenged by the transformation of the international state system. The traditional international relations paradigm, which postulates states as the key actors in the global polity, and war and peace as the central focus of scholarship, is no longer unquestioned. The major alternative approaches – world system or global society theories (which stress a global interdependence that erodes the autonomy and significance of states in world politics), and Marxism and dependency theories commence from different premises and ask different questions. These competing approaches are assessed in K.J. Holsti, *The Dividing Discipline: Hegemony and Diversity in International Theory* (1985).

HISTORY OF IDEAS AND POLITICAL THEORY

The contemporary study of political theory in Canada has been stimulated by the domestic crisis in public authority and by the maturing of a sizeable political science community. An interest in indigenous thought, extending back to the late eighteenth century, lay behind H.D. Forbes's 1985 anthology, *Canadian Political Thought*. A second collection, *Political Thought in Canada* (1984), comp. Stephen Brooks, brings together original contemporary essays dealing with various enduring Canadian concerns.

Much of the constitutional discussion of the 1970s was political philosophy couched in legal language. Political leaders and often polemical commentators addressed issues of citizenship, of the boundaries of community, of democratic participation, and of gender equality both directly and indirectly. An explicit philosophical approach to many of the central issues – the tensions among competing definitions of community, and between community and individual rights – was employed in Stanley French, ed., *Confederation* (1979). Several authors, including Reginald Whitaker, in *Federalism and Democratic Theory* (1983), and Philip Resnick, in *Parliament vs People* (1984), criticized the theory or practice of democratic elitism, and argued for greater individual participation in the major organizations of society. Canadian scholars also made significant contributions to feminist discourse. A 1979 collection of essays edited by Lorenne Clark and Lynda Lange, *The Sexism of Social and Political Theory*,[36] contends that sexist assumptions are so deeply embedded in the Western political tradition that genuine social and political equality is all but precluded short of massive social reorganization. *Feminism in Canada* (1982), edited by Angela Miles and Geraldine Finn, including a vigorous chapter on political science by Jill Vickers, critically examines the 'silencing' of women in the major academic disciplines. Two volumes contribute to the now extensive literature exploring the 'unhappy marriage'[37] between Marxism and feminism: *Women, Class, Family and the State* (1985) by Varda Burstyn and Dorothy Smith with an introduction by Roxanna Ng, and *Feminist Marxism or Marxist Feminism* (1985) by Patricia Armstrong et al., with an introduction by Meg Luxton. Many feminists roundly criticize Marxist theory, in Luxton's words, 'for largely ignoring women, for sex-blindness, and for failing to theorize gender.'

In addition to their explicit contributions to contemporary issues, Canadian scholars published distinguished work on political theory, the history of political concepts and ideas, and the interpretation of the works of previous political thinkers. In the first category of contributions to political theory, the works of C.B. Macpherson, George Grant, and Charles Taylor have a deserved prominence.

In his *Democratic Theory: Essays in Retrieval* (1973), the Marxist theorist C.B. Macpherson extended themes suggested in earlier writings.[38] In *Democratic Theory* he continued his life-long quest of 'retrieving' the ethical values of liberalism, especially the theory of self-realization to be found in the thought of J.S. Mill and T.H. Green, from the 'possessive individualism' of capitalist market society. Macpherson accordingly uses the concept of democracy not to describe a system of government, but to refer to a kind of society, one that ideally should allow us to enjoy our 'human attributes' rather than constrain us to remain mere 'consumers of utilities.' In *The Life and Times of Liberal Democracy* (1977) he argues that if we are to develop into beings capable of exercising our 'powers and capacities,' there must be a transition to a non-capitalist society in which forms of participatory democracy take the place of merely representative institutions.

In *English-Speaking Justice* (1985), George Grant, Canada's foremost conservative philosopher (he died in 1988), also extended a number of themes to be found in earlier writings.[39] This work is a searching critique and profound meditation on the meaning of justice in liberal democratic societies dominated by technology and a purely instrumental notion of rationality and human association.

Charles Taylor, perhaps Canada's most distinguished contemporary political philosopher, is a prominent opponent of those seeking to model the study of politics and society on the theories and assumptions of the natural sciences. Following *The Explanation of Behaviour* (1964), addressed to this concern, Taylor set about to sketch an alternative conception of the self and human agency. The most notable of his recent writings are two important works on Hegel and the 'expressivist' alternative to the 'atomism' that Taylor fears is engulfing contemporary understandings of society (*Hegel*, 1975; *Hegel and Modern Society*, 1979), and two volumes of his philosophical essays, *Human Agency and Language* (1985) and *Philosophy and the Human Sciences* (1985).

Noteworthy work in historical reconstruction and/or analytical clarification of important political concepts and ideas includes David Braybrooke's ongoing philosophical analysis of the role of values such as participation and competing purposes in democratic theory; J.A.W. Gunn's detailed contextual studies of the process of self-recognition or 'social self-knowledge' in eighteenth-century political thought and such key concepts as the public interest, party government, and public opinion; Ronald Beiner's study of political judgment in the thought of twentieth-century thinkers such as Hannah Arendt, Hans-Georg Gadamer, and Jürgen Habermas; several important explorations of domination and the meaning of technology in our times; and some notable attempts to reconceptualize the role of the state in the postwar period. Several volumes of essays appeared on the changing definition and role of the concept of property in the Western tradition. In *Aspects of Political Theory* (1976) and *Approaches to Democracy* (1980), among several other works, W.J. Stankiewicz makes an important contribution to the restoration of such basic classical concepts of political theory as the social contract, the general will, sovereignty, and natural law in a contemporary climate of 'all-pervading relativism.'[40] The latter volume is a critique of current theories of liberal democracy.

Canadian political theorists also valuably interpreted the works of previous political thinkers: Plato and Aristotle by Ellen Meiksins Wood and Neal Wood, several reinterpretations of the thought of Machiavelli, David Kettler's studies of the work of Adam Ferguson and more recently Georg Lukács and Karl Mannheim, C.B. Macpherson's study of Burke, important studies of Locke by James Tully and Neal Wood, as well as explorations of the thought of the French neo-Hegelian, Alexandre Kojève.[41]

While some of the works cited in this section ultimately will be judged to be tracts of the time rather than distinguished contributions to political theory, there are enough of the latter to constitute an impressive performance. Even the former have an appropriate niche in the history of ideas, for recent scholarship suggests that the more popular pamphleteering literature of a period cannot be divorced from more serious contemporary philosophical work. They share vocabularies and concerns and an interdependence such that each illuminates the other.[42]

A major puzzle remains to be explored. While political theory in English Canada is, in Arthur Kroker's phrase, 'typified by a ... highly original and thorough critique of liberalism, old and new,'[43] a 1985 volume by Ronald

Manzer, *Public Policies and Political Development in Canada*, argues convincingly that the principles of policy-making in Canada have been drawn overwhelmingly from the tenets of liberalism.

CONCLUSION

In one sense, the period from the early 1970s to the mid-1980s was one of faculty consolidation after the frantic expansion of the 1960s. However, this was not accompanied by any consensus on the mandate or methodology of the discipline. An expanded faculty in consort with domestic and international political developments greatly enlarged the agenda of political science. Domestically, Quebec nationalism, the women's movement, the entry of the aboriginal peoples into public life, and a generally resurgent ethnicity challenged the dialectic between class, region, and nation which had engaged previous scholarly generations. These centrifugal domestic developments coincided with a similar fragmentation in global politics as the peoples of Africa and Asia became full participants in the world of nation-states.

The proliferation of new subfields in response to these domestic and international events made political scientists ignorant of each other's work. A pluralism of subject-matters was also fed by disciplinary developments, as both political economy and behaviouralism generated enthusiastic disciples with distinctive research agendas.

Cumulatively, these developments seemed to fragment political science, yet the constitutional crisis had an opposite effect, at least for students of domestic politics. Constitutional concerns focused attention on the prospects for Canada's survival, and on how, if at all, constitutional or institutional change might keep the country together. This had the positive academic effect of providing a common focus of attention for many political scientists, and of keeping alive a concern for the relations between states and peoples. Negatively, however, the lure of the contemporary, always strong among political scientists, was reinforced by the apprehension that Canada might not survive. At such times civic concerns consume a disproportionate share of intellectual resources; and more purely scholarly projects, driven by theoretical questions, which may take years to mature, tend to be understudied.

13 Writings in Canadian History

CARL BERGER

In the decade after 1974, Canadian historical research continued to accelerate, as the subject-matter broadened to include neglected groups and regions. At the same time, holistic interpretations of national Canadian experience diminished. Though much of the literature amplified existing traditions of national political history, a sense of the coherence of Canadian history was lost. Historians no longer agreed upon what was central to their field of study and what was peripheral.[1]

This transformation was the consequence of profound changes in the country's social and intellectual life. At the beginning of the boom in higher education there were 160 historians in all colleges and universities in the country; by 1976 there were nearly 1000.[2] In the decade after 1966 the numbers of doctoral and master's theses being written increased from 350 to some 1200. The sheer growth in the numbers of scholars, and the hiring of specialists rather than generalists in Canadian history, led to a tidal wave of publications. Increasingly, moreover, universities justified themselves as pioneers opening up new frontiers of knowledge rather than as transmitters and conservers of it.

The growth in numbers coincided with deep, bewildering changes in Canadian society which impinged upon the consciousness of historians. The later 1960s questioned the directions the country was taking; concomitantly, the postwar feeling of relative self-confidence dissolved. The rise of French-Canadian nationalism, the increasing assertiveness of provincial governments, and economic dependency were only three of the more apparent challenges. In *The Forked Road: Canada, 1939–1957* (1976) Donald Creighton, the country's greatest national historian, continued his personal war against these powerful currents and denounced those who led Canada down the road to subservience to the United States. Written when he was ill with cancer (Creighton died in 1979), the book never did demonstrate that there existed another fork in the road, and it was condemned by most historians. Even those who shared Creighton's nationalist outrage did not know how to cope with his attacks on the welfare state. In some ways this book represented the bankruptcy of a kind of history in which historical forces were personalized and of a nationalist vision of what should have been but had not come to pass.

Where Creighton was driven to despair, others were more hopeful about the possibilities to which social change might lead; for them, the feminist movement, the native peoples' rejection of their 'colonial' position in Canadian society, and, above all, student activism were positive signs. Nowhere was this restlessness and intellectual ferment more pronounced than among the academic supporters of the new left. In Canada as elsewhere this was less a movement than a mood – amorphous, sometimes incoherent, preoccupied with the Vietnam War, civil rights, and the bureaucratic organization of.the multi-university. In so far as it possessed a consistency of feeling, the new left was hostile to hierarchy and authority (including interpretations of history that seemed to justify the flawed present). Those who shared its sentiments were disillusioned with electoral politics, held political history in contempt, and identified, despite their own predominantly middle-class backgrounds, with the victimized and dispossessed – blacks, immigrants, workers, women, and native peoples. Though there was a profoundly anti-historical thrust to the new left, some students searched out critical works of Canadian history that would furnish the counter-culture with independent and authentic roots in the protest movements of the past. Some found these congenial perspectives in Stanley Ryerson's Marxist history of Canada, or Henry Ferns and Bernard Ostry's acerbic life of the young Mackenzie King, or in the 1960 thesis by H. Clare Pentland, *Labour and Capital in Canada 1650–1860*, which was finally published in 1981. Some discovered in such classics of neo-Marxist, British literature as Edward P. Thompson, *The Making of the English Working Class* (1963), models of how to recover anti-capitalist traditions and write alternative histories.

The groups that were rejecting their subordinate positions in society called for new histories that would give them greater recognition in the country's past. These appeals invariably censured the distortions of conventional history and came first from outside the historical establishment, or from young historians just securing a foothold within it. The zeal for certain aspects of social history – the study of women, the working class, native peoples, and immigrants – had numerous roots, including the examples of foreign scholarship and the inevitable recoil against political biography; but it owed much also to contemporary social movements and to their questioning of the legitimacy of institutions. These origins imparted a highly critical spirit: history became a force for remedial action and moral criticism, a weapon for attacking the abuses of the present by exposing their sources and for pointing to better alternatives.

The growth of the professional study and teaching of history was but one aspect of an upsurge of cultural nationalism and an unprecedented popular fascination with the past. Inspired by the celebrations of the centenary of Confederation and sustained by a universal search for roots and genealogy, this wave of nostalgia expressed a hankering for direct contact with a visible, tangible 'living history.' It led to countless private ventures in family history, the vast outpouring of publications on local and regional history, the retrieval of memorabilia and memories, and the creation of many local museums. The promotion of tourism – the selling of the past – was one of the reasons for the expansion of historical investigation in such government agencies as the National Historic Parks and Sites Branch of Parks Canada. The restoration of Fortress Louisbourg generated after 1961 a small library of research reports that provided the basis for several books, including A.B. Johnston's *Religion in Life at Louisbourg, 1713–1758* (1984) and Christopher Moore's *Louisbourg Portraits* (1982). In the latter, the experiences of ordinary people – a widow, merchant, fisherman, a drifter accused of theft – illustrate eighteenth-century strategies of survival, marriage customs, child-rearing practices, and the operations of the judicial system.

The writers who have responded best to the popular curiosity about history have come from the world of journalism, not the university. The appeal of 'popular history' rested on the telling of a dramatic story, entertaining narrative, vivid characterization, or the exposure of human foibles and frailties. Sometimes it could also serve the purposes of national feeling. Pierre Berton's *The Invasion of Canada: 1812–1813* (1980) and *Flames across the Border: 1813–1814* (1981) retold the story of a crucial conflict, its immediacy heightened not only by the grisly detail but also by the use of the present tense throughout. By contrast, Sandra Gwyn's *The Private Capital* (1984) resembled a delightful gossip column: full of personal anecdotes (twice we are told that Sandford Fleming liked marmalade in his porridge) and breathless revelations about Laurier's long affair with his law partner's wife, the social rounds at Rideau Hall, and the sexual escapades and preferences of some of its residents. One of the best popular books was *The Lumberjacks* (1978) by Donald MacKay, a journalist who had worked for United Press, and who graphically recreated the ways of life of the woodcutters, recording their methods of work and camp life, unique language, codes of conduct, songs and folklore, food, and technology.

The expectations of the reading public regarding a work of history and the practice of most academic historians were closer a generation ago than in the 1970s. Historians no longer generally regarded the art of narrative as a model for their work, and they outgrew – or abdicated – the role of interpreters of the national character. Academic scholars increasingly occupied themselves with anonymous social patterns, with groups and classes rather than with individuals; they prized analysis over narrative and description; their most original books did not tell a story but answered questions; and they frequently took as their points of departure evaluations of the corpus of existing literature and its shortcomings. All this tended to make access to the past difficult for the general reader; it was almost as though historians had interposed themselves between the reader and history.

These differences should not obscure the fact that a few scholars did write highly original works of history which found a wide readership beyond the academic profession. Michael Bliss took on the difficult task of recreating the inner history of a scientific breakthrough: *The Discovery of Insulin* (1982) so scintillatingly reconstructed the series of experiments and the clashes of personalities that the book was praised both by the most demanding historians of science and by reviewers who loved a good story. Writers outside the academic establishment, moreover, also wrote well. There was more to be learned, for example, about western Canada in the decade after the Great War from James Gray's *The Roar of the Twenties* (1975) than from any single academic book at the time it was published; a practising lawyer, Patrick Brode, advanced immeasurably an understanding of both the Loyalist tradition and the law in nineteenth-century Ontario in *Sir John Beverley Robinson* (1984); and Murray Peden in *A Thousand Shall Fall* (1979) drew upon his service in an RAF squadron to describe the air war against Nazi Germany. Charles P. Stacey wrote that Peden's was the best book any Canadian has written about his war experiences, and one of the best books about the war that has been written anywhere. Such generous praise was rare. The responses of most academic historians to the surge of popular history were uneasy and critical, as though the confines of a craft guild were violated.

ECONOMIC AND BUSINESS HISTORY

Continuities and discontinuities in academic historical writing were strikingly evident in the literature on economic and business history and in the political economy approach which explored the relationships between economics and politics. The pendulum of academic fashion in the later 1960s led to a rediscovery of the abundant literature on early Canadian economic history. In certain circles Harold Innis became a cult figure. Social scientists attempted to rescue him from the communications theorists, subjected his writings to considerable scrutiny, and reprinted even his inscrutable notebooks.[3] The rehabilitation of Innis and the political economy tradition resulted partly from a general desire to fix upon the material foundations of society and politics. But it owed much also to the resurgence of nationalist concerns with external investment and control, and with the economic basis of regional disparities. Some of his new admirers attempted, without much success, to fuse his work with Marxism. Innis had centred his analysis upon trade relations, on the physical properties of staples of the pre-industrial era, and on the ways in which each commodity had shaped structures and patterns. For the Marxists, the crux of the matter was the process and means of production and the social relations of capital and labour.[4] The marriage of Marx and Innis was a barren union: so much time was expended by the political economists of the left on clarifying paradigms that little history was written. Indeed, the one major contribution of the debate over foreign ownership in the economy, Tom Naylor's two-volume *The History of Canadian Business, 1867–1914* (1975), owed much to Innis, nothing to Marx, and a little to Gustavus Myers, the turn-of-the-century muckraker who had set out to expose the shady origins of Canadian wealth. Naylor argued that Canada's reliance upon staple exports had fashioned a set of commercial institutions and patterns of behaviour that stultified industrial entrepreneurship. While some economic nationalists hailed his study, most historians were skeptical of both his methods and his identification of merchants as the enemies of manufacturing. Even when they recognized that he had fixed upon important problems in Canadian economic history, such as the extent to which banks had actually underwritten industrial ventures, they condemned these volumes as demonologies of the business world, filled with distortions and factual errors.[5]

The Innis tradition inspired two less controversial studies in economic history which did little to support Naylor's assertions regarding the anti-industrial bias of the merchant class. Gerald Tulchinsky's *The River Barons* (1977) investigated entrepreneurs of various ethnic origins who (between 1837 and 1853) were involved in the forwarding trade and ocean shipping, and who built railways to American ports and developed manufacturing around the cheap water-power sites on the Lachine Canal. And in *Unequal Beginnings* (1980), John McCallum contended that Ontario's economic lead over Quebec by 1870 was due to the superior productive capacity of its agriculture: wheat production had brought very high returns which stimulated other sectors of the economy, including transportation and industry. Quebec's more limited industrial growth was due more to lack of virgin land and external markets than to the traits of classes, merchants, or farmers.

One of the most important books of the decade, H. Viv Nelles's *The Politics of Development* (1974), resumed the study of staple production where Innis and his contemporaries had left off and, stimulated by the literature on the activist state generated by American scholars, carried the ramifications of an old subject in surprising directions. This work was both a detailed history of the natural resource industries in Ontario (1849–1940) and the entrepreneurs who developed them, and an incisive and critical appraisal of

the provincial government's development policies. The extension of government activity through regulation and conservation, the promotion of the processing of resources within the province, and the creation of a publicly owned
hydro-electric power system were, according to Nelles, instigated by pressures
from certain segments of the business community, not in opposition to business in general. In fact Nelles claimed that the state became a client of the
business community. Though he did not establish convincingly that feasible
alternatives to what he had condemned existed at the time, his study was
immensely instructive for explaining Ontario's ascendancy within the Canadian economy, continental integration, and what can only be called Ontario's
national policy of development.

Nelles's book contained many new points of reference on state-business
relations, some of which were carried forward by others. In *The State and
Enterprise* (1979) Tom Traves assessed efforts of the newsprint, sugar, steel,
and automobile industries to (between 1917 and 1931) use the state to solve
problems of competition and uncertainty of markets. He found not only that
the government was hardly under the dominant influence of any single interest
but also that business itself was only one among many competing groups
affecting state policy. John Richards and Larry Pratt, in *Prairie Capitalism*
(1979), took up the point that provincial governments had acted as entrepreneurs in staple-led development and examined the efforts of Saskatchewan
and Alberta in promoting the exploitation of natural gas, oil, and potash.
Despite the apparently large ideological differences between the social-dem-
ocratic CCF and the right-wing Social Credit parties, both governments entered
into similar arrangements with foreign companies; in the 1970s, both provinces, again governed by parties with different names, became more activist
in attempting to establish diversified industrial economies based on staples.

Historians who wrote business history – that is, the study of individual
businessmen and firms – tended on the whole to be more sympathetic to
their subjects than those who examined state-business relations. They attempted to write, from the perspective of an individual, of the world in which
he operated and made decisions; they also sometimes set out to rehabilitate
people whose very names had passed into historical folklore as synonyms for
corruption or profiteering. Among the former two case studies dealt with
distinct phases of commerce. Dale Miquelon's *Dugard of Rouen: French
Trade to Canada and the West Indies, 1729–1770* (1975) traced the way a
company raised credit and insurance, arranged return cargoes, and contended
with insecurity in a period of war and piracy. Douglas McCalla's *The Upper
Canada Trade 1834–1872: A Study of the Buchanans' Business* (1979), described, year by year, the business activities of a Hamilton firm of wholesale
importers who were also suppliers of credit to a network of merchants in the
Western Ontario peninsula, and exporters of wheat and flour. The abundance

of records enabled McCalla to comprehend and to explain various business decisions and strategies.

The insecurity of business life also featured prominently in Michael Bliss's *A Living Profit* (1974), essays on the opinions of the business community (during the period 1883–1911) towards success and failure, workers and unions, politics and competition. In his *A Canadian Millionaire: The Life and Business Times of Sir Joseph Flavelle, Bart. 1858–1939* (1978), Bliss replied indirectly to criticisms that he had examined attitudes divorced from practice. Here he presented on a very broad canvas a detailed portrait of a self-made man, his business activities in meat-packing and finance, and his public service as Chairman of the Imperial Munitions Board and in church, hospital, and university. One of the best Canadian biographies, this study escaped the restrictions of the genre to explore the texture of the business culture of turn-of-the-century capitalism: its religious origins in Methodist perfectionism, its complex networks, and its sense of social obligations.

Ted D. Regehr, in *The Canadian Northern Railway* (1976), took on a more difficult task in attempting to restore the reputations of William Mackenzie and Donald Mann. Painstakingly researched, scrupulous in unravelling complex financial dealings, and cautious in interpretation, Regehr claimed that these entrepreneurs were less interested in accumulating wealth than in using their formidable business skills to build something permanent. More convincingly, he demonstrated that their railway (which suffered bankruptcy in the Great War and was taken over by the government) fulfilled real needs of prairie settlers. Duncan McDowall told the uncommon success story of a well-rounded and profitable company that stood in striking contrast to the pattern of dependency upon foreign ownership: *Steel at the Sault: Francis H. Clergue, Sir James Dunn, and the Algoma Steel Corporation, 1901–1956* (1984). This analysis highlighted the interplay of the industry and the three levels of government and was especially effective on the state-regulated and state-controlled capitalism of the World War II period under C.D. Howe, whose presence in the volume seemed as prominent as that of the two title figures. It was Howe who created the crown corporation examined in *Eldorado* (1984) by Robert Bothwell, who recorded the discovery and early exploitation of uranium in the 1930s, the nationalization of the private company in war, and the struggles of the crown corporation for international markets.

MILITARY HISTORY

Historians of politics, government, and external and military policy almost forsook the nineteenth for the twentieth century, extending their investigations to the 1940s and after.[6] The most significant publications tended to cluster in two distinct eras – ages identified with Laurier and Borden, and with

Mackenzie King. The first had been subjected to considerable scrutiny; Robert Craig Brown and Ramsay Cook, in *Canada 1896–1921* (1974), drew upon over sixty theses initiated in the 1960s. A masterful synthesis – a 'progress report' on contemporary Canadian historical scholarship, supplemented by their own independent research – this survey emphasized economic developments, urbanization, western settlement and social movements and, above all, the demands of the war emergency on the social and political system. Thus their analyses of French-English relations, the tensions between East and West, the conscription crisis of 1917, and the upsurge of wartime idealism and reform were all closely related to social changes and group interests. John English put wartime political change into a novel perspective in *The Decline of Politics* (1977), which showed that the Unionist Coalition of 1917 was the climax of efforts predating World War I to modernize the political system, submerge localism and diversity, and establish a national consensus.

Three of the country's most prolific historians collectively demonstrated how profoundly the experience of war shaped Canada's development. In 1977, Charles P. Stacey added to his extensive list of publications in military history the first instalment (1867–1921) of *Canada and the Age of Conflict*. This book emphasized Canada's ambiguous position within the Empire, then traced the efforts to attain some influence over imperial policy, the recognition of autonomous status during World War I, and the final attempt to arrive at a co-operative and co-ordinated imperial policy. In his incisive survey, *Canada and War* (1980), and in *A Peculiar Kind of Politics* (1982), Desmond Morton demonstrated that the recognition of Canada's nationhood depended on the fighting capacity of Canadian soldiers, but no less on the development of effective administrative control over their disposition in Europe. Like Morton, Jack L. Granatstein nurtured his interest in military history in the mid-1960s in the Army Historical Section (then in the process of becoming the Directorate of History, National Defence Headquarters), where he co-operated with J. Mackay Hitsman on a study of manpower policies in both world wars. In *Broken Promises: A History of Conscription in Canada* (1977), these two authors showed scant sympathy for those who had supported compulsory service as a military necessity. They blamed military authorities for miscalculating manpower needs.

Mackenzie King and the politics of his times became an academic growth industry as historians drew upon newly released government records and gained public access to King's private diary. By and large, books published in the 1970s were more favourable to King as a political leader; a generation that was itself conscious of the fragility of Canada showed a greater appreciation of the difficult problems he had confronted in preserving national unity.

That a sympathetic understanding was not always the enemy of detachment should be clear to any reader of Blair Neatby's *William Lyon Mackenzie King, Volume III: 1932–1939 The Prism of Unity* (1976). Its subtitle perfectly conveyed King's deepest conviction that Canada was an association of diverse cultures, regions, and interests, and that the task of statecraft was to encourage a sense of partnership. For King, politics was an endless effort to avoid division (even at the expense of clarity or consistency) and to encourage a sense of commonality: it was this positive belief, combined with his political acuity, not simply luck or opportunism, that guaranteed his improbable success. Neatby was hardly uncritical of King: in fact he devoted so much attention to the development of R.B. Bennett's reform program that he left the impression that King was incapable of responding creatively, if at all, to the emergencies of the early depression years. While Charles Stacey's *A Very Double Life* (1976) reported in profuse detail on King's dreams, his obsessions with money, rich women, and dogs, and his belief in spiritualism, Neatby considered that the biographer could account for King's political decisions exclusively in rational terms. In Jack Granatstein's *Canada's War* (1975), the activities of the prime minister form the central thread of a massively documented account of the conscription crises, the beginnings of the welfare state, fiscal policy, external relations, and the extension of power of the central government between 1939 and 1945. Granatstein emphasized the positive consequences of what King's critics perceived as evasion or dullness. Where King had once been reproached for his timidity in advancing Canada's claim for recognition with the councils of the Allied Powers commensurate with its economic and military contribution, Granatstein attributed the country's marginal position more to the unwillingness of Britain and the United States to share authority. Somewhat surprisingly, this admiration for King's political skills was no less evident in the second volume (1921–48) of Stacey's *Canada and the Age of Conflict* (1981), a book liberally peppered with the author's personal reminiscences. Though Stacey highlighted King's misunderstanding of Hitler, he emphasized that Canada's declaration of war in 1939, with a minimum of internal discord, was King's major political achievement.

These positive explanations of King's contributions to national unity were complemented by extensive examinations of his early career as a labour relations expert, his social thought, and his position as a social reformer. While Paul Craven, in *'An Impartial Umpire'* (1980), was concerned with the development of a distinctive labour relations system between 1900 and 1911, and with the state as mediator of class differences, he also presented the most thorough analysis of King's 'intellectual formation,' explaining the sources of his convictions about society, class, and conflict, and outlining his activities as a conciliator in the Department of Labour during the Laurier period. Similarly, James Struther's *No Fault of Their Own* (1983) was a complex survey of federal government policy relating to the jobless between 1914 and 1941, tracing the changes that led to the adoption of a national unemployment insurance scheme. Though much attention was devoted to the role of the social work profession and to federal-provincial conflict, Struthers also offered telling insights into the reasons for the King government's initiation of unemployment insurance and the limited, indeed conservative, purposes this measure was intended to serve.

In general these studies of King as social scientist, labour relations expert, and reformer were more critical than the political histories in which he was the central actor. One supremely important work that managed to escape the King-centred view of the age was *The Government Party* (1977) by the political scientist Reginald Whitaker. This was by far the best historical examination of the internal make-up and mundane operations of a major party and a perceptive appraisal of the political culture (1930–58) that made possible the virtual identification of the Liberal party and the State. In Whitaker's work, historical detail and analysis took precedence over the application of theoretical models of how parties were supposed to function; the result was a brilliant elucidation of party structure, patronage, appointments, financing, and the important role of advertising agencies. The study was most effective also in showing how the politicians relied upon the civil service for new ideas and initiatives, a point taken up in Granatstein's group portrait of some twenty bureaucrats who exerted an influence disproportionate to their numbers upon the creation of government structures, external policy, and the welfare state, *The Ottawa Men: The Civil Service Mandarins, 1935–1957* (1982).

The most outstanding instance of a single-minded steadiness in the writing of the history of diplomacy and defence policy during this period was James Eayrs's series *In Defence of Canada*, conceived in 1953 when Eayrs was a research assistant on the official biography of Mackenzie King, and to which he added volumes four (*Growing Up Allied*, 1980, on Canada's role in the creation of the North Atlantic alliance) and five (*Indochina*, 1983, on Canada's contradictory involvement in the background to the Vietnam War). In these, as in the preceding volumes, Eayrs was the resolute enemy of both moralism and pretensions to realism: his studies sparkled with striking vignettes of personalities and ironical observations (sometimes at his subjects' expense), and were solidly grounded in documentation.

Few historians took up a revisionist view of the origins of the Cold War, deflating the reality of the Soviet threat and emphasizing the self-interested economic basis of foreign policy. Robert D. Cuff and Jack L. Granatstein in two books – *Canadian-American Relations in Wartime* (1975) and *American Dollars – Canadian Prosperity* (1978) – raised these issues explicitly. In the first they examined several wartime agreements that unintentionally constricted Canada's freedom of action; in the second they thoroughly documented the country's economic dependence upon the American purchases of raw materials and defence requirements.

The major stimulus to the research and writing of military history came from the federal government through the Directorate of History, Department of National Defence, and its predecessor, the Army Historical Section, once directed by Charles Stacey.[7] Many of the historians who published significant studies after 1974 had participated with him in the preparation of the official history of the Canadian Army in World War II, a project he described in his memoirs, *A Date with History* (1982). No one single topic or line of enquiry dominated the research or publication of the twenty or so historians employed there. *North Atlantic Run: The Royal Canadian Navy and the Battle for the Convoys* (1985), by Marc Milner, presented a highly critical view, based on German as well as Canadian sources, of Canada's lack of preparedness and its inefficiencies in fighting the war beneath the sea. In the first of four projected volumes, *Canadian Airmen and the First World War: The Official History of the Royal Canadian Air Force* (1980), Syd F. Wise and his staff solved a unique problem of presenting a coherent account of the many Canadians who were scattered throughout the British air services and were not directly subject to either Canadian authority or policy. The result was a dense history, not only on the development of military aviation and training procedures, but also on the exploits and engagements of individuals. Of more general interest was *Out of the Shadows* (1977) by William A.B. Douglas and Brereton Greenhous, a crisp survey of the war effort, at home and on the fronts between 1939 and 1945, the best non-technical introduction to the subject. Most of the naval veterans, official historians, and maritime scholars who contributed to the excellent collection edited by James A. Boutilier, *The RCN in Retrospect, 1910–1968* (1982), papers both analytical and anecdotal on commanders, warships, and engagements, shared his feeling that Canadians were indifferent to their maritime tradition and that much of it had been lost sight of after the Navy was integrated into the other services in 1968. Reginald H. Roy responded to the fortieth anniversary of the invasion of Europe with *1944: The Canadians in Normandy* (1984) as did Jack Granatstein and Desmond Morton with *Bloody Victory* (1984). Few have done more to document the maritime and imperial dimensions of Canada's colonial history than Barry M. Gough, who completed a trilogy on the British Navy and the North Pacific coast, including *Distant Dominion* (1980), which delineated the role of sea-power and diplomacy in consolidating claims to the territory between 1579 and 1809, and *Gunboat Frontier* (1984), which reported one side of the story of how naval force was used in the later nineteenth century to punish natives for attacks on Europeans, to suppress native warfare and slavery, and to support missionaries.

LOCAL AND REGIONAL HISTORY

The only sustained attempt by historians to interpret recent history, *Canada since 1945* (1981) by Robert Bothwell, Ian Drummond, and John English, set out to correct the bias of the contemporary media towards decline and division by fixing upon undramatic long-term tendencies (the best and most valuable chapters examined economic and population changes and fiscal policy). This book also focused on the postwar developments that sustained the view of Canadian history as a success story, especially the growth of humane social policies, vigorous internationalism, and a richer cultural life. Refreshingly opinionated, if one agrees with them, or, if not, simply ventilating the bias of 'Toronto Whigs,' the authors confessed to a preference for the relatively centralized, outward-looking country of the 1940s and 1950s and – iconoclastic even in this – did not offer any convincing analysis of the roots of 'provincialism' or, more positively, the growth in importance of provincial governments and local identities.

The upsurge of publications in regional history did not represent an abrupt departure from the tradition of Canadian historical writing. The conflict between the search for national consensus and the persistence of local loyalties is an old theme. Indeed, in planning the Canadian Centenary series in the early 1960s, Donald Creighton and William Morton (who died in 1981) highlighted the development of regional communities. Eleven of the projected seventeen volumes addressed the separate histories of old Quebec, Upper and Lower Canada, the Maritimes, the Northwest, and the North.

Regional studies attracted more attention in the 1970s because provincial governments became more prominent and the depths of regional discontent more apparent. A strong identification with, and admiration for, the integrity of local cultures expressed itself in part in the feeling that history was not something that happened somewhere else: rather, it happened in *this* place, and was therefore worthy of attention. This positive appreciation for provincial cultures was often coupled with the conviction that certain parts of the country – usually the Maritimes and the West – continued to pay a disproportionate price for national unity, and that Confederation perpetuated a system of injustice.

Other influences reinforced this trend. Numerous political scientists sought historical patterns in electoral behaviour in order to isolate the major features of provincial or regional political cultures; some (such as David Smith on the Liberal party in Saskatchewan) investigated the histories of provincial political parties. Literary historians, too, such as Patrick O'Flaherty and Dick Harrison, traced the interaction between people and landscape, respectively in Newfoundland and the Prairies.[8] Regional historical writing was enriched also by the late Andrew Hill Clark, who died in 1975, a Canadian-born historical geographer whose studies of Prince Edward Island and old Acadia were emulated by many of his students.[9] Clark was concerned less with the once-fashionable perspective of how climate and landforms influenced the course of events, than with people as active agents who imprint their perceptions and values upon their surroundings. That historical geography was empirical, descriptive, and resolutely regional in focus is exemplified in the finest survey of early Canada, *Canada before Confederation* (1974) by R. Cole Harris and John Warkentin. This study depicted the distinctive features of several separate areas: the localism and diversity of the Maritimes, the seigneurial agriculture of Quebec, the towns and rural landscapes of Ontario, the Indian and fur trade societies of the plains, and the mining community of the West Coast. With reference to nineteenth-century New Brunswick, Graeme Wynn's finely crafted *Timber Colony* (1981) combined the older staples approach to colonial economic development with the geographer's concern with man-land relations; Wynn explored here the economic history of the trade and also demonstrated how it influenced the landscape and the way of life.

Regionalism in historical writing, sustained by the convergence of tendencies within several disciplines and by self-conscious attempts to characterize limited identities, was nourished by non-academic local history as well. Local histories were populist in the sense that they dealt with activities, people, and interests that general readers could readily identify with. One of the most successful of these ventures has been *The Island Magazine*, published since 1976 by the Prince Edward Island Heritage Foundation; its first issue sold almost 6000 copies, and later numbers attained a readership of 3500 to 4000. (Subscribers to the *Canadian Historical Review* numbered about 3000.) Subjects ranged from accounts of outstanding local figures – Sir Andrew Macphail, Lucy Maud Montgomery – to appreciations of church buildings, lists of passengers on immigrant ships, songs once taught at school, folklore, recipes, and a denunciation of daylight saving time.

The printing of books on local history was facilitated by the proliferation of regional publishers – Breakwater Books in St. John's, Ragweed Press in Charlottetown, Western Producer Prairie Books in Saskatoon. This last company, owned by a group of farmers who were members of the Saskatchewan Wheat Pool, brought out its first book in 1954 and thirty years later had a backlist in print of over 150 volumes on such varied subjects as landscape painting on the prairies, Ukrainian folk stories, and the social life of the one-room country school. Not unexpectedly it published studies that were particularly relevant to the province – Charles I. Wilson's mammoth chronicle *A Century of Canadian Grain: Government Policy to 1957* (1978), and John H. Archer's workmanlike survey, *Saskatchewan: A History* (1980). Among its authors were such prolific veterans as Grant MacEwan, who published a life of the meat-packer, *Pat Burns, Cattle King* (1979), and James G. MacGregor, who in *Vision of an Ordered Land* (1984) traced the adventures of the land surveyors whose geometry so decisively marked prairie settlement.

How far the search for a regional or provincial identity superseded the quest for a national identity was apparent in the rationale for one of the most ambitious projects launched in the 1970s. The Ontario Historical Studies series under the editorship of Goldwin French, with Peter Oliver as associate editor, was conceived in 1971 as a group of biographies of the premiers of the province along the lines of Oliver's *G. Howard Ferguson* (1977), and *The Pre-Confederation Premiers* (1980), edited by Maurice Careless, a group of biographical portraits that includes an impressive appraisal of Sir John A. Macdonald by J. Keith Johnson. The series mirrored the changing fashions in historical writing and was eventually projected to thirty-five volumes, including studies of the economy, social structure, labour, minority groups, education, literature, and the arts. It incorporated independently conceived works, such as Christopher Armstrong's *The Politics of Federalism* (1981), which demonstrated how all Ontario premiers extended provincial powers, territories, and control over resources, and also how private interests had successfully played off one level of government against the other. Even though the character of the series changed, the justification for it remained the same: it was claimed that Ontario was imperfectly understood and that its values and convictions were vague, elusive, and baffling. Possessing no tradition of regional grievance, having confidently accepted its dominant role within Confederation, Ontario had simply been confused by historians with the country as a whole.[10]

In the prairie west, a younger generation of historians added to the already rich and mature body of research. Most taught in prairie universities; many contributed to books of essays presented in appreciation to the three men – Lewis G. Thomas, William L. Morton, and Lewis H. Thomas – who had pioneered the field.[11] These youthful scholars frequently published their first research papers in the proceedings of the interdisciplinary Western Canadian Studies Conference and, to a lesser extent, in the biennial *Prairie Forum*, issued from 1973 on by the Great Plains Research Centre at Regina. One of the volumes of papers that resulted from the Calgary conference, *The Canadian West* (1980) ed. Henry Klassen, typified the diversity of prairie studies: it included investigations of utopian ideals and community settlements, women in the Alberta ranching frontier, the Lake of the Woods Milling Company, and Frederick Philip Grove's attitudes to technology.

Unlike any other major region, the prairie west was the creation of old Canada. The best prairie history has always highlighted the interplay of the nation and the region. Doug Owram centred upon a novel dimension of this relationship in *Promise of Eden: The Canadian Expansionist Movement and the Idea of the West, 1856–1900* (1980), which analyzed the writings and assessed the influence of a relatively small Ontario group who advocated the acquisition of the territory and altered the popular image of the area from that of an undesirable wilderness fit only for the fur trade to that of a fertile garden, an agricultural paradise. In the subtlest and most instructive part of his analysis, he showed how (out of the collision of utopian expectations and actual frustrating experience) was born a feeling of regional grievance even among original expansionists. Rod C. Macleod, in *The NWMP and Law Enforcement, 1873–1905* (1976), depicted the police as carriers of the conservative social values of eastern Canada to the frontier and explained their success in preserving order in terms of the recruitment and composition of the force and its organization, military tradition, centralization of authority, and enlightened despotism. The same implanting of British and Canadian cultures was illustrated by David H. Breen in *The Canadian Prairie West and the Ranching Frontier, 1874–1924* (1983). Though mainly concerned with the evolution of land policy, conflicts between farmers and ranchers, and the ranchers as a political lobby, Breen also underlined that the Canadian cattle ranching economy and society was different in origin and character from the cattle kingdoms south of the border.

As the continuing fascination with Louis Riel attested, expansion westwards was hardly an unblemished success story. Riel was accorded scholarly attention extended to no other Canadian figure: in 1978 the University of Alberta launched the Projet Riel Project, under the direction of George F.G. Stanley, which by 1985 reprinted in five volumes every recoverable word that Riel had put on paper. Riel had been as much a symbol as a person and reactions to him were litmus tests of historians' attitudes to more general aspects of Canadian history. He had been portrayed, successively, as a traitor, a victim of Ontario prejudice against French Canadians, a defender of the West, a champion of native peoples, and an early casualty of the way Canada treated dissidents. He was also, as Thomas Flanagan made clear in two books, much more complex in his beliefs and motives. In *Louis 'David' Riel* (1979), Flanagan attempted to make sense of Riel's conviction that he had a divine mission to save his people and to inaugurate a new stage of Christianity. This belief was explained as a compensation for his own feelings of frustration, as an extreme form of ultramontanism, and as a redemptory millenialism that had appealed to other marginalized people in history. While in this account the western rebellion appeared as much a religious as a political movement, in *Riel and the Rebellion of 1885 Reconsidered* (1983) Flanagan challenged directly the claim that the revolt was justified because of the total indifference of the federal government to the reasonable land claims of the Métis. Without exonerating the federal agents for their lack of imagination and will in designing and speedily applying a survey system that would have satisfied most of the Métis, he demonstrated how extensive was Riel's definition of aboriginal rights, and how relentlessly he pursued a private strategy of getting money for himself from the government. Gerald Friesen's *The Canadian Prairies* (1984) devoted a third of the text to the three centuries before 1900 and dealt fully with aboriginal societies, the Métis, and the great crisis of the Plains Indians. In this work of synthesis, which consolidated the more specialized writings of the previous decade, Friesen highlighted those themes which had preoccupied most recent regional historians – immigrant communities, capital and labour, cities and rural society, the depression, and the 'new' West since 1945. John H. Thompson, in *Harvests of War* (1978), examined for a more limited period (1914–18) the impact of national events upon a distinct region. While he found that the effects of World War I were in some respects unique, notably upon the economy and treatment of ethnic minorities, his book also demonstrated that the attitudes of the people of the Prairies towards conscription and war were similar to those in Ontario.

The historians of the Maritime provinces defined their objectives at least partly in reaction to both the existing literature on the region and the once dominant national approach. They inherited a vast body of writing on the colonial period before 1867; but to judge by publications, history seems at that point to have come to an abrupt halt. The period after Confederation was associated with a loss of local control, coercion, and long-term relative decline. As Kenneth G. Pryke, in *Nova Scotia and Confederation, 1864–74* (1979), reminded his readers, union was an inevitable necessity, rather than a desired destiny. Younger historians trained in the late 1960s and early 1970s, whose articles helped make *Acadiensis* (est. 1971) one of the most exciting historical periodicals in the country, tended to concentrate upon social history, especially labour history, and broke through the 1867 barrier. Some of them vigorously protested the relegation of the region to the margins of the historical imagination or – worse – the vague association of the Maritimes in general with an unchanging conservatism and the politics of patronage. And they confronted, far more directly than their predecessors, the task of assessing the position of the seaboard provinces within Confederation.[12]

One of the central themes in their writing was the economic history of underdevelopment and regional disparity. It was clear from T. William Acheson's now classic article, 'The National Policy and the Industrialization of the Maritimes, 1880–1910,'[13] that Nova Scotia and New Brunswick responded positively to the national policy of tariff protection and that in the 1880s they diversified their economies, industrialized, and reduced their dependence on the export of staples. By World War I, however, the Maritimes could no longer compete in the markets of central and western Canada. The economy stagnated, thousands left, and natural products became more important for economic survival. Acheson explained this change as the result of the vulnerability of the family entrepreneurial tradition, the persistence of a colonial attitude among businessmen who had always looked for leadership to metropolitan centres outside the region, and the absence of a strong regional metropolis, all of which facilitated the consolidation movement of the early twentieth century which transferred control of secondary industry and banks to central Canada. This tendency to explain the malaise of the Maritimes in terms of policy (rather than as a sign of shortcomings in resource endowment or economic inevitability) was also at the core of the work of the late David Alexander, a political economist whose essays were collected by Eric W. Sager, Lewis R. Fischer, and Stuart O. Pierson, as *Atlantic Canada and Confederation* (1983). Alexander was in 1976 one of the founders of the Atlantic Shipping Project at Memorial University in Newfoundland. This project assembled an immense body of information from vessel registrations from the files of the British Board of Trade in London and aimed at a comprehensive analysis of both shipbuilding and the shipping trade in five Maritime ports in the nineteenth century. Thus far the results of this enquiry have been published in six collections of articles which have traced the rise and decline of the East Coast shipping economy, recovered much detail on investment and profitability, and contributed new perspectives on both business and labour history.[14] Closely associated with these enquiries into economic history was the discovery of class conflict and a radical tradition that formed part of the region's political culture all too often characterized as historically averse to change. Successive issues of *Acadiensis* reported on the vigorous tenants' rights associations in Prince Edward Island, conflicts in the Cape Breton coal-mining communities, the 1919 general strike at Amherst, and the existence of a lively if small Maritime socialist movement in the early years of the twentieth century.

The most comprehensive and sustained analysis of protest, however, Ernest Forbes's *Maritime Rights: The Maritime Rights Movement, 1919–1927* (1979), emphasized that this progressive attempt to remedy grievances was supported by all classes and that it transcended internal divisions to address the problems of the region as a whole. Forbes's monograph effectively examined the roots of a tradition of regional injustice and also provided a mordant comment on two protest movements – the eastern advocates of Maritime rights and the western agrarian progressives – that operated at cross-purposes in national politics.

The chief virtue of these studies in the histories of the Maritime and Prairie regions was that they focused on the pluralism of experience and applied a multiplicity of viewpoints to the relations of parts of the country to other parts and to the national government. Yet they displayed no unanimity about the basic unit of analysis, the region,[15] not even on what areas were to be included. Unlike political scientists and historical geographers who have their own definitions of region, historians have assumed that a region existed to the extent that people believed that they not only lived in a definite territory but that they possessed a set of common and distinct interests and attributes. Region was in some ways as much an abstraction as nation, for as *The Acadians of the Maritimes* (1982), edited by Jean Daigle, reminded us, there were always limited identities within limited identities. The concept was also ambiguous in that historians equated some regions with individual provinces: provinces were in fact far more precise units of analysis, because their boundaries, constitutional powers, and activist governments were easily identified.

FRENCH CANADA

English-language historical writings on Quebec or French Canada formed a curious commentary on the intellectual history of the 1970s. Despite the prominence of separatism, fewer books were written by English-Canadian historians on Quebec than on, say, the Prairies before 1900, and those that were published were preoccupied with themes that had concerned French-Canadian historians in the 1960s but no longer did so. Over the last two decades French-Canadian scholars shifted their attention away from nationalist themes to social history in general and to the transformation of a rural into an industrial society after the mid-nineteenth century.[16] This priority was fully reflected in a cogent synthesis, *Quebec: A History, 1867–1929* (1979; trans. 1983), by Paul-André Linteau, René Durocher, and Jean-Claude Robert, which gave most weight to the economic base, class structure, role of the state, living conditions, women, labour, and political ideologies and cultural expression. In contrast, *The Dream of Nation* (1983) by Susan Mann Trofimenkoff accentuated the development of a national consciousness and the ideas of political leaders and intellectuals, even though it also incorporated aspects of social history and feminism. Historians writing in English outside the province have tended to concentrate upon the difficulties of maintaining national unity or upon the French-Canadian nationalist tradition and episodes of cultural conflict.

In a study of attitudes based on an intensive reading of the press, *The French-Canadian Idea of Confederation, 1864–1900* (1982), Arthur I. Silver pointed out that the politicians and editors who supported union believed that it would give French Canada a separate, semi-autonomous state. In the following decades, however, French Canadians grew conscious of the contrast between the extensive rights that had been granted to the English minority within Quebec, and the attacks in other parts of the country upon the linguistic and religious rights of Acadians, Franco-Ontarians, and Métis. Out of their identification and involvement with these minorities emerged a rather different view of the meaning of Confederation for French Canada, one that still insisted upon provincial autonomy for Quebec, but that also interpreted Quebec's role as guarantor of minority rights across the country. The idea of Canada as a bicultural community, at least as far as French Canada was concerned, did not originate with Confederation: it was a by-product of the cultural conflicts of the subsequent generation. Two episodes in that pattern of division were investigated by James R. Miller, *Equal Rights: the Jesuits' Estates Act Controversy* (1979), and Paul Crunican, *Priests and Politicians: Manitoba Schools and the Election of 1896* (1974). Miller attributed the public outcry in Ontario in 1889 against Quebec's legislation compensating the Jesuits and the Pope's adjudication of competing claims within the Church not merely to traditional Protestant animosity but also to a feeling of frustration with the unfulfilled hopes inspired by Confederation and an uneasiness about social change and class tension. Crunican subtly explored the divisions within the Church hierarchy and explained the rise of Laurier as a defender of French Canadians' interests.

A later phase of the long history of traditional nationalism was surveyed in Trofimenkoff's *Action Française* (1975). Guided by the priest-historian Abbé Lionel Groulx, this small circle of publicists in the 1920s began with a concern for the purity of the language and ultimately issued a comprehensive program intended to inspire the people and alert them to the dangers of modernity – the city, foreign economic domination, materialism, American movies, the Jew. Somewhat uncertain about the actual influence of the teachings of the group, and disappointing on the myth of the French-Canadian past which was central to Groulx's vision, Trofimenkoff's account brings to the fore the pathetic mismanagement of the organization, underlines its independence from its pro-royalist counterpart in France, and offers a lucid discussion of its ideology, including its persistent appeal for a national leader. *Le chef* soon arrived in an unexpected form and his career has been examined – justified would be a better word – in *Duplessis* (1977) by Conrad Black, who seemed to admire him for all the faults and shortcomings historians have censured. Black (who incidentally was himself the subject of a biography by Peter Newman) wrote a book that was very long, ill-organized, and that wallowed in trivia: but it also presented a highly entertaining impression of Duplessis' personality and the operation of his patronage system, and put in a more positive light his legislative achievements in social policy. For all its defects, it was a necessary antidote to the mythology that held Duplessis personally responsible for the whole political culture of the dark ages of Quebec, a mythology that was embellished by his liberal critics, exponents of the Quiet Revolution, and some historians.

Historians also took up a theme that only came into prominence with the Quiet Revolution: the extent to which French Canadians had participated in the economic development of their own society and the reasons for the peculiar structure of economic power in the province. Some aspects of the subject were touched upon in Tulchinsky's book on mid-nineteenth-century Montreal entrepreneurs and McCallum's comparative analysis of Ontario and Quebec agriculture. It was at the centre of Brian Young's *Promoters and Politicians: The North-Shore Railways in the History of Quebec, 1854–85* (1978), which demonstrated that the provincial government, municipal leaders, and clergymen extended substantial support to this rail network and that clerical leaders in particular did so because they expected the railway would open up lumbering and mining, and thereby facilitate colonization. Paul-André Linteau, in *The Promoters' City: Building the Industrial Town of Maisonneuve, 1883–1918* (1981; trans. 1985), discovered a group of French-Canadian businessmen who gained considerable financial power through real estate development. These monographs have shown that French Canadians were historically more prominent in the economy than was once thought, that they specialized in certain lines of business, and that the Quebec state, and some clerics, were in some instances actively involved in promoting economic growth.

CULTURAL HISTORY

Those historians who treated aspects of cultural history – religion, higher education, and science – tended to dwell upon the ideas and creations of articulate, educated individuals and the institutions with which they were associated. Of all these subfields which accorded priority to ideas, convictions, and values, the history of religion experienced the most curious fate.[17] While historians paid lip service to its pervasive presence in the past, they almost invariably examined religion in conjunction with other subjects. The history of religion as such existed on the margins of Canadian historical scholarship: as for a history that revealed religion as a way of defining self, of feeling and faith, this has hardly been developed at all. In fact, we know more about the religion and world view of the Huron people in the early seventeenth century and the Doukhobors in the 1890s than about popular religion in English Canada at any time.

John Webster Grant took on an exceptionally difficult topic in attempting to explain sympathetically the motivations of Christian missionaries, while at the same time keeping in mind the eventual fate of the native peoples. His synthesis of over four hundred years of interaction between missionaries and Indians, *Moon of Wintertime* (1984), was also an extended reflection upon the ambiguities of the relationship. In his eyes the missionaries were ambivalent about the civilization they represented: of course the values of Christian Europe were central to their programs of conversion, but Europe also represented corruption and evil tendencies. Thus they endeavoured to Christianize and to isolate, to assimilate and to segregate. As for the native peoples, Grant believed that they were introduced to the new religion at the moment when ancestral spirits that had once offered consolation had fled, but that they did not so much abandon traditional beliefs as supplement them with elements of Christian practices.

A similar empathy and a more intense personal engagement entered into George A. Rawlyk's *Ravished by the Spirit: Religious Revivals, Baptists, and Henry Alline* (1984), four lectures on the evangelical tradition in Nova Scotia, New Brunswick, and New England in the late eighteenth and early nineteenth centuries. Rawlyk sympathetically conveyed the meaning of Alline's theological writings and hymns, the experience of conversion and the conviction of salvation; isolated the mystical and pietistic elements of revivalism that permeated Maritime Baptism; and noted that continuing local revivals provided opportunities for oppressed groups, especially women and children, to assert their significance.

That the institutional studies of denominations need not be divorced from social and intellectual history was convincingly demonstrated by John Moir in *Enduring Witness* (1975), occasioned by the centennial of the union of four branches of Presbyterianism into a single General Assembly. Both an examination of internal divisions in the colonial period and a survey of the interaction between one church and the national community, it was most informative on the interplay of the faith and missions abroad and in the West, on social activism, and on the church union of 1925.

Some of the most significant advances in the study of the religious dimension of the past have been made by historians of ideas writing about patterns of thought and philosophies. Brian McKillop began his excellent *A Disciplined Intelligence* (1979) by noting that in the colonial colleges the main purpose of education was the promotion of Christian morality and a comprehension of the will of God. He then analyzed the interplay between this moral purpose and a succession of intellectual currents – among them Scottish common sense philosophy, natural theology, evolution and evolutionary ethics, idealism – and traced the gradual erosion of this combination of the moral imperative and critical enquiry. So strongly, however, had the two been fused that a strain of moralism persisted well beyond the Victorian period. In *The Search for an Ideal* (1976), Sam E.D. Shortt discovered in the beliefs and pronouncements of certain university figures (1890–1930) a pattern of tension between idealism, a faith in an intuitive comprehension of the spiritual order in the world, and an empiricism that depended on the methods of the social sciences. Though *The Faces of Reason* (1981) by Leslie Armour and Elizabeth Trott was a heroic attempt to relate philosophy to national culture between 1850 and 1950, it was also a difficult book for the historian to read, for the authors – both teachers of philosophy – tended to interject their own reflections into the text in distracting ways. Still, it was a storehouse of information about familiar and little-known scholars and thinkers and an essential beginning for a more historically rooted intellectual history. While Michiel Horn's *The League for Social Reconstruction* (1980) was mainly concerned with the eclectic ideology and reformist writings of academic radicals who worked for the CCF (1930–42), it was also a congenial companion to McKillop's book in that it documented the persistence of the moral concerns he had examined.

Historical writing on universities never quite managed to convey adequately the most essential elements in these institutions – the life of the mind, advances in knowledge, and changing perceptions of what was important to preserve and transmit. Though Robin Harris in *A History of Higher Education in Canada, 1663–1960* (1976) surveyed the teaching curriculum and support system for research and scholarship, histories of individual universities were generally chronicles of corporate bodies, based on official records, structured around successive administrations, and obsessed with the achievements of the statesmen of academe. Officially sponsored histories were initiated to commemorate anniversaries, as essays in public relations, and often assigned to either senior professors steeped in local lore or superannuated administrators who were masters at writing communiqués or bland judiciousness. The most that can be said of the generality of such works is that they traced in many cases the transition from church control to lay management and communicated aspects of distinct institutional personalities of, say, the Queen's tradition of state service, or McGill's emphasis on medicine and engineering. There were faint indications in the more recent studies of a more critical approach, or at least less reticence in recognizing cases of fiscal mismanagement, or in reporting candidly cases involving academic freedom. There was also a marked determination to deal more adequately with groups who previously existed only as remote background within the university community, such as students in general and women in particular.[18] Paul Axelrod's *Scholars and Dollars* (1982), explained the growth in the numbers of Ontario institutions from three to fifteen, between 1945 and 1980, mainly as a result of the belief, shared by businessmen and politicians, that universities contributed directly to economic growth. Not only did universities fail to fulfil this function, he argued, but they compromised themselves in the process, for the values that established new universities perverted their true role in society as islands of contemplation and critical thought. How some of the economic and political forces affected an older university was the subject of Claude Bissell's vigorous memoir, *Halfway Up Parnassus: A Personal Account of the University of Toronto, 1932–1971* (1974).

Literature on the history of science in Canada[19] has generally concentrated not on the internal developments of the various sub-specialities but rather on the operations of government agencies and the activities of explorer-scientists, exponents of popular science, and nature writers. By far the most imposing study, *Reading the Rocks: The Story of the Geological Survey of Canada 1842–1972* (1975), by Morris Zaslow, was a densely detailed narrative of the country's premier scientific organization as it struggled to produce immediate practical results and yet to pursue disinterested theoretical knowledge. Within its complex history, Zaslow also skilfully told of advances in geology, and revealed the tangled personal relationships inside the agency and between geologists and politicians. Scientists employed by the federal government also figured prominently in an account of the early conservation movement, Janet Foster's *Working for Wildlife* (1978), which traced the development of policies to protect animal and bird life in the generation after 1880 and attributed the change in attitude to a small group of farsighted Ottawa civil servants.

In the Victorian period, science (especially geology and natural history) were popular and accessible to the educated public. Carl Berger, in *Science, God and Nature* (1984), briefly surveyed some of the reasons for this vogue, traced the association between science and religion, and elucidated some Canadian responses to Darwin. The most satisfying study of the popular culture of science, *David Boyle* (1983) by Gerald Killan, was a biography of a self-taught blacksmith's apprentice who became a teacher of natural science and one of Canada's outstanding archeologists of the Iroquoian peoples. This thoroughly documented study was most impressive for capturing the astonishing range of Boyle's activities and for presenting Boyle as an exemplar of the working-class tradition of self-improvement. John Wadland's *Ernest Thompson Seton* (1978) closely identified with the artist-naturalist, pioneer of the animal story, and originator of the Woodcraft Indians, whose program became the basis for the Boy Scouts. Wadland was most persuasive in revealing the personal roots and intellectual origins of Seton's feeling for the sanctity of all life – the kinship of man and animals – and in demonstrating his admiration for the North American Indians.

Relatively few investigations were conducted into the economic bases of these varied expressions of culture or the means by which ideas, values, and tastes were transmitted. In *A Victorian Authority* (1982), Paul Rutherford focused on the nineteenth-century newspaper as a social and economic institution; he analyzed the structure, financing, and technology of the industry, surveyed the profession of journalism and the emergence of the popular, mass daily, and showed how the press fulfilled certain social needs and selected the news presented. An equally refreshing study, George L. Parker's *The Beginnings of the Book Trade in Canada* (1985), explored the foundations of literary culture up to 1900 – printing technology, book production and distribution, authorship, copyright legislation – and in the process explained much about changing literary tastes.

SOCIAL HISTORY

Most of these works in cultural, political, and economic history represented the persistence – or inertia – of tradition and strong continuities with earlier Canadian historical writing. This was less true of the various species of social history that emerged in the late 1960s, and that since have modified Canadian historical literature. The advocates of social history shared a strong determination to recover the life experiences of 'ordinary' people and reduce the prominence of unrepresentative individuals and elites and past politics. Social history was presented as an all-inclusive approach to the past that would accord priority to transformations in the economic base, the character of institutions, and the interaction of classes and groups. Far more than their predecessors, social historians appreciated the importance of class and class conflict, and of the subtle ways in which membership in an economic, ethnic, or sexual group shaped consciousness and behaviour. They were more aware, too, of patterns of hegemony maintained by such institutions as the public school, more sensitive to the persistence of ethnic feeling, and more sympathetic to groups who had been the victims of history.

Though social history promised a new synthesis that would supersede and not merely supplement existing historical literature, its initial impact was to enhance the diversity of Canadian history in both subject-matter and methods. The biannual journal *Social History* (est. 1967), which did not confine itself to Canadian subjects, early carried articles on such topics as social profiles of the Montreal merchants at the time of the Conquest and of the Boer War contingents; attitudes to improvements in the common schools in Upper Canada and theories of Anglican missionaries regarding the most effective strategies for Christianizing western Indians; trends in female school attendance; and Mennonites' responses to World War II. This diversity of subjects was paralleled by competing claims that history had to be reinterpreted in terms of class, gender, and ethnicity as basic units of analysis. The subfields within social history followed similar life-cycles: first came the manifestoes repudiating 'old' history and arguing for the legitimacy and social utility of the 'new'; then the formation of coteries of the like-minded, networks, and conferences; followed by the publication of newsletters, bibliographical aids, and such specialized journals as *Canadian Ethnic Studies* (est. 1968), *The Urban History Review* (est. 1972), *Atlantis: A Woman's Studies Journal* (est. 1975), and *Labour* (est. 1976). The proponents of each of these subfields came to share a self-conscious identity and enthusiasm, and each field was cultivated in increasing isolation from the others.

Historians of society were also more open to influences from the social sciences – a few would perhaps say the *other* social sciences. There was hardly a better example of the fertile convergence of several disciplines than in the upsurge of writing on Amerindian-European contact and relations. While Indians had been accorded an important place in the historical literature on both the fur trade and New France, they were often treated as homogeneous groups and as passively reacting to European initiatives and economic dictates. Though this European-centred view had been qualified by William Eccles, an informal alliance of historians, anthropologists, historical geographers, and economists began a more systematic effort to explore native cultures, needs, institutions, and motivations. The most impressive contribution was Bruce Trigger's *The Children of Aataentsic: A History of the Huron People to 1660* (1976), a two-volume study that defied tidy classification in any discipline. The most original feature of this comprehensive examination of Huron history and culture from pre-historic times to their dispersal was the application to historical materials of a sensitivity and knowledge gained from the study of other non-literate peoples and the determination to differentiate the various groupings within Huron society just as historians had previously discriminated among French traders, officials, and missionaries. Trigger provided an interior view of this culture that made sense of seemingly inexplicable customs, showed how it had altered even before contact, and illustrated how the Hurons adapted to the fur trade in terms of their customs, experiences, and inter-tribal relations. In the process he reinstated the Hurons into the mainstream of early Canadian history, so that we came to see it, not from the ships and canoes moving westward, but through eyes looking at invading strangers.

In a more limited but no less rewarding book, *Friend and Foe* (1976), Cornelius J. Jaenen unravelled, with a fine sense of irony, the reactions of natives and Europeans to each other's social mores, religions, and styles of warfare. Using European accounts of things that they recorded but could not understand, Jaenen of course noted differences; more intriguing were the parallels he isolated – such as the mystical elements present in Huron religion and seventeenth-century Catholicism.

The fur trade was more than an economic link; it was a cultural interchange between groups that were in the beginning by no means unequal and to which they brought quite different expectations. In *'Give Us Good Measure'* (1978), Arthur J. Ray and Donald R. Freeman investigated native and European trading conventions and economic motivations before 1763. Basing their conclusions on the account books kept at six posts, they did not totally dismiss the importance of exchange in such non-economic behaviour as building alliances, but they treated the Indian as a sophisticated trader, with a critical eye for the quality of goods and a hard bargainer in situations where the British competed with the French. Still, the natives did not in all respects behave according to European conventional wisdom: when prices for furs rose, they brought in fewer pelts.

That Indians in the fur trade period were able to control the scope of change was further amplified in Robin Fisher's *Contact and Conflict: Indian-European Relations in British Columbia, 1778–1890* (1977), and L.F.S. Upton's *Micmacs and Colonists* (1979). The fur trade on the West Coast was a balanced, mutually accommodating system: Europeans did not try to alter Indian patterns of life because they were powerless to do so and because it was in their own economic interest to maintain them. With the Gold Rush in 1859 and subsequent settlement, however, this balance was drastically upset: the 'indolent savages' became obstacles to civilization, missionaries attacked their social practices, and government administrators systematically took away lands that had been allocated to them. In Nova Scotia, New Brunswick, and Prince Edward Island, white settlers blocked the designation of reserves, squatters took up holdings, and colonial authorities encouraged the alienation of freehold lands. In both areas, settlement – in contrast to the fur trade – had devastating consequences, for the Indians lost control over their lives.

How deeply the fur trade affected the personal lives and feelings of those it brought together was reviewed from the perspective of women's and family history. Sylvia Van Kirk, in *'Many Tender Ties'* (1980), explained how native women in western Canada supported the fur trade between 1670 and 1870, as interpreters, guides, and labourers, and how they actively sought connections with the European traders in order to increase their own influence and status. One of the major themes of this sensitive study was the custom governing marriages between native women and white men, the formation of enduring and affectionate families, and the decline and degradation of these practices (and native women) after the 1820s with the arrival of white females. Where Van Kirk centred upon the relatively autonomous role of Indian women and marriage practices, Jennifer Brown, in *Strangers in Blood* (1980), examined the divergent domestic arrangements and family traditions of the traders as a result of the different structures and personnel of the North West Company and the Hudson's Bay Company. As these studies imply, the examination of the encounters of Amerindians and Europeans imperceptibly blended into 'fur trade studies,' another strand of social history, which was less concerned with the trade as a business enterprise than with native societies, recruitment of Company personnel, and even with maps that illustrated Indian conceptions of space, subjects which were developed in a representative collection of nineteen papers, *Old Trails and New Directions* (1980), ed. Carol M. Judd and Arthur J. Ray.

Social history in general represented a more intense involvement with anonymous social processes and structures that underpinned whole ways of life. According to some of its more radical exponents, a history that concentrated upon conscious intentions and actions was quite insufficient; the historian must understand human behaviour in relation to the material framework and structural formations within which they occurred and of which people in the past were unaware. Most social historians were Marxists in the loose sense that they agreed that people made their own history but not in conditions of their own choosing. There was, however, no agreement on how 'conditions' and 'structures' were to be isolated and analyzed.

Fernand Ouellet's two books, *Economic and Social History of Quebec, 1760–1850* and *Lower Canada, 1791–1840* (1966, 1976; trans. 1980), marshalled statistical evidence regarding prices, exports, agricultural production, population, and taxation in order to establish the nature of long-term economic changes and the character of social classes. His discussion of events – especially in the second work, which dealt more fully with the political crisis of the 1837 Rebellion – was at all points related to this material basis and the conflict of classes. Ouellet argued that French-Canadian nationalism was born out of the failure of that society to adjust to economic change, that its leaders deflected attention away from the need to reform or abolish obsolete institutions, and channelled discontent against the British minority. Though this line of argument was challenged in some quarters, Ouellet's works constituted the most compelling demonstrations of how economics, social structures, and political ideologies were bound together, and how they could be analyzed. In English Canada, however, almost no one followed his example.

Another exploration of social structure, one that derived from American social science, was applied by Michael Katz, the director of one of the first large-scale collaborative research undertakings, the Canadian Social History Project, begun at the Ontario Institute for Studies in Education in 1967. This project grew out of the trend among social scientists in the 1960s to measure social mobility as a test of American pretensions to equality of opportunity. It was aided by the discovery of the amazing richness of manuscript censuses, assessment rolls, and marriage and church documents as ways to recover the life experiences of people who left no literary remains, and by the advent of the computer, which made possible the assembly and manipulation of large quantities of statistical information. In his analysis of social mobility in *The People of Hamilton, Canada West* (1975), Katz discovered a striking paradox. There had been an astonishingly high rate of transiency among the population: less than a third of those who lived in the city in 1851 were still there a decade later. But social inequality persisted: the structures which Katz identified according to the division of wealth, property ownership, and distances between people in stratified ranks remained the same. He examined, in addition, family composition, youth, and adolescence, and made a commendable effort at humanizing a history of numbers; but he also seemed as preoccupied with the technical problems of research methods and computation as with the history uncovered. Katz's study was addressed both to American and British scholars who had undertaken similar studies of urban populations to which he compared his own conclusions, and to historians of Canada, most of whom were not familiar with this type of analysis and responded cautiously or critically.

It would be quite unfair to criticize another work in the same genre for not relating numerical analysis to the known context of Canadian history. In *Hopeful Travellers: Families, Land, and Social Change in Mid-Victorian Peel County, Canada West* (1981), David Gagan analyzed the circumstances of life of some 10,000 families in a predominantly rural county between 1850 and 1870. Like Katz, he found a high degree of transiency, but the most original aspect of his work was the explanation of how people adapted to the growing shortage and expense of land and the decline in wheat yields, by devising a new inheritance system for transferring property, restraining family fertility and size, and lengthening the period of children's dependence. Unlike Katz, who had not explained the destinations of the transients, Gagan drew a direct connection between the land crisis in Peel County and the settlement of Manitoba.

These two studies were the most ambitious and original applications of quantitative techniques to social history and they told historians a great deal about how people lived and about the distribution of economic resources. It was not obvious, however, what this information explained or how it was to be related to the more conventional literature. Nor was this history altogether successful in making the inarticulate articulate; from these books we learn more about the conditions of life than about people's thoughts and feelings. Even historians who where sympathetic to social history found Katz's work less than useful: Marxists quarrelled with his definitions of class, complained that his structures were static and frozen, and argued that more was to be learned about society in moments of conflict. Thus even within social history the influence of these works was limited.

LABOUR HISTORY

The most ideologically turbulent department of social history was the study of labour,[20] a subfield which in the 1970s diverged into two distinct strands. Traditional studies of labour concentrated upon the development of unions as the most important institutions controlled by working people, and on conflicts and strikes for union recognition and collective bargaining rights. Eugene Forsey carried forward this approach in *Trade Unions in Canada, 1812-1902* (1982), an encyclopedic archive of information, lovingly and unselectively assembled, on the origins and functions of workers' associations and on their parades, regalia, and rituals. The terminal date of Forsey's study marked the climax in a process – examined by Robert Babcock, in *Gompers in Canada* (1974) – by which the American Federation of Labor came to dominate organized labour in Canada and thereby destroyed both the prospects of a national trade union centre, and forms of unionism other than that based upon the exclusive skilled crafts.

An understanding of labour in wartime, especially in western Canada, was considerably advanced by David J. Bercuson's *Confrontation at Winnipeg* (1974), which explained the conflict of 1919 as the culmination of decades of class polarization and difficult industrial relations in the new prairie city, and censured both the repressive intervention of the federal government and the strike leaders who confused the general strike, a weapon of political revolution, with a large-scale withdrawal of services, and led their followers into predictable defeat. Ross McCormack, in *Reformers, Rebels and Revolutionaries* (1977), tackled the same subject from another angle, and provided a lucid analysis of the three main ideologies and groupings – moderate liberals who sought changes within capitalism, militant industrial unionists, and Marxist revolutionaries – as well as a balanced examination of the complex impact of World War I on the labour movement. The state of labour relations in Canada during World War II was the setting for Laurel S. MacDowell's *'Remember Kirkland Lake'* (1983), which investigated the local and provincial roots and the anatomy of an important but unsuccessful 1941-2 strike, and explained the Canadian and Ontario governments' legislation guaranteeing collective bargaining.

These books only incidentally touched upon conditions of work, standards of living, and institutions other than unions or parties that affected the everyday lives of workers. Some studies during the 1970s, however, more closely approached an understanding of the general structures that shaped working-class existence. In 'The Winter's Tale: The Seasonal Contours of Pre-industrial Poverty in British North America, 1815-1860,'[21] Judith Fingard brilliantly traced the effects of the seasonality of work upon some labourers, and in *Jack in Port* (1982) she isolated the dominant features of the world of the merchant seamen in the age of sail from 1850 to 1880 – including the labour market; rights, contractual obligations, and pay; and the activities of 'crimps,' often boardinghouse keepers, who traded in sailors – and showed how the dockside environments of Quebec, Saint John, and Halifax varied. Two works examined incomes and living conditions of groups of workers in the industrial age and concluded that at least these employees hardly shared its benefits. In *An Anatomy of Poverty* (1974) Terry Copp described and accounted for the features of a 'culture of poverty' – low wages, underemployment, insecurity, and inadequate housing and health services – that encouraged children and women to enter the work force in Montreal between 1897 and 1929. Michael Piva, in *The Condition of the Working Class in Toronto, 1900–1921* (1979), reaffirmed Copp's picture – of a world where the wages of male manual workers were inadequate to support families, and where poor social services, the seasonality of work, and the ineffectuality of early union efforts all compounded the difficulty of people's lives.

Labour history was carried beyond these topics by Marxist scholars who redefined the field as working-class history, enunciated a more comprehensive agenda of research, and at least partly fulfilled their own prescriptions. In the introduction to *Essays in Canadian Workingclass History* (1976) the editors, Greg S. Kealey and Peter Warrian, drew their inspiration from British and American historians who had situated the history of workers in a social matrix and had traced the history of a class in Marxist terms. Working-class history comprised the experiences of all working people, not merely the small number that had engaged in trade union or political activity; and it was to comprehend class not as something fixed but as a changing dialectical relationship of groups in relation to the process of production, in terms of values, beliefs, and class-consciousness. With the possible exception of Kealey's own essay on the Orange Order in Toronto as a working-class organization, few papers in the collection met these new standards which were far better exemplified in two rather different community studies. Bryan Palmer, in *A Culture in Conflict* (1979), centred upon the making of a working-class culture in Hamilton in the late nineteenth century, through efforts to preserve customary rights and control over conditions of work on the shop floor, and especially through such associations as fraternal orders and mechanics' institutes, baseball teams and festivities. Such organizations nurtured and conditioned a sense of solidarity. Against the background of an excellent analysis of industrialization, Kealey's *Toronto Workers Respond to Industrialism, 1867–1892* (1980) also paid considerable attention to the ways in which the conventions of independence, among such skilled artisans as shoemakers, printers, and iron-moulders, persisted into the industrial era and provided these workers with incentives to resist encroachments on their rights as well as a critical perspective on industrial capitalism. Thus behind the early unions and labour politics lay artisan traditions that mediated labour's adjustment to the new order. Kealey and Palmer combined to write *Dreaming of What Might Be: The Knights of Labor in Ontario, 1880–1900* (1982) on an organization that was not quite a union but much more than the self-protective association that historians had previously dismissed as confused and ineffectual. In a work of thick description they analyzed its structure, explained its appeal to both skilled and unskilled women and men, documented involvements in politics and strikes, and reconstructed its reformist ideology. The Knights became, in their account, a real force for societal change in the period, a training ground for later advocates of a more co-operative society, and an expression of a unanimity, a 'movement culture,' that transcended, at least briefly, the internal divisions of the working class.

These 'new' working-class histories sparked a debate among labour historians that was captious, intemperate, and confusing. The flash point of controversy was the concept of working-class culture underlying Palmer's study of the Hamilton workers. Critics questioned the very existence of a free-standing and exclusive culture of workers, both on the grounds that they had always been divided by region, ethnicity, and degrees of skill, and that such institutions as the mechanics' institutes or ideas associated with labour's class consciousness were exclusively working class in neither composition nor origin. Critics also pointed to the large gap between the essays in methodology which defined the new field as one aimed at the recovery of working-class experience in its totality and the omission in all these applications of any consideration of religion in the life of the Victorian worker, or the kind of information about family history uncovered by Katz. The resulting quarrels in some ways perpetuated the warfare of the 1960s between the old left and the new – between the upholders of the social democratic tradition and those who had embraced a humanistic Marxism.[22] These exchanges tended to obscure the substantial similarities between the two types of labour history – including an emphasis upon industrial struggle and politics, and conventional historical methodology. They also obscured the significant achievements of those who had penetrated beyond the political confines. They recovered copious and scarcely suspected details on social life in the Victorian period; they helped move to the centre of attention the social conflict that accompanied the arrival of industrial society and accorded a place to ideas and attitudes in history that belied the commonplace image of Marxist scholarship as materialistic; and they contributed far more to the ultimate clarification of class – and class in history – than the statisticians of social mobility.

ETHNIC STUDIES

Ethnic studies comprised investigations of immigration, the internal histories of distinct groups of people (usually, though not exclusively, those of origins other than Anglo-Celtic or French), the implanting, consolidation, and modification of their cultures and traditions, and the attitudes of the host society towards them. Before the 1960s, ethnic history was usually written either by sociologists primarily interested in immigrant adjustment and assimilation, or

by individuals with strong identifications with particular groups. The exercises
in filial piety written by the latter followed a predictable formula – the reasons
for leaving, the shock on arrival, toil and suffering, and success illustrated
by short biographical sketches of individuals who had done well. In the case
of such highly politically conscious people as the Ukrainians much was made
– by, for example, Michael Evanchuk's *Spruce, Swamp and Stone: A History
of the Pioneer Ukrainian Settlements in the Gimli Area* (1977) – of their
determination to maintain their language and culture, sustain religious institutions, and control schools in the face of both informal and official prejudice
and assimilationist drives. Such histories – literally hundreds of them – continued to be published in the 1970s and early 1980s.

From the late 1960s on, ethnic studies were vigorously advanced by academic historians often working in co-operation with other social scientists
who had come to hold a relativistic concept of culture. The prominence of
the subject was a direct reflection also of drastic changes in attitudes towards
ethnicity, a recognition of the persistence of ethnic identities, and a greater
consciousness of – and praise for – the ethnic variety of Canadian society.[23]
According to the multicultural idea, Canada was an officially bilingual country
with no single official culture and no ethnic group took precedence over others.
In practice this recognition of pluralism meant government financial support
for cultural organizations and for the writing – and rewriting – of history, a
history that would give certain groups a greater prominence in the country's
past. History would expose and thereby expunge the tradition of racial prejudice of the dominant groups. And it would have another therapeutic value,
if written so that members of minority groups would no longer hold their
own pasts in contempt. The Department of the Secretary of State of the
federal government supported a series, Generations: A History of Canada's
Peoples, projected in twenty-five volumes. *A Heritage in Transition: Essays
on the History of the Ukrainians in Canada* (1982), edited by Manoly Lupul,
was typical of the genre in that it was a co-operative venture of writers who
were rooted in that community and who represented several disciplines, and
in that it was a tentative foray rather than a definitive statement. The authors
paid more attention to the urban dimension than was customary in earlier
immigration histories, and focused upon the inner history and organizational
life of the group and its relations with the surrounding society. These latter
themes were especially important in an equally rewarding volume in the
series, *From China to Canada: A History of Chinese Communities in Canada*
(1982), edited by Edgar Wickberg, which showed how restrictive (and then
exclusionist) immigration policies shaped a unique bachelor community with
distinctive cultural and organizational traits that lasted until a generation ago.[24]

The major books by historians in this field fell into two categories. The
first comprised studies of individual groups, often ones with longer histories

in Canada than those usually written about by social scientists. In *The People's Clearance: Highland Emigration to North America, 1770–1815* (1982), Jack M. Bumsted explored in detail the background and motivations of those immigrants who were not an impoverished peasantry but relatively well-off people. For the Highlander, North America offered escape from disadvantages rather than the opportunity to do something new; having escaped change at home they maintained as much of the old life as they possibly could. This conservatism was developed in *Beyond the Atlantic Roar* (1977) by sociologist Douglas Campbell and historian Ray A. Maclean, an impressionistic and discursive survey, informed by many interviews, of the Scots people in four counties in eastern Nova Scotia, their folkways, religious traditions, and political and economic behaviour. Written with a respect for their subjects' integrity and a feeling for the intangibles, they did not gloss over such shortcomings as the indifference to material progress and the transference of loyalties from clan chieftains to political leaders.

In a vigorous and iconoclastic book, *The Irish in Ontario* (1984), Donald H. Akenson reconsidered and revised many generalizations about a group that had settled predominantly in rural districts and villages rather than in cities, were remarkably adaptable and responsive to economic opportunities, and were more successful than the average Canadian-born farmers. The core of Akenson's work was a microstudy of land acquisition, settlement, agricultural production, and the development of a network of social and political institutions in Leeds and Lansdowne township in the early nineteenth century. Though self-styled as a 'contribution to ethnic studies,' this book made it clear that the success of the Irish was due more to social processes than to cultural traditions.

One of the most valuable results of these and other histories of ethnic groups has been the destruction of simplified impressions of them as homogeneous and the revelation of their internal divisions and complexity. Frank H. Epp, in *Mennonites in Canada, 1786–1920* (1974) and *Mennonites in Canada, 1920–1940* (1982), illustrated this point by isolating the two separate streams of Anabaptists that entered Canada (the one from the United States after the Revolution, the other from Russia in the 1870s), exploring the consequences of their tendencies towards fragmentation, and relating their histories to the larger Canadian setting. In a similar fashion, Stephen A. Speisman's *The Jews of Toronto: A History to 1937* (1979) played upon the differences between those who originated in Germany and Britain and those who came later from eastern Europe, between the upholders of reform and orthodox Judaism, and among occupational groups and classes. Ken Adachi, in *The Enemy that Never Was* (1976), delineated the strains within the Japanese-Canadian community occasioned by the second generation's adoption of mores and political involvements quite different from those of their parents, though his main theme was the catastrophic evacuation of the whole group from the West Coast in 1942.

The second type of historical study in this field was the examination of popular attitudes towards ethnic minorities. In general these tell less about individual ethnic communities than about the opinions and feelings of elements of the native-born British-Canadian majority who were able to pressure governments to bend to their wishes. For example, Donald Avery's 'Dangerous Foreigners' (1979) contained a novel account of the changes in immigration policy (1896–1932) that favoured unskilled workers over agricultural settlers, and examined the growth of the legend that equated certain ethnic groups with Bolshevism. It was less satisfactory, however, in dealing with the actual course of radicalism among the Ukrainians and Finns. Two superior examinations of attitudes towards minority ethnic groups dealt with whole provincial societies. Howard Palmer's Patterns of Prejudice (1982) surveyed the permutations of anti-foreign sentiment and discrimination up to World War II, against a background of Alberta's particular mix of peoples and its maverick political traditions. Palmer explored the religious, anti-radical, and Anglo-Saxon roots of prejudice, carefully related expressions of it to such groups as farm leaders and clergymen, and found that there was no simple connection between the undulations of nativism and economic conditions. In White Canada Forever: Popular Attitudes and Public Policy towards Orientals in British Columbia (1978), Peter Ward argued that so strong and pervasive was the desire among whites for an ethnically homogeneous society that anti-orientalism flourished independent of social and economic circumstances. Though other scholars were not convinced by this dismissal of the fears of economic competition as the origins of prejudice, Ward did much to explain the removal of Japanese Canadians during World War II as the culmination of a long-standing drive and not simply as a misguided response to wartime insecurities.

Two important episodes in the tradition Ward assessed were amplified by Hugh Johnston, The Voyage of the Komagata Maru: The Sikh Challenge to Canada's Colour Bar (1979), a succinct, judicious account that emphasized the Indian background, and by Ann Gomer Sunahara, The Politics of Racism (1981), a fine-grained analysis of the federal government's 1942 policy and the varied reactions of the Japanese Canadians themselves. Less well known was the story told by Irving Abella and Harold Troper, in None Is Too Many: Canada and the Jews of Europe 1933–1948 (1982), which implicated Canada in the Holocaust. That the country accepted fewer refugees than almost any other nation in the Western world was attributed to an anti-semitism that permeated society and that was taken into account in Mackenzie King's political calculations and faithfully reflected by the bureaucrats in charge of immigration. These studies of prejudice, nativism, and group conflicts have done much to qualify, if not overturn, the image of Canada as a relatively tolerant community in which a variety of people have intermingled harmoniously in the past.

WOMEN'S HISTORY

Most of the two hundred publications in women's history that appeared in the dozen years before 1982[25] were written or edited by women, and the majority were collections of documents, reprints of early classics, scholarly articles, and anthologies of essays, with few interpretive monographs. These writings have developed two themes. The first, which built upon considerable existing work, was the 'woman question' in the late Victorian period, the emergence of middle-class women as a self-conscious group, their agitation for the suffrage, and support for a many-sided reform program. Veronica Strong-Boag, in *The Parliament of Women* (1976), located the origins of the National Council of Women in many voluntary associations, cultural clubs, and church groups. She set it into the context of the response to industrialism and the extension of a national communications network, and highlighted the ways in which promoting social regeneration and patriotism channelled both the anxieties of the middle class over social change, and the desire of some women to escape the confines of the household. Many of the essays in *A Not Unreasonable Claim: Women and Reform in Canada, 1880–1920* (1979), ed. Linda Kealey, traced the links between emancipation and changes in society at large. They elaborated upon the class-bound nature of suffragette and reform leaders, their negative attitudes to certain immigrant groups, and their differences from working-class and farm women; they displayed a keen appreciation of the restraints upon those few women who entered into such careers as medicine; and they showed how organizations like the Woman's Christian Temperance Union, for all its emphasis upon family life, promoted early feminism.

One effect of these and other enquiries into the ideology of the first wave of Canadian feminists was to underscore the fundamental importance of maternal feminism, the belief that women's special nurturing qualities entitled them to political rights and to a more active role in social reforms that would protect the family. This claim ultimately ensured the acceptance of their case for the franchise, but it also reinforced their separate sphere and continuing subservience. The most severe appraisal of the early feminists was submitted in *Liberation Deferred? The Ideas of the English-Canadian Suffragists, 1877–1918* (1983) by Carol Bacchi, who explored the division between those founders of the earliest women's organizations who advocated female political equality as a principle and as a preliminary to broadening women's spheres of activity, and those who based their case on the late Victorian stereotype of women and subordinated women's interests to puritanical, moralistic re-formism. This account drew too sharp a line between two tendencies, ex-aggerated the influence of the idea of sexual equality, and underestimated the extent to which the demand for the suffrage was a radical step in the context of prevailing views about women in Victorian society.

The second theme that has come in for considerable investigation involved women's employment outside the home. Women's history merged impercep-tibly into labour history in *Women at Work, Ontario, 1850–1930* (1974), ed. Janice Acton, Penny Goldsmith, and Bonnie Shepard, which contained il-luminating studies of women in domestic service, nursing, and school teach-ing. Equally important were the essays in *The Neglected Majority* (1977), edited by Susan M. Trofimenkoff and Alison Prentice, which revealed how substantial was the female work force in the Montreal garment industry in the late nineteenth century, explained the feminization of the teaching profes-sion in the same period, and surveyed the involvement of women in the labour force in World War II and their subsequent withdrawal from it. When these explanations were supplemented by the results of such other enquiries as Veronica Strong-Boag's 'The Girl of the New Day: Canadian Working Women in the 1920s,'[26] patterns in female employment emerged with striking clarity. Not only were working women highly concentrated in certain socially approved and ill-paid sectors of the economy, but not even the entry of women into new fields of work during the world wars was sufficient to advance their equality with men, or to dislodge a tenacious view about their 'proper' (ie, limited) role in society.

These investigations into the sexual bias in the world of work and of the conservatism of the early suffragists were, in effect, encounters with the historical origins and persistence of practices and patterns that the second wave of feminists were bent on overthrowing. By showing these patterns to have been historically rooted – and therefore relative and not preordained – they took the first step in escaping them. This tendency was no less evident in the study of demography, family, and childhood, which some feminist historians associated with the history of women. An awareness of the im-portance of these subjects derived from European and British scholarship on population changes, the lively controversy over the origins of the nuclear family, and a burgeoning literature on the ways in which anonymous eco-nomic and social forces impinged upon the most private and intimate spheres of human activity.

CHILDHOOD AND EDUCATION

In their enquiries into social mobility both Katz and Gagan paid considerable attention to the manner in which class and economic change determined family formation, the ages of the sexes at marriage, family size and household composition, and the shifting definitions and durations of childhood and adolescence. These and parallel topics were developed by others who did not share their enthusiasm for statistical methods but were no less devoted to demonstrating that such apparently biologically determined institutions as family and childhood actually varied enormously in historical experience. Joy Parr, who examined the fates of some eighty thousand boys and girls sent to Canada by philanthropic agencies in *Labouring Children: British Immigrant Apprentices to Canada, 1869–1924* (1980), also edited *Childhood and Family in Canadian History* (1982), which offered glimpses of children in New France, the treatment of juvenile delinquents in late Victorian Toronto, and family survival strategies among the working class in Montreal between 1860 and 1885.

The study of childhood and attitudes towards the young were developed in conjunction with the history of public education as well as with women's history, for an adequate explanation of the origins and evolution of the public school systems necessarily involved an understanding of how perceptions of childhood had drastically altered over time. Up to the 1960s the history of public education had been quite marginal to Canadian historical writing except for those episodes covered by political history in which schools figured in clashes between church and state or in the conflicts of cultures over language and religion. The institutional histories of educational systems and schooling tended to be written by educators as relentless chronicles of improvement. Mainly by way of the example of American writing in the 1960s, the scope of educational history was enlarged to encompass the social, intellectual, and political environments in which these systems originated and developed, and historians turned to enquire more closely into the class and ethnic dimensions of educational institutions.[27] For example, Jean Barman's *Growing Up British in British Columbia* (1984) examined the ideal of the Old World model and the successful transplanting of an ethic summed up by one private school headmaster as Christianity, classics, cricket, cadet corps, cold baths, courtesy, and corporal punishment. Barman not only demonstrated that these institutions sustained a British allegiance but also claimed that schooling based on the separation of classes reinforced the social and economic structure of the province.

Even the apparently more open public school systems were censured by historians such as Michael Katz for their excessive centralization, unresponsiveness to democratic needs, and heavy bureaucracy. Katz, in association with graduate students at the Ontario Institute for Studies in Education, inverted the conventional explanation for the origins of Ontario's school system in the mid-nineteenth century, claiming that it arose not from a commitment to promote individual opportunity or social advancement at large but rather

from the response of a middle class threatened by the urban poor and certain
ethnic groups, and that it was designed to ensure stability, order, and the
continuing hegemony of that class. Like penitentiaries and insane asylums,
schools were instruments of 'social control' intended to impose class values
and discipline. Though some aspects of this interpretation were adumbrated
in *Education and Social Change* (1975), ed. Paul H. Mattingly and Michael
Katz, it was most fully explored in Alison Prentice's *The School Promoters*
(1977). Prentice examined the ideas of Egerton Ryerson and other advocates
of mass public schooling and argued that their primary aim was to prevent
social unrest, criminal behaviour, and class conflicts, and that the system
they designed for Upper Canada was inegalitarian and promoted middle-class
values of respectability and achievement.

In *Children in English-Canadian Society* (1976), Neil Sutherland offered
a more sympathetic interpretation of the motives and accomplishments of
reformers who focused upon the new needs of the young in an industrial,
urban society. He traced their efforts to improve the health and welfare of
children, better the treatment of juvenile delinquents, and extend the scope
of school instruction to include vocational training, physical education, and
(in the prairie provinces) the promotion of unilingualism. To the charge that
reformers had created repressive institutions, he replied that the alternative
at the time to the centralization of education and regulation was not another
strategy of change but simply a device for doing nothing at all. Robert Stamp
in *The Schools of Ontario, 1876–1976* (1982) recognized that educational
reform movements aimed at inculcating desirable behaviour and showed that
their thrusts were essentially conservative; but he also laid to rest the myth
of a centralized system, controlled by an unaccountable bureaucracy, by
demonstrating how responsive it was to local needs and to pressures from
many groups – turn-of-the-century imperialists, progressives, and cultural
nationalists – which sought to use the schools for their particular purposes.

URBAN HISTORY

Of all the aspects of the study of society, urban history was most lacking in
coherence, possibly because it derived from two distinct traditions and had
been influenced by several disciplines.[28] The idea of metropolitanism, which
was rooted in the economic history of the 1930s and was subsequently made
explicit and clarified by Maurice Careless, focused upon the economic dimensions of urban growth and the relations between cities (especially their
business classes) and their hinterlands. The second approach, which dated
from the late 1960s, stressed the internal social texture of urban places: the
segregation of classes and ethnic groups into different districts, social mobility, urban social problems, and reform movements. Alan F.J. Artibise's
Winnipeg (1975) downplayed the relations of the prairie centre to both the

regional economy and eastern business, and instead emphasized the urban environment, class and ethnic structures, and types of social services. Artibise stressed that Winnipeg's growth was energetically promoted by a relatively homogeneous, commercial elite, who employed their own considerable financial resources and undue influence in municipal government to attract railways, industry, and immigration, regardless of the resulting deplorable social conditions. This emphasis upon the promotional activities of civic and business leaders also imparted a degree of unity to the fifteen local studies in Artibise's *Town and City* (1981).

While the city-building process provided some consistency to urban history, the expansion of social history in general made the subfield more diverse. A collection of essays compiled by the chief exponents of the subject, Artibise and Gilbert A. Stelter, was eclectic: *The Canadian City* (1977) encompassed studies of the national tariff policy and the industrialization of the Maritimes, working women in Montreal, the Calgary school system, architectural styles in public buildings in Toronto and private dwellings in Vancouver, and urban reform movements. *Forging a Consensus* (1984), ed. Victor L. Russell, contained fine studies of the Toronto police force and office buildings, and a brilliant essay on the basis and ideology of civic populism by Christopher Armstrong and H.V. Nelles (who had dealt with a portion of this theme in their jocose *The Revenge of the Methodist Bicycle Company: Sunday Street-cars and Municipal Reform in Toronto, 1888–1897*, 1977).

Urban history was evidently a capacious field with an almost unlimited ability to absorb – or assert control over – findings from the other varieties of social history. It was not clear what was regarded as generically urban, and urban history appeared to its more astringent critics as a field in search of a problem. This inclusiveness was only partly brought under control in the History of Canadian Cities series. Its editor, Artibise, attempted to strike a balance between treating individual cities as distinctive places while at the same time isolating such common elements as ethnic relations, regionalism, provincial-municipal interactions, social mobility, labour-management relations, urban planning, and economic development. The five volumes published with the subtitle *An Illustrated History* – Artibise's *Winnipeg* (1977), Max Foran's *Calgary* (1978), Patricia Roy's *Vancouver* (1980), John Weaver's *Hamilton* (1982), and Maurice Careless's *Toronto to 1918* (1984) – were equally divided into text and photographs and in general were models of compression and synthesis. They did not in themselves, however, resolve the problem of diffuseness inherent in the formula to which they were written.

NEW CONTOURS

Social history as a general impulse exercised an influence upon historical writing far beyond these distinct subfields. Historians who did not write of submerged social groups or attempt to isolate structures were still made more sensitive to ethnicity, the significance of class, gender, and the coercive character of social institutions. Such a work as Elinor K. Senior's *British Regulars in Montreal: An Imperial Garrison, 1832–1854* (1981) might have at first sight been mistaken for an old-fashioned military study; in fact it dealt with the military as an institution that intervened in civil conflicts to preserve social order and stability, and that influenced cultural and religious life. Two volumes of papers, *Essays in the History of Canadian Law* (1982, 1983), ed. David H. Flaherty, contained many expositions of the interpenetration of law and society – in, for example, master and servant legislation, law and economic development, and Victorian rape law – though some were weak on the way laws were administered in practice. In a new look at an old subject, *The Rising in Western Upper Canada, 1837–8: The Duncombe Revolt and After* (1982), Colin Read tested – and found wanting – the hypothesis that rebels and loyalists could be differentiated on the basis of landownership and other social traits. These studies did not belong to any exclusive category of social history, but they nonetheless attest to its ramifications and advances on many fronts.

Those historians who reflected on these new contours of historical writing were tempted to describe the significant changes in scope, scale, and subject-matter as little short of revolutionary. Yet in terms of the very crude measurement of books published – including biographies considered in a separate chapter of this *History* – those representing continuity outweighed the literature of the 'new' history (though it should be stressed that the dominant vehicle for publication in social history was the article). Experimentation in novel fields – combined with the relative decline of political history – was greeted by some as a liberation from stultifying formulas and as a step towards a history that corresponded more closely to the needs of contemporary Canada. Others, even those sympathetic to a more pluralistic history, regretted that hyphenated history conveyed an atomistic, one-sided view of the country and that it fostered feelings of differences and injustices wholly disproportionate to any realistic hope of rectification.[29] To regret the loss of coherence, however, was perhaps to judge history by standards that most historians in Canada and elsewhere have abandoned.

14 Life-Writing

SHIRLEY NEUMAN

Biography, autobiography, memoirs, diaries, letters, travel-writing: each establishes a different relationship with the reader. No generic unity encompasses the work that is the subject of this chapter, and, at best, we can claim for it only the broadest thematic unity: each of these genres (like the novel, like poetry) creates a different discourse about 'life.'

Moreover, the Canadian life-writing which is most sophisticated and thoughtful about the problems of inscribing the self in literature, and most innovative in its presentation of auto/biographical content, is not auto/biographical in any strict formal or generic sense at all. Instead it crosses and recrosses the borders between auto/biography and fiction in order to question static and holistic conceptions of the writing subject. Poet and photographer Roy Kiyooka, for example, writes letters that look and sound like poems; later, after having

> re-read/ alter'd/ a-
> mended/ and re-written them ...
> all for the sake of the 'I'/'ME'/'WE,'

he collects them in *transcanada letters* (1975). The process, by fusing the attributes of autobiography and imagination – the letter and the poem – asserts that life-writing is not a construct of facts, memories, and documents but is produced by the conjunction of, as well as the gaps between, the 'selves' inscribed by the conventions of different genres.

Those conjunctions and gaps become the nexus of much of Daphne Marlatt's work, which supplies some of the best evidence available for the thesis that women autobiographers discover and reveal their identity through an 'other.'[1] In her first books, her self-representation was a function of the interdependence of perceiver and perceived. As early as 1968 she wrote of 'the seeping of one's consciousness into other, non-self places (but if every imagining of the other is only a projection of the self?) ... the invasion of self by things.' 'Do we exist,' she asks, 'as crossroads of recognition for things/persons which appear, briefly transparent in all their inter-connectedness, & then disappear into individual and unknowable opacity again?' (*What Matters*, 1980). The question aptly describes the narrative of her Mexican travel book, *Zócalo* (1977), in which the prose poems represent the things seen and the people met on the quest in terms of the narrator's self-referentiality.[2] Beginning with her pregnancy and the birth of her son (1969), Marlatt centres the autobiographical 'other' that is also a self-projection in matrilinearity. The prose poems about her son's birth in *Rings* (1971) are 'autobiological,' as are many of the journal entries in *What Matters*. By the time she writes *How Hug a Stone* (1983) she no longer formally separates journal entries from poems; instead the itinerary and the topography of the English journey stand as symbolic of the autobiological/autobio*graph*ical self reading and writing her life as the 'crossroads' of her mother and her son.[3]

Other 'I'-narrators, clearly identified with their authors and therefore speaking within the conventions of autobiography, turn themselves into the creations of their own fictive discourse by using conventions of structure, characterization, and plot that belong to the short story. In a work such as Michael Ondaatje's *Running in the Family* (1982), the strong narrative line and conventions of characterization familiar from the short story are brought to bear on the author's Sri Lankan background, with the result that, in place of the continuous, coherent, and unary subject assumed by traditional autobiography, we get epiphanic fragments. In other works, the self is no longer one but many resonating selves, constructed through time out of both 'actual' events and imaginative activity, as in the series of lyrical remembrances and short stories that interconnect, then separate, in Stan Dragland's *Journeys through Bookland and Other Passages* (1984). These methods replace the careful exegesis of influences, motives, and character we associate with conventional autobiography by a more fragmented, more allusive, and less logically or mythically coherent construction of the self. 'Self' in these works is as much a function of the stories told about it as of an empirical 'what-happened'; the 'discourses' of life, fiction, and history overlap and blur in what George Bowering has aptly named 'biotext.'

Other works call into question even more radically the unity of the autobiographical self. They may conflate the 'portraits' of two authors as does David Young's *Incognito* (1982), subtitled *A Collection* and labelled 'stories' on the verso of the title page, which Young describes as having grown 'out of my curiosity about the border-blur between autobiography and fiction. I wanted to cross over into that zone and examine the way we use it to remake ourselves and believe in the world. It's worth noting that all the characters were closely shadowed by real people when they entered this book' (Preface). Accompanying the 'border-blur' of fiction and autobiography in *Incognito* is a series of equally metamorphic self-portraits by photographer Jim Lang. The conjunction of photographs with autobiographical stories also questions the blur between selves and self-portraits, between Jim Lang and David Young and between them and their representations. Brian Dedora and bpNichol undertake a more modest exercise of the same sort in *A B.C. Childhood* (1982), in which a photograph of each of two children prefaces twenty childhood memories, but in which neither photographs nor memories are identified as belonging to either of the two 'authors.' The questions of self-definition that arise in such juxtapositions are internalized in Smaro Kamboureli's *in the second person* (1985), a series of journal entries rewritten as prose poems that explore the resonances and the gaps between the Greek 'I' the author has emigrated from and the Canadian 'I' she has immigrated to. Where Kamboureli's title draws attention to a divided/plural self, bpNichol in *Journal* (1978) uses a generic title to signal a writing of the continuous present in which we can clearly hear the influence of Gertrude Stein. Undated, with an 'I'-narrator who is sometimes male, sometimes female, *Journal* points to all writing as simultaneously autobiographical and fictive. 'Self' is self-consciously omnipresent and elusive here, a strategy that can help us read far more conventional memoirs in which the question of 'self' is not foregrounded at all, such as Douglas LePan's *Bright Glass of Memory* (1979). For we can locate 'LePan' neither in his four memoirs, with their emphasis on the characters of General McNaughton, Lord Keynes, T.S. Eliot, and the negotiators of the Colombo Plan, nor in his introductory 'A Letter to My Sons,' with its restrained, but emotionally precise, accounting for himself: the reader finds 'LePan' in the conjunction of the two genres.

Perhaps this blurring of generic distinctions is simply the logical consequence of Cocteau's observation, made many years ago, that every word we write composes part of our self-portrait, an observation reformulated by Clark Blaise and quoted by Eli Mandel as epigraph to *Life Sentence* (1981): 'When autobiography ceases to be, then I shall write from the point of view of a Brazilian General.' Certainly the position that all writing is autobiographical has found justification in and has also partly been impelled by post-structuralist theories which call into question the unity of the speaking/writing subject as well as the referentiality of language.[4] Whatever its impetus, we find this genre-crossing richly exemplified in the recent writing of some of English Canada's better-known poets; indeed, as the work of Marlatt and Fred Wah testifies, much of our most explicit and significant life-writing takes place in 'long poems' rather than in 'autobiography' or 'memoirs.' The autobiographical assumptions common to many of these poems are two: that our 'lives' – or at least our awareness of them – exist only in our cultural representations of them, and that, therefore, they are shaped by those representations. Poetry, for Eli Mandel, becomes a *Life Sentence* in which the poet situates poems and travel diaries contiguously in a manner that he hopes will allow him to avoid the confinement of self within any single discourse and to intimate, in the interstices and intersections of different genres, a more multiple and fluid self which both writes and is rewritten. 'Each new line another line to rewrite / biography. Each poem a new biography, a biography anew.' Robert Kroetsch is less tortuously self-questioning in *Field Notes* (1981) and *Advice to My Friends* (1985), but his point is much the same. By balancing against the autobiographical narrative or the lyric, 'genres' such as ledgers, seed catalogues, and airline tickets, by reading past travel narratives through those of the present, and by writing into the poem diaries, travel logs, postcards, and letters, he creates an auto/biographical narrative that he compares to an archeological dig: the 'self' is both layered and fragmented, inscribed in the discourses he uses and indistinguishable from the white ground of the page that surrounds them.

We can, literally, claim that writers such as Kroetsch, Ondaatje, Young, and Mandel displace the conventional auto/biographical wisdom that writing represents the life; instead the writing *is* the life, the 'poem as long as a life' is also 'lifelost' (Kroetsch, 'The Continuing Poem'). But this is not to follow Oscar Wilde's epigram that life imitates art; rather it is to assert that what we understand as 'life' we understand in terms of the discourses, some of them written, in which we configure it. 'Writing,' as bpNichol puts it in *The Martyrology*, his long poem of the autobiographical present, 'is the thing / we are all part of.' 'What is it makes up the poem,' he asks from the other side of the equation, and answers himself, 'journeyal / a longing work / realating of realationships shape / between the letter & the letter' (*Book 5*, 1982). Within such a poetics of life-writing, to change the life, one must change the writing and it is exactly this that George Bowering undertakes when he rewrites *Duino Elegies* as *Kerrisdale Elegies* (1984). By rewriting Rilke, line by line, in terms of the experience and memory of a middle-aged poet living in Kerrisdale, Vancouver, in the 1980s, Bowering acknowledges the controlling power of the narrative over the life, declares his need to escape the Rilkean narrative, and does so by celebrating a new 'realationship' between his own life and literature.

'Place' can also become the construct of this dialectic between genres, in works that extend the traditional forms of travel-writing. In *Days and Nights in Calcutta* (1977) by Clark Blaise and Bharati Mukherjee, 'Bengal' is not precisely the 'place' of Blaise's narrative, which uses many of the conventions of travel literature in its implicit comparisons of this present time and foreign place with a past time and (partly) native place. Nor is 'Bengal' the 'place' of Mukherjee's more autobiographical narrative with its implicit comparison of Mukherjee the former native and Mukherjee the returned – and altered –

autobiographical perceptions; and Blaise and Mukherjee locate their 'selves' in neither Canada nor India, and in both.

Travel writing, even more than auto/biography, finds its richest and most varied embodiment in recent years in work that conjoins 'travel' and 'autobiographical' genres with more 'literary' forms. A special 'Travel Issue' of *Descant* (1984) institutionalized this phenomenon by including, along with conventional descriptions of places seen and persons encountered, a far greater number of 'travel' poems and short stories. When Gary Geddes edited *Chinada: Memoirs of the Gang of Seven* (1982), a frequently superficial anthology of impressions by the first group of Canadian writers to tour China, he, too, included poems, along with descriptive writing, a diary, and an interview; yet *Chinada* clearly presents itself as travel literature. That most Canadian travel-writing now comes in the guise of other genres is as true of work such as Claire Mowat's *The Outport People* (1983) – directed to the market for popular literature and using narrative conventions from fiction – as it is of the series of travel poems, the 'autobiographillyria,' that make up the bulk of Kroetsch's *Advice to My Friends*. What looks like travel-writing in works such as David McFadden's *A Trip around Lake Erie* (1980) and *A Trip around Lake Huron* (1980) often disguises a more ironic and 'fabulous project': a meditation on Canadian and individual identity, on what it means *to write* 'like myself.'

If biographers have been less radically experimental than these autobiographer/poets, they too have sometimes moved away from the sensitive characterization of the inner man and the precise chronicle of his outer works which we have traditionally thought of as the biographical ideal, in order to acknowledge the fragmentation of the self, or at least of its representation. A very few have chosen to characterize almost entirely through documentation, with only a loose connective thread of narrative, in a biographical mode akin to some of the earliest uses of the genre as simply a compendium of 'facts' about a life. This is Dorothy Livesay's strategy in *Right Hand Left Hand* (1977), a collection of documents from her work with leftist movements in the 1930s. The method, despite appearances, is anything but objective. This volume leaves the reader uncertain as to who – Livesay or editors – assembled it. Moreover, the 'author' is as intrusive here as in more frankly interpretive biographies since 'she' chooses which documents to include, which to omit, and in what narrative context to put them. A good deal, then, depends on the analytic and narrative skill of the person selecting, editing, and arranging these documents. Should they be connected by unanalytic transitions or associations, as they often are in Candace Savage's *Our Nell: A Scrapbook*

Biography of Nellie L. McClung (1979), they prove informative, even entertaining, but the book remains little more than data that could have been the basis for a more conventional biography.

Another variation on the form, far more successful because less fragmented, uses little or no connective narrative but gathers fewer and more substantial documents. This kind of documentary collection can be effective in frankly memorial volumes such as *Glenn Gould: By Himself and His Friends* (ed. John McGreevey, 1983) or James Beveridge's *John Grierson* (1978). The strength of these documentary biographies, however, finally rests on the imaginative intelligence of their collators and on the interest offered by the documents themselves. No one has proved this more wittily than Stan Dragland when he assembled the drawings, newspaper clippings, letters, and poems of *Wilson MacDonald's Western Tour, 1923–24* (1975). Hilariously effective (because done with so little overt interference by Dragland himself), the collage parodies MacDonald, his audiences, and the entire genre of documentary biography.

The auto/biographical genres are almost by definition elitist: few 'ordinary' lives get written, a fact which leaves gaps in our historical and sociocultural understanding. For most aboriginals and poor, and for many immigrants – that is, for the majority of Canadians – life-writing is among the things we are *not* all part of. Even where circumstances and the education available outside the urban middle class have permitted functional literacy, a double bind prevents such people from writing their lives: they are generally too busy making a minimal living to write, and, should they write, the literary conventions that would make their work acceptable to publishers and reviewers are not necessarily those with which they can best frame their experience. When these potential authors do find ways to 'write' their lives, when the narratives are compelling in their integrity, and when editors have the good sense not only to accept them but to resist tampering with them until they no longer stand either within or without our conventional literary expectations, they force us to acknowledge the elitism of those expectations. And while such work, like that of those writers who blur boundaries between genres in order to assert the fragmentation of the self and the pervasiveness of life-writing, brackets more conventional auto/biographical writing, it does so by relying on the referentiality of the written word so radically called into question by most biotexts. Elizabeth Goudie's *Woman of Labrador* (ed. David Zimmerly, 1973) stands as a good example. Written by a woman with a grade four education whose life has been one of exceptional physical and emotional hardship, it is simply and directly told. While there is little 'art' in this telling, Zimmerly has refrained from blunting the directness and force of Goudie's account or from making it the image of all working-class lives; the facts of Goudie's *particular* life, with no literary adornment, are allowed to move the reader. Among the few examples of such life-writing, Marge B. Clement's *My First 30 Years 1920–1950* (1980) may be the most authentically naive autobiography published in Canada (it is certainly among the very few 'ordinary' lives in which we do not suspect a ghostwriter). Clement's story of sexual abuse by her family, alcoholic abuse by her husband, and medical and economic abuse by her society is evidently unedited and is markedly 'unliterary': it suggests virtual illiteracy in its syntax, its refusal or inability to establish causal connections or narrative links between events, and its orthographical and grammatical errors. However, we cannot easily dismiss *My First 30 Years*, for its 'failures' in correctness are consistent with the story Clement tells: social circumstances she herself does not name or analyze are revealed as both subject of and cause behind her naive telling, and the stupefying dailiness of both misery and the resistance to it are the more strongly felt for a style in which climaxes, sensationalism, and analysis all appear equally unavailable to the author. Clement herself refrains from the editorializing of experience that is part of the hidden agenda of every literary convention, and if this restraint will hardly serve to gain her a place in the literary canon, it does give her work an unusual integrity in a genre notable for its manipulations of 'truth.'[5]

'Ordinary' lives are most frequently the products of collaboration, often of transcribed oral history. A book edited from taped interviews, such as *A Man of Our Times: The Life-History of a Japanese-Canadian Fisherman* by Rolf Knight and Maya Koizumi (1976), while undeniably naive in formal terms, manages to transcribe an experience apparently inaccessible to literary convention. Oral history is not without its perils, however, navigating as it must between the Scylla of condescension and the Charybdis of editorial distortion. *No Foreign Land: The Biography of a North American Indian* (1973), a series of taped and edited conversations between Wilfred Pelletier and Ted Poole, negotiates one of the more successful passages, probably because Pelletier brings much prior meditation to the interview's observations about the relations of Indian to white culture (see his *For Every North American Indian Who Begins to Disappear I Also Begin to Disappear*, 1971). The effects of even an oral historian's active editorial hand can sometimes be neutralized when the interviewer is motivated by respect and affection rather than by commercialism, and when s/he allows the interviewee to respond to the transcription: this privilege Rolf Knight grants his mother Phyllis in their *A Very Ordinary Life* (1974), which she concludes by making a distinction between living her life and reading it. The gesture confirms what her transcribed words themselves have testified to: the foregrounding in the book of her vitality and her experience over any preconceived editorial notions about the appropriate literary shape for it.

Increasingly common among collaborative writings is the 'life' of a group or a class rather than of individuals, created sometimes by collecting published documents or a series of biographical sketches, sometimes by using the techniques of oral history. Carole Gerson and Kathy Mezei create a composite portrait of life in Victorian Canada in *The Prose of Life* (1981) by gathering within a volume personal essays and travel sketches of the period. A sophisticated and readable thematic collection of biographies is that of Marian Fowler in *The Embroidered Tent* (1982), which vividly recreates what it meant to be an English gentlewoman armed with 'old-world refinement' in the face of 'frontier roughness' in early Canada. Myrna Kostash et al. in *Her Own Woman: Profiles of Ten Canadian Women* (1975) and Grant MacEwan in *Métis Makers of History* (1981) adopt a vigorous journalistic approach to much larger groups.

Often these collective biographies allow their plural subjects to speak for themselves about a shared experience. Pioneers, the poor, private soldiers, and prisoners of war are their chief subjects.[6] The list itself points to an element of class-consciousness, and sometimes class-condescension, in this approach. Badly used, it denies the individuality of the lives it conscripts into its characterization of a group and reinforces class stereotypes. Rolf Knight's charge that many such works give us 'the old hackneyed views of ordinary people by hucksters on the make,' that all too often their 'Immigrants are colourful and stoic peasants in sheepskin coats, [and their] workers are the horny handed sons of toil' in another 'version of the noble savage,' cannot be set aside. Eliane Leslau Silverman's *The Last Best West: Women on the Alberta Frontier 1880–1930* (1984) does effectively replace picturesque or adventurous stereotypes of pioneering with the far more crushing reality its women speakers recall. But Barry Broadfoot, chief practitioner of the collective autobiography of an historically shared experience, is less successful. In his 'Years' series – *Ten Lost Years 1929–1939* (1973), *Six War Years 1939–1945* (1974), *The Pioneer Years 1895–1914* (1976), and *Years of Sorrow, Years of Shame: The Story of the Japanese Canadians in World War II* (1977) – the sequence of many voices frequently emphasizes their individuality and moves the reader, as does his focus on the detail of his subjects' experience at the expense of the larger configurations of historical events they are participants in and often uncomprehending victims of. Readers, however, have no way of monitoring the distortion introduced by Broadfoot's radical selectivity (sometimes only a few sentences from an interview). The brevity of the speech of many of the 'participants' and the fact that their words often seem to be those best calculated to manipulate our sentiments suggest we be wary; these works are *Broadfoot's* construction of their ostensible subjects whose textual position is one of passive compliance to his narrative.[7] That the narrative is at least as much biotext as *Running in the Family* and at least as much Broadfoot's own autobiography as his *My Own Years* (1983), a work featuring wine and women in the absence of any song, should alert the reader to the exploitation of class stereotypes in all his work.

Writing a chapter such as this, the literary historian confronts not only the biotext's blurring of generic distinctions and the formal experimentation of documentary and collective biographies, but the term 'literary,' which traditionally values text over context. By emphasizing 'literature' over 'history,' literary history contributes to the process by which reviewers, critics, and scholars canonize some works (say, John Glassco's highly artificed *Memoirs of Montparnasse*, 1970). At the same time it writes out of its narrative many other works very much a part of the *history* of our writing (say, to state the case by extremes, Mary Shaver's *The Naked Nun*, 1977). However, that works so sensational, self-serving, and non-'literary' as Shaver's find a trade publisher, a highly marketable packaging, and a larger distribution and readership than many 'canonized' works has repercussions throughout the literary institution. Accounts of our lives do not get published nor are they canonized solely on the basis of their literary merits. *What* gets written and published, and the reception – if any – it gets: these are determined by the literary and cultural institutions in which we find ourselves. In the case of life-writing, the international literary-critical community has effected a reversal in the last fifteen years by reconsidering the formerly 'minor' genres of autobiography and biography as subjects of major literary and critical interest. At the same time, the cultural pressures of international media have combined with specifically Canadian factors to produce some significant expansions – many markedly non-literary – and several lingering deaths in the kinds of life-writing we read.

Much of the cultural and economic impetus to conventional auto/biography in our time clearly comes from media creation of culture heroes which, in its turn, produces a continuous, exploitable demand for their 'life stories.' This leads to journalistic biographies that seldom pretend to psychological complexity or literary merit but that at their best, as in Leslie Scrivener's *Terry Fox* (1981), do recount for a mass market the lives and motivations of popular heroes with a modicum of directness, authority, and restraint. More often, the media serve to intensify a hero worship which creates a market for biographies of young men scarcely escaped from adolescence such as *Gretzky: From the Back Yard Rink to the Stanley Cup* (Walter Gretzky and Jim Taylor, 1984). Dozens upon dozens of these hagiographies, often commissioned, frequently ghostwritten, offer little substantial information about their subjects, psychologize reductively and tolerantly about even the least attractive character traits, rely heavily on improbable dialogue, and assume minimal literacy among their readers. At its worst, our 'media-centricity' has led to a stepped-up opportunism on the part of some writers and publishers, often coupled with the life-writer's desire (prototypical in the genre) to insert him/herself among the famous, to justify his/her life before an avid public, or simply to present a politically expedient image. Examples range from the comparatively discreet *Neil and Me* (Scott Young, 1984, about his son), through the self-justifying confessions of Margaret Trudeau, *Beyond Reason* (1979) and *Consequences* (1982), to many works by and about politicians and civil servants, some of which are the 'instant' writing of electioneering.[8] Titles such as Michael Nolan's 1978 *Joe Clark: The Emerging Leader* speak incisively to the genre's ephemerality.

Not the least of the media-induced compulsions is that in which the teller of its stories – the journalist, the film-maker, the actor – finally must tell his own story. We have a number of memoirs by journalists during this period, many of which rely on the cruder techniques of 'human interest' reportage: dramatic or humorous anecdote, name-dropping, the shorthand communication cliché provides. Most of these would-be autobiographers avoid analyzing the emotional (and often even the political) implications of the events they narrate and of their own lives, and confine themselves to anecdotal, and often opinionated, memoirs. Actors' memoirs can be equally stereotyped. The very title of Patrick Crean's *More Champagne Darling* (1981) suggests an all-too-typical effervescence, and while Ivan Ackery's *Fifty Years on Theatre Row* (1980) offers more theatre history, its format is typically semi-fictional and self-distancing. There are also some partial exceptions to this stereotyped writing. Knowlton Nash, while no stylist, in *History on the Run* (1984) brings more analytic depth to his Washington years than is common among journalists. Although notably reticent about private life, James Gray's *Troublemaker!* (1978) is informed and analytic about newspaper politics and Canadian social history during his years as a journalist. In *The Far Side of the Street* (1976) Bruce Hutchison assesses his personal life and his professional role in relation to Canada through the double perspective by which the autobiographer can both recreate the past and judge it from the vantage of the present. Harry Rasky in *Nobody Swings on Sunday* (1980) presents a series of 'documentaries' of the people he filmed, written with scrupulous attention to the texture of their lives and to his, and their, motivations; and a producer of CBC's 'Stage 44' writes a lively memoir in *Andrew Allan* (1974). The second volume of Raymond Massey's autobiography, *A Hundred Different Lives* (1979), lists the theatre and movie credits, interspersed with an occasional aside to note the birth of a child or the divorce of a wife, that characterizes the minor memoirs of many an actor. However, Massey's first volume, *When I Was Young* (1976), gives us some engaging vignettes of a pre-World War I upbringing in Toronto's well-to-do Rosedale, along with an understated but precisely intimated contrast between the younger Massey, actor-to-be, and his older brother Vincent, governor-general-to-be.

If television in particular has multiplied the demand for the 'life-stories' behind the screen, it has also contributed to the virtual extinction of travel-writing. Armchair travellers now find themselves more immediately served by television documentary with its strong visual representation than by travel literature. At the same time, the number of armchair travellers has been reduced by the availability of tours and cheap fares; the new homogeneous travellers in their turn transform exotic islands into package tours and so rob travel writers of their subject. A result of this cycle is that the only book in Canada between 1972 and 1984 to present with some completeness the history and culture of peoples as well as a description of them and their countries is George Woodcock's *South Sea Journey* (1976). Symptomatically, *that* work is the by-product of Woodcock's contract with the CBC to provide text for a documentary film, and, while replete with information and showing its author as entirely cognizant of the tradition of travel-writing, it nonetheless falls short of the rhetorical achievements of the greatest works in the genre. The very few travel books apart from this are more modest in their aims. Maureen Hynes collects her *Letters from China* (1981) in a volume that, although undistinguished among published letters, presents a new and still compara-tively inaccessible travel experience; it also disturbs in its uncritical acceptance of bureaucratic procedures far from politically innocent. More personal travel-writing often conjoins to description autobiographical meditation. In 'The Village of Melons: Impressions of a Canadian Author in Mexico,' the village provokes George Ryga's enquiry into what it meant to his life and his writing (*Canadian Literature*, 1982). The framing of Gwendolyn MacEwen's *Mer-maids and Ikons: A Greek Summer* (1978) suggests a quest narrative that is more foregrounded in George Galt's *Trailing Pythagoras* (1982). Less ele-gantly written than either of these, Joyce Meyer's *Ricordi* (1982) is unusual among women's travel-writing in that the quest includes an explicitly treated sexuality. In one sense, a work such as Marlatt's *Zócalo* represents a radical extension of this kind of travel-writing into a personal quest plot.

Only the wilderness account, the earliest genre of Canadian travel-writing, endures. The Nahanni generates a stream of autobiographical accounts, most of them romantically coloured; Joanne Ronan Moore's journal of a year at the *Nahanni Trailhead* (1980) stands out among these for its precise descrip-tion. Voyages to the Arctic also still figure; among the best recent examples is *Expedition* (1981), in which David Pelly recapitulates his ancestor's trip.

If technology has contributed to a reduction in travel-writing, it has ef-fectively wiped out the publication of contemporary letters and diaries. One suspects that few diaries in Canadian literary history were actually kept for their authors' private perusal; instead our early literary history yields diaries written as extended and often circulating letters to families and friends. Tele-communications and charter fares have ended this. Similarly, few letters have been published in recent years simply for their epistolary merit. *Prelude to a Marriage: Letters & Diaries of John Coulter & Olive Clare Primrose* (1979) pretends to such merit, but in fact Primrose's descriptions of her letters as hysterical and incoherent all too often prove accurate. More common are scholarly editions of the letters of such canonized writers as Bliss Carman, F.P. Grove, Susanna Moodie, and L.M. Montgomery. Contemporary or near-contemporary writers' letters from recent years include the Pound/Dudek let-ters, Bruce Whiteman's carefully annotated edition of the Gustafson/Ross correspondence,[9] George Woodcock's *Taking It to the Letter* (1981), and selections published in *Line* from the literary correspondence of writers as-sociated with or influenced by Charles Olson and Robert Creeley. Among his contemporaries, Woodcock, although he has edited extensively and al-though his early letters in particular are sometimes graceless, gives by far the richest picture of his activities, documenting both the spirit of his editing of *Canadian Literature* and the friendships he formed through that task. Still, these collections are notable chiefly as anomalies; while many writers now carefully file all their correspondence with an eye to the profit to be derived from the acquisitiveness of librarians, the few contemporary Canadian letters published generally appear rewritten as the 'poems' of works such as Robert Kroetsch's *Letters to Salonika* (1983) or Roy Kiyooka's *transcanada letters*.

The tradition of diary-writing appears equally attenuated. Among the few diaries published and the even fewer published in their entirety, P.K. Page's 'period piece' from the 1950s, *Brazilian Journal* (1987; excerpts published in *Canadian Literature*, 1981, and *Descant*, 1984) stands out for the author's receptiveness to impressions and her gift for lyric and visual imagery. Among diaries not so egocentric and literarily impoverished as to be unreadable, nearly all are either written or edited with an eye on the reader, a gaze that undermines the privacy and frankness basic to the generic contract. This gives us, for example, *The 'Crow' Journals* (1980), a version of the diary Robert Kroetsch kept while writing *What the Crow Said* (1978), but a version with personal remarks excised or rewritten and explanations added, so that we have the impression that he is creating himself as a sketchy character in the novel.

Canada has only one contemporary diarist of importance: the prolific, but reticent, Charles Ritchie. The four volumes to date[10] of his 'undiplomatic diaries' are discreet about both his diplomatic career and his intimate con-versations and emotions. Ritchie's gift lies in the witty, sometimes slightly malicious, character sketch, in what he calls 'mimicry' exercised on the world of socialites, political leaders, and eccentrics in which he moved. Although he occasionally indulges himself at too great length over trivialities, his shrewdest characterizations show us the bearing, tone, or gesture of the politically powerful in order to illustrate, or even to predict, personality traits that will figure in their decisions. When he turns his mimicry on himself, his fellow diplomats, and his fellow Canadians, as he occasionally does to expose our political complacency, he accomplishes the most significant task of the diarist-gone-public: he uses his life to make us question our own.

Cultural policies established in the 1960s and continued into the 1980s also have had an impact on the volume and variety of recent Canadian life-writing. Indeed, the publication between 1972 and 1984 of *at least* 2000 biographies, autobiographies, travel books, journals, and letter collections by or about Canadians has been made possible by the marked increase in the number of nationally owned publishers, large and small, commercial and literary. A new surge of national awareness, given impetus by the centennial celebrations in particular and the Trudeau government's cultural policies in general, combined with a period of increased subsidy from federal and provincial governments, made the lives of Canadian writers, researchers, and publishers less economically precarious while at the same time it created demand for 'Canadian content.'

Changing demographic and educational trends intensified this demand. The children of the baby boom filled classrooms in unprecedented numbers at the same time that many universities inaugurated Canadian Studies programs, a conjunction that has created a new and continually growing readership for Canadian primary texts and archival materials and a growing body of scholars to provide them. At the same time, scholars in many countries began to take life-writing seriously as a genre of literary as well as historical interest. From its place on the outskirts of the literary canon, autobiography has been reconceived as central to our conceptions of narrative and of the self and, therefore, to our literary and cultural consciousness. Nor were publishers slow to respond to this interest in life-writing: the University of Toronto Press and McGill-Queen's published unprecedented numbers of political and literary biographies, as well as archival selections of essays and memoirs. At the same time regional publishing, conducted with professional scholarly and publishing standards, produced biographies and memoirs of historical and cultural importance.

These conditions have produced certain trends in conventional life-writing in recent years. The single most significant undertaking has been the multi-volume *Dictionary of Canadian Biography*, under the general editorship (since 1969 and 1973 respectively) of Francess G. Halpenny and Jean Hamelin. Providing brief scholarly biographies of Canadians from all walks of life, superbly researched, with wide-ranging and carefully cross-referenced entries, and useful appendices, it provides essential biographical reference material, limited only by the fact that it has not been extended to include twentieth-century figures.[11] A minor, but also useful, project generated by the DCB was 'Canadian Biographical Studies,' a series of 'small volumes [which] ... sought to fill a gap in knowledge of figures who seemed often to be secondary in Canada's story, and yet are of importance for an understanding of her social, educational, and economic as well as political history.' Seven volumes were published, including W.L. Morton's *Henry Youle Hind 1823–1908* (1980).

Professional research is also evident in the increasing publication of documentary material relevant to early settler, missionary, and government activities. Reprints abound, many of them prefaced by scholarly and historical introductions, as do editions of archival documents relating to exploration and settlement, and to the fur trade. While the writers of these letters, diaries, and memoirs tended to terseness on one hand and to anecdotal spread on the other, their accounts provide invaluable historical detail. Such valuable detail is perhaps nowhere so evident as in the careful observation recorded in the diaries and sketches of early Canadian explorers and exemplified by C. Stuart Houston's editions of *To the Arctic by Canoe 1819–1821: The Journal and Paintings of Robert Hood Midshipman with Franklin* (1974) and *Arctic Ordeal: The Journal of John Richardson, Surgeon-Naturalist with Franklin 1820–1822* (1984). The high quality of production of these volumes, the completeness and scholarly accuracy of the notes, and the inherent interest of the journals themselves: all these mark a comparatively recent and much-needed maturity in archival study. Fortunately, Houston's work does not stand alone in the quality of its scholarship. The Publications of the Champlain Society continue a tradition of strong scholarly editions of historically significant life-writings. Where the Champlain Society directs its work to the specialist, the University of British Columbia Press has issued an exemplary series of documents relating to the early settlement of British Columbia and directed at a more general readership. Publishing journals such as *Overland from Canada to British Columbia: By Mr Thomas McMicking of Queenston, Canada West* (ed. Joanne Leduc, 1981) or the autobiographical sketches of the first white woman to settle in the Similkameen, *A Pioneer Gentlewoman in British Columbia: The Recollections of Susan Allison* (ed. Margaret A. Ormsby, 1976), this press has found a format that satisfies scholarly needs while remaining accessible to the general reader. Each volume opens with a biographical introduction and the journals or recollections are accompanied by extensive notes, some biographical, some explaining environments, artifacts, and historical events alluded to or assumed by the papers themselves. Both the scholar and the interested lay reader come away informed.[12]

Some of the most important archival publishing has been that surrounding political figures. William D. LeSueur's *William Lyon Mackenzie*, for example, written in 1907–8, finally found publication in 1979, after having been suppressed by the Mackenzie family, even to the third generation. While it lacks biographical artistry, its contemporary analysis of Mackenzie's motivations, character, and policies proves to have been more astute than most that was subsequently written about the leader. But among political figures it is Mackenzie's grandson, William Lyon Mackenzie King, whose life is most revealed by recent archival research. The documentation of spiritualism, ambiguous attachments to a number of women, and plain eccentricity in *The Mackenzie King Diaries* (1973–80, microfiche) made itself felt immediately in historians' recognition of the need to supplement earlier reticent 'political' biographies of the leader with analysis of his private life and personality. C.P. Stacey began this process in *A Very Double Life* (1976), a book that met with several corrections in the most important study of the private, and neurotic, Mackenzie King to date, Joy E. Esberey's *Knight of the Holy Spirit* (1980). Esberey uses the Freudian model of the family romance in an analysis notable for its balanced interpretations of the diary entries. Hers is one of the most convincing *psychological* portraits among recent biographies. What remains to be done in the light of the *Diaries'* revelations is a definitive biography which would bring together the political career and the 'private' Mackenzie King.

At the same time, the scholarly publication of journals and reminiscences by less public figures, about less public events, has aimed to recreate as fully as possible the detail of 'ordinary' lives from Canada's past. When they are well-written, these documents still interest us precisely because they are by those – women and labourers among them – whose capacity and observations are *unofficial*. *Canada Home: Juliana Horatia Ewing's Fredericton Letters 1867–1869* (ed. Margaret Howard Blom and Thomas E. Blom, 1983), for example, while resolutely ignoring the commerce and politics of the Colonies, documents the kind of domestic detail more prestigious figures seldom note. Ewing's keen eye, her witty characterizations, and her sometimes descriptive, sometimes comic sketches and watercolours evoke the life of a colonial town as experienced by the female, non-governing population. Even more private and perhaps revelatory about women's experience in the nineteenth century is *'A Woman with a Purpose': The Diaries of Elizabeth Smith 1872–1884* (ed. Veronica Strong-Boag, 1980), unusual because its author records her public struggle to get a medical education and her private struggle to understand her feelings about male friends. Other letters and journals are less personal but are equally detailed about their time and place, among them *The Edge of the Wilderness* (ed. Cortlandt Schoonover, 1974) by Frank Schoonover, an early twentieth-century illustrator and photographer. The letters of James Thomson, who worked as a baker, lumber-cutter, farmer, and gold prospector, are filled with political observations, many of them of a sort not made by the governing class, and with rare descriptions of tools and methods of work in different areas of the country (*For Friends at Home*, ed. Richard Arthur Preston, 1974). Some of the simplest of these writings, such as Marcel Durieux's *Ordinary Heroes: The Journal of a French Pioneer in Alberta* (trans. Roger Motut and Maurice Legris, 1980), vigorously evoke the hardships their writers lived through.[13] Scholarly biographies involving the fur trade include John S. Galbraith's *The Little Emperor: Governor Simpson of the Hudson's Bay Company* (1976), and Jean Cole's particularly strong *Exile in the Wilderness: The Biography of Chief Factor Archibald McDonald 1790–1853* (1979).

While these 'archival' life-writings cannot tell us much about contemporary writing in the life-genres, the fact that they are being published *now* tells us a good deal about the value the contemporary literary institution places on establishing a tradition with strong historical and sociocultural explanatory power. Moreover, this archival writing provides a context for more contemporary first-hand accounts about the fur trade and pioneering. A country that had, until recently, real frontiers, and which now fills its museums with farm and domestic implements from the childhoods of citizens still only in middle age, Canada proves a receptive milieu for contemporary memoirs of former trappers and settlers now motivated by nostalgia. These accounts come with the odour of the museum on them, but at their best they owe a debt to the tradition of the yarn and preserve lost lives with vigour and exactitude. An autobiographer such as Frank Gilbert Roe in *Getting the Know-How: Homesteading and Railroading in Early Alberta* (1982) combines informal anecdotes with lively and precise detail while Andy Russell in *Memoirs of a Mountain Man* (1984) writes with a dignity that compensates for his lack of narrative sophistication: both are typical of the best popular life-writing about our frontier past.

The commercial success of a biographer like Grant MacEwan also testifies to the popular demand for this kind of material. While his style boasts few rhetorical niceties, and in fact relies heavily on elementary biographical conventions correlating physiognomy and gestures with character, it is also clear, comparatively free of cliché, and marked by the author's own love of his material and respect for his subjects. And although MacEwan shows little inclination to complexity in his presentation of historical contexts or of his subjects' motivations, his biographies are accurately researched, his analyses straightforward, his narrative well-paced. If all this adds up to considerably less than greatness, it is honest in its dealings with both its material and its audience. Its responsibility becomes the more apparent when we look at the lengths to which another popular biographer, James MacGregor, will go to deck out biographical information with anecdote, dramatic incident, crudely rendered conversation, unabashed manipulation of readers' emotions, and clichés that tend to sensationalize rather than explain his protagonists.

However, publishing in the archival spirit, whether of actual papers or of contemporary narratives of disappearing ways of life, is not simply a happy accident produced by the conjunction of available documents or experiences, ready scholars or tale-tellers, and funding for research and publication. Cultural and political trends also determine the moments at which we undertake investigation of given events in our past. The culture producing memoirs about pioneering and fur-trapping values this aspect of its past but, no longer anticipating the endurance of its hardships, turns them into romantic adventure; that same culture does not produce memoirs about living in urban poverty, for the contemporary experience is still too common among Canadians to be looked at comfortably or romantically.

In Canada during the 1970s and 1980s three groups of life-writings are directly connected to the cultural moment: memoirs of two world wars, writings of aboriginals, and writings about the Riel Rebellion. Recent writings about the Canadian war effort are mostly by common soldiers (see note 6 and the discussion of collective biographies), peripheral participants, and prisoners, most of the 'official' – and officers' – stories having been told in the years following the events or – as in the case of the auto/biographies of Jeffry Brock, Hugh Keenleyside, and George Pearkes – having been absorbed in the account of a much longer career and having as much political as military emphasis.[14] Culturally revealing among these is Grace Morris Craig's *But This Is Our War* (1981), written by the sister (and later wife) of World War I officers who quotes extensively from letters written from the front. At first filled with the clichés of men on a romp in service of the Empire, these letters slowly become more halting and precise, gaining in sincerity, dignity, and depth of emotion. Their changing tone, more than what they say, tells a story of courage and suffering so great that the writers will not describe it. However, Craig's own understanding undergoes no such transformation. Her unquestioning imperialism, jingoism, and class-biased certainty that recruitment of the unemployed was in everyone's best interests powerfully (if unselfconsciously) asserts the attitudes of the upper middle class at the time. At the same time, Craig unintentionally provides present readers – more likely than she to enquire into the economic motives of conflict and to question which wars are 'our' wars – with a text they will read against the 'culture' she represents.

Not the jingoists but the involuntary participants – the survivors of internment and concentration camps – have written the most moving of recently published war memoirs. The historical moment is surely crucial here, for the survivors are now in their sixties or older: their intervening life in Canada has put memories of a happier kind between themselves and the war years, in many cases enabling them for the first time to speak publicly of internment experiences. Their age, their awareness of neo-Nazi assertions that the Holocaust never took place, and the fact that a postwar generation knows about World War II in only a general way also compel many of them to publish their stories for didactic social reasons.

Three groups of narratives about non-Nazi internment conveniently reveal the universality of state injustice to civilian populations. Written with measured introspection, Peggy Abkhazi's *A Curious Cage* (ed. S.W. Jackman, 1981) gives a rare portrait of Japanese internment of 'Enemy Subjects' in Shanghai. More plainly told, Takeo Nakano's *Within the Barbed Wire Fence: A Japanese Man's Account of His Internment in Canada* (1980, with Leatrice Nakano) describes a political action Canadians have only recently and shame-facedly acknowledged as part of their past. While the events described in *Within the Barbed Wire Fence* chronicle a particular cultural moment in race relations in Canada, the book's publication marks a more enlightened moment. Also moving, this time in its optimism, is the diary the adolescent Henry Kreisel kept when, after flight from Hitler's invasion of Austria, he found himself interned as an 'Enemy Alien' by the British government, transported to a camp in the Maritimes, and finally released to the benefits of a Canadian education and an academic and literary career. Kept in the broken English of the boy who had just decided to become a writer in his newly adopted tongue, the 'Diary of an Internment' makes few literary claims but does stand as a significant testament to human aspiration and resilience (*White Pelican*, 1974; rpt *Another Country*, ed. Shirley Neuman, 1985).

The reader of Kreisel's diary cannot but recall the concentration camp Hitler had intended for its author. Narratives of survival in those camps are our most harrowing – and miraculous – war literature. The greatest effect of these autobiographies derives from the greatest discipline and chastity of language, from the stark description of the daily events of the camps. Chava Kwinta's *I'm Still Living* (1974), for example, distances the reader by relying on conversations that seem to have become preternaturally stiff either in her memory of them or in their translation from the Hebrew in which she wrote. However Eva Brewster, in *Vanished in Darkness: An Auschwitz Memoir* (1984), and Anita Mayer, in *One Who Came Back* (1981), create compelling and irrefutable narrative out of the directness and restraint with which they write about events and people in the camps.

The public discussion of the Holocaust, the visibility of the civil rights movement in the United States, and the recurrent domestic political concerns with aboriginal rights and human rights legislation have all required Canadians to recognize our own racial prejudices. This is not to say that writing which exploits aboriginals (often while seeming sympathetic) does not still go on. There has been little abatement of popular, heroizing, and ultimately reductive 'biographies' of Indian chiefs; similarly, David F. Raine's *Pitseolak* (1980) uses the Inuit subject to turn genuine hardship to the demands of the journalistic tear-jerker, and, finally, to foreground Raine himself. Yet some writers *are* making important gestures of respect towards the narrative modes that would be used by the subjects of these life-writings themselves. For example, a white anthropologist, Rosamond Vanderburgh, in *I Am Nokomis, Too: The Biography of Verna Patronella Johnston* (1977), takes considerable care to respect the narrative customs of her Indian subject. And Gerard Deagle and Alan Mettrick 'write' *Thrasher ... Skid Row Eskimo* (1976) by using large portions of taped material from Anthony Apakark Thrasher himself.

Some of these subjects write directly, with varying degrees of editorial interference by their publishers. Alice French, *My Name Is Masak* (1976), with matter-of-fact flatness tells about life in her Northwest Territories school, while Jane Willis, *Geniesh: An Indian Girlhood* (1973), tells a comparable story of imperialist miseducation with more narrative skill and much greater anger. Such speech can be invaluable as historical document, as when Margaret B. Blackman combines biographical sketch with oral history in *During My Time: Florence Edenshaw Davidson, a Haida Woman* (1982). Maria Campbell's *Halfbreed* (1973) uses language with greater evocative skill than any of these but, in addition, it points to the thornier cultural issues involved in all this life-writing. At the 1983 Women and Words Conference, Campbell spoke of the excisions her non-Métis editor had insisted on: the 'kind of material most people are not interested in.' The phrase implies that the manuscript was tailored to foreground (and therefore, to some extent, to sensationalize) the story of prostitution and addiction that the editor felt would most interest a non-Métis audience. Jane Willis and Alice French seem to write with less editorial interference; yet their prose speaks to their attempt to confine it within the conventions of written literature whereas (in Inuit and Indian cultures) story-telling is a performance event. Similarly, Vanderburgh or Blackman, while they work with the full co-operation of their subjects and respect their informants' own words, place those words in a context that is alien to aboriginal cultures and even contravenes their own 'copyright' system. Recent life-writing allows aboriginal voices to be 'heard' as never before; it still does not let them speak clearly through their own narrative conventions.

A growing self-consciousness about racism, conjoined to increasingly objective evaluations of the costs of Canadian governmental allegiance to the British empire, has contributed to a third culturally determined moment in Canadian life-writing: a spate of interpretations refusing to accept Louis Riel as a traitor. These range from novelist Rudy Wiebe's *The Scorched-Wood*

People (1977) to numerous popular and scholarly biographies.[15] Buttressed by the spiritual quest and questionings revealed in *The Diaries of Louis Riel* (ed. Thomas Flanagan, 1976), the evidence of familial affection in the letters of Sara Riel (*To Louis from Your Sister Who Loves You*, ed. and trans. Mary Jordan, 1974), and a 1864–6 notebook of Riel's poetry, this re-examination is strongest in Flanagan's *Louis 'David' Riel: 'Prophet of the New World'* (1979). Rather than judge his protagonist 'insane,' Flanagan looks at his writings and religious experience as determinants of his actions, placing him in the context of the millenarianism sometimes found among oppressed peoples 'in dark times.' While Flanagan makes no attempt to detail completely the rebel leader's life, he does question the truth of many of the 'documented' details in previous biographies. And, with a success rare in Canadian biography, he provides a convincing interpretation of Riel's personality and shows how the interaction between the personality and the historical moment produced the Rebellion.

Archival publishing and historical subjects suggest that Canadian life-writing is preoccupied with the 'record' over other auto/biographical concerns. This preoccupation dominates works by and about professionals of every sort. In *The Oxford Companion to Canadian Literature* (1983), George Woodcock puts the matter succinctly: 'biography and autobiography are ... genres in which amateurs, with neither art nor craftsmanship, are most likely to indulge because they think their own experiences are worth recording, or because they believe the same of other people's careers.' The temptation of life-writing proves irresistible to politicians; lawyers follow closely as subjects of biographical renown. Where life-writing about politicians tends to a paradoxical surfeit of both discretion and length, that about lawyers too often exploits the cliché of courtroom drama and engages in special pleading that a judge would throw out of court. Two legal journalists, however, have contributed to the growth of a responsible popular biography, free from the jargon and labyrinthine complexities of scholarly legal writing but thoroughly researched and clear about major issues. Jack Batten's carefully weighed *Robinette* (1984) might stand as model to those wishing to make the issues of the law clear to the non-specialist. While Batten belongs to the school of biographers that prefers to leave the private life private, David Ricardo Williams writes a more completely perceived portrait, both in '...*The Man for a New Country': Sir Matthew Baillie Begbie* (1977), and in *Duff: A Life in the Law* (1984).

For every lawyer's auto/biography we have a jailbird's or an imposter's, most of it mediocre journalism. But David Williams's *Trapline Outlaw: Simon Peter Gunanoot* (1982), is a balanced reading that resists the romanticizing

typical of much writing about 'outlaws.' Two autobiographies about prison
life have also made an appearance. *Go-Boy!* (1978) brought Roger Caron
brief celebrity: his angry articulateness and the horror of his 'insider's' revelations about Canadian penitentiaries contributed to its positive reception. A
more introspective work, Andreas Schroeder's *Shaking It Rough* (1976) is
also more restrained, perhaps because the author (a middle-class writer sen-
tenced for possession of marijuana) regards himself not as a social outcast
but as a victim of a legal archaism, and certainly because his prison circumstances were less desperate.

Life-writing about other professionals shows less consistent trends. That
about contemporary businessmen, for example, includes several corporate
eulogies (eg, Shirley E. Woods, Jr, *The Molson Saga, 1763–1983*, 1983);
their insipidity is countered by the brash egotism of 'self-made' men such
as Lord Thomson (*After I Was Sixty*, 1975). In *Both Sides of the Street*
(1983), publisher and opera-and-theatre benefactor Floyd S. Chalmers writes
with greater frankness than Wood, greater moderation than Thomson, and
greater substance than either. The historical impact of business has received
some attention in Michael Bliss's scholarly, readable biography of Sir Joseph
Flavelle (*A Canadian Millionaire*, 2 vols, 1978), H.B. Timothy's group
biography *The Galts: A Canadian Odyssey* (2 vols, 1977–84), and Brian
Young's corrective *George-Étienne Cartier* (1981) which substitutes for prior
eulogies an examination of the ways in which Cartier's pocketbook, personal
life, and professional, business, and political goals interacted. Each of these
adds to an historical understanding of Canadian society. Dominating the
biographers of businessmen in the popular market is Peter Newman. Titling
his works with a catchy epithet (*Bronfman Dynasty: The Rothschilds of the
New World*, 1978; *The Establishment Man*, 1982, about Conrad Black),
Newman delineates characters in whom intelligence, charm, loyalties, ruth-
lessness, and opportunism compete; while never condoning his characters'
faults, neither does he allow them to alienate the reader. Working within the
limitations living subjects impose, Newman writes strong corporate drama
that owes more to the media profile than to biographical tradition.

Recent medical writing is equally diverse. Much of it describes doctoring
in isolated or foreign communities or in pioneering fields in a reminiscent,
admiring, and naive voice. In contrast *Morgentaler* (1975) by Eleanor Wright
Pelrine damages the abortionist's case by inviting the reader to make a false
analogy between Morgentaler's months in a concentration camp and his experience at the hands of Canada's justice system. More honest, if unexcep-
tional, life-writing about doctors addresses heroes and major figures. Popular
biographies about Norman Bethune proliferate although none matches Roderick Stewart's *Bethune* (1973). Hans Selye inconclusively brings together in
The Stress of My Life (1977) reminiscences about his childhood, questions

about the relation of his professional career to his personal life, egotistic
pitches for his theory of stress, and anecdotes. Valuing modesty and personal
life, Wilder Penfield makes a happier subject of autobiography. *No Man
Alone* (1977) describes his life and career until the opening of the Montreal
Neurological Institute in 1934, including detailed, dramatic accounts of early
neurosurgery. His grandson Jefferson Lewis supplements the autobiography
in *Something Hidden* (1981), which carries the career to its close and dwells
on the sources in private life of Penfield's professional strengths.

The major medical biography is Michael Bliss's *Banting* (1984). A 'study
in the problems of being a hero,' *Banting* draws on Bliss's earlier history,
The Discovery of Insulin (1982), in which he tracks Banting's deductions
from other people's work, his crude experimental procedures, the competitiveness and quarrels among the four 'principal' investigators whose work
led to a Nobel Prize for Banting and J.J. MacLeod, but not for Charles Best.
To this anti-heroic account, Bliss adds the story of Banting's failed scientific
and academic career and scandalously-ended marriage. His thesis – that Banting was 'raw and unequipped to handle either everyday prominence or the
public's expectation of future triumph upon triumph' – he demonstrates con-
clusively, by showing how the man's character, coinciding with circumstances, determined his life and career. Intelligently sensitive and analytic about
personality, working from a premise that character and circumstances are
often mutually determining, scrupulous and thoughtful in his weighing of the
evidence of research, but neither adulatory nor debunking, Bliss writes a rare
important Canadian biography.

Bliss's Banting is, ultimately, a spiritual and scholarly misfit. That the
scholar – to modify Matthew Arnold only slightly – has nominally at least
replaced the man of God as society's spiritual conscience has become increasingly evident in recent life-writings. The decline of religious memoirs
has been steady throughout the century and continues: the only autobiography
of any merit by a man of God during these years is *Unfinished Business*
(1981) and it owes its narrative interest less to W. Gunther Plaut's rabbinical
vocation than to his intelligent responsiveness to historical events, his incisive
characterization of the prominent, and his frank discussions of the intersections of religious and secular politics. Lewis C. Walmsley writes the only
substantial biography of a clerical life, *Bishop in Honan* (1974), which lucidly
and exhaustively chronicles William C. White's career as missionary to China,
professor at the University of Toronto's Chinese Studies Program, and curator
of the Chinese collection at the Royal Ontario Museum.[16] However, museum
is more important than mission in Walmsley's book. And in Gerald Killan's
David Boyle (1983), the central interest is the commitment that led a blacksmith's apprentice to become Canada's first archeologist, important ethnologist, and 'museum man.'

Some scholars relinquish the spurious myth of the ivory tower by writing their own memoirs. These range from modest accounts prepared for circulation among friends (eg, Vincent Bladen, *Bladen on Bladen: Memoirs of a Political Economist*, 1978) to chronicles of high-flying academic careers such as John Kenneth Galbraith's *A Life in Our Times* (1981). Their tone is equally varied. Albert W. Trueman writes ebulliently about his career as university president and instructively about the Canada Council's beginnings in *A Second View of Things* (1982), while chemist John Spinks separates a laboured, though anecdotal, account of his career as university president from a more technical and introspective description of his research and philosophy of science (*Two Blades of Grass*, 1980). H.S. Ferns, in *Reading from Left to Right* (1983), writes with thoughtfulness, strong rhetoric, and feisty riposte, while his fellow historian C.P. Stacey, in *A Date with History* (1983), presents a broader career in a less personalized, more measured manner.

Scholarly quest narratives show divergences at least as broad. Helen Creighton simply goes on record in *A Life in Folklore* (1975). William Blissett adopts the position of an acolyte in *The Long Conversation: A Memoir of David Jones* (1981), which adds to the Blissett-Jones correspondence the memoirist's diary notes and textual emendations to Jones's poems. Blissett's focus remains resolutely fixed on the subject of his scholarly admiration; Kathleen Coburn remains just as resolutely fixed on herself. *In Pursuit of Coleridge* (1977) stresses the labour and luck of manuscript research but is politic in its brevity about the University of Toronto and sometimes ungenerous about the contributions of fellow scholars: several aspects of the account have been questioned.

What these extremes reveal is that educators and scholars have not found an autobiographical mode adequate to the entirety of their experience. Only Galbraith's style flexibly fits his experience. There is no passage in recent Canadian life-writing funnier than his description of his early education at the Ontario Agricultural College, none more scathing than his assessment of Princeton University. Few autobiographers so objectively assess themselves and none so generously acknowledges the contributions of family and staff to his success.

Quoting from his first Canada Council Report, Albert W. Trueman reminds us of what he suspects 'majority opinion' in Canada does not hold: that upon 'the scholar and the creative worker ... largely depend the quality of our people and the image we have of our country.' If we had to rely on the life-writings about 'creative workers,' the 'image' would be non-existent in some fields, decidedly unfocused in others. Literary biographies were the most numerous between 1972 and 1984, whereas there was no significant life-writing relative to dance. To the sparse records which we find in documentary biographies of those working in theatre and film, we can add only *John*

Grierson (1979, by the film-maker's editor, colleague, and friend, Forsyth Hardy). Music fared no better. Biographical information has been limited to the very limited format of the first chapter ('The early years') in each of The Canadian Composers series – volumes that have included *Healey Willan* (F.R.C. Clarke, 1983), *R. Murray Schafer* (Stephen Adams, 1983), *Harry Somers* (Brian Cherney, 1975) and *Barbara Pentland* (Sheila Eastman and Timothy J. McGee, 1983). A discussion for students of 'The Music' and a brief presentation of the 'character' of each composer follows the introductory chapter: the sum hardly makes biography by which we can constitute 'an image of our country.' Autobiographically, the situation is little better. While Harry Adaskin readily acknowledges his literary incapacity, his *A Fiddler's World: Memoirs to 1938* (1977) does reveal a thoughtful man; it also contributes to Canadian music history with its account of the early days of the Hart House String Quartet. A second volume, *A Fiddler's Choice: Memoirs, 1938–1980* (1982), is more garrulous, repetitive, and sometimes inaccurate.

When we turn to the visual arts the shelves do not gape so emptily, but they still reveal the erratic and unrepresentative pattern emerging from contemporary life-writing about Canadian cultural figures. To begin with, the prominent role curators and art dealers play has moved no biographer; the only relevant work here is William R. Watson's *Retrospective* (1974). Among the first dealers to support Canadian art, Watson alludes to many of the famous painters of his time. *Retrospective*, however, is a pastiche of a book, relying heavily on his earlier essays about individual painters. Artists themselves have been represented here and there by the memoirs of relatives and friends. None of these works is critical: some are briefly illuminating in their personal descriptions; some use to advantage access to private papers.[17] Those artists choosing to represent themselves are equally few. An anomaly among them is Humphrey Carver, who turned his British art school training into a career as a Canadian landscape designer and urban planner. Apart from the greeting card 'verse' with which he prefaces the sections of *Compassionate Landscape* (1975), Carver provides a detailed, analytic, hardheaded look at the environmental issues his career raised. Other painter/autobiographers have written three versions of the 'struggling artist' narrative. Naive, but sincere apology, Annora Brown's *Sketches from Life* (1981) interests for its rare treatment of a far-from-rare situation, that of the single daughter made responsible for aged parents with devastating effects on her own artistic career. Introspective and pained, *Someone with Me: The Autobiography of William Kurelek* (1980) opens with the artist's breakdown, backtracks through his early life to trace its genesis, and celebrates his recovery through his conversion to Roman Catholicism. A most promising autobiography by John Davenall Turner, *Sunfield Painter* (1982), remained unfinished when he died. Briefer, therefore, than it might have been about his years as a Calgary dealer

(Turner considerably influenced what became the Glenbow collection), the book never reaches his own late painting career. His work is reproduced in the volume, however, and Jon Whyte contributes a graceful, informative memoir of Turner's last years. The chapter on the projects of the Edmonton Plastic Display Company (by which Turner and his brothers hoped to make a living upon their return from World War I) also makes clear the painter's talents as a humorist.

Nonetheless, artists' autobiographies provide but a scant and scattered offering. The same must be said about their biographers' efforts, most of which appear as brief introductory remarks in exhibition catalogues or in books of plates. More sustained efforts generally address unpromising subjects[18] or fail to transform promising material into major biography.[19] Gerald Finley in *George Heriot* (1983), for example, writes in the guise of biography a very scholarly piece of art history, situating Heriot within eighteenth-century conventions of topographic and picturesque graphics. But as biographer he fails: little is known about Heriot's personal and emotional life, leaving Finley overemphasizing a tedious chronicle of relatives and ancestors and political quarrels. A plethora of documents can pose equal, if opposite, problems, as in the case of the Prince Edward Island Harris family, whose voluminous correspondence has made them the subject of four competent but undistinguished volumes since 1970.[20] Such abundant life-writing about secondary careers, in the context of a paucity of biographies about major careers, seriously distorts the balance of life-writing about Canadian artists.

The one significant biographical effort about a major artist is Maria Tippett's *Emily Carr* (1979). Emphasizing Carr's periods of greatest discovery, change, and productivity, Tippett's account convincingly coheres around her vision of Carr as a woman made unpleasant and difficult by psychological trauma, artistic isolation, fears, poverty, and real and imagined rebuffs. This is not, however, to pose *Emily Carr* as ideal model: it has justifiably been criticized for allowing fact and detail to take 'precedence over the meaning of the life ... and ... analysis of artistic development,'[21] particularly where Carr's response to the Indian villages is concerned. Too ready to accept nineteenth-century medical diagnoses of Carr's sexual 'frigidity' and 'hysteria,' Tippett leaves too many regions of 'Emily's' art and psyche unexamined.

If life-writing by and about most of Canada's professional classes shows diversity and gaps, that about politicians is more monolithic. A glance at the index of occupations in the *Dictionary of Canadian Biography* suggests that the surest paths to auto/biographical immortality before 1900 were those of the politician and the civil servant. We can only regret that this remains true.

Autobiographers who write to forestall or to counter biographers and historians are nothing new, but the failure of frankness and the degree of self-serving they bring to their work seldom matches that of some recent politicians. *I Chose Canada: The Memoirs of the Honourable Joseph R. 'Joey' Smallwood* (1973) stands as a raw, but by no means atypical, example: after brief first chapters devoted to his family origins, Smallwood keeps his private life strictly out of view, while his account of his political life is unremittingly self-aggrandizing; all events appear in either a self-justificatory or self-promoting light. Smallwood's book differs from a good deal of such writing only in that its immodesty is cruder and its vitality greater. John Diefenbaker's three-volume memoir, *One Canada* (1975–7), in spite of his larger and more powerful political arena and his use of research associates to fill in background and smooth out rough edges in the writing, has only a minimum of propriety to recommend it over Smallwood's autobiography. By comparison, those memoirs that rely on candid anecdotes and dramatized conversations, such as Gérard Pelletier's recollections of Lévesque, Marchand, and Trudeau in *Years of Impatience 1950–1960* (trans. Alan Brown, 1984), paradoxically present themselves, to the non-historian at least, far more credibly.[22]

The reader of Canadian political autobiography who has already run the rapids of egocentrism and self-pleading must still face the shoals of tedium. Walter L. Gordon's *A Political Memoir* (1977) is not only limited in its focus but long, long, long. Maxwell Henderson, in *Plain Talk!* (1984), describes his confrontation of government spending as Auditor General in a narrative so dull the reader may well decide to head for the nearest shopping mall. Even Paul Martin, whose virtues include readable prose, reasonable modesty, and comparative objectivity, takes 1200 pages and two volumes to describe his career in elected politics (*A Very Public Life*, 1983–5) and threatens us with more to come about his life as High Commissioner in London. Civil servants, writing from the leisure of retirement, also mar potentially arresting material through garrulousness or banality. While Jeffry V. Brock, in *With Many Voices* (2 vols, 1981–3), writes vigorous anecdotes, he nonetheless falls victim to the desire to use the genre as a form of lengthy self-justification. The *Memoirs of Hugh L. Keenleyside* (2 vols, 1981–2) stands apart from these autobiographies in a number of respects: Keenleyside's diplomatic and administrative career involved some exceptionally important technological and environmental decisions, his account of them foregrounds analysis, principle, and compassion for his fellow human beings, and (rare virtue in these writings) it gestures towards the ways in which the personal and the professional are integrated by presenting Mrs Keenleyside as fully participating in his life. But to find these virtues, one must read over 1100 pages of detail upon detail.

In this context, there is little to wonder at in the praise lavished on Lester B. Pearson's *Mike* (3 vols, 1972–5). Neither in style nor in shapeliness will

Mike ever stand as great literature, but in the Sargasso Sea of recent political autobiography, Pearson and his research associates do let a sense of his personal aims and ambitions filter through the political account. *Mike* is the only autobiography of a politician during these years that manages to be historically informative, modestly self-revealing, meditative, and a little urbane at the same time.

Behind the self-assertions of the politicians lie hundreds of *biographies*. The most negligible could not be less inclined to note failings if their subjects themselves had written them: one date runs into the next, culminating in a eulogy, the whole innocent of any pretensions to either judgment or art. Where the political left is concerned, praise rises to hagiography, presented in a rhetoric that assumes no 'worker' can read past a grade three level.[23] And when a biographer seeks 'objectivity' instead, this all too often means that very little assessment – certainly little *negative* assessment – is ventured at all (Geoffrey Stevens in *Stanfield*, 1973, is typical of many such). Indeed, the cult of personality, and particularly Pierre Trudeau's personality, seems more likely in Canada to lead to assessment of a subject's character than does biography proper. George Radwanski in *Trudeau* (1978) notes Trudeau's influences, personal habits, and weaknesses as well as his political actions, and Richard Gwyn in *The Northern Magus* (1980) provides us with a longer, more detailed, and astute study of the same sort. But both books are character studies of the man still in power; neither author can commit himself to the biographer's mandate to account for the shape of the whole life and its relation to its historical and cultural context.

The two most consistent traits of recent biographies of politicians and civil servants are those which have always characterized such writing in Canada: a pedestrian chronological record of facts fills the gap left by a rigid exclusion of all that is not political in the lives of their subjects. Many a recent Canadian biography begins with dispiriting, if businesslike, banality: 'X was born at Y and went on to become a journalist, parliamentarian, political organizer.' And many a responsible and analytic biographer has – like Reginald H. Roy in his life of Major-General George Pearkes, *For Most Conspicuous Bravery* (1977) – begun promisingly (by introducing his protagonist through a rousing description of a dramatic and initiating moment in his life) but soon foundered. Narrative considerations are overwhelmed by an unwieldy mass of historical detail, and so impoverished by the absence of information about the personal life, that both the narrative and the man inscribed in it leave all but the specialist reader welcoming distraction.

Yet considerable recent political biography is important in scholarly and historical ways. Works like Margaret Prang's *N.W. Rowell: Ontario Nationalist* (1975), Peter Oliver's *G. Howard Ferguson: Ontario Tory* (1977), J.L. Granatstein's *A Man of Influence: Norman A. Robertson and Canadian State-*

craft 1928–68 (1981), and Robert Craig Brown's *Robert Laird Borden* (2 vols, 1975–80), among others, document in exhaustive detail the public lives and the political and historical milieux of their subjects. The balanced reassessment of a political career, supported by extensive documentation and quotation from primary sources, of a work like J. Murray Beck's *Joseph Howe* (2 vols, 1982–3) makes for major political and historical scholarship.

But it does not necessarily make for major biography. The subtitle *A Political Biography*, so frequent on these works, points to their limitations when we consider biography as a literary genre. What many of these biographies account for is a public figure, not a man; historical events, not a life and the ways it is determined by and determinative of those events. This cannot always be avoided. Beck, for example, has no opportunity to chronicle the private Howe in his later years given the absence of private and personal papers; D.J. Hall notes that his *Clifford Sifton* (2 vols, 1981–5), a work well-received for its historical scholarship, is 'of necessity' restricted to being a 'political biography' given that Sifton's papers have been 'stripped' of personal and business correspondence. But George Woodcock tries to turn a limitation into an unreal advantage in his introduction to *Amor De Cosmos* (1975) when he argues that the scarcity of facts about De Cosmos's personal life (or indeed about his life at all except for the years during which he negotiated BC's entry into Confederation) can be construed as better 'enabl[ing] one to place De Cosmos firmly in his historical setting.' This specious argument (Woodcock has repeatedly demonstrated that he knows better) takes up the assumption of much Canadian biography that the personal is somehow historically unreliable, that including it in the biography is to ignore or distort the 'historical setting.' This assumption carries with it a further specious correlative: that historical settings and events are somehow independent of the personal aims and lives of those who bring them about and act in them.

The few exceptions are worth noting. Sometimes a woman subject, because socialized gender roles foreground the difficult balance of her private and public obligations, leads biographers to break the mould of the strictly 'political' biography; this is the case, for example, with an otherwise poorly written biography, Christine Mander's *Emily Murphy* (1985), in which private and public life are made warp and woof of a single fabric. More often the exceptions to the strictly 'political' biography come from writers and scholars who are professional biographers. Robert Bothwell and William Kilbourn, in *C.D. Howe* (1979), manipulate chronology to begin with Howe's being shipwrecked when a British passenger liner is torpedoed, backtrack to account for his being on the ship, and then proceed chronologically. The narrative device would never be cause for comment in a novel; but in Canadian political biography it stands out in its acknowledgment of the need, in addition to historical facts, for the truth that can be revealed by narrative. *C.D. Howe* also stands above the norm by the bluntness with which it insists on balancing its subject's 'integrity, keen intellect, humour, charm, warmth and decency' against the fact that he was 'an utter philistine with respect to an appreciation of the arts and architecture, of religion and of the natural world' or that his 'understanding of British political institutions ... was crude to say the least.' When well-documented, such direct and comprehensive assessments are one of the virtues Canadian biography stands in greatest need of.

A few of the successful political biographers have combined scholarship with stylistic felicity, the personal with the political, while dealing with only a limited period in their protagonists' lives. Elisabeth Batt is one such: in *Monck* (1976), limited to the Governor General's years in Canada, she presents a strong sense of Monck's family and personal life as well as his political life, with the result that the biography of these seven years gives us a far richer sense of the man than many a double-decker account of five decades of strictly political life. Claude Bissell, in *The Young Vincent Massey* (1981), provides another rare proof that a felicitous style and narrative shapeliness are not incompatible with factual accuracy in a biography that (treating Massey's youth) amply proves the instructiveness of describing the private man who lives behind the public figure. Above all these, Joseph Schull stands out as a stylist, a narrator, and an historical interpreter. His *Edward Blake* (2 vols, 1975–6) and his *The Great Scot: A Biography of Donald Gordon* (1979) have been justly praised for their strong narrative and the incisiveness of their style, as well as for their use of contextual information and their political and historical analyses.

Clearly, all is not well with life-writing in Canada, though not for lack of either urging or example. Over thirty years ago Donald Creighton was speaking of biography as a *literary* art, having already acted on his word in *John A. Macdonald* (1952). More recently Donald Swainson, Phyllis Grosskurth, and Ira B. Nadel[24] have written astutely about problems of selection of data, identification with the subject, literary style and structure, and interpretive vision in scholarly biography, Grosskurth speaking in part from her experience writing *Havelock Ellis* (1980). Academics at Canadian universities continue to demonstrate the compatibility of scholarship and narrative art in literary biography: among others, one thinks of Michael Millgate (*Thomas Hardy*, 1982), Michael Collie (*George Gissing*, 1977, and *George Borrow, Eccentric*, 1982), and Paul Delany (*D.H. Lawrence's Nightmare*, 1979). Nonetheless, the quantity of archival publishing and the limitations of Canadian political biography suggest that most auto/biographers still view life-writing *about Canadians* as primarily an historical genre and so direct their attention to the life (*bio*) at the expense of its writing (*graphē*). This situation has led some critics to distinguish two traditions of life-writing – the historical and the literary[25] – and others to protest the monopoly historians have held on our biographical tradition in particular.[26] But even among our literary biographers a number continue to write works in which literature plays a decidedly secondary role: they find an historical chronicle of events and dates sufficient, prefer adulation to evaluation, and fail to enquire into the creative process or to discuss a writer's works critically.[27] Were this the whole story we might lament the long years scholars such as Desmond Pacey and Clara Thomas have spent calling for scholarly and literary biography of Canadian writers. Fortunately, we *have* begun the biographical research these two scholars called for, with results that give cause for some elation.

The very range of literary biographies points to the change. In *An Odd Attempt in a Woman: The Literary Life of Frances Brooke* (1983), Lorraine McMullen adheres rigorously to the position that the biographer can be completely objective and ought to be invisible in the work. She characterizes Brooke largely in terms of her response to her eighteenth-century literary milieu and makes some guarded hypotheses about her personal life. *An Odd Attempt in a Woman* has the lacunae inevitable when 200 years have helped obliterate evidence; nor does it show McMullen giving the same care to style and narrative structure she gives to the documentation of Brooke's career. Nonetheless the thorough scholarship and the critical approach to Brooke's work make this a significant contribution to Canadian, eighteenth-century, and women's studies. Others, such as Mollie Gillen on L.M. Montgomery in *The Wheel of Things* (1975; rpt 1983), Usher Caplan on A.M. Klein in *Like One that Dreamed* (1982), and Douglas Day in *Malcolm Lowry* (1973), bring psychological insights pertinently to bear on biography. Day structures his narrative dramatically to make Lowry's death the end towards which his every act had striven. His Freudian reading effectively explains Lowry's (not) writing although the reader may well resist the psychological predestination of Day's thesis that 'Lowry drank ... because he *had* to.'

Most encouraging in literary biography is the number of scholars who have made a sustained professional commitment to the genre. Among the first of these, Clara Thomas had published in 1967 a pioneering biography of Anna Jameson, *Love and Work Enough* (rpt 1978), well-researched *and* well-written, and perceptive in both literary and psychological terms about the meaning of Jameson's experience as a woman and a writer. She and co-author John Lennox are less successful with *William Arthur Deacon* (1982): their Deacon is a dull man, as perhaps he was in life. Excluding his personal life from their consideration, they break down the professional life into chronologically parallel aspects of his career which they treat in separate chapters for each period of his life. This structure, which creates some overlap and repetition, seems to have been dictated by the volume of the archives available: 18,000 items overwhelm them in detail; they do not always pull together into meaningful pattern. Although the resulting biography might more appropriately have been cast as a study in literary history, their commitment to outlining so fully Deacon's career situates them firmly at the beginnings of genuinely *scholarly* biography about Canadian writers.

Two literary biographers, Betty Keller and Marian Fowler, excel at characterization for a less exclusively scholarly market. The former's lives of Pauline Johnson (*Pauline*, 1981) and Ernest Thompson Seton (*Black Wolf*, 1984)[28] join judicious, though sometimes incomplete, research to narrative vigour. Particularly in *Black Wolf*, Keller often plays her protagonist's accounts of his emotional life against the revelations of an analysis of his motivations. Her own voice constitutes her greatest gift as biographer: a compassion before human frailty allows her to treat her protagonists' difficulties sympathetically while the sensibility of the biographer pushes her to examine critically the sources and effects of those difficulties. Marian Fowler takes the techniques of characterization even further, inventing scenes that *might* have happened and that display her protagonist in a way consistent with what we know from documentary sources. In *Redney: A Life of Sara Jeannette Duncan* (1983), she takes up a biographical position at the opposite pole to McMullen's, opening her narrative, for example, with a telling but *imagined* scene of Duncan in India. Later she imagines Joaquin Miller's attempted seduction of Redney; the scene is a bold interpretive gesture that rings true. Fowler emphasizes the symbolic truths that narrative can convey, and uses existing evidence to dramatize what she believes happened in the life. Scholars quail before the questionable authority of some of her scenes, but the scenes are psychologically convincing.

Elspeth Cameron has most wholeheartedly taken up Pacey's call for scholarly biography of Canadian writers. Her *Hugh MacLennan* (1981) represents a major document in Canadian literary biography, although it will probably prove an apprentice work in her own oeuvre. Along with Fowler's *Redney* and Keller's *Pauline*, published the same year, it is the first attempt to look at the life of a Canadian writer *in toto* in a critical biography, examining MacLennan's childhood, education, marriages, and friendships in relation to his professional career. Like Keller, Cameron relies on perceptive psychological assessment although she shows less stylistic skill in this first work than do either Keller or Fowler. Somewhat constrained by her dependence on the cooperation of a subject still alive, she occasionally soft-pedals negative interpretations. Nonetheless, she does not identify uncritically with her subject; she attends objectively to the unhappy effects on his writing of MacLennan's own constant gauging of the 'market' and of his position as 'spokesman' for Canada. A rather old-fashioned and beleaguered MacLennan emerges.

Writers themselves cannot be said to be keeping pace with the maturing

work of critical biographers. Literary autobiographies run the gamut from cli-
chés of booze-and-broads (Hugh Garner, *One Damn Thing after Another*, 1973)
to the clichés of literary-loyalty-and-nationalism (Wilfrid Eggleston, *Literary
Friends*, 1980); from sincere stories of hardship naively told in clichés (Jessie
Louise Beattie, *A Walk through Yesterday*, 1976, and Edna Jaques, *Uphill
All the Way*, 1977) to stories of success that use sophisticated temporal schema
to keep unpleasant moments at a distance, told in clichés (David Walker,
Lean, Wind, Lean, 1984); from pedestrian narrative chronicling the difficulties
along the road to recognition (Thomas H. Raddall, *In My Time*, 1976) to a
self-justifying round in longstanding literary feuds (Earle Birney, *Spreading
Time*, 1980). In autobiography of literary careers, the most significant writing
has not been autobiography at all, but a group of critical essays examining
the narrative art John Glassco brought to the invention of his self in *Memoirs
of Montparnasse* (1970). Thomas E. Tausky's study of the book (*Canadian
Poetry*, 1983) points particularly well to the complexities surrounding the
issue of historical veracity in autobiography. His examination of Glassco's
manuscripts and journal demonstrates the extensive rewriting and outright lies
Glassco introduced into the *Memoirs*. His discussion of the status of lies in
autobiography, and his conclusion that Glassco's 'artful concealment of identity is itself a defining feature of his identity' marks a decisive moment in
the progress of criticism of Canadian autobiography from naiveté to insight.[29]

Most Canadian writers who turned to autobiography in these years favoured
the subgenre of the childhood. The structure of the 'childhood,' that genre's
only theorist tells us, 'reflects ... the development of the writer's self; beginning often ... with the first light of consciousness, and concluding, quite
specifically, with the attainment of a precise degree of maturity' (Richard
Coe, *When the Grass Was Taller*, 1984). Phenomenal not historical in its
mode, the childhood posits a world of sensation rather than of analysis,
leaving the autobiographer seeking, first, to transform the outer language of
literary description or factual reportage into an inner language of the child's
world and, then, to adapt language and structure to the maturing child's
growing sense of self (and not-self) and his forging of a distinctive identity
in relation to the world around him. The 'classical' examples of the genre
evoke what Coe calls the child's 'small world,' advance through his growing
self-definition, and finally arrive at a portrait of the artist as a young man
(the canonical tradition does not allow for the artist as a young woman).
Since such an account can be historically verified in only trivial ways, the
conviction it carries rests almost entirely on its literary art.

Recent years have seen some exceptional examples of 'childhoods' by
English-Canadian writers, George Woodcock chief among them. He structures

Letter to the Past (1982) around a series of contrasting archetypal metaphors – familiar to readers of literary autobiography and the *Bildungsroman* – for growing up: the bleakness of 'growing up poor' in English row housing and the idyll of his grandparents' farm, that 'great good place that would never change' – so the child believes – and that becomes a lost paradise; the 'time suspended' of his rural vacations and 'time the enemy' in the world of school. 'Death in the family' and the end of his formal education send him into the world to 'years of awakening' and 'new frontiers.' After an apprenticeship as a poet and a theorist of anarchy in the 1930s and 1940s, Woodcock reaches 'a precise degree of maturity' in his decision to emigrate to Canada. His emigration he represents as a double 'going home,' to the country of the first months of his life and to the literary career he will make for himself. The literary success of *Letter to the Past* lies in Woodcock's ability to use metaphor and narrative structure to trace the *meaning of the pattern* he perceives in his life. Clark Blaise takes narrative artifice even further with flashbacks, non-chronological telling, dramatic and epiphanic climaxes in his 'self-seeking – *literally* a seeking after myself' – in his 'Tenants of Unhousement' (*Iowa Review*, 1982). In Blaise's memoirs, his parents – 'English and French, and all the silence that entails' – represent one duality, and a childhood split between the United States and Canada – with Canada always the 'significant blob of otherness in my life' ('Memories of Unhousement,' *Salmagundi*, 1982) – another. The ways in which Blaise uses his narrative of dualities to reveal the self he is seeking make these essays among the richest in Canadian autobiographical literature.

While the contrasting claims of two or more places in the formation of the personality structure many childhoods in the 'classical' tradition of the genre, divergent activities can perform the same function. In his essay 'Noddy and Big Ears Meet Malvolio' (*Kicking Against the Pricks*, 1982), John Metcalf traces his development through his boyhood addictive reading and obsessive collecting, the latter conveyed through a wonderfully disparate list of objects, and both having 'important links with writing,' then through his adolescent 'building the Body Beautiful and snuffling blood and mucus in the ring ... [while] also beginning to burn with a hard, gemlike flame.' If it would be 'quite a long time before [he] *dared* to think of writing,' the entire essay points to that 'precise degree of maturity' when he will think of it. Earle Birney, although he writes less voluptuously of sensation in his brief, thematic 'Child Addict in Alberta' (*Canadian Literature*, 1981), also structures his essay on similarly contrasting activities: his 'reading habit' is the ground from which he strays into boyhood experiences only to return, and the essay's structure shows both reading and experience as formative of the writer-to-be.

Woodcock, Metcalf, and Blaise can claim as part of their inheritance literary conventions which fit in precise ways their sense of their lives. To find a language and a narrative shape becomes more difficult for those whose experience is on the margins of the lives inscribed by literary conventions. For Austin Clarke, for example, the two worlds are, explicitly, village life in Barbados and British-administered school life; implicitly, the two worlds are Barbados and the never-described life in Canada from which he writes the childhood.[30] He structures *Growing Up Stupid under the Union Jack* (1980) in a series of vignettes, each using dialogue to capture the rhythms of Barbados speech, each describing a step in Clarke's choice of which kind of educated 'fool' he will become – 'a mathematics fool,' 'a legal fool,' 'a running fool.' The rite of passage to maturity comes in final exams which translate him into another world. While these and the entire educational system are treated with the seriousness their life-altering power merits, the title, the local dialect, and a hundred other details double the account, ironizing and politicizing what it means to grow up 'educated' in a colony.

Mary Meigs also follows the conventions of the childhood in her description of her parents, of her grandparents' contrasting Philadelphia and rural homes, of the world of sensation she felt herself immersed in, of her awakening to sexuality and her vocation as an artist: all 'inscape' of her life. But when the artist is a woman and the woman a lesbian, just as when he is a black and a colonial, the narrative must be wrenched free of some of the established conventions of the childhood if it is to accommodate the meaning of her experience. Thus Meigs's *Lily Briscoe: A Self-Portrait* (1981), for all that it dwells on the inner life and not on outer events, consistently foregrounds an 'other' as touchstone for introspection and self-knowledge. The critic Edmund Wilson opens the book in the role of this 'other' (important for his intellectual friendship but discomfiting for what he – and through him the world – may know and say about the author's lesbianism), but the most significant 'other' is Virginia Woolf's woman artist, Lily Briscoe. This trope of identification, however, effects a reversal from the classical (male) pattern of the childhood for not the artistic vocation but love takes precedence, in a passage that redirects the integrity that Lily Briscoe brought to her moment of vision while painting: 'When I am in love, I am like Lily Briscoe, making of love a work of art, giving it that totality of attention one gives to painting a picture or writing a poem.'[31] This unconventional search for meaning makes the childhood lifelong and 'lifelost': Meigs's 'precise degree of maturity' arrives when she attains to the 'two chief tasks of my life ... to become an artist and to overcome my [sexual] shame, and, at the age of sixty-one, I am only just beginning to feel that I have accomplished them,' partly through the writing of her 'childhood' in *Lily Briscoe*.

The common structuring of childhoods around two worlds presupposes that the autobiographer's experience *provides* two worlds. In Canada it seldom has. With scattered families and, until recently, the socio-economic homogeneity of parents and children, grandparents' homes seldom provide metaphors for alternative worlds. At the same time the precariousness of cultural endeavours and, until the 1960s, the unavailability of higher education to many Canadians, all prevented easy contacts of writers with their peers. Writers with Canadian childhoods come closest to the classical use of the genre exemplified by Woodcock when their experience has been urban and minimally secure financially. Robert Thomas Allen succeeds best in creating that world in *My Childhood and Yours: Happy Memories of Growing Up* (1977), a colloquial book structured around themes and the passing seasons rather than directed towards any decisive moment of maturity. A lesser example of the genre, Allen's book coheres around his ability to imagine and celebrate the interior life of children. An element of nostalgia for the children-and-the-city-we-were rules most such autobiographies which, like William J. O'Callaghan's *How I Flew the Forties* (1984), tend to end arbitrarily.[32]

The experience described in other childhoods falls more completely outside the genre's conventions. In some, the dwelling in the sensations of a 'small world' that Coe describes as characteristic gives way before a terror that makes the child preternaturally aware of the grown-up world around her and, at the same time, leaves her psychologically isolated from it. Two autobiographies represent such childhoods as a condition to be escaped and end with the 'precise degree of maturity' by which their authors gain the strength to free themselves psychologically and physically. One is Charlotte Vale Allen's *Daddy's Girl* (1980), an autobiographical remembering of incest and her attempts to come to terms with it. The associative structure and flashbacks of *Daddy's Girl* are not always sufficiently controlled to avoid repetition, but the book does convincingly convey the child's sense of coercion, terror, anger, and psychological isolation in the face of abuse about which she was afraid to speak. More stylistically accomplished, and as reasoning and ironic as Allen is circling and subjective, Claire Martin describes her father's verbal and physical beatings and her own developing resistance in *In an Iron Glove* and *The Right Cheek* (trans. Philip Stratford, 1968).

Gentler circumstances also necessitate revision of the conventions of the childhood genre. Moved out of its urban setting into a frontier past, the childhood is no longer well-served by the literary archetypes that George Woodcock employs. 'The North American prairie and the Canadian wilderness,' Richard Coe observes without elaboration, 'produce different, less clearly identifiable, reactions.' One attempt to articulate such a reaction is Fredelle Bruser Maynard's in *Raisins and Almonds* (1972). Her autobiography of her Jewish childhood with shopkeeping parents in a series of small Manitoba towns and later in Winnipeg poses a sameness of place in an immense landscape despite the number of villages lived in. None of the richness of colour and texture, the variety of people, or the travel that gives rise to memorable descriptions in the classic childhoods is available from Maynard's experience. Nonetheless, her chapters are rich with imaginative musings, taking airy life from the more limited stimuli of her father's shop windows and the T. Eaton catalogue – her chapter on this last a tour de force in the genre's use of the list and a superb evocation of the *meaning* to pioneers of a commercial institution lesser writers have reduced to truism. Other writers, less successful in recreating such experience, fall into the historical mould that has dominated Canadian life-writing. Wilfrid Eggleston in *Homestead on the Range* (1982) exemplifies the type; he never really addresses his own experience, choosing instead to write local history under a series of thematic headings. His compassion for the plight of the homesteaders seems pinched because confined to a narrative structure that strings clichés on a chronological thread.

Maynard and Eggleston indicate the two directions writers have taken in attempts to accommodate the genre's literary conventions to isolated childhoods: towards memoirs of parents and towards history. A significant effect of Maynard's childhood is its tribute to her parents; much of its tragedy comes from seeing the diminished health and circumstances of her father. Whereas autobiography, almost as a matter of course, dwells on the child's freeing of himself from his parents, one group of Canadian autobiographies are in fact offerings to parents who endured frontier life with courage and grace. Their forms are as varied as their subjects. Marjorie Wilkins Campbell, in *The Silent Song of Mary Eleanor* (1983), like Fowler, takes biographical licence to present, imaginatively, moments symbolic of her mother's frontier experience: hers is a dignified and psychologically convincing portrait of a pioneer woman whose health finally succumbed to hardship. Jean McKay in *Gone to Grass* (1983) writes with affectionate irony a series of fragmented memories of her childhood, grouped around her minister-father, who figures in each. And Adele Wiseman's non-generic work *Old Woman at Play* (1978), also a series of fragmented memories (of her mother's making dolls and telling stories of her life in Russia), becomes an enquiry into the nature of creativity. *Old Woman at Play* emerges as both a tribute to the novelist's mother and a personal meditation on the creative process.

Where some writers confronted with a 'frontier' past whose imaginative burden is as much historical as personal turn to tributes to their parents rather than to more strictly autobiographical modes, others adapt the form of the childhood to accommodate the history. This has been done most successfully by Helen Meilleur in *A Pour of Rain: Stories from a West Coast Fort* (1980). By extensive use of the fur-trade journals from Port Simpson, Meilleur reconstructs its history from the mid-nineteenth century on. These chapters she intersperses with descriptions of her own childhood at the post where her father was a storekeeper and of its inhabitants as she remembers them. The history of the place and autobiography exist on one continuum in this work, enacting within the genre of the childhood the process of self-identification through identification of site that also characterizes much contemporary Canadian poetry and fiction.

Canadian poets and novelists who write childhoods – Blaise, Clarke, Woodcock – by and large are those who lived those childhoods elsewhere. Writers growing up in Canada who do approach autobiography have typically not pursued the *developmental* aspect of the childhood narrative. Dorothy Livesay, for example, distances the autobiographical self through a transparent fictional veneer in the 'sketches' and 'stories' of *A Winnipeg Childhood* (1973; rpt *Beginnings: A Winnipeg Childhood*, 1975). That veneer permits her to record diverse epiphanic and disjunctive moments without self-reference and without tracing a pattern of development. Al Purdy pays memoiristic tribute to the people of his childhood in sketchy prose amplified by some of his best autobiographical poems in *Morning and It's Summer* (1983), but he refuses self-exploration and self-revelation except through the kaleidoscopically fragmented lens of others. Most frequently, writers with Canadian childhoods behind them produce short autobiographical essays on a theme.[33]

Perhaps this comparative paucity arises from the heavy dependence of childhoods on a convention of alternative worlds not readily available to many Canadians born in Canada. Perhaps the conventions for describing 'small worlds' of the childhood are not readily adaptable to large landscapes. Perhaps the ahistoricism of Canadian communities which paradoxically drives life-writing so relentlessly towards historical narrative does not find conventions suitable to its expression. Whatever the reason, the only Canadian-born writer of an important 'childhood' writes in French, not English, and she writes our best Canadian autobiography to date. In *La détresse et l'enchantement* (1984; *Enchantment and Sorrow*, trans. Patricia Claxton, 1987) Gabrielle Roy finds alternative prairie worlds in St Boniface and Winnipeg, in the French and the English communities; the autobiographical quest for self-identity she narrates as her long, isolated apprenticeship teaching and writing. Upon her return from France, she has reached a 'precise degree of maturity' in her decision, at the volume's end, to stay in Montreal and make her living as a writer. Roy's prose has the simplicity, the directness, and the lyric appropriateness that comes only from long meditation. Events and images open to reveal worlds. In her parents' preparations for the lieutenant-governor's ball and their 'attendance' at it, she epitomizes all the otherness of the poor French-Canadian community in St Boniface. A cat on her father's coffin catches the sense of loss and of life going on that death brings. The Manitoba landscapes bring out the young woman's idealism, yearning, and exhilaration as well as her respect and humility before manifestations of the world's mystery that cannot be summed up in a phrase and set aside. Her closeness to her mother, their mutual sacrifices for each other, her growing need for independence and the anguish that this causes her mother and that the knowledge of having pained her mother causes her: these she details with loving rectitude in as moving an account of the mother-daughter relationship as any in literature. Gabrielle Roy never loses the particularity of her own experience, but she always transforms it into the autobiography of the human condition. Had she alone written autobiography during these years, we might rest content.

15 Writings in Psychology

RAYMOND S. CORTEEN

INTRODUCTION

Each book discussed here has met the following criteria: the author was working in Canada at the time the book was prepared; most of the psychological research referred to in the book was done at a time when the author was resident in Canada; the author was resident in Canada for at least ten years; the author is recognized outside his or her area of specialization as internationally prominent in the field; the book is general enough to be of interest to an educated audience of non-psychologists. No attempt was made to choose on the basis of literary merit. These criteria have their limitations – excluding both francophones and many prominent anglophone psychologists who have written only for a professional readership, in a highly technical language. But francophone universities have been slower in developing independent psychology departments, and it is only in comparatively recent years that they have begun to attain a prominence rivalling that of their anglophone counterparts. My criteria for selection also exclude journal articles; notwithstanding this limitation, I do make some reference to a small number of articles which are particularly significant, which are of general interest, and which are more readable than is usual with this form. I am myself an academic psychologist with a strong bias towards experimental cognitive psychology. Despite strenuous efforts to counteract this bias it will probably be discernible to those with a different background.

Psychology, like most major academic disciplines, does not constitute a unitary body of knowledge. It is divided into several sub-disciplines which interact, but sometimes to a very limited degree. The four main areas of psychology in which Canadians have made significant contributions are animal and physiological psychology, perceptual and cognitive psychology, developmental and social psychology, and personality and clinical psychology. In addition, an increasing and important amount of research is being carried out in the area of gender differences.

ANIMAL AND PHYSIOLOGICAL PSYCHOLOGY

While there were distinguished psychologists at McGill University and the University of Toronto prior to World War II, Canadian psychology first gained international attention through the work of Donald Hebb at McGill University and Wilder Penfield at the Montreal Neurological Institute in the late 1940s and early 1950s. Although Penfield was not a psychologist, several prominent Canadian psychologists did important work with him. The most significant event of those early days was the publication of Hebb's *The Organization of Behavior* (1949). This book proposed a general theory of human behaviour based upon what was then understood of neurophysiological processes. While the theory is no longer regarded as viable it was a genuinely seminal work, generating as it did a vast amount of experimental research, much of it carried out at McGill which, by the late 1950s, had become, at least from an international perspective, the most visible psychology department in Canada. In fact, at that time, it ranked among the best departments in the world. Prominent among Hebb's co-workers was Peter Milner. Milner proposed various extensions and modifications to Hebb's theory and, in 1954, together with James Olds, he discovered areas of the brain in rats which the animals will endlessly self-stimulate, this stimulation apparently producing intense pleasure or satisfaction. Since that time the areas have been known as the 'pleasure centres.' This discovery, which is still felt to be of major importance, projected Milner into considerable prominence, which culminated in the appearance of his book *Physiological Psychology* (1966). This was one of the earliest of the new generation of comprehensive surveys of the field and is regarded as having perpetuated and strengthened that Canadian emphasis on, and reputation in, physiological psychology which Hebb had initiated.

Brenda Milner, Peter Milner's wife, carried out her early work with Wilder Penfield. She has remained at the Montreal Neurological Institute, and has produced a large number of papers on the physiology of memory and on the significance of brain lateralization in humans. The first culmination of this work was the lengthy review article, written with Hans-Lucas Teuber, entitled 'Alteration of Perception and Memory in Man' (in Lawrence Weiskrantz, ed., *Analysis of Behavioural Change*, 1968). In a somewhat unusual division of responsibilities Milner contributed the second half of the paper, which deals with memory, and in reality this constitutes a completely independent piece of work. The paper is an important review of the effect of various brain lesions on memory in humans. Of particular interest is Milner's extensive reference to the tragic case of 'H.M.' (a patient operated on to relieve massive and debilitating epileptic seizures), which has become a classic constantly referred to in that literature which attempts to link brain functioning to memory. The operation involved the partial destruction of an area of the brain known as the hippocampus and had the unfortunate side-effect of producing a severe amnesic syndrome which left the patient incapable of retaining any new information for more than a few seconds. This acquisition amnesia, which has been observed in other patients with brain lesions and also, occasionally, in severe alcoholics, is regarded by some as a malfunctioning of consciousness as it applies to memory storage, a stage sometimes referred to as short-term memory. While we are still far from a complete understanding of these memory processes, Milner's work has been of major importance in advancing our comprehension of this complex topic.

Another area where Brenda Milner has contributed work of major importance is that of hemispheric specialization. It is now widely recognized that the two hemispheres of the brain serve rather different functions. This fact has led to a vast, popular, and sometimes exploitative literature which goes well beyond the available evidence. Milner presented a fair and balanced view in her article 'Hemispheric Specialization,' which appeared in the widely acclaimed publication edited by F.O. Schmitt and F.G. Worden, *The Neurosciences* (1974). This article acknowledges the importance of the left hemisphere in language, at least in most people, but is less certain about the role of the right hemisphere, though Milner accepts the fact that it does seem to play some role in spatial orientation. The way these imperfectly understood hemispheric differences have been exploited by those operating on the fringes of psychology – one example involves the spurious claims made by the proponents of so-called neurolinguistic programming – is a good illustration of the pervasive way in which limited psychological observations, heavily qualified by the original researchers, are distorted beyond reality as they become part of popular knowledge. Reading her lucidly written paper is a good antidote to such excesses. It should be pointed out that Milner's work is only part of a considerable recent Canadian prominence in the study of hemispheric specialization, which is also due to work by Doreen Kimura, Juhn Wada, Phil Bryden, Paul Bakan, and others.

Laterality in hand, ear, eye, and foot (a closely related topic) has been extensively dealt with in *Lateral Preferences and Human Behavior* (1981) by Clare Porac of the University of Victoria and Stanley Coren of the University of British Columbia. Noting that interest in this question, particularly concerning handedness, has been of interest to prominent thinkers from Plato to the present day, the authors present results from a survey of over 20,000 individuals showing the basic pattern of laterality in the population as a whole. Of possibly more interest to the general reader is their review of possible reasons for these patterns of lateralization. They note, in a fascinating section in the first chapter, that lateralization appears to have been a stable characteristic of populations for at least the past 5000 years. They base this conclusion on a survey of 1180 works of art, from pre-3000 BC to the present day, which display an impressive consistency in the portrayal of left-hand-edness. The authors offer several explanations for these consistent patterns of lateralization (among them being genetic factors, social influences, birth stress, and neurological injury), but despite the massive research effort which the book represents, they come to no clear definitive conclusion concerning these differences. Although easily observed and measured, these effects are not amenable to simple explanation. This recognition of causal complexity and ambiguity is becoming more characteristic of contemporary writing in psychology in general. As research methods and theoretical sophistication improve, it is becoming increasingly clear that the questions that psychologists are addressing are very intricate. The absurd simplifications of behaviourism lie far behind us, and ahead loom difficulties which were unimagined only twenty years ago. This understanding is reflected in much of the writing reviewed in this chapter.

Another major Canadian contribution in the field of physiological psychology has been the fascinating work of Ron Melzack, also of McGill University, on the understanding of pain. Melzack has been working on this topic since the mid-1950s and his research culminated in the publication of *The Challenge of Pain* (1983, with P. Wall). The book emphasizes the complex nature of pain, pointing out that the experience of pain is not a simple function of the degree of physical insult but is due to a large number of interacting physiological and psychological factors. Considerable emphasis is placed upon the gate-control theory of pain which Melzack first advanced in 1965. This theory suggests that pain can be controlled at a gate in the spinal cord by the stimulation of certain parts of the nervous system which upset the normal balance of neural impulses signalling pain from the periphery to the brain. The theory has received considerable attention from those interested in the control of chronic and acute pain because it suggests the possibility of pain amelioration by means other than the administration of addictive or debilitative drugs.

This section would not be complete without reference to the work of the animal psychologists Werner Honig of Dalhousie University and Herbert Jenkins of McMaster University. Honig, in *Operant Behaviour* (1966), which he edited, and *Animal Memory* (1971, with P.H.R. James), utilizes Skinnerian methodology in the study of animal cognition. Instead of accepting the 'blind mechanism' approach, which is characteristic of Skinner, Honig accepts the fact that animals, just like humans, are capable of thought and that much of their behaviour in mazes and Skinner boxes can be explained by assuming that they have cognitive capacities. This represents a startling shift in emphasis for animal psychologists. Jenkins, whose work has appeared exclusively in technical articles, must be mentioned for his work on stimulus control and auto-shaping. The latter phenomenon, which exploits the innate tendencies of animals in leading them to produce particular patterns of response, has led behaviourally oriented animal psychologists to pay much more attention to the inborn capacities of the various species they study, and has brought them more into the mainstream of the biological sciences than they were when labouring under the strict, doctrinaire principles of Skinnerian behaviourism. The most accessible of Jenkins's papers, though they are hardly simple popularizations, are 'The Development of Stimulus Control through Differential Reinforcement' (with R.S. Sainsbury, in *Fundamental Issues in Associative Learning*, 1969, ed. N.J. Mackintosh and W.K. Honig) and a monograph *Sign-Tracking: The Stimulus-Reinforcer Relation and Directed Action* (1974, with Eliot Hearst).

PERCEPTUAL AND COGNITIVE PSYCHOLOGY

Canadian contributions to this general area were slow to develop, but by the early 1980s they had reached gratifying levels, both in quantity and quality. Some of the most significant and influential ideas and theories of the past twenty years, particularly in the field of cognition, have emanated from Canadian universities.

Among the pioneers was Daniel Berlyne of the University of Toronto, who researched and developed the concept of physiological arousal and its relation to behaviour, cognition, and aesthetic experience. Arousal can be thought of as a dimension of emotional excitement which ranges from the comatose to extreme emotional experience. Among his extensive writings probably the most interesting of Berlyne's books is *Aesthetics and Psychobiology* (1971), in which he attempts to relate the arousal dimension to novelty which in turn, he maintains, is linked to aesthetic satisfaction. In order to do this he relates novelty to physiological arousal, with very familiar material evoking low arousal and completely unfamiliar items producing high arousal. He then suggests that there is an inverted U-shaped relationship between arousal and aesthetic experience. Very low arousal is associated with indifference, intermediate arousal with pleasure, and very high arousal with aversion and rejection. To take a specific example, we might be bored by a standard rendition of a familiar popular song, intrigued and delighted by a relatively unfamiliar Mozart string quartet (assuming that we have some familiarity with eighteenth- and nineteenth-century classical music), and puzzled and even angered by some of the extremes of twentieth-century atonal music. The theory has some plausibility but there are also some problems. Remaining in the field of music, one might ponder one's continuing pleasure in, say, the Goldberg Variations despite having heard them many times. According to Berlyne one should eventually become indifferent to anything, but this does not seem to happen in all cases. Despite this weakness the theory has received much favourable attention and continues to be the focus of considerable research. (One possible direction for future commentary might be to contrast the psychology of aesthetics with the *philosophy* of aesthetics, such as the 'theory of theory' advanced in Francis Sparshott's *The Theory of the Arts*, 1982, an enquiry into such 'categories' as pleasure, judgment, intuition, and performance.)

Another Canadian pioneer in cognitive psychology is Wallace Lambert of McGill University. He has worked extensively in the field of bilingualism and his most notable contribution has been the demonstration that (holding other factors constant) bilinguals have a more diversified intellectual structure than unilinguals and are more flexible in their thinking. This was a very important and influential finding, especially in a country with two official languages, and in particular because, up to the time of Lambert's extensive work, it was generally considered that bilinguals were at some disadvantage. The clearest summary statement of Lambert's findings is in the article 'The Effects of Bilingualism on the Individual: Cognitive and Sociocultural Consequences' (in P. Hornby, ed., *Bilingualism*, 1977). Also of interest is his book *Bilingual Education of Children: The St Lambert Experiment* (1972, with G. R. Tucker).

Another influential figure in cognitive psychology is Allan Paivio of the University of Western Ontario. At a time when any consideration of mental concepts among experimental psychologists was still largely taboo (thanks to the continuing influence of behaviourism) Paivio, in the mid-1960s, developed extensive research in the field of imagery. He demonstrated the importance of imagery in verbal learning and made the topic, which had been largely ignored for fifty years, respectable again. His book *Imagery and Verbal Processes* (1971) develops and explains his dual-encoding hypothesis. This theory suggests that, when we learn verbal material, there are two possible ways of encoding it, verbal and imaginal. Thus concrete words, which tend to have high imagery content, can be remembered more easily than abstract words, which tend to be associated with little imagery, because there are two routes by which the concrete, high imagery words can be retrieved. While this theory is now considered something of an oversimplification, it served the purpose of all good theories very well in that it generated considerable interest and a vast amount of research. The influence of the book is indicated by the fact that it was in such demand that a second publisher reissued it in 1979. The importance of Paivio's work in general is affirmed by the publication of a Festschrift entitled *Imagery, Memory, and Cognition: Essays in Honour of Allan Paivio* (1983), edited by one of his former students, John Yuille of the University of British Columbia.

Another contribution of major significance has been that of Endel Tulving of the University of Toronto. In his book *Elements of Episodic Memory*

(1983), Tulving elaborates on an idea which he introduced in 1972, namely the need for a distinction between episodic and semantic memory. By episodic memory Tulving means the memory we have for that sequence of events which forms a large part of what we are as individual human beings. In contrast, semantic memory might be regarded as something like general knowledge, knowledge which is not linked to any specific episode in our lives but is just something that we know. Thus our memory for the events of last Christmas is episodic, while the knowledge that Paris is the capital of France is semantic. The distinction is seen by many to be a useful one, though there are others who maintain that the boundary between the two types of memory is so unclear that it is more sensible to regard memory as unitary. Whatever the final conclusion there is no doubt that Tulving's idea that there are two types of memory has attracted a lot of interest and has suggested to many cognitive psychologists the possibility of developing a taxonomy of memory, as an alternative to the idea that memory is a single, undifferentiated mass.

As well as developing the idea of episodic and semantic memory, Tulving has been associated with another important theoretical idea to come from the University of Toronto. This is the 'levels of processing' theory which was primarily the work of Tulving's colleague Fergus Craik. Craik first advanced the idea of levels of processing in 'Levels of Processing: A Framework for Memory Research' (*Journal of Verbal Learning and Verbal Behavior*, 1972, with R.S. Lockhart), which is one of the most heavily cited papers in recent psychological literature. Craik and Tulving further developed the idea in 'Depth of Processing and the Retention of Words in Episodic Memory' (*Journal of Experimental Psychology*, 1975), and it received even fuller expression in *Levels of Processing and Human Memory* (1979), ed. Craik and L.S. Cermack. The theory suggests that our memory for verbal material depends upon the depth of processing which takes place when we are trying to memorize the material. Thus simple acoustical repetition, such as we use when we are trying to remember a telephone number we are about to dial, is shallow processing and is not particularly effective for long-term retention, while taking the numbers and developing some meaningful relationship among them would be deep processing and would be quite effective in long-term retention. The theory is simple and, in many experimental instances, it seems to work. It has certainly generated much related research. It suffers, however, from one serious flaw, and that flaw makes it difficult, if not impossible, to develop a really rigorous test of the theory. Basically the problem is that the theory is circular. Depth of processing is defined by the effect a particular form of processing has on memory. If we achieve good memory then that processing must have been deep, while if we achieve poor memory then the processing must have been shallow. Apart from intuition there is no external measure of depth of processing. This flaw has somewhat diminished the theory's impact in recent years.

An important figure in the field of artificial intelligence is Zenon Pylyshyn of the University of Western Ontario. Pylyshyn, who is a strong advocate of the equivalence between computational processes and human cognition, has published many important articles, but his position is most extensively argued in his book *Computation and Cognition* (1984). He goes further than many psychological proponents of artificial intelligence in that he states that a computational model of cognition must be closely equivalent to the processes that actually occur in the mind. He sees the computational model as a general theory of human cognition which gives psychology the potential for a greater coherence than it currently has – divided, as it is, into a large number of specialized subdivisions, each generating micro-theories with little or no interaction among them. Much of the book presents arguments to support the general position and there is not too much empirical evidence to indicate ways in which the theory relates to actual human cognitive processes. In general (and it shares this flaw with much of the artificial intelligence literature), there seems to be a large and continuing gap between programmatic claims and real achievements, but at least Pylyshyn deserves credit for attempting to formulate a general theory of human cognition. There is little question that psychology requires a more coherent theoretical framework than it currently possesses.

In the field of perception Canadian psychologists have been less prominent than in cognition but there are, nevertheless, some noteworthy figures. Peter Dodwell of Queen's University has been prominent in several areas of perception for the past twenty years. His *Visual Pattern Recognition* (1970) was an important early attempt to understand pattern recognition from a neurophysiological perspective. The chapters on contour coding and adaptation to optically distorted inputs are particularly interesting, and the whole book is useful in the way it attempts to consider the perception of complex patterns by analyzing the process into several distinct stages. This analytic approach contrasts with the global explanations which seem to regard visual perception as a unitary system. Perception may appear unitary to the naive observer because of the ease with which we see and interpret what we see, but it is, in fact, an extremely complex process which we are far from understanding. Dodwell's book marked an important step in really coming to grips with this complexity. This book was complemented by a book of selected papers on pattern recognition, edited by Dodwell, entitled *Perceptual Processing: Stimulus Equivalence and Pattern Recognition* (1971), which traces the development of ideas about pattern recognition over the preceding forty years.

An intriguing contribution, less in the psychological mainstream than Dodwell's work, has been made by Ian Howard of York University. Howard has been interested in the ways in which humans visually perceive the direction and orientation of objects. As with so many questions concerning perception, the problems involved seem, from a naive perspective, intuitively simple. We perceive the direction and orientation of objects so easily and immediately that we do not even seem to be involved in a problem. But it is, in fact, these 'simple' problems which, we have learned, cause the greatest difficulty. Howard's *Human Visual Orientation* (1982) clearly indicates the problems involved. Howard does an excellent job, in the early part of the book, of indicating how we must integrate information from the retina, the head-movement system, and the eye-movement system in order to locate things relative to our current position. But this is only part of the story. We also have to take account of the influence of gravity in deciding upon the orientation of objects and, in addition, we must integrate information from the other senses. Finally, Howard considers the question of how we take location and orientation into account when we recognize familiar objects in unfamiliar positions. The book certainly does not explain how all of these complex accommodations are achieved, but it does pose the problems in an interesting and comprehensible way.

Stanley Coren of the University of British Columbia has already been cited for his work on laterality. He has, however, a considerable number of other research interests, and over the past few years he must rank, in terms of books and papers published, as Canada's most prolific psychologist. One of his major interests has been perceptual illusions, and in his book *Seeing Is Deceiving: The Psychology of Visual Illusions* (1978, with Joan Girgus) Coren explores various theoretical issues concerning illusions. Two general types of illusion theories are presented: structural theories which propose that the structural properties of the optical or neural system are responsible, and strategy theories which propose that the illusions arise during the cognitive processing of the visual information. Neither is seen to be capable of a complete explanation of illusions and the authors feel that illusions are probably due to an interaction of structure and strategy. They emphasize the fact that illusions do not represent a breakdown of normal perceptual processing but are simply the by-product of normal processes operating in particular circumstances. Thus understanding illusions will help us to understand normal perception.

DEVELOPMENTAL AND SOCIAL PSYCHOLOGY

There have been fewer Canadian contributions in this general area, proportionately to other countries, than in the two areas already referred to in this chapter. Some important work has been done, but the work has not been on the same scale, nor has it had the same impact, as the work in physiological psychology or cognition. There is no obvious reason for this, though it may be that the funding patterns in Canadian psychology, growing as they did out of the original strong emphasis on physiological psychology, have been less generous to those areas which are seen by some to be less obviously 'scientific.'

Among the earlier work in developmental psychology was that of David Olson of the Ontario Institute for Studies in Education. In common with many of his contemporaries, Olson worked within a loosely defined Piagetian framework which emphasizes the role of interactive experience in the development of knowledge. This approach characterizes his book *Cognitive Development: The Child's Acquisition of Diagonality* (1970). In general this book maintains that the elaboration of the perceptual world by mastering performatory skills in various media accounts for the development of intelligence. This process is detailed in empirical studies involving the acquisition of the idea of the diagonal, something that young children have surprising difficulty in mastering. Olson makes a reasonable case for his general position, but his emphasis upon performance as a necessary alternative to verbal instruction indicates that this book was written at a time when the belief that children could learn almost without any guidance from others was more prevalent than it is now.

Also working in the Piagetian tradition is Charles Brainerd of the University of Alberta. His book *Piaget's Theory of Intelligence* (1978) gives an overview of Piaget's theory and a detailed examination of the four stages of cognitive development. In this respect the book is not unique, but it does serve a valuable purpose by reviewing several studies in which classroom curricula were developed according to Piagetian theory. Brainerd reaches the surprising conclusion that there is, in these studies, no difference between the Piaget-inspired curricula and regular forms of instruction. This observation is particularly striking because there is usually some beneficial novelty effect whenever any new methods are introduced into the classroom. While Brainerd concludes that the teachers involved in these experiments may have been responsible for the disappointing results, one cannot help but observe that the findings are not inconsistent with the growing skepticism which surround Piaget's theory in general.

Another important contributor to the area of developmental psychology has been John Macnamara of McGill University. His stimulating book *Names for Things* (1982) deals with the extremely difficult topic of meaning and its acquisition by children. Macnamara suggests that categories are useful to the child in discriminating phonological rules, rather than the other way around. He also claims that the idea of reference should be regarded as a cognitive primitive, in that the child does not need to learn the idea of referring. The book tends towards the iconoclastic. For example, Macnamara claims that there is no difference between the child and the adult in the structure of intelligence. This flies in the face of Piagetian orthodoxy, but is is a claim which is gaining increasing empirical support. There is little question that this book will generate much discussion and research.

A major impact in the field of social psychology has been made by John Berry of Queen's University. His particular research interest has been in the area of cross-cultural psychology, where he has been involved in editing three important collections of papers (Berry and P. Dasen, *Culture and Cognition*, 1974; Berry and W.J. Lonner, *Applied Cross-Cultural Psychology*, 1975; H.C. Triandis and Berry, *Handbook of Cross-Cultural Psychology*, Volume II: *Methodology*, 1980) as well as writing many research papers of his own. His *Human Ecology and Cognitive Style* (1976) presents his position on cultural relativism. He argues that the way people perceive and think about the world is influenced by the cultural adaptations they make to environmental demands. Thus perception and thought are not invariable universals but are dependent upon environmental and cultural conditions. While this relativistic position is not supported by all workers in the field, it does provide a framework for research and this is desirable whatever the final outcome.

PERSONALITY AND CLINICAL PSYCHOLOGY

This section can be prefaced by the same general remarks that were used to introduce the previous section. A major contributor in the field of personality has been Norman Endler of York University, whose work on developing an interactional theory of personality is renowned. This work, which seeks to explain personality characteristics through considering the interaction of traits with particular situations, is extensively discussed in *Personality at the Cross-roads: Current Issues in Interactional Psychology* (1977), which Endler edited with D. Magnusson. Endler's important paper in this volume, on the role of person-situation interactions, clearly explains his position. Endler is also the author of a moving book on his experiences when suffering from, and receiving therapy for, extreme clinical depression. *Holiday of Darkness* (1982) is an impressive work which explores depression from the perspective of a trained and experienced psychologist. Particularly interesting is Endler's reaction to the experience of electroconvulsive therapy. This is a controversial technique, with no obvious theoretical basis, which is generally deplored by psychologists. Endler was initially skeptical, but the book describes how he came to admire the effectiveness of the therapy, and he ends by strongly endorsing it. Of all the books referred to in this chapter this is certainly the most accessible to the general reader and possibly the most interesting.

Another major figure in the field of personality theory is Jerry Wiggins of the University of British Columbia. Wiggins is well known for his development of the circumplex approach to personality theory. This is a somewhat technical system which demands, for its full comprehension, extensive statistical knowledge but, simply stated, it involves the arrangement of personality variables into a circle with opposing traits being at opposite ends of diameters of the circle. The best summary of this position is 'A Psychological Taxonomy of Trait-Descriptive Terms: The Interpersonal Domain' (*Journal of Personality and Social Psychology*, 1979), but the material is quite technical. Wiggins is also the author of *Personality and Prediction: Principles of Personality Assessment* (1973), a widely cited account of the rather sophisticated techniques and procedures involved in personality testing. The book is a review of the procedures which might be used to extract the maximum amount of information from data which are inherently 'noisy' or inexact. As with his 1979 paper, the book requires some technical expertise to be fully understood but it is clearly written and many parts are comprehensible to an untrained reader.

Recently much attention has been focused, in the area of clinical psychology, on the work of Donald Meichenbaum of Waterloo University. Meichenbaum's main contribution has been to add a cognitive element to the once-popular behaviour therapy. He propounds his ideas in two books, *Cognitive-Behaviour Modification* (1977) and *Stress Reduction and Prevention* (1982, ed. with M. Jaremko). These books emphasize the importance of thought processes as well as behaviour patterns in therapy: ie, they argue that one should become aware of negative thoughts and think out beforehand beneficial patterns of behaviour. Meichenbaum maintains that attempts to change behaviour without attempting to change the accompanying thought processes are not likely to succeed in many instances. This move, in therapy, away from more rigid behavioural principles parallels a trend in the discipline as a whole towards cognitive interpretations of psychological phenomena. There is, however, a feeling when reading Meichenbaum's work that this is scant advance on the exhortations of Norman Vincent Peale to think positive thoughts. Some may regard this as a sad commentary on the current state of psychotherapy, while others might argue that the intuitions of an earlier age are not necessarily incompatible with scientifically based psychological understanding.

Robert Hare, of the University of British Columbia, has attained an international reputation in the study and diagnosis of psychopathy. His *Psychopathy* (1970) has been translated into several languages. While the author has developed and changed his views since the publication of that book, the work still represents much of the current thinking about psychopaths. These troublesome individuals, who might, at the risk of oversimplification, be characterized as having no conscience, constitute a serious social problem.

They are responsible for more than 50 per cent of crimes in Western society, and almost all the multiple murderers are classic psychopaths. In his book Hare argues that psychopaths suffer from a neurophysiological deficit which manifests itself in low cortical arousal. The condition may be due to early childhood experience or to a more fundamental learning deficit, demonstrated by the fact that psychopaths do not readily develop conditioned fear responses. While Hare argues for the development of long-term treatment programs, involving such things as therapeutic communities, his more recent research has suggested that the long-term prognosis for psychopaths is not good and that the only 'cure' lies in increasing age.

GENDER DIFFERENCES

In the past this topic has been of only intermittent interest to Canadian psychologists, but recently two books have focused attention on this important area. *A World of Difference* (1982) by Esther Greenglass of York University is a useful comprehensive survey of the whole field. The author cites several hundred studies covering such topics as stereotypes, socialization, cognitive ability and achievement, sexuality, the role of the family and employment in reinforcing gender roles, and sex differences in psychopathology. The book, not surprisingly in the light of contemporary wisdom, places a heavy emphasis on social learning as the primary cause of sex-related differences and consequently downplays biological factors. It is certainly reasonable to look for environmental causes for any human differences before invoking immutable biological influences, but there is a tendency in this area to use glib explanations based upon imperfectly understood principles of learning when a more skeptical caution may be in order. As in many topics dealt with by the social sciences, it is difficult to divorce research and explanation in this field from political polemic. This is not to deny that a counterbalance to prior sexist attitudes favouring males is definitely required; the question is whether it should be presented in the form of established scientific fact.

The other book to be mentioned in this area is *Language, the Sexes and Society* (1985) by Philip Smith of the University of British Columbia. In eight carefully argued chapters Smith marshalls a variety of evidence which indicates convincingly that there is a strong masculine bias in everyday English speech and that this bias influences the relations between the sexes. These findings reiterate what many linguists and feminists have long been saying, and while Smith is largely content to define the current situation, he is clearly not unsympathetic to the desirability of change. His book is a useful concentration of material on a topic which has received, in the past, much emotional but sporadic attention.

CONCLUSION

There is obviously no unifying theme or themes in Canadian psychology. The work of all the psychologists cited here is linked into the various streams of research which constitute an international endeavour. The discipline, with the possible exception of research into the intellectual capacities of bilinguals, is not concerned with problems specific to any nation. Thus there is no 'Canadian Psychology' just as there is no 'Canadian Chemistry' or 'Canadian Biology.' It is to be hoped, however, that this chapter demonstrates that the Canadian contribution to psychology as a whole has been, and continues to be, of major importance.

16 From Author to Reader

FRANCESS G. HALPENNY

The previous volumes of the *Literary History*, like this one, concentrated on certain kinds of books written and read, and made only occasional reference to how they were made available to their publics. A significant part of their 'history,' however, has to do with how they fit into the complex action of what can be called the 'book trade': the linked process by which writing, of all kinds, is created, published, printed, sold, distributed, and read. This process has been visualized as an active circle; by it the creations of authors are produced and sent on their way to readers largely through libraries and bookstores, and the reactions of readers to these writings flow back to the authors. Enumerative and descriptive bibliographies record and analyze books as they enter the process. Literary history concerns itself with the results of the process (remembering that authors, who are readers as well, have a place not only at the initiation of the circle but also at its completion). Examinations of the book trade can take in many associated topics: the role of periodicals and magazines in attracting readers and assisting the careers of authors; the literary and artistic culture that surrounds writers and publishers; the dynamics of publishing; the significance of copyright for all actors in the trade (particularly acute in Canada for the period of this volume in such matters as the definition of market territories and the ramifications of photocopying); the technologies of printing, binding, and distribution; the role of reviewers and critics; the activities of bookstores and libraries; the place of reading itself in contemporary culture (who reads? what do they read? how and when do they read?).

Interest in the 'book trade' has developed a noticeable momentum in recent years in several countries. In the United States, for instance, there have been sociological studies of publishing such as *Books: The Culture and Commerce of Publishing* and *Getting into Print: The Decision-Making Process in Scholarly Publishing*, with the names of Lewis A. Cosser and Walter W. Powell prominent. Considerable attention to interrelationships within the trade is demonstrated in such titles as *Reading in the 1980s*, *The Quality of Trade*

Book Publishing in the 1980s, *Publishers and Librarians: A Foundation for Dialogue*, and *The New Publishers*, all of them serious symposia bringing together experience and reflection from various sectors of the book world. Britain has contributed such examinations as those by Peter Mann, which include his *From Author to Reader*. In mounting the World Congress on Books of 1982, UNESCO sponsored a series of 'Studies on Books and Reading,' among which items on *The Future of the Book* take up such topics as the impact of new technologies and the changing role of reading.[1]

This broad theme in a Canadian context lay behind an important symposium of the Royal Society of Canada in 1980; the published proceedings, *The Written Word / Prestige de l'écrit*, with contributions in English and in French, presents a variety of perspectives. Literary authors reflect upon what spurred them to create (D.G. Jones, Antonine Maillet, James Reaney); so do scholars (John F. Bosher, Philippe Sylvain, Ann Saddlemyer); other contributors discuss publishing in relation to authors and readers (Francess G. Halpenny), refer to translation (Naim Kattan), and to libraries, bibliography, and new technologies (Guy Sylvestre, Anne B. Piternick, Basil Stuart-Stubbs), and examine the role of such supporting structures as universities and councils (Alexander G. McKay, Vianney Décarie, Denis M. Shaw). Commenting on the symposium's topic, under the deceptive title 'Nothing but a Book,' George Whalley asserts that artists, scholars, editors, designers, and printers have one common purpose: to ensure and share 'the integrity of the author's glimpse of a shapely possibility.'

But sustained and studious interest in the processes of the book trade in Canada has been slow to develop. Any bibliography of publishing in Canada for the last twenty-five years is largely taken up with reports, briefs, and studies prepared in response to recurring crises in the trade and soon part of grey literature. Conference discussions occur under many auspices but they are too frequently those of panels: brief, slight, ephemeral, repetitive. Nevertheless signs of interest in more solid work are appearing, and materials are being identified or assembled which can relate to all sectors of the trade.[2] Literary biography and autobiography, for instance, more common in recent years, provide valuable insights into the experience of Canadian authors as writers in search of publishers and publics. Biographies of Frances Brooke, Anna Jameson, John Richardson, Gilbert Parker, Sara Jeannette Duncan, Bliss Carman, Charles G.D. Roberts, Pauline Johnson, Hugh MacLennan (significantly subtitled 'A Writer's Life'), A.M. Klein, E.J. Pratt, Roderick Haig-Brown, and Irving Layton are cases in point, whether these authors have published in Canada or elsewhere. So too are the collections of *Letters* by Frederick Philip Grove (1975, ed. Desmond Pacey), Susanna Moodie (1985, ed. Carl Ballstadt, Elizabeth Hopkins, and Michael Peterman) and Bliss Carman (1982, ed. H. Pearson Gundy), as well as the opening volumes of the

Selected Journals of L.M. Montgomery covering 1889–1921 (1985, 1987, ed. Mary Rubio and Elizabeth Waterston): all of these disclose impetuses both internal and external that have led people into the book trade. Kathleen Coburn's *In Pursuit of Coleridge* (1977) makes an autobiographical statement about the interactions of a Canadian environment and international scholarship in the preparation of the Coleridge editions; Earle Birney in *Spreading Time: Remarks on Canadian Writing and Writers* (1980) pungently recalls a poet's career, for the years 1904–49. Charles Stacey invigorates *A Date with History: Memoirs of a Canadian Historian* (1983) with his account of the perils of publishing official history; Irving Layton is characteristically vigorous about life and work in the first volume of his autobiography, *Waiting for the Messiah* (1985). *William Arthur Deacon: A Canadian Literary Life* (1982) by Clara Thomas and John Lennox has much to say about the cultural climate in which Deacon, a reviewer and publicist of Canadian writing, worked from the 1920s to the 1940s. The reminiscences of publishers are few, but two particularly – Lovat Dickson's *The House of Words* (1963) and John Gray's *Fun Tomorrow* (1978) – in recounting the pleasures and pressures of the industry make their readers sense what being 'a publisher' means.

With Canadian writing and attention to Canadian writers on the increase in the decades after 1960, articles, prefaces, and interviews – in print, on the air, and on film – have multiplied. Any study of the intricate relationships that give Canadian authors a sense of place and subject and that link their works to publishing and readers must take all of them into account. As I complete this chapter, for example, I pick up *Books in Canada*'s tenth anniversary issue (May 1986), to read its editors' notes on fifteen years of reviewing and Al Purdy on 'As for Them and Their Houses,' a record of 'One man's adventures in the publishing jungle.' Then I hear Carol Shields on CBC's 'State of the Arts' read from a diary which tells of Winnipeg as the setting in which she writes, of correspondence with her editor while the short stories of *Small Ceremonies* (1976) were shaped into a collection, of the reassurance of meeting other writers and readers in launchings at Mary Scorer Books. The reflections, memories, frustrations, and facts in even such glancing material are to be seized if the book world of Canada is to be felt and understood. They especially inform two anniversary publications (both with contributions in English and in French). The twenty–fifth anniversary issue of *Canadian Literature* (Spring 1984), in itself a tribute to a justified conviction about Canadian writing and its cultural place that overcame the 'disbelief' of 1959, contains moving essays by Henry Kreisel, Jane Rule, Rudy Wiebe, and Daphne Marlatt that provide vivid testimony about the many backgrounds from which Canadian writers have sought their place. *The Arts in Canada: The Last Fifty Years*, edited by W.J. Keith and B.-Z. Shek for the fiftieth anniversary of the *University of Toronto Quarterly* (1980), provides in analysis, memoir, and anecdote – by Northrop Frye, Hugh MacLennan, Ralph Gustafson, Robertson Davies, and George Woodcock for literary arts in English – an appreciation of the development that has made the 1980s so unlike the 1930s for all who write and all who publish and read Canadian books.

A long perspective on the historical interconnections within the book trade has created a new field of scholarly enquiry – France, Great Britain, the United States, and Germany being especially active. France inspired this emphasis (*l'histoire du livre*). As Robert Darnton observes, the new book historians of the 1960s such as Lucien Febvre and Henri-Jean Martin 'tried to uncover the general pattern of book production and consumption over long stretches of time' and for many kinds of publications. Scholars have pursued this interest in 'the book as a force in history' in conferences, new journals (for example, *Publishing History*), new centres (for example, Institut d'Étude du Livre in Paris, Center for the Book in the Library of Congress), and new books. Historians, sociologists, literary scholars, and librarians have become involved, with librarians often protesting that the analytical bibliography in which they have long been engaged is itself an intergral part of the 'history of the book' and not to be regarded as simply a support to textual editing. This expanding, and sometimes confusing, field is outlined in Darnton's 'What Is the History of Books?' (*Daedalus*, 1982) with generous reference notes and indications of necessary research in the circuit of author, publisher, printer, distributor, bookseller, reader, library.[3]

For Canada, little as yet belongs formally to this field of study or connects with it. Historical writing on the trade has usually been fragmentary, intended often to serve some special immediate need, except for such work as H. Pearson Gundy's pioneer monographs and chapters.[4] The weakness of publishing archives had been a concern (McMaster University is now collecting in this area[5]); the international connections from the beginnings pose a special challenge of access and opportunity for scholars; the collections of writers' papers building apace in depositories at the University of Toronto, Queen's, Calgary, UBC, and in the National Library have been used largely for biography rather than for this kind of study. The Canadian Library Association has a section on Library History and has published a set of articles in *Canadian Library Journal* (December 1981) and, in book form, a collection of *Readings* (1986) edited by Peter McNally of the library school at McGill. Canada, however, does have now several centres for the book: the Institut Québécois de recherche sur la culture and the Groupe de Recherche sur l'Édition littéraire au Québec are publishing; in 1984 the Research Institute for Comparative Literature at the University of Alberta set up a program called 'Towards a History of the Literary Institution in Canada'; at Simon Fraser University the Canadian Centre for Studies in Publishing came into official being in 1987 with an advisory board largely drawn from the book trade and with a program for research and education.[6] The year 1985 saw a book–length scholarly study appear which is an essential foundation for future work – George L. Parker's *The Beginnings of the Book Trade in Canada*. Parker takes the story to 1900, demonstrating in detail how 'many of the characteristics and the problems of the twentieth-century book trade had their origins in Canada's unique nineteenth-century situation, first as a group of separate colonies and then as an underpopulated, rather poor, and economically dependent Dominion.' For his chosen period Parker had no precedents; there were only inadequate histories of publishers, and too few biographies and letters, cultural and intellectual studies, statistics, and descriptive bibliographies. Nevertheless his book impressively documents the organization of the trade, the emergence of the colonial and Canadian author, the means of bookselling, the technology of printing, the perils of copyright, and the builders of a national publishing industry. It is a straightforward narrative account, which invites the drawing out of cultural and social implications. Parker makes frequent reference to the Bibliographical Society of Canada's publications, demonstrating the value of its efforts since 1946 to provide research documentation about many aspects of the book trade. The current decade has seen the meticulous work of another scholar of the book trade, Elizabeth Hulse's *A Dictionary of Toronto Printers, Publishers, Booksellers and the Allied Trades 1798–1900* (1982).

The first and second editions of this *Literary History* contained a chapter by H. Pearson Gundy which provides a history of publishing in Canada until 1900; it is especially useful as an introduction to and anticipation of much that followed. Gundy outlines the overlapping relationships between printing, bookselling, and publishing in Canada as the book trade developed by means of imports, reprints, and some original publishing, and he indicates the long-lasting hindrances which were remedied by imperial and dominion copyright legislation in 1875, 1886, and 1900 (Parker's book contains detailed discussion of this topic). Gundy introduces the early firms – headed by such men as John Lovell, George Maclean Rose, William Copp, and William Briggs – and refers to authors such as William Kirby, Susanna Moodie, Sara Jeannette Duncan, Gilbert Parker, Ralph Connor, and May Agnes Fleming, some of whom were very successful commercially and internationally. He describes the threefold division of Canadian publishing activity into agency representation and educational and trade lists. This division and balance are still characteristic of the trade today, although the emphases have shifted.

Publishing in Canada was to undergo many changes particularly after the First World War. These are remarked upon in Volumes I–III of the *Literary*

History of Canada, especially by Gordon Roper dealing with fiction (1880–1920) in Volume ɪ, Desmond Pacey describing 'The Writer and his Public 1920–1960' in Volume ɪɪ, Claude Bissell speaking of 'Politics and Literature in the 1960s,' and W.H. New and George Woodcock of 'Fiction' and 'Poetry' in Volume ɪɪɪ – with echoes in Northrop Frye's two conclusions.

During the 1920s and 1930s original Canadian trade publishing in English, using educational and agency publishing as a base, gradually developed, in firms with their headquarters chiefly in Toronto. In the later 1950s, recovering from the setbacks of World War ɪɪ, publishing began to expand again, and with it the original publishing of Canadian titles. The 1960s strengthened the cultural community of Canada; the new mood and the new energy, symbolized in the Centennial and in Expo '67, had profound effects. New publishing firms were established, often founded by editors or authors with a sole or major interest in Canadian writers; older Canadian firms adjusted their lists to the trend of the times. Owned by Canadians, the new houses, many of them small, were vocal in their commitment to Canadian writing, and to greater recognition by public and government of its cultural importance. They were set up all across the country, and they often responded directly to the work of writers in their region or to the interests of regional audiences. In doing so, they answered and helped to develop a consciousness of regional identities that had actually been characteristic of Canadians from colonial days. They also helped challenge many of the received conventions about Canadian literary models and the quality of Canadian writing. In the two decades following 1965, books and periodicals of Canadian origin, with Canadian authors, from Canadian-owned houses of all sizes, gained greater recognition and acceptance among readers and took an unapologetic place on shelves and stands; in bookstores particularly, Canadian trade books won a greater percentage of sales.

In the same period, and with much of the same energy, various groups – of teachers at all levels, librarians, general public, parents, journalists and publicists, writers, officials – were seriously questioning the way Canada was represented in schools and universities. A major impetus for review of the situation in the universities was provided by the first two volumes of T.H.B. Symons's report for the Commission on Canadian Studies, *To Know Ourselves* (1975). The very title was both a summary of the need the Commission saw and a call to action, engendering country-wide discussion. Changes came in direct response, and then indirectly, as the validity of the argument, and the interests of students themselves, were recognized. The long-delayed acknowledgment of the desirability of studying Canadian subject-matter, and of the credibility of research in Canadian studies in the humanities, social sciences, and science, led to increased instruction and encouraged scholarly investigation. In many universities a course in Canadian literature had by the

1980s become compulsory as part of a program in English literary studies. As Claude Bissell put it in Volume III, 'Canadian literature, as late as the early sixties a nervous and self-conscious visitor in the halls of academe, acquired status and recognition.' By 1986, Canadian literature (as well as history and social studies), had also made a steady appearance in university programs in the United States, Great Britain, Europe, Asia, and the South Pacific (there are thirteen members in the International Council for Canadian Studies); this development continues to startle Canadian citizens, to challenge Canadian politicians, and to nettle those in academic circles who in the name of internationalism still consider professed Canadianists upstarts. The importance of the university and college market for the decisions of Canadian publishers is undoubted – paperbacks have it very much in mind (the New Canadian Library was created originally for it) and a good deal of the publishing of non-fiction depends on use for course or supplementary reading.

Alongside trade and college publishers the university presses should also be mentioned. Their development depended on the development of scholarship in Canada, slow in the years surrounding World War II, and accelerating with the creation of support for it through the research councils and the Canada Council (founded 1957), with the growth in numbers of universities and subject fields, and with the increasing priority ascribed to research from the 1970s on. The University of Toronto Press, instrumental in the 1940s and 1950s in the maintenance of the journals in which research of those years was recorded, expanded its book program from a few titles yearly to an average of one hundred, and moved into fields of scholarship beyond the Canadian history and social sciences that previously had much of its attention. *The University as Publisher* (1961), ed. Eleanor Harman, gives an account of this change. The Press was joined from the 1960s on by the university presses of British Columbia, Alberta, Calgary, Manitoba, Wilfrid Laurier, McGill (later McGill-Queen's), and Carleton, each of which developed a list reflecting a deliberate choice of fields. Titles in Canadian history, social sciences, literary criticism, and biography maintain a significant if varying place on the lists of all these presses, with the university market always in view but with some spillover into trade. In fact they issue some titles with trade sale very much in mind, in hopes of support for their more specialized titles, and responding in some cases to regional interests in history and landscape and writing. The annual number of titles for each press, Toronto excepted, will vary from below ten to around thirty-five. The professionalism of their production has increased along with that of the Canadian book trade generally. The journal *Scholarly Publishing*, initiated by Toronto in 1969, brings an international perspective to the distribution of scholarship.

In one particular area Canadian university press publishing from the 1960s on has won international renown: the creation and support of many-volumed

editions involving teams of editors. These editions have meant close association, over time, of editorial and other press departments with scholars at
many sites. The process has encouraged innovations and refinements of scholarly method. The new knowledge carried by these editions, to be fully appreciated only after they are completed, comes from scholarly interests which
may seem traditional to some but which are undeniable strengths in the
Canadian academic community. One such project, in the Canadian field, is
The Collected Writings of Louis Riel in five volumes (University of Alberta
Press 1985), ed. George F.G. Stanley et al. The work of the Centre for
Editing Early Canadian Texts, under the general editorship of Mary Jane
Edwards, began with *The History of Emily Montague* and *Canadian Crusoes*
(Carleton University Press 1985, 1986); it is effectively encouraging Canadian
literary studies on a path that should lead to authoritative texts and to full
and accurate knowledge of conditions of authorship, opportunities of pub-
lishing, and processes of production. In 1972 the annual Conference on
Editorial Problems of the University of Toronto convened on the topic *Editing
Canadian Texts* (1975), and W.H. New provided then an extended challenge:
'To locate the texts we need in order to articulate [the spirit of our culture]
more clearly is the task we face. To make them available, to ensure as far
as possible their accuracy, to foster an interest in them, and to encourage
further study of the issues they raise are challenges and responsibilities in
which we all share.' The agenda is still full.

The growth in sheer number of Canadian titles published was considerable
in the years covered by volumes III and IV of the *Literary History*. All their
commentators refer to it, and the growth occurred also in types of publications
they do not cover.[7] Numbers in themselves are not significant except in the
sense that, since publishing is an industry, a build-up in traffic assumes a
push behind it and a destination in front of it. But the numbers have other
meanings. An increase in publishing outlets suggests a wider opportunity for
authors to find the kind of publisher they need and want, an important aspect
for the development of literature. More authors able to write and publish add
to the stimulus for all of them in effort and skill. And that advance in skill
is demonstrated not only by the spectrum of successes from traditional to
experimental in the literary genres but also among other publications, where
works stand out more often and more conspicuously from the stodgy and the
inept. Publishers old and new have a maturity and sophistication about what
they are doing in building their lists that simply did not exist in the late
1950s and early 1960s. They now understand better the impulses to authorship
and the dynamics of publishing, especially of publishing in Canada, the
techniques of the book (thus enhancing the physical qualities of book and
periodical production), and the wiles of promotion. The role of senior editors
is given more general attention: in 1981 William Toye of Oxford University

Press was awarded the Eve Orpen Award; 1983 saw the Molson Prize go to Francess G. Halpenny of the University of Toronto Press; in 1985 that patron editor Robert Weaver became the first recipient of University College's Distinguished Visitorship in Canadian Culture; 1986 saw the appearance of 'A Douglas Gibson Book' within the McClelland & Stewart imprint. Authors are, of course, rarely satisfied with what their publishers do at any stage of publication, especially in promotion, but this very tension has often been effective. Most would likely admit that as a group of artists they are in better hands today than many of their predecessors were. To serve their interests and to add to the professionalism of the book trade has come a much more prominent role for the literary agent, advising on manuscripts and selling rights for first book and periodical publication, for paperback or foreign editions, or for translations.

Professionalism is more evident, too, in the movement of Canadian books abroad through special promotional missions, at the Frankfurt and Bologna fairs, and by co-editions: all features of the 1970s and 1980s. Canadian-owned publishers have also been persistent in working for recognition of Canada as a separate market by publishers in Britain and the United States so that they may strengthen their lists here with Canadian editions and be able to sell their original titles as editions abroad. In this climate of exchange Margaret Atwood, Robertson Davies, and Alice Munro are not just familiar names on American and British surveys of active titles but have been on the short list for the Booker Prize; Alice Munro and Mavis Gallant are regulars of *The New Yorker*; and they are only four of the Canadian authors now regularly appearing in editions or periodicals issued beyond Canadian borders. Not so happy is the fact that those teaching Canadian literature, history, and social sciences abroad still find it difficult to obtain the range of titles they need, a gap which certain bookstores specializing in Canadian books, acting as wholesalers, have moved to fill.

A kind of restrained euphoria is understandable for anyone reviewing the developments outlined in the volumes of the *Literary History*, this one included. But these volumes deal only with certain types of presses and certain kinds of books, and their emphasis could be misleading for readers. The book trade brings to the Canadian public many other kinds of books, and depends heavily, especially for its financial survival, on those which are not 'literary' works or specialized studies in the humanities and social sciences. Educational publishing for the schools is one such activity,[8] still highly significant today even though it has been beleaguered in recent years by shifts in attitude to curriculum prescriptions and in priorities for materials to support teaching. The efforts of originating Canadian publishers to respond to the pressure of recent years to increase Canadian subject-matter and Canadian authorship in educational materials (in the face of the many so-called

'Canadian' texts which are basically Canadianized or partly Canadianized versions of foreign texts) are important in the context of the present volume, for such an increase is one means of securing attention to Canadian writing by pupils-become-adults. Publishing trade books created abroad is also still very important, and through the agencies or branch plants of foreign firms is likely to remain so. It is simple fact that Canadians who read in English, sharing a language with two powerful publishing countries and having a history of association with both – and particularly exposed today to the pervasive promotion of American films, television, and magazines – are customers for American or English trade books, in all sorts of subject fields. Answering their interest is a large part of the activity of publishers, booksellers, librarians, book promotion agencies, and reviewers in Canada.[9]

It has also to be noted that a good proportion even of the trade books written and originating in Canada and offered in trade bookstores are not those analyzed in this literary history. Many of the volumes of fiction will show up in these stores, as will most of the biography and history, many of the children's books, a little of the poetry and drama, a sampling of the disciplines (they appear in only slightly larger quantity in most campus stores). What the stock in the trade stores will with certainty include, however, along with the titles from abroad, is Canadian travel and picture books, cookbooks, several levels of local history, popular history, the Pierre Berton-Peter Newman-Robert Bateman-Richard Gwyn bestsellers, and a slowly growing number of popular titles in detective or thriller or romance stories.

Paperbacks are the stuff of success for trade and college bookstores (and they are increasingly apparent in public and school libraries). The very format appeals to a peripatetic society. Foreign titles are a large part of this stock, but Canadian publishers count on paperbacks for original or reprint editions. For some time these usually appeared in quality (or trade) formats; most will continue to do so given the problems of pricing the quantities likely to be sold. Nevertheless agitation grew to get Canadian authors on to the racks. The emergence of imprints such as Bantam-Seal, PaperJacks, General, and NAL in mass market was a significant development of the late 1970s and 1980s. Penguin Canada in the early 1980s took an aggressive interest in a Canadian list of new or reprint fiction; that list is, of course, trade paperback.

In speaking of bookstores it is necessary to distinguish types. The bookstore chains (in 1986 there were 197 stores in the Classics-W.H. Smith chain alone) have a large volume of the sales but also a hard interest in quick and heavy turnover, and they stock sizeable numbers of foreign books. They are not the place to find even all the examples of Canadian writing just designated as usual bookstore stock. It is on the independent bookstores – from A Pair of Trindles in Halifax, to The Double Hook in Montreal, to Longhouse in Toronto (established in 1972, the first store to have an exclusively Canadian stock), to Mary Scorer in Winnipeg, to Duthie Books in Vancouver – that readers must depend for adequate displays (in hardback or paperback) of most Canadian authors. A mix of American, British, and Canadian books similar in kind to that in many trade bookstores is typical of public libraries. These libraries are responding, necessarily, to the reading interests of the local citizens who fund them. It is only in the larger public libraries that the range and richness of contemporary Canadian writing can be met and enjoyed. The large academic libraries particularly are building collections on which much current and future study and research must depend, hampered though they have been in the 1980s by budget cuts. The National Library of Canada, founded only in 1952, now plays a central role.[10] It maintains the national collection through retrospective acquisition and legal deposit, publishes the national record, *Canadiana*, and provides, in association with the larger research libraries, a major support to interlibrary loan.[11]

This cautionary adjunct to an account of publishing developments will perhaps have hinted that the undoubted achievements and new freedoms in Canadian books rest upon a fragile base. That is indeed a chastening truth, as the continually expanding bibliography of official and unofficial reports, briefs, and surveys of Canadian publishing attests. The problem is market: Canada is a large country, with a scattered reading public, which has limited access to good bookstores and which shows a preference for imported material. Canadian books have a share of the total Canadian market which runs at 25–29 per cent.

In a capital intensive industry, Canadian publishers are chronically undercapitalized. Many of the newer ones, brave in their convictions, offer literary works which they have inadequate resources to promote effectively and which do not by kind have a wide sale. The regional titles that have cheered the scene are often difficult to sell other than regionally. Statistics are telling. In a useful study of titles based on *Canadian Books in Print*, Canadian-content books for the years 1979–82 were divided into categories such as biography, description and travel, history, Canadian literature (poetry, fiction, short story, history, and criticism) and assigned to types of publishers. There were 157 publishing companies for these titles, 23 foreign-controlled, 134 Canadian-owned. Of the 134 Canadian-owned, 73 were trade publishers: 12 large (over 20 titles per year), 25 medium (6–20 titles), 36 small (5 titles or fewer). There were 42 literary presses; 10 children's publishers; 9 university presses. The importance of the Canadian-owned group for Canadian-content books, and the size and scope of the firms in that group, should be noted. By genres, the study showed that in fiction the large trade publishers offered 73 titles and the literary presses 24; the foreign-controlled only 14. For the short story, the same groups published 4, 24, and 5; the literary presses stand out. In biography these same three groups report 23, 19 and 10, but the medium trade supply 46; the spread of these figures reflects a strong interest of Canadian readers, but again the identity of the publishers is important. Note poetry. There were 131 titles from Canadian-owned publishers; of these, 113 came from literary presses; none came from foreign-controlled and fewer than 20 from trade publishers. In no other category than poetry did the literary presses move above 24 titles. To put the findings in another way, in 1983 literary publishers accounted for 86 per cent of all poetry published in Canada and 62 per cent of short fiction; however, the 12 large trade houses published 60 per cent of the novels, a better-selling genre. Fragility is palpable in these statistics.[12]

Most of the problems sketched here have always been associated with the publishing of Canadian books. They might have been concealed in the expansionism of the 1960s, but in the 1970s, with declining budgets among institutional puchasers and rising costs, they emerged to full scrutiny by publishers large and small. Recession and retrenchment are still forceful in the 1980s, affecting trade publishers, literary presses, and scholarly houses, and are likely to remain in some form. Inability to finance inventory is a special concern, and the short life of many Canadian books is a problem for bookstores and libraries.[13] Yet though statistics year after year confirm fragility, they also point to the essential contribution made by Canadian-owned publishers, large and small, to the literary world, and also to any general understanding of Canada. Fortunately for authors and readers, they have not lost their nerve. Their importance, underscored again and again by those who have studied publishing of books and periodicals in Canada, makes vital the sometimes uncertain but continued efforts of the federal government through the Canada Council to assist writers with grants, reading tours, and payment for public use, publishers of books and periodicals with block grants and special programs, and through the Department of Communications to provide more stability in the economics of the undertaking; provincial governments move in these directions also. Without such aid, survival would be impossible, and the Canadian voice would be muted.

It is customary in this context to hear a good deal about solutions to problems of production and distribution which new technology is said to provide. There is no question about the effect, and the help, of many modern methods in Canada. Word processors, computers micro mini and main frame, are used by many authors and publishers; discs, magnetic tape, phototypesetting, and offset printing have been accepted as routine in the production of books and periodicals. All have brought distinct advantages in cost and time despite problems of compatibility. Such technology is imperative for large works of reference where correction is integral in creation and updating from edition to edition a necessity. Many of these will be on-line in the future. Presses such as Coach House and Softwords and Frank Davey with

Swift Current have been working with electronic communication of other kinds of text to readers. Nevertheless, however produced, the outward form of books and periodicals in Canada, as elsewhere, remains to all intents and purposes the familiar printed and bound object. A book is, after all, a handy piece of technology which many observers claim may be hard to beat. Machine communication is increasing in an informal way among small groups of scientists, social scientists, and humanists, but there is no indication that transmission of specialized periodicals, even those in science, will largely shift to line in the immediate future.[14] The acceptability is not there among users, and the financial rewards far from certain. With literary works, where form and format and words have had an uncanny association in encouraging response, the page and the volume held in the hand are part of the act of appreciation, and few anticipate a radical shift here. Videodisc is a different communication which suggests intriguing possibilities for image in active combination with word. Its techniques and those of radio, film, and television, which depend on a response to moving sights and sounds, have already had some impact upon authors and publishers, affecting outward forms (eg, ad copy, jacket design) and content. Authors and publishers are transmitters, yet they are also affected by what they see or hear as well as read.

Facing its problems, the Canadian trade from author through to library and bookstores has not been idle in its own behalf: each sector has a professional organization which acts in self-help as well as in lobbying and maintains a liaison through the Book and Periodical Development Council. The Canadian Book Information Centre and the Children's Book Centre spread word of Canadian titles. Publicity about Canadian titles is indeed a key theme of all these support groups, publicity that will arouse the interest of possible readers sufficiently to send them in increasing numbers to bookstores and libraries asking for Canadian titles, which they will then be likely to find there. Canadian books need to be 'news,' and they would become more so if reviews in newspapers appeared steadily and widely across the country rather than being concentrated in a few papers and consolidated in syndicated columns; if the media gave more time to talks, interviews, readings, and dramatizations from the Canadian book trade (the importance of Peter Gzowski's sympathetic and informed response on CBC Radio's 'Morningside' is immense, as has been the effect of such film and television productions as 'Anne of Green Gables' or the 'The Grey Fox' or the series of 'Canadian Short Stories'); if Canada had the kind of full-scale weekly critiques of books and the book world available from London and New York (the nearest we can come is the restricted coverage of *Maclean's* and *Saturday Night* and the fuller columns of the monthlies *Quill & Quire* and *Books in Canada*; the last two are used as buying guides by public libraries or stores but cannot serve the same purpose or public as a *New York Times*). Canada also has need of some concerted program such as that of the Center for the Book in the Library of Congress, which is currently concerned with programs to celebrate reading as a reminder to Americans 'of the fundamental importance of reading in their personal lives and in the life of [their] nation.' The motive is an honourable concern with the values of reading; but practical results mean a better market. The literature is there, concludes W.J. Keith in *Canadian Literature in English* (1985), but the momentum can only be maintained if there is 'a body of educated and discriminating readers.'

Over the years *Quill & Quire*, the journal of the book trade, has provided an invaluable and full running account of ups and downs in Canada. In the 1970s and 1980s a number of book-length treatments of the state of publishing and the book trade appeared which merit attention. The two volumes of the Ontario Royal Commission on Book Publishing are still highly relevant in 1986: the first presents a set of *Background Papers* (1972), and the second, *Canadian Publishers & Canadian Publishing* (1973), a careful discussion of perils and imperatives. The *Summary of Briefs and Hearings* (1981) and the *Report* (1982) of the Federal Cultural Policy Review Committee (the Applebaum-Hébert enquiry) include the book trade and again analyze the challenges to and the cultural necessity of the publication of Canadian books. The report of an enquiry into *Canadian Scholarly Publishing* (1980), issued by the Social Sciences and Humanities Research Council, contains useful information about that activity as do the papers of the *Symposium in Scholarly Communication* (1981) sponsored by the Aid to Scholarly Publications Programme of the federations for the humanities and social sciences. Bernard Ostry's *The Cultural Connection* (McClelland & Stewart 1978) provided information and argument about the relation between culture and government policy. In 1983 Paul Audley published through James Lorimer & Company and the Canadian Institute for Economic Policy a study of *Canada's Cultural Industries: Broadcasting, Publishing, Records and Film* which discusses limitations of impact and the policies aimed at increasing it for Canadian periodicals and books; his study is particularly helpful in its assembly of information on the economic workings of the industry and its summaries in table form, but he makes strong points about cultural relevance as well.

James Lorimer's study of *Book Reading in Canada: The Audience, the Marketplace, and the Distribution System for Trade Books in English Canada* (Association of Canadian Publishers 1983) is a significant study – based on a 1978 government survey of the leisure reading of 17,600 adult Canadians – about the interests and habits of English-language book readers (those who had spent some time reading a book in the previous six weeks). Its wealth of tables and the interpretive text contain a substantial and often surprising profile which points to the importance of bookstores and personal connections as sources of books for leisure reading and for information about them, reveals habits of use for public libraries and book clubs, shows variations for sex, age, and location of readers, and indicates attitudes to Canadian books in general and by genre. History and social science, novels, and biography stand out as preferences among Canadian books. A positive attitude generally to Canadian books was evident among the respondents. Lorimer's suggestions for further research, and for possible adaptations of methods in the sectors of the trade, deserve greater attention than they have so far received. Francess G. Halpenny carried out under the auspices of the Book and Periodical Development Council a first study based on independent statistics of holdings of *Canadian Collections in Public Libraries* (1985), using 4650 titles in a sample of fifteen libraries across Canada, and discussed the findings about procedures in selection and acquisition and about attitudes to Canadian books and periodicals acquired during the study. The titles used for the sampling were those of the late 1970s, and many may now have been weeded from collections, currency being a policy of public libraries; the report's descriptive and reflective sections on the nature of Canadian collections and the attitudes to them of staff and users are as relevant as ever in the context of a literary history.

In 1983 the Association of Canadian Publishers and the Writers' Union convened in Ottawa a policy conference for which a set of background papers was prepared. Roy MacSkimming contributed an excellent study of trade publishing, and his concluding paragraph may serve also as a conclusion to this section of the account of the publishing process for Canadian writing:

At the present time we have in English Canada a trade publishing industry that is diverse, creative and increasingly professional. If there are financial and physical limitations on its capacity to publish, then writers and publishers will have to function creatively within those limitations, while working to improve the overall climate for their profession. The need for everyone who cares about books in Canada, however, is to ensure that those limitations do not become any more restrictive, that they do not silence voices that Canadians need to hear, that Canada's authors have adequate access to an audience in their homeland. That means joint and concerted efforts on several practical fronts: to adapt to electronic ordering systems, to improve physical distribution, to solve the returns problem, to get more Canadian books into libraries and schools, to ensure more long-range and sophisticated commitments of public support from both federal and provincial governments. If all these things are not done, the writing and publishing and reading of Canadian books will all suffer in the 1980s, and the real loser will be the Canadian people.[15]

This chapter will shift its attention now to some recent publications and projects, with a value for literary history, which are particularly, in creation and execution, acts of publishing entrepreneurship but which closely involve authors and editors. It is no coincidence that many of them are large works of reference, resources of information in which material about Canada is brought together; such works require collaboration to begin and to end. One such project is the *Dictionary of Canadian Biography*, established in 1959, with the model of the *DNB* in mind, at the University of Toronto Press; by 1985 it had marshalled hundreds of contributors and library and archival collections for its Volumes I–V, VIII–XI (organized by death dates of individuals), thus recording nearly 5000 lives. Noteworthy is the fact that the *DCB* is also *Dictionnaire biographique du Canada*, for the project is bilingual and bicultural in all aspects of its work. *DCB/DBC* (with Francess G. Halpenny as general editor from 1969 to 1988 and Jean Hamelin as directeur général adjoint from 1973) has won commendation for the scholarly and editorial standards it has set, but also for the readability of its biographies which become together a vast historical novel of Canada (in 1985 it was awarded the University of British Columbia Medal for biography). The project was initiated by means of a bequest from a Toronto businessman, James W. Nicholson, and its major support has come from the Canada Council and then the Social Sciences and Humanities Research Council. In 1970 Hurtig Publishers began the planning of a 'new, comprehensive, affordable encyclopedia of modern Canada' to which the Alberta government and other enterprises gave major support; sited at the University of Alberta, under James H. Marsh as editor-in-chief, it brought together hundreds of consultants and contributors from all subject fields, using manifold resources, to develop its list of articles ('the central creative act in the planning of an encyclopedia') and to compose over 8000 entries. The project was fully automated from first to last. The welcome given to *The Canadian Encyclopedia* in 1985 was instantaneous for its 'intricate sketch of Canada' and the approachability of its accounts; with gratifying sales, it proceeded to a revised and updated four-volume edition in 1988. Another fully automated project is that of the Canadian Institute for Historical Microreproductions. Prompted by the increasingly serious deterioration of library holdings because of acid paper and by the evident fact that the books and periodicals constituting Canada's cultural heritage are held in a miscellany of widely dispersed collections in Canada and abroad, this project set out to make available on microfiche Canadian monographs and pamphlets published before 1901; the total of these is now set at about 52,000. The project has entailed a major effort in locating and photographing titles, during which the dilapidation in collections has been grievously confirmed; in association with the National Library it is also creating detailed bibliographic records of immense value for research and information. CIHM has largely been supported to date by special grants from the Canada Council and the Social Sciences and Humanities Research Council. If funds are available, it will proceed to deal with periodicals before 1901. Ramsay Cook, Guy Sylvestre, and Basil Stuart-Stubbs have in turn chaired its board; Ernest Ingles and Robert Montague have been its executive officers.

At Oxford University Press, William Toye has given a direction to writing, editing, and publication which has provided other essential resources. First came *The Oxford Companion to Canadian History and Literature* of Norah Story (1967), which had a *Supplement* in 1973 with Toye as general editor. *The Oxford Companion to Canadian Literature*, with Toye as general editor and contributions from many writers, appeared in 1983 and at once, with its wide-ranging coverage of French and English authors, titles, genres, movements, and organizations, found a secure place for itself. For French-language works another large effort has resulted, under the editorship of Maurice Lemire, in the *Dictionnaire des œuvres littéraires du Québec* (6 vols, 1978–86). W.H. New has been editing for Bruccoli-Clark-Layman/Gale several volumes of *The Dictionary of Literary Biography* which are devoted to Canadian writers; the first (Volume LIII, *Canadian Writers since 1960*, first series) appeared in 1986 and gave evidence of generous information and comment. The *Encyclopedia of Music in Canada* (1981), ed. Helmut Kallmann, Gilles Potvin, and Kenneth Winters, sponsored with enthusiasm and generosity by Floyd S. Chalmers, and published by University of Toronto Press, was yet another major editorial and authorial effort to tell the full story of an impressive part of Canada's heritage. The *Dictionary of Newfoundland English* (University of Toronto Press 1982) relied on a large team of scholars under the editorship of G.M. Story, W.J. Kirwin, and J.D.A. Widdowson, and on computer work, to create a book of readers' delights that fulfils vividly Emerson's function for a dictionary – to be 'full of suggestion – the raw material of possible poems and histories.'

The appellation 'reference work' can be misleading as applied to almost all these works. They are that, by chief intention, but they become more when they are built on many acts of creative insight in overall pattern and individual parts, for such acts, combined, mean volumes offering not just documented facts but interpretations that will stimulate readers to understanding and enquiry.

Editor-publisher collaborations are also responsible for a number of reference projects acting as resources for information about Canadian writing in general. One of these is *Canadian Books in Print*, established at University of Toronto Press in 1973, now edited by Marian Butler, which provides through its subject and author/title indexes ordering facts about all books 'bearing the imprint of Canadian publishers or originated by the Canadian subsidiaries of international publishing firms'; it also serves as a useful basis for statistics and for enquiry about trends in the trade. *Canadian Book Review Annual* (est. 1975), edited most recently by Leslie and Katherine McGrath, assisted by Dean and Ann Tudor, and published by Simon & Pierre, offers succinct reviews of each year's Canadian publishing and thus a convenient overview. *Canadian Materials for Schools and Libraries* (est. 1971), edited for many years by Adèle Ashby, and published by the Canadian Library Association, is an annotated critical survey whose service extends beyond teachers and librarians. From 1948 the CLA issued the *Canadian Periodical Index*, which reached a coverage of some 135 journals; it was taken on by Info Globe in 1986. The Ontario Ministry of Citizenship and Culture has provided funding for the compilation, at the Faculty of Library and Information Science, University of Toronto, of *Canadian Selection*, an updated, cumulated edition of which was published by University of Toronto Press in 1985 (ed. Mavis Cariou, Sandra Cox, Alvin Bregman); it provides a judicious annotated guide for over 5000 books, published in Canada, about Canada, or written by Canadians, against which Canadian collections can be compared. *Canadiana*, prepared at the National Library, with full bibliographical data, is the ultimate resource for all Canadian material, and is issued in print or microfiche. Individual chapters of this volume of the *Literary History* make reference to published separate bibliographies for their fields. An on-going record has been provided in the articles, short notices, and reviews in *Canadian Literature* since 1959, in 'Letters in Canada' yearly in the *University of Toronto Quarterly* since 1936, in review sections of the long-lived *Dalhousie Review* and *Queen's Quarterly*, and in bibliographies and surveys in the *Journal of Commonwealth Literature* and *Canadian Poetry*.

· It can be stated firmly that, especially if one adds the scattering of reviews in magazines, there is no lack of retrospective information about Canadian writing as it has moved into print (the great problem is the lack of a weekly review of stature to bring information while it is 'news').

Bibliography for research and scholarly purposes, however, has until recently been done largely in fits and starts, so that when Canadian literature, for instance, began to grow as a field in universities and at the senior high school level it had not only few texts with which to work but also a lamentable lack of bibliographical support. Attitudes to bibliography have been a large part of the problem, especially among academics, many of whom still seem to feel it is an exercise for which librarians should be quietly responsible, thus showing not only their own lack of knowledge about the many-sidedness and modernity of Canadian academic librarianship, in which bibliography has, of course, a recognized place, but their unawareness of how fundamental bibliography is to scholarship.[16] It is gradually being recognized that experience of bibliography, starting with the simplest enumerative check list, should begin with students and increase with participation in research. The unevenness of such experience is evident from *Instruction in Bibliography* (1985), the report of a survey of instruction in 1982–3 in selected departments of Canadian universities conducted by the Committee on Bibliography and Information Services for the Social Sciences and Humanities of the National Library Advisory Board. This Committee (disbanded in 1988) owed its origin to a resolution of a major conference to identify the need for bibliographical enterprise in a number of fields in Canadian studies, which was organized by Anne Piternick and held in Vancouver in 1974; to it came those engaged in bibliography and those conscious of gaps in such knowledge. In Halifax in 1981, at the time of a meeting of the International Council of Canadian Studies, the situation was reviewed once more. The published proceedings of both conferences are highly vocal about needs still not met.[17]

A major publishing enterprise in bibliography has been conducted at ECW Press (publishers Robert Lecker and Jack David). It is issuing, in bound collections and individual paper fascicles, a series called 'The Annotated Bibliography of Canada's Major Authors' which for each author provides a bibliography of work published and also of reviews and criticisms with annotations about their content. As of 1987 seven of the planned ten volumes had been published and had received a generally warm and grateful reception, though individual bibliographies vary in inclusiveness. A second series, in twenty volumes, 'Canadian Writers and Their Works: Essays on Form, Context and Development,' begun in 1983, includes in each essay on a novelist or poet a bibliography along with biography, an account of criticism, and the essayist's own new analysis. To this effort, which has demanded immense persistence from the directors, was added in 1987 a *Canadian Literature Index* which will survey some eighty periodicals in a subject and author index. ECW has the college, university, and public library market particularly in mind.

The scholarship of descriptive and analytical bibliography, necessary for any proper understanding of how the books we read came into being as physical facts and as texts, has had few participants as yet. There have been highly respected contributions to this general field, for instance in the work of Marie Tremaine, *A Bibliography of Canadian Imprints 1751–1800* (University of Toronto Press 1952), which was planned 'to bring out through the record of the imprints themselves something of the nature of the society which produced them.' In 1934 the Toronto Public Library issued *A Bibliography of Canadiana* in its holdings, ed. Frances M. Staton and Marie Tremaine, with a first supplement in 1959, and the Metropolitan Toronto Library is in the midst of a large second supplement in three volumes, of which the second and the third, for 1801–49 and 1850–67 imprints, appeared in 1985 and 1986, ed. Sandra Alston and Karen Evans (pre–1867 items in the *Bibliography* will total over 9500). W.F.E. Morley in 1973 provided the first formal description of an author's corpus in his bibliography of John Richardson. The techniques of descriptive bibliography have been well displayed in the *Annotated Bibliography* for A.J.M. Smith by Michael E. Darling

(Véhicule Press 1981) and in *Collected Poems of Raymond Souster: Bibliography* by Bruce Whiteman (Oberon 1984). The work of the CEECT project will, it is hoped, encourage exploration in this mode. Such work will make it possible to understand more fully the writings of Canadian authors and to appreciate their experience of authorship.

And with this call to analytical bibliography we are back at *l'histoire du livre*. The next decades of Canadian literary history can be, promise to be, most interesting for developments in awareness and knowledge of how and what Canadians publish. Challenges abound in accounting, on the basis of research, for the *histoire* of Canadian books, for the past development and present state of the Canadian book trade, for the place of the book in Canadian society. If they are met, we shall know much more about how the passage from author to reader has occurred in Canada and has created our literary history.

Notes

ABBREVIATIONS

Amer   American
Assn   Association
BiC   *Books in Canada*
Can   Canadian
CanD   *Canadian Drama*
CanL   *Canadian Literature*
CCL   *Canadian Children's Literature*
CFM   *Canadian Fiction Magazine*
CHR   *Canadian Historical Review*
CJPS   *Canadian Journal of Political Science*
CPA   *Canadian Public Administration*
CTR   *Canadian Theatre Review*
ECW   *Essays on Canadian Writing*
G&M   *The Globe and Mail* (Toronto)
Hist   Historical
HP   Canadian Historical Assn *Historical Papers*
JCS   *Journal of Canadian Studies*
LHC   *Literary History of Canada*
PerfA   *Performing Arts in Canada*
QQ   *Queen's Quarterly*
R   Review/Revue
SCL   *Studies in Canadian Literature*
Soc   Society
SPE   *Studies in Political Economy: A Socialist Review*
TCL   *Translation in Canadian Literature*
TLS   *The Times Literary Supplement*
UTQ   *University of Toronto Quarterly*

CHAPTER ONE: POETRY

1 See Jonathan Culler's definition of intertextuality, in *The Pursuit of Signs: Semiotics, Literature, Deconstruction* (1981) 38.
2 David McFadden, 'The Blood that Was Used to Boil the Skulls,' *Country of the Open Heart* (1982) 27

3 'Chapter and Verse,' *Amer Poetry R* 7:1 (1978) 27

4 'A Sort of Intro,' *Bursting into Song: An Al Purdy Omnibus* (1982) [11]

5 'The Songs Are Made of Soil,' *G&M* (5 October 1974) 35

6 'The New Surrealism,' in Robert Boyers, ed., *Poetry in America* (1974) 320–5

7 *Introspection and Contemporary Poetry* (1984) 100

8 *The Situation of Poetry* (1976) 83

9 'A Rejected Preface to *New Provinces*, 1936,' *Towards a View of Canadian Letters* (1973) 172

10 'no. xi,' *Under the Thunder* 85. The primary source for the sequence is found in Margaret Coulby Whitridge, ed., *Lampman's Kate: Late Love Poems of Archibald Lampman 1887–1897* (1975).

11 'Sunday Water: Thirteen Anti Ghazals,' in *Selected Poems: The Vision Tree*, ed. Sharon Thesen (1982) 146

12 'Epic and Novel: Toward a Methodology for the Study of the Novel,' in Michael Holquist, ed., *The Dialogic Imagination*, trans. Caryl Emerson and Michael Holquist (1981) 39

13 Culler, 'Apostrophe,' *The Pursuit of Signs* 146

14 *Kerrisdale Elegies* (1984) 12, 125. Quotations from Rilke are taken from Rainer Maria Rilke, *Duino Elegies*, trans. J.B. Leishman and Stephen Spender (1939) 11, 15, 23, 77, 73.

15 'The Documentary Poem: A Canadian Genre,' in Eli Mandel, ed., *Contexts of Canadian Criticism* (1971) 267

16 'Amelia or: Who Do You Think You Are?: Documentary and Identity in Canadian Literature,' *CanL* 100 (1984) 269, 266

17 See, for example, Dewdney's *Fovea Centralis* (1975) 39–43.

18 Gregory Bateson, *Mind and Nature: A Necessary Unity* (1979; rpt 1980) 53

19 John Gribbin, *In Search of Schrodinger's Cat: Quantum Physics and Reality* (1984) 156–8, 259–61

20 Bateson, *Mind and Nature* 53–8

21 Culler, *The Pursuit of Signs* 108

22 Richard Kostelanetz, *The Old Poetries and the New* (1981) 189–90

CHAPTER TWO: SHORT FICTION

1 This period also saw the publication of an aptly titled (at the time) monograph: Clare MacCulloch, *The Neglected Genre: The Short Story in Canada* (1973). Subsequently, various critical works have appeared, including W.H. New, *Dreams of Speech and Violence: The Art of the Short Story in Canada and New Zealand* (1987); and Simone Vauthier, ed., 'La nouvelle canadienne anglophone,' *Ranam* 16 (1983)

2 W.H. New, in *LHC* (2nd ed., 1976), III, noted that 'there were over 1,100 stories by over 550 authors published in Canadian periodicals between 1960 and 1973' (257). According to the annual bibliographies in the *Journal of Canadian Fiction*, nearly 1000 stories were published in the following four years alone. The *Subject Guide to Canadian Books in Print: 1973* listed 86 collections of short fiction; by 1979 the total had almost doubled, and for 1985 there were listed 284 volumes, as *in print*. ECW Press announced for publication in 1989 *A Comprehensive Bibliography of Canadian Short Stories,*

1950–1983, compiled by Allan Weiss, with 20,000 citations of short stories by more than 5300 writers.

The causes of this remarkable increase have not yet been carefully studied. New suggested 'possibly' the influence of film, the development of schools of creative writing, the increased academic study of Canadian literature, and the establishment of new journals and reviews. To this might be added in the years after 1972 the energy of new publishing houses (often supported by funding from the Canada Council – later SSHRCC – and provincial arts organizations), and the increased presentation of short fiction through public readings (with sponsorship again playing an important part). Short fiction may also have better suited an audience whose attention span had been reduced by the artificial programming policies of television. Another possibility is that the short story, in giving its emphasis primarily to a limited number of significant moments in the lives of one or very few characters, appealed more to writers and readers less capable in an age of uncertainty and change of accepting the sense of order and meaning through time offered by the traditional novel. (Canadian fondness for collections of linked short stories – novels deliberately not completed – has often been noted, although the practice, in magazines and in broadcast fiction, was well-established before the 1960s.)

The increasing amount of short fiction was, in addition, not an exclusively Canadian or even North American phenomenon. In his 'Introduction' to *The Australian Short Story* (1986), Laurie Hergenhan, after noting how early in Australian literary history the form had established itself, writes of the 'new wave' that 'enlivened the Australian short story from the later 1960s through 1970s' and of the 'diverse collections' that have 'proliferated' in the early 1980s. Elizabeth Bowen called the short story 'the child of this century,' and while it was relatively slow to flourish in Canada, its development needs to be considered in both national and international contexts.

For an important discussion of the problems facing the literary scholar in dealing with Canadian short fiction, see W.H. New, 'Back to the Future: The Short Story in Canada and the Writing of Literary History,' *Australian-Canadian Studies* 4 (1986)

3 Mavis Gallant had been invited to let one of her stories appear in this anthology. She declined.
4 The four were Garner, Gallant, Munro, and Marshall.
5 'Editing the Best,' in *Kicking Against the Pricks* (1982) 169
6 In his ed., *Illusion Two: Fables, Fantasies and Metafictions* (1983) 7
7 'What Was Canadian Literature? Taking Stock of the Canlit Industry,' *ECW* 30 (1984–5) 32
8 See 'Building Castles,' in Metcalf, ed., *Making It New: Contemporary Canadian Stories* (1982) 43. This quality of Metcalf's work is well treated in Cameron's 'An Approximation of Poetry: The Short Stories of John Metcalf,' *SCL* 2:1 (1977).
9 For a series of reflections on the Group by those who participated in it, see J.R. (Tim) Struthers, ed., *The Montreal Story Tellers: Memoirs, Photographs, Critical Essays* (1985).
10 'Clark Blaise,' in *Canadian Writers and Their Works*, Fiction Series, Vol. 7 (1985) 80
11 See *Here & Now* (1977), *79: Best Canadian Stories* (1979), *80: Best Cana-*

dian Stories (1980). Rooke later became co-editor with Metcalf of *Best Canadian Stories* and subsequently the two co-edited anthologies of new short fiction published by New Press.

12 Geoff Hancock, 'The High-Tech World of Leon Rooke,' *CFM* 38 (1981) 135. For a similar approach see Simone Vauthier, ' "Entering Other Skins" – or, Leon Rooke's "The End of the Revolution",' *The Literary Review* 28:3 (1985).

13 For more on Rooke's concern with voice see Russell Brown, 'Rooke's Move,' *ECW* 30 (1984–5). Rooke's preoccupation with voice invites a connection with an important tradition in the literature of the United States, first significantly established in the work of Whitman and Twain.

14 Geoff Hancock, ['Interview with W.D. Valgardson'], *BiC* 6:9 (1977) 39

15 Barry Cameron, 'Introduction' to *Making It New* ix; Hancock, 'An Interview with Leon Rooke,' *CFM* 38 (1981) 117

16 J.R. (Tim) Struthers, 'The Real Material: An Interview with Alice Munro' in Louis K. MacKendrick, ed., *Probable Fictions: Alice Munro's Narrative Acts* (1983) 17

17 Munro, 'What Is Real?' in *Making It New* 226

18 Bronwen Wallace, 'Women's Lives: Alice Munro' in David Helwig, ed., *The Human Elements: Critical Essays* (1978) 53

19 Eg, Helen Hoy, ' "Dull, Simple, Amazing and Unfathomable": Paradox and Double Vision in Alice Munro's Fiction,' *SCL*, 5:1 (1980). See also the comments on 'The Spanish Lady' in Lorraine M. York, ' "The Other Side of Dailiness": The Paradox of Photography in Alice Munro's Fiction,' *SCL* 8:1 (1983) 56.

20 This and subsequent quotations are from Wayne Grady's interview with Norman Levine, *BiC*, 9:2 (1980) 24–5.

21 D.G. Stephens, 'Looking Homeward' (review article on *Selected Stories*, 1975), *CanL* 70 (1976) 94, 96. This is one of the very few good critical appraisals before the end of the 1970s.

22 'Sandra Birdsell,' in Andrew Garrod, *Speaking for Myself: Canadian Writers in Interview* (1986) 15

23 'Neil Bissoondath,' *Speaking for Myself* 50

24 'Guy Vanderhaeghe,' *Speaking for Myself* 281

25 'Guy Vanderhaeghe,' in Doris Hillis, *Voices & Visions: Interviews with Saskatchewan Writers* (1985) 24

26 Any limited survey of Canadian short fiction published after 1972 will of necessity do less than full justice to many authors. Among those who deserve the considered attention of readers and critics is, for example, Eugene McNamara, whose subtle and ironic depiction of the deceptions and incongruities of contemporary experience is well presented in many of the stories collected in *Salt: Short Stories* (1975) and *The Search for Sarah Grace* (1977). W.P. Kinsella's several collections are of uneven quality. The baseball stories in *Shoeless Joe Jackson Comes to Iowa* (1980) and *The Thrill of the Grass* (1984) are at times sentimental and nostalgic, making an appeal primarily to those who (like me) are true fans of the game; others go far beyond such limits in their insightful, detailed, and moving presentation of the history and cultural significance of the sport and the moral implications of its tradition and form. Kinsella's Indian stories – *Dance Me Outside* (1977), *Scars* (1978), *Born Indian* (1981), and *The Moccasin Telegraph and Other Stories* (1983) – can decline on occasion into mere formula: clever Indians show the shortcom-

NOTES 409

ings of white society in a predictable and superficial way. The better stories make their critical points with telling and comic effectiveness, or show the complexity of relationships between whites and Indians (or between different viewpoints within Indian groups) in stories that are far from superficial in their treatment of characters and situations. Ray Smith's bawdy and high-spirited *Lord Nelson Tavern* (1974), impressive in its authenticity of narrative voices and somewhat disconcerting in its treatment of women by men, has not been followed by another collection. Smith's stories continue to appear in periodicals and anthologies; his development as a writer deserves attention. Graeme Gibson's short fiction has yet to be collected; as with Smith, his work deserves more critical notice than it has received. Andreas Schroeder's *The Late Man* (1972) contains some good stories, written in a style that attempts to blend the plain with the fantastic, of fragmented selves confronting and intruded on by the ambiguities of the external world. Schroeder's work as editor, poet, journalist, and screenwriter made him an important writer in the years after 1972; although he published no collection of short fiction, his stories continued to appear in periodicals and anthologies.

The novelist-poet Kent Thompson's first collection of short fiction, *Shotgun and Other Stories* (1979), brought together an impressively varied and well-crafted number of stories that reveal the unexpected truths lying below the surfaces of seemingly ordinary lives; the title story, in its careful exposure of the terrors suffered in old age by a man whose life has been badly lived, is particularly effective. Elizabeth Spencer is best known for her novels, yet she too has written well in shorter forms. Her first collection, *The Stories of Elizabeth Spencer* (1981), displays an assured treatment, often involving elements of the fantastic and the supernatural, of the difficult but necessary attempt to escape the burdens of the past. There are also several others whose work in this period merits careful consideration: Keath Fraser's mordant humour and ear for the nuances of dialogue, in *Taking Cover* (1982); Don Bailey's abrasive realism in *Making Up* (1981); Greg Hollingshead's whimsy and philosophical wit in *Famous Players* (1982). One could add the names of Ken Mitchell, Martin Avery, Constance Rooke, and David Arnason without exhausting the list of those who have done good work in the form. An insightful treatment of the lives of women and a pointed analysis of human relationships is evident in the best stories in collections by Katherine Govier, Merna Summers, Edna Alford, Daphne Marlatt, Ann Copeland, Leona Gom, Margaret Gilboord Gibson, Carol Shields, and Beth Harvor. These are (relatively) younger writers, or ones who began to publish extensively after 1972. Still other writers began to publish in various anthologies and magazines: Ernest Hekkanen, Veronica Ross, Diane Schoemperlen, Isabel Huggan, Frances Itani, Paulette Jiles, William Bauer, and Sean Virgo. Their development, given their achievement to date, will have to be attended to.

27 'What Was Canadian Literature?' 33

CHAPTER THREE: THE NOVEL

1 This chapter has been prepared with the bibliographic assistance of Ken Durkacz and Heather Jones, and with the editorial help of Laurie Ricou; it was supported by a Leave Fellowship from the Social Sciences and Humanities Research Council of Canada.
2 I should like to thank here all those Canadian publishers who responded to my

enquiries and whose remarks have contributed to my understanding of Canadian publishing. In particular, my gratitude goes to James Polk of the House of Anansi and Jack McClelland of McClelland & Stewart, but also to Robert Lecker of ECW, Glenn Clever and Frank Tierney of Borealis, Ann Reatherford of Porcupine's Quill, and John Harris of Repository Press.

3 See Lee Easton's MA dissertation on 'Patterns of (Af)filiation in the Modern Canadian *Bildungsroman*,' McMaster University 1985.

4 However, one should probably recall Atwood's warning: 'If a man depicts a male character unfavourably, it's The Human Condition; if a woman does it, she's being mean to men' (*Second Words* [1982] 421)

5 For further comments on the Canadian novel during these years, see: Margaret Atwood, *Survival: A Thematic Guide to Canadian Literature* (1972); Jars Balan, ed., *Identifications: Ethnicity and the Writer in Canada* (1982); Paul Cappon, ed., *In Our House: Social Perspectives on Canadian Literature* (1978); Frank Davey, *Surviving the Paraphrase: Eleven Essays on Canadian Literature* (1983); Gaile McGregor, *The Wacousta Syndrome: Explorations in the Canadian Langscape* (1985); Leslie Monkman, *A Native Heritage: Images of the Indian in English-Canadian Literature* (1981); Shirley Neuman and Robert Wilson, *Labyrinths of Voice: Conversations with Robert Kroetsch* (1982); Joseph Pivato, ed., *Contrasts: Comparative Essays on Italian Canadian Writing* (1985); Laurie Ricou, *Vertical Man/Horizontal World: Man and Landscape in Canadian Prairie Fiction* (1973); David Staines, ed., *The Canadian Imagination: Dimensions of a Literary Culture* (1977); Charles Steele, ed., *Taking Stock: The Calgary Conference on the Canadian Novel* (1982).

CHAPTER FOUR: TRANSLATION

1 See *Meta* 22:1 (1977), numéro spécial: 'Histoire de la traduction au Canada,' especially Jean Delisle, 'Les pionniers de l'interprétation au Canada.'

2 David M. Hayne, '*The Golden Dog* and *Le Chien d'or*,' *Papers of the Bibliog Soc of Canada* 20 (1981) 57

3 Ibid. 58

4 David M. Hayne, 'Literary Translation in Nineteenth-Century Canada,' *Translation in Canadian Literature*, ed. Camille La Bossière (1983) 37

5 'Introduction,' *Complete Poems of Saint-Denys-Garneau* (1975) 17

6 'Introduction,' *Poetry of French Canada in Translation*, ed. John Glassco (1970) xxiv

7 Glassco, *Poetry of French Canada* xxii

8 Northrop Frye, 'Foreword' to Anne Hébert and Frank Scott, *Dialogue sur la traduction* (1970) 13

9 Glassco, *Complete Poems of Saint-Denys-Garneau* 16

10 E.D. Blodgett, 'How Do You Say "Gabrielle Roy"?' *Translation in Canadian Literature* 25

11 Ibid. 26n40

12 Ibid. 33, 15

13 Glassco, *Poetry of French Canada* xx

14 Frye, 'Foreword' 14

15 Jacques Brault, 'Remarques sur la traduction de la poésie,' *Ellipse* 21 (1977) 28

16 Blodgett, 'How Do You Say' 29–30

CHAPTER FIVE: THEORY AND CRITICISM: TRENDS IN CANADIAN LITERATURE

1 See also Catherine Belsey, *Critical Practice* (1980), especially Chapter 6.
2 See, too, Henry Kreisel, 'The Prairie: A State of Mind' (1968; rpt in Eli Mandel, ed., *Contexts of Canadian Criticism*, 1971) and Edward A. McCourt, *The
   Canadian West in Fiction* (rev. 1970). These pioneering studies in Western regionalist literature have affected subsequent studies of the subject: Ricou (*Vertical Man*, 1973), Dick Harrison (*Unnamed Country*, 1977), Mandel (*Another
   Time*, 1977), and New (*Articulating West*, 1972) in particular.
3 Homi Bhabha, 'Representation and the Colonial Text,' in *The Theory of Reading*, ed. Frank Gloversmith (1984) 96. Bhabha's discussion of the problematics
   of recognition, mimetic adequacy, and normative fallacies – on which I draw
   later – are informed by the work of Paul Hirst and Pierre Macherey. Many of
   his arguments about ideology complement those of Catherine Belsey, who is
   also indebted to Hirst and Macherey. On the Canadian desire for beginnings,
   see Robert Kroetsch, 'Canada Is a Poem,' *Open Letter* 5th series, no. 4
   (1983).
4 'Economist Abraham Rotstein has described English Canada's brand of nationalism as "mappism," a kind of exaggerated identification of the nation with
   its territory' (Susan Crean and Marcel Rioux, *Two Nations* [1983] 11).
5 See, eg, Eagleton's *Criticism and Ideology* (1986) and Macherey's *A Theory of
   Literary Production* (1978).
6 The term 'corporate,' like the term 'residual' used earlier, derives from the
   English critic Raymond Williams. See his 'Literature in Society' (in Hilda
   Schiff, ed., *Contemporary Approaches to English Studies*, 1977) and *Marxism
   and Literature* (1977). In the latter, Williams uses the term 'dominant' instead
   of 'corporate' to describe a common core of meanings, values, and practices
   in any society. Such a core never includes even all the significant practices:
   hence the need for the concepts of residual and emergent practices. On the
   role of reader as consumer, see 'Literature in Society' 30.
7 See also Davey's introduction to *The Writing Life*, ed. C.H. Gervais (1976)
   15–24.
8 See the third section of the first chapter of Jonathan Culler's *On Deconstruction* (1982), 'Stories of Reading' 64–83.
9 As, eg, in *Another Time*; 'Strange Loops'; 'The Border League: American
   "West" and Canadian "Region",' in Dick Harrison, ed., *Crossing Frontiers*
   (1979); or 'Northrop Frye and the Canadian Literary Tradition,' in Eleanor
   Cook, ed., *Centre and Labyrinth* (1983).
10 This argument could be aligned with Lacanian understanding of textuality and
   perhaps a Bakhtinian notion of polyglossia. Mikhail Bakhtin's *The Dialogic
   Imagination* (trans. 1981) distinguishes between monoglossia – the unified,
   centralized, authoritative language – characterized by hegemony, and polyglossia, characterized by dispersal and differentiation.
11 Roslyn Wallach Bologh, *Dialectical Phenomenology: Marx's Method* (1979) xii
12 See Crean and Rioux, *Two Nations* 29.
13 Of the three broad genres – poetry, prose fiction, and drama – the last has
   received much less attention than the other two in Canadian criticism, although
   there are some fine essays in the periodicals *Canadian Theatre Review* and *Canadian Drama* and occasionally in other periodicals. There is much more theatre history – that is, criticism of drama as performance rather than as text.

Besides the items in the Profiles on Canadian Drama and Twayne series, W.H. New's *Dramatists in Canada* (1972), a collection of essays drawn primarily from *Canadian Literature*, is the only sustained contribution, during the 1972–84 period, to the study of Canadian drama as text, though several works on drama were to appear in 1985 and after.

14 Lowry was the subject of several books, by Canadians and others. W.H. New's *Malcolm Lowry: A Reference Guide* (1978) lists publications on Lowry up to 1976, and is updated in the *Malcolm Lowry Newsletter* (later *Review*); subsequent books include Sherrill Grace, *The Voyage that Never Ends* (1982) and Barry Wood, ed., *Malcolm Lowry* (1980).

15 European criticism on Canadian writing, particularly in Germany, Denmark, Russia, France, and Italy, expanded significantly after 1972. Some of it was critically more sophisticated than commentary produced by Canadians. I find Bonheim's *The Narrative Modes* and Simone Vauthier's work (in *The Literary Review*, 1985) very stimulating. For examples of other foreign work, see the items listed in Barbara Godard's *Inventory of Research in Canadian and Quebec Literatures* (1983), and the essays collected by Robert Kroetsch and Reingard M. Nischik in *Gaining Ground: European Critics on Canadian Literature* (1985), which contains an extensive bibliography.

16 The editorial collective Tessera – consisting of Barbara Godard, Daphne Marlatt, Kathy Mezei, and Gail Scott – is an important agency for feminist literary criticism in Canada. The first issue of the collective appeared in *Room of One's Own* 8:4 (1984), the second in *La nouvelle barre du jour* 157 (1985), the third in *Canadian Fiction Magazine* 57 (1986).

17 See Colin MacCabe, *James Joyce and the Revolution of the Word* (1978) 2–3. 'Every text is ... a weaving together of what has already been produced elsewhere in discontinuous form; every subject, every author, every self is the articulation of an intersubjectivity structured within and around the discourses available to it at any moment in time' (Michael Sprinker, quoted in *Labyrinths of Voice* 207).

CHAPTER SIX: SCHOLARSHIP AND CRITICISM

1 Without the help generously given by many of my colleagues it would not have been possible to write this chapter. I am grateful to all those who assisted me at various points and particularly to the following scholars for guidance: Constance Hieatt and Roberta Frank (Old and Middle English), David Shaw (Victorian Literature). The comments on B. Rajan's work were written by Henry Kreisel.

CHAPTER SEVEN: WRITING FOR RADIO, TELEVISION, AND FILM

1 The vast bulk of Canadian 'media-writing' remains unpublished, but typescripts can be studied in a number of growing archival collections around the country. The Radio Drama Project at Concordia University in Montreal, under the direction of Dr Howard Fink, is the repository of CBC radio drama scripts from the 1930s up to the present. Material up to 1961 is thoroughly organized and catalogued (see Howard Fink and Brian Morrison, *Canadian National Theatre on the Air, 1925–1961: CBC-CRBC-CNR Radio Drama in English: A Descriptive Bibliography and Union List*, 1983). Material after 1961 is at present un-

organized and incomplete, but the next great cataloguing labour started in 1986. Script collections are gradually being shipped to Montreal from the various production centres around the country. York University in Toronto houses the script archives of CBC Television drama, fairly complete and catalogued up to 1977. More recent material remains with the CBC, but will be gradually transferred to York. Audio-tapes of radio drama up to about 1975 are lodged with the National Film, Television and Sound Archives in Ottawa; the rest is either on its way, or awaiting cataloguing, or still in the CBC program archives in Toronto. Videotapes, kinescopes, and movie-prints of TV drama are likewise being transferred to Ottawa from the CBC archives in Toronto. Telefilm Canada retained the scripts of many of the feature films in which it invested, and has deposited them with the Queen's University Archives.

Aside from review journalism, which tends to concentrate on the production rather than on the writing, and which anyway ignores radio drama, the body of critical writing is not large. Typically, the bulk of serious analysis has been addressed to the cinema, much of it in a sociological-thematic vein. Two anthologies edited by Feldman and Nelson have collected a good selection: *Canadian Film Reader* (1977) – relevant contributions include 'Men of Vision' by Peter Harcourt, a study of Don Shebib's films, and 'Coward, Bully or Clown' by Robert Fothergill, on the male image in Canadian cinema – and *Take Two* (1984) – articles by Harcourt, James Leach, and Piers Handling. A valuable reference work, with significant coverage of television as well as cinema, is Peter Morris, *The Film Companion* (1984).

Television drama has been monitored intermittently by Mary Jane Miller, and treated to a critical overview in her article 'Television Drama in English Canada' in Anton Wagner, ed., *Contemporary Canadian Theatre: New World Visions* (1985). Seth Feldman's articles on *Tar Sands* in *Take Two*, and on 'The Electronic Fable: Aspects of the Docudrama in Canada' in *CanD* 9:1 (1983) develop an interesting critique of CBC's 'For the Record' series. Most recently Morris Wolfe's book *Jolts: The TV Wasteland and the Canadian Oasis* (1985) contains a chapter on the distinctive qualities of CBC drama. In the field of broadcast history, Blaine Allan at Queen's University is currently working on a comprehensive, annotated directory of CBC English-language television series, dramatic and non-dramatic, from 1952 to the present.

Of the little that has been written about Canadian radio drama a large proportion is by Howard Fink, including his introduction to his *Bibliography* referred to above, and chapters in Peter Lewis, ed., *Radio Drama* (1981) and in Wagner. *CanD* 9:1 (1983) contains several articles on radio and television drama, including 'From "Stage" to "Sunday Matinee"': Canadian Radio Drama in English' by Malcolm Page. Page also has a paper, 'Canadian Radio Drama,' in Peter Lewis, ed., *Papers of the Radio Literature Conference 1977* (1978). *CTR* 36 (1982) is largely devoted to radio drama, and includes articles by Michael Cook, George Ryga, and Len Peterson. George Woodcock's essay, 'Voices Set Free,' *CanL* 85 (1980) assesses some Vancouver dramatists and the poetry of radio.

2 I have endeavoured, not always with complete consistency, to reserve *italics* for the titles of self-contained works (whether individual plays or serials in many chapters), while employing 'quotation marks' for the umbrella titles of series of more-or-less unrelated works. This is clear enough as long as we are dealing with 'CBC Wednesday Night,' a programming format featuring weekly

radio plays, or *Vanderberg*, a TV serial in six connected parts. The distinction
becomes cloudy, however, between *A Gift to Last*, a series of many chapters
in the life of a single family, and 'Sidestreet,' a series of self-contained episodes in the work of a police department.

3 The phrase is the title of Howard Fink's catalogue of the Concordia Radio
Drama Project, and was first used by Vincent Tovell in a 1948 article in
UTQ.

CHAPTER EIGHT: THEATRE & DRAMA

1 See Michael Tait, 'Drama and Theatre [1920–60],' in Carl F. Klinck, ed.,
LHC (2nd ed., 1976), II, and John Ripley, 'Drama and Theatre [1960–73],'
III.

2 See Don Rubin, 'Creeping Toward a Culture: The Theatre in English Canada
since 1945,' *CTR* 1 (1974) 20.

3 Amateur, university, and semi-professional theatre also continued during 1972–
84, but, since the demise of the Dominion Drama Festival (1970) and the
rapid growth of professional theatre, its importance was greatly reduced. See
Betty Lee, *Love and Whisky: The Story of the Dominion Drama Festival and
the Early Years of Theatre in Canada 1606–1972* (1973) and Mira Friedlander,
'The Enduring Vitality of Community and Grass Roots Theatre,' in Anton
Wagner, ed., *Contemporary Canadian Theatre* (1985).

4 Mark Czarnecki, 'The Regional Theatre System,' in Wagner, 36–7

5 Rubin, 'Celebrating the Nation: History and the Canadian Theatre,' *CTR* 34
(1982) 16

6 'Theatre for Young Audiences in English Canada,' in Wagner, 261. See also
Joyce Doolittle's articles in *CTR* 35 (1982); 10 (1976); 18 (1978); and 41
(1984), as well as her book, co-authored with Zina Barnieh and Hélène Beau-
champ, *A Mirror of Our Dreams: Children and the Theatre in Canada* (1979).
CTR 41 (1984) is a special issue on theatre and the young.

7 Theatre for Young People is to be distinguished from both 'Drama in Educa-
tion' – the use of drama as a teaching mode in schools – and 'Education in
Theatre' – training for theatre skills in school or college. See Wayne Fairhead,
'Drama in Education,' in Wagner, and Mira Friedlander, 'Schools After
Fame,' *CTR* 41 (1984); Susan Duligal, ed., *A Directory of Canadian Theatre
Schools 1982–83* (1982), and Don Rubin, 'Training the Theatre Professional,'
in Wagner. The Vancouver Youth Theatre provides yet another model; it is an
independent company, outside the school system, in which young actors de-
velop and perform their own scripts.

8 Urjo Kareda, quoted in Robert Wallace and Cynthia Zimmerman, 'The Audience and the Season: Four Artistic Directors in Search of a Community,' *CTR*
37 (1983) 29

9 *Canada Council Selected Arts Research Statistics* (3rd ed., 1983) 54

10 Cf. 'In constant 1971 dollars ... corporate support was $3 million in 1972 and
$3 million in 1983 ... ' (Harry Chartrand, Research Director of the Canada
Council, speech at Toronto, 1 October 1984). Yet, as the 1984 Annual Report
of the Continental Bank of Canada pointed out, citing ancillary benefits to
tourism and taxes as proof, 'The irony of the current shortage of financial support is that frequently the arts can be shown to earn their keep' (cited by Mavor Moore, 'An Outlook on the Arts Worth Taking to the Bank,' *G&M* [22
June 1985] E5).

11 For a detailed account of the crisis following Robin Phillips's resignation, see Martin Knelman, *A Stratford Tempest* (1982).

12 George Woodcock, *Strange Bedfellows: The State and the Arts in Canada* (1985) 141

13 For example, Another Theatre Company staged its first repertory season in 1984, and Herbert Whittaker mentions the Wormwood Dog and Monkey, which does workshops for playwrights using professional actors (*G&M* [21 March 1985] E6).

14 For a short account of French theatre in the province, see Michel Vaïs, trans. Audrey Camiré and Mark Czarnecki, 'Quebec,' in Wagner; for francophone theatre elsewhere in Canada, see *CTR* 46 (1986).

15 Ken Gass, 'Toronto's Alternates: Changing Realities,' *CTR* 21 (1979) 127. See also Robert Wallace, 'Growing Pains: Toronto Theatre in the 1970's,' *CanL* 85 (1980).

16 In 1983 the Canada Council gave writer-in-residence grants to thirteen theatres, and most artistic directors claim they devote a lot of time to unsolicited manuscripts from hopeful newcomers (Salem Alaton, 'Canadian Playwrights Keep Plugging,' *G&M* (28 November 1983), 'Stage Canada' 21).

17 On prairie theatre see *CTR* 42 (1985): 'Theatre on the Prairies,' and Ross Stuart's *The History of Prairie Theatre* (1984).

18 For example, Janet Amos from Blyth Theatre Festival to Theatre New Brunswick; James Roy, also from Blyth, to the Manitoba Theatre Centre; Martin Kinch from Toronto Free Theatre to Theatre Calgary; and Bill Glassco from the Tarragon to Toronto's CentreStage Company

19 'Henrik Ibsen on the Necessity of Producing Norwegian Drama,' *CTR* 14 (1977) 52

20 Three areas not considered in this chapter are amateur or semi-professional theatre, community theatre, and 'ethnic' theatre (ie, drama produced by particular racial groups for their own people, not for Canadian audiences at large). Discussion of these areas can be found on pages 216–35 of Wagner. See also: Irene Davis, 'Ethnic Theatre in Canada Struggles for Recognition,' *PerfA* 21:2 (1984); and the special issue 'Salud! Multicultural Theatre,' *Scene Changes* 6:9 (1978).

21 For a comprehensive account of recent women's theatre, see Ann Saddlemyer, 'Circus Feminus: 100 Plays by English-Canadian Women,' *Room of One's Own* 8:2 (1983). *CanD* 5:2 (1979) is a symposium on 'Women in Canadian Drama'; *CTR* 43 (1985) concerns 'Feminism and Canadian Theatre.' See also Rina Fraticelli, 'The Invisibility Factor: Status of Women in Canadian Theatre,' *Fuse* 6:3 (1982).

22 Eg, Peter Colley, *The Donnellys* (1974), with music by Peter Skolnic; Theatre Passe Muraille's *Them Donnellys* (1973), reworked by Ted Johns as *The Death of the Donnellys*; Hugh Graham, *Boys, You Have Done Enough Tonight* (1974); and James Reaney, *Sticks and Stones* (1973), *The St Nicholas Hotel* (1974), and *Handcuffs* (1975).

23 See Neil Carson, 'Canadian Historical Drama: Playwrights in Search of a Myth,' *SCL* 2:2 (1977); Don Rubin, 'Celebrating the Nation: History and the Canadian Theatre,' *CTR* 34 (1982); and Rota H. Lister, 'Canada's Indians and Canadian Drama,' *Amer R Can Studies* 4:1 (1974).

24 See Diane Bessai, Connie Brissenden, and David McCaughna, 'Canada: une dramaturgie récente,' *Jeu* 8 (1978); Diane Bessai, 'The Regionalism of Canadian Drama,' *CanL* 85 (1980); and Robert Wallace, 'Writing the Land Alive:

The Playwrights' Vision in English Canada,' in Wagner. See also Part II of
Wagner: 'Theatre and Drama across Canada' (a province by province survey).

25 *CTR* 42 (1985) is devoted to 'Theatre on the Prairies'; see also Diane Bessai,
'Prairie Playwrights and the Theatre,' in *Prairie Performance*, ed. Diane Bessai (1980) 188.

26 Tremblay plays translated during the period were: *Les Belles Soeurs; Berthe;
Bonjour, là, Bonjour; La Duchesse de Langeais; En Pièces Détachées; For-
ever Yours, Marie-Lou; Gloria Star; Hosanna; Johnny Mangano and His As-
tonishing Dogs; Surprise, Surprise; Damnée Manon, Sacrée Sandra; The
Impromptu of Outremont; Sainte Carmen of the Main*; and *Albertine in Five
Times*. See Catherine McQuaid, 'Michel Tremblay's Seduction of the "Other
Solitude",' *CanD* 2:2 (1976). Other Quebec and Acadian dramatists who had
plays performed in English translation between 1972 and 1984 were: Jean
Barbeau, Michel Garneau, Robert Gurik, Roland Lepage, Antonine Maillet,
Jovette Marchessault, Louise Roy, and the quartet responsible for *Broue/Brew*
– Claude Meunier, Jean-Pierre Plante, Francine Ruel, and Louis Saia. In each
of these cases, only a single play was involved, and their audiences were
much more restricted than Tremblay's. See Marianne Ackerman, 'Bridging the
Two Solitudes: English and French Theatre in Quebec,' in Wagner.

27 See Diane Bessai, 'Canadian Docu-Drama,' *CTR* 16 (1977) and 'Documentary
Theatre in Canada: An Investigation into Questions and Backgrounds,' *CanD*
6:1 (1980); Alan Filewod, 'Collective Creation: Process, Politics and Poetics,'
CTR 34 (1982); Renate Usmiani, *Second Stage* (1983) 43–107. See also Brian
Arnott, 'The Passe-Muraille Alternative' in David Helwig, ed., *The Human
Elements* (1978); and Mary Jane Miller, 'They Shoot! They Score?' *CanD* 4:2
(1978). It is well to remember that collective creations were evolved much
earlier in Europe and the United States, and that George Luscombe of Toronto
Workshop Theatre was specifically influenced by the left-wing English director,
Joan Littlewood, and Paul Thompson of Theatre Passe Muraille and Chris
Brookes of the Newfoundland Mummers by another left-wing English director,
Peter Cheeseman.

28 The collective creations of Toronto Workshop Theatre usually employed a
writer and were always dominated by the personal vision of the company's
founder-director, George Luscombe; for the most part they commented on non-
Canadian political events. Examples from the period are: *You Can't Get Here
from There* (1975), about the Allende crisis in Chile; *Summer '76* (1976), a
history of the Olympics; and *The Wobbly* (1983), about the International
Workers of the World.

29 Jerry Wasserman in his ed., *Modern Canadian Plays* (1985) 19. Besides the
Donnelly trilogy, Reaney's plays in the period were *Baldoon* (1976), *The Dismissal* (1977), *Wacousta!* (1978), *King Whistle* (1979), *Antler River* (1980),
Gyroscope (1981), an opera libretto *The Shivaree* (1982), *The Canadian Brothers* (1983), and *Imprecations* (1984) – a performance poem of invectives for
two voices. In *Fourteen Barrels from Sea to Sea* (1977) Reaney gives an
amusing account of the national tour of the Donnelly trilogy in 1975.

30 See Ross Stuart, 'Song in a Minor Key: Canada's Musical Theatre,' *CTR* 15
(1977); 'They're Playing Our Song: How Canadian Is Our Musical Theatre?'
Scene Changes 8:6 (1980); and J. Frederick Brown, 'The Charlottetown Festival in Review,' *CanD* 9:2 (1983).

31 Besides *Billy Bishop Goes to War*, among the most widely produced plays be-

tween 1972 and 1984 (including amateur productions, productions outside the country, and tours) were: David French, *Leaving Home* (Tarragon Theatre, 1972) and *Jitters* (Tarragon, 1979); Jack Winter et al., *Ten Lost Years* (TWT, 1974); John Murrell, *Waiting for the Parade* (Alberta Theatre Project, 1977); Allan Stratton, *Nurse Jane Goes to Hawaii* (Phoenix Theatre, 1981); Peter Colley, *I'll Be Back before Midnight* (Blyth Festival, 1979); David Fennario, *Balconville* (Centaur Theatre, 1979); and Carol Bolt, *One Night Stand* (Tarragon Theatre, 1977).

32 The almost simultaneous appearance of these three independent anthologies was matched by Ken Gass's attempt to start a Canadian Repertory Theatre in Toronto that same year (see Mira Friedlander, 'A Vision Vanishes: Canadian Rep Theatre Can't Find a Home,' *PerfA* 21:3 [1984]), and by the front page of the Entertainment Section of *G&M* for 9 February 1985, in which nine prominent theatre people were asked to select a repertory of five Canadian plays.

33 We wish to thank Anton Wagner, Ann Saddlemyer, Robert Wallace, Heather MacCallum, Glenn Hunter, Herma Joel, and Ruth Anne MacLennan for help with this chapter. For further listings see Anton Wagner, ed., *The Brock Bibliography of Published Canadian Plays in English 1766–1978* (1980) and the Playwrights Canada publication, *Directory of Canadian Plays and Playwrights* (1981), with a supplement in 1982.

CHAPTER NINE: CHILDREN'S LITERATURE

1 The Centre produces a children's book festival every November; publishes newsletters, information sheets, and 'meet-the-author' kits; provides research assistance, book displays, and speakers; and houses a comprehensive library.

2 New annual awards included the Canadian Association of Children's Librarians' Amelia Frances Howard-Gibbon illustrator's award (established in 1971), the IODE's award to an author or illustrator (1974), the Canada Council's children's literature prizes for authors (1975) and illustrators (1978), the Canadian Booksellers Association's Ruth Schwartz children's book award (1976), the Canadian Authors' Association's Vicky Metcalf award for a body of work (1975) and Vicky Metcalf short-story award (1978), and the Saskatchewan Library Association's Young Adult Canadian Book Award (1981).

3 'Children's Literature,' *LHC* (2nd ed., 1976), III, 205

4 *Galactic Warlord* (1979), *Deathwing over Veynaa* (1980), *Day of the Starwind* (1980), *Planet of the Warlord* (1981), *Young Legionary: The Earlier Adventures of Keill Randor* (1982)

5 See, for example, Mary Alice Downie's *The King's Loon* (1979) and *The Last Ship* (1980).

6 Many of their books have been subsidized by the Multiculturalism Directorate, Government of Canada. See *Publications Supported by the Multiculturalism Directorate, Government of Canada* (2 vols, 1983).

7 Retitled *Who Wants to Be Alone?* in 1974

8 Eg, *Hug Me* (1977), *Bo the Constrictor that Couldn't* (1978), *Sloan and Philamina, or How to Make Friends with Your Lunch* (1979)

9 See Dennis Lee, 'Roots and Play: Writing as a 35-Year-Old Children,' *CCL* 4 (1976).

10 Swede, *Tick Bird* (1983), *Time Is Flies* (1984); Nichol, *Once: A Lullaby* (1983), *The Man Who Loved His Knees* (1983), *To the End of the Block*

(1984); o'huigin, *The Trouble with Stitches* (1981), *Scary Poems for Rotten Kids* (1982), *Well, You Can Imagine* (1983)

11 The Canadian branch of ASSITEJ (Association internationale du théâtre pour l'enfance et la jeunesse) was founded in 1968 but has lacked funding to provide more than archival and information services for its members.

12 Eg, Rolf Kalman, ed., *A Collection of Canadian Plays*, Vol. IV (1975); *Kids Plays: Six Canadian Plays for Children* (1980); Joyce Doolittle, ed., *Eight Plays for Young People* (1984)

13 *OWL* has also reached television. *OWL-TV*, a program designed by the magazine's staff, made its debut on CBC and PBS television in the autumn of 1985.

14 Edited by Mary Rubio and Glenys Stow, then associate editors of *CCL*. In 1980 Rubio became co-editor, with Elizabeth Waterston, of *CCL*.

15 *Great Canadian Adventure Stories* (1979), *Great Canadian Animal Stories* (1978), *Stories from the Canadian North* (1980), *The Princess, the Hockey Player, Magic and Ghosts* (1980)

CHAPTER TEN: FOLKLORE

1 Laval publishes *CELAT – Information*; Laurentian University publishes *La Criée*.

2 Robin Gedalof compiled *An Annotated Bibliography of Canadian Inuit Literature* (1979), and Ralph Maud *A Guide to BC Indian Myth and Legend* (1982), an historical survey of Indian myth-collecting and published texts.

3 *Newfoundland Songs and Ballads in Print 1842–1974* (1979) by Paul Mercer; *A Regional Discography of Newfoundland and Labrador 1904–1971* (1975) by Michael Taft; and *Songs Sung by French Newfoundlanders: A Catalogue of the Holdings of the Memorial University of Newfoundland Folklore and Language Archive* (1978) by Gerald Thomas.

4 Bang-song Song, *The Korean-Canadian Folk Song* (1974); Paul McIntyre, *Black Pentecostal Music in Windsor* (1976); John Michael Glofcheskie, *Folk Music of Canada's Oldest Polish Community* (1980); and Gordon Cox, *Folk Music in a Newfoundland Outport* (1980)

5 These include Marie-Françoise Guedon's *People of the Tetlin, Why Are You Singing?* (1974); Robin Ridington's *Swan People: A Study of the Dunne-za Prophet Dance* (1978); *Eight Inuit Myths* (1979), transcribed and translated by Alex Spalding; *Inuit Songs from Eskimo Point* (1979) by Ramon Pelinski et al.; and *Gambling Music of the Coast Salish Indians* (1973) by Wendy B. Stuart.

CHAPTER ELEVEN: ANTHROPOLOGICAL LITERATURE

1 The best general history of anthropology is Marvin Harris, *The Rise of Anthropological Theory* (1968). Alternative versions are offered by F.W. Voget, *A History of Ethnology* (1975) and J.J. Honigmann, *The Development of Anthropological Ideas* (1976). For the history of prehistoric archeology, see Glyn Daniel, *A Hundred and Fifty Years of Archaeology* (1975) and G.R. Willey and J.A. Sabloff, *A History of American Archaeology* (2nd ed., 1980). The history of Canadian ethnology is examined in *The History of Canadian Anthropology* (1976), a series of papers edited by Michael M. Ames. Its early development is surveyed by Douglas Cole, 'The Origins of Canadian Anthropology,

1850–1910,' *JCS* 8:1 (1973), and work on the West Coast by Ralph Maud, *A Guide to BC Indian Myth and Legend* (1982). The history of Canadian archeology is covered by William C. Noble, 'One Hundred and Twenty-Five Years of Archaeology in the Canadian Provinces,' *Bulletin*, Can. Archaeological Assn 4 (1972), and James V. Wright, 'The Development of Prehistory in Canada, 1935–1985,' *Amer Antiquity* 50:2 (1985).

There is no general textbook or bibliography that can serve as an overall guide to the work of Canadian anthropologists. Recent developments in ethnology and social anthropology are surveyed and bibliographic data provided in *Consciousness and Inquiry: Ethnology and Canadian Realities* (1983), ed. Frank Manning, while anthropology in Quebec is examined in G-H. Lévesque et al., *Continuité et rupture: les sciences sociales au Québec* (2 vols, 1984). Other useful comments are found in David H. Turner, 'Canadian Ethnology Today,' *Anthropology Today* 1:4 (1985). The state of archeology as of the mid-1970s is covered in *New Perspectives in Canadian Archaeology*, ed. A.G. McKay (1977). Many anthropological works relating to native peoples of Canada can be found in G.P. Murdock and T.J. O'Leary, *Ethnographic Bibliography of North America* (5 vols, 1975); T.S. Abler and S.M. Weaver, *A Canadian Indian Bibliography, 1960–1970* (1974); and R.S. Allen, *Native Studies in Canada: A Research Guide* (2nd ed., 1984).

CHAPTER TWELVE: WRITINGS IN POLITICAL SCIENCE

1 See Georges-Henri Lévesque et al., *Continuité et rupture* (1984), for a collection of essays on the social sciences in Quebec, including political science.
2 See also Terence H. Qualter, *Conflicting Political Ideas in Liberal Democracies* (1986), for an even more recent text devoted to an exposition 'of the assumptions and goals of the three major ideologies that co-exist within the broader ideology of liberal democracy: liberalism, conservatism, and democratic socialism.'
3 The Symons Report is indispensable to students of the controversy in Canada. See T.H.B. Symons, *To Know Ourselves: The Report of the Commission on Canadian Studies*, Vols I and II (1975); T.H.B. Symons and James E. Page, *Some Questions of Balance: Human Resources, Higher Education and Canadian Studies*, Vol III (1984); and James E. Page, *Reflections on the Symons Report: The State of Canadian Studies in 1980: A Report Prepared for the Department of the Secretary of State of Canada* (1981).
4 For Canadian work see Jon H. Pammett et al., eds, *Foundations of Political Culture* (1976), and Sylvia B. Bashevkin, ed., *Canadian Political Behaviour* (1985).
5 David J. Elkins and Donald E. Blake, 'Voting Research in Canada: Problems and Prospects,' *CJPS* 8:2 (1975) 322
6 Louis Hartz et al., *The Founding of New Societies* (1964). For a brilliant interpretation of the debate, see H.D. Forbes, 'Hartz-Horowitz at Twenty: Nationalism, Toryism and Socialism in Canada and the United States,' *CJPS* 20:2 (1987).
7 Vols 59 to 70 of the research studies of the Royal Commission on the Economic Union and Development Prospects for Canada, dealing with federalism and the economic union, from the perspectives of law, economics, and political science, and co-ordinated by Mark Krasnick, Kenneth Norrie, and Richard

Simeon, provide an exhaustive survey of federalism for readers wishing more detailed analysis. They are published by the University of Toronto Press, 1985–6.

8 Keith G. Banting, *The Welfare State and Canadian Federalism* (1982); Anthony Careless, *Initiative and Response* (1977); J. Stefan Dupré et al., *Federalism and Policy Development* (1973); Donald J. Savoie, *Federal-Provincial Collaboration* (1981); Richard Schultz, *Federalism, Bureaucracy, and Public Policy* (1980); Neil A. Swainson, *Conflict over the Columbia* (1979); Malcolm G. Taylor, *Health Insurance and Canadian Public Policy* (1978); Hugh G. Thorburn, *Planning and the Economy* (1984)

9 Alan C. Cairns, 'The Governments and Societies of Canadian Federalism,' *CJPS* 10:4 (1977), and 'The Other Crisis of Canadian Federalism,' *CPA* 22:2 (1979)

10 Rainer Knopff and F.L. Morton, 'Nation-Building and the Canadian Charter of Rights and Freedoms,' in Alan Cairns and Cynthia Williams, eds, *Constitutionalism, Citizenship and Society in Canada* (1985); Clare F. Beckton and A. Wayne MacKay, eds, *The Courts and the Charter* (1985)

11. The prolific writings of Edward McWhinney straddled political science and law. He pioneered the introduction of American legal scholarship to Canada in his volume *Judicial Review in the English-Speaking World* (1956) and published extensively on federalism from a comparative perspective.

12 Donald V. Smiley, 'The Case against the Canadian Charter of Human Rights,' *CJPS* 2:3 (1969); 'Courts, Legislatures, and the Protection of Human Rights,' in Martin L. Friedland, ed., *Courts and Trials* (1975); *The Canadian Charter of Rights and Freedoms, 1981* (1981)

13 Jean-Charles Bonenfant exhaustively reviewed the Royal Commission's research in three review articles: 'Les études de la Commission royale d'enquête sur le bilinguisme et le biculturalisme,' *CJPS* 4:3 (1971); 5:2 (1972); 5:3 (1972). The unpublished research is discussed in Christopher R. Adamson et al., 'The Unpublished Research of the Royal Commission on Bilingualism and Biculturalism,' *CJPS* 7:4 (1974).

14 *Report of the Royal Commission of Inquiry on Constitutional Problems* (Quebec 1956)

15 Kenneth McRoberts, 'The Study of English-French Relations in Canada' (mimeo, May 1982, to be published in a forthcoming volume edited by Michael Stein, John Trent, and André Donneur, *Canadian Political Science*). This section on French-English relations owes much to this valuable article.

16 Most of the relevant literature is cited in Donald V. Smiley and Ronald L. Watts, *Intrastate Federalism in Canada* (1985). See also Peter Aucoin, ed., *Party Government and Regional Representation in Canada* (1985) and *Regional Responsiveness and the National Administrative State* (1985).

17 Frank MacKinnon, *The Crown in Canada* (1976); Thomas A. Hockin, ed., *Apex of Power* (2nd ed., 1977); W.A. Matheson, *The Prime Minister and the Cabinet* (1976); Colin Campbell and George Szablowski, *The Superbureaucrats* (1979); Colin Campbell, *Governments under Stress* (1983); Richard D. French, *How Ottawa Decides* (1980; rev. 1984); Robert J. Jackson and Michael M. Atkinson, *The Canadian Legislative System* (2nd rev. ed., 1980); John B. Stewart, *The Canadian House of Commons* (1977); Colin Campbell, *The Canadian Senate* (1978)

18 Banting, ed., *State and Society* (1986); Blais, ed., *Industrial Policy* (1986);

Lermer, ed., *Probing Leviathan* (1984); Sutherland and Doern, *Bureaucracy in Canada* (1985)

19 Robert F. Adie and Paul G. Thomas, *Canadian Public Administration: Problematical Perspectives* (1982); G. Bruce Doern and Richard W. Phidd, *Canadian Public Policy* (1983); O.P. Dwivedi, ed., *The Administrative State in Canada: Essays in Honour of J.E. Hodgetts* (1982); J.E. Hodgetts, *The Canadian Public Service* (1973); Kenneth Kernaghan, ed., *Canadian Public Administration: Discipline and Profession* (1983); V. Seymour Wilson, *Canadian Public Policy and Administration* (1981); Richard W. Phidd and G. Bruce Doern, *The Politics and Management of Canadian Economic Policy* (1978); M.M. Atkinson and M.A. Chandler, eds, *The Politics of Canadian Public Policy* (1983); G. Bruce Doern, ed., *The Politics of Economic Policy* (1985)

20 Thomas R. Berger, *Northern Frontier, Northern Homeland: The Report of the Mackenzie Valley Pipeline Inquiry* (1977); Kenneth M. Lysyk et al., *Report of the Alaska Highway Pipeline Inquiry* (1977)

21 Timothy J. Colton, cited in T.J. Plunkett and Katherine A. Graham, 'Whither municipal government?' *CPA* 25:4 (1982) 618

22 D.J. Higgins, *Urban Canada* (1977); Lionel D. Feldman, ed., *Politics and Government of Urban Canada* (4th ed., 1981); Warren Magnusson and Andrew Sancton, eds, *City Politics in Canada* (1983); C.R. Tindal and S. Nobes Tindal, *Local Government in Canada* (2nd ed., 1984)

23 'Metropolitan Reform in the Capitalist City,' *CJPS* 14:3 (1981); 'Urban Politics and the Local State,' *SPE* 16 (1985); 'The Local State in Canada: Theoretical Perspectives,' *CPA* 28:4 (1985)

24 See the review by Donald E. Blake in *CJPS* 10:1 (1977).

25 See the chapters by Courtney and Leslie Seidle in John C. Courtney, ed., *The Canadian House of Commons: Essays in Honour of Norman Ward* (1985).

26 *The Government Party* (1977); *The L-Shaped Party* (1981); *The Regional Decline of a National Party* (1981); *The Tory Syndrome* (1980); and George C. Perlin, Patrick Martin, and Allan Gregg, *Contenders* (1983)

27 *The Communist Party in Canada* (1975); *Socialism in Canada* (1978). See also Norman Penner, *The Canadian Left* (1977).

28 See also Varda Burstyn, ed., *Women Against Censorship* (1985); Lorenne Clark and Debra Lewis, *Rape: The Price of Coercive Sexuality* (1977); Jean Cochrane, *Women in Canadian Politics* (1977); Heather Menzies, *Women and the Chip* (1981); and Jill M. Vickers, ed., *Taking Sex into Account: The Policy Consequences of Sexist Research* (1984), for useful contributions to this rapidly expanding literature.

29 Canada-US relations are discussed in the following volumes: Andrew Axline et al., eds, *Continental Community?* (1974); Annette Baker Fox et al., eds, *Canada and the United States* (1976); John Holmes, *Life with Uncle* (1981); Doran and Sigler, eds, *Canada and the United States*; Jon H. Pammett and Brian W. Tomlin, eds, *The Integration Question* (1984); Eric Kierans, *Globalism and the Nation-State* (1984).

30 A select bibliography of his works and an evaluation of his scholarship appear in a 1982 Festschrift: Kim Richard Nossal, ed., *An Acceptance of Paradox*.

31 Freda Hawkins, *Canada and Immigration* (1972); Gerald E. Dirks, *Canada's Refugee Policy* (1977)

32 Eg, R.S. Milne, *Politics in Ethnically Bipolar States* (1981); and Anthony H. Birch, *Political Integration and Disintegration in the British Isles* (1977)

33 Work by Herman Bakvis (Netherlands), Anthony H. Birch (United Kingdom), Alberto Ciria (Argentina), Kenneth Heard (South Africa), Jean Laponce (France), Toivo Miljan (Scandinavia), Khalid Bin Sayeed (Pakistan), A.H. Somjee (India), and A. Jeyaratnam Wilson (Sri Lanka) illustrates the phenomenon.

34 Keith Banting, ed., *The State and Economic Interests* (1986), especially the chapters by Banting, Coleman, Fournier, and Panitch

35 See the various works on British government and politics by Keith G. Banting, Anthony H. Birch, R. Kenneth Carty, Colin Leys, and Leo Panitch.

36 The international debate can be followed in Susan Moller Okin, *Women in Western Political Thought* (1979); Jean Bethke Elshtain, ed., *The Family in Political Thought* (1982); and Genevieve Lloyd, *The Man of Reason: 'Male' and 'Female' in Western Philosophy* (1984).

37 See the now classic discussion of Heidi Hartmann, 'The Unhappy Marriage of Marxism and Feminism: Towards a More Progressive Union,' in Lydia Sargent, ed., *Women and Revolution* (1981).

38 *Democracy in Alberta* (1953); *The Political Theory of Possessive Individualism* (1962); *The Real World of Democracy* (1965)

39 *Philosophy in the Mass Age* (1959); *Lament for a Nation* (1965); *Technology and Empire* (1969); *Time as History* (1969). Bibliographies and discussions of Grant's thought can be found in Larry Schmidt, ed., *George Grant in Process* (1978), and in Joan E. O'Donovan, *George Grant and the Twilight of Justice* (1984).

40 Braybrooke, 'The Meaning of Participation and of Demands for It: A Preliminary Survey of the Conceptual Issues,' in J.R. Pennock and J.W. Chapman, eds, Nomos XVI: *Participation in Politics* (1975), and *Three Tests for Democracy: Personal Rights, Human Welfare, Collective Preference* (1968); Gunn, *Beyond Liberty and Property* (1983), *Factions No More* (1972), and *Politics and the Public Interest in the Seventeenth Century* (1969); Beiner, *Political Judgment* (1983); Gad Horowitz, *Repression: Basic and Surplus Repression in Psychoanalytic Theory* (1977); Alkis Kontos, ed., *Domination* (1975); William Leiss, *The Limits to Satisfaction* (1976), and Arthur Kroker, *Technology and the Canadian Mind: Innis, McLuhan, Grant* (1984); David Wolfe, 'State Policy and Politics,' Chap. 23 of Drache and Clement, eds, *New Practical Guide*, and the numerous references in Keith Banting, 'Images of the Modern State: An Introduction' in Banting, ed., *State and Society*; Anthony Parel and Thomas Flanagan, eds, *Theories of Property: Aristotle to the Present* (1979); C.B. Macpherson, ed., *Property: Mainstream and Critical Positions* (1978); W.J. Stankiewicz, ed., *Political Thought since World War II* (1964), and *In Defense of Sovereignty* (1969)

41 Wood and Wood, *Class Ideology and Ancient Political Theory: Socrates, Plato, and Aristotle in Social Context* (1978); Anthony Parel, ed., *The Political Calculus: Essays on Machiavelli's Philosophy* (1972); David Kettler, *The Social and Political Thought of Adam Ferguson* (1965), *Marxismus and Kultur* (1967), subsequently translated by Erich Weck and Tobias Rülcker as 'Culture and Revolution: Lukács in the Hungarian Revolutions of 1918/19,' *Telos* 10 (1971); and (with Volker Meja and Nico Stehr) *Karl Mannheim* (1984) and a translation of Mannheim's *Structures of Thinking* (1982) and *Conservatism* (1985); Macpherson, *Burke* (1980); Tully, *A Discourse on Property: John Locke and His Adversaries* (1980); and Wood, *The Politics of Locke's Philoso-*

phy: A Social Study of 'An Essay Concerning Human Understanding' (1983), and *John Locke and Agrarian Capitalism* (1984); Barry Cooper, *The End of History: An Essay on Modern Hegelianism* (1984); and Tom Darby, *The Feast: Meditations on Politics and Time* (1982)

42 For introductions to this complex issue see J.G.A. Pocock, *Virtue, Commerce, and History* (1985) 1–34; Neal Wood's introductory chapter to *John Locke and Agrarian Capitalism*; Quentin Skinner's seminal article, 'Meaning and Understanding in the History of Ideas,' *History and Theory* 8 (1969); and John G. Gunnell, *Political Theory: Tradition and Interpretation* (1979).

43 Arthur Kroker, 'Canadian Political Theory,' in Drache and Clement, eds, *New Practical Guide* 170

CHAPTER THIRTEEN: WRITINGS IN CANADIAN HISTORY

1 In its fragmentation, Canadian historical writing came to resemble that in Europe and the United States. See Carl Berger, *The Writing of Canadian History* (1976); Serge Gagnon, *Quebec and Its Historians: The Twentieth Century* (1985). Two selective bibliographies are *A Reader's Guide to Canadian History 1: Beginnings to Confederation* (1982), ed. D.A. Muise, and *2: Confederation to the Present* (1982), ed. J.L. Granatstein and Paul Stevens. The most detailed surveys are provided in each issue of *CHR*.

2 Not all were historians of Canada. Indeed, one of the most significant developments in the study of history in general in Canada over the last twenty years has been the increasing prominence, in both teaching and publication, of fields other than Canadian. To those few individuals mentioned by William Kilbourn in Volume I of this *Literary History* (2nd ed., 1976) 518, might be added many others who have published significant monographs on the histories of individual European countries, the Third World, and the United States. This literature was more closely attuned to issues, themes, and approaches shared by international communities of scholars than to Canadian conditions. But indirectly it impinged upon the writing of Canadian history both by broadening the context in which Canadian history was taught and, in some cases, by presenting alternative models of how history could be written.

3 See Robin Neill, *A New Theory of Value* (1977); Innis issue, *JCS* 12:5 (1977); *The Idea File of Harold Adams Innis* (1980), introduced and edited by William Christian.

4 See David McNally, 'Staple Theory as Commodity Fetishism: Marx, Innis and Canadian Political Economy,' *SPE* 6 (1981).

5 Doug McCalla, 'Tom Naylor's *A History of Canadian Business, 1867–1914*: A Comment,' and Naylor, 'Trends in the Business History of Canada, 1867–1914,' both in *HP* (1976). On the special problems of writing corporate history see Duncan McDowall, 'Business History as Public History: One of Canada's Infant Industries,' *JCS* 20:3 (1985).

6 For bibliographies, see Grace Heggie, *Canadian Political Parties, 1867–1968* (1977) and Allan Moscovitch, *The Welfare State in Canada* (1983).

7 See W.A.B. Douglas, 'Filling Gaps in the Military Past: Recent Developments in Canadian Official History,' *JCS* 19:3 (1984); A.M.J. Hyatt, 'Military Studies in Canada: An Overview,' *R Internationale d'Histoire Militaire* 51 (1982); O.A. Cooke, *The Canadian Military Experience 1867–1983: A Bibliography* (1984).

8 See Smith, *Prairie Liberalism* (1975); O'Flaherty, *The Rock Observed* (1979); Harrison, *Unnamed Country* (1977).

9 For an assessment of Clark's work and examples of the writing of the students, see James R. Gibson, ed., *European Settlement and Development in North America* (1978).

10 *Bibliography of Ontario History, 1867–1976: Cultural, Economic, Political, Social* (1980), comp. Olga B. Bishop, Barbara I. Irwin, and Clara G. Miller

11 Lewis H. Thomas, ed., *Essays on Western History in Honour of Lewis Gwynne Thomas* (1976); Carl Berger and Ramsay Cook, eds, *The West and the Nation* (1976); John F. Foster, *The Developing West* (1983); Alan F. Artibise, *Western Canada since 1870: A Select Bibliography and Guide* (1978)

12 See William G. Godfrey, ' "A New Golden Age": Recent Historical Writing on the Maritimes,' *QQ* 91:2 (1984). Philip A. Buckner and David Frank, eds, anthologized some important articles on Atlantic Canada in *The Acadiensis Reader* (2 vols, 1985).

13 *Acadiensis* 1:2 (1972)

14 These books were discussed and preliminary findings summarized in Eric W. Sager and Lewis B. Fischer, 'Atlantic Canada and the Age of Sail Revisited,' *CHR* 63:2 (1982), and Eric W. Sager, 'The Maritime History Group and the History of Seafaring Labour,' *Labour* 15 (1985).

15 See William Westfall, 'On the Concept of Region in Canadian History and Literature,' *JCS* 15:2 (1980).

16 See Ronald Rudin, 'Recent Trends in Quebec Historiography,' *QQ* 92:1 (1985).

17 See John Moir, 'Coming of Age, but Slowly: Aspects of Canadian Religious Historiography since Confederation,' *Study Sessions* of the Can. Catholic Hist. Assn 50 (1983). This journal has since 1964 carried an excellent 'Current Bibliography of Canadian Church History.'

18 See Hilda Neatby, *Queen's University* 1 (1980), ed. Frederick W. Gibson and Roger Graham; Frederick Gibson, *Queen's University* 2 (1983); Charles M. Johnston, *McMaster University* (2 vols, 1970, 1981); Stanley B. Frost, *McGill University* (2 vols, 1980, 1984); John Reid, *Mount Allison University* (2 vols, 1984). For a critical survey, see Paul Axelrod, 'Historical Writing and Canadian Universities: The State of the Art,' *QQ* 89:1 (1982); see also Robin S. Harris, *A Bibliography of Higher Education in Canada: Supplement 1981*.

19 Richard A. Jarrell and Arnold E. Roos, *A Bibliography for Courses in the History of Science, Medicine and Technology* (1979)

20 Peter Weinrich, *Social Protest from the Left in Canada 1870–1970: A Bibliography* (1982); G. Douglas Vaisey, *The Labour Companion: A Bibliography of Canadian Labour History Based on Materials Printed from 1950 to 1975* (1980)

21 *HP* (1974)

22 Gregory S. Kealey, 'Labour and Working-Class History in Canada: Prospects in the 1980s,' *Labour* 7 (1981); Kenneth McNaught, 'E.P. Thompson vs Harold Logan: Writing about Labour and the Left in the 1970s,' *CHR* 62:2 (1981)

23 Allan Smith, 'National Images and National Maintenance: The Ascendancy of the Ethnic Idea in North America,' *CJPS* 14:2 (1981); Howard Palmer, 'History and Present State of Ethnic Studies in Canada,' in W. Isajiw, ed., *Identities* (1977)

24 The other volumes that have appeared are discussed in conjunction with recent article literature in Roberto Perin, 'Clio as an Ethnic: The Third Force in Canadian Historiography,' *CHR* 64:4 (1983).
25 The figure is from Eliane L. Silverman, 'Writing Canadian Women's History, 1970–82: An Historiographical Analysis,' *CHR* 63:4 (1982) 513; see also Beth Light and Veronica Strong-Boag, *True Daughters of the North: Canadian Women's History: An Annotated Bibliography* (1980).
26 *Labour* 4 (1979)
27 J. Donald Wilson, 'Some Observations on Recent Trends in Canadian Educational History,' in his *An Imperfect Past* (1984).
28 Alan F. Artibise and Gilbert A. Stelter, *Canada's Urban Past: A Bibliography to 1980 and Guide to Canadian Urban Studies* (1981)
29 Maurice Careless, 'Limited Identities – Ten Years Later,' *Manitoba History* 1 (1980); Desmond Morton, 'History and Nationality in Canada: Variations on an Old Theme,' *HP* (1979)

CHAPTER FOURTEEN: LIFE-WRITING

1 I paraphrase here the first major theoretical essay on women's autobiography: Mary G. Mason, 'The Other Voice: Autobiographies of Women Writers,' in James Olney, ed., *Autobiography: Essays Theoretical and Critical* (1980), 210. Subsequent writing about women's autobiography has followed this theoretical lead.
2 This is also evident in the 'journal' poems of *In the Month of Hungry Ghosts* (*Net Work* 129: 'I'm finding out more about the taboos I was raised with, the unspoken confines of behaviour, than I am about Penang').
3 The term 'autobiological' I take from George Bowering's *Autobiology*. The notion of 'autobiology' seems to have been one preoccupation of the writers publishing in the *Georgia Straight* Writing Supplement, Vancouver Series. The back cover of Bowering's volume (#7 in the Supplements; Marlatt's *Rings* was #3) echoes Marlatt's with its photograph of Bowering holding his infant daughter; Bowering's focus in his text, however, is more accurately reflected by the front cover's photograph of himself as a child with his mother.
4 These theories, and the questions they raise about genre, have had their effect on colloquia about autobiography in Canada: at both the 1983 ACQL meetings on the topic 'Je est un autre' and at the 1987 University of Ottawa symposium on Canadian autobiography, a significant number of papers were devoted to works that were not autobiographical by conventional generic definition.
5 Critical work on this sort of autobiography is rare; in Canada, see Helen Buss, 'Canadian Women's Autobiography: The Embodiment of a Tradition' (PH D dissertation, University of Manitoba 1987). That this will soon change may be indicated by three events: (1) the publication in *Études littéraires* [Quebec] 17:2 (1984), of theorist Philippe Lejeune's 'La Cote Ln 27' (rpt Lejeune, *Moi aussi*, 1986), which outlines a project to write a social history of all nineteenth-century French autobiographies; (2) the study of the literary institution of Quebec under way for some years at the Centre de recherche en littérature québécoise at Université Laval; and (3) a similar study for the Canadian literatures, undertaken more recently by the History of the Literary Institution in Canada/Histoire de l'institution littéraire au Canada at the University of Al-

berta. Autobiography is only one of many genres looked at by the CRELIQ and the HOLIC/HILAC projects; the interest of both goes beyond those works canonized as 'literary' to the entire written production within this and other genres.

6 Some of the many examples about pioneers include: Harry Piniuta, *Land of Pain Land of Promise: First Person Accounts by Ukrainian Pioneers, 1891–1914* (1978); Bill McNeil, *Voice of the Pioneer* (1978); Moira Farrow, *Nobody Here but Us: Pioneers of the North* (1975); Heather Robertson, *Salt of the Earth* (1974; it is Heather Robertson who is the subject of Knight's remarks [later in my text] about class stereotyping); *A Harvest Yet to Reap* (1976, about women pioneers). The two world wars are addressed in William D. Mathieson, *My Grandfather's War: Canadians Remember the First World War, 1914–1918* (1981); Gordon Reid, ed., *Poor Bloody Murder: Personal Memories of the First World War* (1980); William Repka and Kathleen M. Repka, *Dangerous Patriots: Canada's Unknown Prisoners of War* (1982); and Joyce Hibbert, ed., *The War Brides* (1978). Other examples of the genre include Gloria Montero, *The Immigrants* (1977) and, at the other end of the social scale and using more extended (though in some cases scarcely more literary) written narratives, Margaret Gillett and Kay Sibbald, *A Fair Shake: Autobiographical Essays by McGill Women* (1984).

7 Philippe LeJeune's observation about this mode of 'autobiography' is germane: 'The act of writing assumed by another pushes into view the absence of initiative and of a plan, the fact that this recollection is not a creative act, that it serves no purpose for the one who remembers, even if it awakes nostalgia or fancies. The awakening, the process of analysis and knowledge are the act of the investigator ... and not of the investigated, whom the enquiry leaves unchanged' (*Je est un autre: l'autobiographie de la littérature aux médias*, 1980, 270; my translation).

8 Some 1984 examples: Jack Cahill, *John Turner: The Long Run*; L. Ian MacDonald, *Mulroney: The Making of a Prime Minister*; and Rae Murphy, Robert Chodos, and Nick Auf der Maur, *Brian Mulroney: The Boy from Baie-Comeau*

9 H. Pearson Gundy, ed., *Letters of Bliss Carman* (1981), judiciously selected with usefully concise notes in a handsomely produced volume; Desmond Pacey, ed., *The Letters of Frederick Philip Grove* (1976); Francis W.P. Bolger and Elizabeth R. Epperly, eds, *My dear Mr M: Letters to G.B. MacMillan from L.M. Montgomery* (1980); Carl Ballstadt, Elizabeth Hopkins, and Michael Peterman, eds, *Susanna Moodie: Letters of a Lifetime* (1985), a model edition of letters in terms of its notes and textual apparatus; Louis Dudek, *Dk: Some Letters of Ezra Pound* (1974); Bruce Whiteman, ed., *A Literary Friendship: The Correspondence of Ralph Gustafson and W.W.E. Ross* (1984)

10 *An Appetite for Life: The Education of a Young Diarist, 1924–1927* (1977); *The Siren Years: A Canadian Diplomat Abroad, 1937–1945* (1974); *Diplomatic Passport: More Undiplomatic Diaries, 1946–1962* (1981); and *Storm Signals: More Undiplomatic Diaries, 1962–1971* (1983).

11 At the same time as the DCB volumes have been appearing, more specialized biographical reference works have also been published. The best is William Toye, ed., *The Oxford Companion to Canadian Literature* (1983); Keith MacMillan and John Beckwith, eds, *Contemporary Canadian Composers* (1975) and the poorly written Don Rubin and Alison Cranmer-Byng, eds, *Canada's Playwrights: A Biographical Guide* (1980) also provide information.

12 Other well-edited titles: *The Journal of William Sturgis*, ed. S.W. Jackman

(1978); *The New World Journal of Alexander Graham Dunlop 1845*, ed. David Sinclair and Germaine Warkentin (1976); *Expeditions of Honour: The Journal of John Salusbury in Halifax, Nova Scotia, 1749–53*, ed. Ronald Rompkey (1982); *The Rundle Journals 1840–1848*, ed. Hugh A. Dempsey (1977); Lois Halliday McDonald, *Fur Trade Letters of Francis Ermatinger* (1980); *From Duck Lake to Dawson City: The Diary of Eben McAdam's Journey to the Klondike, 1898–1899*, ed. R.G. Moyles (1977).

13 See also: *Lifelines: The Stacey Letters, 1836–1858*, ed. Jane Vansittart (1976); Helgi Einarsson, *Helgi Einarsson: A Manitoba Fisherman*, trans. George Houser (1982); *Western Canada 1909: Travel Letters by Wilhelm Cohnstaedt*, published as newspaper articles in Germany in 1909, trans. Herta Holle-Scherer, ed. Klaus H. Burmeister (1976); Monica Hopkins, *Letters from a Lady Rancher* (1981); *The Reminiscences of Doctor John Sebastian Helmcken*, ed. Dorothy Blakey Smith (1975); *God's Galloping Girl: The Peace River Diaries of Monica Storrs, 1929–1931*, ed. W.L. Morton (1979; rpt 1984); *A Gentleman Adventurer: The Arctic Diaries of R.H.G. Bonnycastle*, ed. Heather Robertson (1984); Archie Hunter, *Northern Traders* (1983). None will impress by their literariness; all are informative.

14 From World War I: William G. Ogilvie, *Umty-Iddy-Umty: The Story of a Canadian Signaller in the First World War* (1982); Frank J. Shrive, *The Diary of a PBO*, ed. Norman Shrive (1981). The Spanish Civil War is the initiating event in Manuel Alvarez, *The Tall Soldier* (1980) and *Seven Years at Sea* (1983). From World War II: Fred Cederberg, *The Long Road Home: The Autobiography of a Canadian Soldier in Italy in World War II* (1984) and John Patrick Grogan, *Dieppe and Beyond for a Dollar and a Half a Day* (1982), both written with the adventure novel too much in mind; Murray Peden, *A Thousand Shall Fall* (1979), a strong and accurate narrative of a bomber pilot; Robert Buckham, *Forced March to Freedom* (1984), a well-written account based on diaries of a prisoner-of-war's trip out of Germany when hostilities ceased; *Alex Colville: Diary of a War Artist*, comp. Graham Metson and Cheryl Lean (1981), bringing together Colville's diary and visual work from the war years.

15 Other work addressing Riel, his associates, and those with whom he negotiated includes Peter Charlebois, *The Life of Louis Riel* (1975; rev. 1978); George Woodcock, *Gabriel Dumont* (1975; a well-crafted popular biography); and Dale Gibson (with Lee Gibson and Cameron Harvey), *Attorney for the Frontier: Enos Stutsman* (1983).

16 Typical of most Canadian biography, Walmsley's attention to the bishop's personal life is token to a fault: eg, 'So many important public events transpired in the years 1934–48 that developments in his personal life might easily be overlooked. One major episode was the death of his wife and his marriage to Daisy Masters.' Wives go and wives come and good Christian gentlemen evidently neither mourn nor celebrate.

17 Eg: O.J. Firestone, *The Other A.Y. Jackson: A Memoir* (1979); Marjorie Lismer Bridges, *A Border of Beauty: Arthur Lismer's Pen and Pencil* (1977); Peter Varley, *Frederick H. Varley* (1983); Anne McDougall, *Anne Savage: The Story of a Canadian Painter* (1977)

18 Unpromising subjects: Lindner leads Terrence Heath to some telling questions in *Uprooted: The Life and Art of Ernest Lindner* (1983), but leaves his biographer with either too little information or too little substance in the life itself to

provide telling answers. William Blair Bruce, a derivative and unimportant painter, who passed his career in a gentle diminuendo in Europe, unfortunately left letters, which are edited, with a biographical introduction, by Joan Murray (*Letters Home 1859–1906*, 1982); neither the life nor the work justifies the attention.

19 Failure to transform promising material into major biography: Frances K. Smith in *André Biéler* (1980) gives a detailed account of Biéler's professional career in its Canadian context, but does not account convincingly for the man behind the career. G. Blair Laing in *Morrice* (1984) attempts to avoid the dryness of academic biography only to indulge in tourist nostalgia over the places Morrice lived. Jean McGill in *The Joy of Effort: A Biography of R. Tait McKenzie* (1980), while reasonably full about the sculptor's life, attends too little to narrative organization and style. Joan Murray (an important archival scholar and curator), in *Daffodils in Winter: The Life and Letters of Pegi Nicol MacLeod* (1984), provides insufficient information in the narrative connecting the letters; as in her *The Last Buffalo: The Story of Frederick Arthur Verner* (1984), Murray seldom evaluates and is overly reticent about motivations.

20 Architect William Critchlow Harris is the subject of Robert C. Tuck's *Gothic Dreams* (1978) and *The Island Family Harris: Letters of an Immigrant Family in British North America, 1856–1866* (1983). Portrait painter Robert Harris is Moncrieff Williamson's subject in *Robert Harris* (1970), to which he added and deleted material for a popular press version, *Island Painter* (1983).

21 Ira Nadel, 'Canadian Biography and Literary Form,' *ECW* 33 (1986) 152

22 The sense of credibility paradoxically created by dramatizing conversations that could not possibly be remembered verbatim depends to a considerable extent on the complexity of the relations presented in the autobiography and on the intelligence assumed in the reader. Tim Buck's *Yours in the Struggle*, ed. William Bucking and Phyllis Clarke (1977), for example, fails where Pelletier succeeds because the Buck volume is entirely political, giving no sense of the relations between persons that enter into any conversation, and because the style of the volume assumes minimal intelligence in the reader.

23 Eg, Oscar Ryan, *Tim Buck* (1975); Louise Watson, *She Never Was Afraid: The Biography of Annie Buller* (1976); Tom McEwen, *The Forge Glows Red* (1974)

24 Swainson, 'Trends in Canadian Biography: Recent Historical Wriiting,' *QQ* 87:3 (1980); Grosskurth, 'Search and Psyche: The Writing of Biography,' *English Studies in Canada* 11:2 (1985); Ira B. Nadel, *Biography* (1984), and 'Canadian Biography'

25 W.H. New, 'Says Who?' *CanL* 90 (1981); George Woodcock, 'Don't Ever Ask for the True Story; Or, Second Thoughts on Autobiography,' *ECW* 29 (1984)

26 Swainson, 'Trends,' and Nadel, 'Canadian Biography'

27 One or more of these failings can be found in R.H. Macdonald, *Grant MacEwan* (1979); James Doyle, *Annie Howells and Achille Fréchette* (1979); John Coldwell Adams, *Seated with the Mighty: A Biography of Sir Gilbert Parker* (1979); David R. Beasley, *The Canadian Don Quixote: The Life and Works of Major John Richardson, Canada's First Novelist* (1977; inaccurate even in its title); Wayne E. Edmonstone, *Nathan Cohen* (1977); Dorothy Farmiloe, *Isabella Valancy Crawford* (1983).

28 Magdalene Redekop's *Ernest Thompson Seton* (1979) is less ambitious.

29 Two other essays address Glassco's autobiographical self-invention: John Lauber in *CanL* 90 (1981), and Stephen Scobie in *Can Poetry* 13 (1983).

30 An essay by Clarke in *CanL* 95 (1982), 'In the Semi-Colon of the North,' uses an unusual allegory with three musical compositions to describe a Toronto-Timmins journey; a note indicates it is part of a second volume of autobiography to be titled *The Colonial*.

31 An element of 'correction' also enters into this identification with Lily Briscoe which Meigs means to counter Mary McCarthy's depiction of her as Dolly Lamb in *A Charmed Life*. In Meigs's second autobiography, *The Medusa Head* (1983), this element of self-justification proves incompatible with autobiography. Writing about a *ménage-à-trois* which has already been the subject of novels by the other two women, Meigs foregoes, she says, 'the novelist's privilege: to retell the story, to make things fit, to withhold evidence, and finally, to inflict capital punishment' in favour of the autobiographer's 'own personal truth.' The egotism and malice of all three *textes à clef*, however, overcome narrative art.

32 Much less successful attempts of the same type: Shulamis Yelin, *Shulamis* (1983); Harry J. Boyle, *Memories of a Catholic Boyhood* (1973)

33 Among poets and novelists with Canadian childhoods: Irving Layton, with insufficient irony, in 'Waiting for the Messiah,' *CanL* 101 (1984); Roy Daniells, movingly and analytically in 'Plymouth Brother,' and Earle Birney, 'Child Addict in Alberta,' both in *CanL* 90 (1981). Personal essays outside the childhood genre include autobiographical anecdotes by George Woodcock, 'The Dynamite Man,' *CanL* 90 (1981); Clark Blaise, 'Portrait of the Artist as Young Pup' and 'Mentors,' *CanL* 100, 101 (1984), and Daphne Marlatt, 'Entering In: The Immigrant Imagination,' *CanL* 100 (1984).

CHAPTER SIXTEEN: FROM AUTHOR TO READER

1 Lewis A. Cosser, Charles Kadushin, and Walter W. Powell, *Books: The Culture and Commerce of Publishing* (1982); Walter W. Powell, *Getting into Print: The Decision-making Process in Scholarly Publishing* (1985); an influential earlier publication in this field was in the September 1975 *Annals* of the American Academy of Political and Social Science, entitled 'Perspectives on Publishing'; see also John Y. Cole, ed., *Responsibilities of the American Book Community* (1981); Stephen Graubard, ed., *Reading in the 1980s* (1983), reprinted from *Daedalus*; Walter C. Allen, Eleanor Blum, and Ann Heidbreder Eastman, eds, *The Quality of Trade Book Publishing in the 1980s* (*Library Trends* 33:2 [1984]; Mary Biggs, ed., *Publishers and Librarians: A Foundation for Dialogue* (1984); Taylor Hubbard, ed., *The New Publishers* (*Drexel Library Q* 20:3 [1984]; see also Thomas Whiteside, *The Blockbuster Complex: Conglomerates, Show Business, and Book Publishing* (1981); Peter H. Mann, *From Author to Reader: A Social Study of Books* (1982).

2 The research co-operative CANLIT, which was founded on the West Coast in 1973 'to investigate all aspects of Canadian literature, publishing, and culture' and has now disbanded, issued in 1980 an 84-page study called *Paper Phoenix: A History of Book Publishing in English Canada* by Dolores Broten and Peter Birdsall. This study provides a useful overview of developments in the trade. It was preceded by an annotated research bibliography entitled *Studies in the Book Trade*.

3 Other helpful comments about this field of study by those involved in it or with it are John Feather's 'Cross-Channel Currents: Historical Bibliography and *l'histoire du livre*' (*The Library*, 6th series 2:1 [1980]), G. Thomas Tanselle's lecture 'The History of Books as a Field of Study' (*TLS* [5 June 1981] and issued separately by the Hanes Foundation, University of North Carolina at Chapel Hill), and proceedings of two important 1980 conferences, *Books and Society in History* and *Printing and Society in Early America* (reviewed by Thomas R. Adams in *Papers of the Bibliog Soc of America* 79:4 [1985]). Elizabeth Eisenstein's two-volume *The Printing Press as an Agent of Change* (1979) is often referred to at length in discussions about the role of the book, although there are some who have misgivings about her historical method (see a review by Paul Needham in *Fine Print* 6:1 [1980]).

4 In introducing his 'mémoire,' *L'édition au Québec de 1960 à 1977*, Ignace Cau notes that only one monograph on Quebec publishing preceded his own, Jean-Pierre Chalifoux's *L'édition au Québec 1940–1950* (1973). An associate of the sociology department at l'université de Montréal, Cau indicates in his introduction that he has found his approach in the ideas of Robert Escarpit in France (citing Escarpit's *Sociologie de la littérature*, 1958, and later studies), which he analyzes. His study, stretching across tumultuous years of Quebec's cultural and literary history, outlines the evolution of Quebec publishing in those years from an economic and political point of view, then describes the categories of publications which developed, and finally characterizes publishing houses before providing a quantity of statistical tables. He reminds us of an important work in this whole area of discussion, *Littérature et société canadienne-française* by Fernand Dumont and Jean-Charles Falardeau et al. (1964).

5 A result of these acquisitions is *A Bibliography of Macmillan of Canada Imprints 1906–1980* by Bruce Whiteman, Charlotte Stewart, and Catherine Funnell (1985), the kind of study which is essential information for work on publishing, on titles, and on authors.

6 *Scholarly Publishing* 16:1 (1984) contains a useful account by John Dessauer of the founding of the Book Industry Study Group in the United States in 1976 and of the Center for Book Research at the University of Scranton in 1983; the Center established in 1985 a periodical *Book Research Q* to encourage scholarly enquiry. The Center has now closed, but the periodical continues under the Transaction Periodicals Consortium, Rutgers University.

7 *Canadian Books in Print* (1986), listing titles bearing the imprint of Canadian publishers or originated by the Canadian subsidiaries of international publishing houses, has 25,637 entries, 2949 with a 1985 imprint.

8 As a distinguished Canadian educational publisher, Gladys Neale of Macmillan and Clarke Irwin, remarked in accepting the Eve Orpen Award in 1986, she had always been conscious of how important the endeavours of her division were in supporting the original trade titles of her firm.

9 *Letters from Nova Scotia*, ed. Marjory Whitelaw (1986), provides the impressions of an American visitor to a Halifax bookstore in 1856 who finds himself 'once more at home' among the books 'fresh from the teeming presses of the States.' He would still be at home in many a store in Canada.

10 A valuable study of the creation of the National Library is F. Dolores Donnelly's *The National Library of Canada: A Historical Analysis of the Forces which Contributed to Its Establishment and to the Identification of Its Role and Responsibilities* (1973).

11 Since 1984 the National Library has been proceeding with preparation and execution of a National Plan for Collections Inventories which will use collection profiles created by a method known as Conspectus and descriptions of special collections of research value. Greater knowledge of Canadian library resources, including Canadian materials, is intended to improve means of sharing resources, of managing collections, and of preservation. See *National Library News*, October 1985 and 1986.

12 The statistics quoted were prepared by Arden Ford and Harald Bohne for presentation at an annual meeting of the Association of Canadian Publishers in 1984. See also Arden Ford, 'Fashions and Fallacies: What Gets Published in Canada,' *Quill & Quire* (May 1981).

13 *Canadian Selection* (1978) and its supplement (1980) were updated to 31 December 1983 for a new and cumulated edition (see below). Of the book titles listed in the earlier issues, 55% went out of print between 1980 and 1984, 41% of the periodicals listed in the 1978 issue had ceased by 1984, and 35% of those newly listed in the 1980 supplement had gone by that year.

14 For a useful review of state-of-the-art in one area, see May Katzen, 'Electronic Publishing in the Humanities,' *Scholarly Publishing* 18:1 (1986).

15 The problems of the Canadian book trade are in many ways symptoms of life and work in Canada, but problems exist elsewhere and they are often the same. Ken Adachi reported in *The Toronto Star* for 9 August 1986 the gloom of a session of a British Council seminar about the future of 'books of literature' amid the pressure on publishers to turn out 'mainstream books' and the declining budgets of libraries. Michael Hewison, cultural columnist for the *TLS* (1982–5), gave the statistic that a literary novel in a print run of 1500 to 2000 may sell 250 to the public and for the rest is dependent on libraries. A valuable comparison is also available in an issue of an American periodical, *Library Trends* (Fall 1984), on 'The Quality of Trade Book Publishing in the 1980s'; one of the articles, 'Editing: Inside the Enigma,' takes up the implications, in years with rising costs, of a statement by a respected trade editor: 'There is a natural limit on the readership for [new] serious fiction, poetry and nonfiction in America that ranges, I would say, between 500 and 5000 people – roughly a hundred times the number of the publisher's and the author's immediate friends.' The discussions in *Publishers and Librarians: A Foundation for Dialogue* (1984), edited by Mary Biggs for the Graduate Library School of the University of Chicago, are full of pertinent material on 'the publishing culture' and 'the literary one.'

16 See F.G. Halpenny, 'The Bibliographical Temper,' in *Proceedings, National Conference on the State of Canadian Bibliography, 1974* (1977); 'Bibliography: The Foundation of Scholarship,' in *Symposium in Scholarly Communication 1980* (1981).

17 Anne B. Piternick, ed., *National Conference on the State of Canadian Bibliography, 1974* (1977), and *Bibliography for Canadian Studies: Present Trends and Future Needs*, Dalhousie University Conference 1981 (*Can Issues* 4 [1982])

Contributors

CARL BERGER, professor of history, University of Toronto; author of *The Sense of Power* (1970), *The Writing of Canadian History* (rev. 1987), and *Science, God, and Nature in Victorian Canada* (1983).

ALAN C. CAIRNS, professor of political science, University of British Columbia; author of *Prelude to Imperialism* (1965) and editor (with Cynthia Williams) of two volumes of the Macdonald Commission Report (Vol. XXXIII, *Constitutionalism, Citizenship and Society*, and Vol. XXXIV, *The Politics of Gender, Ethnicity and Language in Canada*, 1986).

BARRY CAMERON, professor of English, University of New Brunswick; author of *Clark Blaise and His Work* (1985), *John Metcalf* (1986), and editor of the forthcoming *The Verse Epistles* in the Variorum Edition of the poetry of John Donne.

RAYMOND S. CORTEEN, associate professor of psychology, University of British Columbia; author of several papers on empirical and theoretical issues in cognitive psychology.

ROBERT A. FOTHERGILL, associate professor of English, Atkinson College, York University; author of *Private Chronicles* (1974), articles on film in *A Canadian Film Reader* (1977), and a 1987 play, *Detaining Mr Trotsky*.

EDITH FOWKE, professor emerita, Department of English, York University; author and editor of twenty-one books, including *Sally Go Round the Sun* (1969), *The Penguin Book of Folk Songs* (1973), *Folktales of French Canada* (1979), and (with Carole Carpenter) *Explorations in Canadian Folklore* (1985).

FRANCES FRAZER, professor of English, University of Prince Edward Island; author of several articles in such journals as *Canadian Literature* and *Canadian Children's Literature*.

FRANCESS G. HALPENNY, professor emerita, Faculty of Library and Information Science, University of Toronto; formerly Managing Editor and Associate Director (Academic), University of Toronto Press; Chairman, Book and Periodical Development Council 1984–5; author of *Canadian Collections in Public Libraries* (1985), and general editor (1969–88) of *Dictionary of Canadian Biography/Dictionnaire biographique du Canada*.

LINDA HUTCHEON, professor of English, University of Toronto; author of *Narcissistic Narrative* (1980), *Formalism and the Freudian Aesthetic* (1984), *A Theory of Parody* (1985), and *A Poetics of Postmodernism* (1987).

DAVID JACKEL, associate professor of English, University of Alberta; co-editor with Diane Bessai of a Festschrift for Sheila Watson, and author of many articles.

HENRY KREISEL, University Professor, University of Alberta; formerly chairman of the Department of Comparative Literature; author of several works of fiction including *The Rich Man* (1948), *The Betrayal* (1964), and *The Almost Meeting* (1981), and numerous essays, some of which are collected in *Another Country* (ed. Shirley Neuman, 1985).

DOUGLAS LOCHHEAD, Davidson Professor and former director of the Centre for Canadian Studies, Mount Allison University; editor of *Bibliography of Canadian Bibliographies* (1972), general editor of the Literature of Canada series and the Toronto Reprint Library, and author and editor of numerous other volumes, including his selected poems, *Tiger in the Skull* (1986).

SHIRLEY NEUMAN, professor of English, University of Alberta; author of *Gertrude Stein* (1979), *Some One Myth* (1982), and *Gertrude Stein and the Novel* (1988), and editor of *A Mazing Space* (1987, with Smaro Kamboureli) and books on Kreisel and Kroetsch.

W.H. NEW, professor of English, University of British Columbia, and editor of *Canadian Literature*; author and editor of twenty books, including *Articulating West* (1972), *Among Worlds* (1975), *Malcolm Lowry* (1978), *A Political Art* (1978), *Canadian Short Fiction* (1986), and *Dreams of Speech and Violence* (1987).

BRIAN PARKER, professor of English, Dean of Arts and Vice-Provost, Trinity College, University of Toronto; editor of several plays for New Press, and editor of editions of Thomas Middleton's *A Chaste Maid in Cheapside* (1969), Ben Jonson's *Volpone* (1983), and *Twentieth-Century Interpretations of 'The Glass Menagerie'* (1983).

BALACHANDRA RAJAN, professor emeritus, Department of English, University of Western Ontario; author and editor of more than a dozen books, including *The Lofty Rhyme* (1970), *The Overwhelming Question* (1976), *The Form of the Unfinished* (1985), and two novels, *The Dark Dancer* and *Too Long in the West*.

LAURIE RICOU, professor of English, University of British Columbia, and associate editor of *Canadian Literature*; editor of *Twelve Prairie Poets* (1976) and author of *Vertical Man/Horizontal World* (1973) and *Everyday Magic* (1987).

PHILIP STRATFORD, professor of English, Université de Montréal; author and editor of seven books, including *Faith and Fiction* (1964), *Marie-Claire Blais* (1970), *Stories from Quebec* (1974), and *All the Polarities* (1986), and translator of works by several Quebec and Acadian writers including Claire Martin, André Laurendeau, Félix Leclerc, Antonine Maillet, Robert Melançon, and René Lévesque.

CLARA THOMAS, York University Libraries Canadian Studies Research Fellow, and professor emerita, Department of English, York University; author of several books, including *Love and Work Enough* (1967), *Ryerson of Upper Canada* (1969), *Our Nature – Our Voices* (1972), *The Manawaka World of Margaret Laurence* (1975), and *William Arthur Deacon* (1982, with John Lennox).

BRUCE G. TRIGGER, professor of anthropology, McGill University; author and editor of eleven books, including *Beyond History* (1968), *The Huron* (1969), *The Children of Aataentsic* (1976), *Time and Tradition* (1978), and *Natives and Newcomers* (1985).

DOUGLAS E. WILLIAMS, Canada Research Fellow in political science, Queen's University; author of *Conserving Liberalism* (1988) and editor of *Constitution, Government and Society in Canada* (1988).

CYNTHIA D. ZIMMERMAN, associate professor of English, Glendon College, York University; author of several articles on Canadian drama and co-author (with Robert Wallace) of *The Work: Conversations with English-Canadian Playwrights* (1982).

Index